CONTEMPORARY MORAL PROBLEMS

Fourth Edition

Contemporary Moral Problems

James E. White
St. Cloud State University

West Publishing Company
Minneapolis/St. Paul New York Los Angeles San Francisco

Cover Image: Jackson Pollock *Convergence, 1952, oil on canvas 93-1/2 × 155.* Albright-Knox Art Gallery Buffalo, New York. Gift of Seymour H. Knox, 1956.
Compositor: Parkwood Composition
Index: Terry Casey

610 Opperman Drive
P.O. Box 64526
St. Paul, MN 55164-0526

Printed in the United States of America

01 00 99 98 97 96 95 94 8 7 6 5 4 3 2 1 0

Library of Congress Cataloging-in-Publication Data

Contemporary moral problems / [edited by] James E. White.—4th ed. p. cm.
Includes bibliographical references and index.
ISBN 0–314–02738–6 (soft : alk. paper)
1. Ethical problems. 2. Civilization, Modern —1950– I. White, James E.
BJ1031.C6 1993 93–25928
170–dc20 CIP

West's Commitment to the Environment

In 1906, West Publishing Company began recycling materials left over from the production of books. This began a tradition of efficient and responsible use of resources. Today, up to 95 percent of our legal books and 70 percent of our college texts are printed on recycled, acid-free stock. West also recycles nearly 22 million pounds of scrap paper annually—the equivalent of 181,717 trees. Since the 1960s, West has devised ways to capture and recycle waste inks, solvents, oils, and vapors created in the printing process. We also recycle plastics of all kinds, wood, glass, corrugated cardboard, and batteries and have eliminated the use of Styrofoam book packaging. We at West are proud of the longevity and the scope of our commitment to the environment.

Production, Prepress, Printing and Binding by West Publishing Company.

Contents

PREFACE

The choice of topics for the fourth edition of this text was determined by student surveys and suggestions from instructors who have used the book in class. Students in a class called Contemporary Moral Problems were surveyed to see what moral issues they wished to discuss. Abortion continues to be at or near the top of this list, followed by sex, AIDS, suicide, the death penalty, euthanasia, the environment, animal rights, and welfare. In some classes, the environment was near the top of the list. Instructors who have used the book wanted a chapter on important ethical theories, and several reviewers insisted that the book include feminist theory and women's issues. I have tried to satisfy this demand by putting in two radings on feminist theory in Chapter 1, and adding a separate chapter on women's issues. Also, I have followed the suggestion to replace the chapter on nuclear war and deterrence with a more general chapter on war.

The choice of particular readings for each topic was influenced by a variety of considerations. First there was an attempt to find readings of high quality. As a result, many of the articles included are regarded as "classics" such as Mary Anne Warren's "On the Moral and Legal Status of Abortion." Some of the readings were choosen for their historical importance, e.g., the Supreme Court decisions on abortion and the death penalty. Also, there was an attempt to balance the readings, to have different points of view expressed. On most of these issues, one can discern what might, broadly speaking, be called a conservative view and a more liberal view opposed to it. For example, in the chapter on abortion, John T. Noonan defends the conservative view that abortion is the killing of an innocent human being and as such is almost always wrong; while Mary Anne Warren expounds the liberal view that abortion is not the killing of a person with a right to life and that women have a right to get an abortion when they want to. Whenever possible, a moderate view has been included. For example, in the chapter on abortion, Jane English expresses a view that allows abortion in cases justified by an appeal to self-defense, but certainly not in all cases.

Suitability for students was another important consideration. The book is intended to be an introductory level textbook that can be read and understood by most college students. Many of the readings were assigned in class, and students were tested for comprehension. Some students had difficulty. To alleviate this problem, several students aids have been provided:

1. *Chapter Introductions.* Each chapter begins with a general introduction that explains the issue and supplies background information. When it is necessary, there is a brief survey of the main philosophical issues, arguments, and theories relevant to the moral issue.
2. *Reading Introductions.* An author biography and a short summary of the author's main conclusions and arguments precede each reading.
3. *Study Questions.* Two types of study questions follow each reading. First are the rather detailed and pedestrian review questions that test the student's grasp of the main points in the reading. These are intended for the student who may have difficulty following the text. Second are the more difficult discussion questions that probe deeper into the subject. These are aimed at the student who has understood the reading and is ready to discuss it.
4. *Problem Cases.* The problem cases at the end of each chapter require the student to apply the arguments and theories discussed in the chapter to a hard case, either actual or hypothetical. This case-study method (as they call it in law schools and business schools) produces lively discussion and is a good way to get the students to think about issues from a moral

point of view. The problem cases can also be assigned as short paper topics or used for essay tests. The fourth edition contains a supplementary booklet with additional problem cases.

5. ***Suggested Readings.*** At the end of each chapter, the student can locate a list of specific suggestions for further reading. Usually this consists of books and articles that might have been included in the chapter. It is not intended to take the place of a comprehensive bibliography.

6. ***Glossary.*** A glossary of philosophical terms located at the end of the book defines words that might not be found in an ordinary dictionary, such as those in Arabic language or technical medical terms. It is not meant to take the place of a standard dictionary, but simply to supplement it.

In revising the book for the fourth edition, I have benefited from the help and advice of many people. I learned about feminist theory from my colleague Professor Carolyn G. Hartz. As usual, my friend and colleague Professor Myron Anderson was very helpful. Professor Jordan Curnutt made several useful suggestions. Elena White helped with the research and permissions, and Barbara Seefeldt helped with photocopying. I received advice, corrections, and encouragement from Nancy E. Crochiere, my editor at West Publishing Co. Finally, I am grateful to the following reviewers for their detailed criticisms and suggestions for improving the text:

Jeffrey H. Barker, Albright College; Hollis E. Bishop, McHenry County College; James E. Broyles, Washington State University; Carol Coveney, Trenton State College; David B. Fletcher, Wheaton College; Norris Frederick, Queens College; Bonnie J. Gray, Eastern Kentucky University; Bryan J. Guiot, Arizona Western College; John P. Hittinger, College of St. Francis; Lee Horvitz, Miami University; Claire Elise Katz, Salisbury State University; Beverly Kent, Lakehead University; Robert Larmer, University of New Brunswick; Sanford S. Levy, Montana State University; Richard Lippke, James Madison University; Paul Mattick, Adelphi University; Marcia McKelligan, De Pauw University; Peter Mehl, University of Central Arkansas; Bill Myers, University of Central Arkansas; Roger Paden, George Mason University; Gary Percesepe, Cedarville College; Rebecca J. Potts, Worthington Community College; J. Piers Rawling, University of Missouri-St. Louis; Adrienne Regnier, College of Lake County; Errol G. Rohr, King College; Albert Ruesga, Gettysburg College; Laura Shanner, Georgetown University; Doran Smolkin, Kansas State University; Peter K. Steinfeld, Buena Vista College; Jane Mary Trau, Barry University; Mimi Tucker, Indiana Institute of Technology; Mark Owen Webb, Appalachian State University.

Chapter One

ETHICAL THEORIES

Introduction

The purpose of this chapter is to introduce students to the ethical theories that provide the background for the subsequent readings in the book. The first reading is Aristotle's classic statement of **virtue theory**, followed by Alasdair MacIntyre's version of the theory. The theory of **utilitarianism** is featured in two readings: John Stuart Mill's original statement and a commentary by James Rachels. Equally important is Kant's theory; we have a reading from Kant and a helpful exposition by Onora O'Neill. The selection by W. D. Ross presents an influential alternative theory of moral duty. John Rawls' theory of justice is a **social contract theory** that is often mentioned in current discussions of justice and rights.

Feminist theory has become a focal point in many discussions of moral problems. The general features of feminist ethical theory are explained in the reading by Alison M. Jaggar, and Virginia Held defends one important feminist theory, the ethics of care.

Virtue Theory. Aristotle rejects the popular view that happiness is found in pleasure or honor or wealth. Instead, he holds that true happiness and pleasure derive from virtuous activity, whether moral or intellectual. Moral virtue is said to be a mean between the vices of excess and deficiency, while intellectual virtue is found in contemplation. MacIntyre's view is similar to that of Aristotle, except that he relies more on a distinction between external goods and internal goods (a distinction hinted at by Aristotle). Wealth, status, power, and pleasure that are independent of activity are external goods, while internal goods are those produced by the exercise of virtue. The development of virtue, then, entails the pursuit of internal goods rather than external goods. A major difference between these two types of goods is that external goods such as fame and power can be possessed by only a few people, while internal goods are available to everyone who engages in the practice which produces them.

Utilitarianism. John Stuart Mill, in the next reading, seems to adopt the very view that Aristotle rejects, namely that happiness is pleasure. Mill says, "By happiness is intended pleasure, and the absence of pain." But the most basic principle in utilitarianism is the Principle of Utility which Mill states as follows: "Actions are right in proportion as they tend to promote happiness, wrong as they tend to produce the reverse of happiness."

The most obvious feature of utilitarianism is that it defines acts as right or wrong according to the act's consequences—the happiness or unhappiness it produces. A theory that focuses on consequences is classified as a consequentialist theory or a **teleological theory**, that is, a theory that is concerned with the goal or end of the act. Such a theory is distinguished from nonconsequential or **deontological theories** such as those advanced by Kant and Ross. Of course, not all theories in ethics are either consequentialist or deontological. Virtue theory is not concerned with the rightness or wrongness of acts, but with the traits of character a person should have to be happy or good. Rawl's theory is about justice, not acts or character.

In considering the happiness or unhappiness produced, utilitarianism counts everyone equally (including nonhuman animals). No one's happiness is to be considered more important than anyone else's. This view rejects **ethical egoism**, a rival consequentialist theory holding that people should consider their own happiness above anyone else's. Utilitarianism also seems to be incompatible with Held's feminist theory which places priority on caring for particular people with whom one has a special relationship, for example, a mother caring for her child.

Utilitarianism and Conventional Morality. Determining rightness or wrongness by considering only consequences is a very radical idea that rejects certain features of conventional morality. In deciding what is right or wrong, people sometimes refer to the beliefs of their society and assume the truth of **cultural relativism**, the view that acts generally approved by society are right, and acts disapproved are wrong. But utilitarians and the other moral theorists we are considering reject this view for the simple reason that the moral beliefs of a society can be mistaken. In Mill's time, it was believed that women were inferior to men in intelligence and ability and that women should not be allowed to enter certain occupations such as law and medicine. But as Mill pointed out in his classic feminist work *The Subjection of Women,* these beliefs are mistaken. Women are capable of being doctors and lawyers and should have the opportunity to do so.

Another feature of conventional morality is that people sometimes consult their feelings in deciding what is right or wrong; that is, they accept **subjectivism**, the view that an act is right if a person approves of it, and wrong if a person disapproves of it. This view is similar to cultural relativism, but instead of saying that moral values are relative to the beliefs of society, the subjectivist holds that moral values are relative to subjective feelings. Thus a subjectivist might say, "All abortions are wrong because I very strongly disapprove of them." But utilitarians and the other moral theorists reject subjectivism for the same reason they reject cultural relativism—people can be mistaken in their moral beliefs. The person who believes that abortion is wrong because of negative feelings about it could be mistaken. If a woman with a tubal pregnancy has a life-saving abortion, and this produces more happiness than unhappiness for her and her family, then according to the utilitarian, the abortion is right. The fact that the abortion makes some other person unhappy can be taken into account of course; but if this unhappiness is outweighed by the happiness of the mother and her family, then (in the utilitarian view) the abortion is morally right.

Objections to Utilitarianism. We have seen that utilitarianism sometimes conflicts with conventional morality and can be used as a basis for social criticism and social reform. But these conflicts with conventional morality are also a major source of objection to utilitarianism. Criticisms of utilitarianism are discussed in James Rachels' reading. The basic complaint is that utilitarianism goes too far in its rejection of conventional morality and results in obviously wrong or unjust acts such as punishing an innocent person, violating a person's rights, breaking promises, failing to consider merit, and so on.

Utilitarianism and Religion. Utilitarianism is compatible with belief in God. In fact, Bentham argued that if God is benevolent, then God would command us to follow the Principle of Utility, since this is the best way to be benevolent. But utilitarians cannot accept the **divine command theory**, the deontological theory which says that an act is right if and only if God commands it. Utilitarians do not find the commands commonly attributed to God to be acceptable. For example, consider the basic moral command "Thou shalt not kill." It is easy for a utilitarian to find cases where killing is justified: killing the terrorist who is threatening to blow up an airplane packed with innocent people or even killing an innocent person in order to save many other lives.

Utilitarianism and Moral Problems. The use of utilitarianism for moral criticism and social reform becomes even clearer in the readings when we consider how utilitarianism deals with moral problems, particularly euthanasia, capital punishment, and animal rights. Let us see what the utilitarians have to say about these problems.

The conventional moral rule is that it is wrong to kill innocent people, and this implies that euthanasia is wrong. But in our readings for Chapter 3, Rachels, Singer, and Brandt argue on utilitarian grounds that euthanasia can be morally justified in some cases. Rachels argues that if we allow passive euthanasia (mercifully letting people die) as the American Medical Association does, then we should allow active euthanasia (mercifully killing people) as well, for there is no important moral difference between passive and active euthanasia—both have the same consequences. Singer's argument is more straightforward. According to preference utilitarianism, it is right to maximize the satisfaction of people's preferences; but voluntary euthanasia does this in some cases, namely in those cases where people want to die. So euthanasia is right in some cases. Brandt uses the utilitarian theory to justify the termination of newborn infants whose lives will be unhappy.

What is the justification of capital punishment? In the utilitarian view, killing a criminal can only be justified by appealing to consequences, and the main relevant consequence of capital punishment is to deter other criminals from committing crimes. But does the death penalty deter? In Chapter 4, both Amsterdam and Glover argue that this has not been established, and thus conclude that the death penalty has no utilitarian justification. The view that nonhuman animals should be given equal moral consideration (accepted by Singer and Regan in Chapter 9) is a radical utilitarian idea, found in the writings of Bentham (who is quoted by Singer). Remember that everyone's happiness or unhappiness is to be equally considered; and since nonhuman animals do have the capacity to be happy or unhappy, to feel pleasure and pain, they have a moral standing equal to humans.

Kant's Theory. One of the main rivals to utilitarianism in the readings is Kant's theory. Unlike utilitarianism and ethical egoism, it is a deontological theory that does not consider consequences. Instead, Kant believes that by reasoning we can discover one supreme moral principle that is binding on all rational beings. He calls this principle that Categorical Imperative because it commands absolutely, as distinguished from hypothetical imperatives which command only if you have certain desires.

Kant formulates the Categorical Imperative in several different ways, but commentators usually focus on two distinct versions. The first one is that you should "act only on that maxim which you can at the same time will that it should become a universal law." This principle gives you a way of deciding whether an act is wrong or not. You ask yourself what rule you would be following if you did something; this rule is the "maxim" of your act. If you are not willing to have this rule become a universal law that everyone follows, then the act is wrong. To take one of Kant's examples, suppose you want to lie to someone. The rule you would be proposing (the "maxim" of your act) would be "It is not wrong to lie to someone." But you would not be willing to have everyone follow this rule, Kant claims, because it would be self-defeating. If everyone lied at will, then your lie would be pointless because nobody would believe you. According to Kant, these considerations prove that lying is always wrong.

Many philosophers have thought that this first formulation of the categorical imperative is problematic. One problem is that you can formulate the rule under which an act falls in different ways. Some of these rules could be made universal and others not. For example, instead of a general rule about lying, you could have a more specific rule about lying, such as "It is not wrong to lie to save someone's life." This seems to be a rule about lying that we would be willing to have as a universal law.

Kant formulated the Categorical Imperative in a second way that avoids this problem. His second formulation, called the Formula of the End in Itself, recommends that you should "act in such a way that you always treat humanity, whether in your own person or in the person of any other, never simply as a means, but always at the same time as an end."

This principle is explained by Onora O'Neill in our readings. According to O'Neill, treating others as a mere means is to engage them in an activity to which they could not, in principle, consent, e.g., a deception. Treating people as ends in themselves requires that we treat them not as mere means, but that we help them with their plans and activities. This gives us a duty to help or a duty of beneficence.

Kant's Theory and Moral Problems. Kant's theory and utilitarianism can be used to arrive at similar conclusions in some issues. Singer (a utilitarian) and O'Neill (a Kantian) both agree that we have a moral obligation to help starving people in other countries (although in Chapter 5 Hardin gives utilitarian reasons for not helping). On other matters, however, Kant's theory is opposed to utilitarianism. The difference between the two theories is most clear in the case of capital punishment. In the reading in Chapter 4, Kant condemns the "serpent-windings of Utilitarianism," and insists that murderers must die because they deserve to die; they must be "paid back" for their crimes, and the consequences of the punishment are irrelevant.

Kant also rejects the utilitarian view of nonhuman animals. In the reading in Chapter 9, Tom Regan accurately puts Kant in the anthropocentric tradition that excludes animals from moral concern because they are not supposed to be rational. According to Kant, we do not have any direct duties to animals, but we do have indirect duties based on the effect the treatment of animals has on our treatment of humans. Thus we should not be cruel to animals since this makes us cruel to humans.

Kant does not discuss euthanasia, but in view of his belief that human life is always valuable, even when it is full of suffering, it seems likely he would have condemned euthanasia. He does say that suicide is always wrong because it treats a human life as an animal life, that is, as a life having little or no value in itself.

W. D. Ross's Intuitionism. Ross has provided us with an important deontological theory that is an alternative to both utilitarianism and Kant's theory, and yet combines features of both theories. In the reading titled "What Makes Right Acts Right?" Ross argues that there are various features of an act that can make it right, and not just one, as in utilitarianism and Kant's theory. To use Ross's example, the fact that a person has made a promise is a good reason for saying that he ought to keep the promise, or in Ross's terminology, he has a **prima facie duty** to keep the promise, even if doing so will not produce good consequences. Moral intuition or judgment has to be used to resolve conflicts between prima facie duties, if, for example, keeping the promise results in harming someone. Also, intuition clearly shows us that the general principles of duty are self-evident to the same extent the axioms of mathematics are self-evident.

Rights. Many readings in the book do not appeal to utilitarianism or Kant's theory, but rather to rights. We find references to the rights of fetuses, newborn infants, the terminally ill, animals, future generations, the needy, and the environment. One can debate about who has rights and what those rights are; but what is a right? The analysis of right given by Joel Feinberg in his article "The Rights of Animals and Unborn Generations" in Chapter 12 defines a right as a claim to something against someone. What is the basis for moral rights? The traditional view of Locke and Jefferson is that rights are given to us by God. But most philosophers today do not want to appeal to God; they want a theory that appeals to nonbelievers too. A traditional secular view is the social contract theory of Hobbes and Rousseau—that it is in everyone's self-interest to live together in a society rather than alone in a state of nature. But to live in a society, people must agree to follow certain rules (don't steal, don't murder, etc.), and these rules imply corresponding rights. Every citizen tacitly makes such an agreement (the social contract) in order to get the benefits of living in society. Without this social contract, society would not be possible.

Rawls' Theory of Justice. Rawls' theory is a kind of social contract theory. He imagines that the social contract is made by self-interested, but free and rational persons. In order to ensure impartiality or fairness, the contractors make the agreement in a hypothetical, original position where they are ignorant of all the particular facts about themselves but are aware of general facts about social theory and psychology. According to Rawls, the rational contractors in the original position would agree upon two principles of justice: that "each person is to have an equal right to the most extensive basic liberty compatible with a similar liberty for others," and that "social and economic inequalities are to be arranged so that they are both (a) reasonably expected to be to everyone's advantage, and (b) attached to positions and offices open to all."

This theory is relevant to moral problems about distribution of goods and resources: world hunger, welfare, job discrimination and affirmative action. It is also relevant to problems involving the rights of citizens.

Feminist Theory. The general, feminist theory is critical of all the traditional ethical theories discussed so far. In her discussion of the main features of feminist theory, Alison M. Jaggar notes that these traditional theories all display a male bias that ignores the experience of women and continues their subordination in a male-dominated society. Furthermore, feminist theory challenges most of the basic assumptions of traditional (male) ethical theory. According to feminist theory, impartiality, where everyone is considered morally equal, is not an appropriate or even possible moral ideal. Moral agents are not separate, autonomous, rational beings as Mill, Kant, Ross, and Rawls believe. Despite what traditional male philosophers think, it is not possible to find universally valid moral rules grounded in universal, impartial reason.

Virginia Held presents one popular feminist theory often called the ethics of care. She agrees with Jaggar that an adequate moral theory is not based on abstract principles such as the Mill's Principle of Utility, Kant's Categorical Imperative, or Rawls' Principles of Justice. In Held's view what is needed in the late twentieth century is a feminist theory based on women's experiences in birthing and mothering which emphasizes caring and trusting relations with particular people.

Aristotle

Happiness and Virtue

Aristotle (384–322 B.C.) made important contributions to all areas of philosophy, including the formulation of traditional logic. Along with his teacher Plato, he is regarded as one of the founders of western philosophy.

Aristotle argues that all human beings seek happiness, and that happiness is not pleasure, honor, or wealth, but an activity of the soul in accordance with virtue. Virtue is of two kinds: moral and intellectual. Moral virtue comes from training and habit, and generally is a state of character that is a mean between the vices of excess and deficiency. For example, Aristotle portrays the virtue of courage as a mean between the extremes of rashness (an excess) and cowardness (a deficiency). Intellectual virtue produces the most perfect happiness and is found in the activity of reason or contemplation.

Our discussion will be adequate if it has as much clearness as the subject-matter admits of, for precision is not to be sought for alike in all discussions, any more than in all the products of the crafts. Now fine and just actions, which political science investigates, admit of much variety and fluctuation of opinion, so that they may be thought to exist only by convention, and not by nature. And goods also give rise to a similar fluctuation because they bring harm to many people; for before now men have been undone by reason of their wealth, and others by reason of their courage. We must be content, then, in speaking of such subjects and with such premisses to indicate the truth roughly and in outline, and in speaking about things which are only for the most part true and with premisses of the same kind to reach conclusions that are no better. In the same spirit, therefore, should each type of statement be received; for it is the mark of an educated man to look for precision in each class of things just so far as the nature of the subject admits; it is evidently equally foolish to accept probable reasoning from a mathematician and to demand from a rhetorician scientific proofs.

Now each man judges well the things he knows, and of these he is a good judge. And so the man who has been educated in a subject is a good judge of that subject, and the man who has received an all-round education is a good judge in general. Hence a young man is not a proper hearer of lectures on political science; for he is inexperienced in the actions that occur in life, but its discussions start from these and are about these; and, further, since he tends to follow his passions, his study will be vain and unprofitable, because the end aimed at is not knowledge but action. And it makes no difference whether he is young in years or youthful in character; the defect does not depend on time, but on his living, and pursuing each successive object, as passion directs. For to such persons, as to the incontinent, knowledge brings no profit; but to those who desire and act in accordance with a rational principle knowledge about such matters will be of great benefit.

These remarks about the student, the sort of treatment to be expected, and the purpose of the inquiry, may be taken as our preface.

Let us resume our inquiry and state, in view of the fact that all knowledge and every pursuit aims at some good, what it is that we say political science aims at and what is the highest of all goods achievable by action. Verbally there is very general agreement; for both the general run of men and people of superior refinement say that it is happiness, and identify living well and doing well with being happy; but with regard to what happiness is they differ, and the many do not give the same account as the wise. For the former think it is some plain and obvious thing, like pleasure, wealth, or honour; they differ, however, from one another—and often even the

Aristotle, *Happiness and Virtue,* Books I: 3–5, 7–9, 13; II: 1, 6, 7, 9; and X: 7, 8 from *Ethica Nicomachea* trans. by W. D. Ross in *The Oxford Translation of Aristotle,* Vol. 9 (Oxford: Oxford University Press, 1925). Reprinted by permission of Oxford University Press.

same man identifies it with different things, with health when he is ill, with wealth when he is poor; but, conscious of their ignorance, they admire those who proclaim some great ideal that is above their comprehension. Now some thought that apart from these many goods there is another which is self-subsistent and causes the goodness of all these as well. To examine all the opinions that have been held were perhaps somewhat fruitless; enough to examine those that are most prevalent or that seem to be arguable . . . .

Let us, however, resume our discussion from the point at which we digressed. To judge from the lives that men lead, most men, and men of the most vulgar type, seem (not without some ground) to identify the good, or happiness, with pleasure; which is the reason why they love the life of enjoyment. For there are, we may say, three prominent types of life—that just mentioned, the political, and thirdly the contemplative life. Now the mass of mankind are evidently quite slavish in their tastes, preferring a life suitable to beasts, but they get some ground for their view from the fact that many of those in high places share the tastes of Sardanapallus. A consideration of the prominent types of life shows that people of superior refinement and of active disposition identify happiness with honour; for this is, roughly speaking, the end of the political life. But it seems too superficial to be what we are looking for, since it is thought to depend on those who bestow honour rather than on him who receives it, but the good we divine to be something proper to a man and not easily taken from him. Further, men seem to pursue honour in order that they may be assured of their goodness; at least it is by men of practical wisdom that they seek to be honoured, and among those who know them, and on the ground of their virtue; clearly, then, according to them, at any rate, virtue is better. And perhaps one might even suppose this to be, rather than honour, the end of the political life. But even this appears somewhat incomplete; for possession of virtue seems actually compatible with being asleep, or with life-long inactivity, and, further, with the greatest sufferings and misfortunes; but a man who was living so no one would call happy, unless he were maintaining a thesis at all costs. But enough of this; for the subject has been sufficiently treated even in the current discussions. Third comes the contemplative life, which we shall consider later.

The life of money-making is one undertaken under compulsion, and wealth is evidently not the good we are seeking; for it is merely useful and for the sake of something else. And so one might rather take the aforenamed objects to be ends; for they are loved for themselves. But it is evident that not even these are ends; yet many arguments have been thrown away in support of them . . . .

Let us again return to the good we are seeking, and ask what it can be. It seems different in different actions and arts; it is different in medicine, in strategy, and in the other arts likewise. What then is the good of each? Surely that for whose sake everything else is done. In medicine this is health, in strategy victory, in architecture a house, in any other sphere something else, and in every action and pursuit the end; for it is for the sake of this that all men do whatever else they do. Therefore, if there is an end for all that we do, this will be the good achievable by action, and if there are more than one, these will be the goods achievable by action.

So the argument has by a different course reached the same point; but we must try to state this even more clearly. Since there are evidently more than one end, and we choose some of these (e.g. wealth, flutes, and in general instruments) for the sake of something else, clearly not all ends are final ends; but the chief good is evidently something final. Therefore, if there is only one final end, this will be what we are seeking, and if there are more than one, the most final of these will be what we are seeking. Now we call that which is in itself worthy of pursuit more final than that which is worthy of pursuit for the sake of something else, and that which is never desirable for the sale of something else more final than the things that are desirable both in themselves and for the sake of that other thing, and therefore we call final without qualification that which is always desirable in itself and never for the sake of something else.

Now such a thing happiness, above all else, is held to be; for this we choose always for itself and never for the sake of something else, but honour, pleasure, reason, and every virtue we choose indeed for themselves (for if nothing resulted from them we should still choose each of them), but we choose them also for the sake of happiness, judging that by means of them we shall be happy. Happiness, on the other hand, no one chooses for the sake of these, nor, in general, for anything other than itself . . . .

Presumably, however, to say that happiness is the chief good seems a platitude, and a clearer account of what it is is still desired. This might perhaps be given, if we could first ascertain the function of man. For just as for a fluteplayer, a sculptor, or any artist, and, in general, for all things that have a function or activity, the good and the 'well' is thought to reside in the function, so would it seem to be for man, if he has a function. Have the carpenter, then, and the tanner certain functions or activities, and has man none? Is he born without a function? Or as eye, hand, foot, and in general each of the parts evidently has a function, may one lay it down that man similarly has a function apart from all these? What then can this be? Life seems to be common even to plants, but we are seeking what is peculiar to man. Let us exclude, therefore, the life of nutrition and growth. Next there would be a life of perception, but *it* also seems to be common even to the horse, the ox, and every animal. There remains, then, an active life of the element that has a rational principle; of this, one part has such a principle in the sense of being obedient to one, the other in the sense of possessing one and exercising thought. And, as 'life of the rational element' also has two meanings, we must state that life in the sense of activity is what we mean; for this seems to be the more proper sense of the term. Now if the function of man is an activity of soul which follows or implies a rational principle, and if we say 'a so-and-so' and 'a good so-and-so' have a function which is the same in kind, e. g. a lyre-player and a good lyre-player, and so without qualification in all cases, eminence in respect of goodness being added to the name of the function (for the function of a lyre-player is to play the lyre, and that of a good lyre-player is to do so well): if this is the case, [and we state the function of man to be a certain kind of life, and this to be an activity or actions of the soul implying a rational principle, and the function of a good man to be the good and noble performance of these, and if any action is well performed when it is performed in accordance with the appropriate excellence: if this is the case,] human good turns out to be activity of soul in accordance with virtue, and if there are more than one virtue, in accordance with the best and most complete.

But we must add 'in a complete life.' For one swallow does not make a summer, nor does one day; and so too one day, or a short time, does not make a man blessed and happy . . . .

We must consider it, however, in the light not only of our conclusion and our premisses, but also of what is commonly said about it; for with a true view all the data harmonize, but with a false one the facts soon clash. Now goods have been divided into three classes, and some are described as external, others as relating to soul or to body; we call those that relate to soul most properly and truly goods, and psychical actions and activities we class as relating to soul. Therefore our account must be sound, at least according to this view, which is an old one and agreed on by philosophers. It is correct also in that we identify the end with certain actions and activities; for thus it falls among goods of the soul and not among external goods. Another belief which harmonizes with our account is that the happy man lives well and does well; for we have practically defined happiness as a sort of good life and good action. The characteristics that are looked for in happiness seem also, all of them, to belong to what we have defined happiness as being. For some identify happiness with virtue, some with practical wisdom, others with a kind of philosophic wisdom, others with these, or one of these, accompanied by pleasure or not without pleasure; while others include also external prosperity. Now some of these views have been held by many men and men of old, others by a few eminent persons; and it is not probable that either of these should be entirely mistaken, but rather that they should be right in at least some one respect or even in most respects.

With those who identify happiness with virtue or some one virtue our account is in harmony; for to virtue belongs virtuous activity. But it makes, perhaps, no small difference whether we place the chief good in possession or in use, in state of mind or in activity. For the state of mind may exist without producing any good result, as in a man who is asleep or in some other way quite inactive, but the activity cannot; for one who has the activity will of necessity be acting, and acting well. And as in the Olympic Games it is not the most beautiful and the strongest that are crowned but those who compete (for it is some of these that are victorious), so those who act win, and rightly win, the noble and good things in life.

Their life is also in itself pleasant. For pleasure is a state of *soul,* and to each man that which he is said to be a lover of is pleasant; e. g. not only is a horse pleasant to the lover of horses, and a spectacle to the lover of sights, but also in the same way just acts are pleasant to the lover of justice and in general virtuous acts to the lover of virtue. Now for most men their pleasures are in conflict with one another because these are not by nature pleasant, but the lovers of what is noble find pleasant the things that are by nature pleasant; and virtuous actions are such, so that these are pleasant for such men as well as in their own nature. Their life, therefore, has no further need of pleasure as a sort of adventitious charm, but has its pleasure in itself. For, besides what we have said, the man who does not rejoice in noble actions is not even good; since no one would call a man just who did not enjoy acting justly, nor any man liberal who did not enjoy liberal actions; and similarly in all other cases. If this is so, virtuous actions must be in themselves pleasant. But they are also *good* and *noble,* and have each of these attributes in the highest degree, since the good man judges well about these attributes; his judgment is such as we have described. Happiness then is the best noblest, and most pleasant thing in the world. . . .

Yet evidently, as we said, it needs the external goods as well; for it is impossible, or not easy, to do noble acts without the proper equipment. In many actions we use friends and riches and political power as instruments; and there are some things the lack of which takes the lustre from happiness, as good birth, goodly children, beauty; for the man who is very ugly in appearance or ill-born or solitary and childless is not very likely to be happy, and perhaps a man would be still less likely if he had thoroughly bad children or friends or had lost good children or friends by death. As we said, then, happiness seems to need this sort of prosperity in addition; for which reason some identify happiness with good fortune, though others identify it with virtue.

For this reason also the question is asked, whether happiness is to be acquired by learning or by habituation or some other sort of training, or comes in virtue of some divine providence or again by chance. Now if there is *any* gift of the gods to men, it is reasonable that happiness should be god-given, and most surely god-given of all human things inasmuch as it is the best. But this question would perhaps be more appropriate to another inquiry; happiness seems, however, even if it is not god-sent but comes as a result of virtue and some process of learning or training, to be among the most god-like things; for that which is the prize and end of virtue seems to be the best thing in the world, and something godlike and blessed.

It will also on this view be very generally shared; for all who are not maimed as regards their potentiality for virtue may win it by a certain kind of study and care. But if it is better to be happy thus than by chance, it is reasonable that the facts should be so, since everything that depends on the action of nature is by nature as good as it can be, and similarly everything that depends on art or any rational cause, and especially if it depends on the best of all causes. To entrust to chance what is greatest and most noble would be a very defective arrangement.

The answer to the question we are asking is plain also from the definition of happiness; for it has been said to be a virtuous activity of soul, of a certain kind. Of the remaining goods, some must necessarily pre-exist as conditions of happiness, and others are naturally co-operative and useful as instruments. And this will be found to agree with what we said at the outset; for we stated the end of political science to the best end, and political science spends most of its pains on making the citizens to be of a certain character, viz. good and capable of noble acts.

It is natural, then, that we call neither ox nor horse nor any other of the animals happy; for none of them is capable of sharing in such activity. For this reason also a boy is not happy; for he is not yet capable of such acts, owing to his age; and boys who are called happy are being congratulated by reason of the hopes we have for them. For there is required, as we said, not only complete virtue but also a complete life, since many changes occur in life, and all manner of chances, and the most prosperous may fall into great misfortunes in old age, as is told of Priam in the Trojan Cycle; and one who has experienced such chances and has ended wretchedly no one calls happy . . . .

Since happiness is an activity of soul in accordance with perfect virtue, we must consider the nature of virtue; for perhaps we shall thus see better the nature of happiness . . . .

Virtue, then, being of two kinds, intellectual and moral, intellectual virtue in the main owes both its birth and its growth to teaching (for which reason it requires experience and time), while moral virtue comes about as a result of habit. . . . From this it is also plain that none of the moral virtues arises in us by nature; for nothing that exists by nature can form a habit contrary to its nature. For instance the stone which by nature moves downwards cannot be habituated to move upwards, not even if one tries to train it by throwing it up ten thousand times; nor can fire be habituated to move downwards, nor can anything else that by nature behaves in one way be trained to behave in another. Neither by nature, then, nor contrary to nature do the virtues arise in us; rather we are adapted by nature to receive them, and are made perfect by habit. . . .

We must, however, not only describe virtue as a state of character, but also say what sort of state it is. We may remark, then, that every virtue or excellence both brings into good condition the thing of which it is the excellence and makes the work of that thing be done well; e. g. the excellence of the eye makes both the eye and its work good; for it is by the excellence of the eye that we see well. Similarly the excellence of the horse makes a horse both good in itself and good at running and at carrying its rider and at awaiting the attack of the enemy. Therefore, if this is true in every case, the virtue of man also will be the state of character which makes a man good and which makes him do his own work well.

How this is to happen we have stated already, but it will be made plain also by the following consideration of the specific nature of virtue. In everything that is continuous and divisible it is possible to take more, less, or an equal amount, and that either in terms of the thing itself or relatively to us; and the equal is an intermediate between excess and defect. By the intermediate in the object I mean that which is equidistant from each of the extremes, which is one and the same for all men; by the intermediate relatively to us that which is neither too much nor too little—and this is not one, nor the same for all. For instance, if ten is many and two is few, six is the intermediate, taken in terms of the object; for it exceeds and is exceeded by an equal amount; this is intermediate according to arithmetical proportion. But the intermediate relatively to us is not to be taken so; if ten pounds are too much for a particular person to eat and two too little, it does not follow that the trainer will order six pounds; for this also is perhaps too much for the person who is to take it, or too little—too little for Milo, too much for the beginner in athletic exercises. The same is true of running and wrestling. Thus a master of any art avoids excess and defect, but seeks the intermediate and chooses this—the intermediate not in the object but relatively to us.

If it is thus, then, that every art does its work well—by looking to the intermediate and judging its works by this standard (so that we often say of good works of art that it is not possible either to take away or to add anything, implying that excess and defect destroy the goodness of the works of art, while the mean preserves it; and good artists, as we say, look to this in their work), and if, further, virtue is more exact and better than any art, as nature also is, then virtue must have the quality of aiming at the intermediate. I mean moral virtue; for it is this that is concerned with passions and actions, and in these there is excess, defect, and the intermediate. For instance, both fear and confidence and appetite and anger and pity and in general pleasure and pain may be felt both too much and too little, and in both cases not well; but to feel them at the right times, with reference to the right objects, towards the right people, with the right motive, and in the right way, is what is both intermediate and best, and this is characteristic of virtue. Similarly with regard to actions also there is excess, defect, and the intermediate. Now virtue is concerned with passions and actions, in which excess is a form of failure, and so is defect, while the intermediate is praised and is a form of success; and being praised and being successful are both characteristics of virtue. Therefore virtue is a kind of mean, since, as we have seen, it aims at what is intermediate.

Again, it is possible to fail in many ways (for evil belongs to the class of the unlimited, as the Pythagoreans conjectured, and good to that of the limited), while to succeed is possible only in one way (for which reason also one is easy and the other difficult—to miss the mark easy, to hit it difficult); for these reasons also, then, excess and defect are characteristic of vice, and the mean of virtue;

For men are good in but one way, but bad in many.

Virtue, then, is a state of character concerned with choice, lying in a mean, i. e. the mean relative to us, this being determined by a rational principle, and by that principle by which the man of practical wisdom would determine it. Now it is a mean between two vices, that which depends on excess and that which depends on defect; and again it is a mean because the vices respectively fall short of or exceed what is right in both passions and actions, while virtue both finds and chooses that which is intermediate. Hence in respect of its substance and the definition which states its essence virtue is a mean, with regard to what is best and right an extreme.

But not every action nor every passion admits of a mean; for some have names that already imply badness, e. g. spite, shamelessness, envy, and in the case of actions adultery, theft, murder; for all of these and suchlike things imply by their names that they are themselves bad, and not the excesses or deficiencies of them. It is not possible, then, ever to be right with regard to them; one must always be wrong. Nor does goodness or badness with regard to such things depend on committing adultery with the right woman, at the right time, and in the right way, but simply to do any of them is to go wrong. It would be equally absurd, then, to expect that in unjust, cowardly, and voluptuous action there should be a mean, an excess, and a deficiency; for at that rate there would be a mean of excess and of deficiency, an excess of excess, and a deficiency of deficiency. But as there is no excess and deficiency of temperance and courage because what is intermediate is in a sense an extreme, so too of the actions we have mentioned there is no mean nor any excess and deficiency, but however they are done they are wrong; for in general there is neither a mean of excess and deficiency, nor excess and deficiency of a mean.

We must, however, not only make this general statement, but also apply it to the individual facts. For among statements about conduct those which are general apply more widely, but those which are particular are more genuine, since conduct has to do with individual cases, and our statements must harmonize with the facts in these cases. We may take these cases from our table. With regard to feelings of fear and confidence courage is the mean; of the people who exceed, he who exceeds in fearlessness has no name (many of the states have no name), while the man who exceeds in confidence is rash, and he who exceeds in fear and falls short in confidence is a coward. With regard to pleasures and pains—not all of them, and not so much with regard to the pains—the mean is temperance, the excess self-indulgence. Persons deficient with regard to the pleasures are not often found; hence such persons also have received no name. But let us call them 'insensible'.

With regard to giving and taking of money the mean is liberality, the excess and the defect prodigality and meanness. In these actions people exceed and fall short in contrary ways; the prodigal exceeds in spending and falls short in taking, while the mean man exceeds in taking and falls short in spending. (At present we are giving a mere outline or summary, and are satisfied with this; later these states will be more exactly determined.) With regard to money there are also other dispositions—a mean, magnificence (for the magnificent man differs from the liberal man; the former deals with large sums, the latter with small ones), and excess, tastelessness, and vulgarity, and a deficiency, niggardliness; these differ from the states opposed to liberality . . . .

That moral virtue is a mean, then, and in what sense it is so, and that it is a mean between two vices, the one involving excess, the other deficiency, and that it is such because its character is to aim at what is intermediate in passions and in actions, has been sufficiently stated. Hence also it is no easy task to be good. For in everything it is no easy task to find the middle, e. g. to find the middle of a circle is not for every one but for him who knows; so, too, any one can get angry—that is easy—or give or spend money; but to do this to the right person, to the right extent, at the right time, with the right motive, and in the right way, *that* is not for every one, nor is it easy; wherefore goodness is both rare and laudable and noble . . . .

If happiness is activity in accordance with virtue, it is reasonable that it should be in accordance with the highest virtue; and this will be that of the best thing in us. Whether it be reason or something else that is this element which is thought to be our natural ruler and guide and to take thought of things noble and divine, whether it be itself also divine or only the most divine element in us, the activity of this in accordance with its proper virtue will be perfect happiness. That this activity is contemplative we have already said.

Now this would seem to be in agreement both with what we said before and with the truth. For, firstly, this activity is the best (since not only is reason the best thing in us, but the objects of reason are the best of knowable objects); and, secondly, it is the most continuous, since we can contemplate truth more continuously than we can do anything. And we think happiness has pleasure mingled with it, but the activity of philosophic wisdom is admittedly the pleasantest of virtuous activities; at all events the pursuit of it is thought to offer pleasures marvellous for their purity and their enduringness, and it is to be expected that those who know will pass their time more pleasantly than those who inquire. And the self-sufficiency that is spoken of must belong most to the contemplative activity. For while a philosopher, as well as a just man or one possessing any other virtue, needs the necessaries of life, when they are sufficiently equipped with things of that sort the just man needs people towards whom and with whom he shall act justly, and the temperate man, the brave man, and each of the others is in the same case, but the philosopher, even when by himself, can contemplate truth, and the better the wiser he is; he can perhaps do so better if he has fellow-workers, but still he is the most self-sufficient. And this activity alone would seem to be loved for its own sake; for nothing arises from it apart from the contemplating, while from practical activities we gain more or less apart from the action. And happiness is thought to depend on leisure; for we are busy that we may have leisure, and make war that we may live in peace. Now the activity of the practical virtues is exhibited in political or military affairs, but the actions concerned with these seem to be unleisurely. Warlike actions are completely so (for no one chooses to be at war, or provokes war, for the sake of being at war; any one would seem absolutely murderous if he were to make enemies of his friends in order to bring about battle and slaughter); but the action of the statesman is also unleisurely, and—apart from the political action itself—aims at despotic power and honours, or at all events happiness, for him and his fellow citizens—a happiness different from political action, and evidently sought as being different. So if among virtuous actions political and military actions are distinguished by nobility and greatness, and these are unleisurely and aim at an end and are not desirable for their own sake, but the activity of reason, which is contemplative, seems both to be superior in serious worth and to aim at no end beyond itself, and to have its pleasure proper to itself (and this augments the activity), and the self-sufficiency, leisureliness, unweariedness (so far as this is possible for man), and all the other attributes ascribed to the supremely happy man are evidently those connected with this activity, it follows that this will be the complete happiness of man, if it be allowed a complete term of life (for none of the attributes of happiness is *in*complete).

But such a life would be too high for man; for it is not in so far as he is man that he will live so, but in so far as something divine is present in him; and by so much as this is superior to our composite nature is its activity superior to that which is the exercise of the other kind of virtue. If reason is divine, then in comparison with man, the life according to it is divine in comparison with human life. But we must not follow those who advise us, being men, to think of human things, and, being mortal, of mortal things, but must, so far as we can, make ourselves immortal, and strain every nerve to live in accordance with the best thing in us; for even if it be small in bulk, much more does it in power and worth surpass everything. This would seem, too, to be each man himself, since it is the authoritative and better part of him. It would be strange, then, if he were to choose not the life of his self but that of something else. And what we said before will apply now; that which is proper to each thing is by nature best and most pleasant for each thing; for man, therefore, the life according to reason is best and pleasantest, since reason more than anything else *is* man. This life therefore is also the happiest.

But in a secondary degree the life in accordance with the other kind of virtue is happy; for the activities in accordance with this befit our human estate. Just and brave acts, and other virtuous acts, we do in relation to each other, observing our respective duties with regard to contracts and services and all manner of actions and with regard to passions; and all of these seem to be typically human. Some of them seem even to arise from the body, and virtue of character to be in many ways bound up with the passions. Practical wisdom, too, is linked to virtue of character, and this to practical wisdom, since the principles of practical wisdom are in accordance with the moral virtues and rightness in morals is in accordance with practical wisdom. Being connected with the passions also, the moral virtues must belong to our composite nature; and the virtues of our composite nature are human; so, therefore, are the life and the happiness which correspond to these. The excellence of the reason is a thing apart; we must be content to say this much about it, for to describe it precisely is a task greater than our purpose requires. It would seem, however, also to need external equipment but little, or less than moral virtue does. Grant that both need the necessaries, and do so equally, even if the statesman's work is the more concerned with the body and things of that sort; for there will be little difference there; but in what they need for the exercise of their activities there will be much difference. The liberal man will need money for the doing of his liberal deeds, and the just man too will need it for the returning of services (for wishes are hard to discern, and even people who are not just pretend to wish to act justly); and the brave man will need power if he is to accomplish any of the acts that correspond to his virtue, and the temperate man will need opportunity; for how else is either he or any of the others to be recognized? It is debated, too, whether the will or the deed is more essential to virtue, which is assumed to involve both; it is surely clear that its perfection involves both; but for deeds many things are needed, and more, the greater and nobler the deeds are. But the man who is contemplating the truth needs no such thing, at least with a view to the exercise of his activity; indeed they are, one may say, even hindrances, at all events to his contemplation; but in so far as he is a man and lives with a number of people, he chooses to do virtuous acts; he will therefore need such aids to living a human life.

But that perfect happiness is a contemplative activity will appear from the following consideration as well. We assume the gods to be above all other beings blessed and happy; but what sort of actions must we assign to them? Acts of justice? Will not the gods seem absurd if they make contracts and return deposits, and so on? Acts of a brave man, then, confronting dangers and running risks because it is noble to do so? Or liberal acts? To whom will they give? It will be strange if they are really to have money or anything of the kind. And what would their temperate acts be? Is not such praise tasteless, since they have no bad appetites? If we were to run through them all, the circumstances of action would be found trivial and unworthy of gods. Still, every one supposes that they *live* and therefore that they are active; we cannot suppose them to sleep like Endymion. Now if you take away from a living being action, and still more production, what is left but contemplation? Therefore the activity of God, which surpasses all others in blessedness, must be contemplative; and of human activities, therefore, that which is most akin to this must be most of the nature of happiness.

This is indicated, too, by the fact that the other animals have no share in happiness, being completely deprived of such activity. For while the whole life of the gods is blessed, and that of men too in so far as some likeness of such activity belongs to them, none of the other animals is happy, since they in no way share in contemplation. Happiness extends, then, just so far as contemplation does, and those to whom contemplation more fully belongs are more truly happy, not as a mere concomitant but in virtue of the contemplation; for this is in itself precious. Happiness, therefore, must be some form of contemplation.

But, being a man, one will also need external prosperity; for our nature is not self-sufficient for the purpose of contemplation, but our body also must be healthy and must have food and other attention. Still, we must not think that the man who is to be happy will need many things or great things, merely because he cannot be supremely happy without external goods; for self-sufficiency and action do not involve excess, and we can do noble acts without ruling earth and sea; for even with moderate advantages one can act virtuously (this is manifest enough; for private persons are thought to do worthy acts no less than despots—indeed even more); and it is enough that we should have so much as that; for the life of the man who is active in accordance with virtue will be happy. . . .

Review Questions

1. What is happiness according to Aristotle? How is it related to virtue? How is it related to pleasure?
2. How does Aristotle explain moral virtue? Give some examples.
3. Is it possible for everyone in our society to be happy, as Aristotle explains it? If not, who cannot be happy?

Discussion Questions

1. Aristotle characterizes a life of pleasure as suitable for beasts. But what, if anything, is wrong with a life of pleasure?
2. Aristotle claims that the philosopher will be happier than anyone else. Why is this? Do you agree or not?

Alasdair MacIntyre

The Nature of the Virtues

Alasdair MacIntyre is Professor of Philosophy at Vanderbilt University. He is the author of After Virtue *(1981), from which our reading is taken, and* Whose Justice? Which Rationality *(1988).*

MacIntyre compares and discusses the account of virtues found in Homer, Aristotle, the New Testament, Jane Austen, and Benjamin Franklin. With the exception of Franklin's utilitarian view, these different accounts all contain a core concept of the virtues in MacIntyre's view. This concept has developed in three stages. Our reading contains an account of the first and most basic practice stage. (The other two stages, not discussed here, are a narrative stage and moral tradition stage.) As MacIntyre defines it, a practice is any coherent form of human activity which produces goods in-

From Alasdair MacIntyre, *After Virtue* (Notre Dame, Indiana: University of Notre Dame Press, © 1984). Used by permission.

ternal to the activity. For example, playing chess is regarded as an activity that produces internal goods such as analytic skill and strategic imagination. A virtue is a human quality the exercise of which enables us to achieve goods internal to practices. The three virtues that MacIntyre thinks are essential in any practice with internal goods and standards of excellence are justice, courage, and honesty.

One response to the history which I have narrated so far might well be to suggest that even within the relatively coherent tradition of thought which I have sketched there are just too many different and incompatible conceptions of a virtue for there to be any real unity to the concept or indeed to the history. Homer, Sophocles, Aristotle, the New Testament and medieval thinkers differ from each other in too many ways. They offer us different and incompatible lists of the virtues; they give a different rank order of importance to different virtues; and they have different and incompatible theories of the virtues. If we were to consider later Western writers on the virtues, the list of differences and incompatibilities would be enlarged still further; and if we extended our enquiry to Japanese, say, or American Indian cultures, the differences would become greater still. It would be all too easy to conclude that there are a number of rival and alternative conceptions of the virtues, but, even within the tradition which I have been delineating, no single core conception.

The case for such a conclusion could not be better constructed than by beginning from a consideration of the very different lists of items which different authors in different times and places have included in their catalogues of virtues. Some of these catalogues—Homer's, Aristotle's and the New Testament's—I have already noticed at greater or lesser length. Let me at the risk of some repetition recall some of their key features and then introduce for further comparison the catalogues of two later Western writers, Benjamin Franklin and Jane Austen.

The first example is that of Homer. At least some of the items in a Homeric list of the *aretai* would clearly not be counted by most of us nowadays as virtues at all, physical strength being the most obvious example. To this it might be replied that perhaps we ought not to translate the world *aretê* in Homer by our word 'virtue', but instead by our word 'excellence'; and perhaps, if we were so to translate it, the apparently surprising difference between Homer and ourselves would at first sight have been removed. For we could allow without any kind of oddity that the possession of physical strength is the possession of an excellence. But in fact we would not have removed, but instead would merely have relocated, the difference between Homer and ourselves. For we would now seem to be saying that Homer's concept of an *aretê*, an excellence, is one thing and that our concept of a virtue is quite another since a particular quality can be an excellence in Homer's eyes, but not a virtue in ours and *vice versa.*

But of course it is not that Homer's list of virtues differs only from our own; it also notably differs from Aristotle's. And Aristotle's of course also differs from our own. For one thing, as I noticed earlier, some Greek virtue-words are not easily translated into English or rather out of Greek. Moreover consider the importance of friendship as a virtue in Aristotle's list—how different from us! Or the place of *phronêsis*[1]—how different from Homer and from us! The mind receives from Aristotle the kind of tribute which the body receives from Homer. But it is not just the case that the difference between Aristotle and Homer lies in the inclusion of some items and the omission of others in their respective catalogues. It turns out also in the way in which those catalogues are ordered, in which items are ranked as relatively central to human excellence and which marginal.

Moreover the relationship of virtues to the social order has changed. For Homer the paradigm of human excellence is the warrior; for Aristotle it is the Athenian gentleman. Indeed according to Aristotle certain virtues are only available to those of great riches and of high social status; there are virtues which are unavailable to the poor man, even if he is a free man. And those virtues are on Aristotle's view ones central to human life; magnanimity—and once again, any translation of *megalopsuchia* is unsatisfactory—and munificence are not just virtues, but important virtues within the Aristotelian scheme.

At once it is impossible to delay the remark that the most striking contrast with Aristotle's catalogue is to be found neither in Homer's nor in our own, but in the New Testament's. For the New Testament not only praises virtues of which Aristotle knows nothing—faith, hope and love—and says nothing about virtues such as *phronêsis* which are crucial for Aristotle, but it praises at least one quality as a virtue which Aristotle seems to count as one of the vices relative to magnanimity, namely humility. Moreover since the New Testament quite clearly sees the rich as destined for the pains of Hell, it is clear that the key virtues cannot be available to them; yet they *are* available to slaves. And the New Testament of course differs from both Homer and Aristotle not only in the items included in its catalogue, but once again in its rank ordering of the virtues.

Turn now to compare all three lists of virtues considered so far—the Homeric, the Aristotelian, and the New Testament's—with two much later lists, one which can be compiled from Jane Austen's novels and the other which Benjamin Franklin constructed for himself. Two features stand out in Jane Austen's list. The first is the importance that she allots to the virtue which she calls 'constancy', a virtue about which I shall say more in a later chapter. In some ways constancy plays a role in Jane Austen analogous to that of *phronêsis* in Aristotle; it is a virtue the possession of which is a prerequisite for the possession of other virtues. The second is the fact that what Aristotle treats as the virtue of agreeableness (a virtue for which he says there is no name) she treats as only the simulacrum of a genuine virtue—the genuine virtue in question is the one she calls amiability. For the man who practices agreeableness does so from considerations of honor and expediency, according to Aristotle; whereas Jane Austen thought it possible and necessary for the possessor of that virtue to have a certain real affection for people as such. (It matters here that Jane Austen is a Christian.) Remember that Aristotle himself had treated military courage as a simulacrum of true courage. Thus we find here yet another type of disagreement over the virtues; namely, one as to which human qualities are genuine virtues and which mere simulacra.

In Benjamin Franklin's list we find almost all the types of difference from at least one of the catalogues we have considered and one more. Franklin includes virtues which are new to our consideration such as cleanliness, silence and industry; he clearly considers the drive to acquire itself a part of virtue, whereas for most ancient Greeks this is the vice of *pleonexia*; he treats some virtues which earlier ages had considered minor as major; but he also redefines some familiar virtues. In the list of thirteen virtues which Franklin compiled as part of his system of private moral accounting, he elucidates each virtue by citing a maxim obedience to which *is* the virtue in question. In the case of chastity the maxim is 'Rarely use venery but for health or offspring—never to dullness, weakness or the injury of your own or another's peace or reputation'. This is clearly not what earlier writers had meant by 'chastity'.

We have therefore accumulated a startling number of differences and incompatibilities in the five stated and implied accounts of the virtues. So the question which I raised at the outset becomes more urgent. If different writers in different times and places, but all within the history of Western culture, include such different sets and types of items in their lists, what grounds have we for supposing that they do indeed aspire to list items of one and the same kind, that there is any shared concept at all? A second kind of consideration reinforces the presumption of a negative answer to this question. It is not just that each of these five writers lists different and differing kinds of items; it is also that each of these lists embodies, is the expression of a different theory about what a virtue is.

In the Homeric poems a virtue is a quality the manifestation of which enables someone to do exactly what their well-defined social role requires. The primary role is that of the warrior king and that Homer lists those virtues which he does becomes intelligible at once when we recognize that the key virtues therefore must be those which enable a man to excel in combat and in the games. It follows that we cannot identify the Homeric virtues until we have first identified the key social roles in Homeric society and the requirements of each of them. The concept of *what anyone filling such-and-such a role ought to do* is prior to the concept of a virtue; the latter concept has application only via the former.

On Aristotle's account matters are very different. Even though some virtues are available only to certain types of people, nonetheless virtues attach not to men as inhabiting social roles, but to man as such. It is the *telos* of man as a species which determines what human qualities are virtues. We need to remember however that although Aristotle treats the acquisition and exercise of the virtues as means to an end, the relationship of means to end is internal and not external. I call a means internal to a given end when the end cannot be adequately characterized independently of a characterization of the means. So it is with the virtues and the *telos* which is the good life for man on Aristotle's account. The exercise of the virtues is itself a crucial component of the good life for man. This distinction between internal and external means to an end is not drawn by Aristotle himself in the *Nicomachean Ethics,* as I noticed earlier, but it is an essential distinction to be drawn if we are to understand what Aristotle intended. The distinction *is* drawn explicitly by Aquinas in the course of his defence of St. Augustine's definition of a virtue, and it is clear that Aquinas understood that in drawing it he was maintaining an Aristotelian point of view.

The New Testament's account of the virtues, even if it differs as much as it does in content from Aristotle's—Aristotle would certainly not have admired Jesus Christ and he would have been horrified by St Paul—does have the same logical and conceptual structure as Aristotle's account. A virtue is, as with Aristotle, a quality the exercise of which leads to the achievement of the human *telos. The* good for man is of course a supernatural and not only a natural good, but supernature redeems and completes nature. Moreover the relationship of virtues as means to the end which is human incorporation in the divine kingdom of the age to come is internal and not external, just as it is in Aristotle. It is of course this parallelism which allows Aquinas to synthesize Aristotle and the New Testament. A key feature of this parallelism is the way in which the concept of *the good life for man* is prior to the concept of a virtue in just the way in which on the Homeric account the concept of a social role was prior. Once again it is the way in which the former concept is applied which determines how the latter is to be applied. In both cases the concept of a virtue is a secondary concept.

The intent of Jane Austen's theory of the virtues is of another kind. C. S. Lewis has rightly emphasized how profoundly Christian her moral vision is and Gilbert Ryle has equally rightly emphasized her inheritance from Shaftesbury and from Aristotle. In fact her views combine elements from Homer as well, since she is concerned with social roles in a way that neither the New Testament nor Aristotle are. She is therefore important for the way in which she finds it possible to combine what are at first sight disparate theoretical accounts of the virtues. But for the moment any attempt to assess the significance of Jane Austen's synthesis must be delayed. Instead we must notice the quite different style of theory articulated in Benjamin Franklin's account of the virtues.

Franklin's account, like Aristotle's, is teleological; but unlike Aristotle's, it is utilitarian. According to Franklin in his *Autobiography* the virtues are means to an end, but he envisages the means-ends relationship as external rather than internal. The end to which the cultivation of the virtues ministers is happiness, but happiness understood as success, prosperity in Philadelphia and ultimately in heaven. The virtues are to be useful and Franklin's account continuously stresses utility as a criterion in individual cases: 'Make no expense but to do good to others or yourself; i. e. waste nothing', 'Speak not but what may benefit others or yourself. Avoid trifling conversation' and, as we have already seen, 'Rarely use venery but for health or offspring . . .'. When Franklin was in Paris he was horrified by Parisian architecture: 'Marble, porcelain and gilt are squandered without utility.'

We thus have at least three very different conceptions of a virtue to confront: a virtue is a quality which enables an individual to discharge his or her social role (Homer); a virtue is a quality which enables an individual to move towards the achievement of the specifically human *telos*, whether natural or supernatural (Aristotle, the New Testament and Aquinas); a virtue is a quality which has utility in achieving earthly and heavenly success (Franklin). Are we to take these as three different rival accounts of the same thing? Or are they instead accounts of three different things? Perhaps the moral structures in archaic Greece, in fourth-century Greece, and in eighteenth-century Pennsylvania were so different from each other that we should treat them as embodying quite different concepts, whose difference is initially disguised from us by the historical accident of an inherited vocabulary which misleads us by linguistic resemblance long after conceptual identity and similarity have failed. Our initial question has come back to us with redoubled force . . . .

The question can therefore now be posed directly: are we or are we not able to disentangle from these rival and various claims a unitary core concept of the virtues of which we can give a more compelling account than any of the other accounts so far? I am going to argue that we can in fact discover such a core concept and that it turns out to provide the tradition of which I have written the history with its conceptual unity. It will indeed enable us to distinguish in a clear way those beliefs about the virtues which genuinely belong to the tradition from those which do not. Unsurprisingly perhaps it is a complex concept, different parts of which derive from different stages in the development of the tradition. Thus the concept itself in some sense embodies the history of which it is the outcome.

One of the features of the concept of a virtue which has emerged with some clarity from the argument so far is that it always requires for its application the acceptance for some prior account of certain features of social and moral life in terms of which it has to be defined and explained. So in the Homeric account the concept of a virtue is secondary to that of *a social role,* in Aristotle's account it is secondary to that of *the good life for man* conceived as the *telos* of human action and in Franklin's much later account it is secondary to that of utility. What is it in the account which I am about to give which provides in a similar way the necessary background against which the concept of a virtue has to be made intelligible? It is in answering this question that the complex, historical, multi-layered character of the core concept of virtue becomes clear. For there are no less than three stages in the logical development of the concept which have to be identified in order, if the core conception of a virtue is to be understood, and each of these stages has its own conceptual background. The first stage requires a background account of what I shall call a practice, the second an account of what I have already characterized as the narrative order of a single human life and the third an account a good deal fuller than I have given up to now of what constitutes a moral tradition. Each later stage presupposes the earlier, but not *vice versa.* Each earlier stage is both modified by and reinterpreted in the light of, but also provides an essential constituent of each later stage. The progress in the development of the concept is closely related to, although it does not recapitulate in any straightforward way, the history of the tradition of which it forms the core.

In the Homeric account of the virtues—and in heroic societies more generally—the exercise of a virtue exhibits qualities which are required for sustaining a social role and for exhibiting excellence in some well-marked area of social practice: to excel is to excel at war or in the games, as Achilles does, in sustaining a household, as Penelope does, in giving counsel in the assembly, as Nestor does, in the telling of a tale, as Homer himself does. When Aristotle speaks of excellence in human activity, he sometimes though not always, refers to some well-defined type of human practice: flute-playing, or war, or geometry. I am going to suggest that this notion of a particular type of practice as providing the arena in which the virtues are exhibited and in terms of which they are to receive their primary, if incomplete, definition is crucial to the whole enterprise of identifying a core concept of the virtues. I hasten to add two *caveats* however.

The first is to point out that my argument will not in any way imply that virtues are *only* exercised in the course of what I am calling practices. The second is to warn that I shall be using the word 'practice' in a specially defined way which does not completely agree with current ordinary usage, including my own previous use of that word. What am I going to mean by it?

By a 'practice' I am going to mean any coherent and complex form of socially established cooperative human activity through which goods internal to that form of activity are realized in the course of trying to achieve those standards of excellence which are appropriate to, and partially definitive of, that form of activity, with the result that human powers to achieve excellence, and human conceptions of the ends and goods involved, are systematically extended. Tic-tac-toe is not an example of a practice in this sense, nor is throwing a football with skill; but the game of football is, and so is chess. Bricklaying is not a practice; architecture is. Planting turnips is not a practice; farming is. So are the inquiries of physics, chemistry and biology, and so is the work of the historian, and so are painting and music. In the ancient and medieval worlds the creation and sustaining of human communities—of households, cities, nations—is generally taken to be a practice in the sense in which I have defined it. Thus the range of practices is wide: arts, sciences, games, politics in the Aristotelian sense, the making and sustaining of family life, all fall under the concept. But the question of the precise range of practices is not at this stage of the first importance. Instead let me explain some of the key terms involved in my definition, beginning with the notion of goods internal to a practice.

Consider the example of a highly intelligent seven-year-old child whom I wish to teach to play chess, although the child has no particular desire to learn the game. The child does however have a very strong desire for candy and little chance of obtaining it. I therefore tell the child that if the child will play chess with me once a week I will give the child 50 cents worth of candy; moreover I tell the child that I will always play in such a way that it will be difficult, but not impossible, for the child to win and that, if the child wins, the child will receive an extra 50 cents worth of candy. Thus motivated the child plays and plays to win. Notice however that, so long as it is the candy alone which provides the child with a good reason for playing chess, the child has no reason not to cheat and every reason to cheat, provided he or she can do so successfully. But, so we may hope, there will come a time when the child will find in those goods specific to chess, in the achievement of a certain highly particular kind of analytical skill, strategic imagination and competitive intensity, a new set of reasons, reasons now not just for winning on a particular occasion, but for trying to excel in whatever way the game of chess demands. Now if the child cheats, he or she will be defeating not me, but himself or herself.

There are thus two kinds of good possibly to be gained by playing chess. On the one hand there are those goods externally and contingently attached to chess-playing and to other practices by the accidents of social circumstance—in the case of the imaginary child candy, in the case of real adults such goods as prestige, status and money. There are always alternative ways for achieving such goods, and their achievement is never to be had *only* by engaging in some particular kind of practice. On the other hand there are the goods internal to the practice of chess which cannot be had in any way but by playing chess or some other game of that specific kind. We call them internal for two reasons: first, as I have already suggested, because we can only specify them in terms of chess or some other game of that specific kind and by means of examples from such games (otherwise the meagerness of our vocabulary for speaking of such goods forces us into such devices as my own resort to writing of 'a certain highly particular kind of'); and secondly because they can only be identified and recognized by the experience of participating in the practice in question. Those who lack the relevant experience are incompetent thereby as judges of internal goods. . . .

A practice involves standards of excellence and obedience to rules as well as the achievement of goods. To enter into a practice is to accept the authority of those standards and the inadequacy of my own performance as judged by them. It is to subject my own attitudes, choices, preferences and tastes to the standards which currently and partially define the practice. Practices of course, as I have just noticed, have a history: games, sciences and arts all have histories. Thus the standards are not themselves immune from criticism, but nonetheless we cannot be initiated into a practice without accepting the authority of the best standards realized so far. If, on starting to listen to music, I do not accept my own incapacity to judge correctly, I will never learn to hear, let alone to appreciate, Bartok's last quartets. If, on starting to play baseball, I do not accept that others know better than I when to throw a fast ball and when not, I will never learn to appreciate good pitching let alone to pitch. In the realm of practices the authority of both goods and standards operates in such a way as to rule out all subjectivist and emotivist analyses of judgment. De gustibus *est* disputandum.

We are now in a position to notice an important difference between what I have called internal and what I have called external goods. It is characteristic of what I have called external goods that when achieved they are always some individual's property and possession. Moreover characteristically they are such that the more someone has of them, the less there is for other people. This is sometimes necessarily the case, as with power and fame, and sometimes the case by reason of contingent circumstance as with money. External goods are therefore characteristically objects of competition in which there must be losers as well as winners. Internal goods are indeed the outcome of competition to excel, but it is characteristic of them that their achievement is a good for the whole community who participate in the practice. So when Turner transformed the seascape in painting or W. G. Grace advanced the art of batting in cricket in a quite new way their achievement enriched the whole relevant community.

But what does all or any of this have to do with the concept of the virtues? It turns out that we are now in a position to formulate a first, even if partial and tentative definition of a virtue: *A virtue is an acquired human quality the possession and exercise of which tends to enable us to achieve those goods which are internal to practices and the lack of which effectively prevents us from achieving any such goods*. Later this definition will need amplification and amendment. But as a first approximation to an adequate definition it already illuminates the place of the virtues in human life. For it is not difficult to show for a whole range of key virtues that without them the goods internal to practices are barred to us, but not just barred to us generally, barred in a very particular way.

It belongs to the concept of a practice as I have outlined it—and as we are all familiar with it already in our actual lives, whether we are painters or physicists or quarterbacks or indeed just lovers of good painting or first-rate experiments or a well-thrown pass—that its goods can only be achieved by subordinating ourselves within the practice in our relationship to other practitioners. We have to learn to recognize what is due to whom; we have to be prepared to take whatever self-endangering risks are demanded along the way; and we have to listen carefully to what we are told about our own inadequacies and to reply with the same carefulness for the facts. In other words we have to accept as necessary components of any practice with internal goods and standards of excellence the virtues of justice, courage and honesty. For not to accept these, to be willing to cheat as our imagined child was willing to cheat in his or her early days at chess, so far bars us from achieving the standards of excellence or the goods internal to the practice that it renders the practice pointless except as a device for achieving external goods. . . .

To situate the virtues any further within practices it is necessary now to clarify a little further the nature of a practice by drawing two important contrasts. The discussion so far I hope makes it clear that a practice, in the sense intended, is never just a set of technical skills, even when directed towards some unified purpose and even if the exercise of those skills can on occasion be valued or enjoyed for their own sake. What is distinctive in a practice is in part the way in which conceptions of the relevant goods and ends which the technical skills serve—and every practice does require the exercise of technical skills—are transformed and enriched by these extensions of human powers and by that regard for its own internal goods which are partially definitive of each particular practice or type of practice. Practices never have a goal or goals fixed for all time—painting has no such goal nor has physics—but the goals themselves are transmuted by the history of the activity. It therefore turns out not to be accidental that every practice has its own history and a history which is more and other than that of the improvement of the relevant technical skills. This historical dimension is crucial in relation to the virtues.

To enter into a practice is to enter into a relationship not only with its contemporary practitioners, but also with those who have preceded us in the practice, particularly those whose achievements extended the reach of the practice to its present point. It is thus the achievement, and *a fortiori* the authority, of a tradition which I then confront and from which I have to learn. And for this learning and the relationship to the past which it embodies the virtues of justice, courage and truthfulness are prerequisite in precisely the same way and for precisely the same reasons as they are in sustaining present relationships within practice. . . .

Virtues then stand in a different relationship to external and to internal goods. The possession of the virtues—and not only of their semblance and simulacra—is necessary to achieve the latter; yet the possession of the virtues may perfectly well hinder us in achieving external goods. I need to emphasize at this point that external goods genuinely are goods. Not only are they characteristic objects of human desire, whose allocation is what gives point to the virtues of justice and of generosity, but no one can despise them altogether without a certain hypocrisy. Yet notoriously the cultivation of truthfulness, justice and courage will often, the world being what it contingently is, bar us from being rich or famous or powerful. Thus although we may hope that we can not only achieve the standards of excellence and the internal goods of certain practices by possessing the virtues *and* become rich, famous and powerful, the virtues are always a potential stumbling block to this comfortable ambition. We should therefore expect that, if in a particular society the pursuit of external goods were to become dominant, the concept of the virtues might suffer first attrition and then perhaps something near total effacement, although simulacra might abound.

The time has come to ask the question of how far this partial account of a core conception of the virtues—and I need to emphasize that all that I have offered so far is the first stage of such an account—is faithful to the tradition which I delineated. How far, for example, and in what ways is it Aristotelian? It is—happily—not Aristotelian in two ways in which a good deal of the rest of the tradition also dissents from Aristotle. First, although this account of the virtues is teleological, it does not require any allegiance to Aristotle's metaphysical biology. And secondly, just because of the multiplicity of human practices and the consequent multiplicity of goods in the pursuit of which the virtues may be exercised—goods which will often be contingently incompatible and which will therefore make rival claims upon our allegiance—conflict will not spring solely from flaws in individual character. But it was just on these two matters that Aristotle's account of the virtues seemed most vulnerable; hence if it turns out to be the case that this socially teleological account can support Aristotle's general account of the virtues as well as does his own biologically teleological account, these differences from Aristotle himself may well be regarded as strengthening rather than weakening the case for a generally Aristotelian standpoint.

There are at least three ways in which the account that I have given *is* clearly Aristotelian. First it requires for its completion a cogent elaboration of just those distinctions and concepts which Aristotle's account requires: voluntariness, the distinction between the intellectual virtues and the virtues of character, the relationship of both to natural abilities and to the passions and the structure of practical reasoning. On every one of these topics something very like Aristotle's view has to be defended, if my own account is to be plausible.

Secondly my account can accommodate an Aristotelian view of pleasure and enjoyment, whereas it is interestingly irreconcilable with any utilitarian view and more particularly with Franklin's account of the virtues. We can approach these questions by considering how to reply to someone who, having considered my account of the differences between goods internal to and goods external to a practice enquired into which class, if either, does pleasure or enjoyment fall? The answer is, 'Some types of pleasure into one, some into the other.'

Someone who achieves excellence in a practice, who plays chess or football well or who carries through an inquiry in physics or an experimental mode in painting with success, characteristically enjoys his achievement and his activity in achieving. So does someone who, although not breaking the limit of achievement, plays or thinks or acts in a way that leads toward such a breaking of limit. As Aristotle says, the enjoyment of the activity and the enjoyment of achievement are not the ends at which the agent aims, but the enjoyment supervenes upon the successful activity in such a way that the activity achieved and the activity enjoyed are one and the same state. Hence to aim at the one is to aim at the other; and hence also it is easy to confuse the pursuit of excellence with the pursuit of enjoyment *in this specific sense.* This particular confusion is harmless enough; what is not harmless is the confusion of enjoyment *in this specific sense* with other forms of pleasure.

For certain kinds of pleasure are of course external goods along with prestige, status, power and money. Not all pleasure is the enjoyment supervening upon achieved activity; some is the pleasure of psychological or physical states independent of all activity. Such states—for example that produced on a normal palate by the closely successive and thereby blended sensations of Colchester oyster, cayenne pepper and Veuve Cliquot—may be sought as external goods, as external rewards which may be purchased by money or received in virtue of prestige. Hence the pleasures are categorized neatly and appropriately by the classification into internal and external goods.

It is just this classification which can find no place within Franklin's account of the virtues which is framed entirely in terms of external relationships and external goods. Thus although by this stage of the argument it is possible to claim that my account does capture a conception of the virtues which is at the core of the particular ancient and medieval tradition which I have delineated, it is equally clear that there is more than one possible conception of the virtues and that Franklin's standpoint and indeed any utilitarian standpoint is such that to accept it will entail rejecting the tradition and *vice versa.* . . .

Thirdly my account is Aristotelian in that it links evaluation and explanation in a characteristically Aristotelian way. From an Aristotelian standpoint to identify certain actions as manifesting or failing to manifest a virtue or virtues is never only to evaluate; it is also to take the first step towards explaining why those actions rather than some others were performed. Hence for an Aristotelian quite as much as for a Platonist the fate of a city or an individual can be explained by citing the injustice of a tyrant or the courage of its defenders. Indeed without allusion to the place that justice and injustice, courage and cowardice play in human life very little will be genuinely explicable. It follows that many of the explanatory projects of the modern social sciences, a methodological canon of which is the separation of 'the facts'—this conception of the 'the facts' is the one which I delineated in Chapter 7—from all evaluation, are bound to fail. For the fact that someone was or failed to be courageous or just cannot be recognized as 'a fact' by those who accept that methodological canon. The account of the virtues which I have given is completely at one with Aristotle's on this point. But now the question may be raised: your account may be in many respects Aristotelian, but is it not in some respects false? Consider the following important objection.

I have defined the virtues partly in terms of their place in practices. But surely, it may be suggested, some practices—that is, some coherent human activities which answer to the description of what I have called a practice—are evil. So in discussions by some moral philosophers of this type of account of the virtues it has been suggested that torture and sadomasochistic sexual activities might be examples of practices. But how can a disposition be a virtue if it is the kind of disposition which sustains practices and some practices issue in evil? My answer to this objection falls into two parts.

First I want to allow that there *may* be practices—in the sense in which I understand the concept—which simply *are* evil. I am far from convinced that there are, and I do not in fact believe that either torture or sadomasochistic sexuality answer to the description of a practice which my account of the virtues employs. But I do not want to rest my case on this lack of conviction, especially since it is plain that as a matter of contingent fact many types of practice may on particular occasions be productive of evil. For the range of practices includes the arts, the sciences and certain types of intellectual and athletic game. And it is at once obvious that any of these may under certain conditions be a source of evil: the desire to excel and to win can corrupt, a man may be so engrossed by his painting that he neglects his family, what was initially an honorable resort to war can issue in savage cruelty. But what follows from this?

It certainly is not the case that my account entails *either* that we ought to excuse or condone such evils *or* that whatever flows from a virtue is right. I do have to allow that courage sometimes sustains injustice, that loyalty has been known to strengthen a murderous aggressor and that generosity has sometimes weakened the capacity to do good. But to deny this would be to fly in the face of just those empirical facts which I invoked in criticizing Aquinas' account of the unity of the virtues. That the virtues need initially to be defined and explained with reference to the notion of a practice thus in no way entails approval of all practices in all circumstances. That the virtues—as the objection itself presupposed—*are* defined not in terms of good and right practices, but of practices, does not entail or imply that practices as actually carried through at particular times and places do not stand in need of moral criticism. And the resources for such criticism are not lacking. There is in the first place no inconsistency in appealing to the requirements of a virtue to criticize a practice. Justice may be initially defined as a disposition which in its particular way is necessary to sustain practices; it does not follow that in pursuing the requirements of a practice violations of justice are not to be condemned. Moreover I already pointed out in Chapter 12 that a morality of virtues requires as its counterpart a conception of moral law. Its requirements too have to be met by practices. But, it may be asked, does not all this imply that more needs to be said about the place of practices in some larger moral context? Does not this at least suggest that there is more to the core concept of a virtue than can be spelled out in terms of practices? I have after all emphasized that the scope of any virtue in human life extends beyond the practices in terms of which it is initially defined. What then is the place of the virtues in the larger arenas of human life?

I stressed earlier that any account of the virtues in terms of practices could only be a partial and first account. What is required to complement it? The most notable difference so far between my account and any account that could be called Aristotelian is that although I have in no way restricted the exercise of the virtues to the context of practices, it is in terms of practices that I have located their point and function. Whereas Aristotle locates that point and function in terms of the notion of a type of whole human life which can be called good. And it does seem that the question 'What would a human being lack who lacked the virtues?' must be given a kind of answer which goes beyond anything which I have said so far. For such an individual would not merely fail *in a variety of particular ways* in respect of the kind of excellence which can be achieved through participation in practices and in respect of the kind of human relationship required to sustain such excellence. His own life *viewed as a whole* would perhaps be defective; it would not be the kind of life which someone would describe in trying to answer the question 'What is the best kind of life for this kind of man or woman to live?' And that question cannot be answered without at least raising Aristotle's own question, 'What is the good life for man?' . . .

It is clear therefore that my preliminary account of the virtues in terms of practices captures much, but very far from all, of what the Aristotelian tradition taught about the virtues. It is also clear that to give an account that is at once more fully adequate to the tradition and rationally defensible, it is necessary to raise a question to which the Aristotelian tradition presupposed an answer, an answer so widely shared in the pre-modern world that it never had to be formulated explicitly in any detailed way. This question is: is it rationally justifiable to conceive of each human life as a unity, so that we may try to specify each such life as having its good and so that we may understand the virtues as having their function in enabling an individual to make of his or her life one kind of unity rather than another?

Endnotes

1. Phronêsis can be translated as practical judgement—Ed.

Review Questions

1. Compare the account of virtues given by Homer, Aristotle, the New Testament, Jane Austen, and Benjamin Franklin.
2. Explain the so-called core concept of virtue.
3. In what ways in MacIntyre's account like Aristotle's? How is it different?

Discussion Questions

1. Many people in our society pursue external goods such as wealth, status, and power. What's wrong with doing this? What would MacIntyre say? What is your view?
2. MacIntyre grants that on his account a wicked person, say a Nazi soldier, can have virtues such as courage. But this seems to be a problem. Is courage in a Nazi really a virtue?
3. What is a vice in MacIntyre's view?

John Stuart Mill

Utilitarianism

John Stuart Mill (1806–1873) was one of the most important and influential British philosophers. His most important works in ethics are On Liberty *and* Utilitarianism, *from which the reading is taken.*

Mill sets forth the basic principles of utilitarianism including the Principle of Utility (or the Greatest Happiness Principle) and the hedonistic principle that happiness is pleasure. He explains the theory by replying to various objections, and concludes with an attempt to prove the Principle of Utility.

The creed which accepts as the foundation of morals, Utility, or the Greatest Happiness Principle, holds that actions are right in proportion as they tend to promote happiness, wrong as they tend to produce the reverse of happiness. By happiness is intended pleasure, and the absence of pain; by unhappiness, pain, and the privation of pleasure. To give a clear view of the moral standard set up by the theory, much more requires to be said; in particular, what things it includes in the ideas of pain and pleasure; and to what extent this is left an open question. But these supplementary explanations do not affect the theory of life on which this theory of morality is grounded—namely, that pleasure, and freedom from pain, are the only things desirable as ends; and that all desirable things (which are as numerous in the utilitarian as in any other scheme) are desirable either for the pleasure inherent in themselves, or as means to the promotion of pleasure and the prevention of pain.

Now, such a theory of life excites in many minds, and among them in some of the most estimable in feeling and purpose, inveterate dislike. To suppose that life has (as they express it) no higher end than pleasure—no better and nobler object of desire and pursuit—they designate as utterly mean and grovelling; as a doctrine worthy only of swine, to whom the followers of Epicurus were, at a very early period, contemptuously likened; and modern holders of the doctrine are occasionally made the subject of equally polite comparisons by its German, French, and English assailants.

When thus attacked, the Epicureans have always answered, that it is not they, but their accusers, who represent human nature in a degrading light; since the accusation supposes human beings to be capable of no pleasures ex-

From John Stuart Mill, *Utilitarianism* (1861), Chapters 12 and 14.

cept those of which swine are capable. If this supposition were true, the charge could not be gainsaid, but would then be no longer an imputation; for if the sources of pleasure were precisely the same to human beings and to swine, the rule of life which is good enough for the one would be good enough for the other. The comparison of the Epicurean life to that of beasts is felt as degrading, precisely because a beast's pleasures do not satisfy a human being's conceptions of happiness. Human beings have faculties more elevated than the animal appetites, and when once made conscious of them, do not regard anything as happiness which does not include their gratification. I do not, indeed, consider the Epicureans to have been by any means faultless in drawing out their scheme of consequences from the utilitarian principle. To do this in any sufficient manner, many Stoic, as well as Christian elements require to be included. But there is no known Epicurean theory of life which does not assign to the pleasures of the intellect, of the feelings and imagination, and of the moral sentiments, a much higher value as pleasures than to those of mere sensation. It must be admitted, however, that utilitarian writers in general have placed the superiority of mental over bodily pleasures chiefly in the greater permanency, safety, uncostliness, etc., of the former—that is, in their circumstantial advantages rather than in their intrinsic nature. And on all these points utilitarians have fully proved their case; but they might have taken the other, and, as it may be called, higher ground, with entire consistency. It is quite compatible with the principle of utility to recognize the fact, that some *kinds* of pleasure are more desirable and more valuable than others. It would be absurd that while, in estimating all other things, quality is considered as well as quantity, the estimation of pleasures should be supposed to depend on quantity alone.

If I am asked, what I mean by difference of quality in pleasures, or what makes one pleasure more valuable than another, merely as a pleasure, except its being greater in amount, there is but one possible answer. Of two pleasures, if there be one to which all or almost all who have experience of both give a decided preference, irrespective of any feeling of moral obligation to prefer it, that is the more desirable pleasure. If one of the two is, by those who are competently acquainted with both, placed so far above the other that they prefer it, even though knowing it to be attended with a greater amount of discontent, and would not resign it for any quantity of the other pleasure which their nature is capable of, we are justified in ascribing to the preferred enjoyment a superiority in quality, so far outweighing quantity as to render it, in comparison, of small account.

Now it is an unquestionable fact that those who are equally acquainted with, and equally capable of appreciating and enjoying, both, do give a most marked preference to the manner of existence which employs their higher faculties. Few human creatures would consent to be changed into any of the lower animals, for a promise of the fullest allowance of a beast's pleasures; no intelligent human being would consent to be a fool, no instructed person would be an ignoramus, no person of feeling and conscience would be selfish and base, even though they should be persuaded that the fool, the dunce, or the rascal is better satisfied with his lot than they are with theirs. They would not resign what they possess more than he for the most complete satisfaction of all the desires which they have in common with him. If they ever fancy they would, it is only in cases of unhappiness so extreme, that to escape from it they would exchange their lot for almost any other, however undesirable in their own eyes. A being of higher faculties requires more to make him happy, is capable probably of more acute suffering, and certainly accessible to it at more points, than one of an inferior type; but in spite of these liabilities, he can never really wish to sink into what he feels to be a lower grade of existence. We may give what explanation we pleasure of this unwillingness; we may attribute it to pride, a name which is given indiscriminately to some of the most and to some of the least estimable feelings of which mankind are capable: we may refer it to the love of liberty and personal independence, an appeal to which was with the Stoics one of the most effective means for the inculcation of it; to the love of power, or to the love of excitement, both of which do really enter into and contribute to it:

but its most appropriate appellation is a sense of dignity, which all human beings possess in one form or other, and in some, though by no means in exact, proportion to their higher faculties, and which is so essential a part of the happiness of those in whom it is strong, that nothing which conflicts with it could be, otherwise than momentarily, an object of desire to them. Whoever supposes that this preference takes place at a sacrifice of happiness—that the superior being, in anything like equal circumstances, is not happier than the inferior—confounds the two very different ideas, of happiness, and content. It is undisputable that the being whose capacities of enjoyment are low, has the greatest chance of having them fully satisfied; and a highly endowed being will always feel that any happiness which he can look for, as the world is constituted, is imperfect. But he can learn to bear its imperfections, if they are at all bearable; and they will not make him envy the being who is indeed unconscious of the imperfections, but only because he feels not at all the good which those imperfections qualify. It is better to be a human being dissatisfied than a pig satisfied; better to be Socrates dissatisfied than a fool satisfied. And if the fool, or the pig, are of a different opinion, it is because they only know their own side of the question. The other party to the comparison knows both sides.

It may be objected, that many who are capable of the higher pleasures, occasionally, under the influence of temptation, postpone them to the lower. But this is quite compatible with a full appreciation of the intrinsic superiority of the higher. Men often, from infirmity of character, make their election for the nearer good, though they know it to be the less valuable; and this no less when the choice is between two bodily pleasures, than when it is between bodily and mental. They pursue sensual indulgences to the injury of health, though perfectly aware that health is the greater good. It may be further objected, that many who begin with youthful enthusiasm for everything noble, as they advance in years sink into indolence and selfishness. But I do not believe that those who undergo this very common change, voluntarily choose the lower description of pleasures in preference to the higher. I believe that before they devote themselves exclusively to the one, they have already become incapable of the other. Capacity for the nobler feelings is in most natures a very tender plant, easily killed, not only by hostile influences, but by mere want of sustenance; and in the majority of young persons it speedily dies away if the occupation to which their position in life has devoted them, and the society into which it has thrown them, are not favourable to keeping that higher capacity in exercise. Men lose their high aspirations as they lose their intellectual tastes, because they have not time or opportunity for indulging them; and they addict themselves to inferior pleasures, not because they deliberately prefer them, but because they are either the only ones to which they have access, or the only ones which they are any longer capable of enjoying. It may be questioned whether any one who has remained equally susceptible to both classes of pleasures, ever knowingly and calmly preferred the lower; though many, in all ages, have broken down in an ineffectual attempt to combine both.

From this verdict of the only competent judges, I apprehend there can be no appeal. On a question which is the best worth having of two pleasures, or which of two modes of existence is the most grateful to the feelings, apart from its moral attributes and from its consequences, the judgment of those who are qualified by knowledge of both, or, if they differ, that of the majority among them, must be admitted as final. And there needs be the less hesitation to accept this judgment respecting the quality of pleasures, since there is no other tribunal to be referred to even on the question of quantity. What means are there of determining which is the acutest of two pains, or the intensest of two pleasurable sensations, except the general suffrage of those who are familiar with both? Neither pains nor pleasures are homogeneous, and pain is always heterogeneous with pleasure. What is there to decide whether a particular pleasure is worth purchasing at the cost of a particular pain, except the feelings and judgment of the experienced? When, therefore, those feelings and judgment declare the pleasures derived from the higher faculties to be preferable *in kind*, apart from the question of intensity, to those of which the animal nature, disjoined from the higher faculties, is susceptible, they are entitled on this subject to the same regard.

I have dwelt on this point, as being a necessary part of a perfectly just conception of Utility or Happiness, considered as the directive rule of human conduct. But it is by no means an indispensable condition to the acceptance of the utilitarian stand; for that standard is not the agent's own greatest happiness, but the greatest amount of happiness altogether; and if it may possibly be doubted whether a noble character is always the happier for its nobleness, there can be no doubt that it makes other people happier, and that the world in general is immensely a gainer by it. Utilitarianism, therefore, could only attain its end by the general cultivation of nobleness of character, even if each individual were only benefited by the nobleness of others, and his own, so far as happiness is concerned, were a sheer deduction from the benefit. But the bare enunciation of such an absurdity as this last, renders refutation superfluous.

According to the Greatest Happiness Principle, as above explained, the ultimate end, with reference to and for the sake of which all other things are desirable (whether we are considering our own good or that of other people), is an existence exempt as far as possible from pain, and as rich as possible in enjoyments, both in point of quantity and quality; the test of quality, and the rule for measuring it against quantity, being the preference felt by those who in their opportunities of experience, to which must be added their habits of self-consciousness and self-observation, are best furnished with the means of comparison. This, being, according to the utilitarian opinion, the end of human action, is necessarily also the standard of morality; which may accordingly be defined, the rules and precepts for human conduct, by the observance of which an existence such as has been described might be, to the greatest extent possible, secured to all mankind; and not to them only, but, so far as the nature of things admits, to the whole sentient creation. . . .

I must again repeat, what the assailants of utilitarianism seldom have the justice to acknowledge, that the happiness which forms the utilitarian standard of what is right in conduct, is not the agent's own happiness, but that of all concerned. As between his own happiness and that of others, utilitarianism requires him to be as strictly impartial as a disinterested and benevolent spectator. In the golden rule of Jesus of Nazareth, we read the complete spirit of the ethics of utility. To do as you would be done by, and to love your neighbour as yourself, constitute the ideal perfection of utilitarian morality. As the means of making the nearest approach to this ideal, utility would enjoin, first, that laws and social arrangements should place the happiness, or (as speaking practically it may be called) the interest, of every individual, as nearly as possible in harmony with the interest of the whole; and secondly, that education and opinion, which have so vast a power over human character, should so use that power as to establish in the mind of every individual an indissoluble association between his own happiness and the good of the whole; especially between his own happiness and the practice of such modes of conduct, negative and positive, as regard for the universal happiness prescribes; so that not only he may be unable to conceive the possibility of happiness to himself, consistently with conduct opposed to the general good, but also that a direct impulse to promote the general good may be in every individual one of the habitual motives of action, and the sentiments connected therewith may fill a large and prominent place in every human being's sentient existence. If the impugners of the utilitarian morality represented it to their own minds in this its true character, I know not what recommendation possessed by any other morality they could possibly affirm to be wanting to it; what more beautiful or more exalted developments of human nature any other ethical system can be supposed to foster, or what springs of action, not accessible to the utilitarian, such systems rely on for giving effect to their mandates. . . .

Of What Sort of Proof the Principle of Utility is Susceptible

It has already been remarked, that questions of ultimate ends do not admit of proof, in the ordinary acceptation of the term. To be incapable of proof by reasoning is common to all first principles; to the first premises of our knowledge, as well as to those of our conduct. But the former, being matters of fact, may be the subject of a direct appeal to the faculties which judge of fact—namely, our senses, and our internal consciousness. Can an appeal be made to the same faculties on questions of practical ends? Or by what other faculty is cognizance taken of them?

Questions about ends, in other words, question what things are desirable. The utilitarian doctrine is, that happiness is desirable, and the only thing desirable, as an end; all other things being only desirable as means to that end. What ought to be required of this doctrine—what conditions is it requisite that the doctrine should fulfil—to make good its claim to be believed?

The only proof capable of being given that an object is visible, is that people actually see it. The only proof that a sound is audible, is that people hear it: and so of the other sources of our experience. In like manner, I apprehend, the sole evidence it is possible to produce that anything is desirable, is that people do actually desire it. If the end which the utilitarian doctrine proposes to itself were not, in theory and in practice, acknowledged to be an end, nothing could ever convince any person that it was so. No reason can be given why the general happiness is desirable, except that each person, so far as he believes it to be attainable, desires his own happiness. This, however, being a fact, we have not only all the proof which the case admits of, but all which it is possible to require, that happiness is a good: that each person's happiness is a good to that person, and the general happiness, therefore, a good to the aggregate of all persons. Happiness has made out its title as one of the ends of conduct, and consequently one of the criteria of morality.

But it has not, by this alone, proved itself to be the sole criterion. To do that, it would seem, by the same rule, necessary to show, not only that people desire happiness, but that they never desire anything else. Now it is palpable that they do desire things which, in common language, are decidedly distinguished from happiness. They desire, for example, virtue, and the absence of vice, no less really than pleasure and the absence of pain. The desire of virtue is not as universal, but it is as authentic a fact, as the desire of happiness. And hence the opponents of the utilitarian standard deem that they have a right to infer that there are other ends of human action besides happiness, and that happiness is not the standard of approbation and disapprobation.

But does the utilitarian doctrine deny that people desire virtue, or maintain that virtue is not a thing to be desired? The very reverse. It maintains not only that virtue is to be desired, but that it is to be desired disinterestedly, for itself. Whatever may be the opinion of utilitarian moralists as to the original conditions by which virtue is made virtue; however they may believe (as they do) that actions and dispositions are only virtuous because they promote another end than virtue; yet this being granted, and it having been decided, form considerations of this description, what *is* virtuous, they not only place virtue at the very head of the things which are good as means to the ultimate end, but they also recognise as a psychological fact that possibility of its being, to the individual, a good in itself, without looking to any end beyond it; and hold, that the mind is not in a right state, not in a state conformable to Utility, not in the state most conducive to the general happiness, unless it does love virtue in this manner—as a thing desirable in itself, even although, in the individual instance, it should not produce those other desirable consequences which it tends to produce, and on account of which it is held to be virtue. This opinion is not, in the smallest degree, a departure from the Happiness principle. The ingredients of happiness are very various, and each of them is desirable in itself, and not merely when considered as swelling an aggregate. The principle of utility does not mean that any given pleasure, as music, for instance, or any given exemption from pain, as for example health, is to be looked upon as means to a collective something termed happiness, and to be desired on that account. They are desired and desirable in and for themselves; besides being means, they are a part of the end. Virtue, according to the utilitarian doctrine, is not naturally and originally part of the end, but it is capable of becoming so; and in those who love it disinterestedly it has become so, and is desired and cherished, not as a means to happiness, but as a part of their happiness.

To illustrate this farther, we may remember that virtue is not the only thing, originally a means, and which if it were not a means to anything else, would be and remain indifferent, but which by association with what it is a means to, comes to be desired for itself, and that too with the utmost intensity. What, for example, shall we say of the love of money? There is nothing originally more desirable about money than about any heap of glittering pebbles. Its worth is solely that of the things which it will buy; the desires for other things than itself, which it is a means of gratifying. Yet the love of money is not only one of the strongest moving forces of human life, but money is, in many cases, desired in and for itself; the desire to possess it is often stronger than the desire to use it, and goes on increasing when all the desires which point to ends beyond it, to be compassed by it, are falling off. It may, then, be said truly, that money is desired not for the sake of an end, but as part of the end. From being a means to happiness, it has come to be itself a principal ingredient of the individual's conception of happiness. The same may be said of the majority of the great objects of human life—power, for example, or fame; except that to each of these there is a certain amount of immediate pleasure annexed, which has at least the semblance of being naturally inherent in them; a thing which cannot be said of money. Still, however, the strongest natural attraction, both of power and of fame, is the immense aid they give to the attainment of our other wishes; and it is the strong association thus generated between them and all our objects of desire, which gives to the direct desire of them the intensity it often assumes, so as in some characters to surpass in strength all other desires. In these cases the means have become a part of the end, and a more important part of it than any of the things which they are means to What was once desired as an instrument for the attainment of happiness, has come to be desired for its own sake. In being desired for its own sake it is, however, desired as *part* of happiness. The person is made, or thinks he would be made, happy by its mere possession; and is made unhappy by failure to obtain it. The desire of it is not a different thing from the desire of happiness, any more than the love of music, or the desire of health. They are included in happiness. They are some of the elements of which the desire of happiness is made up. Happiness is not an abstract idea, but a concrete whole; and these are some of its parts. And the utilitarian standard sanctions and approves their being so. Life would be a poor thing, very ill provided with sources of happiness, if there were not this provision of nature, by which things originally indifferent, but conducive to, or otherwise associated with, the satisfaction of our primitive desires, become in themselves sources of pleasure more valuable than the primitive pleasures, both in permanency, in the space of human existence that they are capable of covering, and even in intensity.

Virtue, according to the utilitarian conception, is a good of this description. There was no original desire of it, or motive to it, save its conduciveness to pleasure, and especially to protection from pain. But through the association thus formed, it may be felt a good in itself, and desired as such with as great intensity as any other good; and with this difference between it and the love of money, of power, or of fame, that all of these may, and often do, render the individual noxious to the other members of the society to which he belongs, whereas there is nothing which makes him so much a blessing to them as the cultivation of the disinterested love of virtue. And consequently, the utilitarian standard, while it tolerates and approves those other acquired desires, up to the point beyond which they would be more injurious to the general happiness than promotive of it, enjoins and requires the cultivation of the love of virtue up to the greatest strength possible, as being above all things important to the general happiness.

It results from the preceding considerations, that there is in reality nothing desired except happiness. Whatever is desired otherwise than as a means to some end beyond itself, and ultimately to happiness, is desired as itself a part of happiness, and is not desired for itself until it has become so. Those who desire virtue for its own sake, desire it either because the consciousness of it is a pleasure, or because the consciousness of being without it is a pain, or for both reasons united; as in truth the pleasure and pain seldom exist separately, but almost always together, the same person feeling pleasure in the degree of virtue attained, and pain in not having attained more. If one of these gave him no pleasure, and the other no pain, he would not love or desire virtue, or would desire it only for the other benefits which it might produce to himself or to persons whom he cared for . . . .

Review Questions

1. State and explain the Principle of Utility. Show how it could be used to justify actions that are conventionally viewed as wrong, such as lying and stealing.
2. How does Mill reply to the objection that Epicureanism is a doctrine only worthy of swine?
3. How does Mill distinguish between higher and lower pleasures?
4. According to Mill, whose happiness must be considered?
5. Carefully reconstruct Mill's proof of the Principle of Utility.

Discussion Questions

1. Is happiness nothing more than pleasure, and the absence of pain? What do you think?
2. Does Mill convince you that the so-called higher pleasures are better than the lower ones? What about the person of experience who prefers the lower pleasures over the higher ones?
3. Mill says, "In the golden rule of Jesus of Nazareth, we read the complete spirit of the ethics of utility." Is this true or not?
4. Many commentators have thought that Mill's proof of the Principle of Utility is defective. Do you agree? If so, then what mistake or mistakes does he make? Is there any way to reformulate the proof so that it is not defective?

James Rachels

The Debate over Utilitarianism

James Rachels is University Professor of Philosophy at the University of Alabama of Birmingham. He is the author of The End of Life: Euthanasia and Morality *(1986) and articles on the right to privacy, reverse discrimination, and the treatment of nonhuman animals. The reading is taken from his textbook* The Elements of Moral Philosophy *(1986).*

Rachels presents the main objections to utilitarianism and the replies given by defenders of utilitarianism. His own view is that utilitarianism is correct in telling us to consider the consequences of actions, and in advising us to be impartial, but incorrect in ignoring other important moral considerations such as merit.

From *The Elements of Moral Philosophy*, James Rachels, 1986, McGraw-Hill Publishing Company. Reprinted by permission of McGraw-Hill.

> *The utilitarian doctrine is that happiness is desirable, and the only thing desirable, as an end; all other things being desirable as means to that end.*
>
> *John Stuart Mill,* Utilitarianism *(1861)*

> *Man does not strive after happiness; only the Englishman does that.*
>
> *Friedrich Nietzsch,* Twilight of the Idols *(1889)*

The Resilience of the Theory

Classical Utilitarianism—the theory defended by Bentham and Mill—can be summarized in three propositions:

First, actions are to be judged right or wrong solely in virtue of their consequences. Nothing else matters. Right actions are, simply, those that have the best consequences.

Second, in assessing consequences, the only thing that matters is the amount of happiness or unhappiness that is caused. Everything else is irrelevant. Thus right actions are those that produce the greatest balance of happiness over unhappiness.

Third, in calculating the happiness or unhappiness that will be caused, no one's happiness is to be counted as more important than anyone else's. Each person's welfare is equally important. As Mill put it in his *Utilitarianism,*

> the happiness which forms the utilitarian standard of what is right in conduct, is not the agent's own happiness, but that of all concerned. As between his own happiness and that of others, utilitarianism requires him to be as strictly impartial as a disinterested and benevolent spectator.

Thus right actions are those that produce the greatest possible balance of happiness over unhappiness, with each person's happiness counted as equally important.

The appeal of this theory to philosophers, economists, and others who theorize about human decision making has been enormous. The theory continues to be widely accepted, even though it has been challenged by a number of apparently devastating arguments. These antiutilitarian arguments are so numerous, and so persuasive, that many have concluded the theory must be abandoned. But the remarkable thing is that so many have *not* abandoned it. Despite the arguments, a great many thinkers refuse to let the theory go. According to these contemporary utilitarians, the antiutilitarian arguments show only that the classical theory needs to be *modified;* they say the basic idea is correct and should be preserved, but recast into a more satisfactory form.

In what follows, we will examine some of these arguments against Utilitarianism, and consider whether the classical version of the theory may be revised satisfactorily to meet them. These arguments are of interest not only for the assessment of Utilitarianism but for their own sakes, as they raise some additional fundamental issues of moral philosophy.

Is Happiness the Only Thing That Matters?

The question *What things are good?* is different from the question *What actions are right?* and Utilitarianism answers the second question by referring back to the first one. Right actions, it says, are the ones that produce the most good. But what is good? The classical utilitarian reply is: one thing, and one thing only, namely happiness. As Mill put it, "The utilitarian doctrine is that happiness is desirable, and the only thing desirable, as an end; all other things being desirable as means to that end."

The idea that happiness is the one ultimate good (and unhappiness the one ultimate evil) is known as **Hedonism.** Hedonism is a perennially popular theory that goes back at least as far as the ancient Greeks. It has always been an attractive theory because of its beautiful simplicity, and because it expresses the intuitively plausible notion that things are good or bad only on account of the way they make us *feel.* Yet a little reflection reveals serious flaws in the theory. The flaws stand out when we consider examples like these:

1. A promising young pianist's hands are injured in an automobile accident so that she can no longer play. Why is this a bad thing for her? Hedonism would say it is bad because it causes her unhappiness. She will feel frustrated and upset whenever she thinks of what might have been, and *that* is her misfortune. But this way of explaining the misfortune seems to get things the wrong way around. It is not as though, by feeling unhappy, she has made an otherwise neutral situation into a bad one. On the contrary, her unhappiness is a rational response to a situation that *is* unfortunate. She could have had a career as a concert pianist, and now she cannot. *That* is the tragedy. We could not eliminate the tragedy just by getting her to cheer up.
2. You think someone is your friend, but really he ridicules you behind your back. No one ever tells you, so you never know. Is this situation unfortunate for you? Hedonism would have to say no, because you are never

caused any unhappiness by the situation. Yet we do feel that there is something bad going on here. You *think* he is your friend, and you are "being made a fool," even though you are not aware of it and so suffer no unhappiness.

Both these examples make the same basic point. We value all sorts of things, including artistic creativity and friendship, for their own sakes. It makes us happy to have them, but only because we *already* think them good. (We do not think them good *because* they make us happy—this is what I meant when I said that Hedonism "gets things the wrong way around.") Therefore we think it a misfortune to lose them, independently of whether or not the loss is accompanied by unhappiness.

In this way, Hedonism misunderstands the nature of happiness. Happiness is not something that is recognized as good and sought for its own sake, with other things appreciated only as means of bringing it about. Instead, happiness is a response we have to the attainment of things that we recognize *as* goods, independently and in their own right. We think that friendship is a good thing, and so having friends makes us happy. That is very different from first setting out after happiness, then deciding that having friends might make us happy, and then seeking friends as a means to this end.

Today, most philosophers recognize the truth of this. There are not many contemporary hedonists. Those sympathetic to Utilitarianism have therefore sought a way to formulate their view without assuming a hedonistic account of good and evil. Some, such as the English philosopher G. E. Moore (1873–1958), have tried to compile short lists of things to be regarded as good in themselves. Moore suggested that there are three obvious **intrinsic goods**—pleasure, friendship, and aesthetic enjoyment—and that right actions are those that increase the world's supply of such things. Other utilitarians have tried to bypass the question of how many things are good in themselves, leaving it an open question and saying only that right actions are the ones that have the best results, *however* goodness is measured. (This is sometimes called **Ideal Utilitarianism.**) Still others try to bypass the question in another way, holding only that we should act so as to maximize the satisfaction of people's *preferences*. (This is called **Preference Utilitarianism.**) It is beyond the scope of this book to discuss the merits or demerits of these varieties of Utilitarianism. I mention them only in order to note that although the hedonistic assumption of the classical utilitarians has largely been rejected, contemporary utilitarians have not found it difficult to carry on. They do so by urging that Hedonism was never a necessary part of the theory in the first place.

ARE CONSEQUENCES ALL THAT MATTER?

The claim that only consequences matter *is*, however, a necessary part of Utilitarianism. The most fundamental idea underlying the theory is that in order to determine whether an action would be right, we should look at *what will happen as a result of doing it*. If it were to turn out that some *other* matter is also important in determining rightness, then Utilitarianism would be undermined at its very foundation.

The most serious antiutilitarian arguments attack the theory at just this point: they urge that various other considerations, in addition to utility, are important in determining whether actions are right. We will look briefly at three such arguments.

1. *Justice*. Writing in the academic journal *Inquiry* in 1965, H. J. McCloskey asks us to consider the following case:

> Suppose a utilitarian were visiting an area in which three was racial strife, and that, during his visit, a Negro rapes a white woman, and that race riots occur as a result of the crime, white mobs, with the connivance of the police, bashing and killing Negroes, etc. Suppose too that our utilitarian is in the area of the crime when it is committed such that his testimony would bring about the conviction of a particular Negro. If he knows that a quick arrest will stop the riots and lynchings, surely, as a utilitarian, he must conclude that he has a duty to bear false witness in order to bring about the punishment of an innocent person.

This is a fictitious example, but that makes no difference. The argument is only that *if* someone were in this position, then on utilitarian grounds he should bear false witness against the innocent person. This might have some bad consequences—the innocent man might be executed—but there would be enough good consequences to outweigh them: the riots and lynchings would be stopped. The best consequences would be achieved by lying; therefore, according to Utilitarianism, lying is the thing to do. But, the argument continues, it would be wrong to bring about the execution of the innocent man. Therefore, Utilitarianism, which implies it would be right, must be incorrect.

According to the critics of Utilitarianism, this argument illustrates one of the theory's most serious shortcomings: namely, that it is incompatible with the ideal of justice. Justice requires that we treat people fairly, according to their individual needs and merits. The innocent man has done nothing wrong; he did not commit the rape and so he does not deserve to be punished for it. Therefore, punishing him would be unjust. The example illustrates how the demands of justice and the demands of utility can come into conflict, and so a theory that says utility is the *whole* story cannot be right.

2. *Rights.* Here is a case that is *not* fictitious; it is from the records of the U.S. Court of Appeals, Ninth Circuit (Southern District of California), 1963, in the case of *York v. Story:*

> In October, 1958, appellant [Ms. Angelynn York] went to the police department of Chino for the purpose of filing charges in connection with an assault upon her. Appellee Ron Story, an officer of that police department, then acting under color of his authority as such, advised appellant that it was necessary to take photographs of her. Story then took appellant to a room in the police station, locked the door, and directed her to undress, which she did. Story then directed appellant to assume various indecent positions, and photographed her in those positions. These photographs were not made for any lawful purpose.
>
> Appellant objected to undressing. She stated to Story that there was no need to take photographs of her in the nude, or in the positions she was directed to take, because the bruises would not show in any photograph. . . .
>
> Later that month, Story advised appellant that the pictures did not come out and that he had destroyed them. Instead, Story circulated these photographs among the personnel of the Chino police department. In April, 1960, two other officers of that police department, appellee Louis Moreno and defendant Henry Grote, acting under color of their authority as such, and using police photographic equipment located at the police station made additional prints of the photographs taken by Story. Moreno and Grote then circulated these prints among the personnel of the Chino police department. . . .

Ms. York brought suit against these officers and won. Her *legal* rights had clearly been violated. But what of the *morality* of the officers' behavior?

Utilitarianism says that actions are defensible if they produce a favorable balance of happiness over unhappiness. This suggests that we consider the amount of unhappiness caused to Ms. York and compare it with the amount of pleasure taken in the photographs by Officer Story and his cohorts. It is at least possible that more happiness than unhappiness was caused. In that case, the utilitarian conclusion apparently would be that their actions were morally all right. But this seems to be a perverse way to approach the case. Why should the pleasure afforded Story and his cohorts matter at all? Why should it even count? They had no right to treat Ms. York in that way, and the fact that they enjoyed doing so hardly seems a relevant defense.

To make the point even clearer, consider an (imaginary) related case. Suppose a Peeping Tom spied on Ms. York by peering through her bedroom window, and secretly took pictures of her undressed. Further suppose that he did this without ever being detected and that he used the photographs entirely for his own amusement, without showing them to anyone. Now under these circumstances, it seems clear that the *only* consequence of his action is an increase in his own happiness. No one else, including Ms. York, is caused any unhappiness at all. How, then, could Utilitarianism deny that the Peeping Tom's actions are right? But it is evident to moral common sense that they are not right. Thus, Utilitarianism appears to be an incorrect moral view.

The moral to be drawn from this argument is that Utilitarianism is at odds with the idea that people have *rights* that may not be trampled on merely because one anticipates good results. This is an extremely important notion, which explains why a great many philosophers have rejected Utilitarianism. In the above cases, it is Ms. York's right to privacy that is violated; but it would not be difficult to think of similar cases in which other rights are at issue—the right to freedom of religion, to free speech, or even the right to life itself. It may happen that good purposes are served, from time to time, by ignoring these rights. But we do not think that our rights *should* be set aside so easily. The notion of a personal right is not a utilitarian notion. Quite the reverse: it is a notion that places limits on how an individual may be treated, regardless of the good purposes that might be accomplished.

3. *Backward—Looking Reasons.* Suppose you have promised someone you will do something—say, you promised to meet him downtown this afternoon. But when the time comes to go, you don't want to do it—you need to do some work and would rather stay home. What should you do? Suppose you judge that the utility of getting your work accomplished slightly outweighs the inconvenience your friend would be caused. Appealing to the utilitarian standard, you might then conclude that it is right to stay home. However, this does not seem correct. The fact that *you promised* imposes an obligation on you that you cannot escape so easily. Of course, if the consequences of not breaking the promise were *great*—if, for example, your mother had just been stricken with a heart attack and you had to rush her to the hospital—you would be justified in breaking it. But a *small* gain in utility cannot overcome the obligation imposed by the fact that you promised. Thus Utilitarianism, which says that consequences are the only things that matter, seems mistaken.

There is an important general lesson to be learned from this argument. Why is Utilitarianism vulnerable to this sort of criticism? It is because the only kinds of considerations that the theory holds relevant to determining the rightness of actions are considerations having to do with the *future*. Because of its exclusive concern with consequences, Utilitarianism has us confine our attention to what *will happen* as a result of our actions. However, we normally think that considerations about the *past* also have some importance. The fact that you promised your friend to meet him is a fact about the past, not the future. Therefore, the general point to be made about Utilitarianism is that it seems to be an inadequate moral theory because it excludes what we might call backward-looking considerations.

Once we understand this point, other examples of backward-looking considerations come easily to mind. The fact that someone did not commit a crime is a good reason why he should not be punished. The fact that someone once did you a favor may be a good reason why you should now do him a favor. The fact that you did something to hurt someone may be a reason why you should now make it up to her. These are all facts about the past that are relevant to determining our obligations. But Utilitarianism makes the past irrelevant, and so it seems deficient for just that reason.

The Defense of Utilitarianism

Taken together, the above arguments form an impressive indictment of Utilitarianism. The theory, which at first seemed so progressive and commonsensical, now seems indefensible: it is at odds with such fundamental moral notions as justice and individual rights, and seems unable to account for the place of backward-looking reasons in justifying conduct. The combined weight of these arguments has prompted many philosophers to abandon the theory altogether.

Many thinkers, however, continue to believe that Utilitarianism, in some form, is true. In reply to the arguments, three general defenses have been offered.

The First Line of Defense

The first line of defense is to point out that the examples used in the antiutilitarian arguments are unrealistic and do not describe situations that come up in the real world. Since Utilitarianism is designed as a guide for decision making in the situations we actually face, the fanciful examples are dismissed as irrelevant. . . .

The Second Line of Defense

The first line of defense contains more bluster than substance While it can plausibly be maintained that *most* acts of false witness and the like have bad consequences in the real world, it cannot reasonably be asserted that *all* such acts have bad consequences. Surely, in at least some real-life cases, one can bring about good results by doing things that moral common sense condemns. Therefore, in at least some real-life cases Utilitarianism will come into conflict with common sense. Moreover, even if the antiutilitarian arguments had to rely exclusively on fictitious examples, those arguments would nevertheless retain their power; for showing that Utilitarianism has unacceptable consequences in hypothetical cases is a perfectly valid way of pointing up its theoretical defects. The first line of defense, then, is weak.

The second line of defense admits all this and proposes to save Utilitarianism by giving it a new formulation. In revising a theory to meet criticism, the trick is to identify precisely the feature of the theory that is causing the trouble and to change *that,* leaving the rest of the theory undisturbed as much as possible.

The troublesome aspect of the theory was this: the classical version of Utilitarianism implied that *each individual action* is to be evaluated by reference to its own particular consequences. If on a certain occasion you are tempted to lie, whether it would be wrong is determined by the consequences of *that particular lie.* This, the theory's defenders said, is the point that causes all the trouble; even though we know that *in general* lying has bad consequences, it is obvious that sometimes particular acts of lying can have good consequences.

Therefore, the new version of Utilitarianism modifies the theory so that individual actions will no longer be judged by the Principle of Utility. Instead, *rules* will be established by reference to the principle, and individual acts will then be judged right or wrong by reference to the rules. This new version of the theory is called *Rule–Utilitarianism,* to contrast it with the original theory, now commonly called *Act–Utilitarianism.*

Rule–Utilitarianism has no difficulty coping with the three antiutilitarian arguments. An act-utilitarian, faced with the situation described by McCloskey, would be tempted to bear false witness against the innocent man because the consequences of *that particular act* would be good. But the rule-utilitarian would not reason in that way. He would first ask, "What *general rules of conduct* tend to promote the greatest happiness?" Suppose we imagine two societies, one in which the rule "Don't bear false witness against the innocent" is faithfully adhered to, and one in which this rule is not followed. In which society are people likely to be better off? Clearly, from the point of view of utility, the first society is preferable. Therefore, the rule against incriminating the innocent should be accepted, and *by appealing to this rule,* the rule-utilitarian concludes that the person in McCloskey's example should not testify against the innocent man.

Analogous arguments can be used to establish rules against violating people's rights, breaking promises, lying, and so on. We should accept such rules because following them, as a regular practice, promotes the general welfare. But once having appealed to the Principle of Utility to establish the rules, we do not have to invoke the principle again to determine the rightness of particular actions. Individual actions are justified simply by appeal to the already-established rules.

Thus Rule–Utilitarianism cannot be convicted of violating our moral common sense, or of conflicting with ordinary ideas of justice, personal rights, and the rest. In shifting emphasis from the justification of acts to the justification of rules, the theory has been brought into line with our intuitive judgments to a remarkable degree.

The Third Line of Defense

Finally, a small group of contemporary utilitarians has had a very different response to the antiutilitarian arguments. Those arguments point out that the classical theory is at odds with ordinary notions of justice, individual rights, and so on; to this, their response is, essentially, "So what?" In 1961 the Australian philosopher J. J. C. Smart published a monograph entitled *An Outline of a System of Utilitarian Ethics;* reflecting on his position in that book, Smart said:

> Admittedly utilitarianism does have consequences which are incompatible with the common moral consciousness, but I tended to take the view "so much the worse for the common moral consciousness." That is, I was inclined to reject the common methodology of testing general ethical principles by seeing how they square with our feelings in particular instances.

Our moral common sense is, after all, not necessarily reliable. It may incorporate various irrational elements, including prejudices absorbed from our parents, our religion, and the general culture. Why should we simply assume that our feelings are always correct? And why should we reject a plausible, rational theory of ethics such as Utilitarianism simply because it conflicts with those feelings? Perhaps it is the feelings, not the theory, that should be discarded.

In light of this, consider again McCloskey's example of the person tempted to bear false witness. McCloskey argues that it would be wrong to have a man convicted of a crime he did not commit, because it would be unjust. But wait: such a judgment serves *that man's* interests well enough, but what of the *other* innocent people who will be hurt if the rioting and lynchings are allowed to continue? What of them? Surely we might hope that we never have to face a situation like this, for the options are all extremely distasteful. But if we *must* choose between (a) securing the conviction of one innocent person and (b) allowing the deaths of several innocent people, is it so unreasonable to think that the first option, bad as it is, is preferable to the second?

On this way of thinking, Act–Utilitarianism is a perfectly defensible doctrine and does not need to be modified. Rule–Utilitarianism, by contrast, is an unnecessarily watered-down version of the theory, which gives rules a greater importance than they merit. Act–Utilitarianism is, however, recognized to be a radical doctrine which implies that many of our ordinary moral feelings may be mistaken. In this respect, it does what good philosophy always does—it challenges us to rethink matters that we have heretofore taken for granted.

What is Correct and What is Incorrect in Utilitarianism

There is a sense in which no moral philosopher can completely reject Utilitarianism. The consequences of one's actions—whether they promote happiness, or cause misery—must be admitted by all to be extremely important. John Stuart Mill once remarked that, insofar as we are benevolent, we must accept the utilitarian standard; and he was surely right. Moreover, the utilitarian emphasis on impartiality must also be a part of any defensible moral theory. The question is whether these are the *only* kinds of considerations an adequate theory must acknowledge. Aren't there *other* considerations that are also important?

If we consult what Smart calls our "common moral consciousness," it seems that there are *many* other considerations that are morally important. (In section 8.3 above, we looked at a few examples.) But I believe the radical act-utilitarians are right to warn us that "common sense" cannot be trusted. Many people once felt that there is an important difference between whites and blacks, so that the interests of whites are somehow more important. Trusting the "common sense" of their day, they might have insisted that an adequate moral theory should accommodate this "fact." Today, no one worth listening to would say such a thing. But who knows how many *other* irrational prejudices are still a part of our moral common sense? At the end of his classic study of race relations, *An American Dilemma* (1944), the Swedish sociologist Gunnar Myrdal reminds us:

> There must be still other countless errors of the same sort that no living man can yet detect, because of the fog within which our type of Western culture envelops us. Cultural influences have set up the assumptions about the mind, the body, and the universe

with which we begin; pose the questions we ask; influence the facts we seek; determine the interpretation we give these facts; and direct our reaction to these interpretations and conclusions.

The strength of Utilitarianism is that it firmly resists "corruption" by possibly irrational elements. By sticking to the Principle of Utility as the *only* standard for judging right and wrong, it avoids all danger of incorporating into moral theory prejudices, feelings, and "intuitions" that have no rational basis.

The warning should be heeded. "Common sense" can, indeed, mislead us. At the same time, however, there might be at least some nonutilitarian considerations that an adequate theory *should* accept, because there *is* a rational basis for them. Consider, for example, the matter of what people deserve. A person who has worked hard in her job may deserve a promotion more than someone who has loafed, and it would be unjust for the loafer to be promoted first. This is a point that we would expect any fair-minded employer to acknowledge; we would all be indignant if we were passed over for promotion in favor of someone who had not worked as hard or as well as we. Now utilitarians might agree with this, and say that it can be explained by their theory—they might argue that it promotes the general welfare to encourage hard work by rewarding it. But this does not seem to be an adequate explanation of the importance of desert. The woman who worked harder has a superior claim to the promotion, *not* because it promotes the general welfare for her to get it, but *because she has earned it*. The reason she should be promoted has to do with *her* merits. This does not appear to be the kind of consideration a utilitarian could admit.

Does this way of thinking express a mere prejudice, or does it have a rational basis? I believe it has a rational basis, although it is not one that utilitarians could accept. We ought to recognize individual desert as a reason for treating people in certain ways—for example, as a reason for promoting the woman who has worked harder—because that is the principal way we have of treating individuals as autonomous, responsible beings. If in fact people have the power to choose their own actions, in such a way that they are *responsible* for those actions and what results from them, then acknowledging their deserts is just a way of acknowledging their standing as autonomous individuals. In treating them as they deserve to be treated, we are responding to the way they have freely chosen to behave. Thus in some instances we will not treat everyone alike, because people are not just members of an undifferentiated crowd. Instead, they are individuals who, by their own choices, show themselves to deserve different kinds of responses. . . .

Review Questions

1. Rachels says that classical utilitarianism can be summed up in three propositions. What are they?
2. Explain the problem with hedonism. How do defenders of utilitarianism respond to this problem?
3. What are the objections about justice, rights, and promises?
4. Distinguish between Rule- and Act-Utilitarianism. How does Rule-Utilitarianism reply to the objections?
5. What is the third line of defense?

Discussion Questions

1. Smart's defense of utilitarianism is to reject common moral beliefs when they conflict with utilitarianism. Is this acceptable to you or not? Explain your answer.
2. A utilitarian is supposed to give moral consideration to all concerned. Who must be considered? What about nonhuman animals? How about lakes and streams?
3. Rachels claims that merit should be given moral consideration independent of utility. Do you agree?

Immanuel Kant

The Categorical Imperative

Immanuel Kant (1724–1804), a German, was one of the most important philosophers of all time. He made significant contributions to all areas of philosophy. He wrote many books; the most important ones are Critique of Pure Reason, Prolegomena to All Future Metaphysics, Critique of Practical Reason, Critique of Judgment, and The Foundations of the Metaphysics of Morals, *from which the reading is taken.*

Kant believes that our moral duty can be formulated in one supreme rule, the Categorical Imperative, from which all our duties can be derived. Although he says that there is just one rule, he gives different versions of it, and two of them seem to be distinct. He arrives at the supreme rule or rules by considering the nature of the good will and duty.

THE GOOD WILL

It is impossible to conceive anything at all in the world, or even out of it, which can be taken as good without qualification, except a *good will.* Intelligence, wit, judgment, and any other *talents* of the mind we may care to name, or courage, resolution, and constancy of purpose, as qualities of *temperament,* are without doubt good and desirable in many respects; but they can also be extremely bad and hurtful when the will is not good which has to make use of these gifts of nature, and which for this reason has the term *'character'* applied to its peculiar quality. It is exactly the same with *gifts of fortune.* Power, wealth, honour, even health and that complete well-being and contentment with one's state which goes by the name of *'happiness'*, produce boldness, and as a consequence often over-boldness as well, unless a good will is present by which their influence on the mind—and so too the whole principle of action—may be corrected and adjusted to universal ends; not to mention that a rational and impartial spectator can never feel approval in contemplating the uninterrupted prosperity of a being graced by no touch of a pure and good will, and that consequently a good will seems to constitute the indispensable condition of our very worthiness to be happy.

Some qualities are even helpful to this good will itself and can make its task very much easier. They have none the less no inner unconditioned worth, but rather presuppose a good will which sets a limit to the esteem in which they are rightly held and does not permit us to regard them as absolutely good. Moderation in affections and passions, self-control, and sober reflexion are not only good in many respects: they may even seem to constitute part of the *inner* worth of a person. Yet they are far from being properly described as good without qualification (however unconditionally they have been commended by the ancients). For without the principles of a good will they may become exceedingly bad; and the very coolness of a scoundrel makes him, not merely more dangerous, but also immediately more abominable in our eyes than we should have taken him to be without it.

THE GOOD WILL AND ITS RESULTS

A good will is not good because of what it effects or accomplishes—because of its fitness for attaining some proposed end: it is good through its willing alone—that is, good in itself. Considered in itself it is to be esteemed beyond comparison as far higher than anything it could ever bring about merely in order to favour some in-

From *The Moral Law: Kant's Groundwork of the Metaphysic of Morals,* trans. H. J. Paton (New York, NY: Barnes & Noble, Inc., 1948).

clination or, if you like, the sum total of inclinations. Even if, by some special disfavour of destiny or by the niggardly endowment of stepmotherly nature, this will is entirely lacking in power to carry out its intentions; if by its utmost effort it still accomplishes nothing, and only good will is left (not, admittedly, as a mere wish, but as the straining of every means so far as they are in our control); even then it would still shine like a jewel for its own sake as something which has its full value in itself. Its usefulness or fruitlessness can neither add to, nor subtract from, this value. Its usefulness would be merely, as it were, the setting which enables us to handle it better in our ordinary dealings or to attract the attention of those not yet sufficiently expert, but not to commend it to experts or to determine its value. . . .

The Good Will and Duty

We have now to elucidate the concept of a will estimable in itself and good apart from any further end. This concept, which is already present in a sound natural understanding and requires not so much to be taught as merely to be clarified, always holds the highest place in estimating the total worth of our actions and constitutes the condition of all the rest. We will therefore take up the concept of *duty,* which includes that of a good will, exposed, however, to certain subjective limitations and obstacles. These, so far from hiding a good will or disguising it, rather bring it out by contrast and make it shine forth more brightly.

The Motive of Duty

I will here pass over all actions already recognized as contrary to duty, however useful they may be with a view to this or that end; for about these the question does not even arise whether they could have been done *for the sake of duty* inasmuch as they are directly opposed to it. I will also set aside actions which in fact accord with duty, yet for which men have *no immediate inclination,* but perform them because impelled to do so by some other inclination. For there it is easy to decide whether the action which accords with duty has been done *from duty* or from some purpose of self-interest. This distinction is far more difficult to perceive when the action accords with duty and the subject has in addition an *immediate* inclination to the action. For example, it certainly accords with duty that a grocer should not overcharge his inexperienced customer; and where there is much competition a sensible shopkeeper refrains from so doing and keeps to a fixed and general price for everybody so that a child can buy from him just as well as anyone else. Thus people are served *honestly*; but this is not nearly enough to justify us in believing that the shopkeeper has acted in this way from duty or from principles of fair dealing; his interests required him to do so. We cannot assume him to have in addition an immediate inclination towards his customers, leading him, as it were out of love, to give no man preference over another in the matter of price. Thus the action was done neither from duty nor from immediate inclination, but solely from purposes of self-interest.

On the other hand, to preserve one's life is a duty, and besides this every one has also an immediate inclination to do so. But on account of this the often anxious precautions taken by the greater part of mankind for this purpose have no inner worth, and the maxim of their action is without moral content. They do protect their lives *in conformity with duty,* but not *from the motive of duty.* When on the contrary, disappointments and hopeless misery have quite taken away the taste for life; when a wretched man, strong in soul and more angered at his fate than faint-hearted or cast down, longs for death and still preserves his life without loving it—not from inclination or fear but from duty; then indeed his maxim has a moral content.

To help others where one can is a duty, and besides this there are many spirits of so sympathetic a temper that, without any further motive of vanity or self-interest, they find an inner pleasure in spreading happiness around them and can take delight in the contentment of others as their own work. Yet I maintain that in such a case an action of this kind, however right and however amiable it may be, has still no genuinely moral worth. It stands on the same footing as other inclinations—for example, the inclination for honour, which if fortunate enough to hit on something beneficial and right and consequently honourable, deserves praise and encouragement, but not esteem; for its maxim lacks moral content, namely, the performance of such actions, not from inclination, but *from duty*. Suppose then that the mind of this friend of man were overclouded by sorrows of his own which extinguished all sympathy with the fate of others, but that he still had power to help those in distress, though no longer stirred by the need of others because sufficiently occupied with his own; and suppose that, when no longer moved by any inclination, he tears himself out of this deadly insensibility and does the action without any inclination for the sake of duty alone; then for the first time his action has its genuine moral worth. Still further: if nature had implanted little sympathy in this or that man's heart; if (being in other respects an honest fellow) he were cold in temperament and indifferent to the sufferings of others—perhaps because, being endowed with the special gift of patience and robust endurance in his own sufferings, he assumed the like in others or even demanded it; if such a man (who would in truth not be the worth product of nature) were not exactly fashioned by her to be a philanthropist, would he not still find in himself a source from which he might draw a worth far higher than any that a good-natured temperament can have? Assuredly he would. It is precisely in this that the worth of character begins to show—a moral worth and beyond all comparison the highest—namely, that he does good, not from inclination, but from duty. . . .

Thus the moral worth of an action does not depend on the result expected from it, and so too does not depend on any principle of action that needs to borrow its motive from this expected result. For all these results (agreeable states and even the promotion of happiness in others) could have been brought about by other causes as well, and consequently their production did not require the will of a rational being, in which, however, the highest and unconditioned good can alone be found. Therefore nothing but the *idea of the law* in itself, *which admittedly is present only in a rational being*—so far as it, and not an expected result, is the ground determining the will—can constitute that preeminent good which we call moral, a good which is already present in the person acting on this idea and has not to be awaited merely from the result.

The Categorical Imperative

But what kind of law can this be the thought of which, even without regard to the results expected from it, has to determine the will if this is to be called good absolutely and without qualification? Since I have robbed the will of every inducement that might arise for it as a consequence of obeying any particular law, nothing is left but the conformity of actions to universal law as such, and this alone must serve the will as its principle. That is to say, I ought never to act except in such a way *that I can also will that my maxim should become a universal law*. Here bare conformity to universal law as such (without having as its base any law prescribing particular actions) is what serves the will as its principle, and must so serve it if duty is not to be everywhere an empty delusion and a chimerical concept. The ordinary reason of mankind also agrees with this completely in its practical judgements and always has the aforesaid principle before its eyes. . . .

When I conceive a *hypothetical imperative* in general, I do not know beforehand what it will contain—until its condition is given. But if I conceive a *categorical imperative*, I know at once what it contains. For since besides the law this imperative contains only the necessity that our maxim[1] should conform to this law, while the law, as we have seen, contains no condition to limit it, there remains nothing over to which the maxim has to conform except the universality of a law as such; and it is this conformity alone that the imperative properly asserts to be necessary.

There is therefore only a single categorical imperative and it is this: '*Act only on that maxim through which you can at the same time will that it should become a universal law*'.

Now if all imperatives of duty can be derived from this one imperative as their principle, then even although we leave it unsettled whether what we call duty may not be an empty concept, we shall still be able to show at least what we understand by it and what the concept means. . . .

ILLUSTRATIONS

We will now enumerate a few duties, following their customary division into duties towards self and duties towards others and into perfect and imperfect duties.[2]

1. A man feels sick of life as the result of a series of misfortunes that has mounted to the point of despair, but he is still so far in possession of his reason as to ask himself whether taking his own life may not be contrary to his duty to himself. He now applies the test 'Can the maxim of my action really become a universal law of nature?' His maxim is 'From self-love I make it my principle to shorten my life if its continuance threatens more evil than it promises pleasure'. The only further question to ask is whether this principle of self-love can become a universal law of nature. It is then seen at once that a system of nature by whose law the very same feeling whose function (*Bestimmung*) is to stimulate the furtherance of life should actually destroy life would contradict itself and consequently could not subsist as a system of nature. Hence this maxim cannot possibly hold as a universal law of nature and is therefore entirely opposed to the supreme principle of all duty.

2. Another finds himself driven to borrowing money because of need. He well knows that he will not be able to pay it back; but he sees too that he will get no loan unless he gives a firm promise to pay it back within a fixed time. He is inclined to make such a promise; but he has still enough conscience to ask 'Is it not unlawful and contrary to duty to get out of difficulties in this way?' Supposing, however, he did resolve to do so, the maxim of his action would run thus: 'Whenever I believe myself short of money, I will borrow money and promise to pay it back, though I know that this will never be done'. Now this principle of self-love or personal advantage is perhaps quite compatible with my own entire future welfare; only there remains the question 'Is it right?' I therefore transform the demand of self-love into a universal law and frame my question thus: 'How would things stand if my maxim became a universal law?' I then see straight away that this maxim can never rank as a universal law of nature and be self-consistent, but must necessarily contradict itself. For the universality of a law that every one believing himself to be in need can make any promise he pleases with the intention not to keep it would make promising, and the very purpose of promising, itself impossible, since no one would believe he was being promised anything, but would laugh at utterances of this kind as empty shams.

3. A third finds in himself a talent whose cultivation would make him a useful man for all sorts of purposes. But he sees himself in comfortable circumstances, and he prefers to give himself up to pleasure rather than to bother about increasing and improving his fortunate natural aptitudes. Yet he asks himself further 'Does my maxim of neglecting my natural gifts, besides agreeing in itself with my tendency to indulgence, agree also with what is called duty?' He then sees that a system of nature could indeed always subsist under such a universal law, although (like the South Sea Islanders) every man should let his talents rust and should be bent on devoting his life solely to idleness, indulgence, procreation, and, in a word, to enjoyment. Only he cannot possibly *will* that this should become a universal law of nature or should be implanted in us as such a law by a natural instinct. For as a rational being he necessarily wills that all his powers should be developed, since they serve him, and are given him, for all sorts of possible ends.

4. Yet a *fourth* is himself flourishing, but he sees others who have to struggle with great hardships (and whom he could easily help); and he thinks 'What does it matter to me? Let every one be as happy as Heaven wills or as he can make himself; I won't deprive him of anything; I won't even envy him; only I have no wish to contribute anything to his well-being or to his support in distress!' Now admittedly if such an attitude were a universal law of nature, mankind could get on perfectly well—better no doubt than if everybody prates about sympathy and

goodwill, and even takes pains, on occasion, to practise them, but on the other hand cheats where he can, traffics in human rights, or violates them in other ways. But although it is possible that a universal law of nature could subsist in harmony with this maxim, yet it is impossible to *will* that such a principle should hold everywhere as a law of nature. For a will which decided in this way would be in conflict with itself, since many a situation might arise in which the man needed love and sympathy from others, and in which, by such a law of nature sprung from his own will, he would rob himself of all hope of the help he wants for himself. . . .

The Formula of the End in Itself

The will is conceived as a power of determining oneself to action *in accordance with the idea of certain laws*. And such a power can be found only in rational beings. Now what serves the will as a subjective ground of its self-determination is an *end*; and this, if it is given by reason alone, must be equally valid for all rational beings. What, on the other hand, contains merely the ground of the possibility of an action whose effect is an end is called a *means*. . . .

Now I say that man, and in general every rational being, *exists* as an end in himself, *not merely as a means* for arbitrary use by this or that will: he must in all his actions, whether they are directed to himself or to other rational beings, always be viewed *at the same time as an end*. All the objects of inclination have only a conditioned value; for if there were not these inclinations and the needs grounded on them, their object would be valueless. Inclinations themselves, as sources of needs, are so far from having an absolute value to make them desirable for their own sake that it must rather be the universal wish of every rational being to be wholly free from them. Thus the value of all objects that can *be produced* by our action is always conditioned. Beings whose existence depends, not on our will, but on nature, have none the less, if they are non-rational beings, only a relative value as means and are consequently called *things*. Rational beings, on the other hand, are called *persons* because their nature already marks them out as ends in themselves—that is, as something which ought not to be used merely as a means—and consequently imposes to that extent a limit on all arbitrary treatment of them (and is an object of reverence). Persons, therefore, are not merely subjective ends whose existence as an object of our actions has a value *for us*: they are *objective ends*—that is, things whose existence is in itself an end, and indeed an end such that in its place we can put no other end to which they should serve *simply* as means; for unless this is so, nothing at all of *absolute* value would be found anywhere. But if all value were conditioned—that is, contingent—then no supreme principle could be found for reason at all.

If then there is to be a supreme practical principle and—so far as the human will is concerned—a categorical imperative, it must be such that from the idea of something which is necessarily an end for every one because it is an *end in itself* it forms an *objective* principle of the will and consequently can serve as a practical law. The ground of this principle is: *Rational nature exists as an end in itself.* This is the way in which a man necessarily conceives his own existence: it is therefore so far a *subjective* principle of human actions. But it is also the way in which every other rational being conceives his existence on the same rational ground which is valid also for me; hence it is at the same time an *objective* principle, from which, as a supreme practical ground, it must be possible to derive all laws for the will. The practical imperative will therefore be as follows: *Act in such a way that you always treat humanity, whether in your own person or in the person of any other, never simply as a means, but always at the same time as an end.* . . .

Endnotes

1. A *maxim* is a subjective principle of action and must be distinguished from an *objective principle*—namely, a practical law. The former contains a practical rule determined by reason in accordance with the conditions of the subject (often his ignorance or again his inclinations): it is thus a principle on which the subject *acts*. A law, on the other hand, is an objective principle valid

for every rational being; and it is a principle on which he *ought to act*—that is, an imperative.

2. It should be noted that I reserve my division of duties entirely for a future *Metaphysic of Morals* and that my present division is therefore put forward as arbitrary (merely for the purpose of arranging my examples). Further, I understand here by a perfect duty one which allows no exception in the interests of inclination, and so I recognize among *perfect duties*, not only outer ones, but also inner. This is contrary to the accepted usage of the schools, but I do not intend to justify it here, since for my purpose it is all one whether this point is conceded or not.

Review Questions

1. Explain Kant's account of the good will.
2. Distinguish between hypothetical and categorical imperatives.
3. State the first formulation of the Categorical Imperative (using the notion of a universal law) and explain how Kant uses this rule to derive some specific duties towards self and others.
4. State the second version of the Categorical Imperative (using the language of means and end), and explain it.

Discussion Questions

1. Are the two different versions of the Categorical Imperative just different expressions of one basic rule, or are they two different rules? Defend your view.
2. Kant claims that an action which is not done from the motive of duty has no moral worth. Do you agree or not? If not, give some counter-examples.
3. Some commentators think that the Categorical Imperative (particularly the first formulation) can be used to justify nonmoral or immoral actions. Is this a good criticism?

Onora O'Neill

A Simplified Account of Kant's Ethics

Onora O'Neill teaches philosophy at the University of Essex in Colchester, England. She is the author of Acting on Principle *(1975) and, most recently,* Faces of Hunger *(1986).*

O'Neill interprets and explains the formulation of the Categorical Imperative called the Formula of the End in Itself, and then compares the Kantian and utilitarian moral theories on the value of human life.

Kant's moral theory has acquired the reputation of being forbiddingly difficult to understand and, once understood, excessively demanding in its requirements. I don't believe that this reputation has been wholly earned, and I am going to try to undermine it. . . . I shall try to reduce some of the difficulties. . . . Finally, I shall compare Kantian and utilitarian approaches and assess their strengths and weaknesses.

The main method by which I propose to avoid some of the difficulties of Kant's moral theory is by explaining only one part of the theory. This does not seem to me to be an irresponsible approach in this case. One of the things that makes Kant's moral theory hard to understand is that he gives a number of different versions of the principle that he calls the Supreme Principle of Morality, and these different versions don't look at all like one another. They also don't look at all like the utilitarians' Greatest Happiness Principle. But the Kantian principle is supposed to play a similar role in arguments about what to do.

Kant calls his Supreme Principle the *Categorical Imperative;* its various versions also have sonorous names. One is called the Formula of

---

"A Simplified Account of Kant's Ethics," by Onora O'Neill from *Matters of Life and Death,* ed. Tom Regan, 1986, McGraw-Hill Publishing Company.

Universal Law; another is the Formula of the Kingdom of Ends. The one on which I shall concentrate is known as the *Formula of the End in Itself*. To understand why Kant thinks that these picturesquely named principles are equivalent to one another takes quite a lot of close and detailed analysis of Kant's philosophy. I shall avoid this and concentrate on showing the implications of this version of the Categorical Imperative.

When we want to work out whether an act we propose to do is right or wrong, according to Kant, we should look at our maxims and not at how much misery or happiness the act is likely to produce, and whether it does better at increasing happiness than other available acts. We just have to check that the act we have in mind will not use anyone as a mere means, and, if possible, that it will treat other persons as ends in themselves.

THE FORMULA OF THE END IN ITSELF

Kant states the Formula of the End in Itself as follows:

> Act in such a way that you always treat humanity, whether in your own person or in the person of any other, never simply as a means but always at the same time as an end.[1]

To understand this we need to know what it is to treat a person as a means or as an end. According to Kant, each of our acts reflects one or more *maxims*. The maxim of the act is the principle on which one sees oneself as acting. A maxim expresses a person's policy, or if he or she has no settled policy, the principle underlying the particular intention or decision on which he or she acts. Thus, a person who decides "This year I'll give 10 percent of my income to famine relief" has as a maxim the principle of tithing his or her income for famine relief. In practice, the difference between intentions and maxims is of little importance, for given any intention, we can formulate the corresponding maxim by deleting references to particular times, places, and persons. In what follows I shall take the terms 'maxim' and 'intention' as equivalent.

Whenever we act intentionally, we have at least one maxim and can, if we reflect, state what it is. (There is of course room for self-deception here—"I'm only keeping the wolf from the door" we may claim as we wolf down enough to keep ourselves overweight, or, more to the point, enough to feed someone else who hasn't enough food.)

USING PERSONS AS MERE MEANS

To use someone as a *mere means* is to involve them in a scheme of action *to which they could not in principle consent*. Kant does not say that there is anything wrong about using someone as a means. Evidently we have to do so in any cooperative scheme of action. If I cash a check I use the teller as a means, without whom I could not lay my hands on the cash; the teller in turn uses me as a means to earn his or her living. But in this case, each party consents to her or his part in the transaction. Kant would say that though they use one another as means, they do not use one another as *mere* means. Each person assumes that the other has maxims of his or her own and is not just a thing or a prop to be manipulated.

But there are other situations where one person uses another in a way to which the other could not in principle consent. For example, one person may make a promise to another with every intention of breaking it. If the promise is accepted, then the person to whom it was given must be ignorant of what the promisor's intention (maxim) really is. If one knew that the promisor did not intend to do what he or she was promising, one would, after all, not accept or rely on the promise. It would be as though there had been no promise made. Successful false promising depends on deceiving the person to whom the promise is made about what one's real maxim is. And since the person who is deceived doesn't know that real maxim, he or she can't in principle consent to his or her part in the proposed scheme of action. The person who is deceived is, as it were, a prop or a tool—a mere means—in the false promisor's scheme.

A person who promises falsely treats the acceptor of the promise as a prop or a thing and not as a person. In Kant's view, it is this that makes false promising wrong.

One standard way of using others as mere means is by deceiving them. By getting someone involved in a business scheme or a criminal activity on false pretenses, or by giving a misleading account of what one is about, or by making a false promise or a fraudulent contract, one involves another in something to which he or she in principle cannot consent, since the scheme requires that he or she doesn't know what is going on. Another standard way of using others as mere means is by coercing them. If a rich or powerful person threatens a debtor with bankruptcy unless he or she joins in some scheme, then the creditor's intention is to coerce; and the debtor, if coerced, cannot consent to his or her part in the creditor's scheme. To make the example more specific: If a moneylender in an Indian village threatens not to renew a vital loan unless he is given the debtor's land, then he uses the debtor as a mere means. He coerces the debtor, who cannot truly consent to this "offer he can't refuse." (Of course the outward form of such transactions may look like ordinary commercial dealings, but we know very well that some offers and demands couched in that form are coercive.)

In Kant's view, acts that are done on maxims that require deception or coercion of others, and so cannot have the consent of those others (for consent precludes both deception and coercion), are wrong. When we act on such maxims, we treat others as mere means, as things rather than as ends in themselves. If we act on such maxims, our acts are not only wrong but unjust: such acts wrong the particular others who are deceived or coerced.

Treating Persons as Ends in Themselves

Duties of justice are, in Kant's view (as in many others'), the most important of our duties. When we fail in these duties, we have used some other or others as mere means. But there are also cases where, though we do not use others as mere means, still we fail to use them as ends in themselves in the fullest possible way. To treat someone as an end in him or herself requires in the first place that one not use him or her as mere means, that one respect each as a rational person with his or her own maxims. But beyond that, one may also seek to foster others' plans and maxims by sharing some of their ends. To act beneficently is to seek others' happiness, therefore to intend to achieve some of the things that those others aim at with their maxims. If I want to make others happy, I will adopt maxims that not merely do not manipulate them but that foster some of their plans and activities. Beneficent acts try to achieve what others want. However, we cannot seek everything that others want; their wants are too numerous and diverse, and, of course, sometimes incompatible. It follows that beneficence has to be selective.

There is then quite a sharp distinction between the requirements of justice and of beneficence in Kantian ethics. Justice requires that we act on *no* maxims that use others as mere means. Beneficence requires that we act on *some* maxims that foster others' ends, though it is a matter for judgment and discretion which of their ends we foster. Some maxims no doubt ought not to be fostered because it would be unjust to do so. Kantians are not committed to working interminably through a list of happiness-producing and misery-reducing acts; but there are some acts whose obligatoriness utilitarians may need to debate as they try to compare total outcomes of different choices, to which Kantians are stringently bound. Kantians will claim that they have done nothing wrong if none of their acts is unjust, and that their duty is complete if in addition their life plans have in the circumstances been reasonably beneficent.

In making sure that they meet all the demands of justice, Kantians do not try to compare all available acts and see which has the best effects. They consider only the proposals for action that occur to them and check that these proposals use no other as mere means. If they do not, the act is permissible; if omitting the act would use another as mere means, the act is obligatory. Kant's theory has less scope than utilitarianism. Kantians do not claim to discover whether acts whose maxims they don't know fully are just. They may be reluctant to judge others' acts or policies that cannot be regarded as the maxim of any person or institution. They cannot rank acts in order of merit. Yet, the theory offers more precision than utilitarianism when data are scarce. One can usually tell whether one's act would use others as mere means, even when its impact on human happiness is thoroughly obscure.

The Limits of Kantian Ethics: Intentions and Results

Kantian ethics differs from utilitarian ethics both in its scope and in the precision with which it guides action. Every action, whether of a person or of an agency, can be assessed by utilitarian methods, provided only that information is available about all the consequences of the act. The theory has unlimited scope, but owing to lack of data, often lacks precision. Kantian ethics has a more restricted scope. Since it assesses actions by looking at the maxims of agents, it can only assess intentional acts. This means that it is most at home in assessing individuals' acts; but it can be extended to assess acts of agencies that (like corporations and governments and student unions) have decision-making procedures. It can do nothing to assess patterns of action that reflect no intention or policy, hence it cannot assess the acts of groups lacking decision-making procedures, such as the student movement, the women's movement, or the consumer movement.

It may seem a great limitation of Kantian ethics that it concentrates on intentions to the neglect of results. It might seem that all conscientious Kantians have to do is to make sure that they never intend to use others as mere means, and that they sometimes intend to foster other's ends. And, as we all know, good intentions sometimes lead to bad results and correspondingly, bad intentions sometimes do no harm, or even produce good. If Hardin[2] is right, the good intentions of those who feed the starving lead to dreadful results in the long run. If some traditional arguments in favor of capitalism are right, the greed and selfishness of the profit motive have produced unparalleled prosperity for many.

But such discrepancies between intentions and results are the exception and not the rule. For we cannot just *claim* that our intentions are good and do what we will. Our intentions reflect what we expect the immediate results of our action to be. Nobody credits the "intentions" of a couple who practice neither celibacy nor contraception but still insist "we never meant to have (more) children." Conception is likely (and known to be likely) in such cases. Where people's expressed intentions ignore the normal and predictable results of what they do, we infer that (if they are not amazingly ignorant) their words do not express their true intentions. The Formula of the End in Itself applies to the intentions on which one acts—not to some prettified version that one may avow. Provided this intention—the agent's real intention—uses no other as mere means, he or she does nothing unjust. If some of his or her intentions foster others' ends, then he or she is sometimes beneficent. It is therefore possible for people to test their proposals by Kantian arguments even when they lack the comprehensive causal knowledge that utilitarianism requires. Conscientious Kantians can work out whether they will be doing wrong by some act even though it blurs the implications of the theory. If we peer through the blur, we see that the utilitarian view is that lives may indeed be sacrificed for the sake of a greater good even when the persons are not willing. There is nothing wrong with using another as a mere means provided that the end for which the person is so used is a happier result than could have been achieved any other way, taking into account the misery the means have caused. In utilitarian thought persons are not ends in themselves. Their special moral status derives from their being means to the production of happiness. Human life has therefore a high though derivative value, and one life may be taken for the sake of greater happiness in other lives, or for ending of misery in that life. Nor is there any deep difference between ending a life for the sake of others' happiness by not helping (e.g., by triaging) and doing so by harming. Because the distinction between justice and beneficence is not sharply made within utilitarianism, it is not possible to say that triaging is a matter of not benefiting, while other interventions are a matter of injustice.

Utilitarian moral theory has then a rather paradoxical view of the value of human life. Living, conscious humans are (along with other sentient beings) necessary for the existence of everything utilitarians value. But it is not their being alive but the state of their consciousness that is of value. Hence, the best results may require certain lives to be lost—by whatever means—for the sake of the total happiness and absence of misery that can be produced.

Kant and Respect for Persons

Kantians reach different conclusions about human life. Human life is valuable because humans (and conceivably other beings, e.g., angels or apes) are the bearers of rational life. Humans are able to choose and to plan. This capacity and its exercise are of such value that they ought not to be sacrificed for anything of lesser value. Therefore, no one rational or autonomous creature should be treated as mere means for the enjoyment or even the happiness of another. We may in Kant's view justifiably—even nobly—risk or sacrifice our lives for others. For in doing so we follow our own maxim and nobody uses us as mere means. But no others may use either our lives or our bodies for a scheme that they have either coerced or deceived us into joining. For in doing so they would fail to treat us as rational beings; they would use us as mere means and not as ends in ourselves.

It is conceivable that a society of Kantians, all of whom took pains to use no other as mere means, would end up with less happiness or with fewer persons alive than would some societies of complying utilitarians. For since the Kantians would be strictly bound only to justice, they might without wrongdoing be quite selective in their beneficence and fail to maximize either survival rates or happiness, or even to achieve as much of either as a strenuous group of utilitarians, who they know that their foresight is limited and that they may cause some harm or fail to cause some benefit. But they will not cause harms that they can foresee without this being reflected in their intentions.

Utilitarianism and Respect for Life

From the differing implications that Kantian and utilitarian moral theories have for our actions towards those who do or may suffer famine, we can discover two sharply contrasting views of the value of human life. Utilitarians value happiness and the absence or reduction of misery. As a utilitarian one ought (if conscientious) to devote one's life to achieving the best possible balance of happiness over misery. If one's life plan remains in doubt, this will be because the means to this end are often unclear. But whenever the causal tendency of acts is clear, utilitarians will be able to discern the acts they should successively do in order to improve the world's balance of happiness over unhappiness.

This task is not one for the faint-hearted. First, it is dauntingly long, indeed interminable. Second, it may at times require the sacrifice of happiness, and even of lives, for the sake of a greater happiness. Such sacrifice may be morally required not only when the person whose happiness or even whose life is at stake volunteers to make the sacrifice. It may be necessary to sacrifice some lives for the sake of others. As our control over the means of ending and preserving human life has increased, analogous dilemmas have arisen in many areas for utilitarians. Should life be preserved at the cost of pain when modern medicine makes this possible? Should life be preserved without hope of consciousness? Should triage policies, because they may maximize the number of survivors, be used to determine who should be left to starve? Should population growth be fostered wherever it will increase the total of human happiness—or on some views so long as average happiness is not reduced? All these questions can be fitted into utilitarian frameworks and answered *if* we have the relevant information. And sometimes the answer will be that human happiness demands the sacrifice of lives, including the sacrifice of unwilling lives. Further, for most utilitarians, it makes no difference if the unwilling sacrifices involve acts of injustice to those whose lives are to be lost. It might, for example, prove necessary for maximal happiness that some persons have their allotted rations, or their hard-earned income, diverted for others' benefit. Or it might turn out that some generations must sacrifice comforts or liberties and even lives to rear "the fabric of felicity" for their successors. Utilitarians do not deny these possibilities, though the imprecision of our knowledge of consequences often somehow make the right calculations. On the other hand, nobody will have been made an instrument of others' survival or happiness in the society of complying Kantians.

Endnotes

1. [See the end of the reading from Kant—Ed.]
2. [See the reading by Garett Hardin in Chapter 5—Ed.]

Review Questions

1. According to O'Neill, what is involved in using someone as a mere means? Give some examples. Why is this wrong?
2. On O'Neill's interpretation, how does one treat people as ends in themselves? Give examples.
3. Distinguish between the requirements of justice and beneficence.
4. According to O'Neill, how does Kantian ethics differ from utilitarian ethics?

Discussion Questions

1. Does Kantian ethics require us to help strangers or people in other countries? Why or why not?
2. As O'Neill explains it, Kant's view is that a life is valuable because it is rational. This seems to imply that the life of a fetus or a comatose person is not valuable because it is not rational—it involves no choosing or planning. Do you agree with this?
3. Which theory is more acceptable to you, utilitarianism or Kant's theory? Why?

W. D. Ross

What Makes Right Acts Right?

W. D. Ross (1877–1967) was a British moral philosopher and classical scholar who taught at Oxford University. He is the translator of our reading from Aristotle; his book Aristotle *(1959) explains the general features of Aristotle's ethical theory. Our reading is taken from his best known book,* The Right and the Good *(1930).*

Ross begins by distinguishing between hedonistic utilitarianism (John Stuart Mill's view that the good is pleasure) and ideal utilitarianism (G. E. Moore's theory that other things besides pleasure are good, such as beauty). He then makes a telling objection to these theories: The reason we ought to fulfill a promise is not because this produces good consequences, but simply because it is our prima facie duty (our duty at first view). Ross's definition of prima facie duty is not very clear. Generally speaking, a prima facie duty is an actual duty which may be overridden by some other moral considerations. The basic idea is that we can have conflicts between prima facie duties where we cannot satisfy them all. For example, we may be able to help someone (a duty of beneficence) only if we break a promise. In such cases we can only make a judgement about what to do using moral intuition. Moral intuition also reveals self-evident principles about duty that are more certain than judgements about particular acts. Because Ross appeals to the apprehension of rightness by intuition, his theory is often called intuitionism. *It is also said to be a* pluralistic deontology *because it recognizes different types of duty.*

From W. D. Ross, *The Right and the Good* (Oxford: Clarendon Press, 1930). Reprinted by permission of Oxford University Press.

The real point at issue between hedonism and utilitarianism on the one hand and their opponents on the other is not whether 'right' means 'productive of so and so'; for it cannot with any plausibility be maintained that it does. The point at issue is that to which we now pass, viz. whether there is any general character which makes right acts right, and if so, what it is. Among the main historical attempts to state a single characteristic of all right actions which is the foundation of their rightness are those made by egoism and utilitarianism. But I do not propose to discuss these, not because the subject is unimportant, but because it has been dealt with so often and so well already, and because there has come to be so much agreement among moral philosophers that neither of these theories is satisfactory. A much more attractive theory has been put forward by Professor Moore: that what makes actions right is that they are productive of more *good* than could have been produced by any other action open to the agent.[1]

This theory is in fact the culmination of all the attempts to base rightness on productivity of some sort of result. The first form this attempt takes is the attempt to base rightness on conduciveness to the advantage or pleasure of the agent. This theory comes to grief over the fact, which stares us in the face, that a great part of duty consists in an observance of the rights and a furtherance of the interests of others, whatever the cost to ourselves may be. Plato and others may be right in holding that a regard for the rights of others never in the long run involves a loss of happiness for the agent, that 'the just life profits a man'. But this, even if true, is irrelevant to the rightness of the act. As soon as a man does an action *because* he thinks he will promote his own interests thereby, he is acting not from a sense of its rightness but from self-interest.

To the egoistic theory hedonistic utilitarianism supplies a much-needed amendment. It points out correctly that the fact that a certain pleasure will be enjoyed by the agent is no reason why he *ought* to bring it into being rather than an equal or greater pleasure to be enjoyed by another, though, human nature being what it is, it makes it not unlikely that he *will* try to bring it into being. But hedonistic utilitarianism in its turn needs a correction. On reflection it seems clear that pleasure is not the only thing in life that we think good in itself, that for instance we think the possession of a good character, or an intelligent understanding of the world, as good or better. A great advance is made by the substitution of 'productive of the greatest good' for 'productive of the greatest pleasure'.

Not only is this theory more attractive than hedonistic utilitarianism, but its logical relation to that theory is such that the latter could not be true unless *it* were true, while it might be true though hedonistic utilitarianism were not. It is in fact one of the logical bases of hedonistic utilitarianism. For the view that what produces the maximum pleasure is right has for its bases the views (1) that what produces the maximum good is right, and (2) that pleasure is the only thing good in itself. If they were not assuming that what produces the maximum *good* is right, the utilitarians' attempt to show that pleasure is the only thing good in itself, which is in fact the point they take most pains to establish, would have been quite irrelevant to their attempt to prove that only what produces the maximum *pleasure* is right. If, therefore, it can be shown that productivity of the maximum good is not what makes all right actions right, we shall *a fortiori* have refuted hedonistic utilitarianism.

When a plain man fulfills a promise because he thinks he ought to do so, it seems clear that he does so with no thought of its total consequences, still less with any opinion that these are likely to be the best possible. He thinks in fact much more of the past than of the future. What makes him think it right to act in a certain way is the fact that he has promised to do so—that and, usually, nothing more. That his act will produce the best possible consequences is not his reason for calling it right. What lends colour to the theory we are examining, then, is not the actions (which form probably a great majority of our actions) in which some such reflection as 'I have promised' is the only reason we give ourselves for thinking a certain action right, but the exceptional cases in which the consequences of fulfilling a promise (for instance) would be so disastrous to others that we judge it right not to do so. It must of course be admitted that such cases exist. If I have promised to meet a friend at a particular time for some trivial purpose, I should certainly think myself justified in breaking my engagement if by doing so I could prevent a serious accident or bring relief to the victims of one. And the supporters of the view we are examining hold that my thinking so is due to my thinking that I shall bring more good into existence by the one action than by the other. A different account may, however, be given of the matter, an account which will, I believe, show itself to be the true one. It may be said that besides the duty of fulfilling promises I have and recognize a duty of relieving distress,[2] and that when I think it right to do the latter at the cost of not doing the former, it is not because I think I shall produce more good thereby but because I think it the duty which is in the circumstances more of a duty. This account surely corresponds much more closely with what we really think in such a situation. If, so far as I can see, I could bring equal amounts of good into being by fulfilling my promise and by helping someone to whom I had made no promise, I should not hesitate to regard the former as my duty. Yet on the view that what is right is right because it is productive of the most good I should not so regard it.

There are two theories, each in its way simple, that offer a solution of such cases of conscience. One is the view of Kant, that there are certain duties of perfect obligation, such as those of fulfilling promises, of paying debts, of telling the truth, which admit of no exception whatever in favour of duties of imperfect obligation, such as that of relieving distress. The other is the view of, for instance, Professor Moore and Dr. Rashdall, that there is only the duty of producing good, and that all 'conflicts of duties' should be resolved by asking 'by which action will most good be produced?' But it is more important that our theory fit the facts than that it be simple, and the account we have given above corresponds (it seems to me) better than either of the simpler theories with what we really think, viz. that normally promise-keeping, for example, should come before benevolence, but that when and only when the good to be produced by the benevolent act is very great and the promise comparatively trivial, the act of benevolence becomes our duty.

In fact the theory of 'ideal utilitarianism', if I may for brevity refer so to the theory of Professor Moore, seems to simplify unduly our relations to our fellows. It says, in effect, that the only morally significant relation in which my neighbours stand to me is that of being possible beneficiaries by my action.[3] They do stand in this relation to me, and this relation is morally significant. But they may also stand to me in the relation of promisee to promiser, or creditor to debtor, of wife to husband, of child to parent, of friend to friend, of fellow countryman to fellow countryman, and the like; and each of these relations is the foundation of a *prima facie* duty, which is more or less incumbent on me according to the circumstances of the case. When I am in a situation, as perhaps I always am, in which more than one of these *prima facie* duties is incumbent on me, what I have to do is to study the situation as fully as I can until I form the considered opinion (it is never more) that in the circumstances one of them is more incumbent than any other; then I am bound to think that to do this *prima facie* duty is my duty *sans phrase* in the situation.

I suggest '*prima facie* duty' or 'conditional duty' as a brief way of referring to the characteristic (quite distinct from that of being a duty proper) which an act has, in virtue of being of a certain kind (e.g. the keeping of a promise), of being an act which would be a duty proper if it were not at the same time of another kind which is morally significant. Whether an act is a duty proper or actual duty depends on *all* the morally significant kinds it is an instance of. The phrase '*prima facie* duty' must be apologized for, since (1) it suggests that what we are speaking of is a certain kind of duty, whereas it is in fact not a duty, but something related in a special way to duty. Strictly speaking, we want not a phrase in which duty is qualified by an adjective, but a separate noun. (2) '*Prima' facie* suggests that one is speaking only of an appearance which a moral situation presents at first sight, and which may turn out to be illusory; whereas what I am speaking of is an objective fact involved in the nature of the situation, or more strictly in an element of its nature, though not, as duty proper does, arising from its *whole* nature. I can, however, think of no term which fully meets the case. . . .

There is nothing arbitrary about these *prima facie* duties. Each rests on a definite circumstance which cannot seriously be held to be without moral significance. Of *prima facie* duties I suggest, without claiming completeness or finality for it, the following division.[4]

(1) Some duties rest on previous acts of my own. These duties seem to include two kinds, (a) those resting on a promise or what may fairly be called an implicit promise, such as the implicit undertaking not to tell lies which seems to be implied in the act of entering into conversation (at any rate by civilized men), or of writing books that purport to be history and not fiction. These may be called the duties of fidelity. (b) Those resting on a previous wrongful act. These may be called the duties of reparation. (2) Some rest on previous acts of other men, i.e. services done by them to me. These may be loosely described as the duties of gratitude. (3) Some rest on the fact or possibility of a distribution of pleasure or happiness (or of the means thereto) which is not in accordance with the merit of the persons concerned; in such cases there arises a duty to upset or prevent such a distribution. These are the duties of justice. (4) Some rest on the mere fact that there are other beings in the world whose condition we can make better in respect of virtue, or of intelligence, or of pleasure. These are the duties of beneficence. (5) Some rest on the fact that we can improve our own condition in respect of virtue or of intelligence. These are the duties of self-improvement. (6) I think that we should distinguish from (4) the duties that may be summed up under the title of 'not injuring others'. No doubt to injure others is incidentally to fail to do them good; but it seems to me clear that non-maleficence is apprehended as a duty distinct from that of beneficence, and as a duty of a more stringent character. It will be noticed that this alone among the types of duty has been stated in a negative way. An attempt might no doubt be made to state this duty, like the others, in a positive way. It might be said that it is really the duty to prevent ourselves from acting either from an inclination to harm others or from an inclination to seek our own pleasure, in doing which we should incidentally harm them. But on reflection it seems clear that the primary duty here is the duty not to harm others, this being a duty whether or not we have an inclination that if followed would lead to our harming them; and that when we have such an inclination the primary duty not to harm others gives rise to a consequential duty to resist the inclination. The recognition of this duty of non-maleficence is the first step on the way to the recognition of the duty of beneficence; and that accounts for the prominence of the commands 'thou shalt not kill', 'thou shalt not commit adultery', 'thou shalt not steal', 'thou shalt not bear false witness', in so early a code as the Decalogue. But even when we have come to recognize the duty of beneficence, it appears to me that the duty of non-maleficence is recognized as a distinct one, and as *prima facie* more binding. We should not in general consider it justifiable to kill one person in order to keep another alive, or to steal from one in order to give alms to another.

The essential defect of the 'ideal utilitarian' theory is that it ignores, or at least does not do full justice to, the highly personal character of duty. If the only duty is to produce the maximum of good, the question who is to have the good—whether it is myself, or my benefactor, or a person to whom I have made a promise to confer that good on him, or a mere fellow man to whom I stand in no such special relation—should make no difference to my having a duty to produce that good. But we are all in fact sure that it makes a vast difference.

One or two other comments must be made on this provisional list of the divisions of duty. (1) The nomenclature is not strictly correct. For by 'fidelity' or 'gratitude' we mean, strictly, certain states of motivation; and, as I have urged, it is not our duty to have certain motives, but to do certain acts. By 'fidelity', for instance, is meant, strictly, the disposition to fulfill promises and implicit promises *because we have made them*. We have no general word to cover the actual fulfillment of promises and implicit promises *irrespective of motive*; and I use 'fidelity', loosely but perhaps conveniently, to fill this gap. So too I use 'gratitude' for the returning of services, irrespective of motive. The term 'justice' is not so much confined, in ordinary usage, to a certain state of motivation, for we should often talk of a man as acting justly even when we did not think his motive was the wish to do what was just simply for the sake of doing so. Less apology is therefore needed for our use of 'justice' in this sense. And I have used the word 'beneficence' rather than 'benevolence', in order to emphasize the fact that it is our duty to do certain things, and not to do them from certain motives.

(2) If the objection be made, that this catalogue of the main types of duty is an unsystematic one resting on no logical principle, it may be replied, first, that it makes no claim to being ultimate. It is a *prima facie* classification of the duties which reflection on our moral convictions seems actually to reveal. And if these convictions are, as I would claim that they are, of the nature of knowledge, and if I have not misstated them, the list will be a list of authentic conditional duties, correct as far as it goes though not necessarily complete. The list of *goods* put forward by the rival theory is reached by exactly the same method—the only sound one in the circumstances—viz. that of direct reflection on what we really think. Loyalty to the facts is worth more than a symmetrical architectonic or a hastily reached simplicity. If further reflection discovers a perfect logical basis for this or for a better classification, so much the better.

(3) It may, again, be objected that our theory that there are these various and often conflicting types of *prima facie* duty leaves us with no principle upon which to discern what is our actual duty in particular circumstances. But this objection is not one which the rival theory is in a position to bring forward. For when we have to choose between the production of two heterogeneous goods, say knowledge and pleasure, the 'ideal utilitarian' theory can only fall back on an opinion, for which no logical basis can be offered, that one of the goods is the greater; and this is no better than a similar opinion that one of two duties is the more urgent. And again, when we consider the infinite variety of the effects of our actions in the way of pleasure, it must surely be admitted that the claim which *hedonism* sometimes makes, that it offers a readily applicable criterion of right conduct, is quite illusory.

I am unwilling, however, to content myself with an ***argumentum ad hominem,*** and I would contend that in principle there is no reason to anticipate that every act that is our duty is so for one and the same reason. Why should two sets of circumstances, or one set of circumstances, *not* possess different characteristics, any one of which makes a certain act our *prima facie* duty? When I ask what it is that makes me in certain cases sure that I have a *prima facie* duty to do so and so, I find that it lies in the fact that I have made a promise; when I ask the same question in another case, I find the answer lies in the fact that I have done a wrong. And if on reflection I find (as I think I do) that neither of these reasons is reducible to the other, I must not on any a *priori* ground assume that such a reduction is possible . . . .

Something should be said of the relation between our apprehension of the *prima facie* rightness of certain types of act and our mental attitude towards particular acts. It is proper to use the word 'apprehension' in the former case and not in the latter. That an act, *qua* fulfilling a promise, or *qua* effecting a just distribution of good, or *qua* returning services rendered, or *qua* promoting the good of others, or *qua* promoting the virtue or insight of the agent, is *prima facie* right, is self-evident; not in the sense that it is evident form the beginning of our lives, or as soon as we attend to the proposition for the first time, but in the sense that when we have reached sufficient mental maturity and have given sufficient attention to the proposition it is evident without any need of proof, or of evidence beyond itself. It is self-evident just as a mathematical axiom, or the validity of a form of inference, is evident. The moral order expressed in these propositions is just as much part of the fundamental nature of the universe (and, we may add, of any possible universe in which there were moral agents at all) as is the spatial or numerical structure expressed in the axioms of geometry or arithmetic. In our confidence that these propositions are true there is involved the same trust in our reason that is involved in our confidence in mathematics; and we should have no justification for trusting it in the latter sphere and distrusting it in the former. In both cases we are dealing with propositions that cannot be proved, but that just as certainly need no proof. . . .

The general principles of duty are obviously not self-evident from the beginning of our lives. How do they come to be so? The answer is, that they come to be self-evident to us just as mathematical axioms do. We find by experience that this couple of matches and that couple make four matches, that this couple of balls on a wire and that couple make four balls: and by reflection on these and similar discoveries we come to see that it is of the nature of two and two to make four. In a precisely similar way, we see the *prima facie* rightness of an act which would be the fulfilment of a particular promise, and of another which would be the fulfilment of another promise, and when we have reached sufficient maturity to think in general terms, we apprehend *prima facie* rightness to belong to the nature of any fulfilment of promise. What comes first in time is the apprehension of the self-evident *prima facie* rightness of an individual act of a particular type. From this we come by reflection to apprehend the self-evident general principle of *prima facie* duty . . . .

In what has preceded, a good deal of use has been made of 'what we really think' about moral questions; a certain theory has been rejected because it does not agree with what we really think. It might be said that this is in principle wrong; that we should not be content to expound what our present moral consciousness tells us but should aim at a criticism of our existing moral consciousness in the light of theory. Now I do not doubt that the moral consciousness of men has in detail undergone a good deal of modification as regards the things we think right, at the hands of moral theory. But if we are told, for instance, that we should give up our view that there is a special obligatoriness attaching to the keeping of promises because it is self-evident that the only duty is to produce as much good as possible, we have to ask ourselves whether we really, when we reflect, *are* convinced that this is self-evident, and whether we really *can* get rid of our view that promise-keeping has a bindingness independent of productiveness of maximum good. In my own experience I find that I cannot, in spite of a very genuine attempt to do so; and I venture to think that most people will find the same, and that just because they cannot lose the sense of special obligation, they cannot accept as self-evident, or even as true, the theory which would require them to do so. In fact it seems, on reflection, self-evident that a promise, simply as such, is something that *prima facie* ought to be kept, and it does *not*, on reflection, seem self-evident that production of maximum good is the only thing that makes an act obligatory. And to ask us to give up at the bidding of a theory our actual apprehension of what is right and what is wrong seems like asking people to repudiate their actual experience of beauty, at the bidding of a theory which says 'only that which satisfies such and such conditions can be beautiful'. If what I have called our actual apprehension is (as I would maintain that it is) truly an apprehension, i.e. an instance of knowledge, the request is nothing less than absurd.

I would maintain, in fact, that what we are apt to describe as 'what we think' about moral questions contains a considerable amount that we do not think but know, and that this forms the standard by reference to which the truth of any moral theory has to be tested, instead of having itself to be tested by reference to any theory. I hope that I have in what precedes indicated what in my view these elements of knowledge are that are involved in our ordinary moral consciousness.

It would be a mistake to found a natural science on 'what we really think', i.e. on what reasonably thoughtful and well-educated people think about the subjects of the science before they have studied them scientifically. For such opinions are interpretations, and often misinterpretations, of sense-experience; and the man of science must appeal from these to sense-experience itself, which furnishes his real data. In ethics no such appeal is possible. We have no more direct way of access to the facts about rightness and goodness and about what things are right or good, than by thinking about them; the moral convictions of thoughtful and well-educated people are the data of ethics just as sense-perceptions are the data of a natural science. Just as some of the latter have to be rejected as illusory, so have some of the former; but as the latter are rejected only when they are in conflict with other more accurate sense-perceptions, the former are rejected only when they are in conflict with other convictions which stand better the test of reflection. The existing body of moral convictions of the best people is the cumulative product of the moral reflection of many generations, which has developed an extremely delicate power of appreciation of moral distinctions; and this the theorist cannot afford to treat with anything other than the greatest respect. The verdicts of the moral consciousness of the best people are the foundation on which he must build; though he must first compare them with one another and eliminate any contradictions they may contain . . . .

Endnotes

1. I take the theory which, as I have tried to show, seems to be put forward in Ethics rather than the earlier and less plausible theory put forward in *Principia Ethica*. For the difference, cf. my pp. 8–11.
2. These are not strictly speaking duties, but things that tend to be our duty, or *prima facie* duties.
3. Some will think it, apart from other considerations, a sufficient refutation of this view to point out that I also stand in that relation to myself, so that for this view the distinction of oneself from others is morally insignificant.
4. I should make it plain at this stage that I am *assuming* the correctness of some of our main convictions as to *prima facie* duties, or, more strictly, am claiming that we *know* them to be true. To me it seems as self-evident as anything could be, that to make a promise, for instance, is to create a moral claim on us in someone else. Many readers will perhaps say that they do *not* know this to be true. If so, I certainly cannot prove it to them; I can only ask them to reflect again, in the hope that they will ultimately agree that they also know it to be true. The main moral convictions of the plain man seem to me to be, not opinions which it is for philosophy to prove or disprove, but knowledge from the start; and in my own case I seem to find little difficulty in distinguishing these essential convictions from other moral convictions which I also have, which are merely fallible opinions based on an imperfect study of the working for good or evil or certain institutions or types of action.

Review Questions

1. Distinguish between egoism, hedonistic utilitarianism, and ideal utilitarianism.
2. What criticism does Ross make of utilitarianism?
3. Distinguish between prima facie duty and actual duty or duty proper.
4. Describe the different types of duty.

Discussion Questions

1. Has Ross refuted utilitarianism or not?
2. Is his theory compatible with Kant's theory?
3. Are all the different types of duty equally compelling or are some more important than others?
4. Can you think of any general principles of duty that are really self-evident, as self-evident as axioms in mathematics?

John Rawls

A Theory of Justice

John Rawls is Professor of Philosophy at Harvard University. Our reading is taken from his well-known book A Theory of Justice *(1971).*

Rawls' theory states that there are two principles of justice: The first principle involves equal basic liberties, and the second principle concerns the arrangement of social and economic inequalities. According to Rawls' theory, these are the principles that free and rational persons would accept in a hypothetical original position where there is a veil of ignorance hiding from the contractors all the particular facts about themselves.

The Main Idea of the Theory of Justice

My aim is to present a conception of justice which generalizes and carries to a higher level of abstraction the familiar theory of the social contract as found, say, in Locke, Rousseau, and Kant.[1] In order to do this we are not to think of the original contract as one to enter a particular society or to set up a particular form of government. Rather, the guiding idea is that the principles of justice for the basic structure of society are the object of the original agreement. They are the principles that free and rational persons concerned to further their own interests would accept in an initial position of equality as defining the fundamental terms of their association. These principles are to regulate all further agreements; they specify the kinds of social cooperation that can be entered into and the forms of government that can be established. This way of regarding the principles of justice I shall call justice as fairness.

Thus we are to imagine that those who engage in social cooperation choose together, in one joint act, the principles which are to assign basic rights and duties and to determine the division of social benefits. Men are to decide in advance how they are to regulate their claims against one another and what is to be the foundation charter of their society. Just as each person must decide by rational reflection what constitutes his good, that is, the system of ends which it is rational for him to pursue, so a group of persons must decide once and for all what is to count among them as just and unjust. The choice which rational men would make in this hypothetical situation of equal liberty, assuming for the present that this choice problem has a solution, determines the principles of justice.

In justice as fairness the original position of equality corresponds to the state of nature in the traditional theory of the social contract. This original position is not, of course, thought of as an actual historical state of affairs, much less as a primitive condition of culture. It is understood as a purely hypothetical situation characterized so as to lead to a certain conception of justice.[2] Among the essential features of this situation is that no one knows his place in society, his class position or social status, nor does any one know his fortune in the distribution of natural assets and abilities, his intelligence, strength, and the like. I shall even assume that the parties do not know their conceptions of the good or their special psychological propensities. The principles of justice are chosen behind a **veil of ignorance.** This ensures that no one is advantaged or disadvantaged in the choice of principles by the outcome of natural chance or the contingency of social circumstances. Since all are similarly situated and no one is able to design principles to favor his particular condition, the principles of justice are the result of a fair agreement or bargain. For given the circumstances of the original position, the symmetry of everyone's relations to each other, this initial situation is fair between individuals as moral persons, that is, as rational beings with their own ends and capable, I shall assume, of a sense of justice. The original position is, one might say, the appropriate initial status quo, and thus the fundamental agreements reached in it are fair. This explains the propriety of the name "justice as fairness": it conveys the idea that the principles of justice are agreed to in an initial situation that is fair. The name does not mean that the concepts of justice and fairness are the same, any more than the phrase "poetry as metaphor" means that the concepts of poetry and metaphor are the same.

Justice as fairness begins, as I have said, with one of the most general of all choices which persons might make together, namely, with the choice of the first principles of a conception of justice which is to regulate all subsequent criticism and reform of institutions. Then, having chosen a conception of justice, we can suppose that they are to choose a constitution and a legislature to enact laws, and so on, all in accordance with the principles of justice initially agreed upon. Our social situation is just if it is such that by this sequence of hypothetical agreements we would have contracted into the general system of rules which defines it. Moreover, assuming that the original position does determine a set of principles (that is, that a particular conception of justice would be chosen), it will then be true that whenever social institutions satisfy these principles those engaged in them can say to one another that they are cooperating on terms to which they would agree if they were free and equal persons whose relations with respect to one another were fair. They could all view their arrangements as meeting the stipulations which they would acknowledge in an initial situation that embodies widely accepted and reasonable constraints on the choice of principles. The general recognition of this fact would provide the basis for a public acceptance of the corresponding principles of justice. No society can, of course, be a scheme of cooperation which men enter voluntarily in a literal sense; each person finds himself placed at birth in some particular position in some particular society, and the nature of this position materially affects his life prospects. Yet a society satisfying the principles of justice as fairness comes as close as a society can to being a voluntary scheme, for it meets the principles which free and equal persons would assent to under circumstances that are fair. In this sense its members are autonomous and the obligations they recognize self-imposed.

One feature of justice as fairness is to think of the parties in the initial situation as rational and mutually disinterested. This does not mean that the parties are egoists, that is, individuals with only certain kinds of interests, say in wealth, prestige, and domination. But they are conceived as not taking an interest in one another's interests. They are to presume that even their spiritual aims may be opposed, in the way that the aims of those of different religions may be opposed. Moreover, the concept of rationality must be interpreted as far as possible in the narrow sense, standard in economic theory, of taking the most effective means to given ends. I shall modify this concept to some extent . . . but one must try to avoid introducing into it any controversial ethical elements. The initial situation must be characterized by stipulations that are widely accepted.

In working out the conception of justice as fairness one main task clearly is to determine which principles of justice would be chosen in the original position. To do this we must describe this situation in some detail and formulate with care the problem of choice which it presents. . . . It may be observed, however, that once the principles of justice are thought of as arising from an original agreement in a situation of equality, it is an open question whether the principle of utility would be acknowledged. Offhand it hardly seems likely that persons who view themselves as equals, entitled to press their claims upon one another, would agree to a principle which may require lesser life prospects for some simply for the sake of a greater sum of advantages enjoyed by others. Since each desires to protect his interests, his capacity to advance his conception of the good, no one has a reason to acquiesce in an enduring loss for himself in order to bring about a greater net balance of satisfaction. In the absence of strong and lasting benevolent impulses, a rational man would not accept a basic structure merely because it maximized the algebraic sum of advantages irrespective of its permanent effects on his own basic rights and interests. Thus it seems that the principle of utility is incompatible with the conception of social cooperation among equals for mutual advantage. It appears to be inconsistent with the idea of reciprocity implicit in the notion of a well-ordered society. Or, at any rate, so I shall argue.

I shall maintain instead that the persons in the initial situation would choose two rather different principles: the first requires equality in the assignment of basic rights and duties, while the second holds that social and economic inequalities, for example inequalities of wealth and authority, are just only if they result in compensating benefits for everyone, and in particular for the least advantaged members of society. These principles rule out justifying institutions on the grounds that the hardships of some are offset by a greater good in the aggregate. It may be expedient but it is not just that some should have less in order that others may prosper. But there is no injustice in the greater benefits earned by a few provided that the situation of persons not so fortunate is thereby improved. The intuitive idea is that since everyone's well-being depends upon a scheme of cooperation without which no one could have a satisfactory life, the division of advantages should be such as to draw forth the willing cooperation of everyone taking part in it, including those less well situated. Yet this can be expected only if reasonable terms are proposed. The two principles mentioned seem to be a fair agreement on the basis of which those better endowed, or more fortunate in their social position, neither of which we can be said to deserve, could expect the willing cooperation of others when some workable scheme is a necessary condition of the welfare of all.[3] Once we decide to look for a conception of justice that nullifies the accidents of natural endowment and the contingencies of social circumstance as counters in quest for political and economic advantage, we are led to these principles. They express the result of leaving aside those aspects of the social world that seem arbitrary from a moral point of view.

The problem of the choice of principles, however, is extremely difficult. I do not expect the answer I shall suggest to be convincing to everyone. It is, therefore, worth noting from the outset that justice as fairness, like other contract views, consists of two parts: (1) an interpretation of the initial situation and of the problem of choice posed there, and (2) a set of principles which, it is argued, would be agreed to. One may accept the first part of the theory (or some variant thereof), but not the other, and conversely. The concept of the initial contractual situation may seem reasonable although the particular principles proposed are rejected. To be sure, I want to maintain that the most appropriate conception of this situation does lead to principles of justice contrary to utilitarianism and perfectionism, and therefore that the contract doctrine provides an alternative to these views. . . .

A final remark. Justice as fairness is not a complete contract theory. For it is clear that the contractarian idea can be extended to the choice of more or less an entire ethical system, that is, to a system including principles for all the virtues and not only for justice. Now for the most part I shall consider only principles of justice and others closely related to them; I make no attempt to discuss the virtues in a systematic way. Obviously if justice as fairness succeeds reasonably well, a next step would be to study the more general view suggested by the name "rightness as fairness." But even this wider theory fails to embrace all moral relationships, since it would seem to include only our relations with other persons and to leave out of account how we are to conduct ourselves toward animals and the rest of nature. I do not contend that the contract notion offers a way to approach these questions which are certainly of the first importance; and I shall have to put them aside. We must recognize the limited scope of justice as fairness and of the general type of view that it exemplifies. How far its conclusions must be revised once these other matters are understood cannot be decided in advance. . . .

Two Principles of Justice

I shall now state in a provisional form the two principles of justice that I believe would be chosen in the original position. In this section I wish to make only the most general comments, and therefore the first formulation of these principles is tentative. As we go on I shall run through several formulations and approximate step by step the final statement to be given much later. I believe that doing this allows the exposition to proceed in a natural way.

The first statement of the two principles reads as follows.

First: each person is to have an equal right to the most extensive basic liberty compatible with a similar liberty for others.
Second: social and economic inequalities are to be arranged so that they are both (a) reasonably expected to be to everyone's advantage, and (b) attached to positions and offices open to all. . . .

By way of general comment, these principles primarily apply, as I have said, to the basic structure of society. They are to govern the assignment of rights and duties and to regulate the distribution of social and economic advantages. As their formulation suggests, these principles presuppose that the social structure can be divided into two more or less distinct parts, the first principle applying to the one, the second to the other. They distinguish between those aspects of the social system that define and secure the equal liberties of citizenship and those that specify and establish social and economic inequalities. The basic liberties of citizens are, roughly speaking, political liberty (the right to vote and to be eligible for public office) together with freedom of speech and assembly;

liberty of conscience and freedom of thought; freedom of the person along with the right to hold (personal) property; and freedom from arbitrary arrest and seizure as defined by the concept of the rule of law. These liberties are all required to be equal by the first principle, since citizens of a just society are to have the same basic rights.

The second principle applies, in the first approximation, to the distribution of income and wealth and to the design of organizations that make use of differences in authority and responsibility, or chains of command. While the distribution of wealth and income need not be equal, it must be to everyone's advantage, and at the same time, positions of authority and offices of command must be accessible to all. One applies the second principle by holding positions open, and then, subject to this constraint, arranges social and economic inequalities so that everyone benefits.

These principles are to be arranged in a serial order with the first principle prior to the second. This ordering means that a departure from the institutions of equal liberty required by the first principle cannot be justified by, or compensated for, by greater social and economic advantages. The distribution of wealth and income, and the hierarchies of authority, must be consistent with both the liberties of equal citizenship and equality of opportunity.

It is clear that these principles are rather specific in their content, and their acceptance rests on certain assumptions that I must eventually try to explain and justify. A theory of justice depends upon a theory of society in ways that will become evidence as we proceed. For the present, it should be observed that the two principles (and this holds for all formulations) are a special case of a more general conception of justice that can be expressed as follows.

> All social values—liberty and opportunity, income and wealth, and the bases of self-respect—are to be distributed equally unless an unequal distribution of any, or all, of these values is to everyone's advantage.

Injustice, then, is simply inequalities that are not to the benefit of all. Of course, this conception is extremely vague and requires interpretation.

As a first step, suppose that the basic structure of society distributes certain primary goods, that is, things that every rational man is presumed to want. These goods normally have a use whatever a person's rational plan of life. For simplicity, assume that the chief primary goods at the disposition of society are rights and liberties, powers and opportunities, income and wealth. . . . These are the social primary goods. Other primary goods such as health and vigor, intelligence and imagination, are natural goods; although their possession is influenced by the basic structure, they are not so directly under its control. Imagine, then, a hypothetical initial arrangement in which all the social primary goods are equally distributed: everyone has similar rights and duties, and income and wealth are evenly shared. This state of affairs provides a benchmark for judging improvements. If certain inequalities of wealth and organizational powers would make everyone better off than in this hypothetical starting situation, then they accord with the general conception.

Now it is possible, at least theoretically, that by giving up some of their fundamental liberties men are sufficiently compensated by the resulting social and economic gains. The general conception of justice imposes no restrictions on what sort of inequalities are permissible; it only requires that everyone's position be improved. We need not suppose anything so drastic as consenting to a condition of slavery. Imagine instead that men forego certain political rights when the economic returns are significant and their capacity to influence the course of policy by the exercise of these rights would be marginal in any case. It is this kind of exchange which the two principles as stated rule out; being arranged in serial order they do not permit exchanges between basic liberties and economic and social gains. The serial ordering of principles expresses an underlying preference among primary social goods. When this preference is rational so likewise is the choice of these principles in this order.

In developing justice as fairness I shall, for the most part, leave aside the general conception of justice and examine instead the special case of the two principles in serial order. The advantage of this procedure is that from the first the matter of priorities is recognized and an effort made to find principles to deal with it. One is led to attend throughout to the conditions under which the acknowledgment of the absolute weight of liberty with respect to social and economic advantages, as defined by the lexical order of the two principles, would be reasonable. Offhand, this ranking appears extreme and too special a case to be of much interest; but there is more justification for it than would appear at first sight. Or at any rate, so I shall maintain. . . . Furthermore, the distinction between fundamental rights and liberties and economic and social benefits marks a difference among primary social goods that one should try to exploit. It suggests an important division in the social system. Of course, the distinctions drawn and the ordering proposed are bound to be at best only approximations. There are surely circumstances in which they fail. But it is essential to depict clearly the main lines of a reasonable conception of justice; and under many conditions anyway, the two principles in serial order may serve well enough. When necessary we can fall back on the more general conception.

The fact that the two principles apply to institutions has certain consequences. Several points illustrate this. First of all, the rights and liberties referred to by these principles are those which are defined by the public rules of the basic structure. Whether men are free is determined by the rights and duties established by the major institutions of society. Liberty is a certain pattern of social forms. The first principle simply requires that certain sorts of rules, those defining basic liberties, apply to everyone equally and that they allow the most extensive liberty compatible with a like liberty for all. The only reason for circumscribing the rights defining liberty and making men's freedom less extensive than it might otherwise be is that these equal rights as institutionally defined would interfere with one another.

Another thing to bear in mind is that when principles mention persons, or require that everyone gain from an inequality, the reference is to representative persons holding the various social positions, or offices, or whatever, established by the basic structure. Thus in applying the second principle I assume that it is possible to assign an expectation of well-being to representative individuals holding these positions. This expectation indicates their life prospects as viewed from their social station. In general, the expectations of representative persons depend upon the distribution of rights and duties throughout the basic structure. When this changes, expectations change. I assume, then, that expectations are connected: by raising the prospects of the representative man in one position we presumably increase or decrease the prospects of representative men in other positions. Since it applies to institutional forms, the second principle (or rather the first part of it) refers to the expectations of representative individuals. As I shall discuss below, neither principle applies to distributions of particular goods to particular individuals who may be identified by their proper names. The situation were someone is considering how to allocate certain commodities to needy persons who are known to him is not within the scope of the principles. They are meant to regulate basic institutional arrangements. We must not assume that there is much similarity from the standpoint of justice between an administrative allotment of goods to specific persons and the appropriate design of society. Our common sense intuitions for the former may be a poor guide to the latter.

Now the second principle insists that each person benefit from permissible inequalities in the basic structure. This means that it must be reasonable for each relevant representative man defined by this structure, when he views it as a going concern, to prefer his prospects with the inequality to his prospects without it. One is not allowed to justify differences in income or organizational powers on the ground that the disadvantages of those in one position are outweighed by the greater advantages of those in another. Much less can infringements of liberty be counterbalanced in this way. Applied to the basic structure, the principle of utility would have us maximize the sum of expectations of representative men (weighted by the number of persons they represent, on the classical view); and this would permit us to compensate for the losses of some by the gains of others. Instead, the two principles require that everyone benefit from economic and social inequalities. It is obvious, however, that there are indefinitely many ways in which all may be advantaged when the initial arrangement of equality is taken as a benchmark. How then are we to choose among these possibilities? The principles must be specified so that they yield a determinate conclusion. I now turn to this problem. . . .

Endnotes

1. As the text suggests, I shall regard Locke's *Second Treatise of Government*, Rousseau's *The Social Contract*, and Kant's ethical works beginning with *The Foundations of the Metaphysics of Morals* as definitive of the contract tradition. For all of its greatness, Hobbes's *Leviathan* raises special problems. A general historical survey is provided by J. W. Gough, *The Social Contract*, 2nd ed. (Oxford, The Clarendon Press, 1957), and Otto Gierke, *Natural Law and the Theory of Society*, trans. with an introduction by Ernest Barker (Cambridge, The University Press, 1934). A presentation of the contract view as primarily an ethical theory is to be found in G. R. Grice, *The Grounds of Moral Judgment* (Cambridge, The University Press, 1967). See also § 19, note 30. [The footnotes have been renumbered—Ed.]
2. Kant is clear that the original agreement is hypothetical. See *The Metaphysics of Morals*, pt. I (*Rechtslehre*), especially §§ 47, 52; and pt. II of the essay "Concerning the Common Saying: This May Be True in Theory but It Does Not Apply in Practice," in *Kant's Political Writings*, ed. Hans Reiss and trans. by H. B. Nisbet (Cambridge, The University Press, 1970), pp. 73–87. See Georges Vlachos, *La Pensée politique de Kant* (Paris, Presses Universitaires de France, 1962), pp. 326–335; and J. G. Murphy, *Kant: The Philosophy of Right* (London, Macmillan, 1970), pp. 109–112, 133–136, for a further discussion.
3. For the formulation of this intuitive idea I am indebted to Allan Gibbard.

Review Questions

1. Carefully explain Rawls' conception of the original position.
2. State and explain Rawls' first principle of justice.
3. State and explain the second principle. Which principle has priority such that it cannot be sacrificed?

Discussion Questions

1. On the first principle, each person has an equal right to the most extensive basic liberty as long as this does not interfere with a similar liberty for others. What does this allow people to do? Does it mean, for example, that people have a right to engage in homosexual activities as long as they don't interfere with others? Can people produce and view pornography if it does not restrict anyone's freedom? Are people allowed to take drugs in the privacy of their homes?
2. Is it possible for free and rational persons in the original position to agree upon different principles than those given by Rawls? For example, why wouldn't they agree to an equal distribution of wealth and income rather than an unequal distribution? That is, why wouldn't they adopt socialism rather than capitalism? Isn't socialism just as rational as capitalism?

Alison M. Jaggar

Feminist Ethics: Some Issues for the Nineties

Alison M. Jaggar is Professor of Philosophy at the University of Colorado and the author of Feminist Politics and Human Nature *(1983).*

Jaggar begins by identifying some of the main objectives of feminist theory: to correct the male bias in western ethics; to oppose the subordination of women in a male-dominated society; to offer

From Alison M. Jaggar, "Feminist Ethics: Some Issues for the Nineties", *Journal of Social Philosophy*, Vol. 20, Nos. 1–2 (Spring/Fall 1989). Reprinted by permission of the *Journal of Social Philosophy*.

guidance on all moral issues, both public and private; and to show respect for women's moral experience. In the rest of the article, she surveys five issues that feminists have focused on in their discussions, without always agreeing: impartiality, moral subjectivity, autonomy, and moral epistemology.

Feminist approaches to ethics are distinguished by their explicit commitment to rethinking ethics with a view to correcting whatever forms of male bias it may contain. Feminist ethics, as these approaches are often called collectively, seeks to identify and challenge all those ways, overt but more often and more perniciously covert, in which western ethics has excluded women or rationalized their subordination. Its goal is to offer both practical guides to action and theoretical understandings of the nature of morality that do not, overtly or covertly, subordinate the interests of any woman or group of women to the interests of any other individual or group.

While those whose practice feminist ethics are united by a shared project, they diverge widely in their views as to how this project may be accomplished. These divergences result from a variety of philosophical differences, including differing conceptions of feminism itself, a perennially contested concept. The inevitability of such disagreement means that feminist ethics cannot be identified in terms of a specific range of topics, methods or orthodoxies. For example, it is a mistake, though one to which even some feminists occasionally have succumbed, to identify feminist ethics with any of the following: putting women's interests first; focusing exclusively on so-called women's issues; accepting women (or feminists) as moral experts or authorities; substituting "female" (or "feminine") for "male" (or "masculine") values; or extrapolating directly from women's experience.

. Even though my initial characterization of feminist ethics is quite loose, it does suggest certain minimum conditions of adequacy for any approach to ethics that purports to be feminist.

1. Within the present social context, in which women remain systematically subordinated, a feminist approach to ethics must offer a guide to action that will tend to subvert rather than reinforce this subordination. Thus, such an approach must be practical, transitional and nonutopian, an extension of politics rather than a retreat from it. It must be sensitive, for instance, to the symbolic meanings as well as the practical consequences of any actions that we take as gendered subjects in a male dominated society, and it must also provide the conceptual resources for identifying and evaluating the varieties of resistance and struggle in which women, particularly, have tended to engage. It must recognize the often unnoticed ways in which women and other members of the underclass have refused co-operation and opposed domination, while acknowledging the inevitability of collusion and the impossibility of totally clean hands.

2. Since so much of women's struggle has been in the kitchen and the bedroom, as well as in the parliamentary chamber and on the factory floor, a second requirement for feminist ethics is that it should be equipped to handle moral issues in both the so-called public and private domains. It must be able to provide guidance on issues of intimate relations, such as affection and sexuality, which, until quite recently, were largely ignored by modern moral theory. In so doing, it cannot assume that moral concepts developed originally for application to the public realm, concepts such as impartiality of exploitation, are automatically applicable to the private realm. Similarly, an approach to ethics that is adequate for feminism must also provide appropriate guidance for activity in the public realm, for dealing with large numbers of people, including strangers.

3. Finally, feminist ethics must take the moral experience of all women seriously, though not, of course, uncritically. Though what is *feminist* will often turn out to be very different from what is *feminine,* a basic respect for women's moral experience is necessary to acknowledging women's capacities as moralists and to countering traditional stereotypes of women as less than full moral agents, as childlike or "natural." Furthermore, as Okin [1987], among others, has argued, empirical claims about differences in the moral experience of women and men make it impossible to assume that any approach to ethics will be unanimously

accepted if it fails to consult the moral experience of women. Additionally, it seems plausible to suppose that women's distinctive social experience may make them especially perceptive regarding the implications of domination, especially gender domination, and especially well equipped to detect the male bias that has been shown to pervade so much of male-authored western moral theory.

On the surface, at least, these conditions of adequacy for feminist ethics are quite minimal—although I believe that fulfilling them would have radical consequences for ethics. I think most feminist, and perhaps even many nonfeminist,* philosophers would be likely to find the general statement of these conditions relatively uncontroversial, but that inevitably there will be sharp disagreement over when the conditions have been met. Even feminists are likely to differ over, for instance, just what are women's interests and when they have been neglected, what is resistance to domination and which aspects of which women's moral experience are worth developing and in which directions.

I shall now go on to outline some of these differences as they have arisen in feminist discussions of five ethical and meta-ethical issues. These five certainly are not the only issues to confront feminist ethics; on the contrary, the domain of feminist ethics is identical with that of nonfeminist ethics—it is the whole domain of morality and moral theory. I have selected these five issues both because I believe they are especially pressing in the context of contemporary philosophical debate, and because I myself find them especially interesting. As will shortly become evident, the issues that I have selected are not independent of each other; they are unified at least by recurrent concern about questions of universality and particularity. Nevertheless, I shall separate the issues for purposes of exposition.

1. Equality and Difference

The central insight of contemporary feminism without doubt has been the recognition of gender as a sometimes contradictory but always pervasive system of social norms that regulates the activity of individuals according to their biological sex. Thus individuals whose sex is male are expected to conform to prevailing norms of masculinity, while female individuals are expected to conform to prevailing norms of femininity. In 1970, Shulamith Firestone began her classic *The Dialectic of Sex* with the words "Sex class is so deep as to be invisible" and, for the first decade of the contemporary women's movement, feminists devoted themselves to rendering "sex-class" or gender visible; to exploring (and denouncing) the depth and extent of gender regulation in the life of every individual. Norms of gender were shown to influence not only dress, occupation and sexuality, but also bodily comportment, patterns of speech, eating habits and intellectual, emotional, moral and even physical development—mostly in ways that, practically and/or symbolically, reinforced the domination of men over women.

The conceptual distinction between sex and gender enabled feminists to articulate a variety of important insights. These included recognizing that the superficially nondiscriminatory acceptance of exceptional, i.e., "masculine," women is not only compatible with but actually presupposes a devaluation of "the feminine." The sex/gender distinction also enabled feminists to separate critical reflection on cultural norms of masculinity from antagonism towards actual men.

Useful as the concept of gender has been to feminism, however, more recent feminist reflection has shown that it is neither as simple nor as unproblematic as it seemed when feminists first articulated it. Some feminists have challenged the initially sharp distinction between sex and gender, noting that, just as sex differences have influenced (though not ineluctably determined) the development of gender norms, so gender arrangements may well have influenced the biological evolution of certain secondary sexual characteristics and even of that defining criterion of sex, procreation itself. Other feminists have challenged the distinction between gender and other social categories such as race and class. Recognizing that feminist claims about "women" often had generalized illicitly from the experience of a relatively small group of middle-class white women, feminists in the last ten years have emphasized that gender is a variable rather than a constant, since norms of gender vary not only between but also within cultures, along dimensions such as class, race, age, marital status, sexual preference and so on. Moreover, since every woman is a woman of some determinate age, race, class and marital status, gender is not even an independent variable; there is no concept of pure or abstract gender that can be isolated theoretically and studied independently of class, race, age or marital status. Neither, of course, can these other social categories be understood independently of gender.

Their increasingly sophisticated understandings of gender have complicated feminists' discussions of many moral and social issues. One of these is sexual equality. At the beginning of the contemporary women's movement, in the late 1960s, this seemed to be a relatively straight-forward issue. The nineteenth century feminist preference for "separate spheres" for men and women had been replaced by demands for identity of legal rights for men and women or, as it came to be called, equality before the law. By the end of he 1960s, most feminists in the United States had come to believe that the legal system should be sex-blind, that it should not differentiate in any way between women and men. This belief was expressed in the struggle for an Equal Rights Amendment to the U.S. Constitution, an amendment that, had it passed, would have made any sex-specific law unconstitutional.

By the late 1970s and early 1980s, however, it was becoming apparent that the assimilationist goal of strict equality before the law does not always benefit women, at least in the short term. One notorious example was "no fault" divorce settlements that divided family property equally between husband and wife but invariably left wives in a far worse economic situation than they did husbands. In one study, for instance, ex-husbands' standard of living was found to have risen by 42% a year after divorce, whereas ex-wives' standard of living declined by 73%. This huge discrepancy in the outcome of divorce resulted from a variety of factors, including the fact that women and men typically are differently situated in the job market, with women usually having much lower job qualifications and less work experience. In this sort of case, equality (construed as identity) in the treatment of the sexes appears to produce an outcome in which sexual inequality is increased.

The obvious alternative of seeking equality by providing women with special legal protection continues, however, to be as fraught with dangers for women as it was earlier in the century when the existence of protective legislation was used as an excuse for excluding women from many of the more prestigious and better paid occupations. For instance, mandating special leaves for disability on account of pregnancy or childbirth promotes the perception that women are less reliable workers than men; recognizing "premenstrual syndrome" or post-partum depression as periodically disabling conditions encourages the perception that women are less responsible than men; while attempts to protect women's sexuality through legislation restricting pornography or excluding women from employment in male institutions such as prisons, perpetuate the dangerous stereotypes that women are by nature the sexual prey of men. This cultural myth serves as an implicit legitimation for the prostitution, sexual harassment and rape of women, because it implies that such activities are in some sense natural. In all these cases, attempts to achieve equality between the sexes by responding to perceived differences between men and women seem likely to reinforce rather than reduce existing differences, even differences that are acknowledged to be social rather than biological in origin.

Furthermore, a "sex-responsive," as opposed to "sex-blind," conception of equality ignores differences *between* women, separating all women into a single homogenous category and possibly penalizing one group of women by forcing them to accept protection that another group genuinely may need.

Sooner or later, most feminist attempts to formulate an adequate conception of sexual equality run up against the recognition that the baseline for discussions of equality typically has been a male standard. In Catharine MacKinnon's inimitable words:

> Men's physiology defines most sports, their needs define auto and health insurance coverage, their socially designed biographies define workplace expectations and successful career patterns, their perspectives and concerns define quality in scholarship, their experiences and obsessions define merit, their objectification of life defines art, their military service defines citizenship, their presence defines family, their inability to get along with each other—their wars and rulerships—defines history, their image defines god, and their genitals define sex [MacKinnon 1987:36].

Having once reached this recognition, some feminist theorists have turned away from debating the pros and cons of what MacKinnon calls the "single" versus the "double standard" and begun speculating about the kinds of far-reaching social transformation that would make sex differences "costless." In discussions elaborating such notions as that of "equality as acceptance," feminists seem to be moving towards a radical construal of equality as similarity of individual outcome, equality of condition or effect, a conception quite at odds with traditional liberal understandings of equality as equality of procedure or opportunity.

While some feminists struggle to formulate a conception of sexual equality that is adequate for feminism, others have suggested that the enterprise is hopeless. For them, equality is an integral part of an "ethic of justice" that is characteristically masculine insofar as it obscures human difference by abstracting from the particularity and uniqueness of concrete people in their specific situations and seeks to resolve conflicting interests by applying an abstract rule rather than by responding directly to needs that are immediately perceived. Such feminists suggest that a discourse of responsibility or care may offer a more appropriate model for feminist ethics—even including feminist jurisprudence. Both of these suggestions remain to be worked out in detail.

The tangled debate over equality and difference provides an excellent illustration of one characteristic feature of contemporary feminist ethics, namely, its insistence that gender is often, if not invariably, a morally relevant difference between individuals. Given this insistence, the starting point of much feminist ethics may be different from that of modern moral theory: instead of assuming that all individuals should be treated alike until morally relevant grounds for difference in treatment can be identified, feminist theorists may shift the traditional burden of moral proof by assuming, until shown otherwise, that contemporary men and women are rarely "similarly situated." This leads into a related and equally crucial question for feminist ethics in the nineties, namely, how to characterize and evaluate impartiality.

2. Impartiality

In the modern western tradition, impartiality typically has been recognized as a fundamental value, perhaps even a defining characteristic of morality, distinguishing true morality from tribalism. Impartiality is said to require weighing the interests of each individual equally, permitting differentiation only on the basis of differences that can be shown to be morally relevant. Impartiality thus is linked conceptually with equality and also with rationality and objectivity, insofar as bias often has been defined as the absence of impartiality.

In the last few years, the preeminence traditionally ascribed to impartiality has been challenged both by feminist and nonfeminist philosophers. Nonfeminists have charged that an insistence on impartiality disregards our particular identities, constituted by reference to our particular projects and our unchosen relationships with others; and that it substitutes abstract "variables" for real human agents and patients. Williams [1973, 1981], for instance, has argued that the requirement of impartiality may undermine our personal integrity because it may require us to abandon projects that are central to our identity, and he also suggests that acting from duty may sometimes be less valuable than acting from an immediate emotional response to a particular other. MacIntyre [1981] and Sommers [1986] have argued that impartiality fails to respect tradition, customary expectations and unchosen encumbrances, and may require behavior that is morally repugnant.

While some of the moral intuitions that motivate the nonfeminist critics of impartiality certainly are shared by many feminists, other intuitions most likely are not. It is implausible to suppose, for instance, that most feminists would join Williams in applauding Gaugin's abandonment of his family in order to pursue his art, or that they would join Sommers in accepting without question the claims of customary morality on issues such as women's responsibilities. Instead, the feminist criticisms of impartiality tend to be both less individualistic and less conventionalist. They are quite varied in character.

Nell Noddings [1984] is one of the most extreme opponents of impartiality and her work has been influential with a number of feminists, even though the sub-title of her book makes it clear that she takes herself to be elaborating a feminine rather than a feminist approach to ethics. Noddings views the emotion of caring as the natural basis of morality, a view that would require impartiality to be expressed in universal caring. Noddings claims, however, that we are psychologically able to care only for particular others with whom we are in actual relationships, i.e., relationships that can be "completed" by the cared-for's acknowledgment of our caring. She concludes that pretensions to care for humanity at large are not only hypocritical but self defeating, undermining true caring for those with whom we are in actual relationship. Noddings' arguments, if valid, of course would apply indifferently to caring practised either by men or by women, and so the distinctively feminist interest of Noddings' work might seem to reside solely in her obviously debatable claim that women are "better equipped for caring than men" (97) and therefore less likely to be impartial. As we have noted already, however, feminist ethics is not committed to reproducing the moral practice even of most women and so feminist (and nonfeminist) moral theorists need to evaluate critically all of Noddings' arguments against impartiality, independently of whether her claims about "feminine" morality can be empirically confirmed.

A different criticism of impartiality has been made by those feminist philosophers who assert that, while impartiality is associated historically with individualism, it paradoxically undermines respect for individuality because it treats individuals as morally interchangeable [Code 1988; Sherwin 1987]. Many, though certainly not all, feminists claim that women are less likely than men to commit this alleged moral error because they are more likely to appreciate the special characteristics of particular individuals; again, however, feminist estimates of the soundness or otherwise of Code's and Sherwin's argument must be independent of this empirical claim.

Finally, at least one feminist has extended the claim that women need special protection in the law by recommending that feminist ethics should promote a double standard of morality, limiting moral communities on the basis of gender or perhaps gender solidarity. Susan Sherwin writes that feminists feel a special responsibility to reduce the suffering of women in particular; thus, "(b)y acknowledging the relevance of differences among people as a basis for a difference in sympathy and concern, feminism denies the legitimacy of a central premise of traditional moral theories, namely that all persons should be seen as morally equivalent by us" [Sherwin 1987:26 . . .]. However, since women and even feminists are not homogenous groups, as we have seen, this kind of reasoning seems to push the suggested double standard towards becoming a multiple moral standard—which Enlightenment theorists might well interpret as the total abandonment of impartiality and thus of morality itself.

A variety of responses seems to be available to the foregoing criticisms of impartiality. One alternative is to argue that the criticisms are unwarranted, depending on misrepresentation, misunderstanding and caricature of the impartialist position. If this response can be sustained, it may be possible to show that there is no real conflict between "masculine" impartialism and "feminine" particularism, "masculine" justice and "feminine" care. Another alternative is to bite the bullet of direct moral confrontation, providing arguments to challenge the intuitions of those who criticize impartiality as requiring courses of action that are morally repugnant or politically dangerous. Yet a third alternative may be to reconceive the concept of impartiality and the considerations appropriate for determining our responsibilities toward various individuals and groups. Feminist ethics must find a way of choosing between those or other options and evaluating the proper place of impartiality in ethics for the nineties.

3. Moral Subjectivity

Related to the foregoing questions about impartiality are questions about how to conceptualize individuals, the subjects of moral theory. Feminists and nonfeminists alike have criticized the neo-Cartesian model of the moral self, a disembodied, separate, autonomous, unified, rational being, essentially similar to all other moral selves. Marx challenged the ahistoricism of this model; Freud challenged its claims to rationality; contemporary communitarians, such as Sandel and MacIntyre, challenge the assumption that individuals are "unencumbered," arguing instead that we are all members of communities from which we may be able to distance ourselves to some extent but which nevertheless are deeply constitutive of our identities; postmodernists have deconstructed the model to reveal fractured rather than unitary identities.

The gender bias alleged to contaminate each of the traditions mentioned above means that feminists cannot appropriate uncritically existing critiques of the neo-Cartesian moral self. Nevertheless, in developing their own challenges to this model of the self, feminist theorists often have paralleled and/or built on some nonfeminist work . . . .

Given this burgeoning literature, it is evident that a central concern for feminist ethics in the nineties must be to develop ways of thinking about moral subjects that are sensitive *both* to their concreteness, inevitable particularity and unique specificity, expressed in part through their relations with specific historical communities, *and* to their intrinsic and common value, the ideal expressed in Enlightenment claims about common humanity, equality and impartiality.

4. Autonomy

One aspect of this task is the rethinking of autonomy which, like impartiality (to which it is often conceptually connected), has been a continuing ideal of modern moral theory. (In addition, a closely related concept of autonomy has played a central role in the Cartesian epistemological tradition, which envisions the search for knowledge as a project of the solitary knower.) The core intuition of autonomy is that of independence or self legislation, the self as the ultimate authority in matters of morality or truth. In the Kantian tradition, where the ideal of autonomy is particularly prominent, moral autonomy has been elaborated in terms of disinterest, detachment from particular attachments and interests, and freedom from prejudice and self-deception [Hill 1987].

Contemporary feminists have had a mixed response to the modern ideal of moral autonomy. On the one hand, they have insisted that women are as autonomous in the moral and intellectual sense as men—as rational, as capable of a sense of justice, and so on; and they have also demanded political, social and economic autonomy for women through political representation, the abolition of sex discrimination and respect for women's choices on issues such as abortion. On the other hand, however, some feminists have questioned traditional interpretations of autonomy as masculine fantasies. For instance, they have explored some of the ways in which "choice" is socialized and "consent" manipulated. In addition, they have questioned the possibility of separating ourselves from particular attachments and still retaining our personal identity, and they have suggested that freeing ourselves from particular attachments might result in a cold, rigid, moralistic rather than a truly moral response [Noddings 1984]. Rather than guaranteeing a response that is purely moral, freeing ourselves from particular attachments might instead make us *incapable* of morality if an incliminable part of morality consists in responding emotionally to particular others.

Feminist ethics in the nineties must find ways of conceptualizing moral agency, choice and consent that are compatible with the feminist recognition of the gradual process of moral development, the gendered social construction of the psyche, and the historical constraints on our options. This is one area in which some promising work by feminists exists already.

5. Moral Epistemology and Anti-epistemology

Enlightenment moral theory characteristically assumed that morality was universal—that, if moral claims held, they were valid at all times and in all places. However, the modern abandonment of belief in a teleological and sacred universe rendered the justification of such claims constantly problematic, and much moral theory for the last three centuries has consisted in attempts to provide a rational grounding for morality. At the present time, both the continental European tradition, especially but not only in the form of postmodernism, and the Anglo-American tradition, especially but not only in the form of communitarianism, have developed powerful challenges to the very possibility of the view that morality consists in universally valid rules grounded in universal reason. The inevitable result of these sceptical challenges has been to reinforce normative and **meta-ethical relativism.**

Feminists are ambivalent about these challenges. On the one hand, many of the feminist criticisms of modern moral theory parallel the criticisms made by communitarianism and postmodernism. On the other hand, however, feminists are understandably concerned that their critique of male dominance should not be dismissed as just one point of view. It is therefore crucial for feminist ethics to develop some ways of justifying feminist moral claims. However, moral epistemology is an area in which feminists' critiques are better developed than their alternatives.

Feminist discussions of **moral epistemology** may be divided into two categories, each distinguished by a somewhat different view of the nature of morality. Feminists in the first category do not explicitly challenge the modern conception of morality as consisting primarily in an impartial system of rationally justified rules or principles, though few feminists would assert that it is possible to identify rules that are substantive, specific and hold in all circumstances. Those in the second category, by contrast, deny that morality is reducible to rules and emphasize the impossibility of justifying the claims of ethics by appeal to a universal, impartial reason. The contrast between these two groups of feminists is not as sharp as this initial characterization might suggest: for instance, both share several criticisms of existing decision procedures in ethics. But feminists in the former group are more hopeful of repairing those procedures, while feminists in the latter group seem ready to abandon them entirely.

Feminists in the latter group frequently claim to be reflecting on a moral experience that is distinctively feminine and for this reason they are often—incorrectly—taken to represent a feminist orthodoxy. They include authors such as Gilligan [1982], Noddings [1984], Baier [1987], Blum [1987], Ruddick [1989] and Walker [1989]. While there is considerable variation in the views of these authors, they all reject the view attributed to modern moral theorists that the right course of action can be discovered by consulting a list of moral rules, charging that undue emphasis on the epistemological importance of rules obscures the crucial role of moral insight, virtue and character in determining what should be done. A feminist twist is given to this essentially Aristotelian criticism when claims are made that excessive reliance on rules reflects a juridical-administrative interest that is characteristic of modern masculinity [Blum 1982] while contemporary women, by contrast, are alleged to be more likely to disregard conventionally accepted moral rules because such rules are insensitive to the specificities of particular situations [Gilligan 1982; Noddings 1984]. A morality of rule, therefore, is alleged to devalue the moral wisdom of women, as well as to give insufficient weight to such supposedly feminine virtues as kindness, generosity, helpfulness and sympathy.

Some feminists have claimed that "feminine" approaches to morality contrast with supposedly masculine rule-governed approaches in that they characteristically consist in immediate responses to particular others, responses based on supposedly natural feelings of empathy, care and compassion [Gilligan 1982; Noddings

1984] or loving attention [Murdoch 1970; Ruddick 1989]. However, apart from the difficulties of establishing that such a "particularist" approach to morality [Blum 1987] indeed is characteristically feminine, let alone feminist, attempts to develop a moral epistemology based on such responses face a variety of problems. First, they confront the familiar, though perhaps not insuperable, problems common to all moral epistemologies that take emotion as a guide to right action, namely, the frequent inconsistency, unavailability or plain inappropriateness of emotions. In other words, they face the danger of degenerating into a "do what feels good" kind of subjective relativism. In addition, it is not clear that even our emotional responses to others are not responses to them under some universal description and so in this sense general rather than particular—or, if indeed particular and therefore nonconceptual, then perhaps closer to animal than to distinctively human responses. It is further uncertain how these sorts of particular responses can guide our actions towards large numbers of people, most of whom we shall never meet. Finally, the feminist emphasis on the need for "contextual" reasoning opens up the obvious dangers of *ad hoc*ism, special pleading and partiality.

Not all feminists, of course, are committed to a particularist moral epistemology. Even some of those who take emotions as a proper guide to morality emphasize the intentionality of emotions and discuss the need for their moral education. Additionally, while most feminists criticize certain aspects of the decision procedures developed by modern moral theory, some believe it may be possible to revise and reappropriate some of these procedures. The main candidates for such revision are the methods developed by Rawls and Habermas, each of whom believes that an idealized situation of dialogue (which each describes differently) will both generate and justify morally valid principles. . . .

One possible alternative both to an unwelcome relativism and to what many feminists see as the pretensions of moral rationalism may be the development of a moral standpoint that is distinctively feminist. Sara Ruddick claims that such a standpoint can be found in maternal thinking [1989], but her work has been criticized by some feminists as ethnocentric and overvaluing motherhood. Even if the feminist standpoint were differently identified, however, problems would remain. Standpoint epistemology derives from Marx and, at least in its Lukacian version, it seems to require an objectivist distinction between appearance and reality that is quite alien to the social constructionist tendencies in much contemporary feminism.

The controversy in feminist moral epistemology currently is so sharp that Held [1984] has suggested abandoning the search for a "unified field theory" covering all domains of life activity. However, other authors have pointed to the danger that, if a supposedly feminine "ethic of care" were limited to the realm of personal life, as Kohlberg, for instance has suggested, it would be perceived as subordinate to the supposedly masculine "ethic of justice," just as, in contemporary society, the private is subordinate to the public.

Conclusion

Even such a limited survey as this should make it evident that feminist ethics, far from being a rigid orthodoxy, instead is a ferment of ideas and controversy, many of them echoing and deepening debates in nonfeminist ethics. The centrality of the issues and the liveliness of the on-going discussions suggest that the nineties will be a fruitful period for feminist ethics—and thus for ethics generally.

Reference Notes

Baier, Annette, "The Need for More Than Justice," *Science, Morality and Feminist Theory,* ed. Marsha Hanen and Kai Nielsen, Calgary: University of Calgary Press, 1987.

Blum, Lawrence, "Kant's and Hegel's Moral Rationalism: A Feminist Perspective," *Canadian Journal of Philosophy* 12:2 (June 1982).

Blum, Lawrence, "Particularity and Responsiveness," *The Emergence of Morality in Young Children,* eds. Jerome Kagan and Sharon Lamb, Chicago: University of Chicago Press, 1987.

Code, Lorraine, "Experience, Knowledge and Responsibility," *Feminist Perspectives in Philosophy,* eds. Morwenna Griffiths and Margaret Whitford, Bloomington & Indianapolis: Indiana University Press, 1988.

Gilligan, Carol, *In a Different Voice: Psychological Theory and Women's Development,* Cambridge, MA: Harvard University Press, 1982.

Gilligan, Carol, *In a Different Voice: Psychological Theory and Women's Development*, Cambridge, MA: Harvard University Press, 1982.
Held, Virginia, *Rights and Goods*, New York: The Free Press, 1984.
Hill, Thomas E., Jr., "The Importance of Autonomy," *Women and Moral Theory*, eds. Eva Feder Kittay and Diana T. Meyers, Totowa, NJ: Rowman and Littlefield, 1987.
MacIntyre, Alasdair, *After Virtue: A Study in Moral Theory*, London: Duckworth, 1981.
MacKinnon, Catharine A., *Feminism Unmodified: Discourses on Life and Law*, Cambridge, MA: Harvard University Press, 1987.
Murdoch, Iris, *The Sovereighnty of Good*, London: Routledge & Kegan Paul, 1970.
Noddings, Nell, *Caring: A Feminine Approach to Ethics and Moral Education*, Berkeley: University of California Press, 1984.
Okin, Susan Moller, "Justice and Gender," *Philosophy and Public Affairs* 16:1 (Winter 1987).
Ruddick, Sara, *Maternal Thinking: Toward a Politics of Peace*, Boston: Beacon Press, 1989.
Sherwin, Susan, "A Feminist Approach to Ethics," *Resources for Feminist Research* 16:3, 1987. (Special issue on "Women and Philosophy").
Sommers, Christina Hoff, "Filial Morality," *The Journal of Philosophy 83:8 (August 1986)*.
Walker, Margaret, "Moral Understandings: Alternative 'Epistemology' for a Feminist Ethics," *Hypatia: A Journal of Feminist Philosophy* 4:2 (Summer 1989).
Williams, B., "Morality and the Emotions," *Problems of the Self*, Cambridge: Cambridge University Press, 1973.
Williams, B., "Persons, Character and Morality," "Moral Luck," and "Utilitarianism and Moral Self Indulgence," *Moral Luck*, Cambridge: Cambridge University Press, 1981.

* "Nonfeminist" here refers to philosophers who do not make their feminist concerns explicit in their philosophical work; it is not intended to imply that such philosophers do not demonstrate feminist concern in other ways.

Review Questions

1. Jaggar identifies three minimum conditions that an approach to ethics must have to be feminist. What are they?
2. How do feminists view the issue of sexual equality?
3. Why do feminists challenge the importance of impartiality in morality?
4. Explain the mixed response that feminists have had to the idea of moral autonomy.
5. Jaggar divides discussion of moral epistemology into two categories. What are they?

Discussion Questions

1. What is the sex/gender distinction? Is there a sharp distinction, or are they related?
2. Should the law be sex-blind or sex-responsive?
3. Some philosophers have maintained that feminist ethics is compatible with traditional theories such as utilitarianism or Kant's theory. Do you agree? Why or why not?

Virginia Held

Feminism and Moral Theory

Virginia Held teaches philosophy at the Graduate Center, City University of New York.

Traditional moral theory, Held argues, has ignored the experience of women, particularly their experiences of birthing and mothering. She contends that an adequate moral theory must take these into account. The result is a feminist theory that places its priority on caring and trusting relationships with particular other people rather than on abstract principles and buyer-seller relationships.

The tasks of moral inquiry and moral practice are such that different moral approaches may be

From Virginia Held, "Feminism and Moral Theory," in *Women and Moral Theory*, edited by Eva Feder and Diana T. Meyers (Savage, MD: Rowman and Littlefield Publishers, © 1987).

appropriate for different domains of human activity. I have argued in a recent book that we need a division of moral labor.[1] In *Rights and Goods,* I suggest that we ought to try to develop moral inquiries that will be as satisfactory as possible for the actual contexts in which we live and in which our experience is located. Such a division of moral labor can be expected to yield different moral theories for different contexts of human activity, at least for the foreseeable future. In my view, the moral approaches most suitable for the courtroom are not those most suitable for political bargaining; the moral approaches suitable for economic activity are not those suitable for relations within the family, and so on. The task of achieving a unified moral field theory covering all domains is one we may do well to postpone, while we do our best to devise and to "test" various moral theories in actual contexts and in light of our actual moral experience.

What are the implications of such a view for women? Traditionally, the experience of women has been located to a large extent in the context of the family. In recent centuries, the family has been thought of as a "private" domain distinct not only from that of the "public" domain of the polis, but also from the domain of production and of the marketplace. Women (and men) certainly need to develop moral inquiries appropriate to the context of mothering and of family relations, rather than accepting the application to this context of theories developed for the marketplace or the polis. We can certainly show that the moral guidelines appropriate to mothering are different from those that now seem suitable for various other domains of activity as presently constituted. But we need to do more as well: we need to consider whether distinctively feminist moral theories, suitable for the contexts in which the experience of women has or will continue to be located, are better moral theories than those already available, and better for other domains as well.

The Experience of Women

We need a theory about how to count the experience of women. It is not obvious that it should count equally in the construction or validation of moral theory. To merely survey the moral views of women will not necessarily lead to better moral theories. In the Greek thought that developed into the Western philosophical tradition,[2] reason was associated with the public domain from which women were largely excluded. If the development of adequate moral theory is best based on experience in the public domain, the experience of women so far is less relevant. But that the public domain is the appropriate locus for the development of moral theory is among the tacit assumptions of existing moral theory being effectively challenged by feminist scholars. We cannot escape the need for theory in confronting these issues.

We need to take a stand on what moral experience is. As I see it, moral experience is "the experience of consciously choosing, of voluntarily accepting or rejecting, of willingly approving or disapproving, of living with these choices, and above all of acting and of living with these actions and their outcomes. . . . Action is as much a part of experience as is perception."[3] Then we need to take a stand on whether the moral experience of women is as valid a source or test of moral theory as is the experience of men, or on whether it is more valid.

Certainly, engaging in the process of moral inquiry is as open to women as it is to men, although the domains in which the process has occurred has been open to men and women in different ways. Women have had fewer occasions to experience for themselves the moral problems of governing, leading, exercising power over others (except children), and engaging in physically violent conflict. Men, on the other hand, have had fewer occasions to experience the moral problems of family life and the relations between adults and children. Although vast amounts of moral experience are open to all human beings who make the effort to become conscientious moral inquirers, the contexts in which experience is obtained may make a difference. It is essential that we avoid taking a given moral theory, such as a Kantian one, and deciding that those who fail to develop toward it are deficient, for this procedure imposes a theory on experience, rather than letting experience determine the fate of theories, moral and otherwise.

We can assert that as long as women and men experience different problems, moral theory ought to reflect the experience of women as fully as it reflects the experience of men. The insights and judgments and decisions of women as they engage in the process of moral inquiry should be presumed to be as valid as those of men. In the development of moral theory, men ought to have no privileged position to have their experience count for more. If anything, their privileged position in society should make their experience more suspect rather than more worthy of being counted, for they have good reasons to rationalize their privileged positions by moral arguments that will obscure or purport to justify these privileges.[4]

If the differences between men and women in confronting moral problems are due to biological factors that will continue to provide women and men with different experiences, the experience of women should still count for at least as much as the experience of men. There is no justification for discounting the experience of women as deficient or underdeveloped on biological grounds. Biological "moral inferiority" makes no sense.

The empirical question of whether and to what extent women think differently from men about moral problems is being investigated.[5] If, in fact, women approach moral problems in characteristic ways, these approaches should be reflected in moral theories as fully as are those of men. If the differing approaches to morality that seem to be displayed by women and by men are the result of historical conditions and not biological ones, we could assume that in nonsexist societies, the differences would disappear, and the experience of either gender might adequately substitute for the experience of the other.[6] Then feminist moral theory might be the same as moral theory of any kind. But since we can hardly imagine what a nonsexist society would be like, and surely should not wait for one before evaluating the experience of women, we can say that we need feminist moral theory to deal with the differences of which we are now aware and to contribute to the development of the nonsexist society that might make the need for a distinctively feminist moral theory obsolete. Specifically, we need feminist moral theory to deal with the regions of experience that have been central to women's experience and neglected by traditional moral theory. If the resulting moral theory would be suitable for all humans in all contexts, and thus could be thought of as a human moral theory or a universal moral theory, it would be a feminist moral theory as well if it adequately reflected the experience and standpoint of women.

That the available empirical evidence for differences between men and women with respect to morality is tentative and often based on reportage and interpretation, rather than on something more "scientific," [7] is no problem at all for the claim that we need feminist moral theory. If such differences turn out to be further substantiated, we will need theory to evaluate their implications, and we should be prepared now for this possibility (or, as many think, probability). If the differences turn out to be insignificant, we still need feminist moral theory to make the moral claim that the experience of women is of equal worth to the experience of men, and even more important, that women themselves are of equal worth as human beings. If it is true that the only differences between women and men are anatomical, it still does not follow that women are the moral equals of men. Moral equality has to be based on moral claims. Since the devaluation of women is a constant in human society as so far developed, and has been accepted by those holding a wide variety of traditional moral theories, it is apparent that feminist moral theory is needed to provide the basis for women's claims to equality.

We should never forget the horrors that have resulted from acceptance of the idea that women think differently from men, or that men are rational beings, women emotional ones. We should be constantly on guard for misuses of such ideas, as in social roles that determine that women belong in the home or in educational programs that discourage women from becoming for example, mathematicians. Yet, excessive fear of such misuses should not stifle exploration of the ways in which such claims may, in some measure, be true. As philosophers, we can be careful not to conclude that whatever tendencies exist ought to be reinforced. And if we succeed in making social scientists more alert to the naturalistic fallacy than they would otherwise be, that would be a side benefit to the development of feminist moral theory.

Mothering and Markets

When we bring women's experience fully into the domain of moral consciousness, we can see how questionable it is to imagine contractual relationships as central or fundamental to society and morality. They seem, instead, the relationships of only very particular regions of human activity.[8]

The most central and fundamental social relationship seems to be that between mother or mothering person and child. It is this relationship that creates and recreates society. It is the activity of mothering which transforms biological entities into human social beings. Mothers and mothering persons produce children and empower them with language and symbolic representations. Mothers and mothering persons thus produce and create human culture.

Despite its implausibility, the assumption is often made that human mothering is like the mothering of other animals rather than being distinctively human. In accordance with the traditional distinction between the family and the polis, and the assumption that what occurs in the public sphere of the polis is distinctively human, it is assumed that what human mothers do within the family belongs to the "natural" rather than to the "distinctively human" domain. Or, if it is recognized that the activities of human mothers do not resemble the activities of the mothers of other mammals, it is assumed that, at least, the difference is far narrower than the difference between what animals do and what humans who take part in government and industry and art do. But, in fact, mothering is among the most human of human activities.

Consider the reality. A human birth is thoroughly different form the birth of other animals, because a human mother can choose not to give birth. However extreme the alternative, even when abortion is not a possibility, a woman can choose suicide early enough in her pregnancy to consciously prevent the birth. A human mother comprehends that she brings about the birth of another human being. A human mother is then responsible, at least in an existentialist sense, for the creation of a new human life. The event is essentially different from what is possible for other animals.

Human mothering is utterly different from the mothering of animals without language. The human mother or nurturing person constructs with and for the child a human social reality. The child's understanding of language and of symbols, and of all that they create and make real, occurs in interactions between child and caretakers. Nothing seems more distinctively human than this. In comparison, government can be thought to resemble the governing of ant colonies, industrial production to be similar to the building of beaver dams, a market exchange to be like the relation between a large fish that protects and a small fish that grooms, and the conquest by force of arms that characterizes so much of human history to be like the aggression of packs of animals. But the imparting of language and the creation within and for each individual of a human social reality, and often a new human social reality, seems utterly human.

An argument is often made that art and industry and government create new human reality, while mothering merely "reproduces" human beings, their cultures, and social structures. But consider a more accurate view: in bringing up children, those who mother create new human *persons*. They change persons, the culture, and the social structures that depend on them, by creating the kinds of persons who can continue to transform themselves and their surroundings. Creating new and better persons is surely as "creative" as creating new and better objects or institutions. It is not only bodies that do not spring into being unaided and fully formed; neither do imaginations, personalities, and minds.

Perhaps morality should make room first for the human experience reflected in the social bond between mothering person and child, and for the human projects of nurturing and of growth apparent for both persons in the relationship. In comparison, the transactions of the marketplace seem peripheral; the authority of weapons and the laws they uphold, beside the point.

The relation between buyer and seller has often been taken as the model of all human interactions.[9] Most of the social contract tradition has seen this relation of contractual exchange as fundamental to law and political authority as well as to economic activity. And some contemporary moral philosophers see the contractual relation as the relation on which even morality itself should be based. The marketplace, as a model for relationships, has become so firmly entrenched in our normative theories that it is rarely questioned as a proper foundation for recommendations extending beyond he marketplace. Consequently, much moral thinking is built on the concept of rational economic man. Relationships between human beings are seen as arising, and as justified, when they serve the interests of individual rational contractors.

In the society imagined in the model based on assumptions about rational economic man, connections between people become no more than instrumental. Nancy Hartsock effectively characterizes the worldview of these assumptions, and shows how misguided it is to suppose that the relationship between buyer and seller can serve as a model for all human relations: "the paradigmatic connections between people [on this view of the social world] are instrumental or extrinsic and conflictual, and in a world populated by these isolated individuals, relations of competition and domination come to be substitutes for a more substantial and encompassing community." [10]

Whether the relationship between nurturing person (who need not be a biological mother) and child should be taken as itself paradigmatic, in place of the contractual paradigm, or whether it should be seen only as an obviously important relationship that does not fit into the contractual framework and should not be overlooked, remains to be seen. It is certainly instructive to consider it, at least tentatively, as paradigmatic. If this were done, the competition and desire for domination thought of as acceptable for rational economic man might appear as a very particular and limited human connection, suitable perhaps, if at all, only for a restricted marketplace. Such a relation of conflict and competition can be seen to be unacceptable for establishing the social trust on which public institutions must rest,[11] or for upholding the bonds on which caring, regard, friendship, or love must be based.[12]

The social map would be fundamentally altered by adoption of the point of view here suggested. Possibly, the relationship between "mother" and child would be recognized as a much more promising source of trust and concern than any other, for reasons to be explored later. In addition, social relations would be seen as dynamic rather than as fixed-point exchanges. And assumptions that human beings are equally capable of entering or not entering into the contractual relations taken to characterize social relations generally would be seen for the distortions they are. Although human mothers could do other than give birth, their choices to do so or not are usually highly constrained. And children, even human children, cannot choose at all whether to be born.

It may be that no human relationship should be thought of as paradigmatic for all the others. Relations between mothering persons and children can become oppressive for both, and relations between equals who can decide whether to enter into agreements may seem attractive in contrast. But no mapping of the social and moral landscape can possibly be satisfactory if it does not adequately take into account and provide appropriate guidance for relationships between mothering persons and children.

Between the Self and the Universal

Perhaps the most important legacy of the new insights will be the recognition that more attention must be paid to the domain *between* the self—the ego, the self-interested individual—on the one hand, and the universal—everyone, others in general—on the other hand. Ethics traditionally has dealt with these poles, trying to reconcile their conflicting claims. It has called for impartiality against the partiality of the egoistic self, or it has defended the claims of egoism against such demands for a universal perspective.

In seeing the problems of ethics as problems of reconciling the interests of the self with what would be right or best for everyone, moral theory has neglected the intermediate region of family relations and relations of friendship, and has neglected the sympathy and concern people actually feel for particular others. As Larry Blum has shown, "contemporary moral philosophy in the Anglo-American tradition has paid little attention to [the] morally significant phenomena" of sympathy, compassion, human concern, and friendship.[13]

Standard moral philosophy has construed personal relationships as aspects of the self-interested feelings of individuals, as when a person might favor those he loves over those distant because it satisfies his own desires to do so. Or it has let those close others stand in for the universal "other," as when an analysis might be offered of how the conflict between self and others is to be resolved in something like "enlightened self-interest" or "acting out of respect for the moral law," and seeing this as what should guide us in our relations with those close, particular others with whom we interact.

Owen Flanagan and Jonathan Adler provide useful criticism of what they see as Kohlberg's "adequacy thesis"—the assumption that the more formal the moral reasoning, the better.[14] But they themselves continue to construe the tension in ethics as that between the particular self and the universal. What feminist moral theory will emphasize, in contrast, will be the domain of particular others in relations with one another.

The region of "particular others" is a distinct domain, where it can be seen that what becomes artificial and problematic are the very "self" and "all others" of standard moral theory. In the domain of particular others, the self is already closely entwined in relations with others, and the relation may be much more real, salient, and important than the interests of any individual self in isolation. But the "others" in the picture are not "all others," or "everyone," or what a universal point of view could provide. They are particular flesh and blood others for whom we have actual feelings in our insides and in our skin, not the others of rational constructs and universal principles.

Relationships can be characterized as trusting or mistrustful, mutually considerate or selfish, and so forth. Where trust and consideration are appropriate, we can find ways to foster them. But doing so will depend on aspects of what can be understood only if we look at relations between persons. To focus on either self-interested individuals or the totality of all persons is to miss the qualities of actual relations between actual human beings.

Moral theories must pay attention to the neglected realm of particular others in actual contexts. In doing so, problems of egoism vs. the universal moral point of view appear very different, and may recede to the region of background insolubility or relative unimportance. The important problems may then be seen to be how we ought to guide or maintain or reshape the relationships, both close and more distant, that we have or might have with actual human beings.

Particular others can, I think, be actual starving children in Africa with whom one feels empathy or even the anticipated children of future generations, not just those we are close to in any traditional context of family, neighbors, or friends. But particular others are still not "all rational beings" or "the greatest number."

In recognizing the component of feeling and relatedness between self and particular others, motivation is addressed as an inherent part of moral inquiry. Caring between parent and child is a good example.[15] We should not glamorize parental care. Many mothers and fathers dominate their children in harmful or inappropriate ways, or fail to care adequately for them. But when the relationship between "mother" and child is as it should be, the caretaker does not care for the child (nor the child for the caretaker) because of universal moral rules. The love and concern one feels for the child already motivate much of what one does. This is not to say that morality is irrelevant. One must still decide what one ought to do. But the process of addressing the moral questions in mothering and of trying to arrive at answers one can find acceptable involves motivated acting, not just thinking. And neither egoism nor a morality of universal rules will be of much help.

Mothering is, of course, not the only context in which the salient moral problems concern relations between particular others rather than conflicts between egoistic self and universal moral laws; all actual human contexts may be more like this than like those depicted by Hobbes or Kant. But mothering may be one of the best contexts in which to make explicit why familiar moral theories are so deficient in offering guidance for action. And the variety of contexts within mothering, with the different excellences appropriate of dealing with infants, young children, or adolescents, provide rich sources of insight for moral inquiry.

The feelings characteristic of mothering—that there are too many demands on us, that we cannot do everything that we ought to do—are highly instructive. They give rise to problems different from those of universal rule vs. self-interest. They require us to weigh the claims of one self-other relationship against the claims of other self-other relationships, to try to bring about some harmony between them, to see the issues in an actual temporal context, and to act rather than merely reflect.

For instance, we have limited resources for caring. We cannot care for everyone or do everything a caring approach suggests. We need moral guidelines for ordering our priorities. The hunger of our own children comes before the hunger of children we do not know. But the hunger of children in Africa ought to come before some of the expensive amusements we may wish to provide for our own children. These are moral problems calling to some extent for principled answers. But we have to figure out what we ought to do when actually buying groceries, cooking meals, refusing the requests of our children for the latest toy they have seen advertised, and sending money to UNICEF. The context is one of real action, not of ideal thought.

Principles and Particulars

When we take the context of mothering as central, rather than peripheral, for moral theory, we run the risk of excessively discounting other contexts. It is a commendable risk, given the enormously more prevalent one of excessively discounting mothering. But I think that the attack on principles has sometimes been carried too far by critics of traditional moral theory.

Noddings, for instance, writes that "To say, 'It is wrong to cause pain needlessly,' contributes nothing by way of knowledge and can hardly be thought likely to change the attitude or behavior of one who might ask, ' Why is it wrong?' . . . Ethical caring . . . depends not upon rule or principle" but upon the development of a self "in congruence with one's best remembrance of caring and being cared-for." [16]

We should not forget that an absence of principles can be an invitation to capriciousness. Caring may be a weak defense against arbitrary decisions, and the person cared for may find the relation more satisfactory if both persons, but especially the person caring, are guided, to some extent, by principles concerning obligations and rights. To argue that no two cases are ever alike is to invite moral chaos. Furthermore, for one person to be in a position of caretaker means that that person has the power to withhold care, to leave the other without it. The person cared for is usually in a position of vulnerability. The moral significance of this needs to be addressed along with other aspects of the caring relationship. Principles may remind a giver of care to avoid being capricious or domineering. While most of the moral problems involved in mothering contexts may deal with issues above and beyond the moral minimums that can be covered by principles concerning rights and obligations, that does not mean that these minimums can be dispensed with.

Noddings's discussion is unsatisfactory also in dealing with certain types of questions, for instance those of economic justice. Such issues cry out for relevant principles. Although caring may be needed to motivate us to act on such principles, the principles are not dispensable. Noddings questions the concern people may have for starving persons in distant countries, because she sees universal love and universal justice as masculine illusions. She refrains from judging that the rich deserve less or the poor more, because caring for individuals cannot yield such judgments. But this may amount to taking a given economic stratification as given, rather than as the appropriate object of critical scrutiny that it should be. It may lead to accepting that the rich will care for the rich and the poor for the poor, with the gap between them, however unjustifiably wide, remaining what it is. Some important moral issues seem beyond the reach of an ethic of caring, once caring leads us, perhaps through empathy, to be concerned with them.

On ethical views that renounce principles as excessively abstract, we might have few arguments to uphold the equality of women. After all, as parents can care for children recognized as weaker, less knowledgeable, less capable, and with appropriately restricted rights, so men could care for women deemed inferior in every way. On a view that ethics could satisfactorily be founded on caring alone, men could care for women considered undeserving of equal rights in all the significant areas in which women have been struggling to have their equality recognized. So an ethic of care, essential as a component of morality seems deficient if taken as an exclusive preoccupation.

That aspect of the attack on principles which seems entirely correct is the view that not all ethical problems can be solved by appeal to one or a very few simple principles. It is often argued that all more particular moral rules or principles can be derived from such underlying ones as the Categorical Imperative or the Principle of Utility, and that these can be applied to all moral problems. The call for an ethic of care may be a call, which I share, for a more pluralistic view of ethics, recognizing that we need a division of moral labor employing different moral approaches for different domains, at least for the time being.[17] Satisfactory intermediate principles for areas such as those of international affairs, or family relations, cannot be derived from simple universal principles, but must be arrived at in conjunction with experience within the domains in question.

Attention to particular others will always require that we respect the particularity of the context, and arrive at solutions to moral problems that will not give moral principles more weight than their due. But their due may remain considerable. And we will need principles concerning relationships, not only concerning the actions of individuals, as we will need evaluations of kinds of relationships, not only of the character traits of individuals.

Birth and Valuing

To a large extent, the activity of mothering is potentially open to men as well as to women. Fathers can conceivably come to be as emotionally close, or as close through caretaking, to children as are mothers. The experience of relatedness, of responsibility for the growth and empowerment of new life, and of responsiveness to particular others, ought to be incorporated into moral theory, and will have to be so incorporated for moral theory to be adequate. At present, in this domain, it is primarily the experience of women (and of children) that has not been sufficiently reflected in moral theory and that ought to be so reflected. But this is not to say that it must remain experience available only to women. If men came to share fully and equitable in the care of all persons who need care—especially children, the sick, the old—the moral values that now arise for women in the context of caring might arise as fully for men.

There are some experiences, however, that are open only to women: menstruating, having an abortion, giving birth, suckling. We need to consider their possible significance or lack of significance for moral experience and theory. I will consider here only one kind of experience not open to men but of obviously great importance to women: the experience of giving birth or of deciding not to. Does the very experience of giving birth, or of deciding not to exercise the capacity to do so, make a significant difference for moral experience and moral theory? I think the answer must be: perhaps.

Of course birthing is a social as well as a personal or biological event. It takes place in a social context structured by attitudes and arrangements that deeply affect how women experience it: whether it will be accepted as "natural," whether it will be welcomed and celebrated, or whether it will be fraught with fear or shame. But I wish to focus briefly on the conscious awareness women can have of what they are doing in giving birth, and on the specifically personal and biological aspects of human birthing.

It is women who give birth to other persons. Women are responsible for the existence of new persons in ways far more fundamental than are men. It is not bizarre to recognize that women can, through abortion or suicide, choose not to give birth. A woman can be aware of the possibility that she can act to prevent a new person from existing, and can be aware that if this new person exists, it is because of what she has done and made possible.

In the past we have called attention to the extent to which women do not control their capacity to give birth. They are under extreme economic and social pressure to engage in intercourse, to marry, and to have children. Legal permission to undergo abortion is a recent, restricted, and threatened capacity. When the choice not to give birth requires grave risk to life, health, or well-being, or requires suicide, we should be careful not to misrepresent the situation when we speak of a woman's "choice" to become a mother, or of how she "could have done other" than have a child, or that "since she chose to become a mother, she is responsible for her child." It does not follow that because women are responsible for creating human beings, they should be held responsible by society for caring for them, either alone, primarily, or even at all. These two kinds of responsibility should not be confused, and I am speaking here only of the first. As conscious human beings, women can do other than give birth, and if they do give birth, they are responsible for the creation of other human beings. Though it may be very difficult for women to avoid giving birth, the very familiarity of the literary image of the woman who drowns herself or throws herself from a cliff rather than bear an illegitimate child should remind us that such eventualities are not altogether remote from consciousness.

Women have every reason to be justifiably angry with men who refuse to take responsibility for their share of the events of pregnancy and birth, or for the care children require. Because, for so long, we have wanted to increase the extent to which men would recognize their responsibilities for causing pregnancy, and would share in the long years of care needed to bring a child to independence, we have tended to emphasize the ways in which the responsibilities for creating a new human being are equal between women and men.[18] But in fact, men produce sperm and women produce babies, and the difference is enormous. Excellent arguments can be made that boys and men suffer "womb envy"; indeed, men lack a wondrous capacity that women possess.[19]

Of all the human capacities, it is probably the capacity to create new human beings that is most worth celebrating. We can expect that a woman will care about and feel concern for a child she has created as the child grows and develops, and that she feels responsible for having given the child life. But her concern is more than something to be expected. It is, perhaps, justifiable in certain ways unique to women.

Children are born into actual situations. A mother cannot escape ultimate responsibility for having given birth to this particular child in these particular circumstances. She can be aware that she could have avoided intercourse, or used more effective contraception, or waited to get pregnant until her circumstances were different; that she could have aborted this child and had another later; or that she could have killed herself and prevented this child from facing the suffering or hardship of this particular life. The momentousness of all these decisions about giving or not giving life can hardly fail to affect what she experiences in relation to the child.

Perhaps it might be thought that many of these issues arise in connection with infanticide, and that if one refrains from killing an infant, one is responsible for giving the infant life. Infanticide is as open to men as to women. But to kill or refrain from killing a child, once the child is capable of life with caretakers different from the person who is responsible for having given birth to the child, is a quite different matter from creating or not creating this possibility, and I am concerned in this discussion with the moral significance of giving birth.

It might also be thought that those, including the father, who refrain from killing the mother, or from forcing her to have an abortion, are also responsible for not preventing the birth of the child.[20] But unless the distinction between suicide and murder, and between having an abortion and forcing a woman to have an abortion against her will, are collapsed completely, the issues would be very different. To refrain from murdering someone else is not the same as deciding not to kill oneself. And to decide not to force someone else to have an abortion is different from deciding not to have an abortion when one could. The person capable of giving birth who decides not to prevent the birth is the person responsible, in the sense of "responsible" I am discussing, for creating another human being. To create a new human being is not the same as to refrain from ending the life of a human being who already exists.

Perhaps there is a tendency to want to approve of or to justify what one has decided with respect to giving life. In deciding to give birth, perhaps a woman has a natural tendency to approve of the birth, to believe that the child ought to have been born. Perhaps this inclines her to believe whatever may follow from this: that the child is entitled to care, and that feelings of love for the child are appropriate and justified. The conscious decision to create a new human being may provide women with an inclination to value the child and to have hope for the child's future. Since, in her view, the child ought to have been born, a woman may feel that the world ought to be hospitable to the child. And if the child ought to have been born, the child ought to grow into an admirable human adult. The child's life has, and should continue to have, value that is recognized.

Consider next the phenomenon of sacrifice. In giving birth, women suffer severe pain for the sake of new life. Having suffered for the child in giving the child life, women may have a natural tendency to value what they have endured pain for. There is a tendency, often noted in connection with war, for people to feel that because sacrifices have been made, the sacrifice should have been "worth it," and if necessary, other things ought to be done so that the sacrifice "shall not have been in vain." There may be a similar tendency for those who have suffered to give birth to assure themselves that the pain was for the good reason of creating a new life that is valuable and that will be valued.

Certainly, this is not to say that there is anything good or noble about suffering, or that merely because people want to believe that what they suffered for was worthwhile, it was. A vast amount of human suffering has been in vain, and could and should have been avoided. The point is that once suffering has already occurred and the "price," if we resort to such calculations, has already been paid, it will be worse if the result is a further cost, and better if the result is a clear benefit that can make the price, when it is necessary for the result, validly "worth it."

The suffering of the mother who has given birth will more easily have been worthwhile if the child's life has value. The chance that the suffering will be outweighed by future happiness is much greater if the child is valued by the society and the family into which the child is born. If the mother's suffering yields nothing but further suffering and a being deemed to be of no value, her suffering may truly have been in vain. Anyone can have reasons to value children. But the person who has already undergone the suffering needed to create one has a special reason to recognize that the child is valuable and to want the child to be valued so that the suffering she has already borne will have been, truly, worthwhile.

These arguments can be repeated for the burdens of work and anxiety normally expended in bringing up a child. Those who have already borne these burdens have special reasons for wanting to see the grown human being for whom they have cared as valuable and valued. Traditionally, women have not only borne the burdens of childbirth, but, with little help, the much greater burdens of child rearing. Of course, the burdens of child rearing could be shared fully by men, as they have been partially shared by women other than natural mothers. Although the concerns involved in bringing up a child may greatly outweigh the suffering of childbirth itself, this does not mean that giving birth is incidental.

The decision not to have children is often influenced by a comparable tendency to value the potential child.[21] Knowing how much care the child would deserve and how highly, as a mother, she would value the child, a woman who gives up the prospect of motherhood can recognize how much she is losing. For such reasons, a woman may feel overwhelming ambivalence concerning the choice.

Consider, finally, how biology can affect our ways of valuing children. Although men and women may share a desire or an instinctive tendency to wish to reproduce, and although these feelings may be equally strong for both men and women, such feelings might affect their attitudes toward a given child very differently. In terms of biological capacity, a mother has a relatively greater stake in a child to which she has given birth. This child is about one-twentieth or one twenty-fifth of all the children she could possibly have, whereas a man could potentially have hundreds or thousands of other children. In giving birth, a woman has already contributed a large amount of energy and effort toward the production of this particular child, while a man has, biologically, contributed only a few minutes. To the extent that such biological facts may influence attitudes, the attitudes of the mother and father toward the "worth" or "value" of a particular child may be different. The father might consider the child more easily replaceable in the sense that the father's biological contribution can so easily and so painlessly be repeated on another occasion or with another woman; for the mother to repeat her biological contribution would be highly exhausting and painful. The mother, having already contributed so much more to the creation of this particular child than the father, might value the result of her effort in proportion. And her pride at what she has accomplished in giving birth can be appropriately that much greater. She has indeed "accomplished" far more than has the father.

So even if instincts or desires to reproduce oneself or one's genes, or to create another human being, are equally powerful among men and women, a given child is, from the father's biological standpoint, much more incidental and interchangeable: any child out of the potential thousands he might sire would do. For the mother, on the other hand, if this particular child does not survive and grow, her chances for biological reproduction are reduced to a much greater degree. To suggest that men may think of their children as replaceable is offensive to many men, and women. Whether such biological facts as those I have mentioned have any significant effect on parental attitudes is not known. But arguments from biological facts to social attitudes, and even to moral norms, have a very long history and are still highly popular; we should be willing to examine the sorts of unfamiliar arguments I have suggested that can be drawn from biological facts. If anatomy is destiny, men may be "naturally" more indifferent toward particular children than has been thought.

Since men, then, do not give birth, and do not experience the responsibility, the pain, and momentousness of childbirth, they lack the particular motives to value the child that may spring from this capacity and this fact. Of course, many other reasons for valuing a child are felt by both parents, by caretakers of either gender, and by those who are not parents, but the motives discussed, and others arising from giving birth, may be morally significant. The long years of child care may provide stronger motives for valuing a child than do the relatively short months of pregnancy and hours of childbirth. The decisions and sacrifices involved in bringing up a child can be more affecting than those normally experienced in giving birth to a child. So the possibility for men to acquire such motives through child care may outweigh any long-term differences in motivation between women and men. But it might yet remain that the person responsible for giving birth would continue to have a greater sense of responsibility for how the child develops, and stronger feelings of care and concern for the child.

That adoptive parents can feel as great concern for and attachment to their children as can biological parents may indicate that the biological components in valuing children are relatively modest in importance. However, to the extent that biological components are significant, they would seem to affect men and women in different ways.

Morality and Human Tendencies

So far, I have been describing possible feelings rather than attaching any moral value to them.

That children are valued does not mean that they are valuable, and if mothers have a natural tendency to value their children, it does not follow that they ought to. But if feelings are taken to be relevant to moral theory, the feelings of valuing the child, like the feelings of empathy for other persons in pain, may be of moral significance.

To the extent that a moral theory takes natural male tendencies into account, it would at least be reasonable to take natural female tendencies into account. Traditional moral theories often suppose it is legitimate for individuals to maximize self-interest, or satisfy their preferences, within certain constraints based on the equal rights of others. If it can be shown that the tendency to want to pursue individual self-interest is a stronger tendency among men than among women, this would certainly be relevant to an evaluation of such theory. And if it could be shown that a tendency to value children and a desire to foster the developing capabilities of the particular others for whom we care is a stronger tendency among women than among men, this too would be relevant in evaluating moral theories.

The assertion that women have a tendency to value children is still different from the assertion that they ought to. Noddings speaks often of the "natural" caring of mothers for children.[22] I do not intend to deal here with the disputed empirical question of whether human mothers do or do not have a strong natural tendency to love their children. And I am certainly not claiming that natural mothers have greater skills or excellences in raising children than have others, including, perhaps, men. I am trying, rather, to explore possible "reasons" for mothers to value children, reasons that might be different for mothers and potential mothers than they would be for anyone else asking the question: why should we value human beings? And it does seem that certain possible reasons for valuing living human beings are present for mothers in ways that are different from what they would be for others. The reason, if it is one, that the child should be valued because I have suffered to give the child life is different from the reason, if it is one, that the child should be valued because someone unlike me suffered to give the child life. And both of these reasons are different from the reason, if it is one, that the child should be valued because the continued existence of the child satisfies a preference of a parent, or because the child is a bearer of universal rights, or has the capacity to experience pleasure.

Many moral theories, and fields dependent on them such as economics, employ the assumption that to increase the utility of individuals is a good thing to do. But if asked *why* it is a good thing to increase utility, or satisfy desire, or produce pleasure, or *why* doing so counts as a good reason for something, it is very difficult to answer. The claim is taken as a kind of starting assumption for which no *further* reason can be given. It seems to rest on a view that people seek pleasure, or that we can recognize pleasure as having intrinsic value. But if women recognize quite different assumptions as more likely to be valid, that would certainly be of importance to ethics. We might then take it as one of our starting assumptions that creating good relations of care and concern and trust between ourselves and our children, and creating social arrangements in which children will be valued and well cared for, are more important than maximizing individual utilities. And the moral theories that might be compatible with such assumptions might be very different from those with which we are familiar.

A number of feminists have independently declared their rejection of the Abraham myth.[23] We do not approve the sacrifice of children out of religious duty. Perhaps, for those capable of giving birth, reasons to value the actual life of the born will, in general, seem to be better than reasons justifying the sacrifice of such life.[24] This may reflect an accordance of priority to caring for particular others over abstract principle. From the perspectives of Rousseau, of Kant, of Hegel, and of Kohlberg, this is a deficiency of women. But from a perspective of what is needed for late twentieth century survival, it may suggest a superior morality. Only feminist moral theory can offer a satisfactory evaluation of such suggestions, because only feminist moral theory can adequately understand the alternatives to traditional moral theory that the experience of women requires.

Endnotes

1. See Virginia Held, *Rights and Goods: Justifying Social Action* (New York: Free Press, Macmillan, 1984).
2. See Genevieve Lloyd, *The Man of Reason: "Male" and "Female" in Western Philosophy* (Minneapolis: University of Minnesota Press, 1984).
3. Virginia Held, *Rights and Goods,* p. 272. See also V. Held, "The Political 'Testing' of Moral Theories," *Midwest Studies in Philosophy* 7 (1982): 343–63.
4. For discussion, see especially Nancy Hartsock, *Money, Sex, and Power* (New York: Longman, 1983), chaps. 10, 11.
5. Lawrence Kohlberg's studies of what he claimed to be developmental stages in moral reasoning suggested that girls progress less well and less far than boys through these stages. See his *The Philosophy of Moral Development* (San Francisco: Harper & Row, 1981); and L. Kohlberg and R. Kramer, "Continuities and Discontinuities in Child and Adult Moral Development," *Human Development* 12 (1969): 93–120. James R. Rest, on the other hand, claims in his study of adolescents in 1972 and 1974 that "none of the male-female differences on the Defining Issues Test . . . and on the Comprehension or Attitudes tests were significant." See his "Longitudinal Study of the Defining Issues Test of Moral Judgment: A Strategy for Analyzing Developmental Change," *Developmental Psychology* (Nov. 1975): 738–48; quotation at 741. Carol Gilligan's *In A Different Voice* (Cambridge: Harvard University Press, 1982) suggest that girls and women tend to organize their thinking about moral problems somewhat differently from boys and men; her subsequent work supports the view that whether people tend to construe moral problems in terms of rules of justice or in terms of caring relationships is at present somewhat associated with gender (Carol Gilligan, address at Conference on Women and Moral Thought, SUNY Stony Brook, March 21, 1985). Other studies have shown that females are significantly more inclined than males to cite compassion and sympathy as reasons for their moral positions; see Constance Boucher Holstein, "Irreversible, Stepwise Sequence in the Development of Moral Judgment: A Longitudinal Study of Males and Females." *Child Development* 47, no. 1 (March 1976): 51–61.
6. For suggestions on how Gilligan's stages, like Kohlberg's, might be thought to be historically and culturally, rather than more universally, based, see Linda Nicholson, "Women, Morality, and History," *Social Research* 50, no. 3 (Autumn 1983): 514–36.
7. See, e.g., Debra Nails, "Social-Scientific Sexism: Gilligan's Mismeasure of Man," *Social Research* 50, no. 3 (Autumn 1983): 643–64.
8. I have discussed this in a paper that has gone through several major revisions and changes of title, from its presentation at a conference at Loyola University on April 18, 1983, to its discussion at Dartmouth College, April 2, 1984. I will refer to it as "Non-Contractual Society: A Feminist Interpretation." See also Carole Pateman, "The Fraternal Society Contract: Some Observations on Patriarchy," paper presented at American Political Science Association meeting, Aug. 30–Sept. 2, 1984, and "The Shame of the Marriage Contract," in *Women's Views of the Political World of Men,* edited by Judith Hicks Stiehm (Dobbs Ferry, N.Y.: Transnational Publishers, 1984).
9. For discussion, see especially Nancy Hartsock, *Money, Sex, and Power.*
10. Ibid., p. 39.
11. See Held, *Rights and Goods,* chap. 5.
12. Ibid., chap. 11.
13. Lawrence A. Blum, *Friendship, Altruism and Morality* (London: Routledge and Kegan Paul, 1980), p. 1.
14. Owen J. Flanagan, Jr., and Jonathan E. Alder, "Impartiality and Particularity," *Social Research* 50, no. 3 (Autumn 1983): 576–96.
15. See, e.g., Nell Noddings, *Caring: A Feminine Approach to Ethics and Moral Education* (Berkeley: University of California Press, 1984) pp. 91–94.
16. Ibid., pp. 91–94.
17. Participants in the conference on Women and Moral Theory offered the helpful term "domain relativism" for the version of this view that I defended.
18. See, e.g., Virginia Held, "The Obligations of Mothers and Fathers," repr. in *Mothering: Essays in Feminist Theory,* edited by Joyce Trebilcot (Totowa, N.J.: Rowman and Allanheld, 1984).
19. See Eva Kittay, "Womb Envy: An Explanatory Concept," in *Mothering,* edited by Joyce Trebilcot. To overcome the pernicious aspects of the "womb envy" she skillfully identifies and describes, Kittay argues that boys should be taught that their "procreative contribution is of equal significance" (p. 123). While boys should certainly be told the truth, the truth may remain that, as she states elsewhere, "there is the . . . awesome quality of creation itself—the transmutation performed by the parturient woman" (p. 99).
20. This point was made by Marcia Baron in correspondence with me.
21. In exploring the values involved in birth and mothering, we need to develop views that include women who do not give birth. As Margaret Simons writes, "we must define a feminist maternal ethic that supports a woman's right not to have children." See Margaret A. Simons, "Motherhood, Feminism and Identiy," *Hypatia, Women's Studies International Forum* 7, 5 (1984): 353.
22. E.g., Noddings, *Caring,* pp. 31, 43, 49.
23. See Gilligan, *In a Different Voice,* p. 104; Held, "Non-Contractual Society: A Feminist Interpretation;" and Noddings, *Caring,* p. 43.
24. That some women enthusiastically send their sons off to war may be indicative of a greater than usual acceptance of male myths rather than evidence against this

claim, since the enthusiasm seems most frequent in societies where women have the least influence in the formation of prevailing religious and other beliefs.

Review Questions

1. According to Held, why should moral theory reflect the experience of women rather than just men?
2. Why is mothering the most central and fundamental social relationship in Held's view?
3. What criticism does Held make of standard moral philosophy?
4. What is the moral significance of giving birth according to Held? What sort of ethical perspective results?

Discussions Questions

1. Held says that the activity of mothering is open to men as well as women. Do you agree or not? Is the biological fact that only women give birth relevant or not? Explain your view.
2. Exactly who is included in the category of particular others? For example, could a pet dog or cat be a particular other? Who is excluded?
3. How would Rawls or a utilitarian or a Kantian reply to Held? Do they have a good response?
4. Does feminist ethics ignore the moral experience of men? If so, how does it escape the charge of being arbitrary?

Problem Cases

*1. **Dawn and Denise.*** In New York City, a single woman named Dawn lives with her daughter Denise in a two-room apartment. Dawn works eight hours a day at the check-out counter in the local drug store while Denise goes to elementary school. Denise (age 8) is doing well in school, but suffers from grand mal epileptic seizures, the result of a head injury she received when she was severely beaten by her father two years ago. (The father is now in jail serving a 15-year sentence for armed robbery, and neither Dawn nor Denise have anything to do with him.) The seizures can be controlled by taking anticonvulsant drugs such as Diazepam and Primidone. When Denise takes these drugs, her seizures are rare and of short duration; if she does not take the drugs, the seizures can be very severe. In fact, the last time Denise had a bad seizure, she stopped breathing and almost died. Had she not been given oxygen by the nurse at school, she would have died or had severe brain damage. Unfortunately, the drugs cost over a $100 a month (Denise must take a fairly large dose daily), and Dawn cannot afford to pay for them with her minimum-wage pay from the drugstore. She is barely able to afford the apartment and food and a few used clothes; medical insurance or regular visits to the doctor are out of the question. When Dawn was not working, she qualified for medical assistance—that is how she was able to get a doctor's diagnosis and drug treatment for Denise's condition. But Dawn believes in the value of working and wants to be self-sufficient. She continues working even though it means she is not eligible for medical assistance or Aid to Families with Dependent Children. To get the drugs for Denise, Dawn steals them from the drug store where she works. Thus far she has not been caught; but if she is caught stealing, she will probably lose her job.

Is Dawn a bad person? What would Aristotle or MacIntyre say? What do you think?

Is she doing something wrong? Why or why not? Suppose that Dawn gets another job that enables her to buy the drugs, and she is never caught. In retrospect, do you think she did anything wrong?

Suppose Dawn is caught. Should she be punished? How?

What would you do if you were in Dawn's shoes? Is there a better way to deal with the problem?

*2. **Breaking a Promise and Lying.*** Jane Rachel has been reading about people suffering from famine in Africa and she wants to help. But what can she do? She is unemployed at the moment, having lost her part-time job teaching Introduction to Ethics because of poor student evaluations. (Students complained that she was too demanding and gave low grades.) Despite the fact that Jane has no spare money, she decides to contribute to a famine relief fund. To do this, she asks John, one of he full-time Professors of Philosophy, to loan her $1000. She tells him she needs the money for food and rent because her unemployment compensation has run out (this is not true—she is still getting unemployment compensation checks), and she promises to pay the money back as soon as she can (although she really has no intention of paying the money back—she figures John can afford $1000 because he is a full professor with tenure). John feels sorry for Jane, and he feels guilty because he was partly responsible for the loss of her job, so he gives her the money. Jane promptly gives the money to famine relief, and the money is used to provide food for starving children in Africa. Did Jane do the right thing or not? What would Mill say? How about Kant? What do you think and why?

3. *Protective Punishment.* Genetic research done on male prison inmates, those convicted of violent crimes like assault and murder, reveals that they all have a certain genetic defect, namely a missing y chromosome. Routine blood tests on men in the Army show that one hundred of these men have the genetic defect, making it likely that they will commit violent crimes. Furthermore, clinical studies of these men reveal that in fact they are very aggressive and prone to violence. The genetic researchers and psychologists petition a judge to have these men imprisoned, arguing that they are very likely to commit violent crimes. The judge rules that they are a danger to society, even though they have not yet committed any crimes, and the one hundred men are given life sentences in a maximum security prison. While in prison, thirty of these men commit a murder, and forty have to be placed in solitary confinement because of numerous fights with other inmates. But thirty of the men commit no crimes at all and are eventually released because of their good behavior. Do you agree that these men should have been imprisoned or not? Explain your view.

4. *Should Smoking Be Legal?* In the United States, it is legal for adults to smoke tobacco in cigars, cigarettes, and pipes even though it is unhealthy to do so. Tobacco contains nicotine, a poisonous drug that is as addictive as cocaine and is clearly associated with coronary heart disease and peripheral vascular disease. In addition, the tar in tobacco smoke damages lung tissue and causes lung cancer. Given these facts, do smokers have a right to smoke? If so, should they be allowed to smoke in public? If not, does this mean that smokers do not have a right to smoke in private?

In the United States, it is illegal to smoke marijuana. When smoked, marijuana produces physical effects such as a dry mouth, mild reddening of the eyes, slight clumsiness, and increased appetite. The main psychological effects are feelings of well-being and calmness, and more vivid visual and auditory perceptions. In large doses it may cause panicky states and illusions. In rare cases, large doses may cause psychosis or loss of contact with reality. Prolonged use has been associated with apathy and loss of motivation. All things considered, marijuana is no more dangerous or unhealthy than tobacco, and perhaps is less dangerous and unhealthy. If you agree that it should be legal for adults to smoke tobacco, then why not legalize marijuana for adults? On the other hand, if you think that marijuana should be illegal, then why shouldn't tobacco be illegal too?

SUGGESTED READINGS

1. W. D. Ross explains Aristotle's ethics in his *Aristotle* (New York: Meridan Books, 1959), Chapter 7. John M. Cooper defends Aristotelian ethics in *Reason and the Human Good in Aristotle* (Cambridge, MA: Harvard University Press, 1975).

2. Christina Sommers and Fred Sommers, *Vice and Virtue in Everyday Life,* Third Edition (New York: Harcourt Brace Jovanovich, 1993), Chapters 3 and 4, has articles on virtue and vice by classical and contemporary philosophers. James Rachels, *The Elements of Moral Philosophy* (New York: McGraw-Hill, Inc., 1993), Chapter 12, is an excellent introduction to virtue theory that raises some important objections. Peter Geach discusses classical virtues such as courage in *The Virtues* (Cambridge: Cambridge University Press, 1977).

3. J. J. C. Smart defends Act Utilitarianism and Bernard Williams attacks it in J. J. C. Smart and Bernard Williams, *Utilitarianism: For and Against* (Cambridge University Press, 1973). *Utilitarianism and Beyond,* ed. A. Sen and Bernard Williams (Cambridge: Cambridge University Press, 1973) is a collection of recent articles on utilitarianism.

4. G. E. Moore's nonhedonistic version of utilitarianism is presented in his *Ethics* (London: Oxford University Press, 1912 and his *Principia Ethica* (Cambridge: Cambridge University Press, 1959).

5. Kant's work in ethics is difficult. A good place to begin is his *Lectures on Ethics,* trans. Louis Infield (New York: Harper, 1963). His ethical theory is developed in *Critique of Practical Reason,* trans.

by Lewis White Beck (Indianapolis: Bobbs-Merrill, 1956); *The Metaphysical Elements of Justice,* trans. John Ladd (Indianapolis: Bobbs-Merrill, 1965); and *The Metaphysical Principles of Virtue,* trans. by James Ellington (Indianapolis: Bobbs-Merrill, 1964).

6. For commentaries on Kant's moral philosophy see H. J. Paton, *The Categorical Imperative* (New York: Harper, 1967) and H. B. Acton, *Kant's Moral Philosophy* (London: Macmillan, 1970). Onora O'Neill discusses Kantian ethics in her article "Kant After Virtue," *Inquiry* 26 (1983), pp. 387–405, and in her book, written under the name Onora Nell (instead of O'Neill) *Acting on Principle: An Essay on Kantian Ethics* (New York: Columbia University Press, 1975).

7. The classical formulations of the social contract theory are Thomas Hobbes' *Leviathan* (1651), John Locke's *The Second Treatise of Government* (1690), and Jean-Jacques Rousseau's, *The Social Contract* (1762). These books are available in different editions.

8. Jonathan Dancy, "An ethic of prima facie duties," in Peter Singer, ed., *A Companion to Ethics* (Oxford: Basil Blackwell, 1991), pp. 219–229, gives a clear exposition of Ross's theory of prima facie duty together with some criticisms. The collection in which Dancy's essay appears, Singer's *A Companion to Ethics,* is a comprehensive reference book that has useful articles on all the important moral theories and many moral problems as well.

9. Since it first appeared in 1971, Rawls' theory of justice has been widely discussed. One of the first books on the theory to appear was Brian Barry, *The Liberal Theory of Justice* (Oxford: Oxford University Press, 1973). Another useful critical discussion is Robert Paul Wolff, *Understanding Rawls* (Princeton, N.J.: Princeton University Press, 1977) 1. The journal *Ethics* has devoted its entire July, 1989, issue to a symposium on recent developments in the Rawlsian theory of justice.

10. Feminist theory has been widely discussed in the last ten years. Rosemarie Tong, *Feminist Thought* (Boulder & San Francisco: Westview Press, 1989) is a comprehensive introduction to various feminist theories including liberal feminism, Marxist feminism, radical feminism, psychoanalytic feminism, existentialist feminism, and postmodern feminism. The book from which the reading by Virginia Held was taken, *Women and Moral Theory,* edited by Eva Feder Kittay and Diana T. Meyers (Savage, MD: Rowman and Littlefield Publishers, 1987) has articles on gender differences, autonomy, the theory of care, and challenges to this theory. Marilyn Pearsall, *Women and Values,* Second Edition (Belmont, CA: Wadsworth Publishing Co., 1993), Chapter 8, has a collection of articles on Feminist Ethics. Unlike most books on ethics, all the articles in this book were written by women.

Chapter Two

ABORTION

Introduction

Factual Background. Abortion is the termination of pregnancy involving the death of the fetus. Although the term fetus is often used to describe the prenatal organism from conception to birth, the prenatal organism is, strictly speaking, an embryo until the eighth week, and a zygote when it is a fertilized egg or ovum.

Pregnancy is usually understood as beginning with conception (the fertilization of the egg by the sperm); and an abortion is said to be any artificial termination of the pregnancy from conception to birth. But now some doctors are saying that pregnancy does not begin until the zygote becomes implanted in the lining of the uterus about a week or two after conception. From this perspective, the prevention or termination of pregnancy by means of drugs is not really an abortion, and it is not exactly contraception either. Some doctors call it postcoital contraception; but since conception may have already occurred, others say it is more accurate to call it an interception. This is some of the controversy surrounding the morning-after pill (Ovral, a birth control pill) which is widely prescribed on college campuses. Depending on when a woman takes it, this pill prevents either fertilization or implantation. (For more details on the morning-after pill see the Problem Cases at the end of the chapter.)

In the past, most abortions performed before the tenth week (and after implantation) were done by the medical procedure called dilation and curettage. In this procedure, the cervix is dilated and the fetus is removed from the interior lining of the uterus by scraping it with a curette, a spoon-like instrument. Now abortions are more often done by vacuum aspiration where a suction device is used to remove the fetus rather than a scraping instrument. This involves less risk of internal bleeding than scraping the lining of the uterus. In the future it seems likely that more pregnancies will be terminated by drugs such as Ovral, RU-486, or other drugs under development. Drugs are cheaper, easier, and safer than medical procedures if done early in the pregnancy.

Abortion performed by a qualified doctor is a relatively safe procedure for the mother, particularly if performed in the early stages of pregnancy. (About nine out of ten abortions are done before the twelfth week of pregnancy.) In fact, having an abortion is roughly seven times safer than bearing a child. Abortion is also a common medical procedure. According to the latest statistics available, about 1.6 million abortions are performed each year in the United States. This is more than one abortion for every three babies born alive.

Legal Background. In the 1960s, most states had laws restricting abortion, but all fifty states and the District of Columbia allowed abortion to save the life of the mother. Colorado and New Mexico permitted abortion to prevent serious harm to the mother. In the landmark decision of *Roe* v. *Wade* (1973), which is our first reading in the chapter, the Supreme Court overturned these abortion laws. In its ruling, the Court held that restrictive abortion laws, except in certain narrowly defined circumstances, are unconstitutional. This decision made abortion legally available to women who could afford it. (The average cost of an abortion in 1986 was $213.)

The decision has been controversial, and it has been repeatedly challenged. Opponents of the decision have proposed to amend the Constitution with the Human Life Bill, which affirms that human life begins at conception and that every human life has intrinsic worth and equal value under the Constitution. An important legal challenge to the decision came in the case of *Webster* v. *Reproductive Health Services* (1989). In a 5-4 decision, the Court upheld *Roe* v. *Wade,* but allowed as constitutional certain restrictions placed on abortion by a Missouri law, namely (1) banning the use of public funds for abortion and abortion counseling, (2) banning abortions in public hospitals and clinics, and (3) forbidding public employees to assist in the performance of an abortion.

The latest challenge to *Roe* v. *Wade* was in the case of *Planned Parenthood* v. *Casey* (1992), from which our second reading is taken. In a complicated and controversial decision, the Court again reaffirmed the essential holding of *Roe* that a woman has a right to abortion. However, it permitted states to impose further restrictions on abortion provided they do not impose an undue burden on the woman. The majority of the present Supreme Court has indicated they do not intend to reconsider the basic abortion right, but given the ongoing controversy about abortion, it may well be re-examined by the Court in the future.

The Moral Issue. We shall not concern ourselves with the legal aspects of the abortion controversy, but instead concentrate on the moral issue. The basic moral issue, of course, is whether abortion is morally wrong.

Roughly three positions have been taken on this issue: the conservative view, the liberal view, and the moderate view. The conservative view is that almost all abortions are wrong. The representatives of this view in the readings are Noonan and Marquis. It seems more accurate to label this the conservative view rather than the pro-life view because those who hold it do not usually favor preserving all life, such as would include the lives of murderers or those engaging in an unjust war. Nor is it accurate to call it the anti-abortion view, for conservatives typically allow abortions to save the life of the mother. Noonan mentions the cases of ectopic pregnancy and cancer in the uterus. The most common form of ectopic pregnancy (where the fetus is not in the usual position) is tubal pregnancy; in this condition the zygote does not descend to the uterus, but remains lodged in the fallopian tube. The mother will die if the abortion is not performed in this situation, and there is no hope for the survival of the zygote. Noonan holds that an abortion is not wrong in this case; Marquis simply ignores it, along with other hard cases such as pregnancy due to rape.

The second position, the liberal view, is that abortion is morally permissible whenever the mother chooses it. The only representative of this view in our readings is Mary Anne Warren. It is called the liberal view rather than the pro-abortion or pro-choice view because those who hold it certainly do not recommend that all pregnant women get abortions, nor do they endorse all choices. They are in favor of women having a right to choose an abortion. But why should a pregnant woman want an abortion? There are various answers to this question. If a woman is pregnant due to rape or incest, she may feel justified in getting an abortion. Or a woman may seek an abortion to avoid giving birth to a defective child. A pregnancy that interferes with her career is often cited as a legitimate reason. The liberal insists that abortion is permissible in all of these cases.

Liberals do not agree, however, about infanticide. Some liberals see little difference between abortion and killing newborn infants. Mary Anne Warren does not agree. When responding to the objection that her view allows infanticide, she claims that it does not follow from her view that infanticide is morally permissible in our society. She believes that adoption is a better alternative because many people in our society value the lives of infants.

The third view is the moderate one that abortion is justified in some cases, but not in others. Judith Jarvis Thomson and Jane English are representatives of this position in our readings along with the Supreme Court decisions. Moderates agree in rejecting both the conservative view and the liberal view, but they disagree about when abortion is morally justified. The Supreme Court decisions in *Roe* and *Planned Parenthood* allow abortion merely for the sake of convenience (at least in the early stages of pregnancy), provided the woman can pay for it and is able to get the services of a qualified doctor. But Judith Jarvis Thomson objects to such abortions. She does not think that abortion is justified merely for convenience, say to avoid postponing a trip to Europe. Jane English agrees with Thomson in this circumstance; however, she contends that in the early months of pregnancy, abortion is permissible if it is in the interests of the pregnant woman or her family. This makes English's position slightly more liberal than Thomson's. But English's view is slightly more conservative than that of Justice Blackmun in his opinion in *Roe* because she thinks that we do have a serious obligation not to kill or harm the fetus in the later stages of development when it is more like a baby.

Philosophical Issues. How can we resolve the moral issue about the wrongness of abortion? Most writers agree that settling this issue requires solving some difficult problems in ethics. One is formulating an acceptable moral principle about the wrongness of killing. Such a principle is relevant not only in the abortion controversy, but also in discussions of euthanasia, capital punishment, war, and killing nonhuman animals. But as Marquis points out in his interesting and useful discussion, it is very hard to find a moral principle about killing that is not too broad or too narrow or subject to counter-examples. For example, the conservative principle that it is wrong to take a human life is too broad, since it makes it wrong to kill a human cancer-cell culture (since it is both human and living). The alternative conservative principle that it is wrong to kill a human being is too narrow; it doesn't seem to apply to the fetus in the early stages of development. The liberal principle that it is wrong to kill persons or rational beings has similar problems. Even Marquis' own principle about killing is not without difficulties. His suggested principle forbids killing someone because it inflicts on the victim the loss of a future containing valuable experiences, activities, projects, and enjoyments. The principle may be too broad because it seems to imply that killing nonhuman animals is wrong, and this is problematic in our meat-eating society. (See Chapter 9). Perhaps it is too narrow as well, for it implies that active euthanasia is not morally wrong, and this is debatable. (See Chapter 3).

In the abortion controversy, debate has often centered on the nature and status of the fetus. Is it a person or not, and how do we tell if something is a person or not? Does the fetus have the full moral status of a person, a partial moral status, or none at all? One common approach to these problems is called line drawing, that is, attempting to find a morally significant point or dividing line in the development of the fetus when it becomes a person with rights. Justice Blackmun, for example, thinks that viability is such a point. Viability occurs when the fetus is capable of surviving outside the womb. Just when this occurs is the subject of debate: Blackmun puts viability at the twenty-eighth week of pregnancy, but many doctors say it occurs at twenty-four weeks, or perhaps as early as twenty weeks.

Others have chosen different points in the development of the fetus as significant. Some say that the presence of brain waves, beginning at about the eighth week, is a significant dividing line because their presence marks the beginning of consciousness or the ability to feel pain. This is important for utilitarians who follow Bentham's view that all conscious beings should be given moral consideration. In European common law, abortion is considered killing a person only after quickening, the time when a pregnant woman first feels the fetus move on its own.

Opponents of line drawing between conception and birth, such as Noonan, argue that these lines are always arbitrary and inadequate. Viability is a shifting point. The development of artificial incubation may make the fetus viable at any time, even shortly after conception. Furthermore, the time at which the fetus is viable varies according to circumstances such as its weight, age, and race. Opponents of line drawing often use what are called **slippery slope arguments** to argue that a line cannot be securely drawn at any point in the development of the fetus because such a line inevitably slides down the slope of development to conception; they insist that the only place to draw the line is at conception. This argument is discussed by Thomson in our readings.

Noonan and other conservatives adopt a different approach to the problem of establishing the moral status of the fetus: they try to prove that the fetus is a human being with a right to life from the moment of conception. One argument depends upon the religious **doctrine of ensoulment**. This doctrine states that the soul enters the fetus at the moment of conception. Anything with a soul is a person with a right to life; hence the fetus is a person with a right to life from the moment of conception. This may be the argument that persuades most conservatives, but Noonan avoids it because it appeals to religious doctrines not universally accepted in our pluralistic society. Instead he updates the traditional view by discussing the genetic coding of the zygote. At conception, the zygote receives the full genetic code, twenty-three pairs of chomosomes. Anything with full human genetic coding is a human being with a right to life; hence the zygote is a human being with a right to life from the moment of conception.

Liberals and moderates (and even conservatives such as Marquis) find it very hard to believe that a zygote, a single cell, is a human being with a right to life. For one thing, any human cell has the full genetic coding of a human being but any given human cell is hardly a person. Saying that the zygote is a potential person is no help because the rights of an actual person, the mother, would always outweigh the rights of a merely potential person, assuming that potential persons have rights in the first place.

Warren thinks that conservatives like Noonan confuse two different senses of the word human. There is a genetic sense in which a being is human if it is a member of the biological species *Homo sapiens,* and a moral sense in which a being is human if it is a member of the moral community. Just because the zygote is genetically human does not mean that it is morally human or a member of the moral community. In order to be a person, a being must have at least some of the traits of persons, namely consciousness, reasoning, self-motivated activity, the capacity to communicate, and the presence of self-concepts. Warren contends that the fetus has none of these traits, not even at the later stages of development, and hence it is not a person.

Conservative and moderate critics point out that Warren's position seems to imply that infants are not persons either, since they do not have all of the traits of a person, and thus it can be used to justify infanticide. Because conservatives and moderates both think that babies are undeniably persons with rights, and that infanticide is morally wrong, they find Warren's position unacceptable.

An alternative approach to line drawing is to hold, as English does, that the concept of person has fuzzy borders, that is, there are borderline cases in which we cannot say whether an entity is a person or not. The fetus constitutes just such a case. Another alternative is to hold that the fetus is neither a full-fledged person nor merely an organism with no moral status at all; rather it has some sort of partial moral status.

If we cannot conclusively determine the nature and moral status of the fetus, then how can we answer the moral question about abortion? The tactic of Thomson is to shift the focus of debate from the status of the fetus to the rights of the mother. She argues that even if the fetus is a person with a right to life, it still does not follow that abortions are never justified. The rights of the mother can justify an abortion. English adopts a similar tactic and uses it to attack both the conservative and the liberal views. Even if we assume that the fetus is a person, the mother's right of self-defense is sufficient to justify abortion in a number of cases including rape, serious harm, or great inconvenience. On the other hand, even if we assume that the fetus is not a person, it still has some rights because it is at least personlike. Therefore, we have an obligation to not kill or harm it without a good reason.

The methods of Thomson and English are open to criticism, however. Both of them rely on puzzling imaginary cases, e.g., Thomson's case of the famous violinist who is plugged into another person, and English's case of the mad scientist who hypnotizes people to attack innocent passers-by with knives. They ask us what we would say or think about these cases, that is, they appeal to our moral intuitions. Such an appeal does not always produce agreement, particularly when we are talking about abortion. Conservatives simply do not have the same intuitions about these cases as Thomson and English do. Another problem with appealing to intuitions is that these intuitions may merely reflect different backgrounds, e.g., the different backgrounds of Thomson and Noonan. If so, then they are not an infallible guide to moral conduct.

The Supreme Court

Excerpts from *Roe* v. *Wade* (1973)

Harry A. Blackmun is an associate justice of the United States Supreme Court. He is a graduate of Harvard Law School, and he was appointed to the Court in 1970.

Byron R. White was an associate justice of the United States Supreme Court. He was appointed in 1962 and retired from the Court in 1993. He is a graduate of Yale Law School.

In the case of Roe v. *Wade, a pregnant single woman challenged a Texas abortion law making abortion (except to save the mother's life) a crime punishable by a prison sentence of two to five years. The Court invalidated this law.*

The reading includes excerpts from the majority opinion written by Justice Blackmun (concurred in by six other justices), and from the dissenting opinion written by Justice White (concurred in by Justice William H. Rehnquist).

Justice Blackmun argues that the abortion decision is included in the right of personal privacy. But this right is not absolute. It must yield at some point to the state's legitimate interest in protecting potential life, and this interest becomes compelling at the point of viability.

Justice White in his dissenting opinion holds that the Court has no constitutional basis for its decision, and that it values the convenience of the mother more than the existence and development of human life.

Majority Opinion

A recent review of the common law precedents argues . . . that even post-quickening abortion was never established as a common law crime. This is of some importance because while most American courts ruled, in holding or dictum, that abortion of an unquickened fetus was not criminal under their received common law, others followed Coke in stating that abortion of a quick fetus was a "misprison," a term they translated to mean "misdemeanor." That their reliance on Coke on this aspect of the law was uncritical and, apparently in all the reported cases, dictum (due probably to the paucity of common law prosecutions for post-quickening abortion), makes it now appear doubtful that abortion was ever firmly established as a common law crime even with respect to the destruction of a quick fetus. . . .

It is thus apparent that at common law, at the time of the adoption of our Constitution, and throughout the major portion of the 19th century, abortion was viewed with less disfavor than under most American statutes currently in effect. Phrasing it another way, a woman enjoyed a substantially broader right to terminate a pregnancy than she does in most States today. At least with respect to the early stage of pregnancy, and very possibly without such a limitation, the opportunity to make this choice was present in this country well into the 19th century. Even later, the law continued for some time to treat less punitively an abortion procured in early pregnancy. . . .

Three reasons have been advanced to explain historically the enactment of criminal abortion laws in the 19th century and to justify their continued existence.

It has been argued occasionally that these laws were the product of a Victorian social concern to discourage illicit sexual conduct. Texas, however, does not advance this justification in the present case, and it appears that no court or commentator has taken the argument seriously. . . .

A second reason is concerned with abortion as a medical procedure. When most criminal abortion laws were first enacted, the procedure was a hazardous one for the woman. This was particularly true prior to the development of antisepsis. Antiseptic techniques, of course, were based on discoveries by Lister, Pasteur, and others first announced in 1867, but were not generally accepted and employed until about the turn of the century. Abortion mortality was high. Even after 1900, and perhaps until as late as the development of antibiotics in the 1940s, standard modern techniques such as dilation and curettage were not nearly so safe as they are today. Thus it has been argued that a State's real concern in enacting a criminal abortion law was to protect the pregnant woman, that is, to restrain her from submitting to a procedure that placed her life in serious jeopardy.

Modern medical techniques have altered this situation. Appellants and various *amici* refer to medical data indicating that abortion in early pregnancy, that is, prior to the end of first trimester, although not without its risk, is now relatively safe. Mortality rates for women undergoing early abortions, where the procedure is legal, appear to be as low as or lower than the rates for normal childbirth. Consequently, any interest of the State in protecting the woman from an inherently hazardous procedure, except when it would be equally dangerous for her to forgo it, has largely disappeared. Of course, important state interests in the area of health and medical standards do remain. The State has a legitimate interest in seeing to it that abortion, like any other medical procedure, is performed under circumstances that insure maximum safety for the patient. This interest obviously extends at least to the performing physician and his staff, to the facilities involved, to the availability of aftercare, and to adequate provision for any complication or emergency that might arise. The prevalence of high mortality rates at illegal "abortion mills" strengthens, rather than weakens, the State's interest in regulating the conditions under which abortions are performed. Moreover, the risk to the woman increases as her pregnancy continues. Thus the State retains a definite interest in protecting the woman's own health and safety when an abortion is performed at a late stage of pregnancy.

The third reason is the State's interest—some phrase it in terms of duty—in protecting prenatal life. Some of the argument for this justification rests on the theory that a new human life is present from the moment of conception. . . .

Parties challenging state abortion laws have sharply disputed in some courts the contention that a purpose of these laws, when enacted, was to protect prenatal life. Pointing to the absence of legislative history to support the contention, they claim that most state laws were designed solely to protect the woman. Because medical advances have lessened this concern, at least with respect to abortion in early pregnancy, they argue that with respect to such abortions the laws can no longer be justified by any state interest. There is some scholarly support for this view of original purpose. The few state courts called upon to interpret their laws in the late 19th and early 20th centuries did focus on the State's interest in protecting the woman's health rather than in preserving embryo and fetus. . . .

The Constitution does not explicitly mention any right of privacy. In a line of decisions, however, going back perhaps as far as *Union Pacific R. Co.* v. *Botsford,* 141 U.S. 250, 251 (1891), the Court has recognized that a right of personal privacy, or a guarantee of certain areas or zones of privacy, does exist under the Constitution. In varying contexts the Court or individual Justices have indeed found at least the roots of that right in the First Amendment, . . . in the Fourth and Fifth Amendments . . . in the penumbras of the Bill of Rights . . . in the Ninth Amendment . . . or in the concept of liberty guaranteed by the first section of the Fourteenth Amendment. . . . These decisions make it clear that only personal rights that can be deemed "fundamental" or "implicit in the concept of ordered liberty," . . . are included in this guarantee of personal privacy. They also make it clear that the right has some extension to activities relating to marriage, . . . procreation, . . . contraception, . . . family relationships, . . . and child rearing and education. . . .

This right of privacy, whether it be founded in the Fourteenth Amendment's concept of personal liberty and restrictions upon state action, as well feel it is or, as the District Court determined, in the Ninth Amendment's reservation of rights to the people, is broad enough to encompass a woman's decision whether or not to terminate her pregnancy. . . .

. . . Appellants and some *amici* argue that the woman's right is absolute and that she is entitled to terminate her pregnancy at whatever time, in whatever way, and for whatever reason she alone chooses. With this we do not agree. Appellants' arguments that Texas either has no valid interest at all in regulating the abortion decision, or no interest strong enough to support any limitation upon the woman's sole determination, is unpersuasive. The Court's decisions recognizing a right of privacy also acknowledge that some state regulation in areas protected by that right is appropriate. As noted above, a state may properly assert important interests in safeguarding health, in maintaining medical standards, and in protecting potential life. At some point in pregnancy, these respective interests become sufficiently compelling to sustain regulation of the factors that govern the abortion decision. The privacy right involved, therefore, cannot be said to be absolute. . . .

We therefore conclude that the right of personal privacy includes the abortion decision, but that this right is not unqualified and must be considered against important state interests in regulation.

We note that those federal and state courts that have recently considered abortion law challenges have reached the same conclusion. . . .

Although the results are divided, most of these courts have agreed that the right of privacy, however based, is broad enough to cover the abortion decision; that the right, nonetheless, is not absolute and is subject to some limitations; and that at some point the state interests as to protection of health, medical standards, and prenatal life, become dominant. We agree with this approach.

The appellee and certain *amici* argue that the fetus is a "person" within the language and meaning of the Fourteenth Amendment. In support of this they outline at length and in detail the well-known facts of fetal development. If this suggestion of personhood is established, the appellant's case, of course, collapses, for the fetus' right to life is then guaranteed specifically by the Amendment. The appellant conceded as much on reargument. On the other hand, the appellee conceded on reargument that no case could be cited that holds that a fetus is a person within the meaning of the Fourteenth Amendment.

All this, together with our observation, supra, that throughout the major portion of the 19th century prevailing legal abortion practices were far freer than they are today, persuades us that the word "person," as used in the Fourteenth Amendment, does not include the unborn. . . . Indeed, our decision in *United States* v. *Vuitch,* 402 U.S. 62 (1971), inferentially is to the same effect, for we there would not have indulged in statutory interpretation favorable to abortion in specified circumstances if the necessary consequence was the termination of life entitled to Fourteenth Amendment protection.

. . . As we have intimated above, it is reasonable and appropriate for a State to decide that at some point in time another interest, that of health of the mother or that of potential human life, becomes significantly involved. The woman's privacy is no longer sole and any right of privacy she possesses must be measured accordingly.

. . . We need not resolve the difficult question of when life begins. When those trained in the respective disciplines of medicine, philosophy, and theology are unable to arrive at any consensus, the judiciary, at this point in the development of man's knowledge, is not in a position to speculate as to the answer.

It should be sufficient to note briefly the wide divergence of thinking on this most sensitive and difficult question. There has always been strong support for the view that life does not begin until live birth. This was the belief of the Stoics. It appears to be the predominant, though not the unanimous, attitude of the Jewish faith. It may be taken to represent also the position of a large segment of the Protestant community, insofar as that can be ascertained; organized groups that have taken a formal position on the abortion issue have generally regarded abortion as a matter for the conscience of the individual and her family. As we have noted, the common law found greater significance in quickening. Physicians and their scientific colleagues have regarded that event with less interest and have tended to focus either upon conception or upon live birth or upon the interim point at which the fetus becomes "viable," that is, potentially able to live outside the mother's womb, albeit with artificial aid. Viability is usually placed at about seven months (28 weeks) but may occur earlier, even at 24 weeks. . . .

In areas other than criminal abortion the law has been reluctant to endorse any theory that life, as we recognize it, begins before live birth or to accord legal rights to the unborn except in narrowly defined situations and except when the rights are contingent upon live birth. . . . In short, the unborn have never been recognized in the law as persons in the whole sense.

In view of all this, we do not agree that, by adopting one theory of life, Texas may override the rights of the pregnant woman that are at stake. We repeat, however, that the State does have an important and legitimate interest in preserving and protecting the health of the pregnant woman, whether she be a resident of the State or a nonresident who seeks medical consultation and treatment there, and that it has still *another* important and legitimate interest in protecting the potentiality of human life. These interests are separate and distinct. Each grows in substantiality as the woman approaches term and, at a point during pregnancy, each becomes "compelling."

With respect to the State's important and legitimate interest in the health of the mother, the "compelling" point, in the light of present medical knowledge, is at approximately the end of the first trimester. This is so because of the now established medical fact . . . that until the end of the first trimester mortality in abortion is less than mortality in normal childbirth. It follows that, from and after this point, a State may regulate the abortion procedure to the extent that the regulation reasonably relates to the preservation and protection of maternal health. Examples of permissible state regulation in this area are requirements as to the qualifications of the person who is to perform the abortion; as to the licensure of that person; as to the facility in which the procedure is to be performed, that is, whether it must be a hospital or may be a clinic or some other place of less-than-hospital status; as to the licensing of the facility; and the like.

This means, on the other hand, that, for the period of pregnancy prior to this "compelling" point, the attending physician, in consultation with his patient, is free to determine, without regulation by the State, that in his medical judgment the patient's pregnancy should be terminated. If that decision is reached, the judgment may be effectuated by an abortion free of interference by the State.

With respect to the State's important and legitimate interest in potential life, the "compelling" point is at viability . . . . State regulation protective of fetal life after viability thus has both logical and biological justifications. If the State is interested in protecting fetal life after viability, it may go so far as to proscribe abortion during that period except when it is necessary to preserve the life or health of the mother. . . .

To summarize and repeat:

1. A state criminal abortion statute of the current Texas type, that excepts from criminality only a *life-saving* procedure on behalf of the mother, without regard to pregnancy stage and without recognition of the other interests involved, is violative of the Due Process Clause of the Fourteenth Amendment.
   (a) For the stage prior to approximately the end of the first trimester, the abortion decision and its effectuation must be left to the medical judgment of the pregnant woman's attending physician.
   (b) For the stage subsequent to approximately the end of the first trimester, the State, in promoting its interest in the health of the mother, may, if it chooses, regulate the abortion procedure in ways that are reasonably related to maternal health.
   (c) For the stage subsequent to viability the State, in promoting its interest in the potentiality of human life, may, if it chooses, regulate, and even proscribe, abortion except where it is necessary, in appropriate medical judgment, for the preservation of the life or health of the mother.
2. The State may define the term "physician," as it has been employed in the preceding numbered paragraphs of this Part XI of this opinion, to mean only a physician currently licensed by the State, and may proscribe any abortion by a person who is not a physician as so defined.

. . . The decision leaves the State free to place increasing restrictions on abortion as the period of pregnancy lenghthens, so long as those restrictions are tailored to the recognized state interests. The decision vindicates the right of the physician to administer medical treatment according to his professional judgment up to the points where important state interests provide compelling justifications for intervention. Up to those points the abortion decision in all its aspects is inherently, and primarily, a medical decision, and basic responsibility for it must rest with the physician. If an individual practitioner abuses the privilege of exercising proper medical judgment, the usual remedies, judicial and intraprofessional, are available. . . .

Dissent

At the heart of the controversy in these cases are those recurring pregnancies that pose no danger whatsoever to the life or health of the mother but are nevertheless unwanted for any one or more of a variety of reasons—convenience, family planning, economics, dislike of children, the embarrassment of illegitimacy, etc. The common claim before us is that for any one of such reasons, or for no reason at all, and without asserting or claiming any threat to life or health, any woman is entitled to an abortion at her request if she is able to find a medical advisor willing to undertake the procedure.

The Court for the most part sustains this position: During the period prior to the time the fetus becomes viable, the Constitution of the United States values the convenience, whim or caprice of the putative mother more than the life or potential life of the fetus; the Constitution, therefore, guarantees the right to an abortion as against any state law or policy seeking to protect the fetus from an abortion not prompted by more compelling reasons of the mother.

With all due respect, I dissent. I find nothing in the language or history of hte Constitution to support the Court's judgment. . . . As an exercise of raw judicial power, the Court perhaps has authority to do what it does today; but in my view its judgment is an improvident and extravagant exercise of the power of judicial review which the Constitution extends to this Court.

The Court apparently values the convenience of the pregnant mother more than the continued existence and development of the life or potential life which she carries. . . .

It is my view, therefore, that the Texas statute is not constitutionally infirm because it denies abortions to those who seek to serve only their convenience rather than to protect their life or health. . . .

Review Questions

1. Justice Blackmun discusses three reasons for the enactment of criminal abortion laws. Why doesn't he accept these reasons?
2. Where does the Constitution guarantee a right of privacy according to Justice Blackmun?
3. Is the fetus a person in the legal sense according to Justice Blackmun?
4. According to Justice Blackmun, when is the *compelling* point in the state's interest in the health of the mother?
5. When, according to Justice Blackmun, is the *compelling* point in the state's interest in potential life?
6. Explain Justice Blackmun's conclusions.
7. What are Justice White's objections?

Discussion Questions

1. What is the right to privacy? Try to define it.
2. What do you think is properly included in the right to privacy, and what is properly excluded?
3. Do you think that the fetus has any legal rights or any moral rights? Defend your view.
4. Justice White complains that Justice Blackmun's opinion allows a woman to get an abortion "without asserting or claiming any threat to life or health" provided she is able to find a doctor willing to undertake the procedure. Do you think that women should be allowed to get such abortions? Explain your answer. Do you believe that doctors have any obligation to perform such abortions? Why or why not?

The Supreme Court

Excerpts from *Planned Parenthood of Southeastern Pennsylvania v. Casey* (1992)

The majority opinion in this case was written by Justices O'Connor, Kennedy, and Souter. Several separate opinions agreed in part and dissented in part; we do not have any readings from those separate opinions.

In 1981, Associate Justice Sandra Day O'Connor became the first woman appointed to serve on the Supreme Court. She is a graduate of Stanford University.

Associate Justices Anthony M. Kennedy and David Souter are graduates of Harvard University and were appointed to the Court in 1988 and 1990, respectively.

The majority opinion reaffirmed the essential holding of Roe *that a woman has a right to abortion before viability. This right is protected by a substantive liberty component of the Fourteenth Amendment Due Process Clause. But the abortion right is not absolute; the state may still impose restrictions on abortion provided they do not impose an undue burden on the woman. Using this new undue burden standard, the Justice found that provisions which require the woman: to be informed about the nature and risks of abortion; to wait twenty-four hours after giving her informed consent; and to obtain parental consent if she is a minor are not unconstitutional. The requirement that a married woman notify her husband was found to be an undue burden and was stricken down.*

It must be stated at the outset and with clarity that *Roe*'s essential holding, the holding we reaffirm, has three parts. First is recognition of the right of the woman to choose to have an abortion before viability and to obtain it without undue interference from the State. Before viability, the State's interests are not strong enough to support a prohibition of abortion or the imposition of a substantial obstacle to the woman's effective right to elect the procedure. Second is a confirmation of the State's power to restrict abortions after fetal viability, if the law contains exceptions for pregnancies which endanger a woman's life or health. And third is the principle that the State has legitimate interests from the outset of the pregnancy in protecting the health of the woman and the life of the fetus that may become a child. These principles do not contradict one another; and we adhere to each.

Constitutional protection of the woman's decision to terminate her pregnancy derives from the Due Process Clause of the Fourteenth Amendment. It declares that no State shall "deprive any person of life, liberty, or property, without due process of law." The controlling word in the case before us is "liberty." Although a literal reading of the Clause might suggest that it governs only the procedures by which a State may deprive persons of liberty, for at least 105 years, the Clause has been understood to contain a substantive component as well, one "barring certain government actions regardless of the fairness of the procedures used to implement them."

It is a promise of the Constitution that there is a realm of personal liberty which the government may not enter. We have vindicated this principle before. Marriage is mentioned nowhere in the Bill of Rights and interracial marriage was illegal in most States in the 19th century, but the Court was no doubt correct in finding it to be an aspect of liberty protected against state interference by the substantive component of the Due Process Clause in *Loving v. Virginia* (1967). . . .

In *Griswold,* we held that the Constitution does not permit a State to forbid a married couple to use contraceptives. That same freedom was later guaranteed, under the Equal Protection Clause, for unmarried couples. . . .

The inescapable fact is that adjudication of substantive due process claims may call upon the Court in interpreting the Constitution to exercise that same capacity which by tradition courts always have exercised: reasoned judgment. Its boundaries are not susceptible of expression as a simple rule. That does not mean we are free to invalidate state policy choices with which we disagree; yet neither does it permit us to shrink from the duties of our office. . . .

Men and women of good conscience can disagree, and we suppose some always will disagree, about the profound moral and spiritual implications of terminating a pregnancy, even in its earliest stage. Some of us as individuals find abortion offensive to our most basic principles of morality, but that cannot control our decision. Our obligation is to define the liberty of all, not to mandate our own moral code. The underlying constitutional issue is whether the State can resolve these philosophic questions in such a definitive way that a woman lacks all choice in the matter, except perhaps in those rare circumstances in which the pregnancy is itself a danger to her own life or health, or is the result of rape or incest.

It is conventional constitutional doctrine that where reasonable people disagree the government can adopt one position or the other. . . . That theorem, however, assumes a state of affairs in which the choice does not intrude upon a protected liberty. Thus, while some people might disagree about the proposition that it may not be defiled, we have ruled that a State may not compel or enforce one view or the other. . . .

Our law affords constitutional protection to personal decisions relating to marriage, procreation, contraception, family relationships, child rearing, and education. . . . These matters, involving the most intimate and personal choices a person may make in a lifetime, choices central to personal dignity and autonomy, are central to the liberty protected by the Fourteenth Amendment. At the heart of liberty is the right to define one's own concept of existence, of meaning, of the universe, and of the mystery of human life. Beliefs about these matters could not define the attributes of personhood were they formed under compulsion of the State.

These considerations begin our analysis of the woman's interest in terminating her pregnancy but cannot end it, for this reason: though the abortion decision may originate within the zone of conscience and belief, it is more than a philosophic exercise. Abortion is a unique act. It is an act fraught with consequences for others: for the woman who must live with the implications of her decision; for the persons who perform and assist in the procedure; for the spouse, family, and society which must confront the knowledge that these procedures exist, procedures some deem nothing short of an act of violence against innocent human life; and, depending on one's beliefs, for the life or potential life that is aborted. Though abortion is conduct, it does not follow that the State is entitled to proscribe it in all instances. That is because the liberty of the woman is at take in a sense unique to the human condition and so unique to the law. The mother who carries a child to full term is subject to anxieties, to physical constraints, to pain that only she must bear. That these sacrifices have from the beginning of the human race been endured by woman with a pride that ennobles her in the eyes of others and gives to the infant a bound of love cannot alone be grounds for the State to insist she make the sacrifice. Her suffering is too intimate and personal for the State to insist, without more, upon its own vision of the woman's role, however dominant that vision has been in the course of our history and our culture. The density of the woman must be shaped to a large extent on her own conception of her spiritual imperatives and her place in society.

It should be recognized, moreover, that in some critical respects the abortion decision is of the same character as the decision to use contraception, to which *Griswold v. Connecticut, Eisenstadt v. Baird,* and *Carey v. Population Services International,* afford constitutional protection. We have no doubt as to the correctness of those decisions. They support the reasoning in *Roe* relating to the woman's liberty because they involve personal decisions concerning not only the meaning of procreation but also human responsibility and respect for it. . . .

From what we have said so far it follows that it is a constitutional liberty of the woman to have some freedom to terminate her pregnancy. We conclude that the basic decision in *Roe* was based on a constitutional analysis which we cannot now repudiate. The woman's liberty is not so unlimited, however, that from the outset the State cannot show its concern for the life of the unborn, and at a later point in fetal development the State's interest in life has sufficient force so that the right of the woman to terminate the pregnancy can be restricted.

That brings us, of course, to the point where much criticism has been directed at *Roe*, a criticism that always inheres when the Court draws a specific rule from what in the Constitution is but a general standard. We conclude, however, that the urgent claims of the woman to retain the ultimate control over her destiny and her body, claims implicit in the meaning of liberty, require us to perform that function. Liberty must not be extinguished for want of a line that is clear. And it falls to us to give some real substance to the woman's liberty to determine whether to carry her pregnancy to full term.

The woman's right to terminate her pregnancy before viability is the most central principle of *Roe* v. *Wade*. It is a rule of law and a component of liberty we cannot renounce.

On the other side of the equation is the interest of the State in the protection of potential life. The *Roe* Court recognized the State's "important and legitimate interest in protecting the potentiality of human life." . . . The weight to be given this state interest, not the strength of the woman's interest, was the difficult question faced in *Roe*. . . .

We reject the trimester framework, which we do not consider to be part of the essential holding of *Roe*. See *Webster* v. *Reproductive Health Services*, *supra*, at 518 (opinion of Rehnquist, C. J.); *id.*, at 529 (O'Connor, J., concurring in part and concurring in judgment) (describing the trimester framework as "problematic"). Measures aimed at ensuring that a woman's choice contemplates the consequences for the fetus do not necessarily interfere with the right recognized in *Roe*, although those measures have been found to be inconsistent with the rigid trimester framework announced in that case. A logical reading of the central holding in *Roe* itself, and a necessary reconciliation of the liberty of the woman and the interest of the State in promoting prenatal life, require, in our view, that we abandon the trimester framework as a rigid prohibition on all previability regulation aimed at the protection of fetal life. The trimester framework suffers from these basic flaws: in its formulation it misconceives the nature of the pregnant woman's interest; and in practice it undervalues the State's interest in potential life, as recognized in *Roe*. . . .

The very notion that the State has a substantial interest in potential life leads to the conclusion that not all regulations must be deemed unwarranted. Not all burdens on the right to decide whether to terminate a pregnancy will be undue. In our view, the undue burden standard is the appropriate means of reconciling the State's interest with the woman's constitutionally protected liberty. . . .

The concept of an undue burden has been utilized by the Court as well as individual members of the Court, including two of us, in ways that could be considered inconsistent. See, *e.g.*, *Hodgson* v. *Minnesota*, 497 U. S., at ___ (O'Connor, J., concurring in part and concurring in judgment); *Akron II*, 497 U. S., at ___ (opinion of Kennedy, J.); *Thornburgh* v. *American College of Obstetricians and Gynecologists*, 476 U. S., at 828–829 (O'Connor, J., dissenting); *Akron I*, *supra*, at 461–466 (O'Connor, J., dissenting); *Harris* v. *McRae*, *supra*, at 314; *Maher* v. *Roe*, *supra*, at 473; *Beal* v. *Doe*, 432 U. S. 438, 446 (1977); *Bellotti I*, *supra*, at 147. Because we set forth a standard of general application to which we intend to adhere, it is important to clarify what is meant by an undue burden.

A finding of an undue burden is a shorthand for the conclusion that a state regulation has the purpose or effect of placing a substantial obstacle in the path of a woman seeking an abortion of a nonviable fetus. A statute with this purpose is invalid because the means chosen by the State to further the interest in potential life must be calculated to inform the woman's free choice, not hinder it. And a statute which, while furthering the interest in potential life or some other valid state interest, has the effect of placing a substantial obstacle in the path of a woman's choice cannot be considered a permissible means of serving its legitimate ends. . . .

The Court of Appeals applied what it believed to be the undue burden standard and upheld each of the provisions except for the husband notification requirement. We agree generally with this conclusion, but refine the undue burden analysis in accordance with the principles articulated above. We now consider the separate statutory sections at issue.

We next consider the informed consent requirement. Except in a medical emergency, the statute requires that at least 24 hours before performing an abortion a physician inform the woman of the nature of the procedure, the health risks of the abortion and of childbirth, and the "probable gestational age of the unborn child." The physician or a qualified nonphysician must inform the woman of the availability of printed materials published by the State describing the fetus and providing information about medical assistance for childbirth, information about child support from the father, and a list of agencies which provide adoption and other services as alternatives to abortion. An abortion may not be performed unless the woman certifies in writing that she has been informed of the availability of these printed materials and has been provided them if she chooses to view them.

Our prior decisions establish that as with any medical procedure, the State may require a woman to give her written informed consent to an abortion. See *Planned Parenthood of Central Mo.* v. *Danforth,* 428 U. S., at 67. In this respect, the statute is unexceptional. Petitioners challenge the statute's definition of informed consent because it includes the provision of specific information by the doctor and the mandatory 24—hour waiting period. . . .

We also see no reason why the State may not require doctors to inform a woman seeking an abortion of the availability of materials relating to the consequences to the fetus, even when those consequences have no direct relation to her health. An example illustrates the point. We would think it constitutional for the State to require that in order for there to be informed consent to a kidney transplant operation the recipient must be supplied with information about risks to the donor as well as risks to himself or herself. . . . In short, requiring that the woman be informed of the availability of information relating to fetal development and the assistance available should she decide to carry the pregnancy to full term is a reasonable measure to insure an informed choice, one which might cause the woman to choose childbirth over abortion. This requirement cannot be considered a substantial obstacle to obtaining an abortion, and, it follows, there is no undue burden. . . .

Whether the mandatory 24–hour waiting period is nonetheless invalid because in practice it is a substantial obstacle to a woman's choice to terminate her pregnancy is a closer question. The findings of fact by the District Court indicate that because of the distances many women must travel to reach an abortion provider, the practical effect will often be a delay of much more than a day because the waiting period requires that a woman seeking an abortion make at least two visits to the doctor. The District Court also found that in many instances this will increase the exposure of women seeking abortions to "the harassment and hostility of anti-abortion protestors demonstrating outside a clinic." As a result, the District Court found that for those women who have the fewest financial resources, those who must travel long distances, and those who have difficulty explaining their whereabouts to husbands, employers, or others, the 24–hour waiting period will be "particularly burdensome." . . .

These findings are troubling in some respects, but they do not demonstrate that the waiting period constitutes an undue burden. We do not doubt that, as the District Court held, the waiting period has the effect of "increasing the cost and risk of delay of abortions," *id.,* at 1378, but the District Court did not conclude that the increased costs and potential delays amount to substantial obstacles. Rather, applying the trimester framework's strict prohibition of all regulation designed to promote the State's interest in potential life before viability, see *id.*, at 1374, the District Court concluded that the waiting period does not further the state "interest in maternal health" and "infringes the physician's discretion to exercise sound medical judgment." *Id.*, at 1378. Yet, as we have stated, under the undue burden standard a State is permitted to enact persuasive measures which favor childbirth over abortion, even if those measures do not further a health interest. And while the waiting period does limit a physician's discretion, that is not, standing alone, a reason to invalidate it. In light of the construction given the statute's definition of medical emergency by the Court of Appeals, and the District Court's findings, we cannot say that the waiting period imposes a real health risk.

We also disagree with the District Court's conclusion that the "particularly burdensome" effects of the waiting period on some women require its invalidation. A particular burden is not of necessity a substantial obstacle. Whether a burden falls on a particular group is a distinct inquiry from whether it is a substantial obstacle even as to the women in that group. And the District Court did not conclude that the waiting period is such an obstacle even for the women who are most burdened by it. Hence, on the record before us, and in the context of this facial challenge, we are not convinced that the 24-hour waiting period constitutes an undue burden. . . .

Section 3209 of Pennsylvania's abortion law provides, except in cases of medical emergency, that no physician shall perform an abortion on a married woman without receiving a signed statement from the woman that she has notified her spouse that she is about to undergo an abortion. The woman has the option of providing an alternative signed statement certifying that her husband is not the man who impregnated her; that her husband could not be located; that the pregnancy is the result of spousal sexual assault which she has reported; or that the woman believes that notifying her husband will cause him or someone else to inflict bodily injury upon her. A physician who performs an abortion on a married woman without receiving the appropriate signed statement will have his or her license revoked, and is liable to the husband for damages. . . .

. . .[T]he District Court's findings reinforce what common sense would suggest. In well-functioning marriages, spouses discuss important intimate decisions such as whether to bear a child. But there are millions of women in this country who are the victims of regular physical and psychological abuse at the hands of their husbands. Should these women become pregnant, they may have very good reasons for not wishing to inform their husbands of their decision to obtain an abortion.

The spousal notification requirement is thus likely to prevent a significant number of women from obtaining an abortion. It does not merely make abortions a little more difficult or expensive to obtain; for many women, it will impose a substantial obstacle. We must not blind ourselves to the fact that the significant number of women who fear for their safety and the safety of their children are likely to be deterred from procuring an abortion as surely as if the Commonwealth had outlawed abortion in all cases. . . .

The husband's interest in the life of the child his wife is carrying does not permit the State to empower him with this troubling degree of authority over his wife. The contrary view leads to consequences reminiscent of the common law. A husband has no enforceable right to require a wife to advise him before she exercises her personal choices. If a husband's interest in the potential life of the child outweighs a wife's liberty, the State could require a married woman to notify her husband before she uses a postfertilization contraceptive. Perhaps next in line would be a statute requiring pregnant women to notify their husbands before engaging in conduct causing risks to the fetus. After all, if the husband's interest in the fetus' safety is a sufficient predicate for state regulation, the State could reasonably conclude that pregnant wives should notify their husbands before drinking alcohol or smoking. Perhaps married women should notify their husbands before using contraceptives or before undergoing any type of surgery that may have complications affecting the husband's interest in his wife's reproductive organs. And if a husband's interest justifies notice in any of these cases, one might reasonably argue that it justifies exactly what the *Danforth* Court held it did not justify—a requirement of the husband's consent as well. A State may not give to a man the kind of dominion over his wife that parents exercise over their children.

We next consider the parental consent provision. Except in a medical emergency, an unemancipated young woman under 18 may not obtain an abortion unless she and one of her parents (or guardian) provides informed consent as defined above. If neither a parent nor a guardian provides consent, a court may authorize the performance of an abortion upon a determination that the young woman is mature and capable of giving informed consent and has in fact given her informed consent, or that an abortion would be in her best interests.

We have been over most of this ground before. Our cases establish, and we reaffirm today, that a State may require a minor seeking an abortion to obtain the consent of a parent or guardian, provided that there is an adequate judicial bypass procedure. . . .

Our Constitution is a covenant running from the first generation of Americans to us and then to future generations. It is a coherent succession. Each generation must learn anew that the Constitution's written terms embody ideas and aspirations that must survive more ages than one. We accept our responsibility not to retreat from interpreting the full meaning of the covenant in light of all of our precedents. We invoke it once again to define the freedom guaranteed by the Constitution's own promise, the promise of liberty. . . .

Review Questions

1. According to the Justices, *Roe*'s essential holding has three parts. What are they?
2. What is the constitutional basis for a woman's liberty? In what areas does this right of liberty apply?
3. Why is the trimester framework of *Roe* rejected?
4. Explain the undue burden standard. What restrictions on abortion does it allow? What is not allowed?

Discussion Questions

1. Is this undue burden standard acceptable? Why or why not?
2. Does the mandatory 24-hour waiting period impose an undue burden on a woman?
3. Should a married woman be required to notify her husband of an abortion? What is your view?
4. Should minors be required to get the informed consent of a parent or guardian or judge for an abortion? What do you think?

John T. Noonan, Jr.

An Almost Absolute Value in History

John T. Noonan, Jr., is Professor of Law at the University of California, Berkeley. His books include Contraception: A History of Its Treatment by the Catholic Theologians and Canonists *(1965), (1970), and* Persons and Masks of the Law *(1976).*

Noonan begins with the question, How do you determine the humanity of a being? The answer

Reprinted by permission of the publishers from *The Morality of Abortion: Legal and Historical Perspectives*, ed. by John T. Noonan, Jr., Cambridge, Massachusetts: Harvard Univesity Press, Copyright © 1970 by the President and Fellows of Harvard College.

he defends is what he says is the view of traditional Christian theology, namely that you are human if you are conceived by human parents. This view is compared to other alleged criteria of humanity such as viability, experience, feelings of adults, sensations of adults, and social visibility. Each of these is rejected as inadequate and arbitrary. In his defense of the traditional view, Noonan does not appeal to the medieval theory of ensoulment, that is, the theory that the soul enters the body at conception. Instead, he rests his case on the fact that at conception the fetus (or strictly speaking, the zygote) receives the full genetic code of a human being. He assumes that anything with human genetic coding is a human being with rights equal to those of other humans. It follows that the fetus is a human being with rights from the moment of conception. Once this has been granted, we can see that abortion is morally wrong except in rare cases where it is necessary to save the mother's life.

The most fundamental question involved in the long history of thought on abortion is: How do you determine the humanity of a being? To phrase the question that way is to put in comprehensive humanistic terms what the theologians either dealt with as an explicitly theological question under the heading of "ensoulment" or dealt with implicitly in their treatment of abortion. The Christian position as it originated did not depend on a narrow theological or philosophical concept. It had no relation to theories of infant baptism.[1] It appealed to no special theory of instantaneous ensoulment. It took the world's view on ensoulment as that view changed from Aristotle to Zacchia. There was, indeed, theological influence affecting the theory of ensoulment finally adopted, and, of course, ensoulment itself was a theological concept, so that the position was always explained in theological terms. But the theological notion of ensoulment could easily be translated into humanistic language by substituting "human" for "rational soul"; the problem of knowing when a man is a man is common to theology and humanism.

If one steps outside the specific categories used by the theologians, the answer they gave can be analyzed as a refusal to discriminate among human beings on the basis of their varying potentialities. Once conceived, the being was recognized as man because he had man's potential. The **criterion** for humanity, thus, was simple and all-embracing: if you are conceived by human parents, you are human.

The strength of this position may be tested by a review of some of the other distinctions offered in the contemporary controversy over legalizing abortion. Perhaps the most popular distinction is in terms of viability. Before an age of so many months, the fetus is not viable, that is, it cannot be removed from the mother's womb and live apart from her. To that extent, the life of the fetus is absolutely dependent on the life of the mother. This dependence is made the basis of denying recognition to its humanity.

There are difficulties with this distinction. One is that the perfection of artificial incubation may make the fetus viable at any time: it may be removed and artificially sustained. Experiments with animals already show that such a procedure is possible. This hypothetical extreme case relates to an actual difficulty: there is considerable elasticity to the idea of viability. Mere length of life is not an exact measure. The viability of the fetus depends on the extent of its anatomical and functional development. The weight and length of the fetus are better guides to the state of its development than age, but weight and length vary. Moreover, different racial groups have different ages at which their fetuses are viable. Some evidence, for example, suggests that Negro fetuses mature more quickly than white fetuses. If viability is the norm, the standard would vary with race and with many individual circumstances.

The most important objection to this approach is that dependence is not ended by viability. The fetus is still absolutely dependent on someone's care in order to continue existence; indeed a child of one or three or even five years of age is absolutely dependent on another's care for existence; uncared for, the older fetus or the younger child will die as surely as the early fetus detached from the mother. The unsubstantial lessening in dependence at viability does not seem to signify any special acquisition of humanity.

A second distinction has been attempted in terms of experience. A being who has had experience, has lived and suffered, who possesses memories, is more human than one who has not. Humanity depends on formation by experience. The fetus is thus "unformed" in the most basic human sense.

This distinction is not serviceable for the embryo which is already experiencing and reacting. The embryo is responsive to touch after eight weeks and at least at that point is experiencing. At an earlier stage the zygote is certainly alive and responding to its environment. The distinction may also be challenged by the rare case where aphasia has erased adult memory: has it erased humanity? More fundamentally, this distinction leaves even the older fetus or the younger child to be treated as an unformed inhuman thing. Finally, it is not clear why experience as such confers humanity. It could be argued that certain central experiences such as loving or learning are necessary to make a man human. But then human beings who have failed to love or to learn might be excluded from the class called man.

A third distinction is made by appeal to the sentiments of adults. If a fetus dies, the grief of the parents is not the grief they would have for a living child. The fetus is an unnamed "it" till birth, and is not perceived as personality until at least the fourth month of existence when movements in the womb manifest a vigorous presence demanding joyful recognition by the parents.

Yet feeling is notoriously an unsure guide to the humanity of others. Many groups of humans have had difficulty in feeling that persons of another tongue, color, religion, sex, are as human as they. Apart from reactions to alien groups, we mourn the loss of a ten-year-old boy more than the loss of his one-day-old brother or his 90-year-old grandfather. The difference felt and the grief expressed vary with the potentialities extinguished, or the experience wiped out; they do not seem to point to any substantial difference in the humanity of baby, boy, or grandfather.

Distinctions are also made in terms of sensation by the parents. They embryo is felt within the womb only after about the fourth month. The embryo is seen only at birth. What can be neither seen nor felt is different from what is tangible. If the fetus cannot be seen or touched at all, it cannot be perceived as man.

Yet experience shows that sight is even more untrustworthy than feeling in determining humanity. By sight, color became an appropriate index for saying who was a man, and the evil of racial discrimination was given foundation. Nor can touch provide the test; a being confined by sickness, "out of touch" with others, does not thereby seem to lose his humanity. To the extent that touch still has appeal as a criterion, it appears to be a survival of the old English idea of "quickening"—a possible mistranslation of the Latin *animatus* used in the canon law. To that extent touch as a criterion seems to be dependent on the Aristotelian notion of ensoulment, and to fall when this notion is discarded.

Finally, a distinction is sought in social visibility. The fetus is not socially perceived as human. It cannot communicate with others. Thus, both subjectively and objectively, it is not a member of society. As moral rules are rules for the behavior of members of society to each other, they cannot be made for behavior toward what is not yet a member. Excluded from the society of men, the fetus is excluded from the humanity of men.[2]

By force of the argument from the consequences, this distinction is to be rejected. It is more subtle than that founded on an appeal to physical sensation, but it is equally dangerous in its implications. If humanity depends on social recognition, individuals or whole groups may be dehumanized by being denied any status in their society. Such a fate is fictionally portrayed in *1984* and has actually been the lot of many men in many socieites. In the Roman empire, for example, condemnation to slavery meant the practical denial of most human rights; in the Chinese Communist world, landlords have been classified as enemies of the people and so treated as nonpersons by the state. Humanity does not depend on social recognition, though often the failure of society to recognize the prisoner, the alien, the heterodox as human has led to the destruction of human beings. Anyone conceived by a man and a woman is human. Recognition of this condition by society follows a real event in the objective order, however imperfect and halting the recognition. Any attempt to limit humanity to exclude some group runs the risk of furnishing authority and precedent for excluding other groups in the name of the consciousness or perception of the controlling group in the society.

A philosopher may reject the appeal to the humanity of the fetus because he views "humanity" as a secular view of the soul and because he doubts the existence of anything real and objective which can be identified as humanity. One answer to such a philosopher is to ask how he reasons about moral questions without supposing that there is a sense in which he and the others of whom he speaks are human. Whatever group is taken as the society which determines who may be killed is thereby taken as human. A second answer is to ask if he does not believe that there is a right and wrong way of deciding moral questions. If there is such a difference, experience may be appealed to: to decide who is human on the basis of the sentiment of a given society has led to consequences which rational men would characterize as monstrous.

The rejection of the attempted distinctions based on viability and visibility, experience and feeling, may be buttressed by the following considerations: Moral judgments often rest on distinctions, but if the distinctions are not to appear arbitrary *fiat,* they should relate to some real difference in probabilities. There is a kind of continuity in all life, but the earlier stages of the elements of human life possess tiny probabilities of development. Consider, for example, the spermatozoa in any normal ejaculate: There are about 200,000,000 in any single ejaculate, of which one has a chance of developing into a zygote. Consider the oocytes which may become ova: there are 100,000 to 1,000,000 oocytes in a female infant, of which a maximum of 390 are ovulated. But once spermatozoon and ovum meet and the conceptus is formed, such studies as have been made show that roughly in only 20 percent of the cases will spontaneous abortion occur. In other words, the chances are about 4 out of 5 that this new being will develop. At this stage in the life of the being there is a sharp shift in probabilities, an imense jump in potentialities. To make a distinction between the rights of spermatozoa and the rights of the fertilized ovum is to respond to an enormous shift in possibilities. For about twenty days after conception the egg may split to form twins or combine with another egg to form a chimera, but the probability of either event happening is very small.

It may be asked, What does a change in biological probabilities have to do with establishing humanity? The argument from probabilities is not aimed at establishing humanity but at establishing an objective discontinuity which may be taken into account in moral discourse. As life itself is a matter of probabilities, as most moral reasoning is an estimate of probabilities, so it seems in accord with the structure of reality and the nature of moral thought to found a moral judgment on the change in probabilities at conception. The appeal to probabilities is the most commonsensical of arguments; to a greater or smaller degree all of us base our actions on probabilities, and in morals, as in law, prudence and negligence are often measured by the account one has taken of the probabilities. If the chance is 200,000,000 to 1 that the movement in the bushes into which you shoot is a man's, I doubt if many persons would hold you careless in shooting; but if the chances are 4 out of 5 that the movement is a human being's, few would acquit you of blame. Would the argument be different if only one out of ten children conceived came to term? Of course this argument would be different. This argument is an appeal to probabilities that actually exist, not to any and all states of affairs which may be imagined.

The probabilities as they do exist do not show the humanity of the embryo in the sense of a demonstration in logic any more than the probabilities of the movement in the bush being a man demonstrate beyond all doubt that the being is a man. The appeal is a "buttressing" consideration, showing the plausibility of the standard adopted. The argument focuses on the decisional factor in any moral judgment and assumes that part of the business of a moralist is drawing lines. One evidence of the nonarbitrary character of the line drawn is the difference of probabilities on either side of it. If a spermatozoon is destroyed, one destroys a being which had a chance of far less than 1 in 200 million of developing into a reasoning being, possessed of the genetic code, a heart and other organs, and capable of pain. If a fetus is destroyed, one destroys a being already possessed of the genetic code, organs, and sensitivity to pain, and one which had an 80 percent chance of developing further into a baby outside the womb who, in time, would reason.

The positive argument for conception as the decisive moment of humanization is that at conception the new being receives the genetic code. It is this genetic information which determines his characteristics, which is the biological carrier of the possibility of human wisdom, which makes him a self-evolving being. A being with a human genetic code is man.

This review of current controversy over the humanity of the fetus emphasizes what a fundamental question the theologicans resolved in asserting the inviolability of the fetus. To regard the fetus as possessed of equal rights with other humans was not, however, to decide every case where abortion might be employed. It did decide the case where the argument was that the fetus should be aborted for its own good. To say a being was human was to say it had a destiny to decide for itself which could not be taken from it by another man's decision. But human beings with equal rights often come in conflict with each other, and some decision must be made as to whose claims are to prevail. Cases of conflict involving the fetus are different only in two respects: the total inability of the fetus to speak for itself and the fact that the right of the fetus regularly at stake is the right to life itself.

The approach taken by the theologians to these conflicts was articulated in terms of "direct" and "indirect." Again, to look at what they were doing from outside their categories, they may be said to have been drawing lines or "balancing values." "Direct" and "indirect" are spatial metaphors; "line-drawing" is another. "To weigh" or "to balance" values is a metaphor of a more complicated mathematical sort hinting at the process which goes on in moral judgments. All the metaphors suggest that, in the moral judgments made, comparisons were necessary, that no value completely controlled. The principle of double effect was no doctrine fallen from heaven, but a method of analysis appropriate where two relative values were being compared. In Catholic moral theology, as it developed, life even of the innocent was not taken as an absolute. Judgments on acts affecting life issued from a process of weighing. In the weighing, the fetus was always given a value greater than zero, always a value separate and independent from its parents. This valuation was crucial and fundamental in all Christian thought on the subject and marked it off from any approach which considered that only the parents' interests needed to be considered.

Even with the fetus weighed as human, one interest could be weighed as equal or superior: that of the mother in her own life. The casuists between 1450 and 1895 were willing to weigh this interest as superior. Since 1895, that interest was given decisive weight only in the two special cases of the cancerous uterus and the ectopic pregnancy. In both of these cases the fetus itself had little chance of survival even if the abortion were not performed. As the balance was once struck in favor of the mother whenever her life was endangered, it could be so struck again. The balance reached between 1895 and 1930 attempted prudentially and pastorally to forestall a multitude of exceptions for interests less than life.

The perception of the humanity of the fetus and the weighing of fetal rights against other human rights constituted the work of the moral analysts. But what spirit animated their abstract judgments? For the Christian community it was the injunction of Scripture to love your neighbor as yourself. The fetus as human was a neighbor; his life had parity with one's own. The commandment gave life to what otherwise would have been only rational calculation.

The commandment could be put in humanistic as well as theological terms: Do not injure your fellow man without reason. In these terms, once the humanity of the fetus is perceived, abortion is never right except in self-defense. When life must be taken to save life, reason alone cannot say that a mother must prefer a child's life to her own. With this exception, now of great rarity, abortion violates the rational humanist tennet of the equality of human lives.

For Christians the commandment to love had received a special imprint in that the exemplar proposed of love was the love of the Lord for his disciples. In the light given by this example, self-sacrifice carried to the point of death seemed in the extreme situations not without meaning. In the less extreme cases, preference for one's own interests to the life of another seemed to express cruelty or selfishness irreconcilable with the demands of love.

Endnotes

1. According to Glanville Williams (*The Sanctity of Human Life supra* n. 169, at 193), "The historical reason for the Catholic objection to abortion is the same as for the Christian Church's historical opposition to infanticide: the horror of bringing about the death of an unbaptized child." This statement is made without any citation of evidence. As has been seen, desire to administer baptism could, in the Middle Ages, even be urged as a reason for procuring an abortion. It is highly regrettable that the American Law Institute was apparently misled by Williams' account and repeated after him the same baseless statement. See American Law Institute, *Model Penal Code: Tentative Draft No. 9* (1959), p. 148, n. 12.
2. . . . Thomas Aquinas gave an analogous reason against baptizing a fetus in the womb: "As long as it exists in the womb of the mother, it cannot be subject to the operation of the ministers of the Church as it is not known to men" (*In sententias Petri Lombardi* 4.6 1.1.2).

Review Questions

1. According to Noonan, what is the simple Christian criterion for humanity?
2. Noonan discusses five different distinctions (starting with viability) used by defenders of abortion. Explain Noonan's critique of these distinctions.
3. State and explain Noonan's argument from probabilities.
4. What is Noonan's positive argument for saying that conception is "the decisive moment of humanization?"
5. In Noonan's view, why does the fetus have rights equal to those of other human beings?
6. According to Noonan, how do Christian theologians resolve conflicts of rights such as that between the mother's right to life and the fetus' right to life?
7. According to the traditional view defended by Noonan, in which cases do the fetus' right to life outweigh the mother's right to life?

Discussion Questions

1. Consider the following objection to Noonan's claim that "a being with a human genetic code is a man." A human cell also is a being with a human genetic code, but obviously it is not a man in the sense of being a human being; therefore, Noonan's claim is false. How could Noonan respond to this objection?
2. Is it possible for a nonhuman being, for example an angel or an intelligent alien being, to have rights equal to those of human beings? Defend your answer.
3. Noonan admits that abortion can be justified by appealing to the right of self-defense. Does this right justify an abortion in a case of rape? Why or why not?

Mary Ann Warren

On the Moral and Legal Status of Abortion

Mary Ann Warren teaches at San Francisco State University. She is the author of several articles including "Do Potential People Have Moral Rights?" and "Secondary Sexism and Quota Hiring."

The first part of Warren's article is a response to Thomson. She argues that even though Thomson's argument from analogy is probably conclusive in showing that abortion is justified in the case of pregnancy due to rape, it does not show that abortion is permissible in numerous other cases where pregnancy is not due to rape and is not life-threatening. Warren feels that more argument is needed to show the permissibility of abortion in those cases.

In the second part of the article, Warren presents her case for the liberal view that abortion can be justified in any case. Her argument depends on a distinction between two senses of the word human. *The first sense is a* genetic sense *where something is human if it is a member of the biological species* Homo sapiens; *the second is a* moral sense *where something is human if it is a member of the moral community. She claims that conservatives like Noonan confuse these two senses of human. They fallaciously argue from the fact that fetuses are genetically human to the conclusion that they are morally human, that is, persons with a right to life. But an analysis of the concept of person shows that fetuses are unlike persons in too many areas to have a significant right to life. There are five features central to personhood—consciousness, reasoning, self-motivated activity, the capacity to communicate, and self-awareness. The fetus lacks all of these features in the early stages of development and continues to lack most of them in the later stages. Furthermore, the fetus' potential for becoming a person does not provide us with a good reason for ascribing to it a significant right to life. The rights of a merely potential person, even assuming it has rights, would always be outweighed by the rights of an actual person, in this case, the mother. The mother's right to have an abortion, then, is absolute; it can never be outweighed by the rights of the fetus.*

In the postscript, Warren replies to the objection that her view would justify infanticide. She admits that infants do not have a significant right to life in her view, but she claims that it does not follow that infanticide is permissible for two reasons. First, there may be people willing to adopt the unwanted child and in that case it would be wrong to kill it. Second, many people in our country value infants and would prefer that they be preserved, even if foster parents are not available.

We will be concerned with both the moral status of abortion, which for our purposes we may define as the act which a woman performs in voluntarily terminating, or allowing another person to terminate, her pregnancy, and the legal status which is appropriate for this act. I will argue that, while it is not possible to produce a satisfactory defense of a woman's right to obtain an abortion without showing that a fetus is not a human being, in the morally relevant sense of that term, we ought not to conclude that the difficulties involved in determining whether or not a fetus is human make it impossible to produce any satisfactory solution to the problem of the moral status of abortion. For it is possible to show that, on the basis of intuitions which we may expect even the opponents of abortion to share, a fetus is not a person, and hence not

From "On the Moral and Legal Status of Abortion," *The Monist,* vol. 57, no. 1 (January 1973), p. 43–61. Reprinted with permission from *The Monist* and Dr. Mary Ann Warren, San Francisco State University.

the sort of entity to which it is proper to ascribe full moral rights.

Of course, while some philosophers would deny the possibility of any such proof,[1] others will deny that there is any need for it, since the moral permissibility of abortion appears to them to be too obvious to require proof. But the inadequacy of this attitude should be evident from the fact that both the friends and the foes of abortion consider their position to be morally self-evident. Because pro-abortionists have never adequately come to grips with the conceptual issues surrounding abortion, most if not all, of the arguments which they advance in opposition to laws restricting access to abortion fail to refute or even weaken the traditional antiabortion argument, i.e., that a fetus is a human being, and therefore abortion is murder.

These arguments are typically one of two sorts. Either they point to the terrible side effects of the restrictive laws, e.g., the deaths due to illegal abortions, and the fact that it is poor women who suffer the most as a result of these laws, or else they state that to deny a woman access to abortion is to deprive her of her right to control her own body. Unfortunately, however, the fact that restricting access to abortion has tragic side effects does not, in itself, show that the restrictions are unjustified, since murder is wrong regardless of the consequences of prohibiting it; and the appeal to the right to control one's body, which is generally construed as a property right, is at best a rather feeble argument for the permissibility of abortion. Mere ownership does not give me the right to kill innocent people whom I find on my property, and indeed I am apt to be held responsible if such people injure themselves while on my property. It is equally unclear that I have any moral right to expel an innocent person from my property when I know that doing so will result in his death.

Furthermore, it is probably inappropriate to describe a woman's body as her property, since it seems natural to hold that a person is something distinct from her property, but not from her body. Even those who would object to the identification of a person with his body, or with the conjunction of his body and his mind, must admit that it would be very odd to describe, say, breaking a leg, as damaging one's property, and much more appropriate to describe it as injuring one*self*. Thus it is probably a mistake to argue that the right to obtain an abortion is in any way derived from the right to own and regulate property.

But however we wish to construe the right to abortion, we cannot hope to convince those who consider abortion a form of murder of the existence of any such right unless we are able to produce a clear and convincing refutation of the traditional antiabortion argument, and this has not, to my knowledge, been done. With respect to the two most vital issues which that argument involves, i.e., the humanity of the fetus and its implication for the moral status of abortion, confusion has prevailed on both sides of the dispute.

Thus, both pro-abortionists and antiabortionists have tended to abstract the question of whether abortion is wrong to that of whether it is wrong to destroy a fetus, just as though the rights of another person were not necessarily involved. This mistaken abstraction has led to the almost universal assumption that if a fetus is a human being, with a right to life, then it follows immediately that abortion is wrong (except perhaps when necessary to save the woman's life), and that it ought to be prohibited. It has also been generally assumed that unless the question about the status of the fetus is answered, the moral status of abortion cannot possibly be determined.

Two recent papers, one by B. A. Brody,[2] and one by Judith Thomson,[3] have attempted to settle the question of whether abortion ought to be prohibited apart from the question of whether or not the fetus is human. Brody examines the possibility that the following two statements are compatible: (1) that abortion is the taking of innocent human life, and therefore wrong; and (2) that nevertheless it ought not to be prohibited by law, at least under the present circumstances.[4] Not surprisingly, Brody finds it impossible to reconcile these two statements, since, as he rightly argues, none of the unfortunate side effects of the prohibition of abortion is bad enough to justify legalizing the *wrongful* taking of human life. He is mistaken, however, in concluding that the incompatibility of (1) and (2), in itself, shows that "the legal problem about abortion cannot be resolved independently of the status of the fetus problem" . . . .

What Brody fails to realize is that (1) embodies the questionable assumption that if a fetus is a human being, then of course abortion is morally wrong, and that an attack on *this* assumption is more promising, as a way of reconciling the humanity of the fetus with the claim that laws prohibiting abortion are unjustified, than is an attack on the assumption that if abortion is the wrongful killing of innocent human beings then it ought to be prohibited. He thus overlooks the possibility that a fetus may have a right to life and abortion still be morally permissible, in that the right of a woman to terminate an unwanted pregnancy might override the right of the fetus to be kept alive. The immorality of abortion is no more demonstrated by the humanity of the fetus, in itself, than the immorality of killing in self-defense is demonstrated by the fact that the assailant is a human being. Neither is it demonstrated by the *innocence* of the fetus, since there may be situations in which the killing of innocent human beings is justified.

It is perhaps not surprising that Brody fails to spot this assumption, since it has been accepted with little or no argument by nearly everyone who has written on the morality of abortion. John Noonan is correct in saying that "the fundamental question in the long history of abortion is, How do you determine the humanity of a being?" [5] He summarizes his own antiabortion argument, which is a version of the official position of the Catholic Church, as follows:

> . . . it is wrong to kill humans, however poor, weak, defenseless, and lacking in opportunity to develop their potential they may be. It is therefore morally wrong to kill Biafrans. Similarly, it is morally wrong to kill embryos.[6]

Noonan bases his claim that fetuses are human upon what he calls the theologians' criterion of humanity: that whoever is conceived of human beings is human. But although he argues at length for the appropriateness of this criterion, he never questions the assumption that if a fetus is human then abortion is wrong for exactly the same reason that murder is wrong.

Judith Thomson is, in fact, the only writer I am aware of who has seriously questioned this assumption; she has argued that, even if we grant the antiabortionist his claim that a fetus is a human being, with the same right to life as any other human being, we can still demonstrate that, in at least some and perhaps most cases, a woman is under no moral obligation to complete an unwanted pregnancy.[7] Her argument is worth examining, since if it holds up it may enable us to establish the moral permissibility of abortion without becoming involved in problems about what entitles an entity to be considered human, and accorded full moral rights. To be able to do this would be a great gain in the power and simplicity of the pro-abortion position, since, although I will argue that these problems can be solved at least as decisively as can any other moral problem, we should certainly be pleased to be able to avoid having to solve them as part of the justification of abortion.

On the other hand, even if Thomson's argument does not hold up, her insight, i.e., that it requires *argument* to show that if fetuses are human then abortion is properly classified as murder, is an extremely valuable one. The assumption she attacks is particularly invidious, for it amounts to the decision that it is appropriate, in deciding the moral status of abortion, to leave the rights of the pregnant woman out of consideration entirely, except possibly when her life is threatened. Obviously, this will not do; determining what moral rights, if any, a fetus possesses is only the first step in determining the moral status of abortion. Step two, which is at least equally essential, is finding a just solution to the conflict between whatever rights the fetus may have, and the rights of the woman who is unwillingly pregnant. While the historical error has been to pay far too little attention to the second step, Ms. Thomson's suggestion is that if we look at the second step first we may find that a woman has a right to obtain an abortion *regardless* of what rights the fetus has.

Our own inquiry will also have two stages. In Section I, we will consider whether or not it is possible to establish that abortion is morally permissible even on the assumption that a fetus is an entity with a full-fledged right to life. I will argue that in fact this cannot be established, at least not with the conclusiveness which is essential to our hopes of convincing those who are skeptical about the morality of abortion, and that we therefore cannot avoid dealing with the question of whether or not a fetus really does have the same right to life as a (more fully developed) human being.

In Section II, I will propose an answer to this question, namely, that a fetus cannot be considered a member of the moral community, the set of beings with full and equal moral rights, for the simple reason that it is not a person, and that it is personhood, and not genetic humanity, i.e., humanity as defined by Noonan, which is the basis for membership in this community. I will argue that a fetus, whatever its stage of development, satisfies none of the basic criteria of personhood, and is not even enough *like* a person to be accorded even some of the same rights on the basis of this resemblance. Nor, as we will see, is a fetus's *potential* personhood a threat to the morality of abortion, since, whatever the rights of potential people may be, they are invariably overridden in any conflict with the moral rights of actual people.

I

We turn now to Professor Thomson's case for the claim that even if a fetus has full moral rights, abortion is still morally permissible, at least sometimes, and for some reasons other than to save the woman's life. Her argument is based upon a clever, but I think faulty, analogy. She asks us to picture ourselves waking up one day, in bed with a famous violinist. Imagine that you have been kidnapped, and your bloodstream hooked up to that of the violinist, who happens to have an ailment which will certainly kill him unless he is permitted to share your kidneys for a period of nine months. No one else can save him, since you alone have the right type of blood. He will be unconscious all that time, and you will have to stay in bed with him, but after the nine months are over he may be unplugged, completely cured, that is provided that you have cooperated.

Now then, she continues, what are your obligations in this situation? The antiabortionist, if he is consistent, will have to say that you are obligated to stay in bed with the violinist: for all people have a right to life, and violinists are people, and therefore it would be murder for your to disconnect yourself from him and let him die . . . But this is outrageous, and so there must be something wrong with the same argument when it is applied to abortion. It would certainly be commendable of you to agree to save the violinist, but it is absurd to suggest that your refusal to do so would be murder. His right to life does not obligate you to do whatever is required to keep him alive; nor does it justify anyone else in forcing you to do so. A law which required you to stay in bed with the violinist would clearly be an unjust law, since it is no proper function of the law to force unwilling people to make huge sacrifices for the sake of other people toward whom they have no such prior obligation.

Thomson concludes that, if this analogy is an apt one, then we can grant the antiabortionist his claim that a fetus is a human being, and still hold that it is at least sometimes the case that a pregnant woman has the right to refuse to be a Good Samaritan towards the fetus, i.e., to obtain an abortion. For there is a great gap between the claim that *x* has a right to life, and the claim that *y* is obligated to do whatever is necessary to keep *x* alive, let alone that he ought to be forced to do so. It is *y*'s duty to keep *x* alive only if he has somehow contracted a *special* obligation to do so; and a woman who is unwillingly pregnant, e.g., who was raped, has done nothing which obligates her to make the enormous sacrifice which is necessary to preserve the conceptus.

This argument is initially quite plausible, and in the extreme case of pregnancy due to rape it is probably conclusive. Difficulties arise, however, when we try to specify more exactly the range of cases in which abortion is clearly justifiable even on the assumption that the fetus is human. Professor Thomson considers it a virtue of her argument that it does not enable us to conclude that abortion is *always* permissible. It would, she says, be "indecent" for a woman in her seventh month to obtain an abortion just to avoid having to postpone a trip to Europe. On the other hand, her argument enables us to see that "a sick and desperately frightened schoolgirl pregnant due to rape may *of course* choose abortion, and that any law which rules this out is an insane law" . . . . So far, so good; but what are we to say about the woman who becomes pregnant not through rape but as a result of her own carelessness, or because of contraceptive failure, or who gets pregnant intentionally and then changes her mind about wanting a child? With respect to such cases, the violinist analogy is of much less use to the defender of the woman's right to obtain an abortion.

Indeed, the choice of a pregnancy due to rape, as an example of a case in which abortion is permissible even if a fetus is considered a human being, is extremely significant; for it is only in the case of pregnancy due to rape that the woman's situation is adequately analogous to the violinist case for our intutions about the latter to transfer convincingly. The crucial difference between a pregnancy due to rape and the *normal* case of an unwanted pregnancy is that in the normal case we cannot claim that the woman is in no way responsible for her predicament; she could have remained chaste, or taken her pills more faithfully, or abstained on dangerous days, and so on. If, on the other hand, you are kidnapped by strangers, and hooked up to a strange violinist, then you are free of any shred of responsibility for the situation, on the basis of which it could be argued that you are obligated to keep the violinist alive. Only when her pregnancy is due to rape is a woman clearly just as nonresponsible.[8]

Consequently, there is room for the anti-abortionist to argue that in the normal case of unwanted pregnancy a woman has, by her own actions, assumed responsibility for the fetus. For if *x* behaves in a way which he could have avoided, and which he knows involves, let us say, a 1 percent chance of bringing into existence a human being, with a right to life, and does so knowing that if this should happen then that human being will perish unless *x* does certain things to keep him alive, then it is by no means clear that when it does happen *x* is free of any obligation to what he knew in advance would be required to keep that human being alive.

The plausibility of such an argument is enough to show that the Thomson analogy can provide a clear and persuasive defense of a woman's right to obtain an abortion only with respect to those cases in which the woman is in no way responsible for her pregnancy, e.g., where it is due to rape. In all other cases, we would almost certainly conclude that it was necessary to look carefully at the particular circumstances in order to determine the extent of the woman's responsibility, and hence the extent of her obligation. This is an extremely unsatisfactory outcome, from the viewpoint of the opponents of restrictive abortion laws, most of whom are convinced that a woman has a right to obtain an abortion regardless of how and why she got pregnant.

Of course a supporter of the violinist analogy might point out that it is absurd to suggest that forgetting her pill one day might be sufficient to obligate a woman to complete an unwanted pregnancy. And indeed it *is* absurd to suggest this. As we will see, the moral right to obtain an abortion is not in the least dependent upon the extent to which the woman is responsible for her pregnancy. But unfortunately, once we allow the assumption that a fetus has full moral rights, we cannot avoid taking this absurd suggestion seriously. Perhaps we can make this point more clear by altering the violinist story just enough to make it more analogous to a normal unwanted pregnancy and less to a pregnancy due to rape, and then seeing whether it is still obvious that you are not obligated to stay in bed with the fellow.

Suppose, then, that violinists are pecularily prone to the sort of illness the only cure for which is the use of someone else's blood-stream for nine months, and that because of this there has been formed a society of music lovers who agree that whenever a violinist is stricken they will draw lots and the loser will, by some means, be made the one and only person capable of saving him. Now then, would you be obligated to cooperate in curing the violinist if you had voluntarily joined this society, knowing the possible consequences, and then your name had been drawn and you had been kidnapped? Admittedly, you did not promise ahead of time that you would, but you did deliberately place yourself in a position in which it might happen that a human life would be lost if you did not. Surely this is at least a prima facie reason for supposing that you have an obligation to stay in bed with the violinist. Suppose that you had gotten your name drawn deliberately; surely *that* would be quite a strong reason for thinking that you had such an obligation.

It might be suggested that there is one important disanalogy between the modified violinist case and the case of an unwanted pregnancy, which makes the woman's responsibility significantly less, namely, the fact that the fetus *comes into existence* as the result of the woman's actions. This fact might give her a right to refuse to keep it alive, whereas she would not have had this right had it existed previously, independently, and then as a result of her actions become dependent upon her for its survival.

My own intuition, however, is that *x* has no more right to bring into existence, either deliberately or as a foreseeable result of actions he could have avoided, a being with full moral rights (*y*), and then refuse to do what he knew beforehand would be required to keep that being alive, than he has to enter into an agreement with an existing person, whereby he may be called upon to save that person's life, and then refuse to do so when so called upon. Thus, *x*'s responsibility for *y*'s existence does not seem to lessen his obligation to keep *y* alive, if he is also responsible for *y*'s being in a situation in which only he can save him.

Whether or not this intuition is entirely correct, it brings us back once again to the conclusion that once we allow the assumption that a fetus has full moral rights it becomes an extremely complex and difficult question whether and when abortion is justifiable. Thus the Thomson analogy cannot help us produce a clear and persuasive proof of the moral permissibility of abortion. Nor will the opponents of the restrictive laws thank us for anything less; for their conviction (for the most part) is that abortion is obviously *not* a morally serious and extremely unfortunate, even though sometimes justified act, comparable to killing in self-defense or to letting the violinist die, but rather is closer to being a morally neutral act, like cutting one's hair.

The basis of this conviction, I believe, is the realization that a fetus is not a person, and thus does not have a full-fledged right to life. Perhaps the reason why this claim has been so inadequately defended is that it seems self-evident to those who accept it. And so it is, insofar as it follows from what I take to be perfectly obvious claims about the nature of personhood, and about the proper grounds for ascribing moral rights, claims which ought, indeed, to be obvious to both the friends and foes of abortion. Nevertheless, it is worth examining these claims, and showing how they demonstrate the moral innocuousness of abortion, since this apparently has not been adequately done before.

II

The question which we must answer in order to produce a satisfactory solution to the problem of the moral status of abortion is this: How are we to define the moral community, the set of beings with full and equal moral rights, such that we can decide whether a human fetus is a member of this community or not? What sort of entity, exactly, has the inalienable rights to life, liberty, and the pursuit of happiness? Jefferson attributed these rights to all *men,* and it may or may not be fair to suggest that he intended to attribute them *only* to men. Perhaps he ought to have attributed them to all human beings. If so, then we arrive, first, at Noonan's problem of defining what makes a being human, and, second, at the equally vital question which Noonan does not consider, namely, What reason is there for identifying the moral community with the set of all human beings, in whatever way we have chosen to define that term?

On the Definition of "Human"

One reason why this vital second question is so frequently overlooked in the debate over the moral status of abortion is that the term "human" has two distinct, but not often distinguished, senses. This fact results in a slide of meaning, which serves to conceal the fallaciousness of the traditional argument that since (1) it is wrong to kill innocent human beings, and (2) fetuses are innocent human beings, then (3) it is wrong to kill fetuses. For if "human" is used in the same sense in both (1) and (2) then, which ever of the two senses is meant, one of these premises is question-begging. And if it is used in two different senses then of course the conclusion doesn't follow.

Thus, (1) is a self-evident moral truth,[9] and avoids begging the question about abortion, only if "human being" is used to mean something like "a full-fledged member of the moral community." (It may or may not also be meant to refer exclusively to members of the species *Homo sapiens.*) We may call this the *moral* sense of "human." It is not to be confused with what we will call the *genetic* sense, i.e., the sense in which *any* member of the species is a human being, and no member of any other species could be. If (1) is acceptable only if the moral sense is intended, (2) is non-question-begging only if what is intended is the genetic sense.

In "Deciding Who Is Human," Noonan argues for the classification of fetuses with human beings by pointing to the presence of the full genetic code, and the potential capacity for rational thought . . . . It is clear that what he needs to show, for his version of the traditional argument to be valid, is that fetuses are human in the moral sense, the sense in which it is analytically true that all human beings have full moral rights. But, in the absence of any argument showing that whatever is genetically human is also morally human, and he gives none, nothing more than genetic humanity can be demonstrated by the presence of the human genetic code. And, as we will see, the *potential* capacity for rational thought can at most show that an entity has the potential for *becoming* human in the moral sense.

Defining the Moral Community

Can it be established that genetic humanity is sufficient for moral humanity? I think that there are very good reasons for not defining the moral community in this way. I would like to suggest an alternative way of defining the moral community, which I will argue for only to the extent of explaining why it is, or should be, self-evident. The suggestion is simply that the moral community consists of all and only *people,* rather than all and only human beings;[10] and probably the best way of demonstrating its self-evidence is by considering the concept of personhood, to see what sorts of entity are and are not persons, and what the decision that a being is or is not a person implies about its moral rights.

What characteristics entitle an entity to be considered a person? This is obviously not the place to attempt a complete analysis of the concept of personhood, but we do not need such a full adequate analysis just to determine whether and why a fetus is or isn't a person. All we need is a rough and approximate list of the most basic criteria of personhood, and some idea of which, or how many, of these an entity must satisfy in order to properly be considered a person.

In searching for such criteria, it is useful to look beyond the set of people with whom we are acquainted, and ask how we would decide whether a totally alien being was a person or not. (For we have no right to assume that genetic humanity is necessary for personhood.) Imagine a space traveler who lands on an unknown planet and encounters a race of beings utterly unlike any he has ever seen or heard of. If he wants to be sure of behaving morally toward these beings, he has to somehow decide whether they are people, and hence have full moral rights, or whether they are the sort of thing which he need not feel guilty about treating as, for example, a source of food.

How should he go about making this decision? If he has some anthropological background, he might look for such things as religion, art, and the manufacturing of tools, weapons, or shelters, since these factors have been used to distinguish our human from our prehuman ancestors, in what seems to be closer to the moral than the genetic sense of "human." And no doubt he would be right to consider the presence of such factors as good evidence that the alien beings were people, and morally human. It would, however, be overly anthropocentric of him to take the absence of these things as adequate evidence that they were not, since we can imagine people who have progressed beyond, or evolved without ever developing, these cultural characteristics.

I suggest that the traits which are most central to the concept of personhood, or humanity in the moral sense, are, very roughly, the following:

1. consciousness (of objects and events external and/or internal to the being), and in particular the capacity to feel pain;
2. reasoning (the *developed* capacity to solve new and relatively complex problems);
3. self-motivated activity (activity which is relatively independent of either genetic or direct external control);
4. the capacity to communicate, by whatever means, messages of an indefinite variety of types, that is, not just with an indefinite number of possible contents, but on indefinitely many possible topics;
5. the presence of self-concepts, and self-awareness, either individual or racial, or both.

Admittedly, there are apt to be a great many problems involved in formulating precise definitions of these criteria, let alone in developing universally valid behavioral criteria for deciding when they apply. But I will assume that both we and our explorer know approximately what (1)–(5) mean, and that he is also able to determine whether or not they apply. How, then, should he use his findings to decide whether or not the alien beings are people? We needn't suppose that an entity must have *all* of these attributes to be properly considered a person; (1) and (2) alone may well be sufficient for personhood, and quite probably (1)–(3) are sufficient. Neither do we need to insist that any one of these criteria is *necessary* for personhood, although once again (1) and (2) look like fairly good candidates for **necessary conditions**, as does (3), if "activity" is construed so as to include the activity of reasoning.

All we need to claim, to demonstrate that a fetus is not a person, is that any being which satisfies *none* of (1)–(5) is certainly not a person. I consider this claim to be so obvious that I think anyone who denied it, and claimed that a being which satisfied none of (1)–(5) was a person all the same, would thereby demonstrate that he had no notion at all of what a person is—perhaps because he had confused the concept of a person with that of genetic humanity. If the opponents of abortion were to deny the appropriateness of these five criteria, I do not know what further arguments would convince them. We would probably have to admit that our conceptual schemes were indeed irreconcilably different, and that our dispute could not be settled objectively.

I do not expect this to happen, however, since I think that the concept of a person is one which is very nearly universal (to people), and that it is common to both proabortionists and antiabortionists, even though neither group has fully realized the relevance of this concept to the resolution of their dispute. Furthermore, I think that on reflection even the antiabortionists ought to agree not only that (1)–(5) are central to the concept of personhood, but also that it is a part of this concept that all and only people have full moral rights. The concept of a person is in part a moral concept; once we have admitted that x is a person we have recognized, even if we have not agreed to respect, x's right to be treated as a member of the moral community. It is true that the claim that x is a *human being* is more commonly voiced as part of an appeal to treat x decently than is the claim that x is a person, but this is either because "human being" is here used in the sense which implies personhood, or because the genetic and moral senses of "human" have been confused.

Now if (1)–(5) are indeed the primary criteria of personhood, then it is clear that genetic humanity is neither necessary nor sufficient for establishing that an entity is a person. Some human beings are not people, and there may well be people who are not human beings. A man or woman whose consciousness has been permanently obliterated but who remains alive is a human being which is no longer a person; defective human beings, with no appreciable mental capacity, are not and presumably never will be people; and a fetus is a human being which is not yet a person, and which therefore cannot coherently be said to have full moral rights. Citizens of the next century should be prepared to recognize highly advanced, self-aware robots or computers, should such be developed, and intelligent inhabitants of other worlds, should such be found, as people in the fullest sense, and to respect their moral rights. But to ascribe full moral rights to an entity which is not a person is as absurd as to ascribe moral obligations and responsibilities to such an entity.

Fetal Development and the Right to Life

Two problems arise in the application of these suggestions for the definition of the moral community to the determination of the precise moral status of a human fetus. Given that the paradigm example of a person is a normal adult human being, then (1) How like this paradigm, in particular how far advanced since conception, does a human being need to be before it begins to have a right to life by virtue, not of being fully a person as of yet, but of being *like* a person? and (2) To what extent, if any, does the fact that a fetus has the *potential* for becoming a person endow it with some of the same rights? Each of these questions requires some comment.

In answering the first question, we need not attempt a detailed consideration of the moral rights of organisms which are not developed enough, aware enough, intelligent enough, etc., to be considered people, but which resemble people in some respects. It does seem reasonable to suggest that the more like a person, in the relevant respects, a being is, the stronger is the case for regarding it as having a right to life, and indeed the stronger its right to life is. Thus we ought to take seriously the suggestion that, insofar as "the human individual develops biologically in a continuous fashion . . . the rights of a human person might develop in the same way."[11] But we must keep in mind that the attributes which are relevant in determining whether or not an entity is enough like a person to be regarded as having some of the same moral rights are no different from those which are relevant to determining whether or not it is fully a person—i.e., are no different from (1)–(5)—and that being genetically human, or having recognizably human facial and other physical features, or detectable brain activity, or the capacity to survive outside the uterus, are simply not among these relevant attributes.

Thus it is clear that even though a seven-or eight-month fetus has features which make it apt to arouse in us almost the same powerful protective instinct as is commonly aroused by a small infant, nevertheless it is not significantly more personlike than is a very small embryo. It is *somewhat* more personlike; it can apparently feel and respond to pain, and it may even have a rudimentary form of consciousness, insofar as its brain is quite active. Nevertheless, it seems safe to say that it is not fully conscious, in the way that an infant of a few months is, and that it cannot reason, or communicate messages of indefinitely many sorts, does not engage in self-motivated activity, and has no self-awareness. Thus, in the *relevant* respects, a fetus, even a fully developed one, is considerably less personlike than is the average fish. And I think that a rational person must conclude that if the right to life of a fetus is to be based upon its resemblance to a person, then it cannot be said to have any more right to life than, let us say, a newborn guppy (which also seems to be capable of feeling pain), and that a right of that magnitude could never override a woman's right to obtain an abortion, at any stage of her pregnancy.

There may, of course, be other arguments in favor of placing legal limits upon the stage of pregnancy in which an abortion may be performed. Given the relative safety of the new techniques of artificially inducing labor during the third trimester, the danger to the woman's life or health is no longer such an argument. Neither is the fact that people tend to respond to the thought of abortion in the later stages of pregnancy with emotional repulsion, since mere emotional responses cannot take the place of moral reasoning in determining what ought to be permitted. Nor, finally, is the frequently heard argument that legalizing abortion, especially late in the pregnancy, may erode the level of respect for human life, leading, perhaps, to an increase in unjustified euthanasia and other crimes. For this threat, if it is a threat, can be better met by educating people to the kinds of moral distinctions which we are making here than by limiting access to abortion (which limitation may, in its disregard for the rights of women, be just as damaging to the level of respect for human rights).

Thus, since the fact that even a fully developed fetus is not person-like enough to have any significant right to life on the basis of its person-likeness shows that no legal restrictions upon the stage of pregnancy in which an abortion may be performed can be justified on the grounds that we should protect the rights of the older fetus; and since there is no other apparent justification for such restrictions, we may conclude that they are entirely unjustified. Whether or not it would be *indecent* (whatever that means) for a woman in her seventh month to obtain an abortion just to avoid having to postpone a trip to Europe, it would not, in itself, be *immoral,* and therefore it ought to be permitted.

Potential Personhood and the Right to Life

We have seen that a fetus does not resemble a person in any way which can support the claim that it has even some of the same rights. But what about its *potential,* the fact that if nurtured and allowed to develop naturally it will very probably become a person? Doesn't that alone give it at least some right to life? It is hard to deny that the fact that an entity is a potential person is a strong prima facie reason for not destroying it; but we need not conclude from this that a potential person has a right to life, by virtue of that potential. It may be that our feeling that it is better, other things being equal, not to destroy a potential person is better explained by the fact that potential people are still (felt to be) an invaluable resource, not to be lightly squandered. Surely, if every speck of dust were a potential person, we would be much less apt to conclude that every potential person has a right to become actual.

Still, we do not need to insist that a potential person has no right to life whatever. There may well be something immoral, and not just imprudent, about wantonly destroying potential people, when doing so isn't necessary to protect anyone's rights. But even if a potential person does have some **prima facie right** to life, such a right could not possibly outweigh the right of a woman to obtain an abortion, since the rights of any actual person invariably outweigh those of any potential person, whenever the two conflict. Since this may not be immediately obvious in the case of a human fetus, let us look at another case.

Suppose that our space explorer falls into the hands of an alien culture, whose scientists decide to create a few hundred thousand or more human beings, by breaking his body into its component cells, and using these to create fully developed human beings, with, of course, his genetic code. We may imagine that each of these newly created men will have all of the original man's abilities, skills, knowledge, and so on, and also have an individual self-concept, in short that each of them will be a bona fide (though hardly unique) person. Imagine that the whole project will take only seconds, and that its chances of success are extremely high, and that our explorer knows all of this, and also knows that these people will be treated fairly. I maintain that in such a situation he would have every right to escape if he could, and thus to deprive all of these potential people of their potential lives; for his right to life outweighs all of theirs together, in spite of the fact that they are all genetically human, all innocent, and all have a very high probability of becoming people very soon, if only he refrains from acting.

Indeed, I think he would have a right to escape even if it were not his life which the alien scientists planned to take, but only a year of his freedom, or, indeed, only a day. Nor would he be obligated to stay if he had gotten captured (thus bringing all these people-potentials into existence) because of his own carelessness, or even if he had done so deliberately, knowing the consequences. Regardless of how he got captured, he is not morally obligated to remain in captivity for *any* period of time for the sake of permitting any number of potential people to come into actuality, so great is the margin by which one actual person's right to liberty outweighs whatever right to life even a hundred thousand potential people have. And it seems reasonable to conclude that the rights of a woman will outweigh by a similar margin whatever right to life a fetus may have by virtue of its potential personhood.

Thus, neither a fetus's resemblance to a person, nor its potential for becoming a person provides any basis whatever for the claim that it has any significant right to life. Consequently, a woman's right to protect her health, happiness, freedom, and even her life,[12] by terminating an unwanted pregnancy, will always override whatever right to life it may be appropriate to ascribe to a fetus, even a fully developed one. And thus, in the absence of any overwhelming social need for every possible child, the laws which restrict the right to obtain an abortion, or limit the period of pregnancy during which an abortion may be performed, are a wholly unjustified violation of a woman's most basic moral and constitutional rights.[13]

Postscript on Infanticide

Since the publication of this article, many people have written to point out that my argument appears to justify not only abortion, but infanticide as well. For a new-born infant is not significantly more person-like than an advanced fetus, and consequently it would seem that if the destruction of the latter is permissible so too must be that of the former. Inasmuch as most people, regardless of how they feel about the morality of abortion, consider infanticide a form of murder, this might appear to represent a serious flaw in my argument.

Now, if I am right in holding that it is only people who have a full-fledged right to life, and who can be murdered, and if the criteria of personhood are as I have described them, then it obviously follows that killing a newborn infant isn't murder. It does *not* follow, however, that infanticide is permissible, for two reasons. In the first place, it would be wrong, at least in this country and in this period of history, and other things being equal, to kill a new-born infant, because even if its parents do not want it and would not suffer from its destruction, there are other people who would like to have it, and would, in all probability, be deprived of a great deal of pleasure by its destruction. Thus, infanticide is wrong for reasons analogous to those which make it wrong to wantonly destroy natural resources, or great works of art.

Secondly, most people, at least in this country, value infants, and would much prefer that they be preserved, even if foster parents are not immediately available. Most of us would rather be taxed to support orphanages than allow unwanted infants to be destroyed. So long as there are people who want an infant preserved, and who are willing and able to provide the means of caring for it, under reasonably humane conditions, it is, *ceteris parabis,* wrong to destroy it.

But, it might be replied, if this argument shows that infanticide is wrong, at least at this time and in this country, doesn't it also show that abortion is wrong? After all, many people value fetuses, are disturbed by their destruction, and would much prefer that they be preserved, even at some cost to themselves. Furthermore, as a potential source of pleasure to some foster family, a fetus is just as valuable as an infant. There is, however, a crucial difference between the two cases: so long as the fetus is unborn, its preservation, contrary to the wishes of the pregnant woman, violates her rights to freedom, happiness, and self-determination. Her rights override the rights of those who would like the fetus preserved, just as if someone's life or limb is threatened by a wild animal, his right to protect himself by destroying the animal overrides the rights of those who would prefer that the animal not be harmed.

The minute the infant is born, however, its preservation no longer violates any of its mother's rights, even if she wants it destroyed, because she is free to put it up for adoption. Consequently, while the moment of birth does not mark any sharp discontinuity in the degree to which an infant possesses the right to life, it does mark the end of its mother's right to determine its fate. Indeed, if abortion could be performed without killing the fetus, she would never possess the right to have the fetus destroyed, for the same reasons that she has no right to have an infant destroyed.

On the other hand, it follows from my argument that when an unwanted or defective infant is born into a society which cannot afford and/or is not willing to care for it, then its destruction is permissible. This conclusion will, no doubt, strike many people as heartless and immoral; but remember that the very existence of people who feel this way, and who are willing and able to provide care for unwanted infants, is reason enough to conclude that they should be preserved.

Endnotes

1. For example, Roger Wertheimer, who in "Understanding the Abortion Argument" (*Philosophy and Public Affairs,* 1, No. 1 [Fall 1971], 67–95), argues that the problem of the moral status of abortion is insoluble, in that the dispute over the status of the fetus is not a question of fact at all, but only a question of how one responds to the facts.
2. B. A. Brody, "Abortion and the Law," *The Journal of Philosophy,* 68, No. 12 (June 17, 1971), 357–69.
3. Judith Thomson, "A Defense of Abortion," *Philosophy and Public Affairs,* 1, No. 1 (Fall 1971), 47–66.
4. I have abbreviated these statements somewhat, but not in a way which affects the argument.
5. John Noonan, "Abortion and the Catholic Church: A Summary History," *Natural Law Forum,* 12 (1967), 125.
6. John Noonan, "Deciding Who Is Human," *Natural Law Forum,* 13 (1968), 134.
7. "A Defense of Abortion."
8. We may safely ignore the fact that she might have avoided getting raped, e.g., by carrying a gun, since by similar means you might likewise have avoided getting kidnapped, and in neither case does the victim's failure to take all possible precautions against a highly unlikely event (as opposed to reasonable precautions against a rather likely event) mean that he is morally responsible for what happens.
9. Of course, the principle that it is (always) wrong to kill innocent human beings is in need of many modifications, e.g., that it may be permissible to do so to save a greater number of other innocent human beings, but we may safely ignore these complications here.
10. From here on, we will use "human" to mean genetically human, since the moral sense seems closely connected to, and perhaps derived from, the assumption that genetic humanity is sufficient for membership in the moral community.
11. Thomas L. Hayes, "A Biological View," *Commonweal,* 85 (March 17, 1967), 667–78; quoted by Daniel Callahan, in *Abortion, Law, Choice, and Morality* (London: Macmillan & Co., 1970).
12. That is, insofar as the death rate, for the woman, is higher for childbirth than for early abortion.
13. My thanks to the following people, who were kind enough to read and criticize an earlier version of this paper: Herbert Gold, Gene Glass, Anne Lauterbach, Judith Thomson, Mary Mothersill, and Timothy Binkley.

Review Questions

1. What is the traditional antiabortion argument according to Warren?
2. According to Warren, why are the two typical pro-abortion arguments inadequate?
3. What difficulties does Warren raise in Thomson's argument?
4. Warren claims that the word *human* has two different senses, a *genetic sense* and a *moral sense.* Explain the distinction between the two.
5. Why does Warren think that it is obvious that a fetus is not a person, and why does she expect antiabortionists to agree with her?
6. Warren admits that she has two problems when it comes to applying her account of personhood to human fetuses. What are these two problems, and how does Warren solve them?
7. How does Warren reply to the objection that her position justifies infanticide as well as abortion?

Discussion Questions

1. Warren asserts that neither defective humans with little mental capacity nor permanently comatose humans are persons with moral rights. Do you agree? Why or why not?
2. Warren also claims that there can be nonhuman persons, for example, self-aware robots and alien beings from other planets. Is this possible? Explain your answer.
3. Warren says that an infant of a few months is less personlike than the average fish. Is this true?
4. Warren says, in opposition to Thomson, that a woman in her seventh month of pregnancy ought to be permitted to have an abortion just to avoid postponing a trip to Europe. Do yo agree with this judgment? Defend your answer.

Don Marquis

Why Abortion is Immoral

Don Marquis is Professor of Philosophy at the University of Kansas.

Marquis argues that abortion is seriously immoral, except in some rare or hard cases, because it deprives the fetus of a future having valuable experiences, activities, projects, and enjoyments; this is the same reason why killing an innocent adult human being is wrong.

The view that abortion is, with rare exceptions, seriously immoral has received little support in the recent philosophical literature. No doubt most philosophers affiliated with secular institutions of higher education believe that the anti-abortion position is either a symptom of irrational religious dogma or a conclusion generated by seriously confused philosophical argument. The purpose of this essay is to undermine this general belief. This essay sets out an argument that purports to show, as well as any argument in ethics can show, that abortion is, except possibly in rare cases, seriously immoral, that it is in the same moral category as killing an innocent adult human being.

The argument is based on a major assumption. Many of the most insightful and careful writes on the ethics of abortion—such as Joel Feinberg, Michael Tooley, Mary Anne Warren, H. Tristram Engelhardt, Jr., L. W. Sumner, John T. Noonan, Jr., and Philip Devine[1]—believe that whether or not abortion is morally permissible stands or falls on whether or not a fetus is the sort of being whose life it is seriously wrong to end. The argument of this essay will assume, but not argue, that they are correct.

Also, this essay will neglect issues of great importance to a complete ethics of abortion. Some anti-abortionists will allow that certain abortions, such as abortion before implantation or abortion when the life of a woman is threatened by a pregnancy or abortion after rape, may be morally permissible. This essay will not explore the casuistry of these hard cases. The purpose of this essay is to develop a general argument for the claim that the overwhelming majority of deliberate abortions are seriously immoral.

I.

A sketch of standard anti-abortion and pro-choice arguments exhibits how those arguments possess certain symmetries that explain why partisans of those positions are so convinced of the correctness of their own positions, why they are not successful in convincing their opponents, and why, to others, this issue seems to be unresolvable. An analysis of the nature of this standoff suggests a strategy for surmounting it.

Consider the way a typical anti-abortionist argues. She will argue or assert that life is present from the moment of conception or that fetuses look like babies or that fetuses possess a characteristic such as a genetic code that is both necessary and sufficient for being human. Anti-abortionists seem to believe that (1) the truth of all of these claims is quite obvious, and (2) establishing any of these claims is sufficient to show that abortion is morally akin to murder.

A standard pro-choice strategy exhibits similarities. The pro-choicer will argue or assert that fetuses are not persons or that fetuses are not rational agents or that fetuses are not social beings. Pro-choicers seem to believe that (1) the truth of any of these claims is quite obvious, and (2) establishing any of these claims is sufficient to show that an abortion is not a wrongful killing.

Don Marquis is Professor of Philosophy at the University of Kansas. (Source: Reprinted from *The Journal of Philosophy*, LXXXVI, 4 (April 1989): 183–202, with permission of the author and *The Journal of Philosophy*.

In fact, both the pro-choice and the anti-abortion claims do seem to be true, although the "it looks like a baby" claim is more difficult to establish the earlier the pregnancy. We seem to have a standoff. How can it be resolved?

As everyone who has taken a bit of logic knows, if any of these arguments concerning abortion is a good argument, it requires not only some claim characterizing fetuses, but also some general moral principle that ties a characteristic of fetuses to having or not having the right to life or to some other moral characteristic that will generate the obligation or the lack of obligation not to end the life of a fetus. Accordingly, the arguments of the anti-abortionist and the pro-choicer need a bit of filling in to be regarded as adequate.

Note what each partisan will say. The anti-abortionist will claim that her position is supported by such generally accepted moral principles as "It is always prima facie seriously wrong to take a human life" or "It is always prima facie seriously wrong to end the life of a baby." Since these are generally accepted moral principles, her position is certainly not obviously wrong. The pro-choicer will claim that her position is supported by such plausible moral principles as "Being a person is what gives an individual intrinsic moral worth" or "It is only seriously prima facie wrong to take the life of a member of the human community." Since these are generally accepted moral principles, the pro-choice position is certainly not obviously wrong. Unfortunately, we have again arrived at a standoff.

Now, how might one deal with this standoff? The standard approach is to try to show how the moral principles of one's opponent lose their plausibility under analysis. It is easy to see how this is possible. On the one hand, the anti-abortionist will defend a moral principle concerning the wrongness of killing which tends to be broad in scope in order that even fetuses at an early stage of pregnancy will fall under it. The problem with broad principles is that they often embrace too much. In this particular instance, the principle "It is always prima facie wrong to take a human life" seems to entail that it is wrong to end the existence of a living human cancer-cell culture, on the grounds that the culture is both living and human. Therefore, it seems that the anti-abortionist's favored principle is too broad.

On the other hand, the pro-choicer wants to find a moral principle concerning the wrongness of killing which tends to be narrow in scope in order that fetuses will *not* fall under it. The problem with narrow principles is that they often do not embrace enough. Hence, the needed principles such as "It is prima facie seriously wrong to kill only persons" or "It is prima facie wrong to kill only rational agents" do not explain why it is wrong to kill infants or young children or the severely retarded or even perhaps the severely mentally ill. Therefore, we seem again to have a standoff. The anti-abortionist charges, not unreasonably, that pro-choice principles concerning killing are too narrow to be acceptable; the pro-choicer charges, not unreasonably, that anti-abortionist principles concerning killing are too broad to be acceptable.

Attempts by both sides to patch up the difficulties in their positions run into further difficulties. The anti-abortionist will try to remove the problem in her position by reformulating her principle concerning killing in terms of human beings. Now we end up with: "It is always prima facie seriously wrong to end the life of a human being." This principle has the advantage of avoiding the problem of the human cancer-cell culture counterexample. But this advantage is purchased at a high price. For although it is clear that a fetus is both human and alive, it is not at all clear that a fetus is a human *being*. There is at least something to be said for the view that something becomes a human being only after a process of development, and that therefore first trimetster fetuses and perhaps all fetuses are not yet human beings. Hence, the anti-abortionist, by this move, has merely exchanged one problem for another.[2]

The pro-choicer fares no better. She may attempt to find reasons why killing infants, young children, and the severely retarded is wrong which are independent of her major principle that is supposed to explain the wrongness of taking human life, but which will not also make abortion immoral. This is no easy task. Appeals to social utility will seem satisfactory only to those who resolve not to think of the enormous difficulties with a utilitarian account of the wrongness of killing and the significant social costs of preserving the lives of the unproductive.[3] A pro-choice strategy that extends the definition of 'person' to infants or even to young children seems just as arbitrary as an anti-abortion strategy that extends the definition of 'human being' to fetuses. Again, we find symmetries in the two positions and we arrive at a standoff.

There are even further problems that reflect symmetries in the two positions. In addition to counterexample problems, or the arbitrary application problems that can be exchanged for them, the standard anti-abortionist principle "It is prima facie seriously wrong to kill a human being," or one of its variants, can be objected to on the grounds of ambiguity. If 'human being' is taken to be a *biological* category, then the anti-abortionist is left with the problem of explaining why a merely biological category should make a moral difference. Why, it is asked, is it any more reasonable to base a moral conclusion on the number of chromosomes in one's cells than on the color of one's skin?[4] If 'human being', on the other hand, is taken to be a *moral* category, then the claim that a fetus is a human being cannot be taken to be a premise in the anti-abortion argument, for it is precisely what needs to be established. Hence, either the anti-abortionist's main category is a morally irrelevant, merely biological category, or it is of no use to the anti-abortionist in establishing (noncircularly, of course) that abortion is wrong.

Although this problem with the anti-abortionist position is often noticed, it is less often noticed that the pro-choice position suffers from an analogous problem. The principle "Only persons have the right to life" also suffers from an ambiguity. The term 'person' is typically defined in terms of psychological characteristics, although there will certainly be disagreement concerning with characteristics are most important. Supposing that this matter can be settled, the pro-choicer is left with the problem of explaining why *psychological* characteristics should make a *moral* difference. If the pro-choicer should attempt to deal with this problem by claiming that an explanation is not necessary, that in fact we do treat such a cluster of psychological properties as having moral significance, the sharp-witted anti-abortionist should have a ready response. We do treat being both living and human as having moral significance. If it is legitimate for the pro-choicer to demand that the anti-abortionist provide an explanation of the connection between the biological character of being a human being and the wrongness of being killed (even though people accept this connection), then it is legitimate for the anti-abortionist to demand that the pro-choicer provide an explanation of the connection between psychological criteria for being a person and the wrongness of being killed (even though that connection is accepted).[5]

Feinberg has attempted to meet this objection (he calls psychological personhood "commonsense personhood"):

> The characteristics that confer commonsense personhood are not arbitrary bases for rights and duties, such as race, sex or species membership; rather they are traits that make sense out of rights and duties and without which those moral attributes would have no point or function. It is because people are conscious; have a sense of their personal identities; have plans, goals, and projects; experience emotions; are liable to pains; anxieties, and frustrations; can reason and bargain, and so on—it is because of these attributes that people have values and interests, desires and expectations of their own, including a stake in their own futures, and a personal well-being of a sort we cannot ascribe to unconscious or nonrational beings. Because of their developed capacities they can assume duties and responsibilities and can have and make claims on one another. Only because of their sense of self, their life plans, their value hierarchies, and their stakes in their own futures can they be ascribed fundamental rights. There is nothing arbitrary about these linkages (*op. cit.*, p. 270).

The plausible aspects of this attempt should not be taken to obscure its implausible features. There is a great deal to be said for the view that being a psychological person under some description is a necessary condition for having duties. One cannot have a duty unless one is capable of behaving morally, and a being's capability of behaving morally will require having a certain psychology. It is far from obvious, however, that having rights entails consciousness or rationality, as Feinberg suggests. We speak of the rights of the severely retarded or the severely mentally ill, yet some of these persons are not rational. We speak of the right to the temporarily unconscious. The New Jersey Supreme Court based their decision in the Quinlan case on Karen Ann Quinlan's right to privacy, and she was known to be permanently unconscious at that time. Hence, Feinberg's claim that having rights entails being conscious is, on its face, obviously false.

Of course it might not make sense to attribute rights to a being that would never in its natural history have certain psychological traits. This modest connection between psychological personhood and moral personhood will create a place for Karen Ann Quinlan and the temporarily unconscious. But then it makes a place for fetuses also. Hence, it does not serve Feinberg's pro-choice purposes. Accordingly, it seems that the pro-choicer will have as much difficulty bridging the gap between psychological personhood and personhood in the moral sense as the anti-abortionist has bridging the gap between being a biological human being and being a human being in the moral sense.

Furthermore, the pro-choicer cannot any more escape her problem by making person a purely moral category than the anti-abortionist could escape by the analogous move. For if person is a moral category, then the pro-choicer is left without the resources for establishing (noncircularly, of course) the claim that a fetus is not a person, which is an essential premise in her argument. Again, we have both symmetry and a standoff between pro-choice and anti-abortion views.

Passions in the abortion debate run high. There are both plausibilities and difficulties with the standard positions. Accordingly, it is hardly surprising that partisans of either side embrace with fervor the moral generalizations that support the conclusions they preanalytically favor, and reject with disdain the moral generalizations of their opponents as being subject to inescapable difficulties. It is easy to believe that the counterexamples to one's own moral principles are merely temporary difficulties that will dissolve in the wake of further philosophical research, and that the counterexamples to the principles of one's opponents are as straightforward as the contradiction between *A* and *O* propositions in traditional logic. This might suggest to an impartial observer (if there are any) that the abortion issue is unresolvable.

There is a way out of this apparent dialectical quandry. The moral generalizations of both sides are not quite correct. The generalizations hold for the most part, for the usual cases. This suggests that they are all *accidental* generalizations, that the moral claims made by those on both sides of the dispute do not touch on the *essence* of the matter.

This use of the distinction between essence and accident is not meant to invoke obscure metaphysical categories. Rather, it is intended to reflect the rather atheoretical nature of the abortion discussion. If the generalization a partisan in the abortion dispute adopts were derived from the reason why ending the life of a human being is wrong, then there could not be exceptions to that generalization unless some special case obtains in which there are even more powerful countervailing reasons. Such generalizations would not be merely accidental generalizations; they would point to, or be based upon, the essence of the wrongness of killing, what it is that makes killing wrong. All this suggests that a necessary condition of resolving the abortion controversy is a more theoretical account of the wrongness of killing. After all, if we merely believe, but do not understand, why killing adult human beings such as ourselves is wrong, how could we conceivably show that abortion is either immoral or permissible?

II.

In order to develop such an account, we can start from the following unproblematic assumption concerning our own case: it is wrong to kill *us*. Why is it wrong? Some answers can be easily eliminated. It might be said that what makes killing us wrong is that a killing brutalizes the one who kills. But the brutalization consists of being inured to the performance of an act that is hideously immoral; hence, the brutalization does not explain the immorality. It might be said that what makes killing us wrong is the great loss others would experience due to our absence. Although such hubris is understandable, such an explanation does not account for the wrongness of killing hermits, or those whose lives are relatively independent and whose friends find it easy to make new friends.

A more obvious answer is better. What primarily makes killing wrong is neither its effect on the murderer nor its effect on the victim's friends and relatives, but its effect on the victim. The loss of one's life is one of the greatest losses one can suffer. The loss of one's life deprives one of all the experiences, activities, projects, and enjoyments that would otherwise have constituted one's future. Therefore, killing someone is wrong, primarily because the killing inflicts (one of) the greatest possible losses on the victim. To describe this as the loss of life can be misleading, however. The change in my biological state does not by itself make killing me wrong. The effect of the loss of my biological life is the loss to me of all those activities, projects, experiences, and enjoyments which would otherwise have constituted my future personal life. These activities, projects, experiences, and enjoyments are either valuable for their own sakes or are means to something else that is valuable for its own sake. Some parts of my future are not valued by me now, but will come to be valued by me as I grow older and as my values and capacities change. When I am killed, I am deprived both of what I now value which would have been part of my future personal life, but also what I would come to value. Therefore, when I die, I am deprived of all of the value of my future. Inflicting this loss on me is ultimately what makes killing me wrong. This being the case, it would seem that what makes killing *any* adult human being prima facie seriously wrong is the loss of his or her future.[6]

How should this rudimentary theory of the wrongness of killing be evaluated? It cannot be faulted for deriving an 'ought' from an 'is' for it does not. The analysis assumes that killing me (or you, reader) is prima facie seriously wrong. The point of the analysis is to establish which natural property ultimately explains the wrongness of the killing, given that it is wrong. A natural property will ultimately explain the wrongness of killing, only if (1) the explanation fits with out intuitions about the matter and (2) there is no other natural property that provides the basis for a better explanation of the wrongness of killing. This analysis rests on the intuition that what makes killing a particular human or animal wrong is what it does to that particular human or animal. What makes killing wrong is some natural effect or other of the killing. Some would deny this. For instance, a divine-command theorist in ethics would deny it. Surely this denial is, however, one of those features of divine—command theory which renders it so implausible.

The claim that what makes killing wrong is the loss of the victim's future is directly supported by two considerations. In the first place, this theory explains why we regard killing as one of the worst of crimes. Killing is especially wrong, because it deprives the victim of more than perhaps any other crime. In the second place, people with AIDS or cancer who know they are dying believe, of course, that dying is a very bad thing for them. They believe that the loss of a future to them that they would otherwise have experienced is what makes their premature death a very bad thing for them. A better theory of the wrongness of killing would require a different natural property with killing which better fits with the attitudes of the dying. What could it be?

The view that what makes killing wrong is the loss to the victim of the value of the victim's future gains additional support when some of its implications are examined. In the first place, it is incompatible with the view that it is wrong to kill only beings who are biologically human. It is possible that there exists a different species from another planet whose members have a future like ours. Since having a future like that is what makes killing someone wrong, this theory entails that it would be wrong to kill members of such a species. Hence, this theory is opposed to the claim that only life that is biologically human has great moral worth, a claim which many anti-abortionists have seemed to adopt. This opposition, which this theory has in common with parenthood theories, seems to be a merit of the theory.

In the second place, the claim that the loss of one's future is the wrong-making feature of one's being killed entails the possibility that the futures of some actual nonhuman mammals on our own planet are sufficiently like ours that it is seriously wrong to kill them also. Whether some animals do have the same right to life as human beings depends on adding to the account of the wrongness of killing some additional account of just what it is about my future or the futures of other adult human beings which makes it wrong to kill us. No such additional account will be offered in this essay. Undoubtedly, the provision of such an account would be a very difficult matter. Undoubtedly, any such account would be quite controversial. Hence, it surely should not reflect badly on this sketch of an elementary theory of the wrongness of killing that it is indeterminate with respect to some very difficult issues regarding animal rights.

In the third place, the claim that the loss of one's future is the wrong-making feature of one's being killed does not entail, as sanctity of human life theories do, that active euthanasia is wrong. Persons who are severely and incurably ill, who face a future of pain and despair, and who wish to die will not have suffered a loss if they are killed. It is, strictly speaking, the value of a human's future which makes killing wrong in this theory. This being so, killing does not necessarily wrong some persons who are sick and dying. Of course, there may be other reasons for a prohibition of active euthanasia, but that is another matter. Sanctity-of-human-life theories seem to hold that active euthanasia is seriously wrong even in an individual case where there seems to be good reason for it independently of public policy considerations. This consequence is most implausible, and it is a plus for the claim that the loss of a future of value is what makes killing wrong that it does not share this consequence.

In the fourth place, the account of wrongness of killing defended in this essay does straightforwardly entail that it is prima facie seriously wrong to kill children and infants, for we do presume that they have futures of value. Since we do believe that it is wrong to kill defenseless little babies, it is important that a theory of the wrongness of killing easily account for this. Personhood theories of the wrongness of killing, on the other hand, cannot straightforwardly account for the wrongness of killing infants and young children.[7] Hence, such theories must add special ad hoc accounts of the wrongness of killing the young. The plausibility of such ad hoc theories seems to be a function of how desperately one wants such theories to work. The claim that the primary wrong-making feature of a killing is the loss to the victim of the value of it's future accounts for the wrongness of killing young children and infants directly; it makes the wrongness of such acts as obvious as we actually think it is. This is a further merit of this theory. Accordingly, it seems that this value of a future-like-ours theory of the wrongness of killing shares strengths of both sanctity-of-life and personhood accounts while avoiding weaknesses of both. In addition, it meshes with a central intuition concerning what makes killing wrong.

The claim that the primary wrong-making feature of a killing is the loss of the victim of the values of its future has obvious consequences for the ethics of abortion. The future of a standard fetus includes a set of experiences, projects, activities, and such which are identical with the futures of adult human beings and are identical with the futures of young children. Since the reason that is sufficient to explain why it is wrong to kill human beings after the time of birth is a reason that also applies to fetuses, it follows that abortion is prima facie seriously morally wrong.

This argument does not rely on the invalid inference that, since it is wrong to kill persons, it is wrong to kill potential persons also. The category that is morally central to this analysis is the category of having a valuable future like ours; it is not the category of personhood. The argument to the conclusion that abortion is prima facie seriously morally wrong proceeded independently of the notion of person or potential person or any equivalent. Someone may wish to start with this analysis in terms of the value of a human future, conclude that abortion is, except perhaps in rare circumstances, seriously morally wrong, infer that fetuses have the right to life, and then call fetuses "persons" as a result of their having the right to life. Clearly, in this case, the category of person is being used to state the *conclusion* of the analysis rather than to generate the *argument* of the analysis.

The structure of this anti-abortion argument can be both illuminated and defended by comparing it to what appears to be the best argument for the wrongness of the wanton infliction of pain on animals. This latter argument is based on the assumption that it is prima facie wrong to inflict pain on me (or you, reader). What is the natural property associated with the infliction of pain which makes such infliction wrong? The obvious answer seems to be that the infliction of pain causes suffering and that suffering is a misfortune. The suffering caused by the infliction of pain is what makes the wanton infliction of pain on me wrong. The wanton infliction of pain on other adult humans causes suffering. The wanton infliction of pain on animals causes suffering. Since causing suffering is what makes wanton infliction of pain wrong and since the wanton infliction of pain on animals causes suffering, it follows that the wanton infliction of pain on animals is wrong.

This argument for the wrongness of the wanton infliction of pain on animals shares a number of structural features with the argument for the serious prima facie wrongness of abortion. Both arguments start with an obvious assumption concerning what it is wrong to do to me (or you, reader). Both then look for the characteristic or the consequence of the wrong action which makes the action wrong. Both recognize that the wrong—making feature of these immoral actions is a property of actions sometimes directed at individuals other than postnatal human beings. If the structure of the argument for the wrongness of the wanton infliction of pain on animals is sound, then the structure of the argument for the prima facie serious wrongness of abortion is also sound, for the structure of the two arguments is the same. The structure common to both is the key to the explanation of how the wrongness of abortion can be demonstrated without recourse to the category of person. In neither argument is that category crucial.

This defense of an argument for the wrongness of abortion in terms of a structurally similar argument for the wrongness of the wanton infliction of pain on animals succeeds only if the account regarding animals is the correct account. Is it? In the first place, it seems plausible. In the second place, its major competition is Kant's account. Kant believed that we do not have direct duties to animals at all, because they are not persons. Hence, Kant had to explain and justify the wrongness of inflicting pain on animals on the grounds that "he who is hard in his dealings with animals becomes hard also in his dealing with men."[8] The problem with Kant's account is that there seems to be no reason for accepting this latter claim unless Kant's account is rejected. If the alternative to Kant's account is accepted, then it is easy to understand why someone who is indifferent to inflicting pain on animals is also indifferent to inflicting pain on humans, for one is indifferent to what makes inflicting pain wrong in both cases. But, if Kant's account is accepted, there is no intelligible reason why one who is hard in his dealings with animals (or crabgrass or stones) should also be hard in his dealings with men. After all, men are persons: animals are no more person than crabgrass or stones. Persons are Kant's crucial moral category. Why, in short, should a Kantian accept the basic claim in Kant's argument?

Hence, Kant's argument for the wrongness of inflicting pain on animals rests on a claim that, in a world of Kantian moral agents, is demonstrably false. Therefore, the alternative analysis, being more plausible anyway, should be accepted. Since this alternative analysis has the same structure as the anti-abortion argument being defended here, we have further support for the argument for the immorality of abortion being defended in this essay.

Of course, this value of a future-like-ours argument, if sound, shows only that abortion is prima facie wrong, not that it is wrong in any and all circumstances. Since the loss of the future to a standard fetus, if killed, is, however, at least as great a loss as the loss of the future to a standard adult human being who is killed, abortion, like ordinary killing, could be justified only by the most compelling reasons. The loss of one's life is almost the greatest misfortune that can happen to one. Presumably abortion could be justified in some circumstances, only if the loss consequent on failing to abort would be at least as great. Accordingly, morally permissible abortions will be rare indeed unless, perhaps, they occur so early in pregnancy that a fetus is not yet definitely an individual. Hence, this argument should be taken as showing that abortion is presumptively very seriously wrong, where the presumption is very strong—as strong as the presumption that killing another adult human being is wrong. . . .

In this essay, it has been argued that the correct ethic of the wrongness of killing can be extended to fetal life and used to show that there is a strong presumption that any abortion is morally impermissible. If the ethic of killing adopted here entails, however, that contraception is also seriously immoral, then there would appear to be a difficulty with the analysis of this essay.

But this analysis does not entail that contraception is wrong. Of course, contraception prevents the actualization of a possible future of value. Hence, it follows from the claim that futures of value should be maximized that contraception is prima facie immoral. This obligation to maximize does not exist, however; furthermore, nothing in the ethics of killing in this paper entails that it does. The ethics of killing in this essay would entail that contraception is wrong only if something were denied a human future of value by contraception. Nothing at all is denied such a future by contraception, however.

Candidates for a subject of harm by contraception fall into four categories: (1) some sperm or other, (2) some ovum or other, (3) a sperm and an ovum separately, and (4) a sperm and an ovum together. Assigning the harm to some sperm is utterly arbitrary, for no reason can be given for making a sperm the subject of harm rather than an ovum. Assigning the harm to some ovum is utterly arbitrary, for no reason can be given for making an ovum the subject of harm rather than a sperm. One might attempt to avoid these problems by insisting that contraception deprives both the sperm and the ovum separately of a valuable future like ours. On this alternative, too many futures are lost. Contraception was supposed to be wrong, because it deprived us of one future of value, not two. One might attempt to avoid this problem by holding that contraception deprives the combination of sperm and ovum of a valuable future like ours. But here the definite article misleads. At the time of contraception, there are hundreds of millions of sperm, one (released) ovum and millions of possible combinations of all of these. There is no actual combination at all. Is the subject of the loss to be a merely possible combination? Which one? This alternative does not yield an actual subject of harm either. Accordingly, the immorality of contraception is not entailed by the loss of a future-like-ours argument simply because there is no nonarbitrarily identifiable subject of the loss in the case of contraception.

The purpose of this essay has been to set out an argument for the serious presumptive wrongness of abortion subject to the assumption that the moral permissibility of abortion stands or falls on the moral status of the fetus. Since a fetus possesses a property, the possession of which in adult human beings is sufficient to make killing an adult human being wrong, abortion is wrong. This way of dealing with the problem of abortion seems superior to other approaches to the ethics of abortion, because it rests on an ethics of killing which is close to self-evident, because the crucial morally relevant property clearly applies to fetuses, and because the argument avoids the usual equivocations on 'human life', 'human being,' or 'person'. The argument rests neither on religious claims or on Papal dogma. It is not subject to the objection of "speciesism." Its soundness is compatible with the moral permissibility of euthanasia and contraception. It deals with our intuitions concerning young children.

Finally, this analysis can be viewed as resolving a standard problem—indeed, *the* standard problem—concerning the ethics of abortion.

Clearly, it is wrong to kill adult human beings. Clearly, it is not wrong to end the life of some arbitrarily chosen single human cell. Fetuses seem to be like arbitrarily chosen human cells in some respects and like adult humans in other respects. The problem of the ethics of abortion is the problem of determining the fetal property that settles this moral controversy. The thesis of this essay is that the problem of the ethics of abortion, so understood, is solvable.

Endnotes

1. Feinberg, "Abortion," in *Matters of Life and Death: New Introductory Essays in Moral Philosophy,* Tom Regan, ed. (New York: Random House, 1986), pp. 256–293; Tooley, "Abortion and Infanticide," *Philosophy and Public Affairs,* II, 1 (1972):37–65, Tooley, *Abortion and Infanticide* (New York: Oxford, 1984); Warren, "On the Moral and Legal Status of Abortion," *The Monist,* LVII, 1 (1973):43–61; Engelhardt, "The Ontology of Abortion," *Ethics,* LXXXIV, 3 (1974):217–234; Sumner, *Abortion and Moral Theory* (Princeton: University Press, 1981); Noonan, "An Almost Absolute Value in History," in *The Morality of Abortion: Legal and Historical Perspectives,* Noonan, ed. (Cambridge: Harvard, 1970); and Devine, *The Ethics of Homocide* (Ithaca: Cornell, 1978).
2. For interesting discussions of this issue, see Warren Quinn, "Abortion: Identity and Loss," *Philosophy and Public Affairs,* XIII, 1 (1984):24–54; and Lawrence C. Becker, "Human Being: The Boundaries of the Concept," *Philosophy and Public Affairs,* IV, 4 (1975): 334–359.
3. For example, see my "Ethics and The Elderly: Some Problems," in Stuart Spicker, Kathleen Woodward, and David Van Tassel, eds., *Aging and the Elderly: Humanistic Perspectives in Gerontology* (Atlantic Highlands, NJ: Humanities, 1978), pp. 341–355.
4. See Warren, *op. cit.,* and Tooley, "Abortion and Infanticide."
5. This seems to be the fatal flaw in Warren's treatment of this issue.
6. I have been most influenced on this matter by Jonathan Glover, *Causing Death and Saving Lives* (New York: Penguin, 1977), ch. 3; and Robert Young, "What Is So Wrong with Killing People?" *Philosophy,* LIV, 210 (1979):515–528.
7. Feinberg, Tooley, Warren, and Englehardt have all dealt with this problem.
8. "Duties to Animals and Spirits," in *Lectures on Ethics,* Louis Infeld, trans. (New York: Harper, 1963), p. 239.

Review Questions

1. According to Marquis, what similar problems confront both the standard pro-life and pro-choice positions (as he calls them)?
2. Why is killing wrong according to Marquis?
3. Why is abortion wrong? State and explain Marquis' argument.
4. What is Marquis' position on active euthanasia?

Discussion Questions

1. Marquis allows that there may be rare or hard cases in which abortion is not wrong. What are these cases? Do you agree that abortion is not wrong in these cases?
2. Does Marquis' moral principle about killing imply that killing nonhuman animals is wrong? Is such killing wrong?
3. Is killing a severely defective fetus wrong according to Marquis' moral principle? Do you think it is wrong?
4. Does Marquis convince you that his position does not imply that contraception is wrong?

Judith Jarvis Thomson

A Defense of Abortion

Judith Jarvis Thomson is Professor of Philosophy at Massachusetts Institute of Technology. She is the author of The Realm of Rights *(1990), and numerous articles.*

Thomson assumes, just for the sake of argument, that the fetus is a person from the moment of conception. It does not follow, she argues, that the fetus' right to life always outweighs the moth-

er's rights. Using a series of imaginary examples (such as being plugged into a famous violinist), she tries to convince us that the mother's right to control her own body and her right to self-defense are strong enough to justify abortion in cases of rape, in cases where the mother's life is threatened, and in cases in which the woman has taken reasonable precautions not to get pregnant.

Most opposition to abortion relies on the premise that the fetus is a human being, a person, from the moment of conception. The premise is argued for, but, as I think, not well. Take, for example, the most common argument. We are asked to notice that the development of a human being from conception through birth into childhood is continuous; then it is said that to draw a line, to choose a point in this development and say "before this point the thing is not a person, after this point it is a person" is to make an arbitrary choice, a choice for which in the nature of things no good reason can be given. It is concluded that the fetus is, or anyway that we had better say it is, a person from the moment of conception. But this conclusion does not follow. Similar things might be said about the development of an acorn into an oak tree, and it does not follow that acorns are oak trees, or that we had better say they are. Arguments of this form are sometimes called "slippery slope arguments"—the phrase is perhaps self-explanatory—and it is dismaying that opponents of abortion rely on them so heavily and uncritically.

I am inclined to agree, however, that the prospects for "drawing a line" in the development of the fetus look dim. I am inclined to think also that we shall probably have to agree that the fetus has already become a human person well before birth. Indeed, it comes as a surprise when one first learns how early in its life it begins to acquire human characteristics. By the tenth week, for example, it already has a face, arms and legs, fingers and toes; it has internal organs, and brain activity is detectable.[1] On the other hand, I think that the premise is false, that the fetus is not a person from the moment of conception. A newly fertilized ovum, a newly implanted clump of cells, is no more a person than an acorn is an oak tree. But I shall not discuss any of this. For it seems to me to be of great interest to ask what happens if, for the sake of argument, we allow the premise. How, precisely, are we supposed to get from there to the conclusion that abortion is morally impermissible? Opponents of abortion commonly spend most of their time establishing that the fetus is a person, and hardly any time explaining the step from there to the impermissibility of abortion. Perhaps they think the step too simple and obvious to require much comment. Or perhaps instead they are simply being economical in argument. Many of those who defend abortion rely on the premise that the fetus is not a person, but only a bit of tissue that will become a person at birth; and why pay out more arguments than you have to? Whatever the explanation, I suggest that the step they take is neither easy nor obvious, that it calls for closer examination than it is commonly given, and that when we do give it this closer examination we shall feel inclined to reject it.

I propose, then, that we grant that the fetus is a person from the moment of conception. How does the argument go from here? Something like this, I take it. Every person has a right to life. So the fetus has a right to life. No doubt the mother has a right to decide what shall happen in and to her body; everyone would grant that. But surely a person's right to life is stronger and more stringent than the mother's right to decide what happens in and to her body, and so outweighs it. So the fetus may not be killed; an abortion may not be performed.

It sounds plausible. But now let me ask you to imagine this. You wake up in the morning and find yourself back to back in bed with an unconscious violinist. A famous unconscious violinist. He has been found to have a fatal kidney ailment, and the Society of Music Lovers has canvassed all the available medical records and found that you alone have the right blood type to help. They have therefore kidnapped you, and last night the violinist's circulatory system was plugged into yours, so that your kidneys can be used to extract poisons from his blood as well as your own. The director of the hospital now tells you, "Look, we're sorry the Society of Music Lovers did this to you—we would never have permitted it if we had known. But still, they did it, and the violinist now is plugged into you. To unplug you would be to kill him. But never mind, it's only for nine months. By then he will have recovered from his ailment, and can safely be unplugged from you." Is it morally incumbent on you to accede to this situation? No doubt it would be very nice of you if you did, a great kindness. But do you *have* to accede to it? What if it were not nine months, but nine years? Or longer still? What if the director of the hospital says, "Tough luck, I agree, but you've now got to stay in bed, with the violinist plugged into you, for the rest of your life. Because remember this. All persons have right to life, and violinists are persons. Granted you have a right to decide what happens in and to your body, but a person's right to life outweighs your right to decide what happens in and to your body. So you cannot ever be unplugged from him." I imagine you would regard this as outrageous, which suggests that something really is wrong with that plausible-sounding argument I mentioned a moment ago.

In this case, of course, you were kidnapped; you didn't volunteer for the operation that plugged the violinist into your kidneys. Can those who oppose abortion on the ground I mentioned make an exception for a pregnancy due to rape? Certainly. They can say that persons have a right to life only if they didn't come into existence because of rape; or they can say that all persons have a right to life, but that some have less of a right to life than others, in particular, that those who came into existence because of rape have less. But these statements have a rather unpleasant sound. Surely the question of whether you have a right to life at all, or how much of it you have, shouldn't turn on the question of whether or not you are the product of a rape. And in fact the people who oppose abortion on the ground I mentioned do not make this distinction, and hence do not make an exception in case of rape.

Nor do they make an exception for a case in which the mother has to spend the nine months of her pregnancy in bed. They would agree that would be a great pity, and hard on the mother; but all the same, all persons have a right to life, the fetus is a person, and so on. I suspect, in fact, that they would not make an exception for a case in which, miraculously enough, the pregnancy went on for nine years, or even the rest of the mother's life.

Some won't even make an exception for a case in which continuation of the pregnancy is likely to shorten the mother's life; they regard abortion as impermissible even to save the mother's life. Such cases are nowadays very rare, and many opponents of abortion do not accept this extreme view. All the same, it is a good place to begin; a number of points of interest come out in respect to it.

1. Let us call the view that abortion is impermissible even to save the mother's life "the extreme view." I want to suggest first that it does not issue from the argument I mentioned earlier without the addition of some fairly powerful premises. Suppose a woman has become pregnant, and now learns that she has a cardiac condition such that she will die if she carries the baby to term. What may be done for her? The fetus, being a person, has a right to life, but as the mother is a person too, so has she the right to life. Presumably they have an equal right to life. How is it supposed to come out that an abortion may not be performed? If mother and child have an equal right to life, shouldn't we perhaps flip a coin? Or should we add to the mother's right to life her right to decide what happens in and to her body, which everybody seems to be ready to grant—the sum of her rights now outweighing the fetus' right to life?

The most familiar argument here is the following. We are told that performing the abortion would be directly killing[2] the child, whereas doing nothing would not be killing the mother, but only letting her die. Moreover, in killing the child, one would be killing an innocent person, for the child has committed no crime, and is not aiming at his mother's death. And then there are a variety of ways in which this might be continued: (1) But as directly killing an innocent person is always and absolutely impermissible, an abortion may not be performed. Or (2) as directly killing an innocent person is murder, and murder is always and absolutely impermissible, an abortion may not be performed.[3] Or (3) as one's duty to refrain from directly killing an innocent person is more stringent than one's duty to keep a person from dying, an abortion may not be performed. Or (4) if one's only options are directly killing an innocent person or letting a person die, one must prefer letting the person die, and thus an abortion may not be performed.[4]

Some people seem to have thought that these are not further premises which must be added if the conclusion is to be reached, but that they follow from the very fact that an innocent person has a right to life.[5] But this seems to me to be a mistake, and perhaps the simplest way to show this is to bring out that while we must certainly grant that innocent persons have a right to life, the theses in (1) through (4) are all false. Take (2), for example. If directly killing an innocent person is murder, and thus is impermissible, then the mother's directly killing the innocent person inside her is murder, and this is impermissible. But it cannot seriously be thought to be murder if the mother performs an abortion on herself to save her life. It cannot seriously be said that she *must* refrain, that she *must* sit passively by and wait for her death. Let us look again at the case of you and the violinist. There you are, in bed with the violinist, and the director of the hospital says to you, "It's all most distressing, and I deeply sympathize, but you see this is putting an additional strain on your kidneys, and you'll be dead within the month. But you *have* to stay where you are all the same. Because unplugging you would be directly killing an innocent violinist, and that's murder, and that's impermissible." If anything in the world is true, it is that you do not commit murder, you do not do what is impermissible, if you reach around to your back and unplug yourself from that violinist to save your life.

The main focus of attention in writings on abortion has been on what a third party may or may not do in answer to a request from a woman for an abortion. This is in a way understandable. Things being as they are, there isn't much a woman can safely do to abort herself. So the question asked is what a third party may do, and what the mother may do, if it is mentioned at all, is deduced, almost as an afterthought, from what it is concluded that third parties may do. But it seems to me that to treat the matter in this way is to refuse to grant to the mother that very status of person which is so firmly insisted on for the fetus. For we cannot simply read off what a person may do from what a third party may do. Suppose you find yourself trapped in a tiny house with a growing child. I mean a very tiny house, and a rapidly growing child—you are already up against the wall of the house and in a few minutes you'll be crushed to death. The child on the other hand won't be crushed to death; if nothing is done to stop him from growing he'll be hurt, but in the end he'll simply burst open the house and walk out a free man. Now I could well understand it if a bystander were to say, "There's nothing we can do for you. We cannot choose between your life and his, we cannot be the ones to decide who is to live, we cannot intervene." But it cannot be concluded that you too can do nothing, that you cannot attack it to save your life. However innocent the child may be, you do not have to wait passively while it crushes you to death. Perhaps a pregnant woman is vaguely felt to have the status of house, to which we don't allow the right of self-defense. But if the woman houses the child, it should be remembered that she is a person who houses it.

I should perhaps stop to say explicitly that I am not claiming that people have a right to do anything whatever to save their lives. I think, rather, that there are drastic limits to the right of self-defense. If someone threatens you with death unless you torture someone else to death, I think you have not the right, even to save your life, to do so. But the case under consideration here is very different. In our case there are only two people involved, one whose life is threatened, and one who threatens it. Both are innocent: the one who is threatened is not threatened because of any fault, the one who threatens does not threaten because of any fault. For this reason we may feel that we bystanders cannot intervene. But the person threatened can.

In sum, a woman surely can defend her life against the threat to it posed by the unborn child, even if doing so involves its death. And this shows not merely that the theses in (1) through (4) are false; it shows also that the extreme view of abortion is false, and so we need not canvass any other possible ways of arriving at it from the argument I mentioned at the outset.

2. The extreme view could of course be weakened to say that while abortion is permissible to save the mother's life, it may not be performed by a third party, but only by the mother herself. But this cannot be right either. For what we have to keep in mind is that the mother and the unborn child are not like two tenants in a small house which has, by an unfortunate mistake, been rented to both: the mother *owns* the house. The fact that she does adds to the offensiveness of deducing that the mother can do nothing from the supposition that third parties can do nothing. But it does more than this: it casts a bright light on the supposition that third parties can do nothing. Certainly it lets us see that a third party who says "I cannot choose between you" is fooling himself if he thinks this is impartiality. If Jones has found and fastened on a certain coat, which he needs to keep him from freezing, but which Smith also needs to keep him from freezing, then it is not impartiality that says "I cannot choose between you" when Smith owns the coat. Women have said again and again "This body is *my* body!" and they have reason to feel angry, reason to feel that it has been like shouting into the wind. Smith, after all, is hardly likely to bless us if we say to him, "Of course it's your coat, anybody would grant that it is. But no one may choose between you and Jones who is to have it. . . ."

3. Where the mother's life is not at stake, the argument I mentioned at the outset seems to have a much stronger pull. "Everyone has a right to life, so the unborn person has a right to life." And isn't the child's right to life weightier than anything other than the mother's own right to life, which she might put forward as ground for an abortion?

This argument treats the right to life as if it were unproblematic. It is not, and this seems to me to be precisely the source of the mistake.

For we should now, at long last, ask what it comes to, to have a right to life. In some views having a right to life includes having a right to be given at least the bare minimum one needs for continued life. But suppose that what in fact *is* the bare minimum a man needs for continued life is something he has no right at all to be given? If I am sick unto death, and the only thing that will save my life is the touch of Henry Fonda's cool hand on my fevered brow, then all the same, I have no right to be given the touch of Henry Fonda's cool hand on my fevered brow. It would be frightfully nice of him to fly in from the West Coast to provide it. It would be less nice, though no doubt well meant, if my friends flew out to the West Coast and carried Henry Fonda back with them. But I have no right at all against anybody that he should do this for me. Or again, to return to the story I told earlier, the fact that for continued life that violinist needs the continued use of your kidneys does not establish that he has a right to be given the continued use of your kidneys. He certainly has no right against you that *you* should give him continued use of your kidneys. For nobody has any right to use your kidneys unless you give him such a right; and nobody has the right against you that you shall give him this right—if you do allow him to go on using your kidneys, this is a kindness on your part, and not something he can claim from you as his due. Nor has he any right against anybody else that *they* should give him continued use of your kidneys. Certainly he had no right against the Society of Music Lovers that they should plug him into you in the first place. And if you now start to unplug yourself, having learned that you will otherwise have to spend nine years in bed with him, there is nobody in the world who must try to prevent you, in order to see to it that he is given something he has a right to be given.

Some people are rather stricter about the right to life. In their view, it does not include the right to be given anything, but amounts to, and only to, the right not to be killed by anybody. But here a related difficulty arises. If everybody is to refrain from killing that violinist, then everybody must refrain from doing a great many different sorts of things. Everybody must refrain from slitting his throat, everybody must refrain from shooting him—and everybody must refrain from unplugging you from him. But does he have a right against everybody that they shall refrain from unplugging you from him? To refrain from doing this is to allow him to continue to use your kidneys. It could be argued that he has a right against us that *we* shall allow him to continue to use your kidneys. That is, while he had no right against us that we should give him the use of your kidneys, it might be argued that he anyway has a right against us that we shall not now intervene and deprive him of the use of your kidneys. I shall come back to third-party interventions later. But certainly the violinist has no right against you that *you* shall allow him to continue to use your kidneys. As I said, if you do allow him to use them, it is a kindness on your part, and not something you owe him.

The difficulty I point to here is not peculiar to the right to life. It reappears in connection with all the other natural rights; and it is something which an adequate account of rights must deal with. For present purposes it is enough just to draw attention to it. But I would stress that I am not arguing that people do not have a right to life—quite to the contrary, it seems to me that the primary control we must place on the acceptability of an account of rights is that it should turn out in that account to be a truth that all persons have a right to life. I am arguing only that having a right to life does not guarantee having either a right to be given the use of or a right to be allowed continued use of another person's body—even if one needs it for life itself. So the right to life will not serve the opponents of abortion in the very simple and clear way in which they seem to have thought it would. . . .

Endnotes

1. Daniel Callahan, *Abortion: Law, Choice and Morality* (New York, 1970), p. 373. This book gives a fascinating survey of the available information on abortion. The Jewish tradition is surveyed in David M. Feldman, *Birth Control in Jewish Law* (New York, 1968), Part 5, the Catholic tradition in John T. Noonan, Jr., "An Almost Absolute Value in History," in *The Morality of Abortion*, ed. John T. Noonan, Jr. (Cambridge, Mass., 1970).
2. The term "direct" in the arguments I refer to is a technical one. Roughly, what is meant by "direct killing" is either killing as an end in itself, or killing as a means to some end, for example, the end of saving someone else's life. See note 5, below, for an example of its use.
3. Cf. *Encyclical Letter of Pope Pius XI on Christian Marriage*, St. Paul Editions (Boston, n.d.), p. 32: "however much we may pity the mother whose health and even life is gravely imperiled in the performance of the duty allotted to her by nature, nevertheless what could ever be a sufficient reason for excusing in any way the direct murder of the innocent? This is precisely what we are dealing with here." Noonan (*The Morality of Abortion*, p. 43) reads this as follows: "What cause can ever avail to excuse in any way the direct killing of the innocent? For it is a question of that."
4. The thesis in (4) is in an interesting way weaker than those in (1), (2), and (3): they rule out abortion even in cases in which both mother *and* child will die if the abortion is not performed. By contrast, one who held the view expressed in (4) could consistently say that one needn't prefer letting two persons die to killing one.
5. Cf. the following passage from Pius XII, *Address to the Italian Catholic Society of Midwives:* "The baby in the maternal breast has the right to life immediately from God. Hence there is no man, no human authority, no science, no medical, eugenic, social, economic or moral 'indication' which can establish or grant a valid juridical ground for a direct deliberate disposition of an innocent human life, that is, a disposition which looks to its destruction either as an end or as a means to another end perhaps in itself not illicit. The baby, still not born, is a man in the same degree and for the same reason as the mother" (quoted in Noonan, *The Morality of Abortion*, p. 45).

Review Questions

1. What are slippery slope arguments?
2. Why does Thomson reject them?
3. According to Thomson, does the fetus become a human person before birth or not? Does it become a person at conception?
4. Explain the example about the famous violinist.
5. What is the extreme view?
6. What argument is used to defend this view?
7. How does Thomson attack this argument?
8. What is the point of the example about the tiny house and the growing child?
9. Why do women say, "This body is *my* body?" (Do they say this?)
10. Explain the example about Henry Fonda's cool hand on my fevered brow.

Discussion Questions

1. Does a woman who is pregnant due to rape have a right to get an abortion? Defend your view.
2. Does a woman have a right to have an abortion to save her life? Why, or why not?

3. What are the limits, if any, to the right to self-defense?

4. What obligations, if any, do we have towards people who have a right to life? Do we have an obligation, for example, to feed them?

Jane English

Abortion and the Concept of a Person

Jane English (1947–1978) taught at the University of North Carolina, Chapel Hill, and published several articles in ethics. She was the editor of Sex Equality *(1977).*

English argues that one of the central issues in the abortion debate, whether the fetus is a person or not, cannot be conclusively settled because of the nature of the concept of a person. This concept is said to be a cluster concept because it cannot be defined in terms of necessary and sufficient conditions. Given this lack of defining features, we cannot say whether a fetus is a person or not; it remains in a conceptually fuzzy borderline area.

English argues that regardless of whether or not the fetus is a person we must accept the moderate view that abortion is justified in some cases and not in others. Even if the fetus is a person, as the conservatives hold, it does not follow that abortion is never morally permissible. For the self-defense model not only justifies abortion to save the mother's life, but also justifies abortion to avoid serious harm or injury. On the other hand, the liberal view that the fetus is not a person does not warrant abortion on demand because we still have a duty to not harm or kill nonpersons that are sufficiently personlike. This duty makes late abortions for the sake of convenience (such as the woman who does not want to postpone a trip to Europe) morally wrong.

Reprinted with the permission of the editors from *Canadian Journal of Philosophy*, Vol. V, No. 2, October 1975, pp. 233–243.

The abortion debate rages on. Yet the two most popular positions seem to be clearly mistaken. Conservatives maintain that a human life begins at conception and that therefore abortion must be wrong because it is murder. But not all killings of humans are murders. Most notably, self defense may justify even the killing of an innocent person.

Liberals, on the other hand, are just as mistaken in their argument that since a fetus does not become a person until birth, a woman may do whatever she pleases in and to her own body. First, you cannot do as you please with your own body if it affects other people adversely.[1] Second, if a fetus is not a person, that does not imply that you can do to it anything you wish. Animals, for example, are not persons, yet to kill or torture them for no reason at all is wrong.

At the center of the storm has been the issue of just when it is between ovulation and adulthood that a person appears on the scene. Conservatives draw the line at conception, liberals at birth. In this paper I first examine our concept of a person and conclude that no single criterion can capture the concept of a person and no sharp line can be drawn. Next I argue that if a fetus is a person, abortion is still justifiable in many cases; and if a fetus is not a person, killing it is still wrong in many cases. To a large extent, these two solutions are in agreement. I conclude that our concept of a person cannot and need not bear the weight that the abortion controversy has thrust upon it.

I

The several factions in the abortion argument have drawn battle lines around various proposed criteria for determining what is and what is not a person. For example, Mary Anne Warren[2] lists five features (capacities for reasoning, self-awareness, complex communication, etc.) as her criteria for personhood and argues for the permissibility of abortion because a fetus falls outside this concept. Baruch Brody[3] uses brain waves. Michael Tooley[4] picks having-a-concept-of-self as his criterion and concludes that infanticide and abortion are justifiable, while the killing of adult animals is not. On the other side, Paul Ramsey[5] claims a certain gene structure is the defining characteristic. John Noonan[6] prefers conceived-of-humans and presents counterexamples to various other candidate criteria. For instance, he argues against viability as the criterion because the newborn and infirm would then be nonpersons, since they cannot live without the aid of others. He rejects any criterion that calls upon the sorts of sentiments a being can evoke in adults on the grounds that this would allow us to exclude other races as nonpersons if we could just view them sufficiently unsentimentally.

These approaches are typical: foes of abortion propose **sufficient conditions** for personhood which fetuses satisfy, while friends of abortion counter with necessary conditions for personhood which fetuses lack. But these both presuppose that the concept of a person can be captured in a strait jacket of necessary and/or sufficient conditions.[7] Rather, 'person' is a cluster of features, of which rationality, having a self concept and being conceived of humans are only part.

What is typical of persons? Within our concept of a person we include, first, certain biological factors: descended from humans, having a certain genetic makeup, having a head, hands, arms, eyes, capable of locomotion, breathing, eating, sleeping. There are psychological factors: sentience, perception, having a concept of self and of one's own interests and desires, the ability to use tools, the ability to use language or symbol systems, the ability to joke, to be angry, to doubt. There are rationality factors: the ability to reason and draw conclusions, the ability to generalize and to learn from past experience, the ability to sacrifice present interests for greater gains in the future. There are social factors: the ability to work in groups and respond to peer pressures, the ability to recognize and consider as valuable the interests of others, seeing oneself as one among "other minds," the ability to sympathize, encourage, love, the ability to evoke from others the responses of sympathy, encouragement, love, the ability to work with others for mutual advantage. Then there are legal factors: being subject to the law and protected by it, having the ability to sue and enter contracts, being counted in the census, having a name and citizenship, the ability to own property, inherit, and so forth.

Now the point is not that this list is not that this list is incomplete, or that you can find counterinstances to each of its points. People typically exhibit rationality, for instance, but someone who was irrational would not thereby fail to qualify as a person. On the other hand, something could exhibit the majority of these features and still fail to be a person, as an advanced robot might. There is no single core of necessary and sufficient features which we can draw upon with the assurance that they constitute what really makes a person; there are only features that are more or less typical.

This is not to say that no necessary or sufficient conditions can be given. Being alive is a necessary condition for being a person, and being a U.S. Senator is sufficient. But rather than falling inside a sufficient condition or outside a necessary one, a fetus lies in the penumbra region where our concept of a person is not so simple. For this reason I think a conclusive answer to the question whether a fetus is a person is unattainable.

Here we might note a family of simple fallacies that proceed by stating a necessary condition for personhood and showing that a fetus has that characteristic. This is a form of the **fallacy of affirming the consequent**. For example, some have mistakenly reasoned from the premise that a fetus is human (after all, it is a human fetus rather than, say, a canine fetus), to the conclusion that it is a human. Adding an **equivocation** on 'being', we get the fallacious argument that since a fetus is something both living and human, it is a human being.

Nonetheless, it does seem clear that a fetus has very few of the above family of characteristics, whereas a newborn baby exhibits a much larger proportion of them—and a two-year-old has even more. Note that one traditional anti-abortion argument has centered on pointing out the many ways in which a fetus resembles a baby. They emphasize its development ("It already has ten fingers . . .") without mentioning its dissimilarities to adults (it still has gills and a tail). They also try to evoke the sort of sympathy on our part that we only feel toward other persons ("Never to laugh . . . or feel the sunshine?") This all seems to be a relevant way to argue, since its purpose is to persuade us that a fetus satisfies so many of the important features on the list that it ought to be treated as a person. Also note that a fetus near the time of birth satisfies many more of these factors than a fetus in the early months of development. This could provide reason for making distinctions among the different stages of pregnancy, as the U.S. Supreme Court has done.[8]

Historically, the time at which a person has been said to come into existence has varied widely. Muslims date personhood from fourteen days after conception. Some medievals followed Aristotle in placing ensoulment at forty days after conception for a male fetus and eighty days for a female fetus.[9] In European common law since the Seventeenth Century, abortion was considered the killing of a person only after quickening, the time when a pregnant woman first feels the fetus move on its own. Nor is this variety of opinions surprising. Biologically, a human being develops gradually. We shouldn't expect there to be any specific time or sharp dividing point when a person appears on the scene.

For these reasons I believe our concept of a person is not sharp or decisive enough to bear the weight of a solution to the abortion controversy. To use it to solve that problem is to clarify *obscurum per obscurius.*

II

Next let us consider what follows if a fetus is a person after all. Judith Jarvis Thomson's landmark article, "A Defense of Abortion,"[10] correctly points out that some additional argumentation is needed at this point in the conservative argument to bridge the gap between the premise that a fetus is an innocent person and the conclusion that killing it is always wrong. To arrive at this conclusion, we would need the additional premise that killing an innocent person is always wrong. But killing an innocent person is sometimes permissible, most notably in self-defense. Some examples may help draw out our intuitions or ordinary judgments about self-defense.

Suppose a mad scientist, for instance, hypnotized innocent people to jump out of the bushes and attack innocent passers-by with knives. If you are so attacked, we agree you have a right to kill the attacker in self-defense, if killing him is the only way to protect your life or to save yourself from serious injury. It does not seem to matter here that the attacker is not malicious but himself an innocent pawn, for your killing of him is not done in a spirit of retribution but only in self-defense.

How severe an injury may you inflict in self-defense? In part this depends upon the severity of the injury to be avoided: you may not shoot someone merely to avoid having your clothes torn. This might lead one to the mistaken conclusion that the defense may only equal the threatened injury in severity; that to avoid death you may kill, but to avoid a black eye you may only inflict a black eye or the equivalent. Rather, our laws and customs seem to say that you may create an injury somewhat, but not enormously, greater than the injury to be avoided. To fend off an attack whose outcome would be as serious as rape, a severe beating or the loss of a finger, you may shoot; to avoid having your clothes torn, you may blacken an eye.

Aside from this, the injury you may inflict should only be the minimum necessary to deter or incapacitate the attacker. Even if you know he intends to kill you, you are not justified in shooting him if you could equally well save yourself by the simple expedient of running away. Self-defense is for the purpose of avoiding harms rather than equalizing harms.

Some cases of pregnancy present a parallel situation. Though the fetus is itself innocent, it may pose a threat to the pregnant woman's well-being, life prospects or health, mental or physical. If the pregnancy prevents a slight threat to her interests, it seems self-defense cannot justify abortion. But if the threat is on a par with a serious beating or the loss of a finger, she may kill the fetus that poses such a threat, even if it is an innocent person. If a lesser harm to the fetus could have the same defensive effect, killing it would not be justified. It is unfortunate that the only way to free the woman from the pregnancy entails the death of the fetus (except in very late stages of pregnancy). Thus a self-defense model supports Thomson's point that the woman has a right only to be freed from the fetus, not a right to demand its death.[11]

The self-defense model is most helpful when we take the pregnant woman's point of view. In the pre-Thomson literature, abortion is often framed as a question for a third party: do you, a doctor, have a right to choose between the life of the woman and that of the fetus? Some have claimed that if you were a passer-by who witnessed a struggle between the innocent hypnotized attacker and his equally innocent victim, you would have no reason to kill either in defense of the other. They have concluded that the self defense model implies that a woman may attempt to abort herself, but that a doctor should not assist her. I think the position of the third party is somewhat more complex. We do feel some inclination to intervene on behalf of the victim rather than the attacker, other things equal. But if both parties are innocent, other factors come into consideration. You would rush to the aid of your husband whether he was attacker or attackee. If a hypnotized famous violinist were attacking a skid row bum, we would try to save the individual who is of more value to society. These considerations would tend to support abortion in some cases.

But suppose you are a frail senior citizen who wishes to avoid being knifed by one of these innocent hypnotics, so you have hired a bodyguard to accompany you. If you are attacked, it is clear we believe that the bodyguard, acting as your agent, has a right to kill the attacker to save you from a serious beating. Your rights of self defense are transferred to your agent. I suggest that we should similarly view the doctor as the pregnant woman's agent in carrying out a defense she is physically incapable of accomplishing herself.

Thanks to modern technology, the cases are rare in which a pregnancy poses as clear a threat to a woman's bodily health as an attacker brandishing a switchblade. How does self defense fare when more subtle, complex and long-range harms are involved?

To consider a somewhat fanciful example, suppose you are a highly trained surgeon when you are kidnapped by the hypnotic attacker. He says he does not intend to harm you but to take you back to the mad scientist who, it turns out, plans to hypnotize you to have a permanent mental block against all your knowledge of medicine. This would automatically destroy your career which would in turn have a serious adverse impact on your family, your personal relationships and your happiness. It seems to me that if the only way you can avoid this outcome is to shoot the innocent attacker, you are justified in so doing. You are defending yourself from a drastic injury to your life prospects. I think it is no exaggeration to claim that unwanted pregnancies (most obviously among teenagers) often have such adverse life-long consequences as the surgeon's loss of livelihood.

Several parallels arise between various views on abortion and the self-defense model. Let's suppose further that these hypnotized attackers only operate at night, so that it is well known that they can be avoided completely by the considerable inconvenience of never leaving your house after dark. One view is that since you could stay home at night, therefore if you go out and are selected by one of these hypnotized people, you have no right to defend yourself. This parallels the view that abstinence is the only acceptable way to avoid pregnancy. Others might hold that you ought to take along some defense such as mace which will deter the hyponotized person without killing him, but that if this defense fails, you are obliged to submit to the resulting injury, no matter how severe it is. This parallels the view that contraception is all right but abortion is always wrong, even in cases of contraceptive failure.

A third view is that you may kill the hyponotized person only if he will actually kill you, but not if he will only injure you. This is like the position that abortion is permissible only if it is required to save a woman's life. Finally we have the view that it is all right to kill the attacker, even if only to avoid a very slight inconvenience to yourself and even if you knowingly walked down the very street where all these incidents have been taking place without taking along any mace or protective escort. If we assume that a fetus is a person, this is the analogue of the view that abortion is always justifiable, "on demand."

The self-defense model allows us to see an important difference that exists between abortion and infanticide, even if a fetus is a person from conception. Many have argued that the only way to justify abortion without justifying infanticide would be to find some characteristic of personhood that is acquired at birth. Michael Tooley, for one, claims infanticide is justifiable because the really significant characteristics of person are acquired some time after birth. But all such approaches look to characteristics of the developing human and ignore the relation between the fetus and the woman. What if, after birth, the presence of an infant or the need to support it posed a grave threat to the woman's sanity or life prospects? She could escape this threat by the simple expedient of running away. So a solution that does not entail the death of the infant is available. Before birth, such solutions are not available because of the biological dependence of the fetus on the woman. Birth is the crucial point not because of any characteristics the fetus gains, but because after birth the woman can defend herself by a means less drastic than killing the infant. Hence self-defense can be used to justify abortion without necessarily thereby justifying infanticide.

III

On the other hand, supposing a fetus is not after all a person, would abortion always be morally permissible? Some opponents of abortion seem worried that if a fetus is not a full-fledged person, then we are justified in treating it in any way at all. However, this does not follow. Nonpersons do get some consideration in our moral code, though of course they do not have the same rights as persons have (and in general they do not have moral responsibilities), and though their interests may be overridden by the interests of persons. Still, we cannot just treat them in any way at all.

Treatment of animals is a case in point. It is wrong to torture dogs for fun or to kill wild birds for no reason at all. It is wrong Period, even though dogs and birds do not have the same rights persons do. However, few people think it is wrong to use dogs as experimental animals, causing them considerable suffering in some cases, provided that the resulting research will probably bring discoveries of great benefit to people. And most of us think it all right to kill birds for food or to protect our crops. People's rights are different from the consideration we give to animals, then, for it is wrong to experiment on people, even if others might later benefit a great deal as a result of their suffering. You might volunteer to be a subject, but this would be supererogatory; you certainly have a right to refuse to be a medical guinea pig.

But how do we decide what you may or may not do to nonpersons? This is a difficult problem, one for which I believe no adequate account exists. You do not want to say, for instance, that torturing dogs is all right whenever the sum of its effects on people is good—when it doesn't warp the sensibilities of the torturer so much that he mistreats people. If that were the case, it would be all right to torture dogs if you did it in private, or if the torturer lived on a desert island or died soon afterward, so that his actions had no effect on people. This is an inadequate account, because whatever moral consideration animals get, it has to be indefeasible, too. It will have to be a general proscription of certain actions, not merely a weighing of the impact on people on a case-by-case basis.

Rather, we need to distinguish two levels on which consequences of actions can be taken into account in moral reasoning. The traditional objections to Utilitarianism focus on the fact that it operates solely on the first level, taking all the consequences into account in particular cases only. This Utilitarianism is open to "desert island" and "lifeboat" counterexamples because these cases are rigged to make the consequences of actions severely limited.

Rawls' theory could be described as a teleological sort of theory, but with teleology operating on a higher level.[12] In choosing the principles to regulate society from the original position, his hypothetical choosers make their decision on the basis of the total consequences of various systems. Furthermore, they are constrained to choose a general set of rules which people can readily learn and apply. An ethical theory must operate by generating a set of sympathies and attitudes toward others which reinforces the functioning of that set of moral principles. Our prohibition against killing people operates by means of certain moral sentiments including sympathy, compassion and guilt. But if these attitudes are to form a coherent set, they carry us further: we tend to perform supererogatory actions, and we tend to feel similar compassion toward person-like nonpersons.

It is crucial that psychological facts play a role here. Our psychological constitution makes it the case that for our ethical theory to work, it must prohibit certain treatment of nonpersons which are significantly person-like. If our moral rules allowed people to treat some person-like nonpersons in ways we do not want people to be treated, this would undermine the system of sympathies and attitudes that makes the ethical system work. For this reason, we would choose in the original position to make mistreatment of some sorts of animals wrong in general (not just wrong in the cases with public impact), even though animals are not themselves parties in the original position. Thus it makes sense that it is those animals whose appearance and behavior are most like those of people that get the most consideration in our moral scheme.

It is because of "coherence of attitudes," I think, that the similarity of a fetus to a baby is very significant. A fetus one week before birth is so much like a newborn baby in our psychological space that we cannot allow any cavalier treatment of the former while expecting full sympathy and nurturative support for the latter. Thus, I think that anti-abortion forces are indeed giving their strongest arguments when they point to the similarities between a fetus and a baby, and when they try to evoke our emotional attachment to and sympathy for the fetus. An early horror story from New York about nurses who were expected to alternate between caring for six-week premature infants and disposing of viable 24-week aborted fetuses is just that—a horror story. These beings are so much alike that no one can be asked to draw a distinction and treat them so very differently.

Remember, however, that in the early weeks after conception, a fetus is very much unlike a person. It is hard to develop these feelings for a set of genes which doesn't yet have a head, hands, beating heart, response to touch or the ability to move by itself. Thus it seems to me that the alleged "slippery slope" between conception and birth is not so very slippery. In the early stages of pregnancy, abortion can hardly be compared to murder for psychological reasons, but in the latest stages it is psychologically akin to murder.

Another source of similarity is the bodily continuity between fetus and adult. Bodies play a surprisingly central role in our attitudes toward persons. One has only to think of the philosophical literature on how far physical identity suffices for personal identity or Wittgenstein's remark that the best picture of the human soul is the human body. Even after death, when all agree the body is no longer a person, we still observe elaborate customs of respect for the human body; like people who torture dogs, necrophiliacs are not to be trusted with people.[13] So it is appropriate that we show respect to a fetus as the body continuous with the body of a person. This is a degree of resemblance to persons that animals cannot rival.

Michael Tooley also utilizes a parallel with animals. He claims that it is always permissible to drown newborn kittens and draws conclusions about infanticide.[14] But it is only permissible to drown kittens when their survival would cause some hardship. Perhaps it would be a burden to feed and house six more cats or to find other homes for them. The alternative of letting them starve produces even more suffering than the drowning. Since the kittens get their rights second-hand, so to speak, *via* the need for coherence in our attitudes, their interests are often overridden by the interests of full-fledged persons. But if their survival would be no inconvenience to people at all, then it is wrong to drown them, *contra* Tooley.

Tooley's conclusions about abortion are wrong for the same reason. Even if a fetus is not a person, abortion is not always permissible, because of the resemblance of a fetus to a person. I agree with Thomson that it would be wrong for a woman who is seven months pregnant to have an abortion just to avoid having to postpone a trip to Europe. In the early months of pregnancy when the fetus hardly resembles a baby at all, then, abortion is permissible whenever it is in the interests of the pregnant woman or her family. The reasons would only need to outweigh the pain and inconvenience of the abortion itself. In the middle months, when the fetus comes to resemble a person, abortion would be justifiable only when the continuation of the pregnancy or the birth of the child would cause harms—physical, psychological, economic or social—to the woman. In the late months of pregnancy, even on our current assumption that a fetus is not a person, abortion seems to be wrong except to save a woman from significant injury or death.

The Supreme Court has recognized similar gradations in the alleged slippery slope stretching between conception and birth. To this point, the present paper has been a discussion of the moral status of abortion only, not its legal status. In view of the great physical, financial and sometimes psychological costs of abortion, perhaps the legal arrangement most compatible with the proposed moral solution would be the absence of restrictions, that is, so-called abortion "on demand."

So I conclude, first, that application of our concept of a person will not suffice to settle the abortion issue. After all, the biological development of a human being is gradual. Second, whether a fetus is a person or not, abortion is justifiable early in pregnancy to avoid modest harms and seldom justifiable late in pregnancy except to avoid significant injury or death.[15]

Endnotes

1. We also have paternalistic laws which keep us from harming our own bodies even when no one else is affected. Ironically, anti-abortion laws were originally designed to protect pregnant women from a dangerous but tempting procedure.
2. Mary Anne Warren, "On the Moral and Legal Status of Abortion," *Monist* 57 (1973), [*supra,* pp. 102–119].
3. Baruch Brody, "Fetal Humanity and the Theory of Essentialism," in Robert Baker and Frederick Elliston (eds.), *Philosophy and Sex* (Buffalo, N.Y., 1975).
4. Michael Tooley, "Abortion and Infanticide," *Philosophy and Public Affairs* 2 (1971). [Revised version *supra,* pp. 120–134.
5. Paul Ramsey, "The Morality of Abortion," in James Rachels, ed., *Moral Problems* (New York, 1971).
6. John Noonan, "Abortion and the Catholic Church: A Summary History," *Natural Law Forum* 12 (1967), pp. 125–131.
7. Wittgenstein has argued against the possibility of so capturing the concept of a game, *Philadelphia Investigations* (New York, 1958), § 66–71.
8. Not because the fetus is partly a person and so has some of the rights of persons, but rather because of the rights of person-like non-persons. This I discuss in part III below.
9. Aristotle himself was concerned, however, with the different question of when the soul takes form. For historical data, see Jimmye Kimmey, "How the Abortion Laws Happened," *Ms* 1 (April, 1973), pp. 48ff, and John Noonan, *loc. cit.*
10. J. J. Thomson, "A Defense of Abortion," *Philosophy and Public Affairs* 1 (1971). [*Infra,* pp. 173–187.]
11. *Ibid.* [p. 187].
12. John Rawls, *A Theory of Justice* (Cambridge, Mass., 1971), § 3–4.
13. On the other hand, if they can be trusted with people, then our moral customs are mistaken. It all depends on the facts of psychology.
14. *Op. cit.,* pp. 40, 60–61.
15. I am deeply indebted to Larry Crocker and Arthur Kuflik for their constructive comments.

Review Questions

1. What is wrong with the conservative view according to English?
2. What two objections does she make to the liberal argument?
3. According to English, why do the various attempts to find the necessary and/or sufficient conditions for personhood all fail?
4. Explain English's own account of the concept of person including the biological, psychological, rationality, social, and legal factors.
5. According to English, in what cases does the self-defense model justify abortion, as distinguished from merely extracting the fetus and keeping it alive?
6. English discusses four different views of abortion and self-defense. Distinguish between these four different views.

7. According to English, why isn't abortion always morally permissible even if the fetus is not a person?

Discussion Questions

1. Is English's analysis of the concept of person correct? To find out, try to state necessary and sufficient conditions for being a person.
2. English never commits herself to one of the four views on abortion and self-defense. Which of these do you think is the most plausible? Why?
3. English asserts that it is wrong—period—to kill wild birds for no reason at all. Do you agree? Why or why not?

Problem Cases

*1. **The Morning-After Pill.*** (Discussed in "The Morning-After Pill," by Jan Hoffman in *The New York Times Magazine,* January 10, 1993.) Depending on when a woman takes it, the morning-after pill prevents either fertilization (occurring up to eighteen hours after intercourse) or implantation of the fertilized egg in the lining of the uterus (occurring about a week or two after conception). Since pregnancy tests do not register positive until a day or two after implantation, a woman who takes the pill after intercourse will not know if she has prevented conception or implantation.

The drug most often used as a morning-after pill is Ovral. It is also used as a birth-control pill, and it was approved as such by the F.D.A. (the Federal Food and Drug Administration) in 1968. Other lower-dose pills that can be used as morning-after pills are Lo/Ovral, Nordette, Levlen, Triphasil and Tri Levlen. All these pills combine estrogen and progestin, and they affect a woman's hormones in such a way that the egg cannot be fertilized; or if it is, it cannot become implanted in the lining of the uterus. Instead the egg is sloughed off during menstruation.

The morning-after pill can be effectively taken up to seventy-two hours after intercourse, and it reduces the likelihood of pregnancy to below eight percent. (On her most fertile day, a woman's chance of becoming pregnant is at most about twenty-five percent.) Although it certainly reduces the chances of becoming pregnant, it is not completely effective because it does not prevent tubal pregnancies. The side effects of the morning-after pill include temporary nausea and breast tenderness, and it is not recommended for women who should not take oral contraceptives.

According to the *Times* article, the morning-after pill is widely prescribed on college campuses, and it has been part of standard care for rape victims for more than a decade. Planned Parenthood affiliates have been offering it for about three years. Use of birth-control pills as morning-after pills has not received the approval of the F.D.A., largely because no drug company has sought approval, and without F.D.A. approval they cannot be dispensed in federally supported Title X clinics which serve poor women.

Doctors estimate that by making the morning-after pill widely available, the number of unwanted pregnancies could be reduced by 1.7 million annually, and the number of abortions could be reduced by 800,000 annually. Currently there are about 3.5 million unwanted pregnancies per year in the United States, and about 1.6 million abortions.

The morning-after pill raises several interesting questions:

Is preventing implantation an abortion, contraception, interception, or what?

Is the zygote or fertilized egg a person with rights before it becomes implanted?

The IUD (inter-uterine device) also prevents fertilization or implantation. Does using it amount to getting an abortion?

In the one or two weeks before implantation, many fertilized eggs are naturally sloughed off, and women don't usually think of this as miscarriage. So why should a woman think of preventing implantation as an abortion?

*2. **Mrs. Sherri Finkbine and Thalidomide.*** In 1962, Mrs. Sherri Finkbine, the mother of four normal children, became pregnant. During the pregnancy, Mrs. Finkbine had trouble sleeping, so without consulting her physician, she took some tranquilizers containing the drug thalidomide which her husband had brought back from a trip to Europe. In Europe, the sedative was widely used.

Later Mrs. Finkbine read that a number of severely deformed children had been born in Europe. These children's limbs failed to develop, or developed in malformed ways; some were born blind and deaf, or had seriously defective internal organs. The birth defects were traced to the use in pregnancy of a widely used tranquilizer whose active ingredient was thalidomide, the very tranquilizer that she had taken.

Mrs. Finkbine went to her physician, and he confirmed her fears. The tranquilizer did contain thalidomide, and she had a very good chance of delivering a seriously deformed baby. The physician recommended an abortion. Mrs. Finkbine then presented her case to the three-member medical board of Phoenix, and they granted approval for the abortion.

In her concern for other women who might have taken thalidomide, Mrs. Finkbine told her story to a local newspaper. The story made the front page, and it wasn't long before reporters had discovered and published Mrs. Finkbine's identity. She became the object of an intense anti-abortion campaign, and she was condemned as a murderer by the Vatican newspaper.

As a result of the controversy, the medical board decided that their approval for an abortion would not survive a court test because the Arizona statute at that time allowed abortion only to save the mother's life. So the board withdrew their approval.

Eventually Mrs. Finkbine found it necessary to get an abortion in Sweden. After the abortion, Mrs. Finkbine asked if the fetus was a boy or a girl. The doctor could not say because the fetus was too badly deformed.

Do you think that Mrs. Finkbine acted wrongly in having an abortion? Explain your answer.

Do you think that the government has a right to prohibit abortions in such cases? Why or why not?

3. A Cancer Case. (This is an actual case, but the name has been changed.) Mrs. Jones was a devout Catholic, a wonderful wife, and the mother of eight children. She did not use any artificial method of birth control and became pregnant for the ninth time. Tragically, it was discovered that she had cancer of the uterus. Rather than getting an abortion to save her life, she decided to have the child and risk dying of cancer. She delivered the child successfully and died a short time later, leaving her husband with nine children.

Do you think that Mrs. Jones made the morally correct decision? Explain your answer.

4. A Minor. In Alabama, state law forbids a minor (anyone under eighteen) to have an abortion without the parent's consent. Kathy is a seventeen-year-old woman who is accidentally pregnant after having sex once with her boyfriend. Her parents are divorced, and she lives with her mother and an alcoholic stepfather who frequently abuses Kathy and her mother. She does not want to tell her mother or her stepfather about the problem because she is afraid she will be beaten by the stepfather. She wants to have an abortion and decides to consult an abortion clinic. The people at the clinic are eager to challenge the law about minors, offering to give her free legal representation if she takes the case to court. She goes to court, but the judge rules against her—she cannot get a legal abortion without her parent's consent. Her lawyer wants to appeal the case to a higher court, but by the time she gets to court again, the fetus will be viable, and Kathy does not want to abort a viable fetus.

What should Kathy do? Should she get an illegal abortion? What is your advice?

Suggested Readings

1. Sissela Bok, "Ethical Problems of Abortion," *Hastings Center Studies* 2 (January 1974), pp. 33–52, rejects attempts to define "humanity" and suggests that various reasons for not getting an abortion become stronger as the fetus develops.

2. Baruch Brody, "On the Humanity of the Fetus," in *Abortion: Pro and Con,* Robert L. Perkins, ed. (Cambridge, MA: Schenkman, 1974), pp. 69–90. After critically examining various proposals for "drawing the line" on the humanity of the fetus, Brody suggests that the most defensible view is to draw the line at the point when fetal brain waves can be detected, at about the eighth week of development.

3. Daniel Callahan, *Abortion: Law, Choice and Morality* (New York: Macmillan, 1970), provides factual material relevant to medical, social, and legal questions about abortion. He defends the moderate view that the fetus has what he calls a "partial moral status."

4. Marshall Cohen, Thomas Nagel, and Thomas Scanlon, eds., *The Rights and Wrongs of Abortion* (Princeton, NJ: Princeton University Press, 1974). This short anthology has five articles including two by Judith Jarvis Thomson; all originally appeared in the journal *Philosophy and Public Affairs*.

5. Angela Davis, *Women, Race, and Class* (New York: Random House, 1981), Chapter 12, discusses the abortion rights movement in the context of race, class, and the women's liberation movement.

6. Phillip E. Devine, *The Ethics of Homicide* (Ithaca and London: Cornell University Press, 1978). Devine discusses killing fetuses and the comatose in Chapter III.

7. Tristram H. Engelhardt, Jr., "The Ontology of Abortion," *Ethics* 84 (April 1974), pp. 217–234, deals with the question of whether or not the fetus is a person. He decides that it is not a person until the later stages of infancy, but after viability the fetus can be treated as if it were a person.

8. Fred Feldman, *Confrontations with the Reaper* (New York: Oxford University Press, 1992), Chapter 12, defends a utilitarian theory called Justicized Act Utilitarianism which entails that abortion is morally right in cases of rape, a severely deformed fetus, and possibly in other cases where universal justice level is maximized.

9. Joel Feinberg, ed., *The Problem of Abortion* (Belmont, CA: Wadsworth, 1984). This is the best anthology available on the subject with a wide range of good articles representing different points of view.

10. Joel Feinberg, "Abortion," in *Matters of Life and Death,* 2nd ed., edited by Tom Regan (New York: Random House, 1985) provides a sophisticated discussion of various issues connected to abortion including the status of the fetus. Feinberg ends up with a liberal position since he finds that fetuses are not "people" in the ordinary meaning of the term, and not moral persons either.

11. Germain Grisez, *Abortion: The Myths, The Realities, and the Arguments* (New York: Corpus Books, 1970). This is a long and difficult book; Grisez defends the conservative view on abortion in Chapter VI.

12. R. M. Hare, "Abortion and the Golden Rule," *Philosophy and Public Affairs* 4 (Spring 1975), pp. 201–222, attacks those who appeal to intuition, such as Thomson, and replies on the Golden Rule as a basic ethical principle to support a roughly moderate view of abortion.

13. Susan Nicholson, *Abortion and the Roman Catholic Church* (Knoxville, Tenn.: Religious Ethics, 1974), explains the position of the Church on abortion.

14. Robert L. Perkins, ed., *Abortion: Pro and Con* (Cambridge, MA: Schenkman, 1974). This anthology contains a variety of articles representing different positions on abortion.

15. Peter Singer, *Practical Ethics* (Cambridge: Cambridge University Press, 1979), Chapter 6, discusses abortion from a utilitarian point of view. The version of utilitarianism that Singer accepts is preference utilitarianism.

16. Brenda Timmins, "What about Us?" in *Gender Basics,* Anne Minas, ed. (Belmont, CA: Wadsworth Publishing Co., 1993), pp. 432–436, argues that because of the difficulties in caring for handicapped children, women should have unrestricted access to abortion.

17. Michael Tooley, "Abortion and Infanticide," *Philosophy and Public Affairs* 1 (Fall 1971), pp. 47–66, presents a classic defense of the extreme liberal view that neither a fetus nor a newborn infant have a serious right to continued existence, and that both abortion and infanticide are morally acceptable. Tooley also has a book titled *Abortion and Infanticide* (New York: Oxford University Press, 1983) in which he develops his position.

18. Alan Zaitchik, "Viability and the Morality of Abortion," *Philosophy & Public Affairs,* 10:1 (1981), pp. 18–24, defends the view that viability is a morally significant dividing line against criticisms made by conservatives.

Chapter Three

SUICIDE AND EUTHANASIA

Introduction

Suicide is the taking of one's own life, and euthanasia is killing someone for the sake of mercy to relieve great suffering. But when a doctor helps an injured or ill person commit suicide, as Dr. Jack Kevorkian does (See the first Problem Case), it seems that there is little difference between assisted suicide and euthanasia. This point is made clear by Singer in the readings. Gay-Williams goes even further. He implies that suicide, whether assisted or not, can be the same as euthanasia. According to his definition of euthanasia, a person who takes her life because she is suffering from a presumably hopeless illness or injury has committed an act of euthanasia.

The distinction between suicide and euthanasia, then, may be fuzzy or even nonexistent in some cases. To clarify matters, it is customary to distinguish between different types of euthanasia. *Voluntary euthanasia* is mercy killing with the consent of the terminally ill person. This is the type of euthanasia that includes suicide, at least in the view of Gay-Williams. For example, a patient suffering from very painful and terminal cancer may ask to be killed with a fatal injection of morphine. Or the patient may turn a switch that triggers the fatal injection as in one of Dr. Kevorkian's suicide devices. *Nonvoluntary euthanasia,* by contrast, is mercy killing without the consent of the person who is ill (although the consent of others such as parents or relatives can be obtained). This type of euthanasia does not include suicide. Authors who discuss nonvoluntary euthanasia usually have in mind the killing of those who are unable to give consent, for example a comatose person such as Karen

Ann Quinlan or a defective infant. Obviously, such a person cannot commit suicide. There is another possibility, however, and that is the mercy killing of a person who is able to give consent but is not asked. If the person killed does not wish to die, it might be more accurate to call this *involuntary euthanasia*. Certainly it could not be called suicide.

A further distinction is often made between active and passive euthanasia, or between killing and letting die for the sake of mercy. Just how this distinction should be drawn is a matter of some debate. As Rachels explains it in the reading, active euthanasia is taking a direct action designed to kill the patient, such as giving the patient a lethal injection. Passive euthanasia, by contrast, is allowing the patient to die by withholding treatment—not performing life-saving surgery on a defective infant, for example.

Rachels believes that this distinction has no moral significance, and that using it leads to confused moral thinking. But Tom L. Beauchamp defends the distinction, and argues that it should play an important role in our moral reasoning.

In the third reading for the chapter, J. Gay-Williams objects to making any distinction between active and passive euthanasia. He claims that the phrase passive euthanasia is misleading and mistaken. In his view, what is called passive euthanasia is not really euthanasia at all because it is not intentional killing. Either the killing is an unintended consequence, a side effect of the real intention—elimination of the suffering—or the cause of death is the person's injuries or disease, not the failure to receive treatment.

The traditional position that Gay-Williams adopts rests on a distinction between the intended consequence of an act and the foreseen but unintended consequence. Although Gay-Williams does not discuss it, it is worth noting that this distinction is part of the traditional **doctrine of double effect**. According to this doctrine, as long as the intended consequence of an act is good, a bad forseen consequence (such as death) can be morally allowed provided it is not intended and prevents a greater evil (such as great suffering). To use Gay-William's example, suppose that a doctor gives a terminal cancer patient an overdose of morphine, that is, an amount sufficient to kill the patient. If the doctor intends only to reduce or eliminate the patient's pain, and not to kill the patient, and if the death of the patient is not as bad as the patient's suffering, then according to the doctrine of double effect, the doctor's action is not wrong, even though the doctor foresees that the patient will die from the overdose.

The Moral Issue. The moral issue is whether suicide and euthanasia are wrong. The issue is complicated by the fact that parties do not always agree on the meaning of the term euthanasia. It seems accurate to say that the traditional conservative view is that active euthanasia and suicide are always wrong (unless God commands it—this exception is mentioned by Brandt). The representatives of the conservative view in our readings are St. Thomas Aquinas, Gay-Williams, and the AMA statement (discussed by Rachels). St. Thomas argues that suicide is wrong because it is contrary to **natural law** and charity, harms the community, and destroys God's gift to us. Gay-Williams makes similar objections to euthanasia; it is unnatural, it is contrary to self-interest, it produces bad effects on others, and it violates the nature and dignity of humans.

But conservatives such as Gay-Williams grant that patients may be morally allowed to die or even indirectly killed in some cases. Gay-Williams also argues that allowing a patient with no chance of recovery to die by failing to treat his or her injuries or disease results in the cause of death being the injuries or disease, not the failure to provide treatment. Therefore, it is not properly regarded as passive euthanasia.

The AMA position is somewhat different. It allows the cessation of extraordinary means of treatment; and in some cases, this seems to be passive euthanasia, even though the AMA statement does not make any distinction between passive and active euthanasia.

The liberal view on euthanasia and suicide, as distinguished from what we are calling the traditional conservative view, is that active euthanasia and suicide can be morally right in some cases and is even preferable to passive euthanasia when a quick and painless death avoids suffering by the patient. This view is defended by Brandt in two readings in the chapter. In the first one on suicide, he argues that suicide is both rational and morally right when a patient is suffering from a painful and terminal illness. In the second article, Brandt uses similar arguments to justify the active termination of defective newborn infants. Rachels and Singer also defend active euthanasia to avoid suffering.

Philosophical Issues. As far as voluntary euthanasia and suicide are concerned, one basic issue is whether or not terminally ill persons who are rational and fully informed should be free to decide to die, and then to bring about that decision by themselves or with another's help. Singer argues that such active voluntary euthanasia is morally permissible, even in those cases where it is basically the same as assisted suicide. Brandt agrees that suicide in such a case is rational and morally permissible. Gay-Williams does not agree. He argues that a person who chooses to die, whether by suicide or by active euthanasia, is acting contrary to nature and contrary to self-interest.

Another issue is whether or not there is a morally significant difference between killing and letting die. There is also controversy about the doctrine of double effect. Critics complain that no clear distinction can be made between the two effects, the intended one and the unintended but foreseen one. Furthermore, assuming that a distinction between the two effects can be made, then it seems to follow that the doctrine can be used to defend any evil act provided it is merely foreseen and not intended. All that is required is an appropriate manipulation of intentions. Defenders of the doctrine insist that a clear distinction between the two effects in question can be made, in some important cases anyway, and that it does not allow any evil act, but only those that prevent an even greater evil.

Another matter of controversy is the distinction between ordinary and extraordinary means of prolonging life. This distinction is found in the AMA statement. Rachels thinks that the cessation of extraordinary means of treatment amounts to passive euthanasia because it is the intentional termination of life. But is this true? Perhaps the reason for stopping extraordinary treatment is to avoid treatment that causes more discomfort than the disease. In that case the reason for doing this is not to terminate life, but to avoid excessive suffering.

Another important issue is how to make life-or-death decisions. One standard answer, given by Rachels and Brandt, is to appeal to the quality of a person's life: If a person will have a bad life, then his or her life should be ended; but if a person will have a good life, then his or her life should be continued. But how do we distinguish between good and bad lives? That is a classical problem in ethics that resists easy solution. One answer is that we should ask ourselves if we would want to live the life in question. But it seems unlikely that everyone will agree about which lives are or are not worth living. Taking surveys may not be the answer. Brandt's suggestion is that we use a "happiness criterion." A life is good or worth living if over the whole lifetime there are more moments of happiness (moments of experience that are liked) than moments of unhappiness (moments of experience that are disliked). But is happiness the only thing to be considered? What about other things like knowledge and achievement? Perhaps an unhappy life could still be good because of achievements or knowledge.

St. Thomas Aquinas

Suicide is Unnatural and Immoral

St. Thomas Aquinas (1225–1274), a member of the Dominican Order, was one of the greatest medieval philosophers. As an Angelic Doctor of the Roman Catholic Church, his teachings have a position of special authority, but this does not mean that all Catholic thinkers agree with him on every point of doctrine.

St. Thomas employs the scholastic style of presenting objections to his own position, and then replying to each objection in turn. After stating five arguments for the moral permissibility of suicide, St. Thomas presents three arguments against suicide, and then replies to each of the first five arguments. (St. Thomas refers to Artistotle as the Philosopher, and to Aristotle's Nichomachean Ethics *as Ethic.)*

We proceed thus to the Fifth Article:

Objection 1. It would seem lawful for a man to kill himself. For murder is a sin in so far as it is contrary to justice. But no man can do an injustice to himself, as is proved in *Ethic.* v. 11.[1] Therefore no man sins by killing himself.

Obj. 2. Further, It is lawful, for one who exercises public authority, to kill evildoers. Now he who exercises public authority is sometimes an evildoer. Therefore he may lawfully kill himself.

Obj. 3. Further, It is lawful for a man to suffer spontaneously a lesser danger that he may avoid a greater. Thus it is lawful for a man to cut off a decayed limb even from himself, that he may save his whole body. Now sometimes a man, by killing himself, avoids a greater evil, for an example an unhappy life, or the shame of sin. Therefore a man may kill himself.

Obj. 4. Further, Sampson killed himself, as related in Judges xvi, and yet he is numbered among the saints (Heb. xi). Therefore it is lawful for a man to kill himself.

Obj. 5. Further, It is related (2 Mach. xiv. 42) that a certain Razias killed himself, *choosing to die nobly rather than to fall into the hands of the wicked, and to suffer abuses unbecoming his noble birth.* Now nothing that is done nobly and bravely is unlawful. Therefore suicide is not unlawful.

On the contrary, Augustine says (*De Civ. Dei* i. 20): *Hence it follows that the words "Thou shalt not kill" refer to the killing of a man; not another man; therefore, not even thyself. For he who kills himself, kills nothing else than a man.*

I answer that, It is altogether unlawful to kill oneself, for three reasons. First, because everything naturally loves itself, the result being that everything naturally keeps itself in being, and resists corruption so far as it can. Wherefore suicide is contrary to the inclination of nature and to charity, whereby every man should love himself. Hence suicide is always a mortal sin, as being contrary to the natural law and to charity.

Secondly, because every part, as such, belongs to the whole. Now every man is part of the community, and so, as such, he belongs to the community. Hence by killing himself he injures the community, as the Philosopher declares (*Ethic* v. ii).

Thirdly, because life is God's gift to man, and is subject to His power, Who kills and makes to live. Hence whoever takes his own life sins against God, even as he who kills another's slave sins against that slave's master, and as he who usurps himself judgment of a matter not entrusted to him. For it belongs to God alone to pronounce sentence of death and life, according to Duet. xxxii. 39, *I will kill and I will make to live.*

Reply Obj. 1. Murder is a sin, not only because it is contrary to justice, but also because it is opposed to charity, which a man should

---

From *Summa Theologica,* Vol. II, (New York: Benziger Brothers, 1925) Part II, Question 64, A5.

have towards himself; in this respect suicide is a sin in relation to oneself. In relation to the community and to God, it is sinful, by reason also to its opposition to justice.

Reply Obj. 2. One who exercises public authority may lawfully put to death an evildoer, since he can pass judgment on him. But no man is judge of himself. Wherefore it is not lawful for one who exercises public authority to put himself to death for any sin whatever, although he may lawfully commit himself to the judgment of others.

Reply Obj. 3. Man is made master of himself through his **free will:** wherefore he can lawfully dispose of himself as to those matters which pertain to this life, which is ruled by man's free will. But the passage from this life to another and happier one is subject not to man's free will but to the power of God. Hence it is not lawful for a man to take his own life that he may pass to a happier life, nor that he may escape any unhappiness whatsoever to the present life, because the ultimate and most fearsome evil of this life is death, as the Philosopher states (*Ethic.* iii. 6). Therefore to bring death upon oneself in order to escape the other afflictions of this life is to adopt a greater evil in order to avoid a lesser. In like manner it is unlawful to take one's own life on account of one's having committed a sin, both because by so doing one does oneself a very great injury, by depriving oneself of the time needful for repentance, and because it is not lawful to slay an evildoer except by the sentence of the public authority. Again it is unlawful for a woman to kill herself lest she be violated, because she ought not to commit on herself the very great sin of suicide to avoid the lesser sin of another. For she commits no sin in being violated by force, provided she does not consent, since *without consent of the mind there is no stain on the body,* as the Blessed Lucy declared. Now it is evident that fornication and adultery are less grievous sins than taking a man's, especially one's own, life, since the latter is most grievous, because one injures oneself, to whom one owes the greatest love. Moreover it is most dangerous since no time is left wherein to expiate it by repentance. Again it is not lawful for anyone to take his own life for fear he should consent to sin, because *evil must not be done that good may come* (Rom. iii. 8) or that evil maybe avoided, especially if the evil be of small account and an uncertain event, for it is uncertain whether one will at some future time consent to a sin, since God is able to deliver man from sin under any temptation whatever.

Reply Obj. 4. As Augustine says (*De Civ. Dei* i. 21), *not even Samson is to be excused that he crushed himself together with his enemies under the ruins of the house, except the Holy Ghost, Who had wrought many wonders through him, had secretly commanded him to do this.* He assigns the same reason in the case of certain holy women who at the time of persecution took their own lives and who are commemorated by the Church.

Reply Obj. 5. It belongs to fortitude that a man does not shrink from being slain by another, for the sake of the good of virtue and that he may avoid sin. But that a man take his own life in order to avoid penal evils has indeed an appearance of fortitude (for which reason some . . . have killed themselves, thinking to act from fortitude), yet it is not true fortitude, but rather a weakness of soul unable to bear penal evils, as the Philosopher (*Ethic.* iii. 7) and Augustine (*De Civ. Dei* i. 22, 23) declare.

Review Questions

1. State and explain the five arguments for the lawfulness of suicide, and St. Thomas' replies.
2. What are St. Thomas' arguments against suicide?

Discussion Question

1. Does St. Thomas convince you that suicide is wrong? Why or why not?

Richard Brandt

On the Morality and Rationality of Suicide

Richard Brandt is Professor Emeritus of Philosophy at the University of Michigan. He is the author of **Ethical Theory** *(1959) and* **A Theory of the Good and the Right** *(1979).*

Brandt discusses three questions about suicide: Is it morally blameworthy? Is it objectively wrong? and Is is rational? He finds that in some cases, for example, where a person is suffering from a painful terminal illness, suicide is not blameworthy, not wrong, and not irrational.

From the point of view of contemporary philosophy, suicide raises the following distinct questions: whether a person who commits suicide (assuming that there is suicide if and only if there is intentional termination of one's own life) is morally blameworthy, reprehensible, sinful in all circumstances; whether suicide is objectively right or wrong, and in what circumstances it is right or wrong, from a moral point of view; and whether, or in which circumstances, suicide is the best or the rational thing to do from the point of view of the agent's personal welfare.

The Moral Blameworthiness of Suicide

In former times the question of whether suicide is sinful was of great interest because the answer to it was considered relevant to how the agent would spend eternity. At present the practical issue is not as great, although a normal funeral service may be denied a person judged to have committed suicide sinfully. The chief practical issue now seems to be that persons may disapprove of a decedent for having committed suicide, and his friends or relatives may wish to defend his memory against moral charges.

The question of whether an act of suicide was sinful or morally blameworthy is not apt to arise unless it is already believed that the agent morally ought not to have done it: for instance, if he really had very poor reason for doing so, and his act foreseeably had catastrophic consequences for his wife and children. But, even if a given suicide is morally wrong, it does not follow that it is morally reprehensible. For, while asserting that a given act of suicide was wrong, we may still think that the act was hardly morally blameworthy or sinful if, say, the agent was in a state of great emotional turmoil at the time. We might then say that, although what he did was wrong, his action is *excusable*, just as in the criminal law it may be decided that, although a person broke the law, he should not be punished because he was *not responsible*, that is, was temporarily insane, did what he did inadvertently, and so on.

The foregoing remarks assume that to be morally blameworthy (or sinful) on account of an act is one thing, and for the act to be wrong is another. But, if we say this, what after all does it *mean* to say that a person is morally blameworthy on account of an action? We cannot say there is agreement among philosophers on this matter, but I suggest the following account as being safe from serious objection: "*X* is morally blameworthy on account of an action *A*" may be taken to mean "*X* and *A*, and *X* would not have done *A* had not his character been in some respect below standard; and in view of this it is fitting or justified for *X* to have some disapproving attitudes including remorse toward himself, and for some other persons *Y* to have some disapproving attitudes toward *X* and to express them in behavior." Traditional thought would include God as one of the "other persons" who might have and express disapproving attitudes.

From Richard Brandt, "On the Morality and Rationality of Suicide," in *A Handbook for the Study of Suicide*, ed. Seymour Perlin.

In case the foregoing definition does not seem obviously correct, it is worthwhile pointing out that it is usually thought that an agent is not blameworthy or sinful for an action unless it is a *reflection on him;* the definition brings this fact out and makes clear why.

If someone charges that a suicide was sinful, we may now properly ask, "What defect of character did it show?" Some writers have claimed that suicide is blameworthy because it is *cowardly*, and since being cowardly is generally conceded to be a defect of character, if an act of suicide is admitted to be both objectively wrong and also cowardly, the claim to blameworthiness might be warranted in terms of the above definition. Of course, many people would hesitate to call taking one's own life a cowardly act, and there will certainly be controversy about which acts are cowardly and which are not. But at least we can see part of what has to be done to make a change of blameworthiness valid.

The most interesting question is the general one: which types of suicide in general are ones that, even if objectively wrong (in a sense to be explained below) are not sinful or blameworthy? Or, in other words, when is a suicide *morally excused* even if it is objectively wrong? We can at least identify some types that are morally excusable.

1. Suppose I *think* I am morally bound to commit suicide because I have a terminal illness and continued medical care will ruin my family financially. Suppose, however, that I am mistaken in this belief, and that suicide in such circumstances is not right. But surely I am not morally blameworthy; for I may be doing, out of a sense of duty to my family, what I would personally prefer not to do and is hard for me to do. What defect of character might my action show? Suicide from a genuine sense of duty is not blameworthy, even when the moral conviction in question is mistaken.

2. Suppose that I commit suicide when I am temporarily of unsound mind, either in the sense of the M'Naghten rule that I do not know that what I am doing is wrong, or of the Durham rule that, owing to a mental defect, I am substantially unable to do what is right. Surely, any suicide in an unsound state of mind is morally excused.

3. Suppose I commit suicide when I could not be said to be temporarily of unsound mind, but simply because I am not myself. For instance, I may be in an extremely depressed mood. Now a person may be in a very depressed mood, and commit suicide on account of being in that mood, when there is nothing the matter with his character—or, in other words, his character is not in any relevant way below standard. What are other examples of being "not myself," or emotional states that might be responsible for a person's committing suicide, and that might render the suicide excusable even if wrong? Being frightened; being distraught; being in almost any highly emotional frame of mind (anger, frustration, disappointment in love); perhaps just being terribly fatigued.

So there are at least three types of suicide which can be morally excused even if they are objectively wrong. The main point is this: Mr. *X* may commit suicide and it may be conceded that he ought not to have done so, but it is another step to show that he is sinful, or morally blameworthy, for having done so. To make out that further point, it must be shown that his act is attributable to some substandard trait of character. So, Mrs. *X* after the suicide can concede that her husband ought not to have done what he did, but she can also point out that it is no reflection on his character. The distinction, unfortunately, is often overlooked. St. Thomas Aquinas, who recognizes the distinction in other places, seems blind to it in his discussion of suicide.

The Moral Reasons for and Against Suicide

Persons who say suicide is morally wrong must be asked which of two positions they are affirming: Are they saying that *every* act of suicide is wrong, *everything considered;* or are they merely saying that there is always *some* moral obligation—doubtless of serious weight—not to commit suicide, so that very often suicide is wrong, although it is possible that there are *countervail-*

ing considerations which in particular situations make it right or even a moral duty? It is quite evident that the first position is absurd; only the second has a chance of being defensible.

In order to make clear what is wrong with the first view, we may begin with an example. Suppose an army pilot's single-seater plane goes out of control over a heavily populated area; he has the choice of staying in the plane and bringing it down where it will do little damage but at the cost of certain death for himself, and of bailing out and letting the plane fall where it will, very possibly killing a good many civilians. Suppose he chooses to do the former, and so, by our definition, commits suicide. Does anyone want to say that his action is morally wrong? Even Immanuel Kant, who opposed suicide in all circumstances, apparently would not wish to say that it is; he would, in fact, judge that this act is not one of suicide, for he says, "It is no suicide to risk one's life against one's enemies, and even to sacrifice it, in order to preserve one's duties toward oneself."[1] St. Thomas Aquinas, in his discussion of suicide, may seem to take the position that such an act would be wrong, for he says, "It is altogether unlawful to kill oneself," admitting as an exception only the case of being under special command of God. But I believe St. Thomas would, in fact, have concluded that the act is right because the basic intention of the pilot was to save the lives of civilians, and whether an act is right or wrong is a matter of basic intention.[2]

In general, we have to admit that there are things with some moral obligation to avoid which, on account of other morally relevant considerations, it is sometimes right or even morally obligatory to do. There may be some obligation to tell the truth on every occasion, but surely in many cases the consequences of telling the truth would be so dire that one is obligated to lie. The same goes for promises. There is some moral obligation to do what one has promised (with a few exceptions); but, if one can keep a trivial promise only at serious cost to another person (i.e., keep an appointment only by failing to give aid to someone injured in an accident), it is surely obligatory to break the promise.

The most that the moral critic of suicide could hold, then, is that there is *some* moral obligation not to do what one knows will cause one's death; but he surely cannot deny that circumstances exist in which there are obligations to do things which, in fact, will result in one's death. If so, then in principle it would be possible to argue, for instance, that in order to meet my obligation to my family, it might be right for me to take my own life as the only way to avoid catastrophic hospital expenses in a terminal illness. Possibly the main point that critics of suicide on moral grounds would wish to make is that it is never right to take one's own life *for reasons of one's own personal welfare,* of any kind whatsoever. Some of the arguments used to support the immorality of suicide, however, are so framed that if they were supportable at all, they would prove that suicide is *never* moral.

One well-known type of argument against suicide may be classified as *theological.* St. Augustine and others urged that the Sixth Commandment ("Thou shalt not kill.") prohibits suicide, and that we are bound to obey a divine commandment. To this reasoning one might first reply that it is arbitrary exegesis of the Sixth Commandment to assert that it was intended to prohibit suicide. The second reply is that if there is not some consideration which shows on the merits of the case that suicide is morally wrong, God had no business prohibiting it. It is true that some will object to this point, and I must refer them elsewhere for my detailed comments on the **divine-will theory of morality.**[3]

Another theological argument with wide support was accepted by John Locke, who wrote: ". . . Men being all the workmanship of one omnipotent and infinitely wise Maker; all the servants of one sovereign Master, sent into the world by His order and about His business; they are His property, whose workmanship they are made to last during His, not one another's pleasure. . . . Every one . . . is bound to preserve himself, and not to quit his state on wilfully. . . ."[4] And Kant: "We have been placed in this world under certain conditions and for specific purposes. But a suicide opposes the purpose of his Creator; he arrives in the other world as one who has deserted his post; he must be looked upon as a rebel against God. So long as we remember the truth that it is God's intention to preserve life, we are bound to regulate our activities in conformity with it. This duty is upon us until the time comes when God expressly commands us to leave this life. Human beings are sentinels on earth and may not leave their posts until relieved by another beneficent hand."[5] Unfortunately, however, even if we grant that it is the duty of human beings to do what God commands or intends them to do, more argument is required to show that God does *not* permit human beings to quit this life when their own personal welfare would be maximized by so doing. How does one draw the requisite inference about the intentions of God? The difficulties and contradictions in arguments to reach such a conclusions are discussed at length and perspicaciously by David Hume in his essay "On Suicide," and in view of the unlikelihood that readers will need to be persuaded about these, I shall merely refer those interested to that essay."[6]

A second group of arguments may be classed as arguments *from natural law*. St. Thomas says: "It is altogether unlawful to kill oneself, for three reasons. First, because everything naturally loves itself, the result being that everything naturally keeps itself in being, and resists corruptions so far as it can. Wherefore suicide is contrary to the inclination of nature, and to charity whereby every man should love himself. Hence suicide is always a mortal sin, as being contrary to the natural law and to charity."[7] Here St. Thomas ignores two obvious points. First, it is not obvious why a human being is morally bound to do what he or she has some inclination to do. (St. Thomas did not criticize chastity.) Second, while it is true that most human beings do feel a strong urge to live, the human being who commits suicide obviously feels a stronger inclination to do something else. It is natural for a human being to dislike, and to take steps to avoid, say, great pain, as it is to cling to life.

A somewhat similar argument by Immanuel Kant may seem better. In a famous passage Kant writes that the maxim of a person who commits suicide is "From self-love I make it my principle to shorten my life if its continuance threatens more evil than it promises pleasure. The only further question to ask is whether this principle of self-love can become a universal law of nature. It is then seen at once that a system of nature by whose law the very same feeling whose function is to stimulate the furtherance of life should actually destroy life would contradict itself and consequently could not subsist as a system of nature. Hence this maxim cannot possibly hold as a universal law of nature and is therefore entirely opposed to the supreme principle of all duty."[8] What Kant finds contradictory is that the motive of self-love (interest in one's own long-range welfare) should sometimes lead one to struggle to preserve one's life, but at other times to end it. But where is the contradiction? One's circumstances change, and, if the argument of the following section in this chapter is correct, one sometimes maximizes one's own long-range welfare by trying to stay alive, but at other times by bringing about one's demise.

A third group of arguments, a form of which goes back at least to Aristotle, has a more modern and convincing ring. These are arguments to show that, in one way or another, a suicide necessarily does harm to other persons, or to society at large. Aristotle says that the suicide treats the *state* unjustly.[9] Partly following Aristotle, St. Thomas says: "Every man is part of the community, and so, as such, he belongs to the community. Hence by killing himself he injures the community."[10] Blackstone held that a suicide is an offense against the king "who hath an interest in the preservation of all his subjects," perhaps following Judge Brown in 1563, who argued that suicide cost the king a subject—"he being the head has lost one of his mystical members."[11] The premise of such arguments is, as Hume pointed out, obviously mistaken in many instances. It is true that Freud would perhaps have injured society had he, instead of finishing his last book, committed suicide to escape the pain of throat cancer. But surely there have been many suicides whose demise was not a noticeable loss to society; an honest man could only say that in some instances society was better off without them.

It need not be denied that suicide is often injurious to other persons, especially the family of a suicide. Clearly it sometimes is. But, we should notice what this fact establishes. Suppose we admit, as generally would be done, that there is some obligation not to perform any action which will probably or certainly be injurious to other people, the strength of the obligation being dependent on various factors, notably the seriousness of the expected injury. Then there is *some* obligation not to commit suicide, when that act would probably or certainly be injurious to other people. But, as we have already seen, many cases of *some* obligation to do something nevertheless are *not* cases of duty to do that thing, *everything considered.* So it could sometimes be morally justified to commit suicide, even if the act will harm someone. Must a man with terminal illness undergo excruciating pain because his death will cause his wife sorrow—when she will be caused sorrow a month later anyway, when he is dead of natural causes? Moreover, to repeat, the fact that an individual has some obligation not to commit suicide when that act will probably injure other persons does not imply that, everything considered, it is wrong for him to do it, namely, that in all circumstances suicide *as such* is something there is some obligation to avoid.

Is there any sound argument, convincing to the modern mind, to establish that there is (or is not) *some moral obligation* to avoid suicide *as such,* an obligation, of course, which might be overridden by other obligations in some or many cases? (Captain Oates may have had a moral obligation not to commit suicide as such, but his obligation not to stand in the way of his comrades' getting to safety might have been so strong that, everything considered, he was justified in leaving the polar camp and allowing himself to freeze to death.)

To present all the arguments necessary to answer this question convincingly would take a great deal of space. I shall, therefore, simply state one answer to it which seems plausible to some contemporary philosophers. Suppose it could be shown that it would maximize the long-run welfare of everybody affected if people were taught that there is a moral obligation to avoid suicide—so that people would be motivated to avoid suicide just because they thought it wrong (would have anticipatory guilt feelings at the very idea), and so that other people would be inclined to disapprove of persons who commit suicide unless there were some excuse (such as those mentioned in the first section). One might ask: how could it **maximize utility** to mold the conceptual and motivational structure of persons in this way? To which the answer might be: feeling in this way might make persons who are impulsively inclined to commit suicide in a bad mood, or a fit of anger or jealousy, take more time to deliberate; hence, some suicides that have bad effects generally might be prevented. In other words, it might be a good thing in its effects for people to feel about suicide in the way they feel about breach of promise or injuring others, just as it might be a good thing for people to feel a moral obligation not to smoke, or to wear seat belts. However, it might be that negative moral feelings about suicide as such would stand in the way of action by those persons whose welfare really is best served by suicide and whose suicide is the best thing for everybody concerned.

When a Decision to Commit Suicide is Rational From the Person's Point of View

The person who is contemplating suicide is obviously making a choice between future world-courses; the world-course that includes his demise, say, an hour from now, and several possible ones that contain his demise at a later point. One cannot have precise knowledge about many features of the latter group of world-courses, but it is certain that they will all end with death some (possibly short) finite time from now.

Why do I say the choice is between *world*-courses and not just a choice between future life-courses of the prospective suicide, the one shorter than the other? The reason is that one's suicide has some impact on the world (and one's continued life has some impact on the world), and that conditions in the rest of the world will often make a difference in one's evaluation of the possibilities. One is interested in things in the world other than just oneself and one's own happiness.

The basic question a person must answer, in order to determine which world-course is best or rational for him to choose, is which he *would* choose under conditions of optimal use of information, when *all* of his desires are taken into account. It is not just a question of what we prefer *now*, with some clarification of all the possibilities being considered. Our preferences change, and the preferences of tomorrow (assuming we can know something about them) are just as legitimately taken into account in deciding what to do now as the preferences of today. Since any reason that can be given today for weighting heavily today's preference can be given tomorrow for weighting heavily tomorrow's preference, the preferences of any time-stretch have a rational claim to an equal vote. Now the importance of that fact is this: we often know quite well that our desires, aversions, and preferences may change after a short while. When a person is in a state of despair—perhaps brought about by a rejection in love or discharge from a long held position—nothing but the thing he cannot have seems desirable; everything else is turned to ashes. Yet we know quite well that the passage of time is likely to reverse all this; replacements may be found or other types of things that are available to use may begin to look attractive. So, if we were to act on the preferences of today alone, when the emotion of despair seems more than we can stand, we might find death preferable to life; but if we allow for the preferences of the weeks and years ahead, when many goals will be enjoyable and attractive, we might find life much preferable to death. So, if a choice of what is best is to be determined by what we want not only now but later (and later desires on an equal basis with the present ones)—as it should be—then what is the best or preferable world-course will often be quite different from what it would be if the choice, or what is best for one, were fixed by one's desires and preferences now.

Of course, if one commits suicide there are no future desires or aversions that may be compared with present ones and that should be allowed an equal vote in deciding what is best. In that respect the course of action that results in death is different from any other course of action we may undertake. I do not wish to suggest the rosy possibility that it is often or always reasonable to believe that next week "I shall be more interested in living than I am today, if today I take a dim view of continued existence." On the contrary, when a person is seriously ill, for instance, he may have no reason to think that the preference-order will be reversed—it may be that tomorrow he will prefer death to life more strongly.

The argument is often used that one can never be *certain* what is going to happen, and hence one is never rationally justified in doing anything as drastic as committing suicide. But we always have to live by probabilities and make our estimates as best we can. As soon as it is clear beyond reasonable doubt not only that death is now preferable to life, but also that it will be every day from now until the end, the rational thing is to act promptly.

Let us not pursue the question of whether it is rational for a person with a painful terminal illness to commit suicide; it is. However, the issue seldom arises, and few terminally ill patients do commit suicide. With such patients matters usually get worse slowly so that no particular time seems to call for action. They are often so heavily sedated that it is impossible for the mental processes of decision leading to action to occur; or else they are incapacitated in a hospital and the very physical possibility of ending their lives is not available. Let us leave this grim topic and turn to a practically more important problem: whether it is rational for persons to commit suicide for some reason other than painful terminal physical illness. Most persons who commit suicide do so, apparently, because they face a nonphysical problem that depresses them beyond their ability to bear.

Among the problems that have been regarded as good and sufficient reasons for ending life, we find (in addition to serious illness) the following: some event that has made a person feel ashamed or lose his prestige and status; reduction from affluence to poverty; the loss of a limb or of physical beauty; the loss of sexual capacity;

some event that makes it seem impossible to achieve things by which one sets store; loss of a loved one; disappointment in love; the infirmities of increasing age. It is not to be denied that such things can be serious blows to a person's prospects of happiness.

Whatever the nature of an individual's problem, there are various plain errors to be avoided—errors to which a person is especially prone when he is depressed—in deciding whether, everything considered, he prefers a world-course containing his early demise to one in which his life continues to its natural terminus. Let us forget for a moment the relevance to the decision of preferences that he may have tomorrow, and concentrate on some errors that may infect his preference as of today, and for which correction or allowance must be made.

In the first place, depression, like any severe emotional experience, tends to primitivize one's intellectual processes. It restricts the range of one's survey of the possibilities. One thing that a rational person would do is compare the world-course containing his suicide with his *best* alternative. But his best alternative is precisely a possibility he may overlook if, in a depressed mood, he thinks only of how badly off he is and cannot imagine any way of improving his situation. If a person is disappointed in love, it is possible to adopt a vigorous plan of action that carries a good chance of acquainting him with someone he likes at least as well; and if old age prevents a person from continuing the tennis game with his favorite partner, it is possible to learn some other game that provides the joys of competition without the physical demands.

Depression has another insidious influence on one's planning: it seriously affects one's judgment about probabilities. A person disappointed in love is very likely to take a dim view of himself, his prospects, and his attractiveness; he thinks that because he has been rejected by one person he will probably be rejected by anyone who looks desirable to him. In a less gloomy frame of mind he would make different estimates. Part of the reason for such gloomy probability estimates is that depression tends to repress one's memory of evidence that supports a nongloomy prediction. Thus, a rejected lover tends to forget any cases in which he has elicited enthusiastic response from ladies in relation to whom he has been the one who has done the rejecting. Thus his pessimistic self-image is based upon a highly selected, and pessimistically selected, set of data. Even when he is reminded of the data, moreover, he is apt to resist an optimistic inference.

Another kind of distortion of the look of future prospects is not a result of depression, but is quite normal. Events distant in the future feel small, just as objects distant in space look small. Their prospect does not have the effect on motivational processes that it would have if it were of an event in the immediate future. Psychologists call this the "goal-gradient" phenomenon; a rat, for instance, will run faster toward a perceived food box than a distant unseen one. In the case of a person who has suffered some misfortune, and whose situation now is an unpleasant one, this reduction of the motivational influence of events distant in time has the effect that present unpleasant states weigh far more heavily than probable future pleasant ones in any choice of world-courses.

If we are trying to determine whether we now prefer, or shall later prefer, the outcome of the world-course to that of another (and this is leaving aside the questions of the weight of the votes of preferences at a later date), we must take into account these and other infirmities of our "sensing" machinery. Since knowing that the machinery is out of order will not tell us what results it would give if it were working, the best recourse might be to refrain from making any decision in a stressful frame of mind. If decisions have to be made, one must recall past reactions, in a normal frame of mind, to outcomes like those under assessment. But many suicides seem to occur in moments of despair. What should be clear from the above is that a moment of despair, if one is seriously contemplating suicide, ought to be a moment of reassessment of one's goals and values, a reassessment which the individual must realize is very difficult to make objectively, because of the very quality of his depressed frame of mind.

A decision to commit suicide may in certain circumstances be a rational one. But a person who wants to act rationally must take into account the various possible "errors" and make appropriate rectification of his initial evaluations.

Endnotes

1. Immanuel Kant, *Lectures on Ethics* (New York: Harper Torchbook, 1963), p. 150.
2. See St. Thomas Aquinas, *Summa Theologica,* Second Part of the Second Part, Q. 64, Art. 5. In Article 7, he says: "Nothing hinders one act from having two effects, only one of which is intended, while the other is beside the intention. Now moral acts take their species according to what is intended, and not according to what is beside the intention, since this is accidental as explained above" (Q. 43, Art. 3: I–II, Q. 1, Art. 3, as 3). Mr. Norman St. John-Stevas, the most articulate contemporary defender of the Catholic view, writes as follows: "Christian thought allows certain exceptions to its general condemnation of suicide. That covered by a particular divine inspiration has already been noted. Another exception arises where suicide is the method imposed by the State for the execution of a just death penalty. A third exception is *altruistic* suicide, of which the best known example is Captain Oates. Such suicides are justified by involving the principles of double effect. The act from which death results must be good or at least morally indifferent; some other good effect must result: The death must not be directly intended or the real means to the good effect: and a grave reason must exist for adopting the course of action" [*Life, Death and the Law* (Bloomington, Ind.: Indiana University Press, 1961), pp. 250–51]. Presumably the Catholic doctrine is intended to allow suicide when this is required for meeting strong moral obligations; whether it can do so consistently depends partly on the interpretation given to "real means to the good effect." Readers interested in pursuing further the Catholic doctrine of double effect and its implications for our problem should read Philippa Foot, "The Problem of Abortion and the Doctrine of Double Effect," *The Oxford Review,* 5 (Trinity 1967), 5–15.
3. R. B. Brandt, *Ethical Theory* (Englewood Cliffs, N.J.: Prentice-Hall, Inc., 1959), pp. 61–82.
4. John Locke, *The Second Treatise on Civil Government,* Chap. 2.
5. Kant, *Lectures on Ethics,* p. 154.
6. This essay appears in collections of Hume's works.
7. For an argument similar to Kant's, see also St. Thomas Aquinas, *Summa Theologica,* II, II, Q. 64, Art. 5.
8. Immanuel Kant, *The Fundamental Principles of the Metaphysic of Morals,* trans. H. J. Paton (London: The Hutchinson Group, 1948), Chap. 2.
9. Aristotle, *Nicomachaean Ethics,* Bk. 5, Chap. 10, p. 1138a.
10. St. Thomas Aquinas, *Summa Theologica,* II, II, Q. 64, Art. 5.
11. Sir William Blackstone, *Commentaries,* 4:189, Brown in *Hales* v. *Petit.* I Plow. 253, 75 E.R. 387 (C.B. 1563). Both cited by Norman St. John-Stevas, *Life, Death and the Law,* p. 235.

Review Questions

1. What reasons does Brandt give for saying that suicide is not morally blameworthy?
2. When is suicide permissible according to Brandt?
3. How does he reply to theological arguments, the argument from natural law, and the arguments claiming that suicide necessarily harms others?
4. When is suicide rational in Brandt's view? When is it irrational?

Discussion Questions

1. Do you agree with Brandt that it is rational for a person with a painful terminal illness to commit suicide? Why or why not?
2. Is it morally right for a person to commit suicide to save the lives of others? If so, is this morally required, that is, a duty?

J. Gay-Williams

The Wrongfulness of Euthanasia

J. Gay-Williams has requested that no biographical information be provided.

Gay-Williams defines "euthanasia" as intentionally taking the life of a presumably hopeless person. Suicide can count as euthanasia, but not "passive euthanasia" because the latter does not involve intentional killing. Three main arguments are presented to show that euthanasia is wrong: the argument from nature, the argument from self-interest, and the argument from practical effects.

My impression is that euthanasia—the idea, if not the practice—is slowly gaining acceptance within our society. Cynics might attribute this to an increasing tendency to devalue human life, but I do not believe this is the major factor. The acceptance is much more likely to be the result of unthinking sympathy and benevolence. Well-publicized, tragic stories like that of Karen Quinlan elicit from us deep feelings of compassion. We think to ourselves, "She and her family would be better off if she were dead." It is an easy step from this very human response to the view that if someone (and others) would be better off dead, then it must be all right to kill that person.[1] Although I respect the compassion that leads to this conclusion, I believe the conclusion is wrong. I want to show that euthanasia is wrong. It is inherently wrong, but it is also wrong judged from the standpoints of self-interest and of practical effects.

Before presenting my arguments to support this claim, it would be well to define "euthanasia." An essential aspect of euthanasia is that it involves taking a human life, either one's own or that of another. Also, the person whose life is taken must be someone who is believed to be suffering from some disease or injury from which recovery cannot reasonably be expected. Finally, the action must be deliberate and intentional. Thus, euthanasia is intentionally taking the life of a presumably hopeless person. Whether the life is one's own or that of another, the taking of it is still euthanasia.

It is important to be clear about the deliberate and intentional aspect of the killing. If a hopeless person is given an injection of the wrong drug by mistake and this causes his death, this is wrongful killing but not euthanasia. The killing cannot be the result of accident. Furthermore, if the person is given an injection of a drug that is believed to be necessary to treat his disease or better his condition and the person dies as a result, then this is neither wrongful killing nor euthanasia. The intention was to make the patient well, not kill him. Similarly, when a patient's condition is such that it is not reasonable to hope that any medical procedures or treatments will save his life, a failure to implement the procedures or treatments is not euthanasia. If the person dies, this will be as a result of his injuries or disease and not because of his failure to receive treatment.

The failure to continue treatment after it has been realized that the patient has little chance of benefiting from it has been characterized by some as "passive euthanasia." This phrase is misleading and mistaken.[2] In such cases, the person involved is not killed (the first essential aspect of euthanasia), nor is the death of the person intended by the withholding of additional treatment (the third essential aspect of euthanasia). The aim may be to spare the person additional and unjustifiable pain, to save him from the indignities of hopeless manipulations, and to avoid increasing the financial and emotional burden on his family. When I buy a pencil it is so that I can use it to write, not to contribute to an increase in the gross national product. This may be the unintended consequence of my action, but it is not the aim of my action. So it is with failing to continue the treatment of a dying person. I intend his death no more than I intend to reduce the GNP by not using medical supplies. His is an unintended dying, and so-called "passive euthanasia" is not euthanasia at all.

The Argument from Nature

Every human being has a natural inclination to continue living. Our reflexes and responses fit us to fight attackers, flee wild animals, and dodge out of the way of trucks. In our daily lives we exercise the caution and care necessary to protect ourselves. Our bodies are similarly structured for survival right down to the molecular level. When we are cut, our capillaries seal shut, our blood clots, and fibrogen is produced to start the process of healing the wound. When we are invaded by bacteria, antibodies are produced to fight against the alien organisms, and their remains are swept out of the body by special cells designed for clean-up work.

Euthanasia does violence to this natural goal of survival. It is literally acting against nature because all the processes of nature are bent towards the end of bodily survival. Euthanasia defeats these subtle mechanisms in a way that, in a particular case, disease and injury might not.

It is possible, but not necessary, to make an appeal to revealed religion in this connection.[3] Man as trustee of his body acts against God, its rightful possessor, when he takes his own life. He also violated the commandment to hold life sacred and never to take it without just and compelling cause. But since this appeal will persuade only those who are prepared to accept that religion has access to revealed truths, I shall not employ this line of argument.

It is enough, I believe, to recognize that the organization of the human body and our patterns of behavioral responses make the continuation of life a natural goal. By reason alone, then, we can recognize that euthanasia sets us against our own nature.[4] Furthermore, in doing so, euthanasia does violence to our dignity. Our dignity comes from seeking our ends. When one of our goals is survival, and actions are taken that eliminate that goal, then our natural dignity suffers. Unlike animals, we are conscious through reason of our nature and our ends. Euthanasia involves acting as if this dual nature—inclination towards survival and awareness of this as an end—did not exist. Thus, euthanasia denies our basic human character and requires that we regard ourselves or others as something less than fully human.

The Argument From Self-Interest

The above arguments are, I believe, sufficient to show that euthanasia is inherently wrong. But there are reasons for considering it wrong when judged by standards other than reason. Because death is final and irreversible, euthanasia contains within it the possibility that we will work against our own interest if we practice it or allow it to be practiced on us.

Contemporary medicine has high standards of excellence and a proven record of accomplishment, but it does not possess perfect and complete knowledge. A mistaken diagnosis is possible, and so is a mistaken prognosis. Consequently, we may believe that we are dying of a disease when, as a matter of fact, we may not be. We may think that we have no hope of recovery when, as a matter of fact, our chances are quite good. In such circumstances, if euthanasia were permitted, we would die needlessly. Death is final and the chance of error too great to approve the practice of euthanasia.

Also, there is always the possibility that an experimental procedure or a hitherto untried technique will pull us through. We should at least keep this option open, but euthanasia closes it off. Furthermore, spontaneous remission does occur in many cases. For no apparent reason, a patient simply recovers when those all around him, including his physicians, expected him to die. Euthanasia would just guarantee their expectations and leave no room for the "miraculous" recoveries that frequently occur.

Finally, knowing that we can take our life at any time (or ask another to take it) might well incline us to give up too easily. The will to live is strong in all of us, but it can be weakened by pain and suffering and feelings of hopelessness. If during a bad time we allow ourselves to be killed, we never have a chance to reconsider. Recovery from a serious illness requires that we fight for it, and anything that weakens our determination by suggesting that there is an easy way out is ultimately against our own interest. Also, we may be inclined towards euthanasia because of our concern for others. If we see our sickness and suffering as an emotional and financial burden on our family, we may feel that to leave our life is to make their lives easier.[5] The very presence of the possibility of euthanasia may keep us from surviving when we might.

The Argument From Practical Effects

Doctors and nurses are, for the most part, totally committed to saving lives. A life lost is, for them, almost a personal failure, an insult to their skills and knowledge. Euthanasia as a practice might well alter this. It could have a corrupting influence so that in any case that is severe doctors and nurses might not try hard enough to save the patient. They might decide that the patient would simply be "better off dead" and take the steps necessary to make that come about. This attitude could then carry over to their dealings with patients less seriously ill. The result would be an overall decline in the quality of medical care.

Finally, euthanasia as a policy is a slippery slope. A person apparently hopelessly ill may be allowed to take his own life. Then he may be permitted to deputize others to do it for him should he no longer be able to act. The judgment of others then becomes the ruling factor. Already at this point euthanasia is not personal and voluntary, for others are acting "on behalf of" the patient as they see fit. This may well incline them to act on behalf of other patients who have not authorized them to exercise their judgment. It is only a short step, then, from voluntary euthanasia (self-inflicted or authorized), to directed euthanasia administered to a patient who has given no authorization, to involuntary euthanasia conducted as part of a social policy.[6] Recently many psychiatrists and sociologists have argued that we define as "mental illness" those forms of behavior that we disapprove of.[7] This gives us license then to lock up those who display the behavior. The category of the "hopelessly ill" provides the possibility of even worse abuse. Embedded in a social policy, it would give society or its representatives the authority to eliminate all those who might be considered too "ill" to function normally any longer. The dangers of euthanasia are too great to all to run the risk of approving it in any form. The first slippery step may well lead to a serious and harmful fall.

I hope that I have succeeded in showing why the benevolence that inclines us to give approval of euthanasia is misplaced. Euthanasia is inherently wrong because it violates the nature and dignity of human beings. But even those who are not convinced by this must be persuaded that the potential personal and social dangers inherent in euthanasia are sufficient to forbid our approving it either as a personal practice or as a public policy.

Suffering is surely a terrible thing, and we have a clear duty to comfort those in need and to ease their suffering when we can. But suffering is also a natural part of life with values for the individual and for others that we should not overlook. We may legitimately seek for others and for ourselves an easeful death, as Arthur Dyck has pointed out.[8] Euthanasia, however, is not just an easeful death. It is a wrongful death. Euthanasia is not just dying. It is killing.

Endnotes

1. For a sophisticated defense of this position see Philippa Foot, "Euthanasia," *Philosophy and Public Affairs* 6 (1977): 85–112. Foot does not endorse the radical conclusion that euthanasia, voluntary and involuntary, is always right.
2. James Rachels rejects the distinction between active and passive euthanasia as morally irrelevant in his "Active and Passive Euthanasia," *New England Journal of Medicine*, 292: 78–80. But see the criticism by Foot, pp. 100–103.
3. For a defense of this view see J. V. Sullivan, "The Immorality of Euthanasia," in *Beneficent Euthanasia*, ed. Marvin Kohl (Buffalo, NY: Prometheus Books, 1975), pp. 34–44.
4. This point is made by Ray V. McIntyre in "Voluntary Euthanasia: The Ultimate Perversion," *Medical Counterpoint* 2: 26–29.
5. See McIntyre, p. 28.
6. See Sullivan, "Immorality of Euthanasia," pp. 34–44, for a fuller argument in support of this view.
7. See, for example, Thomas S. Szasz, *The Myth of Mental Illness*, rev. ed. (New York: Harper & Row, 1974).
8. Arthur Dyck, "Beneficent Euthanasia and Benemortasia," Kohl, op. cit., pp. 117–129.

Review Questions

1. How does Gay-Williams define euthanasia?
2. Why does he object to the phrase passive euthanasia?
3. Explain the three arguments he uses to show that euthanasia is wrong.

Discussion Questions

1. Is Gay-Williams' definition of euthanasia acceptable? Defend your view.
2. Are his arguments sound or not?

James Rachels

Active and Passive Euthanasia

For biographical information on Rachels, see his reading in Chapter 1.

Here Rachels attacks the distinction between active and passive euthanasia, and the doctrine apparently accepted by the American Medical Association that taking direct action to kill a patient (active euthanasia) is wrong, but withholding treatment and allowing a patient to die (passive euthanasia) is allowable. Rachels makes three criticisms of this doctrine. First, it results in unnecessary suffering for patients who die slowly and painfully rather than quickly and painlessly. Second, the doctrine leads to moral decisions based on irrelevant considerations. Third, the distinction between killing and letting die assumed by the doctrine is of no moral significance.

The distinction between active and passive euthanasia is thought to be crucial for medical ethics. The idea is that it is permissible, at least in some cases, to withhold treatment and allow a patient to die, but it is never permissible to take any direct action designed to kill the patient. This doctrine seems to be accepted by most doctors, and it is endorsed in a statement adopted by the House of Delegates of the American Medical Association on December 4, 1973:

> The intentional termination of the life of one human being by another—mercy killing—is contrary to that for which the medical profession stands and is contrary to the policy of the American Medical Association. The cessation of the employment of extraordinary means to prolong the life of the body when there is irrefutable evidence that biological death is imminent is the decision of the patient and/or his immediate family. The advice and judgment of the physician should be freely available to the patient and/or his immediate family.

However, a strong case can be made against this doctrine. In what follows I will set out some of the relevant arguments, and urge doctors to reconsider their views on this matter.

To begin with a familiar type of situation, a patient who is dying of incurable cancer of the throat is in terrible pain, which can no longer be satisfactorily alleviated. He is certain to die within a few days, even if present treatment is continued, but he does not want to go on living for those days since the pain is unbearable. So he asks the doctor for an end to it, and his family joins in the request.

Suppose the doctor agrees to withhold treatment, as the conventional doctrine says he may. The justification for his doing so is that the patient is in terrible agony, and since he is going to die anyway, it would be wrong to prolong his suffering needlessly. But now notice this. If one simply withholds treatment, it may take the patient longer to die, and so he may suffer more than he would if more direct action were taken and a lethal injection given. This fact provides strong reason for thinking that, once the initial decision not to prolong his agony has been made, active euthanasia is actually preferable to passive euthanasia, rather than the reverse. To say otherwise is to endorse the option that leads to more suffering rather than less, and is contrary to the humanitarian impulse that prompts the decision not to prolong his life in the first place.

Part of my point is that the process of being "allowed to die" can be relatively slow and painful, whereas being given a lethal injection is relatively quick and painless. Let me give a different sort of example. In the United States about one in 600 babies is born with Down's syndrome. Most of these babies are otherwise healthy—that is, with only the usual pediatric

From James Rachels, "Active and Passive Euthanasia," *The New England Journal of Medicine*, Vol. 292, No. 2, 9 January 1975, pp. 78–80.

care, they will proceed to an otherwise normal infancy. Some, however, are born with congenital defects such as intestinal obstructions that require operations if they are to live. Sometimes, the parents and the doctor will decide not to operate, and let the infant die. Anthony Shaw describes what happens then:

> . . . When surgery is denied [the doctor] must try to keep the infant from suffering while natural forces sap the baby's life away. As a surgeon whose natural inclination is to use the scalpel to fight off death, standing by and watching a salvageable baby die is the most emotionally exhausting experience I know. It is easy at a conference, in a theoretical discussion, to decide that such infants should be allowed to die. It is altogether different to stand by in the nursery and watch as dehydration and infection wither a tiny being over hours and days. This is a terrible ordeal for me and the hospital staff—much more so than for the parents who never set foot in the nursery.[1]

I can understand why some people are opposed to all euthanasia, and insist that such infants must be allowed to live. I think I can also understand why other people favor destroying these babies quickly and painlessly. But why should anyone favor letting "dehydration and infection wither a tiny being over hours and days?" The doctrine that says that a baby may be allowed to dehydrate and wither, but may not be given an injection that would end its life without suffering, seems so patently cruel as to require no further refutation. The strong language is not intended to offend, but only to put the point in the clearest possible way.

My second argument is that the conventional doctrine leads to decisions concerning life and death made on irrelevant grounds.

Consider again the case of the infants with Down's syndrome who need operations for congenital defects unrelated to the syndrome to live. Sometimes, there is no operation, and the baby dies, but when there is no such defect, the baby lives on. Now, an operation such as that to remove an intestinal obstruction is not prohibitively difficult. The reason why such operations are not performed in these cases is, clearly, that the child has Down's syndrome and the parents and doctor judge that because of that fact it is better for the child to die.

But notice that this situation is absurd, no matter what view one takes of the lives and potentials of such babies. If the life of such an infant is worth preserving, what does it matter if it needs a simple operation? Or, if one thinks it better that such a baby should not live on, what difference does it make that it happens to have an unobstructed intestinal tract? In either case, the matter of life and death is being decided on irrelevant grounds. It is the Down's syndrome, and not the intestines, that is the issue. The matter should be decided, if at all, on that basis, and not be allowed to depend on the essentially irrelevant question of whether the intestinal tract is blocked.

What makes this situation possible, of course, is the idea that when there is an intestinal blockage, one can "let the baby die," but when there is no such defect there is nothing that can be done, for one must not "kill" it. The fact that this idea leads to such results as deciding life or death on irrelevant grounds is another good reason why the doctrine should be rejected.

One reason why so many people think that there is an important moral difference between active and passive euthanasia is that they think killing someone is morally worse than letting someone die. But is it? Is killing, in itself, worse than letting die? To investigate this issue, two cases may be considered that are exactly alike except that one involves killing whereas the other involves letting someone die. Then, it can be asked whether this difference makes any difference to the moral assessments. It is important that the cases be exactly alike, except for this one difference, since otherwise one cannot be confident that it is this difference and not some other that accounts for any variation in the assessments of the two cases. So, let us consider this pair of cases:

In the first, Smith stands to gain a large inheritance if anything should happen to his six-year-old cousin. One evening while the child is taking his bath, Smith sneaks into the bathroom and drowns the child, and then arranges things so that it will look like an accident.

In the second, Jones also stands to gain if anything should happen to his six-year-old cousin. Like Smith, Jones sneaks in planning to drown the child in his bath. However, just as he enters the bathroom Jones sees the child slip and hit his head, and fall face down in the water. Jones is delighted; he stands by, ready to push the child's head back under if it is necessary, but it is not necessary. With only a little thrashing about, the child drowns all by himself, "accidentally," as Jones watches and does nothing.

Now Smith killed the child, whereas Jones "merely" let the child die. That is the only difference between them. Did either man behave better, from a moral point of view? If the difference between killing and letting die were in itself a morally important matter, one should say that Jones's behavior was less reprehensible than Smith's. But does one really want to say that? I think not. In the first place, both men acted from the same motive, personal gain, and both had exactly the same end in view when they acted. It may be inferred from Smith's conduct that he is a bad man, although that judgment may be withdrawn or modified if certain further facts are learned about him—for example, that he is mentally deranged. But would not the very same thing be inferred about Jones from his conduct? And would not the same further considerations also be relevant to any modification of this judgment? Moreover, suppose Jones pleaded, in his own defense, "After all, I didn't do anything except just stand there and watch the child drown. I didn't kill him; I only let him die." Again, if letting die were in itself less bad than killing, this defense should have at least some weight. But it does not. Such a "defense" can only be regarded as a grotesque perversion of moral reasoning. Morally speaking, it is no defense at all.

Now, it may be pointed out, quite properly, that the cases of euthanasia with which doctors are concerned are not like this at all. They do not involve personal gain or the destruction of normal healthy children. Doctors are concerned only with cases in which the patient's life is of no further use to him, or in which the patient's life has become or will soon become a terrible burden. However, the point is the same in these cases: the bare difference between killing and letting die does not, in itself, make a moral difference. If a doctor lets a patient die, for humane reasons, he is in the same moral position as if he had given the patient a lethal injection for humane reasons. If his decision was wrong—if, for example, the patient's illness was in fact curable—the decision would be equally regrettable no matter which method was used to carry it out. And if the doctor's decision was the right one, the method used is not in itself important.

The AMA policy statement isolates the crucial issue very well; the crucial issue is "the intentional termination of the life of one human being by another." But after identifying this issue, and forbidding "mercy killing," the statement goes on to deny that the cessation of treatment is the intentional termination of a life. This is where the mistake comes in, for what is the cessation of treatment, in these circumstances, if it is not "the intentional termination of the life of one human being by another?" Of course it is exactly that, and if it were not, there would be no point to it.

Many people will find this judgment hard to accept. One reason, I think, is that it is very easy to conflate the question of whether killing is, in itself, worse than letting die, with the very different question of whether most actual cases of killing are more reprehensible than most actual cases of letting die. Most actual cases of killing are clearly terrible (think, for example, of all the murders reported in the newspapers), and one hears of such cases every day. On the other hand, one hardly ever hears of a case of letting die, except for the actions of doctors who are motivated by humanitarian reasons. So one learns to think of killing in a much worse light than of letting die. But this does not mean that there is something about killing that makes it in itself worse than letting die, for it is not the bare difference between killing and letting die that makes the difference in these cases. Rather, the other factors—the murderer's motive of personal gain, for example, contrasted with the doctor's humanitarian motivation—account for different reactions to the different cases.

I have argued that killing is not in itself any worse than letting die; if my contention is right, it follows that active euthanasia is not any worse than passive euthanasia. What arguments can be given on the other side? The most common, I believe, is the following:

> The important difference between active and passive euthanasia is that, in passive euthanasia, the doctor does not do anything to bring about the patient's death. The doctor does nothing, and the patient dies of whatever ills already afflict him. In active euthanasia, however, the doctor does something to bring about the patient's death: he kills him. The doctor who gives the patient with cancer a lethal injection has himself caused his patient's death; whereas if he merely ceases treatment, the cancer is the cause of the death.

A number of points need to be made here. The first is that it is not exactly correct to say that in passive euthanasia the doctor does nothing, for he does do one thing that is very important: he lets the patient die. "Letting someone die" is certainly different, in some respects, from other types of action—mainly in that it is a kind of action that one may perform by way of not performing certain other actions. For example, one may let a patient die by way of not giving medication, just as one may insult someone by way of not shaking his hand. But for any purpose of moral assessment, it is a type of action nonetheless. The decision to let a patient die is subject to moral appraisal in the same way that a decision to kill him would be subject to moral appraisal: it may be assessed as wise or unwise, compassionate or sadistic, right or wrong. If a doctor deliberately let a patient die who was suffering from a routinely curable illness, the doctor would certainly be to blame for what he had done, just as he would be to blame if he had needlessly killed the patient. Charges against him would then be appropriate. If so, it would be no defense at all for him to insist that he didn't "do anything." He would have done something very serious indeed, for he let his patient die.

Fixing the cause of death may be very important from a legal point of view, for it may determine whether criminal charges are brought against the doctor. But I do not think that this notion can be used to show a moral difference between active and passive euthanasia. The reason why it is considered bad to be the cause of someone's death is that death is regarded as a great evil—and so it is. However, if it has been decided that euthanasia—even passive euthanasia—is desirable in a given case, it has also been decided that in this instance death is no greater an evil than the patient's continued existence. And if this is true, the usual reason for not wanting to be the cause of someone's death simply does not apply.

Finally, doctors may think that all of this is only of academic interest—the sort of thing that philosophers may worry about but that has no practical bearing on their own work. After all, doctors must be concerned about the legal consequences of what they do, and active euthanasia is clearly forbidden by the law. But even so, doctors should also be concerned with the fact that the law is forcing upon them a moral doctrine that may well be indefensible, and has a considerable effect on their practices. Of course, most doctors are not now in the position of being coerced in this matter, for they do not regard themselves as merely going along with what the law requires. Rather in statements such as the A.M.A. policy statement that I have quoted, they are endorsing this doctrine as a central point of medical ethics. In that statement, active euthanasia is condemned not merely as illegal but as "contrary to that for which the medical profession stands," whereas passive euthanasia is approved. However, the preceding considerations suggest that there is really no moral difference between the two, considered in themselves (there may be important moral differences in some case in their *consequences,* but, as I pointed out, these differences may make active euthanasia, and not passive euthanasia, the morally preferable option). So, whereas doctors may have to discriminate between active and passive euthanasia to satisfy the law, they should not do any more than that. In particular, they should not give the distinction any added authority and weight by writing it into official statements of medical ethics.

Endnote

1. A. Shaw, "Doctor, Do We Have a Choice?" *The New York Times Magazine,* January 30, 1972, p. 54.

Review Questions

1. According to Rachels, what is the distinction between active and passive euthanasia?

2. Why does Rachels think that being allowed to die is worse in some cases than a lethal injection?
3. What is Rachels' second argument against the conventional doctrine?
4. According to Rachels, why isn't killing worse than letting die?

Discussion Questions

1. The AMA statement quoted by Rachels does not use the terminology of active and passive euthanasia. Furthermore, so-called passive euthanasia could be the intentional termination of life rejected by the AMA. Does the AMA really accept this distinction? Why or why not?
2. Is the distinction between killing and letting die morally relevant? What do you think?
3. Should the law be changed to allow active euthanasia or not? Defend your view.

Tom L. Beauchamp

A Reply to Rachels on Active and Passive Euthanasia

Tom L. Beauchamp is a member of the philosophy department at Georgetown University. He is the author of Philosophical Ethics *(1982) and coauthor of* Medical Ethics *and* Principles of Biomedical Ethics *(1989).*

Beauchamp agrees with Rachels that the active/passive distinction is sometimes morally insignificant. But it does not follow, he argues, that the distinction is always morally irrelevant in our moral thinking about euthanasia. He presents utilitarian arguments for saying that the best consequences for society might result (he is cautious about predicting consequences) if passive euthanasia is allowed and active euthanasia is not. The resulting ethical position is in substantial but not total agreement with the AMA position, which does seem to endorse a limited form of passive euthanasia.

James Rachels has recently argued that the distinction between active and passive euthanasia is neither appropriately used by the American Medical Association nor generally useful for the resolution of moral problems of euthanasia.[1] Indeed he believes this distinction—which he equates with the killing/letting die distinction—does not in itself have any moral importance. The chief object of his attack is the following statement adopted by the House of Delegates of the American Medical Association in 1973:

> The intentional termination of the life of one human being by another—mercy killing—is contrary to that for which the medical profession stands and is contrary to the policy of the American Medical Association. The cessation of the employment of extraordinary means to prolong the life of the body when there is irrefutable evidence that biological death is imminent is the decision of the patient and/or his immediate family. The advice and judgment of the physician should be freely available to the patient and/or his immediate family (241).

Rachels constructs a powerful and interesting set of arguments against this statement. In this paper I attempt the following: (1) to challenge his views on the grounds that he does not appreciate the moral reasons which give weight to the active/passive distinction; and (2) to provide a constructive account of the moral relevance of the active/passive distinction; and (3) to offer reasons showing that Rachels may nonetheless be correct in urging that we *ought* to abandon

This paper is a heavily revised version of an article by the same title first published in T. Mappes and J. Zembaty, eds. *Social Ethics* (N.Y.: McGraw-Hill, 1976).

the active/passive distinction for purposes of moral reasoning.

I would concede that the active/passive distinction is *sometimes* morally irrelevant. Of this Rachels convinces me. But it does not follow that it is *always* morally irrelevant. What we need, then, is a case where the distinction is a morally relevant one and an explanation why it is so. Rachels himself uses the method of examining two cases which are exactly alike except that "one involves killing whereas the other involves letting die" (243). We may profitably begin by comparing the kinds of cases governed by the AMA's doctrine with the kinds of cases adduced by Rachels in order to assess the adequacy and fairness of his cases.

The second paragraph of the AMA statement is confined to a narrowly restricted range of passive euthanasia cases, viz., those (a) where the patients are on extraordinary means, (b) where irrefutable evidence of imminent death is available, and (c) where patient or family consent is available. Rachels' two cases involve conditions notably different from these:

> In the first, Smith stands to gain a large inheritance if anything should happen to his six-year-old cousin. One evening while the child is taking his bath, Smith sneaks into the bathroom and drowns the child, and then arranges things so that it will look like an accident.
>
> In the second, Jones also stands to gain if anything should happen to his six-year-old cousin. Like Smith, Jones sneaks in planning to drown the child in his bath. However, just as he enters the bathroom Jones sees the child slip and hit his head, and fall face down in the water. Jones is delighted; he stands by, ready to push the child's head back under if it is necessary, but it is not necessary. With only a little thrashing about, the child drowns all by himself, "accidentally," as Jones watches and does nothing.
> Now Smith killed the child, whereas Jones "merely" let the child die. That is the only difference between them (243).

Rachels says there is no moral difference between the cases in terms of our moral assessments of Smith and Jones' behavior. This assessment seems fair enough, but what can Rachels' cases be said to prove, as they are so markedly disanalogous to the sorts of cases envisioned by the AMA proposal? Rachels concedes important disanalogies, but thinks them irrelevant:

> The point is the same in these cases: the bare difference between killing and letting die does not, in itself, make a moral difference. If a doctor lets a patient die, for humane reasons, he is in the same moral position as if he had given the patient a lethal injection for humane reasons (244).

Three observations are immediately in order. First, Rachels seems to infer that from such cases we can conclude that the distinction between killing and letting die is *always* morally irrelevant. This conclusion is fallaciously derived. What the argument in fact shows, being an analogical argument, is only that in all *relevantly similar* cases the distinction does not in itself make a moral difference. Since Rachels concedes that other cases are disanalogous, he seems thereby to concede that his argument is as weak as the analogy itself. Second, Rachels' cases involve two *unjustified* actions, one of killing and the other of letting die. The AMA statement distinguishes one set of cases of unjustified killing and another of *justified* cases of allowing to die. Nowhere is it claimed by the AMA that what makes the difference in these cases is the active/passive distinction itself. It is only implied that one set of cases, the justified set, *involves* (passive) letting die while the unjustified set *involves* (active) killing. While it is said that justified euthanasia cases are passive ones and unjustified ones active, it is not said either that what makes some acts justified is the fact of their being passive or that what makes others unjustified is the fact of their being active. This fact will prove to be of vital importance.

The third point is that in both of Rachels' cases the respective moral agents—Smith and Jones—are morally responsible for the death of the child and are morally blameworthy—even though Jones is presumably not causally responsible. In the first case death is caused by the agent, while in the second it is not; yet the second agent is no less morally responsible.

While the law might find only the first homicidal, morality condemns the motives in each case as equally wrong, and it holds that the duty to save life in such cases is as compelling as the duty not to take life. I suggest that it is largely because of this equal degree of moral responsibility that there is no morally relevant difference in Rachels' cases. In the cases envisioned by the AMA, however, an agent is held to be responsible for taking life by actively killing but is not held to be morally required to preserve life, and so not responsible for death, when removing the patient from extraordinary means (under conditions a–c above). I shall elaborate this latter point momentarily. My only conclusion thus far is the negative one that Rachels' arguments rest on weak foundations. His cases are not relevantly similar to euthanasia cases and do not support his apparent conclusion that the active/passive distinction is *always* morally irrelevant.

I wish first to consider an argument that I believe has powerful intuitive appeal and probably is widely accepted as stating the main reason for rejecting Rachels' views. I will maintain that this argument fails, and so leaves Rachels' contentions untouched.

I begin with an actual case, the celebrated Quinlan case.[2] Karen Quinlan was in a coma, and was on a mechanical respirator which artificially sustained her vital processes and which her parents wished to cease. At least some physicians believed there was irrefutable evidence that biological death was imminent and the coma irreversible. This case, under this description, closely conforms to the passive cases envisioned by the AMA. During an interview the father, Mr. Quinlan, asserted that he did not wish to kill his daughter, but only to remove her from the machines in order to see whether she would live or would die a natural death.[3] Suppose he had said—to envision now a second and hypothetical, but parallel case—that he wished only to see her die painlessly and therefore wished that the doctor could induce death by an overdose of morphine. Most of us would think the second act, which involves active killing, morally unjustified in these circumstances, while many of us would think the first act morally justified. (This is not the place to consider whether in fact it is justified, and if so under what conditions.) What accounts for the apparent morally relevant difference?

I have considered these two cases together in order to follow Rachels' method of entering parallel cases where the only difference is that the one case involves killing and the other letting die. However, there is a further difference, which crops up in the euthanasia context. The difference rests in our judgments of medical fallibility and moral responsibility. Mr. Quinlan seems to think that, after all, the doctors might be wrong. There is a remote possibility that she might live without the aid of a machine. But whether or not the medical prediction of death turns out to be accurate, if she dies then no one is morally responsible for directly bringing about or causing her death, as they would be if they caused her death by killing her. Rachels finds explanations which appeal to causal conditions unsatisfactory; but perhaps this is only because he fails to see the nature of the causal link. To bring about her death is by that act to preempt the possibility of life. To "allow her to die" by removing artificial equipment is to allow for the possibility of wrong diagnosis or incorrect prediction and hence to absolve oneself of moral responsibility for the taking of life under false assumptions. There may, of course, be utterly no empirical possibility of recovery in some cases since recovery would violate a law of nature. However, judgments of empirical impossibility in medicine are notoriously problematic—the reason for emphasizing medical fallibility. And in all the hard cases we do not *know* that recovery is empirically impossible, even if good *evidence* is available.

The above reason for invoking the active/passive distinction can now be generalized: Active termination of life removes all possibility of life for the patient, while passively ceasing extraordinary means may not. This is not trivial since patients have survived in several celebrated cases where, in knowledgeable physicians' judgments, there was "irrefutable" evidence that death was imminent.[4]

One may, of course, be entirely responsible and culpable for another's death either by killing him or by letting him die. In such cases, of which Rachels' are examples, there is no morally significant difference between killing and letting die precisely because whatever one does, omits, or refrains from doing does not absolve one of responsibility. Either active or passive involvement renders one responsible for the death of another, and both involvements are equally wrong for the same principled moral reason: it is (prima facie) morally wrong to bring about the death of an innocent person capable of living whenever the causal intervention or negligence is intentional. (I use causal terms here because causal involvement need not be active, as when by one's negligence one is nonetheless causally responsible.) But not all cases of killing and letting die fall under this same moral principle. One is sometimes culpable for killing, because morally responsible as the agent for death, as when one pulls the plug on a respirator sustaining a recovering patient (a murder). But one is sometimes not culpable for letting die because not morally responsible as agent, as when one pulls the plug on a respirator sustaining an irreversibly comatose and unrecoverable patient (a routine procedure, where one is *merely* causally responsible).[5] Different degrees and means of involvement assess different degrees of responsibility, and our assessments of culpability can become intricately complex. The only point which now concerns us, however, is that because different moral principles may govern very similar circumstances, we are sometimes morally culpable for killing but not for letting die. And to many people it will seem that in passive cases we are not morally responsible for causing death, though we are responsible in active cases.

This argument is powerfully attractive. Although I was once inclined to accept it in virtually the identical form just developed,[6] I now think that, despite its intuitive appeal, it cannot be correct. It is true that different degrees and means of involvement entail different degrees of responsibility, but it does not follow that we are *not* responsible and therefore are absolved of possible culpability in *any* case of intentionally allowing to die. We are responsible and *perhaps* culpable in either active or passive cases. Here Rachels' argument is entirely to the point: It is not primarily a question of greater or lesser responsibility by an active or a passive means that should determine culpability. Rather, the question of culpability is decided by the moral *justification* for choosing either a passive or an active means. What the argument in the previous paragraph overlooks is that one might be unjustified in using an active means or unjustified in using a passive means, and hence be culpable in the use of either; yet one might be justified in using an active means or justified in using a passive means, and hence not be culpable in using either. Fallibility might just as well be present in a judgment to use one means as in a judgment to use another. (A judgment to allow to die is just as subject to being based on *knowledge which is fallible* as a judgment to kill.) Moreover, in either case, it is a matter of what one knows and believes, and not a matter of a particular kind of causal connection or causal chain. If we kill the patient, then we are certainly causally responsible for his death. But, similarly, if we cease treatment, and the patient dies, the patient might have recovered if treatment had been continued. The patient might have been saved in either case, and hence there is no morally relevant difference between the two cases. It is, therefore, simply beside the point that "one is sometimes culpable for killing . . . but one is sometimes not culpable for letting die"—as the above argument concludes.

Accordingly, despite its great intuitive appeal and frequent mention, this argument from responsibility fails.

There may, however, be more compelling arguments against Rachels, and I wish now to provide what I believe is the most significant argument that can be adduced in defense of the active/passive distinction. I shall develop this argument by combining (1) so-called wedge or slippery slope arguments with (2) recent arguments in defense of rule utilitarianism. I shall explain each in turn and show how in combination they may be used to defend the active/passive distinction.

(1) *Wedge arguments* proceed as follows: if killing were allowed, even under the guise of a merciful extinction of life, a dangerous wedge would be introduced which places all "undesir-

able" or "unworthy" human life in a precarious condition. Proponents of wedge arguments believe the initial wedge places us on a slippery slope for at least one of two reasons: (i) It is said that our justifying principles leave us with no principled way to avoid the slide into saying that all sorts of killings would be justified under similar conditions. Here it is thought that once killing is allowed, a firm line between justified and unjustified killings cannot be securely drawn. It is thought best not to redraw the line in the first place, for redrawing it will inevitably lead to a downhill slide. It is then often pointed out that as a matter of historical record this is precisely what has occurred in the darker regions of human history, including the Nazi era, where euthanasia began with the best intentions for horribly ill, non-Jewish Germans and gradually spread to anyone deemed an enemy of the people. (ii) Second, it is said that our basic principles against killing will be gradually eroded once some form of killing is legitimated. For example, it is said that permitting voluntary euthanasia will lead to permitting involuntary euthanasia, which will in turn lead to permitting euthanasia for those who are a nuisance to society (idiots, recidivist criminals, defective newborns, and the insane, e.g.). Gradually other principles which instill respect for human life will be eroded or abandoned in the process.

I am not inclined to accept the first reason (i).[7] If our justifying principles are themselves justified, then any action they warrant would be justified. Accordingly, I shall only be concerned with the second approach (ii).

(2) *Rule utilitarianism* is the position that a society ought to adopt a rule if its acceptance would have better consequences for the common good (greater social utility) than any comparable rule could have in that society. Any action is right if it conforms to a valid rule and wrong if it violates the rule. Sometimes it is said that alternative rules should be measured against one another, while it has also been suggested that whole moral *codes* (complete sets of rules) rather than individual rules should be compared. While I prefer the latter formulation (Brandt's), this internal dispute need not detain us here. The important point is that a particular rule or a particular code of rules is morally justified if and only if there is no other competing rule or moral code whose acceptance would have a higher utility value for society, and where a rule's acceptability is contingent upon the consequences which would result if the rule were made current.

Wedge arguments, when conjoined with rule utilitarian arguments, may be applied to euthanasia issues in the following way. We presently subscribe to a no-active-euthanasia rule (which the AMA suggests we retain). Imagine now that in our society we make current a restricted-active-euthanasia rule (as Rachels seems to urge). Which of these two moral rules would, if enacted, have the consequence of maximizing social utility? Clearly a restricted-active-euthanasia rule would have *some* utility value, as Rachels notes, since some intense and uncontrollable suffering would be eliminated. However, it may not have the highest utility value in the structure of our present code or in any imaginable code which could be made current, and therefore may not be a component in the ideal code for our society. If wedge arguments raise any serious questions at all, as I think they do, they rest in this area of whether a code would be weakened or strengthened by the addition of active euthanasia principles. For the disutility of introducing legitimate killing into one's moral code (in the form of active euthanasia rules) may, in the long run, outweigh the utility of doing so, as a result of the eroding effect such a relaxation would have on rules in the code which demand respect for human life. If, for example, rules permitting active killing were introduced, it is not implausible to suppose that destroying defective newborns (a form of involuntary euthanasia) would become an accepted and common practice, that as population increases occur the aged will be even more neglectable and neglected than they now are, that capital punishment for a wide variety of crimes would be increasingly tempting, that some doctors would have appreciably reduced fears of actively injecting fatal doses whenever it seemed to them propitious to do so, and that laws of war against killing would erode in efficacy even beyond their already abysmal level.

A hundred such possible consequences might easily be imagined. But these few are sufficient to make the larger point that such rules permitting killing could lead to a general reduction of respect for human life. Rules against killing in a moral code are not *isolated* moral principles; they are pieces of a web of rules against killing which forms the code. The more threads one removes, the weaker the fabric becomes. And if, as I believe, moral principles against active killing have the deep and continuously civilizing effect of promoting respect for life, and if principles which allow passively letting die (as envisioned in the AMA statement) do not themselves cut against this effect, then this seems an important reason for the maintenance of the active/passive distinction. (By the logic of the above argument passively letting die would also have to be prohibited if a rule permitting it had the serious adverse consequence of eroding acceptance of rules protective of respect for life. While this prospect seems to me improbable, I can hardly claim to have refuted those conservatives who would claim that even rules which sanction letting die place us on a precarious slippery slope.)

A troublesome problem, however, confronts my use of utilitarian and wedge arguments. Most all of us would agree that both killing and letting die are justified under some conditions. Killings in self-defense and in "just" wars are widely accepted as justified because the conditions excuse the killing. If society can withstand these exceptions to moral rules prohibiting killing, then why is it not plausible to suppose society can accept another excusing exception in the form of justified active euthanasia? This is an important and worthy objection, but not a decisive one. The defenseless and the dying are significantly different classes of persons from aggressors who attack individuals and/or nations. In the case of aggressors, one does not confront the question whether their lives are no longer *worth living*. Rather, we reach the judgment that the aggressors' morally blameworthy actions justify counteractions. But in the case of the dying and the otherwise ill, there is no morally blameworthy action to justify our own. Here we are required to accept the judgment that their lives are no longer *worth living* in order to believe that the termination of their lives is justified. It is the latter sort of judgment which is feared by those who take the wedge argument seriously. We do not now permit and never have permitted the taking of morally blameless lives. I think this is the key to understanding why recent cases of intentionally allowing the death of defective newborns (as in the now famous case at the Johns Hopkins Hospital) have generated such protracted controversy. Even if such newborns could not have led meaningful lives (a matter of some controversy), it is the wedged foot in the door which creates the most intense worries. For if we once take a decision to allow a restricted infanticide justification or any justification at all on grounds that a life is not meaningful or not worth living, we have qualified our moral rules against killing. That this qualification is a matter of the utmost seriousness needs no argument. I mention it here only to show why the wedge argument may have moral force even though we already allow some very different conditions to justify intentional killing.

There is one final utilitarian reason favoring the preservation of the active/passive distinction.[8] Suppose we distinguish the following two types of cases of wrongly diagnosed patients:

1. Patients wrongly diagnosed as hopeless, and who will survive even if a treatment *is* ceased (in order to allow a natural death).
2. Patients wrongly diagnosed as hopeless, and who will survive only if the treatment is *not ceased* (in order to allow a natural death).

If a social rule permitting only passive euthanasia were in effect, then doctors and families who "allowed death" would lose only patients in class 2, not those in class 1; whereas if active euthanasia were permitted, at least some patients in class 1 would be needlessly lost. Thus, the consequence of a no-active-euthanasia rule would be to save some lives which could not be saved if both forms of euthanasia were allowed. This reason is not a *decisive* reason for favoring a policy of passive euthanasia, since these classes (1 and 2) are likely to be very small and since there might be counterbalancing reasons (extreme pain, autonomous expression of the patient, etc.) in favor of active euthanasia. But certainly it is *a* reason favoring only passive euthanasia and one which is morally relevant and ought to be considered along with other moral reasons. . . .

There remains, however, the important question as to whether we *ought* to accept the distinction between active and passive euthanasia, now that we are clear about (at least one way of drawing) the moral grounds for its invocation. That is, should we employ the distinction in order to judge some acts of euthanasia justified and others not justified? Here, as the hesitant previous paragraph indicates, I am uncertain. This problem is a substantive moral issue—not merely a conceptual one—and would require at a minimum a lengthy assessment of wedge arguments and related utilitarian considerations. In important respects empirical questions are involved in this assessment. We should like to know, and yet have hardly any evidence to indicate, what the consequences would be for our society if we were to allow the use of active means to produce death. The best hope for making such an assessment has seemed to some to rest in analogies to suicide and capital punishment statutes. Here it may reasonably be asked whether recent liberalizations of laws limiting these forms of killing have served as the thin end of a wedge leading to a breakdown of principles protecting life or to widespread violations of moral principles. Nonetheless, such analogies do not seem to me promising, since they are still fairly remote from the pertinent issue of the consequences of allowing active humanitarian killing of one person by another.

It is interesting to notice the outcome of the Kamisar-Williams debate on euthanasia—which is almost exclusively cast by both writers in a consequential, utilitarian framework.[9] At one crucial point in the debate, where possible consequences of laws permitting euthanasia are under discussion, they exchange "perhaps" judgments:

> I [Williams] will return Kamisar the compliment and say: "Perhaps." We are certainly in an area where no solution is going to make things quite easy and happy for everybody, and all sorts of embarrassments may be conjectured. But these embarrassments are not avoided by keeping to the present law: we suffer from them already.[10]

Because of the grave difficulties which stand in the way of making accurate predictions about the impact of liberalized euthanasia laws—especially those that would permit active killing—it is not surprising that those who debate the subject would reach a point of exchanging such "perhaps" judgments. And that is why, so it seems to me, we are uncertain whether to perpetuate or to abandon the active-passive distinction in our moral thinking about euthanasia. I think we *do* perpetuate it in medicine, law, and ethics because we are still somewhat uncertain about the conditions under which *passive* euthanasia should be permitted by law (which is one form of social *rule*). We are unsure about what the consequences will be of the California "Natural Death Act" and all those similar acts passed by other states which have followed in its path. If no untoward results occur, and the balance of the results seems favorable, then we will perhaps be less concerned about further liberalizations of euthanasia laws. If untoward results do occur (on a widespread scale), then we would be most reluctant to accept further liberalizations and might even abolish natural death acts.

In short, I have argued in this section that euthanasia in its active and its passive forms presents us with a dilemma which can be developed by using powerful consequentialist arguments on each side, yet there is little clarity concerning the proper resolution of the dilemma precisely because of our uncertainty regarding proclaimed consequences. . . .

Endnotes

1. "Active and Passive Euthanasia," *New England Journal of Medicine* 292 (January 9, 1975), 78–80.
2. As recorded in the Opinion of Judge Robert Muir, Jr., Docket No. C-201-75 of the Superior Court of New Jersey, Chancery Division, Morris County (November 10, 1975).
3. See Judge Muir's Opinion, p. 18—a slightly different statement but on the subject.
4. This problem of the strength of evidence also emerged in the Quinlan trial, as physicians disagreed whether

the evidence was "irrefutable." Such disagreement, when added to the problems of medical fallibility and causal responsibility just outlined, provides in the eyes of some one important argument against the *legalization* of active euthanasia, as perhaps the AMA would agree.

5. Among the moral reasons why one is held to be responsible in the first sort of case and not responsible in the second sort are, I believe, the moral grounds for the active/passive distinction under discussion in this section.
6. In *Social Ethics,* as cited in the permission note to this article.
7. An argument of this form, which I find unacceptable for reasons given below, is Arthur Dyck, "Beneficient Euthanasia and Benemortasia: Alternative Views of Mercy," in M. Kohl, ed., *Beneficent Euthanasia* (Buffalo: Prometheus Books, 1975), pp. 120f.
8. I owe most of this argument to James Rachels, whose comments on an earlier draft of this paper led to several significant alterations.
9. Williams bases his pro-euthanasia argument on the prevention of two consequences: (1) loss of liberty and (2) cruelty. Kamisar bases his anti-enthanasia position on three projected consequences of euthanasia laws: (1) mistaken diagnosis, (2) pressured decisions by seriously ill patients, and (3) the wedge of the laws will lead to legalized involuntary euthanasia. Kamisar admits that individual acts of euthanasia are sometimes justified. It is the rule that he opposes. He is thus clearly a rule-utilitarian, and I believe Williams is as well (cf. his views on children and the senile). Their assessments of wedge arguments are, however, radically different.
10. Glanville Williams, "Mercy-Killing Legislation—A Rejoinder," *Minnesota Law Review,* 43, no. 1 (1958), 5.

Review Questions

1. Beauchamp begins with three criticisms of Rachels. What are they?
2. What is the widely accepted argument for rejecting Rachels' position? Why doesn't Beauchamp accept it?
3. Explain the wedge or slippery slope argument that is used to defend the active/passive distinction.
4. Explain the utilitarian arguments that Beauchamp uses to defend the active/passive distinction.

Discussion Questions

1. Are Beauchamp's utilitarian arguments persuasive? Why or why not?
2. Should we accept the distinction between active and passive euthanasia or not? What is your view?

Peter Singer

Justifying Voluntary Euthanasia

Peter Singer is Professor of Philosophy at Monash University in Australia. He is the author of Animal Liberation *(1975) and* Practical Ethics, *(1980) from which our reading is taken.*

Singer argues that voluntary euthanasia and assisted suicide (which is very similar) are morally justified in cases where a patient is suffering from an incurable and painful or very distressing condition. In such cases, the fear of death, preference utilitarianism, the theory of rights, and respect for autonomy all provide reasons for allowing voluntary euthanasia or assisted suicide.

From Peter Singer, *Practical Ethics* (Cambridge: Cambridge University Press, 1979).

Voluntary Euthanasia

Most of the groups currently campaigning for changes in the law to allow euthanasia are campaigning for voluntary euthanasia—that is, euthanasia carried out at the request of the person killed.

Sometimes voluntary euthanasia is scarcely distinguishable from assisted suicide. In *Jean's Way,* Derek Humphry has told how his wife

Jean, when dying of cancer, asked him to provide her with the means to end her life swiftly and without pain. They had seen the situation coming and discussed it beforehand. Derek obtained some tablets and gave them to Jean, who took them and died soon afterwards.

In other cases, people wanting to die may be unable to kill themselves. In 1973 George Zygmaniak was injured in a motorcycle accident near his home in New Jersey. He was taken to the hospital, where he was found to be totally paralyzed from the neck down. He was also in considerable pain. He told his doctor and his brother, Lester, that he did not want to live in this condition. He begged them both to kill him. Lester questioned the doctor and hospital staff about George's prospects of recovery; he was told that they were nil. He then smuggled a gun into the hospital, and said to his brother: 'I am here to end your pain, George. Is it all right with you?' George, who was now unable to speak because of an operation to assist his breathing, nodded affirmatively. Lester shot him through the temple.

The Zygmaniak case appears to be a clear instance of voluntary euthanasia, although without some of the procedural safeguards that advocates of the legalization of voluntary euthanasia propose. For instance, medical opinions about the patient's prospects of recovery were obtained only in an informal manner. Nor was there a careful attempt to establish, before independent witnesses, that George's desire for death was of a fixed and rational kind, based on the best available information about his situation. The killing was not carried out by a doctor. An injection would have been less distressing to others than shooting. But these choices were not open to Lester Zygmaniak, for the law in New Jersey, as in most other places, regards mercy killing as murder, and if he had made his plans known, he would not have been able to carry them out.

Euthanasia can be voluntary even if a person is not able, as Jean Humphry and George Zygmaniak were able, to indicate the wish to die right up to the moment the tablets are swallowed or the trigger pulled. A person may, while in good health, make a written request for euthanasia if, through accident or illness, she should come to be incapable of making or expressing a decision to die, in pain, or without the use of her mental faculties, and there is no reasonable hope of recovery. In killing a person who has made such a request, has re-affirmed it from time to time, and is now in one of the states described, one could truly claim to be acting with her consent. . . .

Justifying Voluntary Euthanasia

Under existing laws people suffering unrelievable pain or distress from an incurable illness who ask their doctors to end their lives are asking their doctors to become murderers. Although juries are extremely reluctant to convict in cases of this kind the law is clear that neither the request, nor the degree of suffering, nor the incurable condition of the person killed, is a defence to a charge of murder. Advocates of voluntary euthanasia propose that this law be changed so that a doctor could legally act on a patient's desire to die without further suffering.

The case for voluntary euthanasia has some common ground with the case for nonvoluntary euthanasia, in that the reason for killing is to end suffering. The two kinds of euthanasia differ, however, in that voluntary euthanasia involves the killing of a person, a rational and self-conscious being and not a merely conscious being. (To be strictly accurate it must be said that this is not always so, because although only rational and self-conscious beings can consent to their own deaths, they may not be rational and self-conscious at the time euthanasia is contemplated—the doctor may, for instance, be acting on a prior written request for euthanasia if, through accident or illness, one's rational faculties should be irretrievably lost. For simplicity we shall, henceforth, disregard this complication.)

We have seen that it is possible to justify nonvoluntary euthanasia, when the being killed lacks the capacity to consent. We must now ask in what way the ethical issues are different when the being is capable of consenting, and does in fact consent.

Let us return to the general principles about killing. . . . I [have] argued . . . that the wrongness of killing a conscious being which is not self-conscious, rational or autonomous, depends on utilitarian considerations. It is on this basis that I have defended nonvoluntary euthanasia. On the other hand it is, as we saw, plausible to hold that killing a self-conscious being is a more serious matter than killing a merely conscious being. We found four distinct grounds on which this could be argued:

i. The classical utilitarian claim that since self-conscious beings are capable of fearing their own death, killing them has worse effects on others.
ii. The preference utilitarian calculation which counts the thwarting of the victim's desire to go on living as an important reason against killing.
iii. A theory of rights according to which to have a right one must have the ability to desire that to which one has a right, so that to have a right to life one must be able to desire one's own continued existence.
iv. Respect for the autonomous decisions of rational agents.

Now suppose we have a situation in which a person suffering from a painful and incurable disease wishes to die. If the individual were not a person—not rational or self-conscious—euthanasia would, as I have said, be justifiable. Do any of the four grounds for holding that it is normally worse to kill a person provide reasons against killing when the individual is a person?

The classical utilitarian objection does not apply to killing that takes place only with the genuine consent of the person killed. That people are killed under these conditions would have no tendency to spread fear or insecurity, since we have no cause to be fearful of being killed with our own genuine consent. If we do not wish to be killed, we simply do not consent. In fact, the argument from fear points in favour of voluntary euthanasia, for if voluntary euthanasia is not permitted we may, with good cause, be fearful that our deaths will be unnecessarily drawn-out and distressing.

Preference utilitarianism also points in favour of, not against, voluntary euthanasia. Just as preference utilitarianism must count a desire to go on living as a reason against killing, so it must count a desire to die as a reason for killing.

Next, according to the theory of rights we have considered, it is an essential feature of a right that one can waive one's rights if one so chooses. I may have a right to privacy; but I can, if I wish, film every detail of my daily life and invite the neighbours to my home movies. Neighbours sufficiently intrigued to accept my invitation could do so without violating my right to privacy, since the right has on this occasion been waived. Similarly, to say that I have a right to life is not to say that it would be wrong for my doctor to end my life, if she does so at my request. In making this request I waive my right to life.

Lastly, the principle of respect for autonomy tells us to allow rational agents to live their own lives according to their own autonomous decisions, free from coercion or interference; but if rational agents should autonomously choose to die, then respect for autonomy will lead us to assist them to do so as they choose.

So, although there are reasons for thinking that killing a self-conscious being is normally worse than killing any other kind of being, in the special case of voluntary euthanasia most of these reasons count for euthanasia rather than against. Surprising as this result might at first seem, it really does no more than reflect the fact that what is special about self-conscious beings is that they can know that they exist over time and will, unless they die, continue to exist. Normally this continued existence is fervently desired; when the foreseeable continued existence is dreaded rather than desired however, the desire to die may take the place of the normal desire to live, reversing the reasons against killing based on the desire to live. Thus the case for voluntary euthanasia is arguably much stronger than the case for nonvoluntary euthanasia.

Some opponents of the legalization of voluntary euthanasia might concede that all this follows, if we have a genuinely free and rational decision to die; but, they add, we can never be sure that a request to be killed is the result of a free and rational decision. Will not the sick and elderly be pressured by their relatives to end their lives quickly? Will it not be possible to commit outright murder by pretending that a person has requested euthanasia? And even if there is no pressure of falsification, can anyone who is ill, suffering pain, and very probably in a drugged and confused state of mind, make a rational decision about whether to live or die?

These questions raise technical difficulties for the legalization of voluntary euthanasia, rather than objections to the underlying ethical principles; but they are serious difficulties nonetheless. Voluntary euthanasia societies in Britain and elsewhere have sought to meet them by proposing that euthanasia should be legal only for a person who:

i. is diagnosed by two doctors as suffering from an incurable illness expected to cause severe distress or the loss of rational faculties;

and

ii. has, at least 30 days before the proposed act of euthanasia, and in the presence of two independent witnesses, made a written request for euthanasia in the event of the situation described in (i) occurring.

Only a doctor could administer euthanasia, and if the patient was at the time still capable of consenting, the doctor would have to make sure that the patient still wished the declaration to be acted upon. A declaration could be revoked at any time.

These provisions, though in some respects cumbersome, appear to meet most of the technical objections to legalization. Murder in the guise of euthanasia would be farfetched. Two independent witnesses to the declaration, the 30 day waiting period, and—in the case of a mentally competent person—the doctor's final investigation of the patient's wishes would together do a great deal to reduce the danger of doctors acting on requests which did not reflect the free and rational decisions of their patients.

It is often said, in debates about euthanasia, that doctors can be mistaken. Certainly some patients diagnosed by competent doctors as suffering from an incurable condition have survived. Possibly the legalization of voluntary euthanasia would, over the years, mean the deaths of one or two people who would otherwise have recovered. This is not, however, the knockdown argument against euthanasia that some imagine it to be. Against a very small number of unnecessary deaths that might occur if euthanasia is legalized we must place the very large amount of pain and distress that will be suffered by patients who really are terminally ill if euthanasia is not legalized. Longer life is not such a supreme good that it outweighs all other considerations. (If it were, there would be many more effective ways of saving life—such as a ban on smoking, or on cars that can drive faster than 10 m.p.h.—than prohibiting voluntary euthanasia.) The possibility that two doctors may make a mistake means that the person who opts for euthanasia is deciding on the balance of probabilities, and giving up a very slight chance of survival in order to avoid suffering that will almost certainly end in death. This may be a perfectly rational choice. Probability is, as Bishop Butler said, the guide of life, and we must follow its guidance right to the end. Against this, some will reply that improved care for the terminally ill has eliminated pain and made voluntary euthanasia unnecessary. Elisabeth Kübler-Ross, whose *On Death and Dying* is perhaps the best-known book on care for the dying, has claimed that none of her patients request euthanasia. Given personal attention and the right medication, she says, people come to accept their deaths and die peacefully without pain.

Kübler-Ross may be right. It may be possible, now, to eliminate pain. It may even be possible to do it in a way which leaves patients in possession of their rational faculties and free from vomiting, nausea, or other distressing side-effects. Unfortunately only a minority of dying patients now receive this kind of care. Nor is physical pain the only problem. There can also be other distressing conditions, like bones so fragile they fracture at sudden movements, slow starvation due to a cancerous growth, inability to control one's bowels or bladder, difficulty in breathing and so on.

Take the case of Jean Humphry, as described in *Jean's Way*. This is not a case from the period before effective painkillers: Jean Humphry died in 1975. Nor is it the case of someone unable to get good medical care: she was treated at an Oxford hospital and if there were anything else that could have been done for her, her husband, a well-connected Fleet St. journalist, would have been better placed than most to obtain it. Yet Derek Humphry writes:

> when the request for help in dying meant relief from relentless suffering and pain and I had seen the extent of this agony, the option simply could not be denied . . . And certainly Jean deserved the dignity of selecting her own ending. She must die soon—as we both now realized—but together we would decide when this would be.

Perhaps one day it will be possible to treat all terminally ill patients in such a way that no one requests euthanasia and the subject becomes a non-issue; but this still distant prospect is no reason to deny euthanasia to those who die in less comfortable conditions. It is, in any case, highly paternalistic to tell dying patients that they are now so well looked after they need not be offered the option of euthanasia. It would be more in keeping with respect for individual freedom and autonomy to legalize euthanasia and let patients decide whether their situation is bearable—let them, as Derek Humphry puts it, have the dignity of selecting their own endings. Better than voluntary euthanasia be an unexercised legal right than a prohibited act which, for all we know, some might desperately desire.

Finally, do these arguments for voluntary euthanasia perhaps give too much weight to individual freedom and autonomy? After all, we do not allow people free choices on matters like, for instance, the taking of heroin. This is a restriction of freedom but, in the view of many, one that can be justified on paternalistic grounds. If preventing people becoming heroin addicts is justifiable paternalism, why isn't preventing people having themselves killed?

The question is a reasonable one, because respect for individual freedom can be carried too far. John Stuart Mill thought that the state should never interfere with the individual except to prevent harm to others. The individual's own good, Mill thought, is not a proper reason for state intervention. But Mill may have had too high an opinion of the rationality of a human being. It may occasionally be right to prevent people making choices which are obviously not rationally based and which we can be sure they will later regret. The prohibition of voluntary euthanasia cannot be justified on paternalistic grounds, however, for voluntary euthanasia is, by definition, an act for which good reasons exist. Voluntary euthanasia occurs only when, to the best of medical knowledge, a person is suffering from an incurable and painful or distressing condition. In these circumstances one cannot say that to choose to die quickly is obviously irrational. The strength of the case for voluntary euthanasia lies in this combination of respect for the preferences, or autonomy, of those who decide for euthanasia; and the clear rational basis of the decision itself. . . .

Review Questions

1. Distinguish between the cases of Jean Humphry and George Zygmaniak.
2. What are the four grounds for holding that killing a person, a rational and self-conscious being, is wrong?
3. According to Singer, how do these grounds provide reasons for allowing voluntary euthanasia or assisted suicide?
4. What objections does Singer discuss? How does he reply to these objections?

Discussion Questions

1. Was Jean Humphry morally justified in committing suicide or not? Would it make any moral difference if her husband had killed her instead?
2. Was Lester Zygmaniak justified in killing his brother? Why or why not? If not, then should Lester be punished? Explain your view.
3. Do you think that the law should be changed to allow voluntary euthanasia or assisted suicide for terminally ill patients? Defend your answer.

Richard B. Brandt

Defective Newborns and the Morality of Termination

For biographical information on Brandt, see the second reading in this chapter.

Brandt argues that it is morally right to actively or passively terminate the life of a defective newborn if its life is bad according to a "happiness criterion". Consent is irrelevant; the infant cannot give consent, and it will be indifferent to continued life. But the cost of caring for the infant is relevant to the decision to terminate in addition to the quality of the prospective life.

The *legal* rights of a fetus are very different from those of a newborn. The fetus may be aborted, legally, for any reason or no reason up to twenty-four or twenty-eight weeks (U.S. Supreme Court, *Roe* v. *Wade*). But, at least in theory, immediately after birth an infant has all the legal rights of the adult, including the right to life.

The topic of this paper, however, is to identify the moral rights of the newborn, specifically whether *defective* newborns have a right to life. But it is simpler to talk, not about "rights to life," but about when or whether it is *morally right* either actively or passively (by withdrawal of life-supportive measures) to terminate defective newborns. It is also better because the conception of a right involves the notion of a sphere of autonomy—something is to be done or omitted, but only if the subject of the rights wants or consents—and this fact is apt to be confusing or oversimplifying. Surely what we want to know is whether termination is morally right or wrong, and nothing can turn on the **semantics** of the concept of a "right."[1]

What does one have to do in order to support some answers to these questions? One thing we can do is ask—and I think myself that the answer to this question is definitive for our purposes—whether rational or fully informed persons would, in view of the total consequences, support a moral code for a society in which they expected to live, with one or another, provision on this matter. (I believe a fully rational person will at least normally have some degree of benevolence, or positive interest in the welfare or happiness of others; I shall not attempt to specify how much.) Since, however, I do not expect that everyone else will agree that answering this question would show what is morally right, I shall, for their benefit, also argue that certain moral principles on this matter are coherent with strong moral convictions of reflective people; or, to use Rawls's terminology, that a certain principle on the matter would belong to a system of moral principles in "reflective equilibrium."

Historically, many writers, including Pope Pius XI in *Casti Connubii* (1930), have affirmed an absolute prohibition against killing anyone who is neither guilty of a capital crime nor an unjust assailant threatening one's life (self-defense), except in case of "extreme necessity." Presumably the prohibition is intended to include withholding of food or liquid from a newborn, although strictly speaking this is only *failing* to do something, not actually *doing* something to bring about a death. (Would writers in this tradition demand, on moral grounds, that complicated and expensive surgery be undertaken to save a life? Such surgery is going beyond normal care, and in some cases beyond what earlier writers even conceived.) However the intentions of these writers may be, we should observe that historically their moral condemnation of all killing (except for the cases mentioned) derives from the Biblical injunction, "Thou shalt not kill," which, as it stands and without interpretation, may be taken to forbid

---

From *Infanticide and the Value of Life*, ed. by Marvin Kohl (Prometheus Books, 1978). Reprinted with permission.

suicide, killing of animals, perhaps even plants, and hence cannot be taken seriously.

Presumably a moral code that is coherent with our intuitions and that rational persons would support for their society would include some prohibition of killing, but it is another matter to identify the exact class to which such a prohibition is to apply. For one thing, I would doubt that killing one's self would be included—although one might be forbidden to kill one's self if that would work severe hardship on others, or conflict with the discharge of one's other moral obligations. And, possibly, defective newborns would *not* be included in the class. Further, a decision has to be made whether the prohibition of killing is *absolute* or only ***prima facie,*** meaning by "prima facie" that the duty not to kill might be outweighed by some other duty (or right) stronger in the circumstances, which could be fulfilled only by killing. In case this distinction is made, we would have to decide whether defective newborns fall within the scope of even a prima facie moral prohibition against killing. I shall, however, not attempt to make this fine distinction here, and shall simply inquire whether, everything considered, defective newborns—or some identifiable group of them—are excluded from the moral prohibition against killing.

THE PROSPECTIVE QUALITY OF LIFE OF DEFECTIVE NEWBORNS

Suppose that killing a defective newborn, or allowing it to die, would not be an *injury,* but would rather be doing the infant a favor. In that case we should feel intuitively less opposed to termination of newborns, and presumably rational persons would be less inclined to support a moral code with a prohibition against such action. In that case we would feel rather as we do about a person's preventing a suicide attempt from being successful, in order that the person be elaborately tortured to death at a later stage. It is no favor to the prospective suicide to save his life; similarly, if the prospective life of defective newborns is bad we are doing them a favor to let them die.

It may be said that we have no way of knowing what the conscious experiences of defective children are like, and that we have no competence in any case to decide when or what kind of life is bad or not worth living. Further, it may be said that predictions about a defective newborn's prospects for the future are precarious, in view of possible further advances of medicine. It does seem, however, that here, as everywhere, the rational person will follow the evidence about the present or future facts. But there is a question how to decide whether a life is bad or not worth living.

In the case of *some* defective newborns, it seems clear that their prospective life is bad. Suppose, as sometimes happens, a child is hydrocephalic with an extremely low I.Q., is blind and deaf, has no control over its body, can only lie on its back all day and have all its needs taken care of by others, and even cries out with pain when it is touched or lifted. Infants born with spina bifida—and these number over two per one thousand births—are normally not quite so badly off, but are often nearly so.

But what criterion are we using if we say that such a life is bad? One criterion might be called a "happiness" criterion. If a person *likes* a moment of experience while he is having it, his life is so far good; if a person *dislikes* a moment of experience while he is having it, his life is so far bad. Based on such reactions, we might construct a "happiness curve" for a person, going up above the indifference axis when a moment of experience is liked—and how far above depending on how strongly it is liked—and dipping down below the line when a moment is disliked. Then this criterion would say that a life is worth living if there is a net balance of positive area under the curve over a lifetime, and that it is bad if there is a net balance of negative area. One might adopt some different criterion: for instance, one might say that a life is worth living if a person would *want* to live it over again given that, at the end, he could remember the whole of it with perfect vividness in some kind of grand intuitive awareness. Such a response to this hypothetical holistic intuition, however, would likely be affected by the state of the person's drives or moods at the time, and the conception strikes me as unconvincing, compared with the moment-by-moment reaction to what is going on. Let us, for the sake of the argument, adopt the happiness criterion.[2]

Is the prospective life of the seriously defective newborn, like the one described above, bad or good according to this criterion? One thing seems clear: that it is *less* good than is the prospective life of a normal infant. But is it bad?

We have to do some extrapolating from what we know. For instance, such a child will presumably suffer from severe sensory deprivation; he is simply not getting interesting stimuli. On the basis of laboratory data, it is plausible to think the child's experience is at best boring or uncomfortable. If the child's experience is painful, of course, its moments are, so far, on the negative side. One must suppose that such a child hardly suffers from disappointment, since it will not learn to expect anything exciting, beyond being fed and fondled, and these events will be regularly forthcoming. One might expect such a child to suffer from isolation and loneliness, but insofar as this is true, the object of dislike probably should be classified as just sensory deprivation; dislike of loneliness seems to depend on the deprivation of past pleasures of human company. There are also some positive enjoyments: of eating, drinking, elimination, seeing the nurse coming with food, and so on. But the brief enjoyments can hardly balance the long stretches of boredom, discomfort, or even pain. On the whole, the lives of such children are bad according to the happiness criterion.

Naturally we cannot generalize about the cases of all "defective" newborns; there are all sorts of defects, and the cases I have described are about the worst. A child with spina bifida may, if he survives the numerous operations, I suppose, adjust to the frustration of immobility; he may become accustomed to the embarrassments of no bladder or bowel control; he may have some intellectual enjoyments like playing chess; he will suffer from observing what others have but he cannot, such as sexual satisfactions, in addition to the pain of repeated surgery. How does it all balance out? Surely not as very good, but perhaps above the indifference level.

It may fairly be said, I think, that the lives of some defective newborns are destined to be bad on the whole, and it would be a favor to them if their lives were terminated. Contrariwise, the prospective lives of many defective newborns are modestly pleasant, and it would be some injury to them to be terminated, albeit the lives they will live are ones some of us would prefer not to live at all.

Consent

Let us now make a second suggestion, not this time that termination of a defective newborn would be doing him a favor, but this time that he *consents* to termination, in the sense of expressing a rational deliberated preference for this. In that case I suggest that intuitively we would be *more* favorably inclined to judge that it is right to let the defective die, and I suggest also that for that case rational persons would be more ready to support a moral code permitting termination. Notice that we think that if an ill person has signified what we think a rational and deliberated desire to die, we are morally better justified in withdrawing life-supporting measures than we otherwise would be.

The newborn, however, is incapable of expressing his preference (giving consent) at all, much less expressing a rational deliberated preference. There could in theory be court-appointed guardians or proxies, presumably disinterested parties, authorized to give such consent on his behalf, but even so this would not be *his* consent.

Nevertheless, there is a fact about the mental life of the newborn (defective or not) such that, if he could understand the fact, it seems he would not object—even rationally or after deliberation, if that were possible—to his life being terminated, or to his parents substituting another child in his place. This suggestion may seem absurd, but let us see. The explanation runs along the lines of an argument I once used to support the morality of abortion. I quote the paragraph in which this argument was introduced.[3]

Suppose I were seriously ill, and were told that, for a sizeable fee, an operation to save "my life" could be performed, of the following sort: my brain would be removed to another body which could provide a normal life, but the unfortunate result would be that

> my memory and learned abilities would be wholly erased, and that the forming of memory brain traces must begin again from scratch, as in a newborn baby. Now, how large a fee would I be willing to pay for this operation, when the alternative is my peaceful demise? My own answer would be: None at all. I would take no interest in the continued existence of "myself" in that sense, and I would rather add the sizeable fee to the inheritance of my children. . . . I cannot see the point of forfeiting my children's inheritance in order to start off a person who is brand new except that he happens to enjoy the benefit of having my present brain, without the memory traces. It appears that some continuity of memory is a necessary condition for personal identity in an important sense.

My argument was that the position of a fetus, at the end of the first trimester, is essentially the same as that of the person contemplating this operation: he will consider that the baby born after six months will not be *he* in any *important* and *motivating* sense (there will be no continuity of memory, and, indeed, maybe nothing to have been remembered), and the later existence of this baby, in a sense bodily continuous with his present body, would be a matter of indifference to him. So, I argued, nothing is being done to the fetus that he would object to having done if he understood the situation.

What do I think is necessary in order for the continuation of my body with its conscious experiences to be worthwhile? One thing is that it is able to remember the events I can now remember; another is that it takes some interest in the projects I am now planning and remembers them as my projects; another is that it recognizes my friends and has warm feelings for them, and so on. Reflection on these states of a future continuation of my body with its experiences is what makes the idea motivating. But such motivating reflection for a newborn is impossible: he has no memories that he wants recalled later; he has no plans to execute; he has no warm feelings for other persons. He has simply not had the length of life necessary for these to come about. Not only that: the conception of these things cannot be motivating because the concept of some state of affairs being motivating requires roughly a past experience in which similar states of affairs were satisfying, and he has not lived long enough for the requisite conditioning to have taken place. (The most one could say is that the image of warm milk in his mouth is attractive; he might answer affirmatively if it could be put to him whether he would be aversive to the idea of no more warm milk.) So we can say not merely that the newborn does not want the continuation of himself as a subject of experiences (he has not the conceptual framework for this), he does not want *anything* that his own survival would promote. It is like the case of the operation: there is nothing I want that the survival of my brain with no memory would promote. Give the newborn as much *conceptual* framework as you like; the *wants* are not there, which could give significance to the continuance of his life.

The newborn, then, is bound to be *indifferent* to the idea of a continuation of the stream of his experiences, even if he clearly has the idea of that. It seems we can know this about him.

The truth of all this is still not for it to be the case that the newborn, defective or not, gives *consent* to, or expresses a preference for, the termination of his life. *Consent* is a performance, normally linguistic, but always requiring some conventional *sign*. A newborn, who has not yet learned how to signalize consent, cannot give consent. And it may be thought that this difference makes all the difference.

In order to see what difference it does make in this case, we should ask what makes adult consent morally important. Why is it that we think euthanasia can be practiced on an adult only if he gives his consent, at least his implied consent (e.g., by previous statements)? There seem to be two reasons. The first is that a person is more likely to be concerned with his own welfare, and to take steps to secure it, than are others, even his good friends. Giving an individual control over his own life, and not permitting others to take control except when he consents, is normally to promote his welfare. An individual may, of course, behave stupidly or shortsightedly, but we think that on the whole a person's welfare is best secured if decisions about it are in his hands; and it is best for society in the normal case (not for criminals, etc.)

if persons' own lives are well-served. The second reason is the feeling of security a person can have if he knows the major decisions about himself are in his own hands. When they are not, a person can easily, and in some cases very reasonably, suppose that other persons may well be able to do something to him that he would very much like them not to do. He does not have to worry about that if he knows they cannot do it without his consent.

Are things different with the newborn? At least he, like the fetus, is not yet able to suffer from insecurity; he cannot worry about what others may do to him. So the second reason for requiring consent cannot have any importance in his case. His situation is thus very unlike that of the senile adult, for an adult can worry about what others may do to him if they judge him senile. And this worry can well cast a shadow over a lot of life. But how about the first reason? Here matters are more complex. In the case of children, we think their own lives are better cared for if certain decisions are in the hands of others; the child may not want to visit the dentist, but the parents know that his best interests are served by going, and they make him go. The same for compulsory school attendance. And the same for the newborn. But there is another point: that society has an interest, at certain crucial points, that may not be served by doing just exactly what is for the lifelong interest of the newborn. There are huge costs that are relevant, in the case of the defective newborn. I shall go into that problem in a moment. It seems, then, that in the case of the newborn, *consent* cannot have the moral importance that it has in the case of adults.

On the other hand, then, the newborn will not *care* whether his life is terminated, even if he understands his situation perfectly; and, on the other hand, consent does not have the moral importance in his case that it has for adults. So, while it seems true that we would feel better about permitting termination of defective newborns if only they could give rational and deliberated consent and gave it, nevertheless when we bear the foregoing two points in mind, the absence of consent does not seem morally crucial in their case. We can understand why rational persons deciding which moral code to support for their society would not make the giving of consent a necessary condition for feeling free to terminate an infant's life when such action was morally indicated by the other features of the situation.

Replacement In Order to Get a Better Life

Let us now think of an example owing to Derek Parfit. Suppose a woman wants a child, but is told that if she conceives a child now it will be defective, whereas if she waits three months she will produce a normal child. Obviously we think it would be wrong for the mother not to delay. (If she delays, the child she will have is not the *same* child as the one she would have had if she had not delayed, but it will have a better life.) This is the sole reason why we think she should delay and have the later-born child.

Suppose, however, a woman conceives but discovers only three months later that the fetus will become a defective child, but that she can have a normal child if she has an abortion and tries again. Now this time there is still the same reason for having the abortion that there formerly was for the delay: that she will produce a child with a better life. Ought she not then to have the abortion? If the child's life is bad, he could well complain that he had been injured by deliberately being brought to term. Would he complain if he were aborted, in favor of the later normal child? Not if the argument of the preceding section is correct.

But now suppose the woman does not discover until after she gives birth, that the child is severely defective, but that she could conceive again and have a normal child. Are things really different, in the first few days? One might think that a benevolent person would want, in each of these cases, the substitution of a normal child for the defective one, of the better life for the worse one.

The Cost and its Relevance

It is agreed that the burden of care for a defective infant, say one born with spina bifida, is huge. The cost of surgery alone for an infant with spina bifida has been estimated to be around $275,000.[4] In many places this cost must be met by the family of the child, and there is the additional cost of care in an institution, if the child's condition does not permit care at home—and a very modest estimate of the monthly cost at present is $1,100. To meet even the surgical costs, not to mention monthly payments for continuing care, the lives of members of the family must be at a most spartan level for many years. The psychological effects of this, and equally, if not more so, of care provided at home, are far-reaching; they are apt to destroy the marriage and to cause psychological problems for the siblings. There is the on-going anxiety, the regular visits, the continuing presence of a caretaker if the child is in the home. In one way or another the continued existence of the child is apt to reduce dramatically the quality of life of the family as a whole.

It can be and has been argued that such costs, while real, are irrelevant to the moral problem of what should be done.[5] It is obvious, however, that rational persons, when deciding which moral code to support, would take these human costs into account. As indeed they should: the parents and siblings are also human beings with lives to live, and any sacrifices a given law or moral system might call on them to make must be taken into account in deciding between laws and moral codes. Everyone will feel sympathy for a helpless newborn; but everyone should also think, equally vividly, of all the others who will suffer and just how they will suffer—and, of course, as indicated above, of just what kind of life the defective newborn will have in any case. There is a choice here between allowing a newborn to die (possibly a favor to it, and in any case not a serious loss), and imposing a very heavy burden on the family for many years to come.

Philosophers who think the cost to others is irrelevant to what should be done should reflect that we do not accept the general principle that lives should be saved at no matter what cost. For instance, ships are deliberately built with only a certain margin of safety; that could be built so that they would hardly sink in any storm, but to do so would be economically unfeasible. We do not think we should require a standard of safety for automobiles that goes beyond a certain point of expense and inconvenience; we are prepared to risk a few extra deaths. And how about the lives we are willing to lose in war, in order to assure a certain kind of economic order or democracy or free speech? Surely there is a point at which the loss of a life (or the abbreviation of a life) and the cost to others become comparable. Is it obvious that the continuation of a marginal kind of life for a child takes moral precedence over providing a college education for one or more of his siblings? Some comparisons will be hard to make, but continuing even a marginally pleasant life hardly has absolute priority.

Drawing Lines

There are two questions that must be answered in any complete account of what is the morally right thing to do about defective newborns.

The first is: If a decision to terminate is made, how soon must it be made? Obviously it could not be postponed to the age of five, or of three, or even a year and a half. At those ages, all the reasons for insisting on consent are already cogent. And at those ages, the child will already care what happens to him. But ten days is tolerable. Doubtless advances in medicine will permit detection of serious prospective defects early in pregnancy, and this issue of how many days will not arise.

Second, the argument from the quality of the prospective life of the defective newborn requires that we decide which defects are so serious that the kind of life the defective child can have gives it no serious claim as compared with the social costs. This issue must be thought through, and some guidelines established, but I shall not attempt this here.

One might argue that, if the newborn cannot rationally care whether its life ends or not, the parents are free to dispose of a child irrespective of whether he is defective, if they simply do not want it. To this there are two replies. First, in practice there are others who want a child if the parents do not, and they can put it up for adoption. But second, the parents are *injuring* a child if they prevent it from having the good life it could have had. We do not in general accept the argument that a person is free to injure another, for no reason, even if he has that person's consent. In view of these facts, we may expect that rational, benevolent persons deciding which moral code to support would select one that required respect for the life of a normal child, but would permit the termination of the life of a seriously defective child.

Active and Passive Procedures

There is a final question: that of a choice between withdrawal of life-supporting measures (such as feeding), and the active, painless taking of life. It seems obvious, however, that once the basic decision is made that an infant is not to receive the treatment necessary to sustain life beyond a few days, it is mere stupid cruelty to allow it to waste away gradually in a hospital bed—for the child to suffer, and for everyone involved also to suffer in watching the child suffer. If death is the outcome decided upon, it is far kinder for it to come quickly and painlessly.

Endnotes

1. Here I disagree with Michael Tooley, "Abortion and Infanticide," *Philosophy and Public Affairs* 2 (1972): 37–65, especially pp. 44–49.
2. Professor P. Foot has made interesting remarks on when a life is worth living. See her "Euthanasia," *Philosophy and Public Affairs,* 6 (1977): 85–112, especially pp. 95–96. She suggests that a good life must "contain a minimum of basic goods," although not necessarily a favorable balance of good over evil elements. When does she think this minimum fails? For one thing, in extreme senility or severe brain damage. She also cites as examples of conditions for minimum goods that "a man is not driven to work far beyond his capacity; that he has the support of a family or community; that he can more or less satisfy his hunger; that he has hopes for the future; that he can lie down to rest at night." Overwhelming pain or nausea, or crippling depression, she says, also can make life not worth living. All of these, of course, except for cases of senility and brain damage, are factors fixing whether stretches of living are highly unpleasant.

   If a person thinks that life is not good unless it realizes certain human potentialities, he will think life can be bad even if liked—and so far sets a higher standard than the happiness criterion. But Foot and such writers may say that even when life is not pleasant on balance, it can still be good if human potentialities are being realized or these basic minimal conditions are met; and in that sense they set a lower standard.
3. Richard B. Brandt, "The Morality of Abortion," in an earlier form in *The Monist* 56 (1972): 504–526, and in revised form in R. L. Perkins, ed., *Abortion: Pro and Con* (Cambridge, MA: Schenkman Publishing Co., 1974).
4. See A. M. Shaw and I. A. Shaw, in S. Gorovitz, et al., *Moral Problems in Medicine* (Englewood Cliffs, NJ: Prentice-Hall, Inc., 1976), pp. 335–341.
5. See, for instance, Philippa Foot; "Euthanasia," especially pp. 109–111. She writes: "So it is not for their sake but to avoid trouble to others that they are allowed to die. When brought out into the open this seems unacceptable; at least we do not easily accept the principle that adults who need special care should be counted too burdensome to be kept alive." I would think that "to avoid trouble to others" is hardly the terminology to describe the havoc that is apt to be produced. I agree that adults should not be allowed to die, or actively killed, without their consent, possibly except when they cannot give consent but are in great pain; but the reasons that justify different behavior in the two situations have appeared in the section, "Consent."

Review Questions

1. According to Brandt, how should one answer questions about moral rightness?
2. According to Brandt, why can't the Biblical injunction "Thou shalt not kill" be taken seriously?
3. Explain Brandt's happiness criterion.
4. In Brandt's view, in what cases would the life of a defective infant be bad?
5. Why would a newborn be indifferent to continued life according to Brandt?
6. In Brandt's view, why is it better to replace a defective child with a normal one?
7. According to Brandt, why is active euthanasia better than passive euthanasia in some cases?

Discussion Questions

1. Is Brandt's happiness criterion acceptable? Defend your view.
2. Is the cost of caring for a defective infant morally relevant? Defend your position.
3. Do you agree that in some cases active euthanasia is better than passive euthanasia? Why or why not?

PROBLEM CASES

1. ***Dr. Jack Kevorkian.*** Dr. Kevorkian is a retired Michigan pathologist who has become famous for assisting suicides. In the past three years, he has helped many people commit suicide.

Kevorkian's standard method of assisted suicide is to provide patients with one of several suicide devices he has made. Some inject a lethal drug and others allow the patient to breath a lethal gas. The lethal drug device allows the patient to push a button or switch forcing a lethal drug (potassium chloride for example) through a tube and into a vein in the arm producing a quick and relatively painless death.

Perhaps the most famous case involved Janet Adkins, a woman suffering from Alzheimer's disease who killed herself by lethal injection using one of Kevorkian's suicide devices. The next day, Kevorkian appeared on practically every talk show and news program in the country. Although Adkins was not terminally ill in the usual sense of the term, a Michigan judge did not prosecute Kevorkian for murder because the state had no laws against assisted suicide. There is a court injunction forbidding Kevorkian to use his devices, but he has continued to use them.

Is Dr. Kevorkian doing something wrong? If so, what? And why is it wrong?

Should there be a law against assisted suicide? How should the law read?

2. ***The Case of Karen Quinlan.*** On the night of April 15, 1975, for reasons still unclear, Karen Quinlan ceased breathing. She had been at a birthday party, and after a few drinks, passed out. Her friends thought she was drunk and put her to bed. Later, they found that she had stopped breathing. Her friends gave her mouth-to-mouth resuscitation and took her to the nearest hospital. She had a temperature of 100 degrees, her pupils were unreactive and she was unresponsive even to deep pain.

Blood and urine tests showed that Karen had not consumed a dangerous amount of alcohol. A small amount of aspirin and the tranquillizer Valium were present, but not enough to be toxic or lethal. Why Karen had stopped breathing was a mystery. It was clear that part of her brain had died from oxygen deprivation.

After a week of unconsciousness, she was moved to St. Clare's Hospital in nearby Denville, where she was examined by Dr. Robert J. Morse, a neurologist. Dr. Morse found that she was in a "chronic persistent vegetative state" but not **brain dead** by the ordinary medical standard. It was judged that no form of treatment could restore her to cognitive life.

Nevertheless, she was kept breathing by means of a respirator that pumped air through a tube in her throat, and fed by means of a nasal-gastro tube. Her condition began to deteriorate. Her weight dropped to seventy pounds, and her five-foot two-inch frame bent into a rigid fetal position about three feet in length. After a few months, her father, Joseph Quinlan, asked to be appointed her legal guardian with the express purpose of requesting that the respirator be discontinued. Experts testified that there was a strong likelihood that death would follow the removal of the respirator. The lower court refused his request that the respirator be discontinued; it said that "to do so would be homicide and an act of euthanasia." But in a famous decision (Supreme Court of New Jersey 355 A.2d 647), the Supreme Court of New Jersey granted the request on the condition that: (1) attending physicians of Joseph Quinlan's choice conclude that there was no reasonable possibility of Karen being restored to cognitive life, and (2) the ethics committee of the institution where Karen was hospitalized concur in the physician's judgement.

Do you agree with the Supreme Court of New Jersey decision? Why or why not?

3. ***The Case of Karen Quinlan Continued.*** Six weeks after the court decision, the respirator still had not been turned off because the attending physicians, Dr. Robert Morse (a neurologist) and Dr. Javed (a pulmonary internist) were reluctant to do so. After Mr. Quinlan demanded that they remove her from the respirator, they agreed to wean her slowly from the machine. Soon she was breathing without mechanical assistance and moved to a chronic-care hospital. For about ten years Karen was kept alive in the Morris View Nursing Home with high-nutrient feedings and regular doses of antibiotics to prevent infections. During this time, she never regained consciousness, but sometimes she made reflexive responses to touch and sound. After about ten years of comatose existence, Karen Quinlan died.

Would it have been morally right, during this long comatose period, to withhold antibiotics so that she would die from infections?

Would it have been wrong to give her a fatal injection? Why or why not?

Was it a good idea to keep her alive all this time? Why or why not?

4. The Case of Baby Jane Doe. In October 1983, Baby Jane Doe (as the infant was called by the court to protect her anonymity) was born with spina bifida and a host of other congenital defects. According to the doctors consulted by the parents, the child would be severely mentally retarded, bedridden, and suffer considerable pain. After consultations with doctors and religious counselors, Mr. and Mrs. A (as the parents were called in the court documents) decided not to consent to life-saving surgery.

Did the parents make the right decision or not? Explain and defend your position.

5. The Baby Doe Case Continued. A right-to-life activist lawyer tried to legally force life-saving surgery in the Baby Doe case, but two New York appeals courts and a state children's agency decided not to override the parent's right to make a decision in the case. At this point, the U.S. Justice Department intervened in the case. It sued to obtain records from the University Hospital in Stony Brook, New York, to determine if the hospital had violated a federal law that forbids discrimination against the handicapped. Dr. C. Everett Koop, the U.S. Surgeon General, appeared on television to express the view that the government has the moral obligation to intercede on behalf of such infants in order to protect their right to life.

Two weeks later, Federal District Judge Leonard Wexler threw out the Justice Department's unusual suit. Wexler found no discrimination. The hospital had been willing to do the surgery, but had failed to do so because the parents refused to consent to the surgery. Wexler found the parent's decision to be a reasonable one in view of the circumstances.

The day after the ruling, the Justice Department appealed. On January 9, 1984, federal regulations were issued preventing federally funded hospitals from withholding treatment in such cases.

Do parents have a right to make life and death decisions for their defective children? Why or why not?

Do you agree with Dr. Koop that the government has a moral obligation to save the lives of such infants, even when their parents do not wish it? Explain your position.

If the government forces us to save the lives of defective infants like Baby Doe, then should it assume the responsibility for the cost of surgery, intensive care, and so on? If so, then how much money should be spent on this program? If not, then who is going to pay the bills?

SUGGESTED READINGS

1. Albert Camus, *The Myth of Sisyphus,* trans by J. O'Brien (New York: Vintage Books, 1955), argues that we should not commit suicide even if life seems meaningless or without value.

2. Margaret Pabst Battin and David J. Mayo, eds., *Suicide: The Philosophical Issues* (New York: St. Martin's Press, 1980) has a useful collection of contemporary articles on suicide.

3. Tristram H. Englehardt, Jr., "Ethical Issues in Aiding the Death of Young Children," in *Beneficient Euthanasia,* Marvin Kohl, ed. (Buffalo, NY: Prometheus Books, 1975), pp. 180–192. Englehardt distinguishes between adult euthanasia and euthanasia of children. He assumes that adult euthanasia can be justified by the appeal to freedom. Adults have a right to choose to die. But, Englehardt claims, children do not have this right because they are not persons in a strict sense; they are persons only in a social sense. He argues that child euthanasia is justified when parents decide that the child has little chance of a full human life and a great chance of suffering, when the cost of prolonging life is great.

4. Philippa Foot, "Euthanasia," *Philosophy and Public Affairs* 6 (Winter 1977), pp. 85–112. Foot defines euthanasia as producing a death (by act or omission) that is good for the one who dies. She distinguishes between voluntary and nonvoluntary euthanasia, and between active and passive euthanasia. The latter distinction is based on the right to life and the correlative duty of noninterference. This duty is usually violated by active euthanasia, but not by passive euthanasia. She finds that nonvoluntary active euthanasia is never justified; however, she allows that the other types can be justified in some cases.

5. Philipa Foot, "The Problem of Abortion and the Doctrine of the Double Effect," *Oxford Review,* No. 5, pp. 5–15. Foot gives a classic discussion of

the doctrine of double effect. As Foot defines it, this doctrine maintains that it is sometimes permissible to bring about by oblique intention what is wrong to directly intend. Appealing to this doctrine, conservatives hold that it is permissible to perform an abortion to save the mother's life since the direct intention is to save the mother's life. The death of the fetus is only indirectly or obliquely intended, that is, foreseen as a consequence, but not directly intended.

6. Jonathan Glover, *Causing Death and Saving Lives* (Harmondsworth, Middlesex, England: Penguin Books, 1977), pp. 182–189. Glover applies utilitarianism to the problem of euthanasia and to other problems of killing such as abortion and capital punishment.

7. Marvin Kohl, ed., *Beneficent Euthanasia* (Buffalo, NY: Prometheus Books, 1975). This anthology has a number of excellent articles on euthanasia.

8. Marvin Kohl, ed., *Infanticide and the Value of Life* (Buffalo, NY: Prometheus Books, 1978). This anthology concentrates on the morality of euthanasia for severely defective newborns.

9. John Ladd, "Positive and Negative Euthanasia," in *Ethical Issues Relating to Life & Death,* John Ladd, ed. (Oxford: Oxford University Press, 1979), pp. 164–186. Ladd prefers to talk about positive and negative euthanasia rather than active and passive euthanasia. He rejects two positions: the absolutist position that a clear-cut and absolute distinction can be made between killing and letting die, and the consequentialist position that the consequences of killing and letting die are the same, and so there is no significant moral difference between the two. His own position is called a contextual position; it is the view that the distinction always depends on the context.

10. James Rachels, "Euthanasia," in *Matters of Life and Death,* 3d ed., Tom Regan, ed. (New York: Random House, 1993), pp. 30–68. Rachels discusses the history of euthanasia, the arguments for and against active euthanasia, and concludes with a proposal on how to legalize active euthanasia.

11. James Rachels, *The End of Life: Euthanasia and Morality* (Oxford: Oxford University Press, 1986). Rachels develops a liberal view on euthanasia and defends it from criticism.

12. John A. Robertson, "Involuntary Euthanasia of Defective Newborns," *Stanford Law Review,* vol. 27 (Jan. 1975), pp. 213–261. In opposition to Engelhardt, Brandt, and others, Robertson argues that the utilitarian or consequentialist defense of euthanasia for defective newborns does not succeed in showing that it is justified.

13. Seneca, "On Suicide," *Epistles,* trans. by E. Barker (Oxford: Clarendon Press, 1932). The Roman Stoic gives a classical discussion of suicide.

14. Bonnie Steinbock, "The Intentional Termination of Life," *Ethics in Science and Medicine,* No. 315 (1979), pp. 59–64. Steinbock defends the AMA statement on euthanasia from the attacks made by Rachels. She claims that the AMA statement does not make any distinction between active and passive euthanasia. She argues that cessation of extraordinary means of treatment is not the same as passive euthanasia.

15. Thomas D. Sullivan, "Active and Passive Euthanasia: An Impertinent Distinction?" *Human Life Review* III (Summer 1977), pp. 40–46, defends the AMA statement against Rachels attack in "Active and Passive Euthanasia." He argues that Rachels' distinction between active and passive euthanasia is impertinent and irrelevant. Rachels' reply to Sullivan is entitled "More Impertinent Distinctions," in *Biomedical Ethics,* ed. by T. A. Mappes and J. S. Zembaty (New York: McGraw-Hill, 1981), pp. 355–359.

16. Donald Van DeVeer, "Whither Baby Doe?" in *Matters of Life and Death,* 2d ed. Tom Regan, ed. (New York: Random House, 1986), pp. 213–255. Van DeVeer begins a detailed discussion of the famous Baby Doe case (see the Problem Cases). Then he examines various moral issues raised by the case, including the relevance of defects, the neonatal right to life, neonatal moral standing, and questions of public policy on the treatment or nontreatment of defective newborns.

17. Robert Young, "Voluntary and Nonvoluntary Euthanasia," *The Monist* 59 (April 1976), pp. 264–282. Young reviews a number of arguments used to show that voluntary active euthanasia is not justified and concludes that none of them is successful.

18. Robert F. Weir, *Selective Nontreatment of Handicapped Newborns: Moral Dilemmas in Neonatal Medicine* (New York: Oxford University Press, 1984). Weir discusses moral issues relating to the care and treatment of defective or handicapped newborns.

Chapter Four

CAPITAL PUNISHMENT

Introduction

Legal Background. The Eighth Amendment to the Constitution of the United States prohibits cruel and unusual punishment. For example, the medieval punishment of cutting off the hands of thieves seems to be cruel and unusual. Is the death penalty another example of cruel and unusual punishment, and thus unconstitutional? This is a matter of debate. In the case of *Furman* v. *Georgia* (1972), the Supreme Court ruled (by a five-to-four majority) that the death penalty was unconstitutional because it was being administered in an arbitrary and capricious manner. Juries were allowed to inflict the death sentence without any explicit guidelines or standards, and the result was that blacks were much more likely to receive the death penalty than whites.

After the *Furman* decision, states wishing to retain the death penalty reacted in two ways. One was to correct the arbitrary discretion of juries by making the death penalty mandatory for certain crimes. But in *Woodson* v. *North Carolina* (1976), the court ruled (again by a mere five-to-four majority) that mandatory death sentences were unconstitutional.

The second attempt to counter the objection raised in *Furman* was to provide standards for juries. Georgia specified in its law ten statutory aggravating circumstances, one of which the jury had to find beyond a reasonable doubt in order to render a death sentence. This second approach proved to be successful. In *Gregg* v. *Georgia* (1976), the first reading for the chapter, the majority ruled, with Justice Marshall and Justice Brennan dissenting, that the death penalty is not unconstitutional for the crime of murder, provided there are safeguards against any arbitrary or capricious imposition by juries.

But why isn't the death penalty cruel and unusual? In their majority opinion, Justices Stewart, Powell, and Stevens answered this important question. First, they gave an explanation of the concept of cruel and unusual. In their view, a punishment is cruel and unusual if it either fails to accord with evolving standards of decency or fails to accord with the dignity of man that is the basic concept underlying the Eighth Amendment. This second stipulation rules out excessive punishment that involves unnecessary pain or is disproportionate to the crime. They argued that the death penalty does not satisfy either of these stipulations. It is acceptable to the majority of the people, since thirty-five states have statutes providing for the death penalty, and it is not excessive because it achieves two important social purposes, **retribution** and **deterrence.**

Retribution. To fully understand the appeal to retribution, it is necessary to examine the theory on which it is based, namely **retributivism.** The classical formulation of this theory is given by Immanuel Kant in the second reading. According to Kant, the only justification for punishing a person is guilt. If a person is guilty of a crime, then justice requires that he or she be punished; and if a person is not guilty, then no punishment is justified. In other words, guilt is both a necessary and a sufficient condition for justified punishment. Furthermore, in Kant's view the punishment must fit the crime (be proportionate) according to the traditional principle of retaliation (**lex talionis**) that says, "life for life, eye for eye, tooth for tooth." Now what punishment fits the crime of murder using this principle? Kant insists that death, and only death, is the proper punishment for murder; no other punishment will satisfy the requirements of legal justice.

Various objections have been made to the retributive view. Glover (in the last reading of the chapter) claims that it is open to the objection that it leads to what he considers to be pointless suffering, that is, suffering without any real benefits, either to the person punished or to other people. But the retributivist such as Kant or van den Haag (see the fourth reading for the chapter) can reply that punishment does provide an important benefit, namely that justice is served by giving the criminal the punishment he or she deserves. If punishment is not given, then people will not be held accountable for their actions nor will they realize the consequences of their deeds.

In the third reading for the chapter, Anthony G. Amsterdam rejects the principle of strict retaliation according to which there must be "an eye for an eye, a life for a life." He claims that appealing to this principle does not justify capital punishment because of the simple fact that most murderers are sent to prison, not executed. Obviously we think that many crimes of murder do not deserve the death penalty; for example, we do not have the death sentence for homicides that are unpremeditated or accidental. Another objection to the strict principle of retaliation is that we do have the death sentence for nonhomicidal crimes such as treason. This shows that the death sentence can be justified for crimes other than murder.

The principle of strict retaliation can be revised to say that the punishment should fit the crime, so that serious crimes are severely punished. But as Amsterdam points out, this does not tell us how severely we ought to punish any particular crime. Should we punish vicious murderers by burning them at the stake or boiling them in oil? Now it seems that retributivism can be used to justify punishment that is indeed cruel.

But retributivism can be defended against the charge that it justifies cruel and unusual punishment. We can agree with retributivism that criminals should be punished, but insist there be limits to the severity of the punishment. We shouldn't, for example, torture criminals. We must treat the criminal with the respect due to a member of the community (as Kant would say). But Kant and van den Haag both think that the death penalty is compatible with respectful treatment. They think that the death penalty actually treats the criminal with humanity and dignity because it affirms the criminal's rationality and responsibility for action.

Deterence. The principle of deterence is an appeal to the social benefits of punishment. The particular social benefits claimed for the death penalty by its defenders are deterrence and prevention: It deters other potential criminals from killing, and it prevents the criminal who is executed from committing further crimes. No doubt an executed criminal can commit no more crimes; but does the death penalty actually deter other potential criminals? This is a factual question that is much debated.

Without going into the details, the Supreme Court Justices note that statistical attempts to prove that the death penalty is a deterrent have been inconclusive. However, the Justices think that the death penalty is undoubtedly a significant deterrent for some potential murderers, for example, those who carefully contemplate their actions.

Amsterdam reviews some of the evidence for the death penalty as a deterrent and finds it to be inconclusive—it does not show that the death penalty is a better deterrent than life imprisonment for murder. Amsterdam also discusses and rejects the appeal to intuition, namely, that the fear of death would intuitively seem to deter potential murderers.

Ernest van den Haag agrees that there is no conclusive statistical evidence that the death penalty is a better deterrent than alternative punishments. But he uses a subtle argument, called the best-bet argument by Glover, to show that we should use the death penalty rather than alternative punishments because it might save innocent victims whose lives are more valuable than the murderers who are executed. Glover discusses this argument, as well as the intuitive argument, and attempts to refute them both.

Glover's own view is that capital punishment has not been shown to be a substantial deterrent and that there is a strong presumption against it because of its special evils and bad side effects.

The Supreme Court

Gregg v. Georgia (1976)

Potter Stewart, Lewis F. Powell, Jr., and John Paul Stevens are Associate Justices of the United States Supreme Court. Justice Stewart, a graduate of Yale Law School, was appointed to the Court in 1958. Justice Powell, LL.M (Harvard), was appointed in 1971. Justice Stevens graduated from Northwestern University School of Law, and was appointed to the Court in 1975. Thurgood Marshall, associate justice of the United States Supreme Court, was appointed in 1967; he was the first black person ever to be appointed. (He is now deceased.)

The main issue before the Court in the case of Gregg v. Georgia *(1976) was whether or not the death penalty violates the Eighth Amendment prohibition of cruel and unusual punishment. The majority of the Court, with Justice Marshall and Justice Brennan dissenting, held that the death penalty does not violate the Eighth Amendment because it is in accord with contemporary standards of decency. It serves both a deterrent and retributive purpose, and in the case of the Georgia law being reviewed, it is no longer arbitrarily applied.*

In his dissenting opinion, Justice Marshall objects that the death sentence is excessive because a less severe penalty—life imprisonment—would accomplish the legitimate purposes of punishment. In reply to the claim that the death sentence is necessary for deterrence, Marshall asserts that the available evidence shows that this is not the case. As for the appeal to retribution, Marshall argues that the purely retributive justification for the death penalty is not consistent with human dignity.

The issue in this case is whether the imposition of the sentence of death for the crime of murder under the law of Georgia violates the Eighth and Fourteenth Amendments.

I

The petitioner, Troy Gregg, was charged with committing armed robbery and murder. In accordance with Georgia procedure in capital cases, the trial was in two stages, a guilt stage and a sentencing stage. . . .

. . . The jury found the petitioner guilty of two counts of murder.

At the penalty stage, which took place before the same jury, . . . the trial judge instructed the jury that it could recommend either a death sentence or a life prison sentence on each count. . . . The jury returned verdicts of death on each count.

The Supreme Court of Georgia affirmed the convictions and the imposition of the death sentences for murder. . . . The death sentences imposed for armed robbery, however, were vacated on the grounds that the death penalty had rarely been imposed in Georgia for that offense. . . .

II

. . . The Georgia statute, as amended after our decision in *Furman* v. *Georgia* (1972), retains the death penalty for six categories of crime: murder, kidnapping for ransom or where the victim is harmed, armed robbery, rape, treason, and aircraft hijacking. . . .

III

We address initially the basic contention that the punishment of death for the crime of murder is, under all circumstances, "cruel and unusual" in violation of the Eighth and Fourteenth Amendments of the Constitution. In Part IV of this opinion, we will consider the sentence of death imposed under the Georgia statutes at issue in this case.

The Court on a number of occasions has both assumed and asserted the constitutionality of capital punishment. In several cases that assumption provided a necessary foundation for the decision, as the Court was asked to decide whether a particular method of carrying out a capital sentence would be allowed to stand under the Eighth Amendment. But until *Furman* v. *Georgia* (1972), the Court never confronted squarely the fundamental claim that the punishment of death always, regardless of the enormity of the offense or the procedure followed in imposing the sentence, is cruel and unusual punishment in violation of the Constitution. Although this issue was presented and addressed in *Furman,* it was not resolved by the Court. Four Justices would have held that capital punishment is not unconstitutional *per se;* two Justices would have reached the opposite conclusion; and three Justices, while agreeing that the statutes then before the Court were invalid as applied, left open the question whether such punishment may ever be imposed. We now hold that the punishment of death does not invariably violate the Constitution.

A

The history of the prohibition of "cruel and unusual" punishment already has been reviewed at length. The phrase first appeared in the English Bill of Rights of 1689, which was drafted by Parliament at the accession of William and Mary. The English version appears to have been directed against punishments unauthorized by statute and beyond the jurisdiction of the sentencing court, as well as those disproportionate to the offense involved. The American draftsmen, who adopted the English phrasing in drafting the Eighth Amendment, were primarily concerned, however, with proscribing "tortures" and other "barbarous" methods of punishment.

In the earliest cases raising Eighth Amendment claims, the Court focused on particular methods of execution to determine whether they were too cruel to pass constitutional muster. The constitutionality of the sentence of death itself was not at issue, and the criterion used to evaluate the mode of execution was its similarity to "torture" and other "barbarous" methods. . . .

But the Court has not confined the prohibition embodied in the Eighth Amendment to "barbarous" methods that were generally outlawed in the 18th century. Instead, the Amendment has been interpreted in a flexible and dynamic manner. The Court early recognized that "a principle to be vital must be capable of wider application than the mischief which gave it birth." Thus the clause forbidding "cruel and unusual" punishments "is not fastened to the obsolete but may acquire meaning as public opinion becomes enlightened by a humane justice." . . .

It is clear from the foregoing precedents that the Eighth Amendment has not been regarded as a static concept. As Mr. Chief Justice Warren said, in an oftquoted phrase, "[t]he Amendment must draw its meaning from the evolving standards of decency that mark the progress of a maturing society." Thus, an assessment of contemporary values concerning the infliction of a challenged sanction is relevant to the application of the Eighth Amendment. As we develop below more fully, this assessment does not call for a subjective judgment. It requires, rather, that we look to objective indicia that reflect the public attitude toward a given sanction.

But our cases also make clear that public perceptions of standards of decency with respect to criminal sanctions are not conclusive. A penalty also must accord with "the dignity of man," which is the "basic concept underlying the Eighth Amendment." This means, at least, that the punishment not be "excessive." When a form of punishment in the abstract (in this case, whether capital punishment may ever be imposed as a sanction for murder) rather than in the particular (the propriety of death as a penalty to be applied to a specific defendant for a specific crime) is under consideration, the inquiry into "excessiveness" has two aspects. First, the punishment must not involve the unnecessary and wanton infliction of pain. Second, the punishment must not be grossly out of proportion to the severity of the crime.

B

Of course, the requirements of the Eighth Amendment must be applied with an awareness of the limited role to be played by the courts. This does not mean that judges have no role to play, for the Eighth Amendment is a restraint upon the exercise of legislative power. . . .

But, while we have an obligation to ensure that constitutional bounds are not over-reached, we may not act as judges as we might as legislators. . . .

Therefore, in assessing a punishment selected by a democratically elected legislature against the constitutional measure, we presume its validity. We may not require the legislature to select the least severe penalty possible so long as the penalty selected is not cruelly inhumane or disproportionate to the crime involved. And a heavy burden rests on those who would attack the judgment of the representatives of the people.

This is true in part because the constitutional test is intertwined with an assessment of contemporary standards and the legislative judgment weighs heavily in ascertaining such standards. "[I]n a democratic society legislatures, not courts, are constituted to respond to the will and consequently the moral values of the people."

The deference we owe to the decisions of the state legislatures under our federal system is enhanced where the specification of punishments is concerned, for "these are peculiarly questions of legislative policy." Caution is necessary lest this Court become, "under the aegis of the Cruel and Unusual Punishment Clause, the ultimate arbiter of the standards of criminal responsibility . . . throughout the country." A decision that a given punishment is impermissible under the Eighth Amendment cannot be reversed short of a constitutional amendment. The ability of the people to express their preference through the normal democratic processes, as well as through the normal democratic processes, as well as through ballot referenda, is shut off. Revisions cannot be made in the light of further experience.

C

In the discussion to this point we have sought to identify the principles and considerations that guide a court in addressing an Eighth Amendment claim. We now consider specifically whether the sentence of death for the crime of murder is a *per se* violation of the Eighth and Fourteenth Amendments to the Constitution. We note first that history and precedent strongly support a negative answer to this question.

The imposition of the death penalty for the crime of murder has a long history of acceptance both in the United States and in England. . . .

It is apparent from the text of the Constitution itself that the existence of capital punishment was accepted by the Framers. At the time the Eighth Amendment was ratified, capital punishment was a common sanction in every State. Indeed, the First Congress of the United States enacted legislation providing death as the penalty for specified crimes. . . .

For nearly two centuries, this Court, repeatedly and often expressly, has recognized that capital punishment is not invalid *per se*. . . .

Four years ago, the petitioners in *Furman* and its companion cases predicated their argument primarily upon the asserted proposition that standards of decency had evolved to the point where capital punishment no longer could be tolerated. The petitioners in those cases said, in effect, that the evolutionary process had come to an end, and that standards of decency required that the Eighth Amendment be construed finally as prohibiting capital punishment for any crime regardless of its depravity and impact on society. This view was accepted by two Justices. Three other Justices were unwilling to go so far; focusing on the procedures by which convicted defendants were selected for the death penalty rather than on the actual punishment inflicted, they joined in the conclusion that the statutes before the Court were constitutionally invalid.

The petitioners in the capital cases before the Court today renew the "standards of decency" argument, but developments during the four years since *Furman* have undercut substantially the assumptions upon which their argument rested. Despite the continuing debate, dating back to the nineteenth century, over the morality and utility of capital punishment, it is now evident that a large proportion of American society continues to regard it as an appropriate and necessary criminal sanction.

The most marked indication of society's endorsement of the death penalty for murder is the legislative response to *Furman*. The legislatures of at least thirty-five States have enacted new statutes that provide for the death penalty for at least some crimes that result in the death of another person. And the Congress of the United States, in 1974, enacted a statute providing the death penalty for aircraft piracy that results in death. These recently adopted statutes have attempted to address the concerns expressed by the Court in *Furman* primarily (i) by specifying the factors to be weighed and the procedures to be followed in deciding when to impose a capital sentence, or (ii) by making the death penalty mandatory for specified crimes. But all of the post-*Furman* statutes make clear that capital punishment itself has not been rejected by the elected representatives of the people. . . .

The jury also is a significant and reliable objective index of contemporary values because it is so directly involved. The Court has said that "one of the most important functions any jury can perform in making . . . a selection [between life imprisonment and death for a defendant convicted in a capital case] is to maintain a link between contemporary community values and the penal system." It may be true that evolving standards have influenced juries in recent decades to be more discriminating in imposing the sentence of death. But the relative infrequency of jury verdicts imposing death sentence does not indicate rejection of capital punishment *per se*. Rather, the reluctance of juries in many cases to impose the sentence may well reflect the humane feeling that this most irrevocable of sanctions should be reserved for a small number of extreme cases. Indeed, the actions of juries in many states since *Furman* are fully compatible with the legislative judgments, reflected in the new statutes, as to the continued utility and necessity of capital punishment in appropriate cases. At the close of 1974 at least 254 persons had been sentenced to death since *Furman,* and by the end of March 1976, more than 460 persons were subject to death sentences.

As we have seen, however, the Eighth Amendment demands more than that a challenged punishment be acceptable to contemporary society. The Court also must ask whether it comports with the basic concept of human dignity at the core of the amendment. Although we cannot "invalidate a category of penalties because we deem less severe penalties adequate to serve the ends of penology," the sanction imposed cannot be so totally without penological justification that it results in the gratuitous infliction of suffering.

The death penalty is said to serve two principal social purposes: retribution and deterrence of capital crimes by prospective offenders.[1]

In part, capital punishment is an expression of society's moral outrage at particularly offensive conduct. This function may be unappealing to many, but it is essential in an ordered society that asks its citizens to rely on legal processes rather than self-help to vindicate their wrongs.

> The instinct for retribution is part of the nature of man, and channeling that instinct in the administration of criminal justice serves an important purpose in promoting the stability of a society governed by law. When people begin to believe that organized society is unwilling or unable to impose upon criminal offenders the punishment they "deserve," then there are sown the seeds of anarchy—if self-help, vigilante justice, and lynch law. Furman v. Georgia (Stewart, J., concurring).

Retribution is no longer the dominant objective of the criminal law," but neither is it a forbidden objective nor one inconsistent with our respect for the dignity of men. Indeed, the decision that capital punishment may be the appropriate sanction in extreme cases is an expression of the community's belief that certain crimes are themselves so grievous an affront to humanity that the only adequate response may be the penalty of death.

Statistical attempts to evaluate the worth of the death penalty as a deterrent to crimes of potential offenders have occasioned a great deal of debate. The results simply have been inconclusive. . . .

Although some of the studies suggest that the death penalty may not function as a significantly greater deterrent than lesser penalties, there is no convincing empirical evidence either supporting or refuting this view. We may nevertheless assume safely that there are murderers, such as those who act in passion, for whom the threat of death has little or no deterrent effect. But for many others, the death penalty undoubtedly is a significant deterrent. There are carefully contemplated murders, such as murder for hire, where the possible penalty of death may well enter into the cold calculus that precedes the decision to act. And there are some categories of murder, such as murder by a life prisoner, where other sanctions may not be adequate.

The value of capital punishment as a deterrent of crime is a complex factual issue the resolution of which properly rests with the legislatures, which can evaluate the results of statistical studies in terms of their own local conditions and with a flexibility of approach that is not available to the courts. Indeed, many of the post-*Furman* statutes reflect just such a responsible effort to define those crimes and those criminals for which capital punishment is most probably an effective deterrent.

In sum, we cannot say that the judgment of the Georgia Legislature that capital punishment may be necessary in some cases is clearly wrong. Considerations of federalism, as well as respect for the ability of a legislature to evaluate, in terms of its particular State, the moral consensus concerning the death penalty and its social utility as a sanction, require us to conclude, in the absence of more convincing evidence, that the infliction of death as a punishment for murder is not without justification and thus is not constitutionally severe.

Finally, we must consider whether the punishment of death is disproportionate in relation to the crime for which it is imposed. There is no question that death as a punishment is unique in its severity and irrevocability. When a defendant's life is at stake, the Court has been particularly sensitive to insure that every safeguard is observed. But we are concerned here only with the imposition of capital punishment for the crime of murder, and when a life has been taken deliberately by the offender,[2] we cannot say that the punishment is invariably disproportionate to the crime. It is an extreme sanction, suitable to the most extreme of crimes.

We hold that the death penalty is not a form of punishment that may never be imposed, regardless of the circumstances of the offense, regardless of the character of the offender, and regardless of the procedure followed in reaching the decision to impose it.

IV

We now consider whether Georgia may impose the death penalty on the petitioner in this case.

A

While *Furman* did not hold that the infliction of the death penalty *per se* violates the Constitution's ban on cruel and unusual punishments, it did recognize that the penalty of death is different in kind from any other punishment imposed under our system of criminal justice. Because of the uniqueness of the death penalty, *Furman* held that it could not be imposed under sentencing procedures that created a substantial risk that it would be inflicted in an arbitrary and capricious manner. . . .

Furman mandates that where discretion is afforded a sentencing body on a matter so grave as the determination of whether a human life should be taken or spared, that discretion must be suitably directed and limited so as to minimize the risk of wholly arbitrary and capricious action.

It is certainly not a novel proposition that discretion in the area of sentencing be exercised in an informed manner. We have long recognized that "[f]or the determination of sentences, justice generally requires . . . that there be taken into account the circumstances of the offense together with the character and propensities of the offender." . . .

Jury sentencing has been considered desirable in capital cases in order "to maintain a link between contemporary community values and the penal system—a link without which the determination of punishment could hardly reflect 'the evolving standards of decency that mark the progress of a maturing society.' " But it creates special problems. Much of the information that is relevant to the sentencing decision may have no relevance to the question of guilt, or may even be extremely prejudicial to a fair determination of that question. This problem, however, is scarcely insurmountable. Those who have studied the question suggest that a bifurcated procedure—one in which the question of sentence is not considered until the determination of guilt has been made—is the best answer. . . . When a human life is at stake and when the jury must have information prejudicial to the question of guilt but relevant to the question of penalty in order to impose a rational sentence, a bifurcated system is more likely to ensure elimination of the constitutional deficiencies identified in *Furman*.

But the provision of relevant information under fair procedural rules is not alone sufficient to guarantee that the information will be properly used in the imposition of punishment, especially if sentencing is performed by a jury. Since the members of a jury will have had little, if any, previous experience in sentencing, they are unlikely to be skilled in dealing with the information they are given. To the extent that this problem is inherent in jury sentencing, it may not be totally correctable. It seems clear, however, that the problem will be alleviated if the jury is given guidance regarding the factors about the crime and the defendant that the State, representing organized society, deems particularly relevant to the sentencing decision. . . .

While some have suggested that standards to guide a capital jury's sentencing deliberations are impossible to formulate, the fact is that such standards have been developed. When the drafters of the Model Penal Code faced this problem, they concluded "that it is within the realm of possibility to point to the main circumstances of aggravation and of mitigation that should be weighed *and weighed against each other* when they are presented in a concrete case." [3] While such standards are by necessity somewhat general, they do provide guidance to the sentencing authority and thereby reduce the likelihood that it will impose a sentence that fairly can be called capricious or arbitrary. Where the sentencing authority is required to specify the factors it relied upon in reaching its decision, the further safeguard of meaningful appellate review is available to ensure that death sentences are not imposed capriciously or in a freakish manner.

In summary, the concerns expressed in *Furman* that the penalty of death not be imposed in an arbitrary or capricious manner can be met by a carefully drafted statute that ensures that the sentencing authority is given adequate information and guidance. As a general proposition these concerns are best met by a system that provides for a bifurcated proceeding at which the sentencing authority is apprised of the information relevant to the imposition of sentence and provided with standards to guide its use of the information.

We do not intend to suggest that only the above-described procedures would be permissible under *Furman* or that any sentencing system constructed along these general lines would inevitably satisfy the concerns of *Furman*, for each distinct system must be examined on an individual basis. Rather, we have embarked upon this general exposition to make clear that it is possible to construct capital-sentencing systems capable of meeting *Furman*'s constitutional concerns.

B

We now turn to consideration of the constitutionality of Georgia's capital-sentencing procedures. In the wake of *Furman*, Georgia amended its capital punishment statute, but chose not to narrow the scope of its murder provisions. Thus, now as before *Furman*, in Georgia "[a] person commits murder when he unlawfully and with malice aforethought, either express or implied, causes the death of another human being." All persons convicted of murder "shall be punished by death or by imprisonment for life."

Georgia did act, however, to narrow the class of murderers subject to capital punishment by specifying ten statutory aggravating circumstances, one of which must be found by the jury to exist beyond a reasonable doubt before a death sentence can ever be imposed. In addition, the jury is authorized to consider any other appropriate aggravating or mitigating circumstances. The jury is not required to find any mitigating circumstance in order to make a recommendation of mercy that is binding on the trial court, but it must find a *statutory* aggravating circumstance before recommending a sentence of death.

These procedures require the jury to consider the circumstances of the crime and the criminal before it recommends sentence. No longer can a Georgia jury do as Furman's jury did: reach a finding of the defendant's guilt and then, without guidance or direction, decide whether he should live or die. Instead, the jury's attention is directed to the specific circumstances of the crime: Was it committed in the course of another capital felony? Was it committed for money? Was it committed on a peace officer or judicial officer? Was it committed in a particularly heinous way or in a manner that endangered the lives of many persons? In addition, the jury's attention is focused on the characteristics of the person who committed the crime: Does he have a record of prior convictions for capital offenses? Are there any special facts about this defendant that mitigate against imposing capital punishment (*e.g.*, his youth, the extent of his cooperation with the police, his emotional state at the time of the crime)? As a result, while some jury discretion still exists, "the discretion to be exercised is controlled by clear and objective standards so as to produce nondiscriminatory application."

As an important additional safeguard against arbitrariness and caprice, the Georgia statutory scheme provides for automatic appeal of all death sentences to the State's Supreme Court. That court is required by statute to review each sentence of death and determine whether it was imposed under the influence of passion or prejudice, whether the evidence supports the jury's finding of statutory aggravating circumstance, and whether the sentence is disproportionate compared to those sentences imposed in similar cases.

In short, Georgia's new sentencing procedures require as a prerequisite to the imposition of the death penalty, specific jury findings as to the circumstances of the crime or the character of the defendant. Moreover, to guard further against a situation comparable to that presented in *Furman*, the Supreme Court of Georgia compares each death sentence with the sentences imposed on similarly situated defendants to ensure that the sentence of death in a particular case is not disproportionate. On their face these procedures seem to satisfy the concerns of *Furman*. No longer should there be "no meaningful basis for distinguishing the few cases in which [the death penalty] is imposed from the many cases in which it is not." . . .

V

The basic concern of *Furman* centered on those defendants who were being condemned to death capriciously and arbitrarily. Under the procedures before the Court in that case, sentencing authorities were not directed to give attention to the nature or circumstances of the crime committed or to the character or record of the defendant. Left unguided, juries imposed the death sentence in a way that could only be called freakish. The new Georgia sentencing procedures, by contrast, focus the jury's attention on the particularized nature of the crime and the particularized characteristics of the individual defendant. While the jury is permitted to consider any aggravating or mitigating circumstances, it must find and identify at least one statutory aggravating factor before it may impose a penalty of death. In this way the jury's discretion is channeled. No longer can a jury wantonly and freakishly impose the death sentence; it is always circumscribed by the legislative guidelines. In addition, the review function of the Supreme Court of Georgia affords additional assurance that the concerns that prompted our decision in *Furman* are not present to any significant degree in the Georgia procedure applied here.

For the reasons expressed in this opinion, we hold that the statutory system under which Gregg was sentenced to death does not violate the Constitution. Accordingly, the judgment of the Georgia Supreme Court is affirmed.

Dissenting Opinion

In *Furman* v. *Georgia* (1972) (concurring opinion), I set forth at some length my views on the basic issue presented to the Court in [this case]. The death penalty, I concluded, is a cruel and unusual punishment prohibited by the Eighth and Fourteenth Amendments. That continues to be my view.

I have no intention of retracing the "long and tedious journey" that led to my conclusion in *Furman*. My sole purposes here are to consider the suggestion that my conclusion in *Furman* has been undercut by developments since then, and briefly to evaluate the basis for my Brethren's holding that the extinction of life is a permissible form of punishment under the Cruel and Unusual Punishments Clause.

In *Furman*, I concluded that the death penalty is constitutionally invalid for two reasons. First, the death penalty is excessive. And second, the American people, fully informed as to the purposes of the death penalty and its liabilities, would in my view reject it as morally unacceptable.

Since the decision in *Furman*, the legislatures of thirty-five States have enacted new statutes authorizing the imposition of the death sentence for certain crimes, and Congress has enacted a law providing the death penalty for air piracy resulting in death. I would be less than candid if I did not acknowledge that these developments have a significant bearing on a realistic assessment of the moral acceptability of the death penalty to the American people. But if the constitutionality of the death penalty turns, as I have urged, on the opinion of an *informed* citizenry, then even the enactment of new death statutes cannot be viewed as conclusive. In *Furman*, I observed that the American people are largely unaware of the information critical to a judgment on the morality of the death penalty, and concluded that if they were better informed they would consider it shocking, unjust, and unacceptable. A recent study, conducted after the enactment of the post-*Furman* statutes, has confirmed that the American people know little about the death penalty, and that the opinions of an informed public would differ significantly from those of a public unaware of the consequences and effects of the death penalty.

Even assuming, however, that the post-*Furman* enactment of statutes authorizing the death penalty renders the prediction of the views of an informed citizenry an uncertain basis for a constitutional decision, the enactment of those statutes has no bearing whatsoever on the conclusion that the death penalty is unconstitutional because it is excessive. An excessive penalty is invalid under the Cruel and Unusual Punishments Clause "even though popular sentiment may favor" it. The inquiry here, then, is simply whether the death penalty is necessary to accomplish the legitimate legislative purposes in punishment, or whether a less severe penalty—life imprisonment—would do as well.

The two purposes that sustain the death penalty as nonexcessive in the Court's view are general deterrence and retribution. In *Furman*, I canvassed the relevant data on the deterrent effect of capital punishment. The state of knowledge at that point, after literally centuries of debate, was summarized as follows by a United Nations Committee:

> It is generally agreed between the retentionists and abolitionists, whatever their opinions about the validity of comparative studies of deterrence, that the data which now exist show no correlation between the existence of capital punishment and lower rates of capital crime.

The available evidence, I concluded in *Furman*, was convincing that "capital punishment is not necessary as a deterrent to crime in our society." . . .

The evidence I reviewed in *Furman* remains convincing, in my view, that "capital punishment is not necessary as a deterrent to crime in our society." The justification for the death penalty must be found elsewhere.

The other principal purpose said to be served by the death penalty is retribution. The notion that retribution can serve as a moral justification for the sanction of death finds credence in the opinion of my Brothers Stewart, Powell, and Stevens. . . . It is this notion that I find to be the most disturbing aspect of today's unfortunate [decision].

The concept of retribution is a multifaceted one, and any discussion of its role in the criminal law must be undertaken with caution. On one level, it can be said that the notion of retribution or reprobation is the basis of our insistence that only those who have broken the law be punished, and in this sense the notion is quite obviously central to a just system of criminal sanctions. But our recognition that retribution plays a crucial role in determining who may be punished by no means requires approval of retribution as a general justification for punishment. It is the question whether retribution can provide a moral justification for punishment—in particular, capital punishment—that we must consider.

My Brothers Stewart, Powell, and Stevens offer the following explanation of the retributive justification for capital punishments:

> The instinct for retribution is part of the nature of man, and channeling that instinct in the administration of criminal justice serves an important purpose in promoting the stability of a society governed by law. When people begin to believe that organized society is unwilling or unable to impose upon criminal offenders the punishment they "deserve," then there are sown the seeds of anarchy—of self-help, vigilante justice, and lynch law.

This statement is wholly inadequate to justify the death penalty. As my Brother Brennan stated in *Furman*, "[t]here is no evidence whatever that utilization of imprisonment rather than death encourages private blood feuds and other disorders." It simply defies belief to suggest that the death penalty is necessary to prevent the American people from taking the law into their own hands.

In a related vein, it may be suggested that the expression of moral outrage through the imposition of the death penalty serves to reinforce basic moral values—that it marks some crimes as particularly offensive and therefore to be avoided. The argument is akin to a deterrence argument, but differs in that it contemplates the individual's shrinking from antisocial conduct, not because he fears punishment, but because he has been told in the strongest possible way that the conduct is wrong. This contention, like the previous one, provides no support for the death penalty. It is inconceivable that any individual concerned about conforming his conduct to what society says is "right" would fail to realize that murder is "wrong" if the penalty were simply life imprisonment.

The foregoing contentions—that society's expression of moral outrage through the imposition of the death penalty preempts the citizenry from taking the law into its own hands and reinforces moral values—are not retributive in the purest sense. They are essentially utilitarian in that they portray the death penalty as valuable because of its beneficial results. These justifications for the death penalty are inadequate because the penalty is, quite clearly I think, not necessary to the accomplishment of those results.

There remains for consideration, however, what might be termed the purely retributive justification for the death penalty—that the death penalty is appropriate, not because of its beneficial effect on society, but because the taking of the murderer's life is itself morally good. Some of the language of the opinion of my Brothers Stewart, Powell, and Stevens . . . appears positively to embrace this notion of retribution for its own sake as a justification for capital punishment. They state:

> [T]he decision that capital punishment may be the appropriate sanction in extreme cases is an expression of the community's belief that certain crimes are themselves so grievous an affront to humanity that the only adequate response may be the penalty of death.

They then quote with approval from Lord Justice Denning's remarks before the British Royal Commission on Capital Punishment:

> The truth is that some crimes are so outrageous that society insists on adequate punishment, because the wrong-doer deserves it, irrespective of whether it is a deterrent or not.

Of course, it may be that these statements are intended as no more than observations as to the popular demands that it is thought must be responded to in order to prevent anarchy. But the implication of the statements appears to me to be quite different—namely, that society's judgment that the murderer "deserves" death must be respected not simply because the preservation of order requires it, but because it is appropriate that society make the judgment and carry it out. It is the latter notion, in particular, that I consider to be fundamentally at odds with the Eighth Amendment. The mere fact that the community demands the murderer's life in return for the evil he has done cannot sustain the death penalty, for as Justices Stewart, Powell, and Stevens remind us, "the Eighth Amendment demands more than that a challenged punishment be acceptable to contemporary society." To be sustained under the Eighth Amendment, the death penalty must "compor[t] with the basic concept of human dignity at the core of the Amendment;" the objective in imposing it must be "[consistent] with our respect for the dignity of [other] men." Under these standards, the taking of life "because the wrongdoer deserves it" surely must fail, for such a punishment has as its very basis the total denial of the wrongdoer's dignity and worth.

The death penalty, unnecessary to promote the goal of deterrence or to further any legitimate notion of retribution, is an excessive penalty forbidden by the Eighth and Fourteenth Amendments. I respectfully dissent from the Court's judgment upholding the [sentence] of death imposed upon the [petitioner in this case].

Endnotes

1. Another purpose has been discussed in the incapacitation of dangerous criminals and the consequent prevention of crimes that they may otherwise commit in the future.
2. We do not address here the question whether the taking of the criminal's life is a proportionate sanction where no victim has been deprived of life—for example, when capital punishment is imposed for rape, kidnapping, or armed robbery that does not result in the death of any human being.
3. The Model Penal Code proposes the following standards:

   "(3) Aggravating Circumstances.

   "(a) The murder was committed by a convict under sentence of imprisonment.

   "(b) The defendant was previously convicted of another murder or of a felony involving the use or threat of violence to the person.

   "(c) At the time the murder was committed the defendant also committed another murder.

   "(d) The defendant knowingly created a great risk of death to many persons.

   "(e) The murder was committed while the defendant was engaged or was an accomplice in the commission of, or an attempt to commit, or flight after committing or attempting to commit robbery, rape or deviate sexual intercourse by force or threat of force, arson, burglary or kidnapping.

   "(f) The murder was committed for the purpose of avoiding or preventing a lawful arrest or effecting an escape from lawful custody.

   "(g) The murder was committed for pecuniary gain.

   "(h) The murder was especially heinous, atrocious or cruel, manifesting exceptional depravity.

   "(4) Mitigating Circumstances.

   "(a) The defendant has no significant history of prior criminal activity.

   "(b) The murder was committed while the defendant was under the influence of extreme mental or emotional disturbance.

   "(c) The victim was a participant in the defendant's homicide conduct or consented to the homicidal act.

   "(d) The murder was committed under circumstances which the defendant believed to provide a moral justification or extenuation for his conduct.

   "(e) The defendant was an accomplice in a murder committed by another person and his participation in the homicide act was relatively minor.

   "(f) The defendant acted under duress or under the domination of another person.

   "(g) At the time of the murder, the capacity of the defendant to appreciate the criminality [wrongfulness] of his conduct or to conform his conduct to the requirements of law was impaired as a result of mental disease or defect or intoxication.

   "(h) The youth of the defendant at the time of the crime." ALI Model Penal Code §210.6 (Proposed Official Draft 1962).

Review Questions

1. How did the justices rule in *Furman* v. *Georgia* (1972), and by contrast, how do they rule in this case?
2. According to the justices, what is the basic concept underlying the Eighth Amendment?
3. According to the justices, in what two ways may a punishment be excessive?
4. According to the justices, why doesn't the death penalty violate contemporary standards of decency?
5. The justices say that the death penalty serves two principal social purposes. What are they, and how are they supposed to work?
6. What safeguards against the arbitrary and capricious application of the death sentence are suggested by the justices?
7. Explain Justice Marshall's objections and his criticisms of the majority opinion.

Discussion Questions

1. The Georgia statute retains the death penalty for six crimes, including rape, armed robbery, and treason. Do you agree that persons guilty of these crimes should receive the death sentence? Explain your view.
2. Try to give a precise definition of the phrase "cruel and unusual." Can you do it?
3. How could it be conclusively proven that the death penalty deters potential criminals better than life imprisonment?
4. Should the instinct for retribution be satisfied? Defend your answer.

Immanual Kant

The Retributive Theory of Punishment

For biographical information on Kant, see his reading in Chapter 1.

In Kant's retributive theory of punishment, punishment is not justified by any good results, but simply by the criminal's guilt. Criminals must pay for their crimes; otherwise an injustice has occurred. Furthermore, the punishment must fit the crime. Kant asserts that the only punishment that is appropriate for the crime of murder is the death of the murderer. As he puts it, "Whoever has committed a murder must die."

Judicial or juridical punishment (*poena forensis*) is to be distinguished from natural punishment (*poena naturalis*), in which crime as vice punishes itself, and does not as such come within the cognizance of the legislator. Juridical punishment can never be administered merely as a means for promoting another good, either with regard to the criminal himself or to civil society, but must in all cases be imposed only because the individual on whom it is inflicted *has committed a crime*. For one man ought never to be dealt with merely as a means subservient to the purpose of another, nor be mixed up with the subjects of real right. Against such treatment his inborn personality has a right to protect him, even although he may be condemned to lose his civil personality. He must first be found guilty and *punishable*, before there can be any thought of drawing from his punishment any benefit for himself or his fellow-citizens. The penal law is a categorical imperative; and woe to him who creeps through the serpent-windings of utilitarianism to discover some advantage that may discharge him from the justice of punishment, or even from the due measure of it, according to the pharisaic maxim: 'It is better that *one* man should die than that the whole people should perish.' For if justice and righteousness perish, human life would no longer have any value in the world. What, then, is to be said of such a proposal as to keep a criminal alive who has been condemned to death, on his being given to understand that if he agreed to certain dangerous experiments being performed upon him, he would be allowed to survive if he came happily through them? It is argued that physicians might thus obtain new information that would be of value to the commonweal. But a court of justice would repudiate with scorn any proposal of this kind if made to it by the medical faculty; for justice would cease to be justice, if it were bartered away for any consideration whatever.

But what is the mode and measure of punishment which public justice takes as its principle and standard? It is just the principle of equality, by which the pointer of the scale of justice is made to incline no more to the one side than the other. It may be rendered by saying that the undeserved evil which any one commits on another, is to be regarded as perpetrated on himself. Hence it may be said: 'If you slander another, you slander yourself; if you steal from another, you steal from yourself; if you strike another, you strike yourself; if you kill another, you kill yourself.' This is the right of retaliation (*jus talionis*); and properly understood, it is the only principle which in regulating a public court, as distinguished from mere private judgment, can definitely assign both the quality and the quantity of a just penalty. All other standards are wavering and uncertain; and on account of other considerations involved in them, they contain no principle comformable to the sentence of pure and strict justice. It may appear, however, that difference of social status would not admit the application of the principal of retaliation, which is that of 'like with like.'

Immanuel Kant, *The Philosophy of Law*, Part II trans. W. Hastie (1887).

But although the application may not in all cases be possible according to the letter, yet as regards the effect it may always be attained in practice, by due regard being given to the disposition and sentiment of the parties in the higher social sphere. Thus a pecuniary penalty on account of a verbal injury, may have no direct proportion to the injustice of slander; for one who is wealthy may be able to indulge himself in this offense for his own gratification. Yet the attack committed on the honor of the party aggrieved may have its equivalent in the pain inflicted upon the pride of the aggressor, especially if he is condemned by the judgment of the court, not only to retract and apologize, but to submit to some meaner ordeal, as kissing the hand of the injured person. In like manner, if a man of the highest rank has violently assaulted an innocent citizen of the lower orders, he may be condemned not only to apologize but to undergo a solitary and painful imprisonment, whereby, in addition to the discomfort endured, the vanity of the offender would be painfully affected, and the very shame of his position would constitute an adequate retaliation after the principle of like with like. But how then would we render the statement: 'If you *steal* from another, you steal from yourself'? In this way, that whoever steals anything makes the property of all insecure; he therefore robs himself of all security in property, according to the right of retaliation. Such a one has nothing, and can acquire nothing, but he has the will to live; and this is only possible by others supporting him. But as the state should not do this gratuitously, he must for this purpose yield his powers to the state to be used in penal labour; and thus he falls for a time, or it may be for life, into a condition of slavery. But whoever has committed murder, must *die*. There is, in this case, no juridical substitute or surrogate, that can be given or taken for the satisfaction of justice. There is no *likeness* or proportion between life, however painful, and death; and therefore there is no equality between the crime of murder and the retaliation of it but what is judicially accomplished by the execution of the criminal. His death, however, must be kept free from all maltreatment that would make the humanity suffering in his person loathsome or abominable. Even if a civil society resolved to dissolve itself with the consent of all its members—as might be supposed in the case of a people inhabiting an island resolving to separate and scatter themselves throughout the whole world—the last murderer lying in the prison ought to be executed before the resolution was carried out. This ought to be done in order that every one may realize the desert of his deeds, and that bloodguiltiness may not remain upon the people; for otherwise they might all be regarded as participators in the murder as a public violation of justice.

The equalization of punishment with crime, is therefore only possible by the cognition of the judge extending even to the penalty of death, according to the right of retaliation.

Review Questions

1. According to Kant, who deserves judicial punishment?
2. Why does Kant reject the maxim "It is better that *one* man should die than that the whole people should perish"?
3. How does Kant explain the principle of retaliation?

Discussion Questions

1. Does Kant have any good reason to reject the "serpent-windings of utilitarianism"?
2. Is death always a just punishment for murder? Can you think of any exceptions?

Anthony G. Amsterdam

Capital Punishment

Anthony G. Amsterdam is a lawyer who has represented many clients who have received the death sentence.

Amsterdam begins by asserting that capital punishment is a great evil simply because it is intentionally killing a person. Furthermore, it is wrong because it results in killing people in error, and these errors cannot be corrected. Moreover, it is unfairly applied. The death sentence is disproportionately imposed on the poor and blacks.

Armstrong concludes with a discussion of retribution and deterrence. He argues that neither the appeal to retribution nor the appeal to deterrence justifies capital punishment.

My discussion of capital punishment will proceed in three stages.

First, I would like to set forth certain basic factual realities about capital punishment, like the fact that capital punishment is a fancy phrase for legally killing people. Please forgive me for beginning with such obvious and ugly facts. Much of our political and philosophical debate about the death penalty is carried on in language calculated to conceal these realities and their implications. The implications, I will suggest, are that capital punishment is a great evil—surely the greatest evil except for war that our society can intentionally choose to commit.

This does not mean that we should do away with capital punishment. Some evils, like war, are occasionally necessary, and perhaps capital punishment is one of them. But the fact that it is a great evil means that we should not choose to do it without some very good and solid reason of which we are satisfactorily convinced upon sufficient evidence. The conclusion of my first point simply is that the burden of proof upon the question of capital punishment rightly rests on those who are asking us to use our laws to kill people with, and that this is a very heavy burden.

Second, I want to review the justifications that have been advanced to support capital punishment. I want to explore with you concepts such as retribution and deterrence, and some of the assumptions and evidence about them. The conclusion of my second point will be that none of these reasons which we like to give ourselves for executing criminals can begin to sustain the burden of proof that rightfully rests upon them.

Third, I would like to say a word about history—about the slow but absolutely certain progress of maturing civilization that will bring an inevitable end to punishment by death. That history does not give us the choice between perpetrating and abolishing capital punishment, because we could not perpetuate it if we wanted to. A generation or two within a single nation can retard but not reverse a long-term, worldwide evolution of this magnitude. Our choice is narrower although it is not unimportant: whether we shall be numbered among the last generations to put legal killing aside. I will end by asking you to cast your choice for life instead of death. But, first, let me begin with some basic facts about the death penalty.

I. The most basic fact, of course, is that capital punishment means taking living, breathing men and women, stuffing them into a chair, strapping them down, pulling a lever, and exterminating them. We have almost forgotten this fact because there have been no executions in this country for more than ten years, except for Gary Gilmore whose combined suicide and circus were so wildly extravagant as to seem unreal. For many people, capital punishment has become a sanitized and symbolic issue: Do you or do you not support your local police? Do you

From the *Stanford Magazine*, Fall/Winter 1977.

or do you not care enough about crime to get tough with criminals? These abstractions were never what capital punishment was about, although it was possible to think so during the ten-year moratorium on executions caused by constitutional challenges to the death penalty in the courts. That is no longer possible. The courts have now said that we can start up executions again, if we want to. Today, a vote for capital punishment is a vote to kill real, live people.

What this means is, first, that we bring men or women into court and put them through a trial for their lives. They are expected to sit back quietly and observe decent courtroom decorum throughout a proceeding whose purpose is systematically and deliberately to decide whether they should be killed. The jury hears evidence and votes; and you can always tell when a jury has voted for death because they come back into court and they will not look the defendant or defense counsel in the eyes. The judge pronounces sentence and the defendant is taken away to be held in a cell for two to six years, hoping that his appeals will succeed, not really knowing what they are all about, but knowing that if they fail, he will be taken out and cinched down and put to death. Most of the people in prison are reasonably nice to him, and even a little apologetic; but he realizes every day for that 700 or 2,100 days that they are holding him there helpless for the approaching slaughter; and that, once the final order is given, they will truss him up and kill him, and that nobody in that vast surrounding machinery of public officials and servants of the law will raise a finger to save him. This is why Camus once wrote that an execution

> . . . is not simply death. It is just as different . . . from the privation of life as a concentration camp is from prison. . . . It adds to death a rule, a public premeditation known to the future victim, an organization . . . which is itself a source of moral sufferings more terrible than death . . . *[Capital punishment] is . . . the most premeditated of murders, to which no criminal's deed, however calculated . . . can be compared. . . . For there to be an equivalency, the death penalty would have to punish a criminal who had warned his victim of the date at which he would inflict a horrible death on him and who, from that moment onward, had confined him at his mercy for months. Such a monster is not encountered in private life.*

I will spare you descriptions of the execution itself. Apologists for capital punishment commonly excite their readers with descriptions of extremely gruesome, gory murders. All murders are horrible things, and executions are usually a lot cleaner physically—although, like Camus, I have never heard of a murderer who held his victim captive for two or more years waiting as the minutes and hours ticked away toward his preannounced death. The clinical details of an execution are as unimaginable to me as they are to most of you. We have not permitted public executions in this country for over 40 years. The law in every state forbids more than a few people to watch the deed done behind prison walls. In January of 1977, a federal judge in Texas ruled that executions could be photographed for television, but the attorneys general of 25 states asked the federal Court of Appeals to set aside that ruling, and it did. I can only leave to your imagination what they are trying so very hard to hide from us. Oh, of course, executions are too hideous to put on television; we all know that. But let us not forget that it is the same hideous thing, done in secret, which we are discussing under abstract labels like "capital punishment" that permit us to talk about the subject in after-dinner conversation instead of spitting up.

In any event, the advocates of capital punishment can and do accentuate their arguments with descriptions of the awful physical details of such hideous murders as that of poor Sharon Tate. All of us naturally and rightly respond to these atrocities with shock and horror. You can read descriptions of executions that would also horrify you (for example, in Byron Eshelman's 1962 book, *Death Row Chaplain,* particularly pages 160–61), but I prefer not to insult your intelligence by playing "can you top this" with issues of life and death. I ask you only to remember two things, if and when you are exposed to descriptions of terrifying murders.

First, the murders being described are not murders that are being done by us, or in our name, or with our approval; and our power to stop them is exceedingly limited even under the most exaggerated suppositions of deterrence, which I shall shortly return to question. Every execution, on the other hand, is done by our paid servants, in our collective name, and we can stop them all. Please do not be bamboozled into thinking that people who are against executions are in favor of murders. If we had the individual or the collective power to stop murders, we would stop them all—and for the same basic reason that we want to stop executions. Murders and executions are both ugly, vicious things, because they destroy the same sacred and mysterious gift of life which we do not understand and can never restore.

Second, please remember therefore that descriptions of murders are relevant to the subject of capital punishment only on the theory that two wrongs make a right, or that killing murderers can assuage their victims' sufferings or bring them back to life, or that capital punishment is the best deterrent to murder. The first two propositions are absurd, and the third is debatable—although as I shall later show, the evidence is overwhelmingly against it. My present point is only that deterrence *is* debatable, whereas we *know* that persons whom we execute are dead beyond recall, no matter how the debate about deterrence comes out. That is a sufficient reason, I believe, why the burden of proof on the issue of deterrence should be placed squarely upon the executioners.

There are other reasons too. Let me try to state them briefly.

Capital punishment not merely kills people, it also kills some of them in error, and these are errors which we can never correct. When I speak about legal error, I do not mean only the question whether "they got the right man" or killed somebody who "didn't do it." Errors of that sort do occur: Timothy Evans, for example, an innocent man whose execution was among the reasons for the abolition of the death penalty in Great Britain. If you read Anthony Scaduto's recent book, *Scapegoat,* you will come away with unanswerable doubts whether Bruno Richard Hauptmann was really guilty of the kidnapping of the Lindbergh infant for which he was executed, or whether we killed Hauptmann, too, for a crime he did not commit.

In 1975, the Florida Cabinet pardoned two black men, Freddie Lee Pitts and Wilbert Lee, who were twice tried and sentenced to death and spent 12 years apiece on death row for a murder committed by somebody else. This one, I am usually gliby told, "does not count," because Pitts and Lee were never actually put to death. Take comfort if you will but I cannot, for I know that only the general constitutional attack which we were then mounting upon the death penalty in Florida kept Pitts and Lee alive long enough to permit discovery of the evidence of their innocence. Our constitutional attack is now dead, and so would Pitts and Lee be if they were tried tomorrow. Sure, we catch some errors. But we often catch them by extremely lucky breaks that could as easily not have happened. I represented a young man in North Carolina who came within a hair's breadth of being the Gary Gilmore of his day. Like Gilmore, he became so depressed under a death sentence that he tried to dismiss his appeal. He was barely talked out of it, his conviction was reversed, and on retrial a jury acquitted him in 11 minutes.

We do not know how many "wrong men" have been executed. We think and pray that they are rare—although we can't be sure because, after a man is dead, people seldom continue to investigate the possibility that he was innocent. But that is not the biggest source of error anyway.

What about *legal* error? In 1968, the Supreme Court of the United States held that it was unconstitutional to exclude citizens from capital trial juries simply because they had general conscientious or religious objections to the death penalty. That decision was held retroactive; and I represented 60 or 70 men whose death sentences were subsequently set aside for constitutional errors in jury selection. While researching their cases, I found the cases of at least as many more men who had already been executed on the basis of trials infected with identical errors. On June 29, 1977, we finally won a decision from the Supreme Court of the United States that the death penalty is excessively harsh and therefore unconstitutional for the crime of rape. Fine, but it comes too late for the 455 men executed for rape in this country since 1930—405 of them black.

In 1975, the Supreme Court held that the constitutional presumption of innocence forbids a trial judge to tell the jury that the burden of proof is on a homicide defendant to show provocation which reduces murder to manslaughter. On June 17, 1977, the Court held that this decision was also retroactive. Jury charges of precisely that kind were standard forms for more than a century in many American states that punished murder with death. Can we even begin to guess how many people were unconstitutionally executed under this so-called retroactive decision?

Now what about errors of fact that go to the degree of culpability of a crime? In almost every state, the difference between first and second-degree murder—or between capital and noncapital murder—depends on whether the defendant acted with something called "premeditation" as distinguished from intent to kill. Premeditation means intent formed beforehand, but no particular amount of time is required. Courts tell juries that premeditation "may be as instantaneous as successive thoughts in the mind." Mr. Justice Cardozo wrote that *he* did not understand the concept of premeditation after several decades of studying and trying to apply it as a judge. Yet this is the kind of question to which a jury's answer spells out life or death in a capital trial—this, and the questions of whether the defendant had "malice aforethought," or "provocation and passion," or "insanity," or the "reasonableness" necessary for killing in self-defense.

I think of another black client, Johnny Coleman, whose conviction and death sentence for killing a white truck driver named "Screwdriver" Johnson we twice got reversed by the Supreme Court of the United States. On retrial a jury acquitted him on the grounds of self-defense upon exactly the same evidence that an earlier jury had had when it sentenced him to die. When ungraspable legal standards are thus applied to intangible mental states, there is not merely the possibility but the actuarial certainty that juries deciding substantial volumes of cases are going to be wrong in an absolutely large number of them. If you accept capital punishment, you must accept the reality—not the risk, but the reality—that we shall kill people whom the law says that it is not proper to kill. No other outcome is possible when we presume to administer an infallible punishment through a fallible system.

You will notice that I have taken examples of black defendants as some of my cases of legal error. There is every reason to believe that discrimination on grounds of race and poverty fatally infect the administration of capital justice in this country. Since 1930, an almost equal number of white and black defendants has been executed for the crime of murder, although blacks constituted only about a tenth of the nation's population during this period. No sufficiently careful studies have been done of these cases, controlling variables other than race, so as to determine exactly what part race played in the outcome. But when that kind of systemic study *was* done in rape cases, it showed beyond the statistical possibility of a doubt that black men who raped white women were disproportionately sentenced to die on the basis of race alone. Are you prepared to believe that juries which succumbed to conscious or unconscious racial prejudices in rape cases were or are able to put those prejudices wholly aside where the crime charged is murder? Is it not much more plausible to believe that even the most conscientious juror—or judge, or prosecuting attorney—will be slower to want to inflict the death penalty on a defendant with whom he can identify as a human being; and that the process of identification in our society is going to be very seriously affected by racial identity?

I should mention that there have been a couple of studies—one by the *Stanford Law Review* and the other by the Texas Judicial Council—which found no racial discrimination in capital sentencing in certain murder cases. But both of these studies had methodological problems and limitations; and both of them also found death-sentencing discrimination against the economically poor, who come disproportionately from racial minorities. The sum of the evidence still stands where the National Crime Commission found it ten years ago, when it described the following discriminatory patterns. "The death sentence," said the Commission, "is disproportionately imposed and carried out on the poor, the Negro, and members of unpopular groups."

Apart from discrimination, there is a haphazard, crazy-quilt character about the administration of capital punishment that every knowledgeable lawyer or observer can describe but none can rationally explain. Some juries are hanging juries, some counties are hanging counties, some years are hanging years; and men live or die depending on these flukes.

However atrocious the crime may have been for which a particular defendant is sentenced to die, "[e]xperienced wardens know many prisoners serving life or less whose crimes were equally, or more atrocious." This is a quotation, by the way, from former Attorney General Ramsey Clark's statement to a congressional subcommittee; and wardens Lewis Lawes, Clinton Duffy, and others have said the same thing.

With it I come to the end of my first point. I submit that the deliberate judicial extinction of human life is intrinsically so final and so terrible an act as to cast the burden of proof for its justification upon those who want us to do it. But certainly when the act is executed through a fallible system which assures that we kill some people wrongly, others because they are black or poor or personally unattractive or socially unacceptable, and all of them quite freakishly in the sense that whether a man lives or dies for any particular crime is a matter of luck and happenstance, *then,* at the least, the burden of justifying capital punishment lies fully and heavily on its proponents.

II. Let us consider those justifications. The first and the oldest is the concept of *retribution:* an eye for an eye, a life for a life. You may or may not believe in this kind of retribution, but I will not waste your time debating it because it cannot honestly be used to justify the only form of capital punishment that this country has accepted for the past half-century. Even before the judicial moratorium, executions in the United States had dwindled to an average of about 30 a year. Only a rare, sparse handful of convicted murderers are being sentenced to die or executed for the selfsame crimes for which many, many times as many murderers were sent away to prison. Obviously, as Professor Herbert Wechsler said a generation ago, the issue of capital punishment is no longer "whether it is fair or just that one who takes another person's life should lose his own. . . . [W]e do not and cannot act upon . . . [that proposition] generally in the administration of the penal law. The problem rather is whether a small and highly random sample of people who commit murder. . . . ought to be despatched, while most of those convicted of . . . [identical] crimes are dealt with by imprisonment."

Sometimes the concept of retribution is modernized a little with a notion called *moral reinforcement*—the ideal that we should punish very serious crimes very severely in order to demonstrate how much we abhor them. The trouble with *this* justification for capital punishment, of course, is that it completely begs the question, which is *how severely* we ought to punish any particular crime to show appropriate abhorrence for it. The answer can hardly be found in a literal application of the eye-for-an-eye formula. We do not burn down arsonists' houses or cheat back at bunco artists. But if we ought not punish all crimes exactly according to their kind, then what is the fit moral reinforcement for murder? You might as well say burning at the stake or boiling in oil is as simple as gassing or electrocution.

Or is it not more plausible—if what we really want to say is that the killing of a human being is wrong and ought to be condemned as clearly as we can—that we should choose the punishment of prison as the fitting means to make this point? So far as moral reinforcement goes, the difference between life imprisonment and capital punishment is precisely that imprisonment continues to respect the value of human life. The plain message of capital punishment, on the other hand, is that life ceases to be sacred whenever someone with the power to take it away decides that there is a sufficiently compelling pragmatic reason to do so.

But there is still another theory of a retributive sort which is often advanced to support the death penalty, particularly in recent years. This is the argument that *we*—that is, the person making the argument—no longer believe in the outworn concept of retribution, but the *public*—they believe in retribution, and so we must let them have their prey or they will lose respect for law. Watch for this argument because it is the surest sign of demogragic depravity. It is disgusting in its patronizing attribution to "the public" of a primitive, uneducable bloodthirstiness which the speaker is unprepared to defend but is prepared to exploit as a means of sidestepping the rational and moral limitations of a *just* theory of retribution. It out-judases Judas in its abnegation of governmental responsibility to respond to popular misinformation with enlightenment, instead of seizing on it as a pretext for atrocity. This argument asserts that the proper way to deal with a lynch mob is to string its victim up before the mob does.

I don't think "the public" is a lynch mob or should be treated as one. People today are troubled and frightened by crime, and legitimately so. Much of the apparent increase of violent crime in our times is the product of intensified statistics keeping, massive and instantaneous and graphic news reporting, and manipulation of figures by law enforcement agencies which must compete with other sectors of the public economy for budget allocations. But part of the increase is also real, and very disturbing. Murders ought to disturb us all, whether or not they are increasing. Each and every murder is a terrible human tragedy. Nevertheless, it is irresponsible for public officials—particularly law enforcement officials whom the public views as experts—first to exacerbate and channel legitimate public concern about crime into public support for capital punishment by advertising unsupportable claims that capital punishment is an answer to the crime problem, and then to turn around and cite public support for capital punishment as justification when all other justifications are shown to be unsupportable. Politicians do this all the time, for excellent political reasons. It is much easier to advocate simplistic and illusory solutions to the crime problem than to find real and effective solutions. Most politicians are understandably afraid to admit that our society knows frighteningly little about the causes or cure of crime, and will have to spend large amounts of taxpayers' money even to begin to find out. The facile politics of crime do much to explain our national acceptance of capital punishment, but nothing to justify it.

Another supposed justification for capital punishment that deserves equally brief treatment is the notion of *isolation or specific deterrence*—the idea that we must kill a murderer to prevent him from murdering ever again. The usual forms that this argument takes are that a life sentence does not mean a life sentence—it means parole after 7, or 12, or 25 years; and that, within prisons themselves, guards and other prisoners are in constant jeopardy of death at the hands of convicted but unexecuted murderers.

It amazes me that these arguments can be made or taken seriously. Are we really going to kill a human being because we do not trust other people—the people whom we have chosen to serve on our own parole boards—to make a proper judgment in his case at some future time? We trust this same parole board to make far more numerous, difficult, and dangerous decisions: hardly a week passes when they do not consider the cases of armed robbers, for example, although armed robbers are much, much more likely statistically to commit future murders than any murderer is to repeat his crime. But if we really do distrust the public agencies of law—if we fear that they may make mistakes—then surely that is a powerful argument *against* capital punishment. Courts which hand out death sentences because they predict that a man will still be criminally dangerous 7 or 25 years in the future cannot conceivably make fewer mistakes than parole boards who release a prisoner after 7 or 25 years of close observation in prison have convinced them that he is reformed and no longer dangerous.

But pass this point. If we refuse to trust the parole system, then let us provide by law that the murderers whose release we fear shall be given sentences of life imprisonment without parole which *do* mean life imprisonment without parole. I myself would be against that, but it is far more humane than capital punishment, and equally safe.

As for killings inside prisons, if you examine them you will find that they are very rarely done by convicted murderers, but are almost always done by people imprisoned for crimes that no one would think of making punishable by death. Warden Lawes of Sing Sing and Governor Wallace of Alabama, among others, regularly employed murder convicts as house servants because they were among the very safest prisoners. There are exceptions, of course; but these can be handled by adequate prison security. You cannot tell me or believe that a society which is capable of putting a man on the moon is incapable of putting a man in prison, keeping him there, and keeping him from killing while he is there. And if anyone says that this is costly, and that we should kill people in order to reduce government expenditures, I can only reply that the cost of housing a man for life in prison is considerably less than the cost of putting the same man through all of the extraordinary legal proceedings necessary to kill him.

That brings me to the last supposed justification for the death penalty: *deterrence*. This is the subject that you most frequently hear debated, and many people who talk about capital punishment talk about nothing else. I have done otherwise here, partly for completeness, partly because it is vital to approach the subject of deterrence knowing precisely what question you want to ask and have answered. I have suggested that the proper question is *whether there is sufficiently convincing evidence that the death penalty deters murder better than does life imprisonment so that you are willing to accept responsibility for doing the known evil act of killing human beings—with all of the attending ugliness that I have described—on the faith of your conviction in the superior deterrent efficacy of capital punishment*.

If this is the question, then I submit that there is only one fair and reasonable answer. When the Supreme Court of the United States reviewed the evidence in 1976, it described that evidence as "inconclusive." Do not let anybody tell you—as death-penalty advocates are fond of doing—that the Supreme Court held the death penalty justifiable as a deterrent. What the Court's plurality opinion said, exactly, was that "there is no convincing evidence *either supporting or refuting* . . . [the] view" that "the death penalty may not function as a significantly greater deterrent than lesser penalties." *Because* the evidence was inconclusive, the Court held that the Constitution did not forbid judgment either way. But if the evidence is inconclusive, is it *your* judgment that we should conclusively kill people on a factual theory that the evidence does not conclusively sustain?

I hope not. But let us examine the evidence more carefully because—even though it is not conclusive—it is very, very substantial; and the overwhelming weight of it refutes the claims of those who say that capital punishment is a better deterrent than life imprisonment for murder.

For more than 40 years, criminologists have studied this question by a variety of means. They have compared homicide rates in countries and states that did and did not have capital punishment, or that actually executed people more and less frequently. Some of these studies compared large aggregates of abolitionist and retentionist states; others compared geographically adjacent pairs or triads of states, or states that were chosen because they were comparable in other socio-economic factors that might affect homicide. Other studies compared homicide rates in the same country or state before and after the abolition or reinstatement of capital punishment, or they compared homicide rates for the same geographic area during periods preceding and following well publicized executions. Special comparative studies were done relating to police killings and prison killings. All in all, there were dozens of studies. Without a single exception, *none* of them found that the death penalty had any statistically significant effect upon the rate of homicide or murder. Often I have heard advocates of capital punishment explain away its failures by likening it to a great lighthouse: "We count the ships that crash," they say, "but we never know how many saw the light and were saved." What these studies show, however, is that coastlines of the same shape and depth and tidal structure, with and without lighthouses, invariably have the same number of shipwrecks per year. On that evidence, would you invest your money in a lighthouse, or would you buy a sonar if you really wanted to save lives?

In 1975, the first purportedly scientific study ever to find that capital punishment *did* deter homicides was published. This was done by Issac Ehrlich of Chicago, who is not a criminologist but an economist. Using regression analysis involving an elaborate mathematical model, Ehrlich reported that every execution deterred something like eight murders. Naturally supporters of capital punishment hurriedly clambered on the Ehrlich bandwagon.

Unhappily, for them, the wagon was a factory reject. Several distinguished econometricians—including a team headed by Lawrence Klein, president of the American Economy Association—reviewed Ehrlich's work and found it fatally flawed with numerous methodological errors. Some of these were technical: it appeared, for example, that Ehrlich had produced his results by the unjustified and unexplained use of a logarithmic form of regression equation instead of the more conventional linear form—which made his findings of deterrence vanish. Equally important, it was shown that Ehrlich's findings depended entirely on data from the post-1962 period, when executions declined and the homicide rate rose *as a part of a general rise, in the overall crime rate that Ehrlich incredibly failed to consider.*

Incidentally, the nonscientific proponents of capital punishment are also fond of suggesting that the rise in homicide rates in the 1960s and the 1970s, when executions were halted, proves that executions used to deter homicides. This is ridiculous when you consider that crime as a whole has increased during this period; that homicide rates have increased about *half* as much as the rates for all other FBI Index crimes; and that whatever factors are affecting the rise of most noncapital crimes (which *cannot* include cessation of executions) almost certainly affect the homicide-rate rise also.

In the event, Ehrlich's study was discredited and a second, methodologically inferior study by a fellow named Yunker is not even worth criticizing here. These are the only two scientific studies in 40 years, I repeat, which have ever purported to find deterrence. On the other hand, several recent studies have been completed by researchers who adopted Ehrlich's basic regression-analysis approach but corrected its defects. Peter Passell did such a study finding no deterrence. Kenneth Avio did such a study finding no deterrence. If you want to review all of these studies yourselves, you may find them discussed and cited in an excellent article in the 1976 *Supreme Court Review* by Hans Zeisel, on page 317. The conclusion you will have to draw is that—during 40 years and today—the scientific community has looked and looked and looked for any reliable evidence that capital punishment deters homicide better than does life imprisonment, and it has found no such evidence at all.

Proponents of capital punishment frequently cite a different kind of study, one that was done by the Los Angeles Police Department. Police officers asked arrested robbers who did not carry guns, or did not use them, *why* they did not; and the answers, supposedly, were frequently that the robber "did not want to get the death penalty." It is noteworthy that the Los Angeles Police Department has consistently refused to furnish copies of this study and its underlying data to professional scholars, apparently for fear of criticism. I finally obtained a copy of the study from a legislative source, and I can tell you that it shows two things. First, an arrested person will tell a police officer anything that he thinks the police officer wants to hear. Second, police officers, like all other human beings, hear what they want to hear. When a robber tries to say that he did not carry or use a gun because he did not wish to risk the penalties for homicide, he will describe those penalties in terms of whatever the law happens to be at the time and place. In Minnesota, which has no death penalty, he will say, "I didn't want to get life imprisonment." In Los Angeles, he will say, "I didn't want to get the death penalty." Both responses mean the same thing; neither tells you that death is a superior deterrent to life imprisonment.

The real mainstay of deterrence thesis, however, is not evidence but intuition. You and I ask ourselves: Are we not afraid to die? Of course! Would the threat of death, then, not intimidate us to forbear from a criminal act? Certainly! *Therefore,* capital punishment must be a deterrent. The trouble with this intuition is that the people who are doing the reasoning and the people who are doing the murdering are not the same people. You and I do not commit murder for a lot of reasons other than the death penalty. The death penalty might perhaps also deter us from murdering—but altogether needlessly, since we would not murder with it or without it. Those who are sufficiently dissocialized to murder are not responding to the world in the same way that we are, and we simply cannot "intuit" their thinking processes from ours.

Consider, for example, the well-documented cases of persons who kill *because* there is a death penalty. One of these was Pamela Watkins, a babysitter in San Jose who had made several unsuccessful suicide attempts and was frightened to try again. She finally strangled two children so that the state of California would execute her. In various bizarre forms, this "suicide-murder" syndrome is reported by psychiatrists again and again. (Parenthetically, Gary Gilmore was probably such a case.) If you intuit that somewhere, sometime, the death penalty *does* deter some potential murders, are you also prepared to intuit that their numbers mathematically exceed the numbers of these wretched people who are actually induced to murder by the existence of capital punishment?

Here, I suggest, our intuition does—or should—fail, just as the evidence certainly does fail, to establish a deterrent justification for the death penalty. There is simply no credible evidence, and there is no rational way of reasoning about the real facts once you know them, which can sustain this or any other justification with the degree of confidence that should be demanded before a civilized society deliberately extinguishes human life.

III. I have only a little space for my final point, but it is sufficient because the point is perfectly plain. Capital punishment is a dying institution in this last quarter of the twentieth century. It has already been abandoned in law or in fact throughout most of the civilized world. England, Canada, the Scandinavian countries, virtually all of Western Europe except for France and Spain have abolished the death penalty. The vast majority of countries in the Western Hemisphere have abolished it. Its last strongholds in the world—apart from the United States—are in Asia and Africa, particularly South Africa. Even the countries which maintain capital punishment on the books have almost totally ceased to use it in fact. In the United States, considering only the last half century, executions have plummeted from 199 in 1935 to approximately 29 a year during the decade before 1967, when the ten-year judicial moratorium began.

Do you doubt that this development will continue? Do you doubt that it will continue because it is the path of civilization—the path up out of fear and terror and the barbarism that terror breeds, into self-confidence and decency in the administration of justice? The road, like any other built by men, has its detours, but over many generations it has run true, and will run true. And there will therefore come a time—perhaps in 20 years, perhaps in 50 or 100, but very surely and very shortly as the lifetime of nations is measured—when our children will look back at us in horror and unbelief because of what we did in their names and for their supposed safety, just as we look back in horror and unbelief at the thousands of crucifixions and beheadings and live disembowelments that our ancestors practiced for the supposed purpose of making our world safe from murderers and robbers, thieves, shoplifters, and pickpockets.

All of these kinds of criminals are still with us, and will be with our children—although we can certainly decrease their numbers and their damage, and protect ourselves from them a lot better, if we insist that our politicians stop pounding on the whipping boy of capital punishment and start coming up with some real solutions to the real problems of crime. Our children will cease to execute murderers for the same reason that we have ceased to string up pickpockets and shoplifters at the public crossroads, although there are still plenty of them around. Our children will cease to execute murderers because executions are a self-deluding, self-defeating, self-degrading, futile, and entirely stupid means of dealing with the crime of murder, and because our children will prefer to be something better than murderers themselves. Should we not—can we not—make the same choice now?

Review Questions

1. Why does Amsterdam think that capital punishment is a great evil?
2. What additional reasons does Amsterdam give for saying that capital punishment is wrong?
3. Why does Amsterdam reject the oldest concept of retribution, an eye for an eye, a life for a life?
4. What is the notion of moral reinforcement, and why doesn't Amsterdam accept it?
5. How does Amsterdam reply to the argument that the public's desire for retribution must be satisfied?
6. What is wrong with the notion of specific deterrence according to Amsterdam?
7. How does Amsterdam deal with the appeal to deterrence?

Discussion Questions

1. Do you agree with Amsterdam that capital punishment is a great evil? Why or why not?
2. Has Amsterdam successfully defeated the appeal to retribution?
3. Are you convinced that capital punishment is not a better deterrent than life imprisonment? Explain your answer.

Ernest van den Haag

The Ultimate Punishment: A Defense

Ernest van den Haag is Professor of Jurisprudence and Public Policy at Fordham University, and a prominent defender of capital punishment. He is the author of The Fabric of Society *(1957),* Political Violence and Civil Disobedience *(1973), and* Punishing Criminals: Concerning a Very Old and Painful Question *(1975).*

In this article, van den Haag replies to various objections to capital punishment, including most of the ones raised by Amsterdam in the previous reading. These objections include the following: Capital punishment is discriminatory; innocents are executed; it has not been proven to be a deterrent; it is too costly; it is an excessive punishment; it violates the right to life; and it is inconsistent with human dignity.

From Ernest van den Haag, "The Ultimate Punishment: A Defense," *Harvard Law Review* 99 (1986).

In an average year about 20,000 homicides occur in the United States. Fewer than 300 convicted murderers are sentenced to death. But because no more than thirty murderers have been executed in any recent year, most convicts sentenced to death are likely to die of old age.[1] Nonetheless, the death penalty looms large in discussions: it raises important moral questions independent of the number of executions.

The death penalty is our harshest punishment.[2] It is irrevocable: it ends the existence of those punished, instead of temporarily imprisoning them. Further, although not intended to cause physical pain, execution is the only corporal punishment still applied to adults.[3] These singular characteristics contribute to the perennial, impassioned controversy about capital punishment.

I. Distribution

Consideration of the justice, morality, or usefulness of capital punishment is often conflated with objections to its alleged discriminatory or capricious distribution among the guilty. Wrongly so. If capital punishment is immoral *in se*, no distribution among the guilty could make it moral. If capital punishment is moral, no distribution would make it immoral. Improper distribution cannot affect the quality of what is distributed, be it punishments or rewards. Discriminatory or capricious distribution thus could not justify abolition of the death penalty. Further, maldistribution inheres no more in capital punishment than in any other punishment.

Maldistribution between the guilty and the innocent is, by definition, unjust. But the injustice does not lie in the nature of the punishment. Because of the finality of the death penalty, the most grievous maldistribution occurs when it is imposed upon the innocent. However, the frequent allegations of discrimination and capriciousness refer to maldistribution among the guilty and not to the punishment of the innocent.

Maldistribution of any punishment among those who deserve it is irrelevant to its justice or morality. Even if poor or black convicts guilty of capital offenses suffer capital punishment, and other convicts usually guilty of the same crimes do not, a more equal distribution, however desirable, would merely be more equal. It would not be more just to the convicts under sentence of death.

Punishments are imposed on persons, not on racial or economic groups. Guilt is personal. The only relevant question is: does the person to be executed deserve the punishment? Whether or not others who deserved the same punishment, whatever their economic or racial group, have avoided execution is irrelevant. If they have, the guilt of the executed convicts would not be diminished, nor would their punishment be less deserved. To put the issue starkly, if the death penalty were imposed on guilty blacks, but not on guilty whites, or, if it were imposed by a lottery among the guilty, this irrationally discriminatory or capricious distribution would neither make the penalty unjust, nor cause anyone to be unjustly punished, despite the undue impunity bestowed on others.[4]

Equality, in short, seems morally less important than justice. And justice is independent of distributional inequalities. The ideal of equal justice demands that justice be equally distributed, not that it be replaced by equality. Justice requires that as many of the guilty as possible be punished, regardless of whether others have avoided punishment. To let these others escape the deserved punishment does not do justice to them, or to society. But it is not unjust to those who could not escape.

These moral considerations are not meant to deny that irrational discrimination, or capriciousness, would be inconsistent with constitutional requirements. But I am satisfied that the Supreme Court has in fact provided for adherence to the constitutional requirement of equality as much as is possible. Some inequality is indeed unavoidable as a practical matter in any system.[5] But, *ultra posse nemo obligatur*. (Nobody is bound beyond ability.)

Recent data reveal little direct racial discrimination in the sentencing of those arrested and convicted of murder.[6] The abrogation of the death penalty for rape has eliminated a major source of racial discrimination. Concededly, some discrimination based on the race of murder victims may exist; yet, this discrimination affects criminal victimizers in an unexpected way. Murderers of whites are thought more likely to be executed than murderers of blacks. Black victims, then, are less fully vindicated than white ones. However, because most black murderers kill blacks, black murderers are spared the death penalty more often than are white murderers. They fare better than most white murderers. The motivation behind unequal distribution of the death penalty may well have been to discriminate against blacks, but the result has favored them. Maldistribution is thus a straw man for empirical as well as analytical reasons.

II. Miscarriages of Justice

In a recent survey Professors Hugo Adam Bedau and Michael Radelet found that 7000 persons were executed in the United States between

1900 and 1985 and that 25 were innocent of capital crimes.[7] Among the innocents they list Sacco and Vanzetti as well as Ethel and Julius Rosenberg. Although their data may be questionable, I do not doubt that, over a long enough period, miscarriages of justice will occur even in capital cases.

Despite precautions, nearly all human activities, such as trucking, lighting, or construction, cost the lives of some innocent bystanders. We do not give up those activities, because the advantages, moral or material, outweigh the unintended losses. Analogously, for those who think the death penalty just, miscarriages of justice are offset by the moral benefits and the usefulness of doing justice. For those who think the death penalty unjust even when it does not miscarry, miscarriages can hardly be decisive.

III. Deterrence

Despite much recent work, there has been no conclusive statistical demonstration that the death penalty is a better deterrent than are alternative punishments.[8] However, deterrence is less than decisive for either side. Most abolitionists acknowledge that they would continue to favor abolition even if the death penalty were shown to deter more murders than alternatives could deter.[9] Abolitionists appear to value the life of a convicted murderer or, at least, his nonexecution, more highly than they value the lives of the innocent victims who might be spared by deterring prospective murderers.

Deterrence is not altogether decisive for me either. I would favor retention of the death penalty as retribution even if it were shown that the threat of execution could not deter prospective murderers not already deterred by the threat of imprisonment.[10] Still, I believe the death penalty, because of its finality, is more feared than imprisonment, and deters some prospective murderers not deterred by the threat of imprisonment. Sparing the lives of even a few prospective victims by deterring their murderers is more important than preserving the lives of convicted murderers because of the possibility, or even the probability, that executing them would not deter others. Whereas the lives of the victims who might be saved are valuable, that of the murderer has only negative value, because of his crime. Surely the criminal law is meant to protect the lives of potential victims in preference to those of actual murderers.

Murder rates are determined by many factors; neither the severity nor the probability of the threatened sanction is always decisive. However, for the long run, I share the view of Sir James Fitzjames Stephen: "Some men, probably, abstain from murder because they fear that if they committed murder they would be hanged. Hundreds of thousands abstain from it because they regard it with horror. One great reason why they regard it with horror is that murderers are hanged." [11] Penal sanctions are useful in the long run for the formation of the internal restraints so necessary to control crime. The severity and finality of the death penalty is appropriate to the seriousness and the finality of murder.[12]

IV. Incidental Issues: Cost, Relative Suffering, Brutalization

Many nondecisive issues are associated with capital punishment. Some believe that the monetary cost of appealing a capital sentence is excessive.[13] Yet most comparisons of the cost of life imprisonment with the cost of execution, apart from their dubious relevance, are flawed at least by the implied assumption that life prisoners will generate no judicial costs during their imprisonment. At any rate, the actual monetary costs are trumped by the importance of doing justice.

Others insist that a person sentenced to death suffers more than his victim suffered, and that this (excess) suffering is undue according to the *lex talionis* (rule of retaliation).[14] We cannot know whether the murderer on death row suffers more than his victim suffered; however, unlike the murderer, the victim deserved none of the suffering inflicted. Further, the limitations of the *lex talionis* were meant to restrain private vengeance, not the social retribution that has taken its place. Punishment—regardless of the motivation—is not intended to revenge, offset, or compensate for the victim's suffering or to be measured by it. Punishment is to vindicate the law and the social order undermined by the crime. This is why a kidnapper's penal confinement is not limited to the period for which he imprisoned his victim; nor is a burglar's confinement meant merely to offset the suffering or the harm he caused his victim; nor is it meant only to offset the advantage he gained.[15]

Another argument heard at least since Beccaria is that, by killing a murderer, we encourage, endorse, or legitimize unlawful killing. Yet, although all punishments are meant to be unpleasant, it is seldom argued that they legitimize the unlawful imposition of identical unpleasantness. Imprisonment is not thought to legitimize kidnapping; neither are fines thought to legitimize robbery. The difference between murder and execution, or between kidnapping and imprisonment, is that the first is unlawful and undeserved, the second a lawful and deserved punishment for an unlawful act. The physical similarities of the punishment to the crime are irrelevant. The relevant difference is not physical, but social.[16]

V. Justice, Excess, Degradation

We threaten punishments in order to deter crime. We impose them not only to make the threats credible but also as retribution (justice) for the crimes that were not deterred. Threats and punishments are necessary to deter and deterrence is a sufficient practical justification for them. Retribution is an independent moral justification.[17] Although penalties can be unwise, repulsive, or inappropriate, and those punished can be pitiable, in a sense the infliction of legal punishment on a guilty person cannot be unjust. By committing the crime, the criminal volunteered to assume the risk of receiving a legal punishment that he could have avoided by not committing the crime. The punishment he suffers is the punishment he voluntarily risked suffering and, therefore, it is no more unjust to him than any other event for which one knowingly volunteers to assume the risk. Thus, the death penalty cannot be unjust to the guilty criminal.[18]

There remain, however, two moral objections. The penalty may be regarded as always excessive as retribution and always morally degrading. To regard the death penalty as always excessive, one must believe that no crime—no matter how heinous—could possibly justify capital punishment. Such a belief can be neither corroborated nor refuted; it is an article of faith.

Alternatively, or concurrently, one may believe that everybody, the murderer no less than the victim, has an imprescriptible (natural?) right to life. The law therefore should not deprive anyone of life. I share Jeremy Bentham's view that any such "natural and imprescriptible rights" are "nonsense upon stilts." [19]

Justice Brennan has insisted that the death penalty is "uncivilized," "inhuman," inconsistent with "human dignity" and with "the sanctity of life," [20] that it "treats members of the human race as nonhumans, as objects to be toyed with and discarded," [21] that it is "uniquely degrading to human dignity" [22] and "by its very nature, [involves] a denial of the executed person's humanity." [23] Justice Brennan does not say why he thinks execution "uncivilized." Hitherto most civilizations have had the death penalty, although it has been discarded in Western Europe, where it is currently unfashionable probably because of its abuse by totalitarian regimes.

By "degrading," Justice Brennan seems to mean that execution degrades the executed convicts. Yet philosophers, such as Immanual Kant and G. W. F. Hegel have insisted that, when deserved, execution, far from degrading the executed convict, affirms his humanity by affirming his rationality and his responsibility for his actions. They thought that execution, when deserved, is required for the sake of the convict's dignity. (Does not life imprisonment violate human dignity more than executions, by keeping alive a prisoner deprived of all autonomy?) [24]

Common sense indicates that it cannot be death—our common fate—that is inhuman. Therefore, Justice Brennan must mean that death degrades when it comes not as a natural or accidental event, but as a deliberate social imposition. The murderer learns through his punishment that his fellow men have found him unworthy of living; that because he has murdered, he is being expelled from the community of the living. The degradation is self-inflicted. By murdering, the murderer has so dehumanized himself that he cannot remain among the living. The social recognition of self-degradation is the punitive essence of execution. To believe, as Justice Brennan appears to, that the degradation is inflicted by the execution reverses the direction of causality.

Execution of those who have committed heinous murders may deter only one murder per year. If it does, it seems quite warranted. It is also the only fitting retribution for murder I can think of.

Endnotes

1. Death row as a semipermanent residence is cruel, because convicts are denied the normal amenities of prison life. Thus, unless death row residents are integrated into the prison population, the continuing accumulation of convicts on death row should lead us to accelerate either the rate of execution or the rate of commutations. I find little objection to integration.
2. Some writers, for example, Cesare Bonesana, Marchese di Beccaria, have thought that life imprisonment is more severe. *See* C. Beccaria, *Dei Delitti c Delle Pene* 62-70 (1764). More recently, Jacques Barzum has expressed this view. *See* Barzun, *In Favor of Capital Punishment,* in *The Death Penalty of America* 154. (H. Bedau ed. 1964). However, the over-whelming majority of both abolitionists and of convicts under death sentence prefer life imprisonment to execution.
3. For a discussion of the sources of opposition to corporal punishment, see E. van den Haag, *Punishing Criminals* 196-206 (1975).
4. Justice Douglas, concurring in Furman v. Georgia, 408 U.S. 238 (1972), wrote that "a law which . . . reaches that [discriminatory] result in practice has no more sanctity than a law which in terms provides the same." *Id.* at 256 (Douglas, J., concurring). Indeed, a law legislating this result "in terms" would be inconsistent with the "equal protection of the laws" provided by the fourteenth amendment, as would the discriminatory result reached in practice. But that result could be changed by changing the distributional practice. Thus, Justice Douglas notwithstanding, a discriminatory result does not make the death penalty unconstitutional, unless the penalty ineluctably must produce that result to an unconstitutional degree.
5. The ideal of equality, unlike the ideal of retributive justice (which can be approximated separately in each instance), is clearly unattainable unless all guilty persons are apprehended, and thereafter tried, convicted and sentenced by the same court, at the same time. Unequal justice is the best we can do; it is still better than the injustice, equal or unequal, which occurs if, for the sake of equality, we deliberately allow some who could be punished to escape.

†It barely need be said that any discrimination *against* (for example, black murderers of whites) must also be discrimination *for* (for example, black murderers of blacks).

6. *See* Bureau of Justice Statistics, U.S. Dept. of Justice, Bulletin No. NCJ-98, 399, *Capital Punishment 1984,* at 9 (1985); Johnson, *The Executioner's Bias, Nat'l Rev.*, Nov. 15, 1985, at 44.
7. Bedau & Radelet, *Miscarriages of Justice in Potentially Capital Cases* (1st draft, Oct. 1985) (on file at Harvard Law School Library).
8. For a sample of conflicting views on the subject, see Baldus & Cole, *A Comparison of the Work of Thorsten Sellin and Isaac Ehrlich on the Deterrent Effect of Capital Punishment,* 85 *Yale L. J.* 170 (1975); Bowers & Pierce, *Deterrence or Brutilization: What Is the Effect of Executions?,* 26 *Crime & Delinq.* 453 (1980); Bowers & Pierce, *The Illustration of Deterrence in Isaac Ehrlich's Research on Capital Punishment,* 85 *Yale L. J.* 187 (1975); Ehrlich, *Fear of Deterrence: A Critical Evaluation of the "Report of the Panel on Research on Deterrent and Incapacitative Effects,"* 6 *J. Legal Stud.* 293 (1977); Ehrlich, *The Deterrent Effect of Capital Punishment: A Question of Life and Death,* 65 *Am. Econ. Rev.* 397, 415-16 (1975); Ehrlich & Gibbons, *On the Measurement of the Deterrent Effect of Capital Punishment and the Theory of Deterrence,* 6 *J. Legal Stud.* 35 (1977).
9. For most abolitionists, the discrimination argument, *see supra* pp. [410-411], is similarly nondecisive: they would favor abolition even if there could be no racial discrimination.
10. If executions were shown to increase the murder rate in the long run, I would favor abolition. Sparing the innocent victims who would be spared, *ex hypothesi,* by the nonexecution of murderers would be more important to me than the execution, however just, of murderers. But although there is a lively discussion of the subject, no serious evidence exists to support the hypothesis that executions produce a higher murder rate. *Cf.*, Phillips, *The Deterrent Effect of Capital Punishment: New Evidence on an Old Controversy,* 86 *Am. J. Soc.* 139 (1980) (arguing that murder rates drop immediately after executions of criminals.
11. H. Gross, *A Theory of Criminal Justice* 489 (1979) (attributing this passage to Sir James Fitzjames Stephen).
12. Weems v. United States, 217 U.S. 349 (1910), suggests that penalties be proportionate to the seriousness of the crime—a common theme of the criminal law. Murder, therefore, demands more than life imprisonment, if, as I believe, it is a more serious crime than other crimes punished by life imprisonment. In modern times, our sensibility requires that the range of punishments be narrower than the range of crimes—but not so narrow as to exclude the death penalty.
13. *Cf.* Kaplan, *Administering Capital Punishment,* 36 *U. Fla. L. Rev.* 177, 178, 190-91 (1984) (noting the high cost of appealing a capital sentence).
14. For an example of this view, see A. Camus, *Reflections on the Guillotine* 24-30 (1959). On the limitations al-

legedly imposed by the *lex talionis*, see Reiman, *Justice, Civilization, and the Death Penalty: Answering van den Haag*, 14 *Phil. & Pub. Aff.* 115, 119-34 (1985).

15. Thus restitution (a civil liability) cannot satisfy the punitive purpose of penal sanctions, whether the purpose be retributive or deterrent.
16. Some abolitionists challenge: if the death penalty is just and serves as a deterrent, why not televise executions? The answer is simple. The death even of a murderer, however well-deserved, should not serve as public entertainment. It so served in earlier centuries. But in this respect our sensibility has changed for the better, I believe. Further, television unavoidably would trivialize executions, wedged in, as they would be, between game shows, situation comedies, and the like. Finally, because televised executions would focus on the physical aspects of the punishment, rather than the nature of the crime and the suffering of the victim, a televised execution would present the murderer as the victim of the state. Far from communicating the moral significance of the execution, television would shift the focus to the pitiable fear of the murderer. We no longer place in cages those sentenced to imprisonment to expose them to public view. Why should we so expose those sentenced to execution?
17. *See* van de Haag, *Punishment as a Device for Controlling the Crime Rate*, 33 *Rutgers L. Rev.* 706, 719 (1981) (explaining why the desire for retribution, although independent, would have to be satisfied even if deterrence were the only purpose of punishment).
18. An explicit threat of punitive action is necessary to the justification of any legal punishment: *nulla poena sine lege* (no punishment without [preexisting] law). To be sufficiently justified, the threat must in turn have a rational and legitimate purpose. "Your money or your life" does not qualify; nor does the threat of an unjust law; nor, finally, does a threat that is altogether disproportionate to the importance of its purpose. In short, preannouncement legitimizes the threatened punishment only if the threat is warranted. But this leaves a very wide range of justified threats. Furthermore, the punished person is aware of the penalty for his punishment. His victim, however, did not volunteer to risk anything. The question whether any self-inflicted injury—such as a legal punishment—ever can be unjust to a person who knowingly risked it is a matter that requires more analysis than is possible here.
19. *The Works of Jeremy Bentham* 105 (J. Bowring ed. 1972). However, I would be more polite about prescriptible natural rights, which Bentham described as "simple nonsense." *Id.* (It does not matter whether natural rights are called "moral" or "human" rights as they currently are by most writers.)
20. *The Death Penalty in America* 256-63 (H. Bedau ed., 3d ed. 1982) quoting Furman v. Georgia, 408 U.S. 238, 286, 305 (1972) (Brennan, J., concurring).
21. *Id.* at 272-73; *see also* Gregg v. Georgia, 428 U.S. 153, 230 (1976) (Brennan, J., dissenting).
22. Furman v. Georgia, 408 U.S. 238, 291 (1972) (Brennan, J., concurring).
23. *Id.* at 290.
24. *See* Barzun, *supra* [footnote p. 410], *passim*.

Review Questions

1. How does van den Haag reply to the objection that capital punishment is discriminatory?
2. What is his response to the claim that innocent people are mistakenly executed?
3. According to van den Haag, why does the possibility or probability of deterrence support the use of the death penalty?
4. How does he reply to the objections about cost, excessive suffering, legitimizing killing, the right to life, and human dignity?

Discussion Questions

1. Do you agree that the death penalty is the harshest punishment? Can you think of worse punishments?
2. Are you willing to accept the execution of innocent people as van den Haag does? Why or why not?
3. Are you convinced by van den Haag's argument about deterrence? (You may want to wait until you have read Glover's attack on this argument in the next reading.)

Jonathan Glover

Execution and Assassination

Johnathan Glover is a Fellow and Tutor in Philosophy at New College, Oxford, and has written Responsibility *(1970), and* Causing Death and Saving Lives, *(1977).*

Glover begins with a discussion of Kant's retributive view and the absolutist rejection of capital punishment. He finds both of these to be unacceptable from a utilitarian point of view. The utilitarian approach is that the death penalty is justified if the number of lives saved exceeds the number of executions. But due to the bad side effects of execution on the person executed and on others, as well as other undesirable features, the death penalty is not justified unless it has a substantial deterrent effect. After considering arguments for this deterrent effect, Glover concludes that the case for capital punishment as a substantial deterrent fails.

The Penal Law is a Categorical Imperative; and woe to him who creeps through the serpent-windings of Utilitarianism to discover some advantage that may discharge him from the Justice of Punishment, or even from the due measure of it . . . For if Justice and Righteousness perish, human life would no longer have any value in the world . . . Whoever has committed murder must die.

Immanuel Kant, The Philosophy of Law

It is curious, but till that moment I had never realized what it means to destroy a healthy, conscious man. When I saw the prisoner step aside to avoid the puddle I saw the mystery, the unspeakable wrongness, of cutting a life short when it is in full tide. This man was not dying, he was alive just as we are alive. All the organs of his body were working—bowels digesting food, skin renewing itself, nails growing, tissues forming—all toiling away in solemn foolery. His nails would still be growing when he stood on the drop, when he was falling through the air with a tenth of a second to live. His eyes saw the yellow gravel and the gray walls, and his brain still remembered, foresaw, reasoned, even about puddles. He and we were a party of men walking together, seeing, hearing, feeling, understanding the same world; and in two minutes, with a sudden snap, one of us would be gone—one mind less, one world less.

George Orwell, "A Hanging," Adelphi, *1931*

The debate about capital punishment for murder is, emotionally at least, dominated by two absolutist views. On the retributive view, the murderer must be given the punishment he deserves, which is death. On the other view, analogous to pacifism about war, there is in principle no possibility of justifying capital punishment; in execution there is only "the unspeakable wrongness of cutting a life short when it is in full tide." Supporters of these two approaches agree only in rejecting the serpent-windings of utilitarianism.

Let us look first at the retributive view. According to retributivism in its purest form, the aim of punishment is quite independent of any beneficial social consequences it may have. To quote Kant again:

> Even if a Civil Society resolved to dissolve itself with the consent of all its members—as might be supposed in the case of a people inhabiting an island resolving to separate and scatter themselves throughout the whole world—the last Murderer lying in the prison ought to be executed before the resolution was carried out. This ought to be done in order that everyone may realize the desert of his deeds, and that blood-guiltiness may not remain upon the people; for otherwise they might all be regarded as participants in the murder as a public violation of justice.

This view of punishment, according to which it has a value independent of its contribution to

From Jonathan Glover: *Causing Death & Savings Lives* (Pelican Books 1977) pp. 228-245.

reducing the crime rate, is open to the objection that acting on it leads to what many consider to be pointless suffering. To impose suffering or deprivation on someone, or to take his life, is something that those of us who are not retributivists think needs very strong justification in terms of benefits, either to the person concerned or to other people. The retributivist has to say either that the claims of justice can make it right to harm someone where no one benefits, or else to cite the curiously **metaphysical** "benefits" of justice being done, such as Kant's concern that we should have "blood-guiltiness" removed. I have no way of refuting these positions, as they seem to involve no clear intellectual mistake. I do not expect to win the agreement of those who hold them, and I am simply presupposing the other view, that there is already enough misery in the world, and that adding to it requires a justification in terms of nonmetaphysical benefits to people.

This is not to rule out retributive moral principles perhaps playing a limiting role in a general theory of punishment. There is a lot to be said for the retributive restrictions that *only* those who deserve punishment should receive it and that they should never get more punishment than they deserve. (The case for this, which at least partly rests on utilitarian considerations, has been powerfully argued by H. L. A. Hart.[1]) But the approach to be adopted here rules out using retributive considerations to justify any punishment not already justifiable in terms of social benefits. In particular it rules out the argument that capital punishment can be justified, whether or not it reduces the crime rate, because the criminal deserves it.

This approach also has the effect of casting doubt on another way of defending capital punishment, which was forthrightly expressed by Lord Denning: "The ultimate justification of any punishment is not that it is a deterrent, but that it is the emphatic denunciation by the community of a crime: and from this point of view, there are some murders which, in the present state of public opinion, demand the most emphatic denunciation of all, namely the death penalty."[2] The question here is whether the point of the denunciation is to reduce the murder rate, in which case this turns out after all to be a utilitarian justification, or whether denunciation is an end in itself. If it is an end in itself, it starts to look like the retributive view in disguise, and should be rejected for the same reasons.

If we reject retribution for its own sake as a justification for capital punishment we are left with two alternative general approaches to the question. One is an absolute rejection in principle of any possibility of capital punishment being justified, in the spirit of Orwell's remarks. The other is the rather more messy approach, broadly utilitarian in character, of weighing up likely social costs and benefits.

The Absolutionist Rejection of Capital Punishment

To some people, it is impossible to justify the act of killing a fellow human being. They are absolute pacifists about war and are likely to think of capital punishment as "judicial murder." They will sympathize with Beccaria's question: "Is it not absurd that the laws which detest and punish homicide, in order to prevent murder, publicly commit murder themselves?"

The test of whether an opponent of capital punishment adopts this absolutionist position is whether he would still oppose it if it could be shown to save many more lives than it cost, if, say, every execution deterred a dozen potential murderers. The absolutist, unlike the utilitarian opponent of the death penalty, would be unmoved by any such evidence. This question brings out the links between the absolutionist position and the **acts and omissions doctrine.** For those of us who reject the acts and omissions doctrine, the deaths we fail to prevent have to be given weight, as well as the deaths we cause by execution. So those of us who do not accept the acts and omissions doctrine cannot be absolutist opponents of capital punishment.

There is a variant on the absolutist position that at first sight seems not to presuppose the acts and omissions doctrine. On this view, while saving a potential murder victim is in itself as important as not killing a murderer, there is something so cruel about the kind of death involved in capital punishment that this rules out the possibility of its being justified. Those of us who reject the acts and omissions doctrine have to allow that sometimes there can be side effects associated with an act of killing, but not with failure to save a life, which can be sufficiently bad to make a substantial moral difference between the two. When this view is taken of the cruelty of the death penalty, it is not usually the actual method of execution that is objected to, though this can seem important, as in the case where international pressure on General Franco led him to substitute shooting for the garrote. What seems peculiarly cruel and horrible about capital punishment is that the condemned man has the period of waiting, knowing how and when he is to be killed. Many of us would rather die suddenly then linger for weeks or months knowing we were fatally ill, and the condemned man's position is several degrees worse than that of the person given a few months to live by doctors. He has the additional horror of knowing exactly when he will die, and of knowing that his death will be in a ritualized killing by other people, symbolizing his ultimate rejection by the members of his community. The whole of his life may seem to have a different and horrible meaning when he sees it leading up to this end.

For reasons of this kind, capital punishment can plausibly be claimed to fall under the United States Constitution's ban on "cruel and unusual punishments," so long as the word unusual is not interpreted too strictly. The same reasons make the death penalty a plausible candidate for falling under a rather similar ethical ban, which has been expressed by H. L. A. Hart: "There are many different ways in which we think it morally incumbent on us to *qualify* or *limit* the pursuit of the utilitarian goal by methods of punishment. Some punishments are ruled out as too barbarous to use *whatever their social utility*" [3] (final italics mine). Because of the extreme cruelty of capital punishment, many of us would, if forced to make a choice between two horrors, prefer to be suddenly murdered than be sentenced to death and executed. This is what makes it seem reasonable to say that the absolutist rejection of the death penalty need not rest on the acts and omissions doctrine.

But this appearance is illusory. The special awfulness of capital punishment may make an execution even more undesirable than a murder (though many would disagree on the grounds that this is outweighed by the desirability that the guilty rather than the innocent should die). Even if we accept that an execution is worse than an average murder, it does not follow from this that capital punishment is too barbarous to use *whatever its social utility*. For supposing a single execution deterred many murders? Or suppose that some of the murders deterred would themselves have been as cruel as an execution? When we think of the suffering imposed in a famous kidnapping case, where the mother received her son's ear through the post, we may feel uncertain even that capital punishment is more cruel than some "lesser" crimes than murder. The view that some kinds of suffering are too great to impose, whatever their social utility, rules out the possibility of justifying them, however much more suffering they would prevent. And this does presuppose the acts and omissions of us even from this version of absolutism.

A Utilitarian Approach

It is often supposed that the utilitarian alternative to absolutism is simply one of adopting an unqualified maximizing policy. On such a view, the death penalty would be justified if, and only if, it was reasonable to think the number of lives saved exceeded the number of executions. (The question of what to do where the numbers exactly balance presupposes a fineness of measurement that is unattainable in these matters.) On any utilitarian view, numbers of lives saved must be a very important consideration. But there are various special features that justify the substantial qualification of a maximizing policy.

The special horror of the period of waiting for execution may not justify the absolutist rejection of the death penalty, but it is a powerful reason for thinking that an execution may normally cause more misery than a murder, and so for thinking that, if capital punishment is to be justified, it must do better than break even when lives saved through deterrence are compared with lives taken by the executioner.

This view is reinforced when we think of some of the other side effects of the death penalty. It must be appalling to be told that your husband, wife, or child has been murdered, but this is surely less bad than the experience of waiting a month or two for your husband, wife, or child to be executed. And those who think that the suffering of the murderer himself matters less than that of an innocent victim will perhaps not be prepared to extend this view to the suffering of the murderer's parents, wife, and children.

There is also the possibility of mistakenly executing an innocent man, something which it is very probable happened in the case of Timothy Evans. The German Federal Ministry of Justice is quoted in the Council of Europe's report on *The Death Penalty in European Countries* as saying that in the hundred years to 1953, there were twenty-seven death sentences "now established or presumed" to be miscarriages of justice. This point is often used as an argument against capital punishment, but what is often not noticed is that its force must depend on the special horrors of execution as compared with other forms of death, including being murdered. For the victim of murder is innocent too, and he also has no form of redress. It is only the (surely correct) assumption that an innocent man faces something much worse in execution than in murder that gives this argument its claim to prominence in this debate. For, otherwise, the rare cases of innocent men being executed would be completely overshadowed by the numbers of innocent men being murdered. (Unless, of course, the acts and omissions doctrine is again at work here, for execution is something that we, as a community, *do* while a higher murder rate is something, we at most *allow*.

The death penalty also has harmful effects on people other than the condemned man and his family. For most normal people, to be professionally involved with executions, whether as judge, prison warden, chaplain, or executioner, must be highly disturbing. Arthur Koestler quotes the case of the executioner Ellis, who attempted suicide a few weeks after he executed a sick woman "whose insides fell out before she vanished through the trap."[4] (Though the chances must be very small of the experience of Mr. Pierrepoint, who describes in his autobiography how he had to execute a friend with whom he often sang duets in a pub.[5]) And there are wider effects on society at large. When there is capital punishment, we are all involved in the horrible business of a long-premeditated killing, and most of us will to some degree share in the emotional response George Orwell had so strongly when he had to be present. It cannot be good for children at school to know that there is an execution at the prison down the road. And there is another bad effect, drily stated in the *Report of the Royal Commission on Capital Punishment:* "No doubt the ambition that prompts an average of five applications a week for the post of hangman, and the craving that draws a crowd to the prison where a notorious murderer is being executed, reveal psychological qualities that no state would wish to foster in its citizens."

Capital punishment is also likely to operate erratically. Some murderers are likely to *go* free because the death penalty makes juries less likely to convict. (Charles Dickens, in a newspaper article quoted in the 1868 Commons debate, gave the example of a forgery case, where a jury found a £10 note to be worth thirty-nine shillings, in order to save the forger's life.) There are also great problems in operating a reprieve system without arbitrariness, say, in deciding whether being pregnant or having a young baby should qualify a woman for a reprieve.

Finally, there is the drawback that the retention or reintroduction of capital punishment contributes to a tradition of cruel and horrible punishment that we might hope would wither away. Nowadays we never think of disemboweling people or chopping off their hands as a punishment. Even if these punishments would be especially effective in deterring some very serious crimes, they are not regarded as a real possibility. To many of us, it seems that the utilitarian benefits from this situation outweigh the loss of any deterrent power they might have if reintroduced for some repulsive crime like kidnapping. And the longer we leave capital punishment in abeyance, the more its use will seem as out of the question as the no more cruel punishment of mutilation. (At this point, I come near to Hart's view that some punishments are too barbarous to use whatever their social utility. The difference is that I think that arguments for and against a punishment should be based on social utility, but that a wide-spread view that some things are unthinkable is itself of great social utility.)

For these reasons, a properly thought-out utilitarianism does not enjoin an unqualified policy of seeking the minimum loss of life, as the no trade-off view does. Capital punishment has its own special cruelties and horrors, which change the whole position. In order to be justified, it must be shown, with good evidence, that it has a deterrent effect not obtainable by less awful means, and one that is quite substantial rather than marginal.

Deterrence and Murder

The arguments over whether capital punishment deters murder more effectively than less drastic methods are of two kinds: statistical and intuitive. The statistical arguments are based on various kinds of comparisons of murder rates. Rates are compared before and after abolition in a country, and where possible, further comparisons are made with rates after reintroduction of capital punishment. Rates are compared in neighboring countries, or neighboring states of the U.S.C.A., with and without the death penalty. I am not a statistician and have no special competence to discuss the issue, but will merely purvey the received opinion of those who have looked into the matter. Those who have studied the figures are agreed that there is no striking correlation between the absence of capital punishment and any alteration in the curve of the murder rate. Having agreed on this point they then fall into two schools. On one view, we can conclude that capital punishment is not a greater deterrent to murder than the prison sentences that are substituted for it. On the other, more cautious, view, we can only conclude that we do not know that capital punishment is a deterrent. I shall not attempt to choose between these interpretations. For, given that capital punishment is justified only where there is good evidence that it is a substantial deterrent, either interpretation fails to support the case for it.

If the statistical evidence were conclusive that capital punishment did not deter more than milder punishments, this would leave no room for any further discussion. But, since the statistical evidence may be inconclusive, many people feel there is room left for intuitive arguments. Some of these deserve examination. The intuitive case was forcefully stated in 1864 by Sir James Fitzjames Stephen: [6]

> No other punishment deters men so effectually from committing crimes as the punishment of death. This is one of those propositions which it is difficult to prove, simply because they are in themselves more obvious than any proof can make them. It is possible to display ingenuity in arguing against it, but that is all. The whole experience of mankind is in the other direction. The threat of instant death is the one to which resort has always been made when there was an absolute necessity for producing some result. . . . No one goes to certain inevitable death except by compulsion. Put the matter the other way. Was there ever yet a criminal who, when sentenced to death and brought out to die, would refuse the offer of a commutation of his sentence for the severest secondary punishment? Surely not. Why is this? It can only be because "All that a man has will he give for his life." In any secondary punishment, however terrible, there is hope; but death is death; its terrors cannot be described more forcibly.

These claims turn out when scrutinized to be much more speculative and doubtful than they at first sight appear.

The first doubt arises when Stephen talks of "certain inevitable death." The Royal Commission, in their *Report,* after quoting the passage from Stephen above, quote figures to show that, in the fifty years from 1900 to 1949, there was in England and Wales one execution for every twelve murders known to the police. In Scotland in the same period there was less than one execution for every twenty-five murders known to the police. Supporters of Stephen's view could supplement their case by advocating more death sentences and fewer reprieves, or by optimistic speculations about better police detection or greater willingness of juries to convict. But the reality of capital punishment as it was in these countries, unmodified by such recommendations and speculations, was not one where the potential murderer faced certain, inevitable death. This may incline us to modify Stephen's estimate of its deterrent effect, unless we buttress his view with the further speculation that a fair number of potential murderers falsely believed that what they would face was certain, inevitable death.

The second doubt concerns Stephen's talk of "the threat of instant death." The reality again does not quite fit this. By the time the police conclude their investigation, the case is brought to trial, and verdict and sentence are followed by appeal, petition for reprieve, and then execution, many months have probably elapsed, and when this time factor is added to the low probability of the murderers being executed, the picture looks very different. For we often have a time bias, being less affected by threats of future catastrophes than by threats of instant ones. The certainty of immediate death is one thing; it is another thing merely to increase one's chances of death in the future. Unless this were so, no one would smoke or take on such high-risk jobs as diving in the North Sea.

There is another doubt when Stephen very plausibly says that virtually all criminals would prefer life imprisonment to execution. The difficulty is over whether this entitles us to conclude that it is therefore a more effective deterrent. For there is the possibility that, compared with the long term of imprisonment that is the alternative, capital punishment is what may appropriately be called an "overkill." It may be that, for those who will be deterred by threat of punishment, a long prison sentence is sufficient deterrent. I am not suggesting that this is so, but simply that it is an open question whether a worse alternative here generates any additional deterrent effect. The answer is *not* intuitively obvious.

Stephen's case rests on the speculative psychological assumptions that capital punishment is not an overkill compared with a prison sentence, and that its additional deterrent effect is not obliterated by time bias, nor by the low probability of execution, nor by a combination of these factors. Or else it must be assumed that, where the additional deterrent effect would be obliterated by the low probability of death, either on its own or in combination with time bias, the potential murderer thinks the probability is higher than it is. Some of these assumptions may be true, but, when they are brought out into the open, it is by no means obvious that the required combination of them can be relied upon.

Supporters of the death penalty also sometimes use what David A. Conway, in his valuable discussion of this issue, calls "the best-bet argument." [7] On this view, since there is no certainty whether or not capital punishment reduces the number of murders, either decision about it involves gambling with lives. It is suggested that it is better to gamble with the lives of murderers than with the lives of their innocent potential victims. This presupposes the attitude, rejected here, that a murder is a greater evil than the execution of a murderer. But, since this attitude probably has overwhelmingly widespread support, it is worth noting that, even if it is accepted, the best-bet argument is unconvincing. This is because, as Conway has pointed out, it overlooks the fact that we are not choosing between the chance of a murderer dying and the chance of a victim dying. In leaving the death penalty, we are opting for the certainty of the murderer dying that we hope will give us a chance of a potential victim being saved. This would look like a good bet only if we thought an execution substantially preferable to a murder and either the statistical evidence or the intuitive arguments made the effectiveness of the death penalty as a deterrent look reasonably likely.

Since the statistical studies do not give any clear indication that capital punishment makes any difference to the number of murders committed, the only chance of its supporters discharging the heavy burden of justification would be if the intuitive arguments were extremely powerful. We might then feel justified in supposing that other factors distorted the murder rate, masking the substantial deterrent effect of capital punishment. The intuitive arguments, presented as the merest platitudes, turn out to be speculative and unobvious. I conclude that the case for capital punishment as a substantial deterrent fails.

Deterrence and Political Crimes by Opposition Groups

It is sometimes suggested that the death penalty may be an effective deterrent in the case of a special class of "political" crimes. The "ordinary" murder (killing one's wife in a moment of rage, shooting a policeman in panic after a robbery, killing someone in a brawl) may not be particularly sensitive to different degrees of punishment. But some killings for political purposes have a degree of preparation and thought that may allow the severity of the penalty to affect the calculation. Two different kinds of killing come to mind here. There are killings as part of a political campaign, ranging from assassination through terrorist activities up to full-scale guerrilla war. And then there are policies carried out by repressive governments, varying from "liquidation" of individual opponents with or without "trial" to policies of wholesale extermination, sometimes, but not always, in wartime.

Let us look first at killings by groups opposed to governments. Would the various sectarian terrorist groups in Ireland stop their killings if those involved were executed? Would independence movements in countries like Algeria or Kenya have confined themselves to nonviolent means if more executions had taken place? Could the Nazis have deterred the French resistance by more executions? Could the Americans have deterred guerrillas war in Vietnam by more executions?

To ask these questions is to realize both the variety of different political situations in which the question of deterrent killing arises, and also to be reminded, if it is necessary, that moral right is not always on the side of the authorities trying to do the deterring. But let us, for the sake of argument, assume a decent government is trying to deal with terrorists or guerrillas whose cause has nothing to be said for it. People have always gone to war knowing they risk their lives, and those prepared to fight in a guerrilla war seem scarcely likely to change their mind because of the marginal extra risk of capital punishment if they are arrested. If the case is to be made, it must apply to lower levels of violence than full-scale guerrilla war.

Given the death penalty's drawbacks, is there any reason to think it would be sufficiently effective in deterring a campaign of terrorist violence to be justified? The evidence is again inconclusive. In many countries there have been terrorist campaigns where the authorities have responded with executions without stopping the campaign. It is always open to someone to say that the level of terrorist activity might have been even higher but for the executions, but it is hard to see why this should be likely. Those who do the shooting or the planting of bombs are not usually the leaders and can be easily replaced by others willing to risk their lives. Danger to life does not deter people from fighting in wars, and a terrorist gunman may be just as committed to his cause as a soldier. And executions create martyrs, which helps the terrorist cause. They may even raise the level of violence by leading to reprisals.

But it may be that a sufficiently ruthless policy of executions would be effective enough to overcome these drawbacks. It has been claimed that the policy of the Irish government in 1922-3 is an instance of this. David R. Bates describes it as follows: [8]

> In the turbulent period following the establishment of the Irish Free State, military courts with power to inflict the death penalty were set up to enable the Irregulars (opposing the Treaty) to be crushed. These powers were first used on 17 November 1922, when four young men were arrested in Dublin and, on being found to be armed, were executed. Shortly afterwards the Englishman, Erskine Childers, captured while carrying a revolver, was also executed. On 7 December two Deputies were shot (one fatally) by the Irregulars. The Minister for Defense, with the agreement of the Cabinet, selected four Irregular leaders who had been in prison since the fall of the Four Courts on 29 June. They were wakened, told to prepare themselves, and were executed by firing

squad at dawn. During a six-month period, almost twice as many Irregular prisoners were executed as had been executed by the British from 1916 to 1921. At the end of April '1923, the Irregulars sought a cease fire to discuss terms. The Free State Government refused. In May 1924, the Irregulars conceded military defeat.

This is an impressive case, and it may be that this degree of ruthlessness by the government involved fewer deaths than would have taken place during a prolonged terrorist campaign. But against this must be set some doubts. What would have happened if the terrorists had been as ruthless in reprisal as the government, perhaps announcing that for every man executed there would be two murders? Is it clear that after a period of such counter-retaliation it would have been the Irregulars rather than the government who climbed down? Does not any net saving of lives by the government's ruthless policy depend on the terrorists refraining from counter-retaliation, and can this be relied on in other cases? And is there not something dangerous in the precedent set when a government has prisoners executed without their having been convicted and sentenced for a capital offense? And, in this case, is it even clear that the defeat of the Irregulars ended once and for all the violence associated with the issues they were campaigning about? I raise these questions, not to claim that the government policy was clearly wrong, but to show how even a case like this is ambiguous in the weight it lends to the argument for using the death penalty against terrorism.

I do not think that the chance of a net saving of lives will in general outweigh the combination of the general drawbacks of capital punishment combined with the danger of its merely leading to a higher level of violence in a terrorist situation. But this is a matter of judgment rather than proof, and I admit that it *may* be that the opposite view had better results than mine would have had in 1922.

Deterrence and Political Crimes by the Authorities

The other category of political crimes that sometimes seems so special as to justify the death penalty is atrocities committed by governments or their agents. The executions of leading Nazis after the Nuremberg trials and the execution of Eichmann after his trial in Jerusalem come to mind. The justification usually advanced for these executions is retributive, and it is hard to imagine any more deserving candidates for the death penalty. But, for those of us who do not consider retribution an acceptable aim of punishment, the question must be whether executing them made their kind of activity less likely to happen again in the future. For, if not, we have no answer to the question asked by Victor Gollancz at the time of the Eichmann trial: why should we think we improve the world by turning six million deaths into six million and one?

The chances of people who design or carry out governmental policies of murder being tried and sentenced must often be very small. Sometimes this happens as the result of revolution or defeat in war, but those in power stand a fairly good chance of being killed under these circumstances anyway, and the additional hazard of capital punishment may not have much deterrent effect. As with "ordinary" murderers, the hope of not being caught reduces the punishment's terrors. Some of those who murdered for Hitler were executed; their opposite numbers under Stalin paid no penalty. The torturers who worked for the Greek colonels were brought to trial, but those now at work in Chile, Brazil, and South Africa have every expectation of not being punished.

When considering isolated cases of governmental murder (perhaps the assassination of a troublesome foreign leader by a country's intelligence agency, or the single killing of a political opponent) there seems no reason to think capital punishment more of a deterrent than it is of "ordinary" nonpolitical murder. If anything, it is likely to be less of a deterrent because of the reduced chance of a murder charge ever being brought. So there seems no case for treating these crimes as other than ordinary murders. But when considering large-scale atrocities, on the scale of those of Hitler or Stalin, or even on the scale of Lyndon Johnson in Vietnam or General Gowon in Nigeria, a version of the best-bet argument comes into play. There are two possible advantages to the death penalty here. One is simply that of totally eliminating the chance of the same mass murderer occupying a position of leadership again. Suppose Hitler had been captured at the end of the Second World War and the question of executing him had arisen. If he had not been executed, it is overwhelmingly probable that he would have spent the rest of his life in Spandau prison, writing his memoirs and giving increasingly senile lectures on world history to visiting journalists. But there would always be the very slight risk of an escape and return to power in the style of Napoleon. This slight risk is removed by execution. The other advantage of the death penalty is the chance, which we have seen to be probably very slight, of deterring repetition of such policies by other leaders.

The best-bet argument in these cases can be used by someone who accepts that the dangers of a defeated leader returning to power are very small and that the chances of execution deterring future leaders from similar policies are also very small. The argument is simply that, where the prevention of such enormous atrocities is in question, even an extremely small probability of prevention is valuable. Consider a case in which numbers and probabilities are parallel, but in which act and omission are reversed. Suppose someone in the hospital can have his life saved only by the making of some organism that has previously been banned. The reason for the ban is that there is a danger, but only a very faint one, of the organism getting out of control. If it does this, the death rate will run into millions. Let us suppose that our intuitive estimate of the unquantifiable risk here is the same as our intuitive estimate of the unquantifiable reduction of risk caused by executing the murdering leader. Those who would rather let the hospital patient die than breach the ban on the dangerous organism must either rely on the acts and omissions doctrine, or else rely on some difference of side effects, if they are not prepared to support executing the murdering politician or official.

Part of the difficulty in interpreting comparisons of this sort arises from the fact that we are dealing with probabilities that cannot be measured. And, even if they could be measured, most of us are unclear what sacrifices are worth making for the reduction of some risk that is already very small. But if we make the highly artificial assumption that the alterations in probability of risk are the same in the medical case as in the executions case, the dilemma remains. Let us suppose that the risk is one that we would not take in the medical case to save a single life. Those of us who do not accept the acts and omissions doctrine must then either find some difference of side effects or else support the execution.

Side effects do go some way towards separating the two cases. For, to breach the ban on producing the organism, even if it does no harm itself, contributes by example to a less strict observance of that ban (and possibly others) in cases in which the risk may be much greater. In the case of the Nazi leaders, such bad side effects as exist follow from execution rather than from saving their lives. These side effects include the contribution made to a climate of opinion where the death penalty seems more acceptable in other contexts, and the precedent that may encourage politicians to have their overthrown rivals, at home or abroad, executed. This last effect could be mitigated by more effort than was made at Nuremberg to remove the impression of the defeated being tried by the victors. It would be possible to set up a court of a genuinely international kind, independent of governmental pressure, to which prosecutions for a large-scale murder could be brought. But the general effect on the public consciousness of having capital punishment as a series of possibility would remain. I am uncertain how to weigh this against the small chance of helping to avert a great evil. For this reason my own views on this question are undecided.

Endnotes

1. H. L. A. Hart, "Prolegomenon to the Principles of Punishment," *Proceedings of the Aristotelian Society*, 1959–60.
2. Quoted in the *Report of the Royal Commission on Capital Punishment*, 1953.
3. H. L. A. Hart, "Murder and the Principles of Punishment," *Northwestern Law Review*, 1958.
4. Arthur Koestler, *Reflections on Hanging*, London, 1956.
5. Albert Pierrepoint, *Executioner: Pierrepoint*, London, 1974.

6. James Fitzjames Stephen, "Capital Punishments," *Fraser's Magazine,* 1864.
7. David A. Conway, "Capital Punishment and Deterrence," *Philosophy and Public Affairs,* 1974.
8. Professor David R. Bates, Letter to *The Times,* 14 October 1975.

Review Questions

1. Why doesn't Glover accept Kant's view of capital punishment?
2. What is the other view that Glover is presupposing?
3. Why doesn't Glover accept the absolutist rejection of capital punishment?
4. Why does Glover think that capital punishment can plausibly be claimed to be a "cruel and unusual punishment?"
5. According to Glover, in what cases can capital punishment be justified even if it is cruel?
6. State the maximizing policy, and the considerations that Glover introduces to qualify it.
7. According to Glover, how can capital punishment be justified?
8. Glover discusses three arguments (beginning with the statistical argument) that are used to defend capital punishment. What are these arguments, and why doesn't Glover accept them?
9. What is Glover's position on capital punishment for political crimes?

Discussion Questions

1. "Whoever has committed murder must *die.*" Do you agree with this statement? Explain your view.
2. Is the death penalty a cruel and unusual punishment? Explain your answer.
3. Glover concludes that the case for capital punishment as a substantial deterrent fails. Do you agree? Defend your position.
4. Can you think of any cases in which capital punishment would be justified? What are they?

Problem Cases

1. Death for Rape. In the case of *Coker* v. *Georgia* (1977), the Supreme Court ruled that the death sentence could not be imposed for rape, because such a punishment is grossly disproportionate to the injury caused the victim. Yet the following states allow the death penalty for the crime of rape in certain circumstances: Florida, Georgia, Louisiana, Mississippi, North Carolina, Oklahoma, and Tennessee.

Is capital punishment justified for the crime of rape? If so, in what cases?

2. The Case of Troy Gregg (*Gregg* v. *Georgia,* 428 U.S. 153, 1976). Troy Gregg and Floyd Allen were hitchhiking when they were picked up by Fred Simmons and Bob Moore. Simmons and Moore left the car at a rest stop. According to the testimony of Allen, Gregg said that they were going to rob Simmons and Moore. He fired at them when they came back to the car, then shot each of them in the head, robbed them, and finally drove away with Allen. Gregg first admitted that Allen's account was accurate, but later denied it. Gregg's story was that Simmons had attacked him and that he had killed the two men in self-defense. The jury found Gregg guilty of two counts of murder, and determined that the murders were committed for the purpose of robbery.

Should Gregg be given the death sentence or not? Defend you answer.

3. The Case of Paul Crump. (See Ronald Bailey, "Facing Death: A New Life Perhaps Too Late," *Life,* July 27, 1962, pp. 28-29.) In the early 1950s, Paul Crump was convicted of a vicious murder, sentenced to death, and put in an Illinois prison. At his trial, he was said to be full of hatred, "animalistic and belligerent," and a danger to society. Yet under the influence of Warden Jack Johnson and his prison reforms, Crump became rehabilitated. Even though he had only a ninth-grade education, he took courses in reading and writing. Soon he was reading poetry, fiction, and philosophy, and writing stories, articles and poems which were published in small magazines. He wrote an autobiographical novel, *Burn, Killer, Burn.* Eventually, he began to help his fellow prisoners and was put in charge of caring for the sick and disabled in the convalescent section of the jail hospital. All this did not happen overnight, but took a period of seven years. At the end of this time, Warden Johnson claimed that Crump was "completely rehabilitated," and on August 1, 1962, Illinois Governor Otto Kerner commuted Crump's death sentence to 199 years with the possibility of parole.

Do you think that Governor Kerner made the right decision or not? Explain your answer.

Would it have been morally right to free Crump? Why or why not?

Would it have been morally justifiable to execute Crump despite his rehabilitation? What do you think?

4. *The Sacco-Vanzetti Case.* On April 15, 1920, a paymaster for a shoe company in South Braintree, MA, and his guard were shot and killed by two men who escaped with over $15,000. Witnesses thought the two men were Italians, and Nicola Sacco and Bartolomeo Vanzetti were arrested. Both men were anarchists and had evaded the army draft. Upon their arrest, they made false statements. Both carried firearms; but neither had a criminal record, nor was there any evidence that they had the money. In July 1921, they were found guilty and sentenced to death. The conduct of the trial by Judge Webster Thayer was criticized, and indeed much of the evidence against them was later discredited. The court denied their appeal for a new trial, and Governor Alvan T. Fuller, after postponing the execution, allowed them to be executed on August 22, 1927. Many regarded them as innocent, prompting worldwide sympathy demonstrations. The case has been the subject of many books, most of which agree that Vanzetti was innocent, but that Sacco may have been guilty. The gun found on Sacco was tested with modern ballistics equipment in 1961, and these tests seem to show that the gun had been used to kill the guard.

Was it morally right to execute these two men? Why or why not?

5. *William Alvin Smith.* (Reported in *Time,* July 19, 1989.) William Alvin Smith robbed and killed the owner of a grocery store in rural Georgia when he was twenty years old. Smith turned himself into the police and signed a confession. A local jury condemned Smith to death in the electric chair, but in July 1989, a Federal judge ordered a new sentencing hearing for Smith on the grounds that he lacked the ability to understand the significance of waiving his rights to remain silent and to have an attorney present. Smith has the mental capacity of a ten-year-old.

Does he deserve the death sentence?

It is estimated that about 30 percent of the 2,200 convicts on death row are mentally retarded or mentally impaired. Should they be executed?

Suggested Readings

1. Anthony G. Amsterdam "Race and the Death Penalty," *Criminal Justice Ethics,* Vol. 7, No. 1 (Winter/Spring 1988), pp. 82-86, argues that the Supreme Court ruling in *McCleskey* allowing the discriminatory practice of imposing the death sentence on African American males in Georgia amounts to a license to discriminate against people of color.

2. Hugo Adam Bedau, "Capital Punishment," in *Matters of Lie and Death,* 3d ed., Tom Regan, ed., (New York: Random House, 1993), pp. 160-194. Bedau is an abolitionist who argues that neither the appeal to retribution nor deterrence justifies the death penalty as opposed to the lesser penalty of life imprisonment. He claims that scientists who have studied the issue determined the deterrence achieved by the death penalty is not measurably greater than the deterrence achieved by life imprisonment. As for preventing convicted murderers from killing again, Bedau holds that the death sentence is unnecessary, since less than one convicted murderer in a hundred commits another murder.

3. Hugo Adam Bedau, ed., *The Death Penalty in America,* 3d ed., (New York: Oxford, 1982). This excellent anthology provides a number of useful articles on factual data relevant to the death penalty, and articles both for and against.

4. Walter Berns, *For Capital Punishment* (New York: Basic Books, 1979). Berns presents a retributivist justification of capital punishment.

5. Albert Camus, *Reflections on the Guillotine: An Essay on Capital Punishment,* trans. By Richard Howard (Michigan City, IN: Fridtjof-Karla Press, 1959). Camus expresses his opposition to the death penalty.

6. Gertrude Ezorsky, ed., *Philosophical Perspectives on Punishment* (Albany: State University of New York Press, 1972). This anthology covers capi-

tal punishment and general philosophical questions about punishment.

7. Robert S. Gerstein, "Capital Punishment—'Cruel and Unusual?': A Retributivist Response," *Ethics,* vol. 85, no. 1, pp. 75-79. Gerstein argues that retributivism is not vengeance, but rather the view that punishment restores the balance of advantages to a just community. The punishment must be proportionate to the offense, but also it must treat the offender with the respect due a member of a community founded on principles of justice.

8. Steven Goldberg, "On Capital Punishment," *Ethics* 85 (October 1974), pp. 67-74. Goldberg examines the factual issue of whether or not the death penalty is a uniquely effective deterrent. A revised version entitled "Does Capital Punishment Deter?" appears in *Today's Moral Problems,* 2d ed., Richard A. Wasserstrom, ed. (New York: Macmillan, 1979), pp. 538-551.

9. Ernest van den Haag and John P. Conrad, *The Death Penalty: A Debate* (New York: Plenum, 1983). Conrad is against the death penalty and van den Haag is for it; each presents his case and critically responds to the other's arguments.

10. Sidney Hook, "The Death Sentence," *The Death Penalty in America,* rev. ed., in Hugo Adam Bedau, ed. (Garden City, NY: Doubleday, 1967). Hook supports the retention of the death penalty in two cases: (1) defendants convicted of murder who choose the death sentence rather than life imprisonment, and (2) those who have been sentenced to prison for premeditated murder and then murder again. Since the publication of the original essay, Professor Hook advises that he is now prepared to extend the scope of discretionary death sentences in cases of multiple and aggravated capital crimes.

11. Robert Johnson, "This Man Has Expired: Witness to an Execution," *Commonweal,* January 13, 1989, pp. 9-13, gives a very detailed and graphic description of an electric-chair execution as well as the events before and after the event.

12. Thomas Long, "Capital Punishment—'Cruel and Unusual'?" *Ethics* 83 (April 1973), pp. 214-223. Long discusses various arguments for the view that capital punishment is cruel and unusual.

13. Jeffrie B. Murphy, ed. *Punishment and Rehabilitation,* 2d ed. (Belmont, CA: Wadsworth, 1985). This anthology covers various philosophical aspects of punishment including capital punishment.

14. Stephen Nathanson, *An Eye for an Eye? The Morality of Punishing by Death* (Totawa, NJ: Rowman & Littlefield, 1987) discusses issues surrounding the death penalty and develops a case for abolishing it.

Chapter Five

HUNGER AND WELFARE

Introduction

The World Health Organization conservatively estimates that ten million children in the world under the age of five suffer chronic malnourishment. If these children survive at all, they will endure the lasting effects—stunted growth and brain damage from lack of protein. In addition, if we assume there are 7 adults for every child, we get a total of about seventy million chronically malnourished people in the world. This is a very conservative estimate; the Overseas Development Council puts the number of malnourished at two billion—out of a global population of about five billion. Ten thousand people starve to death every day.

Some of these needy people are in rich countries such as the United States. According to recent reports, the United States has about thirty million people living below the poverty level, including an increasing number of homeless people. In 1989, the Coalition for the Homeless estimated a homeless population of three to four million in the United States. Dealing with the needs of these poor people is part of the welfare problem.

The majority of needy people, however, are in other countries—countries on the subcontinent (India, Pakistan, and Bangladesh) and in poor nations of the Caribbean, Latin America, Southeast Asia, and Africa. Dealing with the starving people in other countries is the world hunger problem.

Before turning to these two related problems, we should briefly discuss two factual issues: 1) Can some countries provide welfare for their needy citizens, and 2) Is it possible to feed all the hungry people in the world?

The first question is easily answered: No doubt some poor countries cannot provide welfare for their citizens; that is one reason why we have the problem of world hunger. But rich countries like the United States can and do provide welfare for some of their poor citizens. They could provide welfare for *all* their needy citizens if they considered it as important as national defense. The main issue of welfare is not whether it is actually possible in rich countries—obviously it is. Rather, the moral question is whether needy citizens in rich countries have a right to welfare, and the governments a corresponding duty to provide it.

The second factual question is not so easy to answer. Is it even possible to feed all the hungry people in the world? To determine the amount of aid actually required to do this, we need to know how many people need food, what their nutritional requirements are, how distribution can be made, what population growth will be, and other facts relevant to the problem. If there are two billion people to be fed, as the Overseas Development Council claims, then the task is difficult but perhaps not impossible. Statistics on world grain production show that the world's farmers produce enough grain to provide every human being with 3,600 calories a day—more than enough for healthy men or women. Given some international cooperation, everyone could be fed, at least in principle. Furthermore, even more food could be produced by using available land. According to the Worldwatch Institute, less than sixty percent of the world's farmland is under cultivation, and in almost every country where there is widespread hunger and environmental destruction, much of the best agricultural land is used to raise export crops or livestock. These countries could produce more food by growing grain instead of raising livestock and growing exports crops.

But if enough food is produced to feed everyone, then why do people starve to death? The standard answer is that the rich nations consume more than their fair share of the food; specifically, the rich nations (e.g., the United States, European countries, and Japan) consume seventy percent more protein than the rest of the world. They do this by consuming grain indirectly via feedstocks converted into animal protein rather than directly in the form of bread, noodles, rice, and so on. In other words, the problem is the result of unequal food distribution rather than inadequate food production.

The World Hunger Problem. Let us assume that it is at least theoretically possible to feed all of the world's hungry people. Is there any moral obligation to do this? Do rich nations have any moral obligation to help people from starving to death in poor countries?

One view of the problem, expressed by Foot (see her article "Euthanasia," cited in the Suggested Readings for Chapter 2) and others who distinguish between killing and letting die, is that we have a negative duty not to kill people, but not a positive duty to prevent people from dying of starvation. To be sure, it is a good thing to give to charity to prevent this, but this is optional—it is not required by morality.

The view that giving aid to needy people is a morally optional charity and not a moral duty is attacked by Singer in our first reading for the chapter. He argues that the traditional distinction between duty and charity cannot be drawn, or at least not in the way that Foot and others draw it. He thinks that helping starving people in other countries should not be viewed as optional charity, but as a morally required duty. According to Singer, this duty derives from intuitively obvious moral principles.

Garrett Hardin does not agree. He objects to welfare-style transfers from rich nations to poor ones. In his view, nations are lifeboats with limited carrying capacity: they cannot afford to feed poor nations. Besides, aid to poor nations just makes matter worse—the result is a vicious cycle of overpopulation, starvation, more aid, and so on until there is ecological disaster. The implication is that we should let people in poor nations die.

Robert N. Van Wyk objects to the utilitarian approach used by both Singer and Hardin. Singer expands the area of our moral duty to the point of eliminating the moral supererogatory and fails to take seriously the bad long-term consequences of keeping everybody alive. Hardin's use of metaphor is inappropriate—rich countries are more like luxury liners than lifeboats, and even most poor countries have the resources to feed its people if the resources were only used for that purpose. Instead of a utilitarian approach, Van Wyk suggests a Kantian ethic to solve the problem of world hunger. From Kant's principle of respect for persons, we can derive a duty of reparation to poor countries for past harms committed against them by rich countries and a duty of the affluent to do their fair share to help those who are needy.

The Welfare Problem. Even if we agree that rich nations should not help people in poor nations, there remains the question of what to do about the poor people in the rich nations themselves. Peter Marin gives a graphic description of some of the most needy people in the United States—the homeless. The homeless include Vietnam veterans, the mentally and physically ill, the elderly, single mothers, abused runaway children, immigrants, and traditional hobos. Some (such as the hobos) may choose to be homeless, but it seems clear that most of them have had homelessness forced on them and would like to escape it. Marin adopts a social contract view of the problem. People who have worked have fulfilled their obligation to society, and in return, society owes them aid when they are no longer able to work. But he thinks that we have some obligation to help even those who choose not to work; this shows respect for the right to be left alone and for the freedom that Americans cherish.

Trudy Govier does not discuss the social contract view; instead she examines three other positions on the welfare problem: the individualist position which holds that no one has a right to welfare, the permissive view that everyone in a rich country has a right to welfare, and the more moderate puritan view that the right to welfare in an affluent society is conditional on one's willingness to work. She formulates these positions in terms of rights rather than obligations but agrees that rights imply obligations. If a person in a rich country has a legal or moral right to welfare, then the country has a moral obligation to provide welfare benefits. Which position does Govier accept? After a careful evaluation of the three positions with respect to social justice and consequences, Govier concludes that the permissive view is the most acceptable.

These views are not just hypothetical. One could accurately say that the United States follows a puritan type system of welfare, while Canada (where Govier lives) has a more permissive system. Which system works best? According to statistics cited in *The New York Times* (September 24, 1989), the Canadian system is more efficient when it comes to medical care. The United States spends about twelve percent of its gross national product on health care, while ignoring 31 million Americans with no health insurance. By contrast, Canada spends less than nine percent of its G.N.P. providing health care for *all* its citizens. In the Canadian system, the government is responsible for practically all health care expenses, paying hospitals at a negotiated rate and doctors according to a binding fee schedule.

In vivid contrast to Marin and Govier, Charles Murray proposes that the United States eliminate all federal welfare for working-aged people except unemployment insurance. He argues that this radical cutting of the welfare knot would have good consequences for almost everyone. The majority of the population will gain savings from tax cuts, and those presently on welfare will be strongly encouraged to improve their lives by working or making new arrangements. The hard-core welfare-dependent people who really can't survive without assistance will be taken care of by local and private services.

In the last reading for the chapter, Nancy Fraser presents a feminist analysis of the United States' social-welfare system. She gives some disturbing facts about the system: most of the welfare recipients and employees are women; programs like Aid to Families with Dependent Children keep mothers poor and on welfare; the system assumes that women should be care-givers and domestic workers; it treats women as dependent clients rather than bearers of rights; and important political issues about the interpretation of people's needs and social roles have been reduced to mere legal, administrative and/or therapeutic matters.

Peter Singer

Famine, Affluence, and Morality

For biographical information on Singer, see his reading in Chapter 3.

In this reading, Singer begins with two moral principles. The first is that suffering and death from lack of food, shelter, and medical care are bad. He expects us to accept this principle without argument. The second principle is more controversial, and is formulated in a strong and a weak version. The strong version is that if we can prevent something bad from happening "without thereby sacrificing anything of comparable moral importance," then we should do it. The weak version is that we ought to prevent something bad from happening "unless we have to sacrifice something morally significant." It follows from those two moral principles, Singer argues, that it is a moral duty, and not just a matter of charity, for affluent nations to help starving people in countries like East Bengal.

As I write this, in November 1971, people are dying in East Bengal from lack of food, shelter, and medical care. The suffering and death that are occurring there now are not inevitable, not unavoidable in any fatalistic sense of the term. Constant poverty, a cyclone, and a civil war have turned at least nine million people into destitute refugees; nevertheless, it is not beyond the capacity of the richer nations to give enough assistance to reduce any further suffering to very small proportions. The decisions and actions of human beings can prevent this kind of suffering. Unfortunately, human beings have not made the necessary decisions. At the individual level, people have, with very few exceptions, not responded to the situation in any significant way. Generally, speaking, people have not given large sums to relief funds; they have not written to their parliamentary representatives demanding increased government assistance; they have not demonstrated in the streets, held symbolic fasts, or done anything else directed toward providing the refugees with the means to satisfy their essential needs. At the government level, no government has given the sort of massive aid that would enable the refugees to survive for more than a few days. Britain, for instance, has given rather more than most countries. It has, to date, given £14,750,000. For comparative purposes, Britain's share of the nonrecoverable development costs of the Anglo-French Concorde project is already in excess of £275,000,000, and on present estimates will reach £440,000,000. The implication is that the British government values a supersonic transport more than thirty times as highly as it values the lives of the nine million refugees. Australia is another country which, on a per capita basis, is well up in the "aid to Bengal" table. Australia's aid, however, amounts to less than one-twelfth of the cost of Sydney's new opera house. The total amount given, from all sources, now stands at about £65,000,000. The estimated cost of keeping the refugees alive for one year is £464,000,000. Most of the refugees have now been in the camps for more than six months. The World Bank has said that India

From Peter Singer, "Famine, Affluence, and Morality," *Philosophy & Public Affairs*, Vol. 1, No. 3 (Spring 1972).

needs a minimum of £300,000,000 in assistance from other countries before the end of the year. It seems obvious that assistance on this scale will not be forthcoming. India will be forced to choose between letting the refugees starve or diverting funds from her own development program, which will mean that more of her own people will starve in the future.[1]

These are the essential facts about the present situation in Bengal. So far as it concerns us here, there is nothing unique about this situation except its magnitude. The Bengal emergency is just the latest and most acute of series of major emergencies in various parts of the world, arising both from natural and from man-made causes. There are also many parts of the world in which people die from malnutrition and lack of food independent of any special emergency. I take Bengal as my example only because it is the present concern, and because the size of the problem has ensured that it has been given adequate publicity. Neither individuals nor governments can claim to be unaware of what is happening there.

What are the moral implications of a situation like this? In what follows, I shall argue that the way people in relatively affluent countries react to a situation like that in Bengal cannot be justified; indeed, the whole way we look at moral issues—our moral conceptual scheme—needs to be altered, and with it, the way of life that has come to be taken for granted in our society.

In arguing for this conclusion I will not, of course, claim to be morally neutral. I shall, however, try to argue for the moral position that I take, so that anyone who accepts certain assumptions, to be made explicit, will, I hope, accept my conclusion.

I begin with the assumption that suffering and death from lack of food, shelter, and medical care are bad. I think most people will agree about this, although one may reach the same view by different routes. I shall not argue for this view. People can hold all sorts of eccentric positions, and perhaps from some of them it would not follow that death by starvation is in itself bad. It is difficult, perhaps impossible, to refute such positions, and so for brevity I will henceforth take this assumption as accepted. Those who disagree need read no further.

My next point is this: if it is in our power to prevent something bad from happening, without thereby sacrificing anything of comparable moral importance, we ought, morally, to do it. By "without sacrificing anything of comparable moral importance" I mean without causing anything else comparably bad to happen, or doing something that is wrong in itself, or failing to promote some moral good, comparable in significance to the bad thing that we can prevent. This principle seems almost as uncontroversial as the last one. It requires us only to prevent what is bad, and not to promote what is good, and it requires this of us only when we can do it without sacrificing anything that is, from the moral point of view, comparably important. I could even, as far as the application of my argument to the Bengal emergency is concerned, qualify the point so as to make it: if it is in our power to prevent something very bad from happening, without thereby sacrificing anything morally significant, we ought, morally, to do it. An application of this principle would be as follows: if I am walking past a shallow pond and see a child drowning in it, I ought to wade in and pull the child out. This will mean getting my clothes muddy, but this is insignificant, while the death of the child would presumably be a very bad thing.

The uncontroversial appearance of the principle just stated is deceptive. If it were acted upon, even in its qualified form, our lives, our society, and our world would be fundamentally changed. For the principle takes, firstly, no account of proximity or distance. It makes no moral difference whether the person I can help is a neighbor's child ten yards from me or a Bengali whose name I shall never know, ten thousand miles away. Secondly, the principle makes no distinction between cases in which I am the only person who could possibly do anything and cases in which I am just one among millions in the same position.

I do not think I need to say much in defense of the refusal to take proximity and distance into account. The fact that a person is physically near to us, so that we have personal contact with him, may make it more likely that we *shall* assist him, but this does not show that we *ought* to help him rather than another who happens to be further away. If we accept any principle of impartiality, universalizability, equality, or whatever, we cannot discriminate against someone merely because he is far away from us (or we are far away from him). Admittedly, it is possible that we are in a better position to judge what needs to be done to help a person near to us than one far away, and perhaps also to provide the assistance we judge to be necessary. If this were the case, it would be a reason for helping those near to us first. This may once have been a justification for being more concerned with the poor in one's own town than with famine victims in India. Unfortunately for those who like to keep their moral responsibilities limited, instant communication and swift transportation have changed the situation. From the moral point of view, the development of the world into a "global village" has made an important, though still unrecognized, difference to our moral situation. Expert observers and supervisors, sent out by famine relief organizations or permanently stationed in famine-prone areas, can direct our aid to a refugee in Bengal almost as effectively as we could get it to someone in our own block. There would seem, therefore, to be no possible justification for discriminating on geographical grounds.

There may be a greater need to defend the second implication of my principle—that the fact that there are millions of other people in the same position, in respect to the Bengali refugees, as I am, does not make the situation significantly different from a situation in which I am the only person who can prevent something very bad from occurring. Again, of course, I admit that there is a psychological difference between the cases; one feels less guilty about doing nothing if one can point to others, similarly placed, who have also done nothing. Yet this can make no real difference to our moral obligations.[2] Should I consider that I am less obliged to pull the drowning child out of the pond if on looking around I see other people, no further away than I am, who have also noticed the child but are doing nothing? One has only to ask this question to see the absurdity of the view that numbers lessen obligation. It is a view that is an ideal excuse for inactivity; unfortunately most of the major evils—poverty, overpopulation, pollution—are problems in which everyone is almost equally involved.

The view that numbers do make a difference can be made plausible if stated in this way: if everyone in circumstances like mine gave £5 to the Bengal Relief Fund, there would be enough to provide food, shelter, and medical care for the refugees; there is no reason why I should give more than anyone else in the same circumstances as I am; therefore I have no obligation to give more than £5. Each premise in this argument is true, and the argument looks sound. It may convince us, unless we notice that it is based on a hypothetical premise, although the conclusion is not stated hypothetically. The argument would be sound if the conclusion were: if everyone in circumstances like mine were to give £5, I would have no obligation to give more than £5. If the conclusion were so stated, however, it would be obvious that the argument has no bearing on a situation in which it is not the case that everyone else gives £5. This, of course, is the actual situation. It is more or less certain that not everyone in circumstances like mine will give £5. So there will not be enough to provide the needed food, shelter, and medical care. Therefore by giving more than £5 I will prevent more suffering than I would if I gave just £5.

It might be thought that this argument has an absurd consequence. Since the situation appears to be that very few people are likely to give substantial amounts, it follows that I and everyone else in similar circumstances ought to give as much as possible, that is, at least up to the point at which by giving more one would begin to cause serious suffering for oneself and one's dependents—perhaps even beyond this point to the point of marginal utility, at which by giving more one would cause oneself and one's dependents as much suffering as one would prevent in Bengal. If everyone does this, however, there will be more than can be used for the benefit of the refugees, and some of the sacrifice will have been unnecessary. Thus, if everyone does what he ought to do, the result will not be as good as it would be if everyone did a little less than he ought to do, or if only some do all that they ought to do.

The paradox here arises only if we assume that the actions in question—sending money to the relief funds—are performed more or less simultaneously, and are also unexpected. For if it is to be expected that everyone is going to contribute something, then clearly each is not obliged to give as much as he would have been obliged to had others not been giving too. And if everyone is not acting more or less simultaneously, then those giving later will know how much more is needed, and will have no obligation to give more than is necessary to reach this amount. To say this is not to deny the principle that people in the same circumstances have the same obligations, but to point out that the fact that others have given, or may be expected to give, is a relevant circumstance: those giving after it has become known that many others are giving and those giving before are not in the same circumstances. So the seemingly absurd consequence of the principle I have put forward can occur only if people are in error about the actual circumstances—that is, if they think they are giving when others are not, but in fact they are giving when others are. The result of everyone doing what he really ought to do cannot be worse than the result of everyone doing less than he ought to do, although the result of everyone doing what he reasonably believes he ought to do could be.

If my argument so far has been sound, neither our distance from a preventable evil nor the number of other people who, in respect to that evil, are in the same situation as we are, lessens our obligation to mitigate or prevent that evil. I shall therefore take as established the principle I asserted earlier. As I have already said, I need to assert it only in its qualified form: if it is in our power to prevent something very bad from happening, without thereby sacrificing anything else morally significant, we ought, morally, to do it.

The outcome of this argument is that our traditional moral categories are upset. The traditional distinction between duty and charity cannot be drawn, or at least, not in the place we normally draw it. Giving money to the Bengal Relief Fund is regarded as an act of charity in our society. The bodies which collect money are known as "charities." These organizations see themselves in this way—if you send them a check, you will be thanked for your "generosity." Because giving money is regarded as an act of charity, it is not thought that there is anything wrong with not giving. The charitable man may be praised, but the man who is not charitable is not condemned. People do not feel in any way ashamed or guilty about spending money on new clothes or a new car instead of giving it to famine relief. (Indeed, the alternative does not occur to them.) This way of looking at the matter cannot be justified. When we buy new clothes not to keep ourselves warm but to look "well-dressed" we are not providing for any important need. We would not be sacrificing anything significant if we were to continue to wear our old clothes, and give the money to famine relief. By doing so, we would be preventing another person from starving. It follows from what I have said earlier that we ought to give money away, rather than spend it on clothes which we do not need to keep us warm. To do so is not charitable, or generous. Nor is it the kind of act which philosophers and theologians have called "supererogatory"—an act which it would be good to do, but not wrong not to do. On the contrary, we ought to give the money away, and it is wrong not to do so.

I am not maintaining that there are no acts which are charitable, or that there are no acts which it would be good to do but not wrong not to do. It may be possible to redraw the distinction between duty and charity in some other place. All I am arguing here is that the present way of drawing the distinction, which makes it an act of charity for a man living at the level of affluence which most people in the "developed nations" enjoy to give money to save someone else from starvation, cannot be supported. It is beyond the scope of my argument to consider whether the distinction should be redrawn or abolished altogether. There would be many other possible ways of drawing the distinction—for instance, one might decide that it is good to make other people as happy as possible, but not wrong not to do so.

Despite the limited nature of the revision in our moral conceptual scheme which I am proposing, the revision would, given the extent of both affluence and famine in the world today, have radical implications. These implications may lead to further objections, distinct from those I have already considered. I shall discuss two of these.

One objection to the position I have taken might be simply that it is too drastic a revision of our moral scheme. People do not ordinarily judge in the way I have suggested they should. Most people reserve their moral condemnation for those who violate some moral norm, such as the norm against taking another person's property. They do not condemn those who indulge in luxury instead of giving to famine relief. But given that I did not set out to present a morally neutral description of the way people make moral judgments, the way people do in fact judge has nothing to do with the validity of my conclusion. My conclusion follows from the principle which I advanced earlier, and unless that principle is rejected, or the arguments shown to be unsound, I think the conclusion must stand, however strange it appears.

It might, nevertheless, be interesting to consider why our society, and most other societies, do judge differently from the way I have suggested they should. In a well-known article, J. O. Urmson suggests that the imperatives of duty, which tell us what we must do, as distinct from what it would be good to do but not wrong not to do, function so as to prohibit behavior that is intolerable if men are to live together in society.[3] This may explain the origin and continued existence of the present division between acts of duty and acts of charity. Moral attitudes are shaped by the needs of society, and no doubt society needs people who will observe the rules that make social existence tolerable. From the point of view of a particular society, it is essential to prevent violations of norms against killing, stealing, and so on. It is quite inessential, however, to help people outside one's own society.

If this is an explanation of our common distinction between duty and **supererogation**, however, it is not a justification of it. The moral point of view requires us to look beyond the interests of our own society. Previously, as I have already mentioned, this may hardly have been feasible, but it is quite feasible now. From the moral point of view, the prevention of the starvation of millions of people outside our society must be considered at least as pressing as the upholding of property norms within our society.

It has been argued by some writers, among them Sidgwick and Urmson, that we need to have a basic moral code which is not too far beyond the capacities of the ordinary man, for otherwise there will be a general breakdown of compliance with the moral code. Crudely stated, this argument suggests that if we tell people that they ought to refrain from murder and give everything they do not really need to famine relief, they will do neither, whereas if we tell them that they ought to refrain from murder and that it is good to give to famine relief but not wrong not to do so, they will at least refrain from murder. The issue here is: Where should we drawn the line between conduct that is required and conduct that is good although not required, so as to get the best possible result? This would seem to be an empirical question, although a very difficult one. One objection to the Sidgwick-Urmson line of argument is that it takes insufficient account of the effect that moral standards can have on the decisions we make. Given a society in which a wealthy man who gives five percent of his income to famine relief is regarded as most generous, it is not surprising that a proposal that we all ought to give away half our incomes will be thought to be absurdly unrealistic. In a society which held that no man should have more than enough while others have less than they need, such a proposal might seem narrow-minded. What it is possible for a man to do and what he is likely to do are both, I think, very greatly influenced by what people around him are doing and expecting him to do. In any case, the possibility that by spreading the idea that we ought to be doing very much more than we are to relieve famine we shall bring about a general breakdown of moral behavior seems remote. If the stakes are an end to widespread starvation, it is worth the risk. Finally, it should be emphasized that these considerations are relevant only to the issue of what we should require from others, and not to what we ourselves ought to do.

The second objection to my attack on the present distinction between duty and charity is one which has from time to time been made against utilitarianism. It follows from some forms of utilitarian theory that we all ought, morally, to be working full time to increase the balance of happiness over misery. The position I have taken here would not lead to this conclusion in all circumstances, for if there were no bad occurrences that we could prevent without sacrificing something of comparable moral importance, my argument would have no application. Given the present conditions in many parts of the world, however, it does follow from my argument that we ought, morally, to be working full time to relieve great suffering of the sort that occurs as a result of famine or other disasters. Of course, mitigating circumstances can be adduced—for instance, that if we wear ourselves out through overwork, we shall be less effective than we would otherwise have been. Nevertheless, when all considerations of this sort have been taken into account, the conclusion remains: we ought to be preventing as much suffering as we can without sacrificing something else of comparable moral importance. This conclusion is one which we may be reluctant to face. I cannot see, though, why it should be regarded as a criticism of the position for which I have argued, rather than a criticism of our ordinary standards of behavior. Since most people are self-interested to some degree, very few of us are likely to do everything that we ought to do. It would, however, hardly be honest to take this as evidence that it is not the case that we ought to do it.

It may still be thought that my conclusions are so wildly out of line with what everyone else thinks and has always thought that there must be something wrong with the argument somewhere. In order to show that my conclusions, while certainly contrary to contemporary Western moral standards, would not have seemed so extraordinary at other times and in other places, I would like to quote a passage from a writer not normally thought of as a way-out radical, Thomas Aquinas.

> Now, according to the natural order instituted by divine providence, material goods are provided for the satisfaction of human needs. Therefore the division and appropriation of property, which proceeds from human law, must not hinder the satisfaction of man's necessity from such goods. Equally, whatever a man has in super-abundance is owed, of natural right, to the poor for their sustenance. So Ambrosius says, and it is also to be found in the *Decretum Gratiani:* "The bread which you withhold belongs to the hungry; the clothing you shut away, to the naked; and the money you bury in the earth is the redemption and freedom of the penniless." [4]

I now want to consider a number of points, more practical than philosophical, which are relevant to the application of the moral conclusion we have reached. These points challenge not the idea that we ought to be doing all we can to prevent starvation, but the idea that giving away a great deal of money is the best means to this end.

It is sometimes said that overseas aid should be a government responsibility, and that therefore one ought not to give to privately run charities. Giving privately, it is said, allows the government and the noncontributing members of society to escape their responsibilities.

This argument seems to assume that the more people there are who give to privately organized famine relief funds, the less likely it is that the government will take over full responsibility for such aid. This assumption is unsupported, and does not strike me as at all plausible. The opposite view—that if no one gives voluntarily, a government will assume that its citizens are uninterested in famine relief and would not wish to be forced into giving aid—seems more plausible. In any case, unless there were a definite probability that by refusing to give one would be helping to bring about massive government assistance, people who do refuse to make voluntary contributions are refusing to prevent a certain amount of suffering, without being able to point to any tangible beneficial consequence of their refusal. So the onus of showing how their refusal will bring about government action is on those who refuse to give.

I do not, of course, want to dispute the contention that governments of affluent nations should be giving many times the amount of genuine, no-strings-attached aid that they are giving now. I agree, too, that giving privately is not enough, and that we ought to be campaigning actively for entirely new standards for both public and private contributions to famine relief. Indeed, I would sympathize with someone who thought that campaigning was more important than giving oneself, although I doubt whether preaching what one does not practice would be very effective. Unfortunately, for many people the idea that "it's the government's responsibility" is a reason for not giving which does not appear to entail any political action either.

Another more serious reason for not giving to famine relief funds is that until there is effective population control, relieving famine merely postpones starvation. If we save the Bengal refugees now, others, perhaps the children of these refugees, will face starvation in a few years' time. In support of all this, one may cite the now well-known facts about the population explosion and the relatively limited scope for expanded production.

This point, like the previous one, is an argument against relieving suffering that is happening now, because of a belief about what might happen in the future; it is unlike the previous point in that very good evidence can be adduced in support of this belief about the future. I will not go into the evidence here. I accept that the earth cannot support indefinitely a population rising at the present rate. This certainly poses a problem for anyone who thinks it important to prevent famine. Again, however, one could accept the argument without drawing the conclusion that it absolves one from any obligation to do anything to prevent famine. The conclusion that should be drawn is that the best means of preventing famine, in the long run, is population control. It would then follow from the position reached earlier that one ought to be doing all one can to promote population control (unless one held that all forms of population control were wrong in themselves, or would have significantly bad consequences). Since there are organizations working specifically for population control, one would then support them rather than more orthodox methods of preventing famine.

A third point raised by the conclusion reached earlier relates to the question of just how much we all ought to be giving away. One possibility, which has already been mentioned, is that we ought to give until we reach the level of marginal utility—that is, the level at which, by giving more, I would cause as much suffering to myself or my dependents as I would relieve by my gift. This would mean, of course, that one would reduce one-self to very near the material circumstances of a Bengali refugee. It will be recalled that earlier I put forward both a strong and a moderate version of the principle of preventing bad occurrences. The strong version, which required us to prevent bad things from happening unless in doing so we would be sacrificing something of comparable moral significance, does seem to require reducing ourselves to the level of marginal utility. I should also say that the strong version seems to me to be the correct one. I proposed the more moderate version—that we should prevent bad occurrences unless, to do so, we had to sacrifice something morally significant—only in order to show that even on this surely undeniable principle a great change in our way of life is required. On the more moderate principle, it may not follow that we ought to reduce ourselves to the level of marginal utility, for one might hold that to reduce oneself and one's family to this level is to cause something significantly bad to happen. Whether this is so I shall not discuss, since, as I have said, I can see no good reason for holding the moderate version of the principle rather than the strong version. Even if we accepted the principle only in its moderate form, however, it should be clear that we would have to give away enough to ensure that the consumer society, dependent as it is on people spending on trivia rather than giving to famine relief, would slow down and perhaps disappear entirely. There are several reasons why this would be desirable in itself. The value and necessity of economic growth are now being questioned not only by conservationists, but by economists as well.[5] There is no doubt, too, that the consumer society has had a distorting effect on the goals and purposes of its members. Yet looking at the matter purely from the point of view of overseas aid, there must be a limit to the extent to which we should deliberately slow down our economy; for it might be the case that if we gave away, say, forty percent of our Gross National Product, we would slow down the economy so much that in absolute terms we would be giving less than if we gave twenty-five percent of the much larger GNP than we would have if we limited our contribution to this smaller percentage.

I mention this only as an indication of the sort of factor that one would have to take into account in working out an ideal. Since Western societies generally consider one percent of the GNP an acceptable level for overseas aid, the matter is entirely academic. Nor does it affect the question of how much an individual should give in a society in which very few are giving substantial amounts.

It is sometimes said, though less often now than it used to be, that philosophers have no special role to play in public affairs, since most public issues depend primarily on an assessment of facts. On questions of fact, it is said, philosophers as such have no special expertise, and so it has been possible to engage in philosophy without committing oneself to any position on major public issues. No doubt there are some issues of social policy and foreign policy about which it can truly be said that a really expert assessment of the facts is required before taking sides or acting, but the issue of famine is surely not one of these. The facts about the existence of suffering are beyond dispute. Nor, I think, is it disputed that we can do something about it, either through orthodox methods of famine relief or through population control or both. This is therefore an issue on which philosophers are competent to take a position. The issue is one which faces everyone who has more money than he needs to support himself and his dependents, or who is in a position to take some sort of political action. These categories must include practically every teacher and student of philosophy in the universities of the Western world. If philosophy is to deal with matters that are relevant to both teachers and students, this is an issue that philosophers should discuss.

Discussion, though, is not enough. What is the point of relating philosophy to public (and personal) affairs if we do not take our conclusions seriously? In this instance, taking our conclusion seriously means acting upon it. The philosopher will not find it any easier than anyone else to alter his attitudes and way of life to the extent that, if I am right, is involved in doing everything that we ought to be doing. At the very least, though, one can make a start. The philosopher who does so will have to sacrifice some of the benefits of the consumer society, but he can find compensation in the satisfaction of a way of life in which theory and practice, if not yet in harmony, are at least coming together.

Endnotes

1. There was also a third possibility: that India would go to war to enable the refugees to return to their lands. Since I wrote this paper, India has taken this way out. The situation is no longer that described above, but this does not affect my argument, as the next paragraph indicates.
2. In view of the special sense philosophers often give to the term, I should say that I use "obligation" simply as the abstract noun derived from "ought," so that "I have an obligation to" means no more, and no less, than "I ought to." This usage is in accordance with the definition of "ought" given by the *Shorter Oxford English Dictionary:* "the general verb to express duty or obligation." I do not think any issue of substance hangs on the way the term is used; sentences in which I use "obligation" could all be rewritten, although somewhat clumsily, as sentences in which a clause containing "ought" replaces the term "obligation."
3. J. O. Urmson, "Saints and Heroes," in *Essays in Moral Philosophy,* ed., Abraham I. Melden (Seattle and London, 1958), p. 214. For a related but significantly different view see also Henry Sidgwick, *The Methods of Ethics,* 7th edn. (London, 1907), pp. 220-221, 492-493.
4. *Summa Theologica,* II-II, Question 66, Article 7, in *Aquinas, Selected Political Writings,* ed. A. P. d'Entreves, trans. J. G. Dawson (Oxford, 1948), p. 171.
5. See, for instance, John Kenneth Galbraith, *The New Industrial State* (Boston, 1967); and E. J. Mishan, *The Costs of Economic Growth* (London, 1967).

Review Questions

1. According to Singer, what are the moral implications of the situation that occurred in East Bengal?
2. What is Singer's first moral principle?

3. What is the second principle? Distinguish between the two different versions of this principle.
4. Explain Singer's view of the distinction between duty and charity.
5. What is the Sidgwick-Urmson line of argument? How does Singer respond to it?
6. What is the criticism of utilitarianism? How does Singer reply?
7. What are Singer's conclusions?

Discussion Questions

1. Towards the end of his essay, Singer says that it would be desirable in itself if the consumer society would disappear. Do you agree? Why or why not?
2. What does the phrase "morally significant" in the weak version of the second principle mean? See if you can give a clear definition of this crucial phrase.
3. Singer grants that "until there is effective population control, relieving famine merely postpones starvation." Is this a good reason for not giving aid to countries that refuse to adopt any measures to control population? What is your view?
4. Singer attacks the traditional distinction between duty and charity. Is there any way to save the distinction? How?
5. Is Singer a utilitarian? Why or why not?

John Arthur

Rights and Duty to Bring Aid

John Arthur is Associate Professor of Philosophy and Director of the Law and Society Program at the State University of New York at Binghamton. He is the author of The Unfinished Constitution *(1989), and several articles on social and political philosophy.*

Arthur attacks Singer's two utilitarian principles about helping others. Singer's weak principle wrongly implies that we have little or no duty of benevolence since any aid to others might require a sacrifice of something morally significant. The strong principle ignores the rights and interests of the affluent. Arthur concludes with an alternative principle of benevolence that makes the obligation to help others dependent on a person's psychological nature.

From John Arthur, "Rights and Duty to Bring Aid," in *World Hunger and Moral Obligation,* William Aiken and Hugh LaFollette, eds. (Englewood Cliffs, NJ: Prentice-Hall, 1977).

There is no doubt that the large and growing incidence of world hunger constitutes a major problem, both moral and practical, for the fortunate few who have surpluses of cheap food. Our habits regarding meat consumption exemplify the magnitude of the moral issue. Americans now consume about two and one-half times the meat they did in 1950 (currently about 125 lbs. per capita per year). Yet, meat is extremely ineffective as a source of food. Only a small portion of the total calories consumed by the animal remains to be eaten in the meat. As much as 95 per cent of the food is lost by feeding and eating cattle rather than producing the grain for direct human consumption. Thus, the same amount of food consumed by Americans largely indirectly in meat form could feed one and a half billion persons on a (relatively meatless) Chinese diet. Much, if not all, of the world's food crisis could be resolved if Americans were simply to change their eating habits by moving toward direct consumption of grain and at the same time providing the surpluses for the hungry. Given this, plus the serious moral problems associated with animal suffering,[1] the overall case for vegetarianism seems strong.

I want to discuss here only one of these two related problems, the obligations of the affluent few to starving people. I begin by considering a recent article on the subject by Peter Singer, entitled "Famine, Affluence, and Morality".[2] I argue that Singer fails to establish the claim that such an obligation exists. This is the case for both the strong and weak interpretations of his view. I then go on to show that the role of rights needs to be given greater weight than utilitarian theories like Singer's allow. The rights of both the affluent and the starving are shown to be morally significant but not in themselves decisive, since obligations of benevolence can and often do override rights of others (e.g., property rights). Finally, I argue that under specific conditions the affluent are obligated not to exercise their rights to consume at the expense of others' lives.

II

Singer's argument is in two stages. First, he argues that two general moral principles ought to be accepted. Then he claims the principles imply an obligation to eliminate starvation. The first principle is simply that "suffering and death from lack of food, shelter and medical care are bad." [3] This principle seems obviously true and I will have little to say about it. Some may be inclined to think that the existence of an evil in itself places an obligation on others, but that is, of course, the problem which Singer addresses. I take it that he is not begging the question in this obvious way and will argue from the existence of evil to the obligation of others to eliminate it. But how, exactly, does he establish the connection? It is the second principle which he thinks shows that connection.

The necessary link is provided by either of two versions of this principle. The first (strong) formulation which Singer offers of the second principle is as follows:

> if it is in our power to prevent something bad from happening, without thereby sacrificing anything of comparable moral importance, we ought, morally, to do it.[4]

The weaker principle simply substitutes for "comparable moral importance" the phrase "any moral significance." He goes on to develop these notions, saying that:

> By 'without sacrificing anything of comparable moral importance' I mean without causing anything else comparably bad to happen, or doing something that is wrong in itself, or failing to promote some moral good, comparable in significance to the bad thing we can prevent.[5]

These remarks can be interpreted for the weaker principle by simply eliminating "comparable" in the statement.

One question is, of course, whether either of these two principles ought to be accepted. There are two ways in which this could be established. First, they could be shown, by philosophical argument, to follow from reasonably well established premises or from a general theory. Second, they might be justified because they are principles which underlie particular moral judgments the truth of which is accepted. Singer doesn't do either of these explicitly, although he seems to have the second in mind. He first speaks of what he takes to be the "uncontroversial appearance" of the principles. He then applies the principles to a similar case in which a drowning child requires help. Singer argues, in essence, that since the drowning is bad and it can be avoided without sacrificing something of moral significance, it is obligatory that the child be saved. He claims further that both the strong and weak versions are sufficient to establish the duty. Dirtying one's clothes, for example, is not of "moral significance" and so does not justify failure to act. The last part of his paper is devoted to the claim that the analogy between the case of the child and starving people is apt in that geographical distance and others' willingness to act are not acceptable excuses for inaction.

III

My concern here is not with these latter issues. Rather, I want to focus on the two versions of the second principle, discussing each in terms of (1) whether it is plausible, and (2) if true, whether it establishes the duty to provide aid. I will deal with the weak version first, arguing that it fails at step (2) in the argument.

This version reads, "if it is in our power to prevent something bad from happening without thereby sacrificing *anything* morally significant we ought morally to do it." Singer later claims that:

> Even if we accept the principle in its moderate form, however, it should be clear that we would have to give away enough to ensure that the consumer society, dependent as it is on people spending on trivia rather than giving to famine relief, would slow down and perhaps disappear entirely.[6]

The crucial idea of "morally significant" is left largely unanalyzed. Two examples are given: dirtying one's clothes and being "well dressed." Both are taken to be morally *in*significant.

It could perhaps be argued against Singer that these things *are* morally significant. Both, for example, would be cases of decreasing aesthetic value, and if you think aesthetic values are intrinsic you might well dispute the claim that being "well dressed" is without moral significance. There is, however, a more serious objection to be raised. To see this, we need to distinguish between the possible value of the *fact* of being "well dressed" and the value of the *enjoyment* some persons receive and create by being "well dressed" (and, of course, the unhappiness avoided by being "badly dressed").

That such enjoyment and unhappiness are of some moral significance can be seen by the following case. Suppose it were possible that, by simply singing a chorus of "Dixie" you could eliminate all the unhappiness and embarrassment that some people experience at being badly dressed. Surely, doing that would be an act of moral significance. Similarly, throwing mud on people's clothes, though not a great wrong, is surely not "without *any* moral significance."

It seems then, that the weak principle (while perhaps true) does not generally establish a duty to provide aid to starving people. Whether it does in specific instances depends on the nature of the cost to the person providing the aid. If *either* the loss to the giver is in itself valuable or the loss results in increased unhappiness or decreased happiness to someone, then the principle does not require that the burden be accepted.

(It is interesting to ask just how much giving *would* be required by this principle. If we can assume that givers would benefit in some minimal way by giving—and that they are reasonable—then perhaps the best answer is that the level of giving required is the level that is actually given. Otherwise, why would people *not* give more if there is no value to them in things they choose to keep?)

In addition to the moral significance of the costs that I just described, there is a further problem which will become particularly significant in considering the strong principle. For many people it is part of their moral sense that they and others have a special relationship to their own goals or projects. That is, in making one's choices a person may properly weigh the outcome that one desires more heavily than the goals that others may have. Often this is expressed as a right or entitlement.[7] Thus, for example, if *P* acquires some good (*x*) in a just social arrangement without violating others' rights, then *P* has a special title to *x* that *P* is entitled to weigh against the desires of others. P need not, in determining whether he ought to give *x* to another, overlook the fact that *x* is his; he acquired it fairly, and so has special say in what happens to it. If this is correct, it is a fact of some moral significance and thus would also block the inference from the weak principle to the obligation to give what one has to others. I will pursue this line of argument in the following section while considering the strong version of the principle.

IV

Many people, especially those inclined toward utilitarianism, would probably accept the preceding, believing that it is the stronger of the two principles that should be used. "After all," they might argue, "the real issue is the great *disparity* between the amount of good which could be produced by resources of the rich if applied to problems of starvation as against the small amount of good produced by the resources if spent on second cars and houses, fancy clothes, etc." I will assume that the facts are just as the claim suggests. That is, I will assume that it can *not* be plausibly argued that there are, for example, artistic or cultural values which (1) would be lost by such redistribution of wealth and (2) are equal in value to the starvation which would be eliminated. Thus, if the strong principle is true, then it (unlike the weak version) would require radical changes in our common understanding of the duties of the wealthy to starving people.

But is it true, as Singer suggests, that "if it is in our power to prevent something bad from happening without thereby sacrificing something of comparable moral significance we ought morally to do it?" Here the problem with the meaning of "moral significance" is even more acute than in the weak version. All that was required for the weak principle was that we be able to distinguish courses of action that have moral significance from those that do not. Here, however, the moral significance of alternative acts must be both *recognized* and *weighed*. And how is this to be done, according to Singer? Unfortunately he provides little help here, though this is crucial in evaluating his argument.

I will discuss one obvious interpretation of "comparable moral significance," argue it is inadequate, and then suggest what I take to be some of the factors an adequate theory would consider.

Assuming that giving aid is not "bad in itself," the only other facts which Singer sees as morally significant in evaluating obligations are the good or bad consequences of actions. Singer's strong version obviously resembles the act utilitarian principle. With respect to starvation, this interpretation is open to the objection raised at the end of part III above, since it takes no account of a variety of important factors, such as the apparent right to give added weight to one's own choices and interests, and to ownership. I now wish to look at this claim in more detail.

Consider the following examples of moral problems which I take to be fairly common. One obvious means by which you could aid others is with your body. Many of your extra organs (eye, kidney) could be given to another with the result that there is more good than if you kept both. You wouldn't see as well or live as long, perhaps, but that is not of comparable significance to the benefit others would receive. Yet, surely the fact that it is your eye and you need it is not insignificant. Perhaps there could be cases where one is obligated to sacrifice one's health or sight, but what seems clear is that this is not true in every case where (slightly) more good would come of your doing so. Second, suppose a woman has a choice between remaining with her husband or leaving. As best she can determine, the morally relevant factors do not indicate which she should do (the consequences of each seem about equally good and there is no question of broken promises, deception, or whatever). But, suppose in addition to these facts, it is the case that by remaining with her husband the woman will be unable to pursue important aspects of the plan of life she has set for herself. Perhaps by remaining she will be forced to sacrifice a career which she wishes to pursue. If the *only* facts that are of moral significance are the consequences of her choice, then she ought, presumably, to flip a coin (assuming there is some feature of her staying that is of equal importance to the unhappiness at the loss of the career *she* will experience). Surely, though, the fact that some goals are ones *she* chooses for herself (assuming she doesn't violate the others' rights) is of significance. It is, after all, *her* life and *her* future and she is entitled to treat it that way. In neither of these cases is the person required to accept as equal to his or her own goals and well-being the welfare of even his or her family, much less the whole world. The fact that others may benefit even slightly more from their pursuing another course is not in itself sufficient to show they ought to act other than they choose. Servility, though perhaps not a vice, is certainly not an obligation that all must fulfill.[8]

The above goes part way, I think, in explaining the importance we place on allowing people maximal latitude in pursuing their goals. Rights or entitlements to things that are our own reflect important facts about people. Each of us has only one life and it is uniquely valuable to each of us. Your choices do not constitute my life, nor do mine yours. The purely utilitarian interpretation of "moral significance" provides for assigning no special weight to the goals and interests of individuals in making their choices. It provides no basis for saying that though there may be greater total good done by one course, still a person could be entitled for some reason to pursue another.

It seems, then, that determining whether giving aid to starving persons would be sacrificing something of comparable moral significance demands weighing the facts that the persons are entitled to give special weight to their own interests where their future or (fairly acquired) property is at issue. Exactly *how much* weight may be given is a question that I will consider shortly. The point here is that the question of the extent of the obligation to eliminate starvation has not been answered. My argument was that however "moral significance" is best understood, it is far too simple to suggest that *only* the total good produced is relevant. If providing quality education for one's children is a goal, then (assuming the resources were acquired fairly) the fact that it is a goal *itself* provides additional weight against other ways the resources might be used, including the one that maximizes the total good. Further, if the resources to be used for the purpose are legitimately owned, then that too is something that the parent is entitled to consider.

Returning to the case of the drowning child, the same point may be made. Suppose it is an important part of a person's way of life that he not interfere. Perhaps the passer-by believes God's will is being manifested in this particular incident and strongly values noninterference with God's working out of His plan. Surely, this is especially relevant to the question of whether the person is obligated to intervene, even when the greatest good would be promoted by intervention. When saying that a person is obligated to act in some way, the significance *to the person* of the act must not only be considered along with all the other features of the act, but is also of special moral significance in determining that person's duty. More, however, needs to be said here.

Suppose, for instance, that the case were like this: A passer-by sees a child drowning but fails to help, not for the sake of another important goal but rather out of lack of interest. Such situations are not at all uncommon, as when people fail to report violent crimes they observe in progress. I assume that anyone who fails to act in such circumstances is acting wrongly. As with the case of the utilitarian principle discussed earlier, the drowning child also represents a limiting case. In the former, *no* significance is assigned to the woman's choice by virtue of its being *hers*. Here, however, the interests of *others* are not weighed. An acceptable principle of benevolence would fall between the two limiting cases. The relative moral significance of alternative acts could then be determined by applying the principle, distinguishing acts which are obligatory from charitable ones.

In summary, I have argued that neither the strong nor the weak principle advanced by Singer provides an adequate solution to the issue of affluence and hunger. The essential problem is with his notion of "moral significance." I argued that the weak principle fails to show any obligations, given the normal conception of factors which possess such significance. I then argued that the strong principle (which is close to act utilitarianism) is mistaken. The basic objection to this principle is that it fails to take into account of certain aspects of the situation which must be considered in any adequate formulation of the principle.

V

As I suggested earlier, a fully adequate formulation of the principle of benevolence depends on a general theory of right. Such a theory would not only include a principle of benevolence but also give account of the whole range of rights and duties and a means to weigh conflicting claims. In this section, I discuss some of the various problems associated with benevolence, obligation, and rights. In the final section, I offer what I believe to be an adequate principle of benevolence.

One view, which has been criticized recently by Judith Thomson,[9] suggests that whenever there is a duty or obligation there must be a corresponding right. I presume we want to say that in some cases (e.g., the drowning child) there is an obligation to benevolence, but does this also mean that the child has a *right* to be aided? Perhaps there is only a semantic point here regarding "right," but perhaps also there is a deeper disagreement.

I suggest that, whether we call it a "right" or not, there are important differences between obligations based upon benevolence and other obligations. Two differences are significant. First, the person who has the obligation to save the drowning child did not *do anything* that created the situation. But, compare this case with a similar one of a lifeguard who fails to save someone. Here there is a clear sense in which the drowning victim may claim a right to have another do his utmost to save him. An agreement was reached whereby the lifeguard *accepted* the responsibility for the victim's welfare. The guard, in a sense, took on the goals of the swimmers as his own. To fail to aid is a special sort of injustice that the passer-by does not do. It seems clearly appropriate to speak of the lifeguard's failure to act as a case of a right being violated.

A second important point regarding the drowning child example and rights is that the passer-by is not *taking positive steps* in reference to the child. This can be contrasted with an action that might be taken to drown a child who would not otherwise die. Here, again, it is appropriate to describe this act as a violation of a right (to life). Other violations of rights also seem to require that one act, not merely fail to take action—for example, property rights (theft) and privacy rights (listening without leave). The drowning child and starvation cases are wrong not because of acts but the failure to act.

Thus, there are important differences between duties of benevolence and others where a right is obviously at issue. Cases of failing to aid are not (unlike right violations) either instances of positive actions that are taken or ones in which the rich or the passer-by has taken responsibility by a previous act. It does not follow from this, however, that strong obligations are not present to save other persons. Obviously, one ought to aid a drowning child (at least) in cases where there is no serious risk or cost to the passer-by. This is true even though there is no obvious right that the child has to be aided.

Furthermore, if saving a drowning child requires using someone's boat without their permission (a violation of property right), then it still ought to be done. Duties to bring aid can override duties not to violate rights. The best thing to say here is that, depending on the circumstances, duties to aid and not to violate rights can each outweigh the other. Where actions involve both violation of rights and failing to meet duties to aid (the lifeguard's failing to save), the obligation is stronger than either would be by itself. Describing the situation in this way implies that although there is a sense in which the boat owner, the affluent spender, and the passer-by have a right to fail to act, still they are obligated not to exercise that right because there is a stronger duty to give aid.

Some may be inclined to say, against this, that in fact the passer-by does not have such a right not to help. But this claim is ambiguous. If what is meant is that they ought to help, then I agree. There is, however, still a point in saying owners of food have the right to use the food as they see fit. It serves to emphasize that there is a moral difference between these cases and ones where the object of need is *not* legitimately owned by anyone (as, for example, if it's not another's boat but a log that the drowning child needs). To say that the property right is *lost* where the principle of benevolence overrides is to hide this difference, though it is morally significant.

Other people might be inclined to say about these situations that the point of saying someone has a right to their food, time, boat or whatever is that others ought not to intervene to force them to bring aid. A person defending this view might accept my claim that in fact the person ought to help. It might then be argued that because they are not violating a right of another (to be saved) and they have a (property) right to the good, others can't, through state authority, force them to bring aid.

This claim obviously raises a variety of questions in legal and political philosophy, and is outside the scope of the present paper. My position does not preclude good samaritan laws, nor are they implied, This is a further question which requires further argument. That one has a moral right to *x*, but is obligated for other reasons not to exercise the right, leaves open the issue of whether others either can or should make that person fulfill the obligation.

If what I have said is correct, two general points should be made about starvation. First, even though it may be that the affluent have a right to use resources to pursue their own goals, and not provide aid, they may also be strongly obligated not to exercise the right. This is because, in the circumstances, the duty to benevolence is overriding. The existence and extent of such an obligation can be determined only by discovering the relative weight of these conflicting principles. In the final section, I consider how this should be done.

Second, even if it is also true that the passerby and the affluent do not violate a right of another in failing to help, it may still be the case that they strongly ought not do so. Of course, their behavior could also be even worse than it is (by drowning the child or sending poisoned food to the hungry and thus violating their rights). All that shows, however, is that the failure to help is not the *most* morally objectionable course that can be imagined in the circumstances. This point hardly constitutes justification for failing to act.

VI

I argued earlier that neither Singer's weak principle nor the utilitarian one is what we are after. The former would imply (wrongly) little or no duty of benevolence, and the latter does not take seriously enough the rights and interests of the affluent. What is needed is a principle which we may use to determine the circumstances in which the needs of others create a duty to bring aid which is more stringent than the rights of the affluent to pursue their own interests and use their property as they desire.

The following principle, while similar to the utilitarian one, seems to be most adequate: "If it is in our power to prevent death of an innocent without sacrificing anything of *substantial* significance then we ought morally to do it." The problem, of course, is to determine exactly what is meant by "substantial significance." I assume there are no duties present that arise out of others' rights, as, for example, those of one's children to be provided for. Considerations of that sort would lead beyond the present paper. My concern here is limited to instances in which there is a question of bringing aid (where no obvious right to the aid is present) or using resources for other (preferred) ends.

There are two questions which are important in deciding whether what is being given up by the affluent is of substantial significance. First, we might specify *objectively* the needs which people have, and grant that the duty to bring aid is not present unless these needs have already been met. Included among the needs which are of substantial significance would be those things without which a person cannot continue to function physically—for example, food, clothing, health care, housing, and sufficient training to provide these for oneself.

It also, however, seems reasonable that certain psychological facts ought to be weighed before a person is obligated to help others meet their needs. For example, if you cannot have an even modestly happy life without some further good, then surely that, too, is something to which you are entitled. This suggests a second, *subjective* standard that should also be employed to determine whether something is of no substantial significance and so ought not be consumed at the expense of others' basic needs. The best way to put this, I believe, is to say that "if the lack of *x* would not affect the long-term happiness of a person, then *x* is of no substantial significance." By "long-term happiness" I mean to include anything which, if not acquired, will result in unhappiness over an extended period of one's life, not just something the lack of which is a source of momentary loss but soon forgotten. Thus, in a normal case, dirtying one's clothes to save a drowning child is of no substantial significance and so the duty of benevolence is overriding. If, however, selling some possession for famine relief would mean the person's life *really is* (for a long period) less happy, then the possessions are of substantial significance and so the person is not wrong in exercising the right of ownership instead of providing aid. If the possessions had been sold, it would have been an act of charity, not fulfillment of a duty. The same analysis can be provided for other choices we make—for example, how our time is spent and whether to donate organs. If doing so would result in your not seeing well and this would make your life less happy over time, then you are not obligated to do so.

If what I have said is correct, then duties of benevolence increase as one's dependence on possession for living a happy life decreases. If a person's long-term happiness does not depend on (second?) cars and fancy clothes, then that person ought not to purchase those goods at the expense of others' basic needs being unfulfilled. Thus, depending on the psychological nature of persons, their duties of benevolence will vary.

The question of the actual effect of not buying a new car, house, clothes, or whatever on one's long-term happiness is of course a difficult one. My own feeling is that if the principle were to be applied honestly, those of us who are relatively affluent would discover that a substantial part of the resources and time we expend should be used to bring aid. The extent of the obligation must, finally, be determined by asking whether the lack of some good *really would* result in a need not being met or in a less happy life for its owner, and that is a question between each of us and our conscience.

In summary, I have argued that Singer's utilitarian principle is inadequate to establish the claim that acts to eliminate starvation are obligatory, but that such an obligation still exists. The rights of both the affluent and the hungry are considered, and a principle is defended which clarifies the circumstances in which it is a duty and not merely charitable to provide aid to others whose basic needs are not being met.

Endnotes

1. Peter Singer, *Animal Liberation* (New York: New York Review of Books/Random House, 1975).
2. Peter Singer, "Famine, Affluence, and Morality," *Philosophy and Public Affairs,* I, no. 3 (Spring 1972).
3. Ibid.
4. Ibid.
5. Ibid. I assume 'importance' and 'significance' are synonymous.
6. Ibid.
7. In a recent book (*Anarchy, State, and Utopia,* New York: Basic Books, 1974), Robert Nozick argues that such rights are extensive against state authority.
8. For an argument that servility is wrong, see Thomas Hill, "Servility and Self-Respect," *The Monist,* VII, no. 4 (January 1973).
9. Judith Jarvis Thomson, "The Right to Privacy," *Philosophy and Public Affairs,* IV, no. 4 (Summer 1975).

Review Questions

1. What criticisms does Arthur make of Singer's weak principle?
2. How does Arthur attack Singer's strong principle?
3. State and explain Arthur's alternative principle of benevolence and its implications for the duty of benevolence.

Discussion Questions

1. In Arthur's view, the duty of benevolence varies according to a person's psychological nature. This implies that a greedy person who craves luxury items like fur coats and BMWs has little or no obligation to help others. Is this an acceptable view of our obligation to others?
2. How would Singer reply to Arthur?

Garrett Hardin

Living on a Lifeboat

Garrett Hardin is Professor of Biology at the University of California at Santa Barbara. He is the author of many books, including The Limits of Altruism: An Ecologist's View of Survival *(1977).*

Hardin uses the metaphor of a lifeboat to argue that rich nations such as the United States do not have a moral obligation to help poor nations. In fact, he claims, aid in the form of food makes matters worse; it results in more population growth, and eventually the ruin of natural resources such as oceans.

Susanne Langer (1942) has shown that it is probably impossible to approach an unsolved problem save through the door of metaphor. Later, attempting to meet the demands of rigor, we may achieve some success in cleansing theory of metaphor, though our success is limited if we are unable to avoid using common language, which is shot through and through with fossil metaphors. (I count no less than five in the preceding two sentences.)

Since metaphorical thinking is inescapable it is pointless merely to weep about our human limitations. We must learn to live with them, to understand them, and to control them. "All of us," said George Eliot in *Middlemarch,* "get our thoughts entangled in metaphors, and act fatally on the strength of them." To avoid unconscious suicide we are well advised to pit one metaphor against another. From the interplay of competitive metaphors, thoroughly developed, we may come closer to metaphor-free solutions to our problems.

No generation has viewed the problem of the survival of the human species as seriously as we have. Inevitably, we have entered this world of concern through the door of metaphor. Environmentalists have emphasized the image of the earth as a spaceship—Spaceship Earth. Kenneth Boulding (1966) is the principal architect of this metaphor. It is time, he says, that we replace the wasteful "cowboy economy" of the past with the frugal "spaceship economy" required for continued survival in the limited world we now see ours to be. The metaphor is notably useful in justifying pollution-control measures.

Unfortunately, the image of a spaceship is also used to promote measures that are suicidal. One of these is a generous immigration policy, which is only a particular instance of a class of policies that are in error because they lead to the tragedy of the commons (Hardin 1968). These suicidal policies are attractive because they mesh with what we unthinkingly take to be the ideals of "the best people." What is missing in the idealistic view is an insistence that rights and responsibilities must go together. The "generous" attitude of all too many people results in asserting inalienable rights while ignoring or denying matching responsibilities.

For the metaphor of a spaceship to be correct the aggregate of people on board would have to be under unitary sovereign control (Ophuls 1974). A true ship always has a captain. It is conceivable that a ship could be run by a committee. But it could not possibly survive if its course were determined by bickering tribes that claimed rights without responsibilities.

What about Spaceship Earth? It certainly has no captain, and no executive committee. The United Nations is a toothless tiger, because the signatories of its charter wanted it that way. The spaceship metaphor is used only to justify spaceship demands on common resources without acknowledging corresponding spaceship responsibilities.

An understandable fear of decisive action leads people to embrace "incrementalism"—moving toward reform by tiny stages. As we shall see, this strategy is counterproductive in the area discussed here if it means accepting rights before responsibilities. Where human survival is at stake, the acceptance of responsibilities is a precondition to the acceptance of rights, if the two cannot be introduced simultaneously.

Lifeboat Ethics

Before taking up certain substantive issues let us look at an alternative metaphor, that of a lifeboat. In developing some relevant examples the following numerical values are assumed. Approximately two-thirds of the world is desperately poor, and only one-third is comparatively rich. The people in poor countries have an average per capita GNP (Gross National Product) of about $200 per year; the rich, of about $3,000. (For the United States it is nearly $5,000 per year.) Metaphorically, each rich nation amounts to a lifeboat full of comparatively rich people. The poor of the world are in other, much more crowded lifeboats. Continuously, so to speak, the poor fall out of their lifeboats and swim for a while in the water outside, hoping to be admitted to a rich lifeboat, or in some other way to benefit from the "goodies" on board. What should the passengers on a rich lifeboat do? This is the central problem of "the ethics of a lifeboat."

First we must acknowledge that each lifeboat is effectively limited in capacity. The land of every nation has a limited carrying capacity. The exact limit is a matter for argument, but the energy crunch is convincing more people every day that we have already exceeded the carrying capacity of the land. We have been living on "capital"—stored petroleum and coal—and soon we must live on income alone.

Let us look at only one lifeboat—ours. The ethical problem is the same for all, and is as follows. Here we sit, say fifty people in a lifeboat. To be generous, let us assume our boat has a capacity of ten more, making sixty. (This, however, is to violate the engineering principle of the "safety factor." A new plant disease or a bad change in the weather may decimate our population if we don't preserve some excess capacity as a safety factor.)

The fifty of us in the lifeboat see 100 others swimming in the water outside, asking for admission to the boat, or for handouts. How shall we respond to their calls? There are several possibilities.

One. We may be tempted to try to live by the Christian ideal of being "our brother's keeper," or by the Marxian ideal (Marx 1875) of "from each according to his abilities, to each according to his needs." Since the needs of all are the same, we take all the needy into our boat, making a total of 150 in a boat with a capacity of sixty. The boat is swamped, and everyone drowns. Complete justice, complete catastrophe.

Two. Since the boat has an unused excess capacity of ten, we admit just ten more to it. This has the disadvantage of getting rid of the safety factor, for which action we will sooner or later pay dearly. Moreover, *which* ten do we let in? "First come, first served?" The best ten? The neediest ten? How do we *discriminate?* And what do we say to the ninety who are excluded?

Three. Admit no more to the boat and preserve the small safety factor. Survival of the people in the lifeboat is then possible (though we shall have to be on our guard against boarding parties).

The last solution is abhorrent to many people. It is unjust, they say. Let us grant that it is.

"I feel guilty about my good luck," say some. The reply to this is simple: *Get out and yield your place to others.* Such a selfless action might satisfy the conscience of those who are addicted to guilt but it would not change the ethics of the lifeboat. The needy person to whom a guilt-addict yields his place will not himself feel guilty about his sudden good luck. (If he did he would not climb aboard.) The net result of conscience-stricken people relinquishing their unjustly held positions is the elimination of their kind of conscience from the lifeboat. The lifeboat, as it were, purifies itself of guilt. The ethics of the lifeboat persist, unchanged by such momentary aberrations.

This then is the basic metaphor within which we must work out our solutions. Let us enrich the image step by step with substantive additions from the real world.

Reproduction

The harsh characteristics of lifeboat ethics are heightened by reproduction, particularly by reproductive differences. The people inside the lifeboats of the wealthy nations are doubling in numbers every eighty-seven years; those outside are doubling every thirty-five years, on the average. And the relative difference in prosperity is becoming greater.

Let us, for a while, think primarily of the U.S. lifeboat. As of 1973 the United States had a population of 210 million people, who were increasing by 0.8% per year, that is, doubling in number every eighty-seven years.

Although the citizens of rich nations are outnumbered two to one by the poor, let us imagine an equal number of poor people outside our lifeboat—a mere 210 million poor people reproducing at a quite different rate. If we imagine these to be the combined populations of Columbia, Venezuela, Ecuador, Morocco, Thailand, Pakistan, and the Philippines, the average rate of increase of the people "outside" is 3.3% per year. The doubling time of this population is twenty-one years.

Suppose that all these countries, and the United States, agreed to live by the Marxian ideal, "to each according to his needs," the ideal of most Christians as well. Needs, of course, are determined by population size, which is affected by reproduction. Every nation regards its rate of reproduction as a sovereign right. If our lifeboat were big enough in the beginning it might be possible to live *for a while* by Christian-Marxian ideals. *Might.*

Initially, in the model given, the ratio of non-Americans to Americans would be one to one. But consider what the ratio would be eighty-seven years later. By this time Americans would have doubled to a population of 420 million. The other group (doubling every twenty-one years) would now have swollen to 3,540 million. Each American would have more than eight people to share with. How could the lifeboat possibly keep afloat?

All this involves extrapolation of current trends into the future, and is consequently suspect. Trends may change. Granted: but the change will not necessarily be favorable. If—as seems likely—the rate of population increase falls faster in the ethnic group presently inside the lifeboat than it does among those now outside, the future will turn out to be even worse than mathematics predicts, and sharing will be even more suicidal.

Ruin in the Commons

The fundamental error of the sharing ethics is that it leads to the tragedy of the commons. Under a system of private property the man (or group of men) who own property recognize their responsibility to care for it, for if they don't they will eventually suffer. A farmer, for instance, if he is intelligent, will allow no more cattle in a pasture than its carrying capacity justifies. If he overloads the pasture, weeds take over, erosion sets in, and the owner loses in the long run.

But if a pasture is run as a common open to all, the right of each to use it is not matched by an operational responsibility to take care of it. It is no use asking independent herdsmen in a commons to act responsibility, for they dare not. The considerate herdsman who refrains from overloading the commons suffers more than a selfish one who says his needs are greater. (As Leo Durocher says, "Nice guys finish last.") Christian-Marxian idealism is counterproductive. That it *sounds* nice is no excuse. With distribution systems, as with individual morality, good intentions are no substitute for good performance.

A social system is stable only if it is insensitive to errors. To the Christian-Marxian idealist a selfish person is a sort of "error." Prosperity in the system of the commons cannot survive errors. If *everyone* would only restrain himself, all would be well; but it takes *only one less than everyone* to ruin a system of voluntary restraint. In a crowded world of less than perfect human beings—and we will never know any other—mutual ruin is inevitable in the commons. This is the core of the tragedy of the commons.

One of the major tasks of education today is to create such an awareness of the dangers of the commons that people will be able to recognize its many varieties, however disguised. There is pollution of the air and waste because these media are treated as commons. Further growth of population and growth in the per capita conversion of natural resources into pollutants require that the system of the commons be modified or abandoned in the disposal of "externalities."

The fish populations of the oceans are exploited as commons, and ruin lies ahead. No technological invention can prevent this fate; in fact, all improvements in the art of fishing merely hasten the day of complete ruin. Only the replacement of the system of the commons with a responsible system can save oceanic fisheries.

The management of western range lands, though nominally rational, is in fact (under the steady pressure of cattle ranchers) often merely a government-sanctioned system of the commons, drifting toward ultimate ruin for both the rangelands and the residential enterprisers.

World Food Banks

In the international arena we have recently heard a proposal to create a new commons, namely an international depository of food reserves to which nations will contribute according to their abilities, and from which nations may draw according to their needs. Nobel laureate Norman Borlaug has lent the prestige of his name to this proposal.

A world food bank appeals powerfully to our humanitarian impulses. We remember John Donne's celebrated line, "Any man's death diminishes me." But before we rush out to see for whom the bell tolls let us recognize where the greatest political push for international granaries comes from, lest we be disillusioned later. Our experience with Public Law 480 clearly reveals the answer. This was the law that moved billions of dollars worth of U.S. grain to food-short, population-long countries during the past two decades. When P.L. 480 first came into being, a headline in the business magazine *Forbes* (Paddock and Paddock 1970) revealed the power behind it: "Feeding the World's Hungry Millions: How it will mean billions for U.S. business."

And indeed it did. In the years 1960 to 1970 a total of $7.9 billion was spent on the "Food for Peace" program, as P.L. 480 was called. During the years 1948 to 1970 an additional $49.9 billion were extracted from American taxpayers to pay for other economic aid programs, some of which went for food and food-producing machinery. (This figure does *not* include military aid.) That P.L. 480 was a giveaway program was concealed. Recipient countries went through the motions of paying for P.L. 480 food—with IOUs. In December 1973 the charade was brought to an end as far as India was concerned when the United States "forgave" India's $3.2 billion debt (Anonymous 1974). Public announcement of the cancellation of the debt was delayed for two months; one wonders why.

"Famine—1974!" (Paddock and Paddock 1970) is one of the few publications that points out the commercial roots of this humanitarian attempt. Though all U.S. taxpayers lost by P.L. 480, special interest groups gained handsomely. Farmers benefited because they were not asked to contribute the grain—it was bought from them by the taxpayers. Besides the direct benefit there was the indirect effect of increasing demand and thus raising prices of farm products generally. The manufacturers of farm machinery, fertilizers, and pesticides benefited by the farmers' extra efforts to grow more food. Grain elevators profited from storing the grain for varying lengths of time. Railroads made money hauling it to port, and shipping lines by carrying it overseas. Moreover, once the machinery for P.L. 480 was established an immense bureaucracy had a vested interest in its continuance regardless of its merits.

Very little was ever heard of these selfish interests when P.L. 480 was defended in public. The emphasis was always on its humanitarian effects. The combination of multiple and relatively silent selfish interests with highly vocal humanitarian apologists constitutes a powerful lobby for extracting money from taxpayers. Foreign aid has become a habit that can apparently survive in the absence of any known justification. A news commentator in a weekly magazine (Lansner 1974), after exhaustively going over all the conventional arguments for foreign aid—self-interest, social justice, political advantage, and charity—and concluding that none of the known arguments really held water, concluded: "So the search continues for some logically compelling reasons for giving aid. . . ." In other words, *Act now, justify later*—if ever. (Apparently a quarter of a century is too short a time to find the justification for expending several billion dollars yearly).

The search for a rational justification can be short-circuited by interjecting the word "emergency." Borlaug uses this word. We need to look sharply at it. What is an "emergency?" It is surely something like an accident, which is correctly defined as *an event that is certain to happen, though with a low frequency* (Hardin 1972a). A well-run organization prepares for everything that is certain, including accidents and emergencies. It budgets for them. It saves for them. It expects them—and mature decision-makers do not waste time complaining about accidents when they occur.

What happens if some organizations budget for emergencies and others do not? If each organization is solely responsible for its own well-being, poorly managed ones will suffer. But they should be able to learn from experience. They have a chance to mend their ways and learn to budget for infrequent but certain emergencies. The weather, for instance, always varies and periodic crop failures are certain. A wise and competent government saves out of the production of the good years in anticipation of bad years that are sure to come. This is not a new idea. The Bible tells us that Joseph taught this policy to Pharaoh in Egypt more than 2,000 years ago. Yet it is literally true that the vast majority of the governments of the world today have no such policy. They lack either the wisdom or the competence, or both. Far more difficult than the transfer of wealth from one country to another is the transfer of wisdom between sovereign powers or between generations.

"But it isn't their fault! How can we blame the poor people who are caught in an emergency? Why must we punish them?" The concepts of blame and punishment are irrelevant. The question is, what are the operational consequences of establishing a world food bank? If it is open to every country every time a need develops, slovenly rulers will not be motivated to take Joseph's advice. Why should they? Others will bail them out whenever they are in trouble.

Some countries will make deposits in the world food bank and others will withdraw from it; there will be almost no overlap. Calling such a depository-transfer unit a "bank" is stretching the metaphor of *bank* beyond its elastic limits. The proposers, of course, never call attention to the metaphorical nature of the word they use.

The Ratchet Effect

An "international food bank" is really, then, not a true bank but a disguised one-way transfer device for moving wealth from rich countries to poor. In the absence of such a bank, in a world inhabited by individually responsible sovereign nations, the population of each nation would repeatedly go through a cycle of the sort shown in Exhibit A. P_2 is greater than P_1, either in absolute numbers or because a deterioration of the food supply has removed the safety factor and produced a dangerously low ratio of resources to population. P_2 may be said to represent a state of overpopulation, which becomes obvious upon the appearance of an "accident," e.g., a crop failure. If the "emergency" is not met by outside help, the population drops back to the "normal" level—the "carrying capacity" of the environment—or even below. In the absence of population control by a sovereign, sooner or later the population grows to P_2 again and the cycle repeats. The long-term population curve (Hardin 1966) is an irregularity fluctuating one, equilibrating more or less about the carrying capacity.

A demographic cycle of this sort obviously involves great suffering in the restrictive phase, but such a cycle is normal to any independent country with inadequate population control. The third century theologian Tertullian (Hardin 1969a) expressed what must have been the recognition of many wise men when he wrote: "The scourges of pestilence, famine, wars, and earthquakes have come to be regarded as a blessing to overcrowded nations, since they serve to prune away the luxuriant growth of the human race."

Only under a strong and farsighted sovereign—which theoretically could be the people themselves, democratically organized—can a population equilibrate at some set point below the carrying capacity, thus avoiding the pains normally caused by periodic and unavoidable disasters. For this happy state to be achieved it is necessary that those in power be able to contemplate with equanimity the "waste" of surplus food in times of bountiful harvests. It is essential that those in power resist the temptation to convert extra food into extra babies. On the public relations level it is necessary that the phrase "surplus food" be replaced by "safety factor."

But wise sovereigns seem not to exist in the poor world today. The most anguishing problems are created by poor countries that are governed by rulers insufficiently wise and powerful. If such countries can draw on a world food bank in times of "emergency," the population *cycle* of Exhibit A will be replaced by the population *escalator* of Exhibit B. The input of food from a food bank acts as the pawl of a ratchet, preventing the population from retracting its steps to a lower level. Reproduction pushes the population upward, inputs from the world bank prevent its moving downward. Population size escalates, as does the absolute magnitude of "accidents" and "emergencies." The process is brought to an end only by the total collapse of the whole system, producing a catastrophe of scarcely imaginable proportions.

Such are the implications of the well-meant sharing of food in a world of irresponsible reproduction.

I think we need a new word for systems like this. The adjective "melioristic" is applied to systems that produce continual improvement; the English word is derived from the Latin *meliorare,* to become or make better. Parallel with this it would be useful to bring in the word *pejoristic* (from the Latin *pejorare,* to become or make worse). This word can be applied to those systems that by their very nature, can be relied upon to make matters worse. A world food bank coupled with sovereign state irresponsibility in reproduction is an example of a pejoristic system.

This pejoristic system creates an unacknowledged commons. People have more motivation to draw from than to add to the common store.

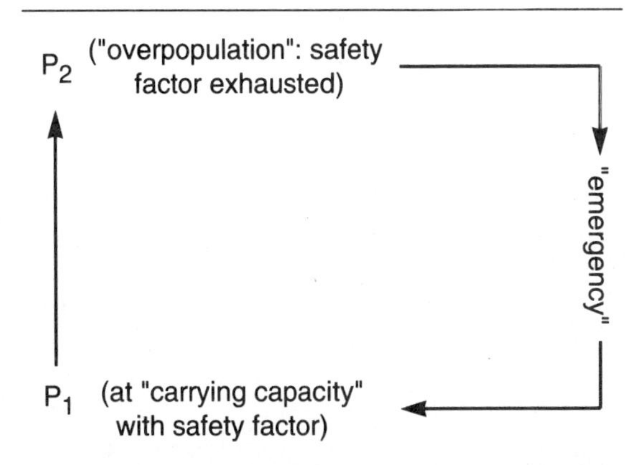

Exhibit A. The population cycle of a nation that has no effective conscious population control, and which receives no aid from the outside. P_2 is greater than P_1.

The license to make such withdrawals diminishes whatever motivation poor countries might otherwise have to control their populations. Under the guidance of this ratchet, wealth can be steadily moved in one direction only, from the slowly-breeding rich to the rapidly-breeding poor, the process finally coming to a halt only when all countries are equally and miserably poor.

All this is terribly obvious once we are acutely aware of the persuasiveness and danger of the commons. But many people still lack this awareness and the euphoria of the "benign demographic transition" (Hardin 1973) interferes with the realistic appraisal of pejoristic mechanisms. As concerns public policy, the deductions drawn from the benign demographic transition are these:

1. If the per capital GNP rises the birth rate will fall; hence, the rate of population increase will fall, ultimately producing ZPG (Zero Population Growth).
2. The long-term trend all over the world (including the poor countries) is of a rising per capita GNP (for which no limit is seen).
3. Therefore, all political interference in population matters is unnecessary; all we need to

do is foster economic "development"—*note the metaphor*—and population problems will solve themselves.

Those who believe in the benign demographic transition dismiss the pejoristic mechanism of Exhibit B in the belief that each input of food from the world outside fosters development within a poor country thus resulting in a drop in the rate of population increase. Foreign aid has proceeded on this assumption for more than two decades. Unfortunately it has produced no indubitable instance of the asserted effect. It has, however, produced a library of excuses. The air is filled with plaintive calls for more massive foreign aid appropriations so that the hypothetical melioristic process can get started. The doctrine of demographic laissez-faire implicit in the hypothesis of the benign demographic transition is immensely attractive. Unfortunately there is more evidence against the melioristic system than there is for it (Davis 1963). On the historical side there are many counter-examples. The rise in per capita GNP in France and Ireland during the past century has been accompanied by a rise in population growth. In the twenty years following the Second World War the same positive correlation was noted almost everywhere in the world. Never in world history before 1950 did the worldwide population growth reach one percent per annum. Now the average population growth is over two percent and shows no signs of slackening.

On the theoretical side, the denial of the pejoristic scheme of Exhibit B probably springs from the hidden acceptance of the "cowboy economy" that Boulding castigated. Those who recognize the limitations of a spaceship, if they are unable to achieve population control at a safe and comfortable level, accept the necessity of the corrective feedback of the population

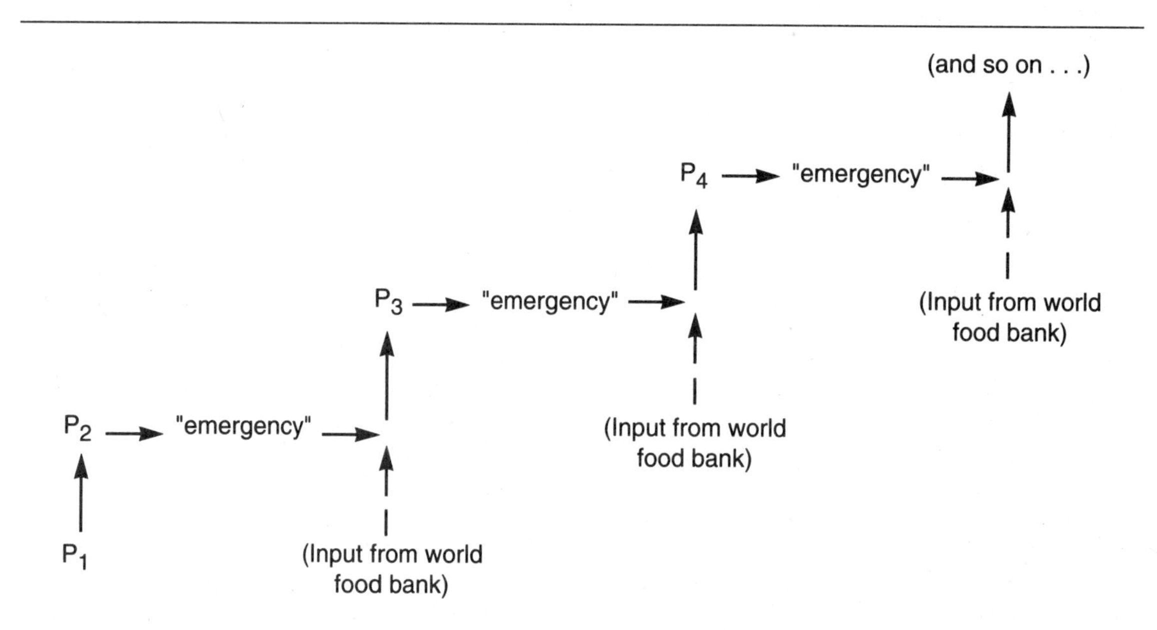

Exhibit B. The population escalator. Note that input from a world food bank acts like the pawl of a ratchet, preventing the normal population cycle shown in Exhibit A from being completed. P_{n+1} is greater than P_n, and the absolute magnitude of the "emergencies" escalates. Ultimately the entire system crashes. The crash is not shown, and few can imagine it.

cycle shown in Exhibit A. No one who knew in his bones that he was living on a true spaceship would countenance political support of the population escalator shown in Exhibit B.

Eco-Destruction via the Green Revolution

The demoralizing effect of charity on the recipient has long been known. "Give a man a fish and he will eat for a day; teach him how to fish and he will eat for the rest of his days." So runs an ancient Chinese proverb. Acting on this advice the Rockefeller and Ford Foundations have financed a multipronged program for improving agriculture in the hungry nations. The result, known as the "Green Revolution," has been quite remarkable. "Miracle wheat" and "miracle rice" are splendid technological achievements in the realm of plant genetics.

Whether or not the Green Revolution can increase food production is doubtful (Harris 1972, Paddock 1970, Wilkes 1972), but in any event not particularly important. What is missing in this great and well-meaning humanitarian effort is a firm grasp of fundamentals. Considering the importance of the Rockefeller Foundation in this effort it is ironic that the late Alan Gregg, a much-respected vice-president of the Foundation, strongly expressed his doubts of the wisdom of all attempts to increase food production some two decades ago. (This was before Borlaug's work—supported by Rockefeller—had resulted in the development of "miracle wheat.") Gregg (1955) likened the growth and spreading of humanity over the surface of the earth to the metastasis of cancer in the human body, wryly remarking that "Cancerous growths demand food; but, as far as I know, they have never been cured by getting it."

"Man does not live by bread alone"—the scriptural statement has a rich meaning even in the material realm. Every human being born constitutes a draft on all aspects of the environment—food, air, water, unspoiled scenery, occasional and optional solitude, beaches, contact with wild animals, fishing, hunting—the list is long and incompletely known. Food can, perhaps, be significantly increased, but what about clean beaches, unspoiled forests, and solitude? If we satisfy the need for food in a growing population we necessarily decrease the supply of other goods, and thereby increase the difficulty of equitably allocating scarce goods (Hardin 1969b, 1972b).

The present population of India is 600 million, and it is increasing by fifteen million per year. The environmental load of this population is already great. The forests of India are only a small fraction of what they were three centuries ago. Soil erosion, floods, and the psychological costs of crowding are serious. Every one of the net fifteen million lives added each year stresses the Indian environment more severely. *Every life saved this year in a poor country diminishes the quality of life for subsequent generations.*

Observant critics have shown how much harm we wealthy nations have already done to poor nations through our well-intentioned but misguided attempts to help them (Paddock and Paddock 1973). Particularly reprehensible is our failure to carry out post-audits of these attempts (Farver and Milton 1972). Thus have we shielded our tender consciences from knowledge of the harm we have done. Must we Americans continue to fail to monitor the consequences of our external "do-gooding?" If, for instance, we thoughtlessly make it possible for the present 600 million Indians to swell to 1,200 million by the year 2001—as their present growth rate promises—will posterity in India thank *us* for facilitating an even greater destruction of *their* environment? Are good intentions ever a sufficient excuse for bad consequences?

Immigration Creates a Commons

I come now to the final example of a commons in action, one for which the public is least prepared for rational discussion. The topic is at present enveloped by a great silence that reminds me of a comment made by Sherlock Holmes in A. Conan Doyle's story, "Silver Blaze." Inspector Gregory had asked, "Is there any point to which you wish to draw my attention?" To this Holmes responded:

"To the curious incident of the dog in the night-time."
"The dog did nothing in the night-time," said the Inspector.
"That was the curious incident," remarked Sherlock Holmes.

By asking himself what would repress the normal barking instinct of a watch dog Holmes realized that it must be the dog's recognition of his master as the criminal trespasser. In a similar way we should ask ourselves what repression keeps us from discussing something as important as immigration?

It cannot be that immigration is numerically of no consequence. Our government acknowledges a *net* inflow of 400,000 a year. Hard data are understandably lacking on the extent of illegal entries, but a not implausible figure is 600,000 per year. (Buchanan 1973). The natural increase of the resident population is now about 1.7 million per year. This means that the yearly gain from immigration is at least nineteen percent and may be thirty-seven percent, of the total increase. It is quite conceivable that educational campaigns like that of Zero Population Growth, Inc., coupled with adverse social and economic factors—inflation, housing shortage, depression, and loss of confidence in national leaders—may lower the fertility of American women to a point at which all of the yearly increase in population would be accounted for by immigration. Should we not at least ask if that is what we want? How curious it is that we so seldom discuss immigration these days!

Curious, but understandable—as one finds out the moment he publicly questions the wisdom of the status quo in immigration. He who does so is promptly charged with *isolationism, bigotry, prejudice,* **ethnocentrism**, *chauvinism,* and *selfishness.* These are hard accusations to bear. It is pleasanter to talk about other matters, leaving immigration policy to wallow in the crosscurrents of special interests that take no account of the good of the whole—*or of the interests of posterity.*

We Americans have a bad conscience because of things we said in the past about immigrants. Two generations ago the popular press was rife with references to *Dagos, Wops, Pollacks, Japs, Chinks,* and *Krauts*—all pejorative terms that failed to acknowledge our indebtedness to Goya, Leonardo, Copernicus, Hiroshige, Confuscius, and Bach. Because the implied inferiority of foreigners was *then* the justification for keeping them out, it is *now* thoughtlessly assumed that restrictive policies can only be based on the assumption of immigrant inferiority. *This is not so.*

Existing immigration laws exclude idiots and known criminals; future laws will almost certainly continue this policy. But should we also consider the quality of the average immigrant, as compared with the quality of the average resident? Perhaps we should, perhaps we shouldn't. (What is "quality" anyway?) But the quality issue is not our concern here.

From this point on, *it will be assumed that immigrants and native-born citizens are of exactly equal quality,* however, quality may be defined. The focus in only on quantity. The conclusions reached depend on nothing else, so all charges of ethnocentrism are irrelevant.

World food banks move food to the people, thus facilitating the exhaustion of the environment of the poor. By contrast, unrestricted immigration moves people to the food, thus speeding up the destruction of the environment in rich countries. Why poor people should want to make this transfer is no mystery, but why should rich hosts encourage it:? This transfer, like the reverse one, is supported by both selfish interests and humanitarian impulses.

The principal selfish interest in unimpeded immigration is easy to identify: it is the interest of the employers of cheap labor, particularly that needed for degrading jobs. We have been deceived about the forces of history by the lines of Emma Lazarus inscribed on the Statute of Liberty:

Give me your tired, your poor,
Your huddled masses yearning to breath free,
The wretched refuse of your teeming shore,
Send these, the homeless, tempest-tossed to me:
I lift my lamp beside the golden door.

The image is one of an infinitely generous earth-mother, passively opening her arms to hordes of immigrants who come here on their own initiative. Such an image may have been adequate for the early days of colonization, but by the time these lines were written (1886) the force for immigration was largely manufactured inside our own borders by factory and mine owners who sought cheap labor not to be found among laborers already here. One group of foreigners after another was thus enticed into the United States to work at wretched jobs for wretched wages.

At present, it is largely the Mexicans who are being so exploited. It is particularly to the advantage of certain employers that there be many illegal immigrants. Illegal immigrant workers dare not complain about their working conditions for fear of being repatriated. Their presence reduces the bargaining power of all Mexican-American laborers. Cesar Chavez has repeatedly pleaded with congressional committees to close the doors to more Mexicans so that those here can negotiate effectively for higher wages and decent working conditions. Chavez understands the ethics of a lifeboat.

The interests of the employers of cheap labor are well served by the silence of the intelligentsia of the country. WASPS—White Anglo-Saxon Protestants—are particularly reluctant to call for a closing of the doors to immigration for fear of being called ethnocentric bigots. It was, therefore, an occasion of pure delight for this particular WASP to be present at a meeting when the points he would like to have made were made better by a non-WASP speaking to other non-WASPS. It was in Hawaii, and most of the people in the room were second-level Hawaiian officials of Japanese ancestry. All Hawaiians are keenly aware of the limits of their environment, and the speaker had asked how it might be practically and constitutionally possible to close the doors to more immigrants to the islands. (To Hawaiians, immigrants from the other forty-nine states are as much of a threat as those from other nations. There is only so much room in the islands, and the islanders know it. Sophistical arguments that imply otherwise do not impress them.)

Yet the Japanese-Americans of Hawaii have active ties with the land of their origin. This point was raised by a Japanese-American member of the audience who asked the Japanese-American speaker: "But how can we shut the doors now? We have many friends and relations in Japan that we'd like to bring to Hawaii some day so that they can enjoy this beautiful land."

The speaker smiled sympathetically and responded slowly, "Yes, but we have children now and someday we'll have grandchildren. We can bring more people here from Japan only by giving away some of the land that we hope to pass on to our grandchildren some day. What right do we have to do that?"

To be generous with one's own possessions is one thing; to be generous with posterity's is quite another. This, I think, is the point that must be gotten across to those who would, from a commendable love of **distributive justice**, institute a ruinous system of the commons, either in the form of a world food bank or that of unrestricted immigration. Since every speaker is a member of some ethnic group it is always possible to charge him with ethnocentrism. But even after purging an argument of ethnocentrism the rejection of the commons is still valid and necessary if we are to save at least some parts of the world from environmental ruin. It is not desirable that at least some of the grandchildren of people now living should have a decent place in which to live?

The Asymmetry of Door-Shutting

We must now answer this telling point: "How can you justify slamming the door once you're inside? You say that immigrants should be kept out. But aren't we all immigrants, or the descendants of immigrants? Since we refuse to leave, must we not, as a matter of justice and symmetry, admit all others?"

It is literally true that we Americans of non-Indian ancestry are the descendants of thieves. Should we not, then, "give back" the land to the Indians, that is, give it to the now-living Americans of Indian ancestry? As an exercise in pure logic I see no way to reject this proposal. Yet I am unwilling to live by it, and I know no one who is. Our reluctance to embrace pure justice may spring from pure selfishness. On the other hand, it may arise from an unspoken recognition of consequences that have not yet been clearly spelled out.

Suppose, becoming intoxicated with pure justice, we "Anglos" should decide to turn our land over to the Indians. Since all our other wealth has also been derived from the land, we would have to give that to the Indians, too. Then what would we non-Indians do? Where would we go? There is no open land in the world on which men without capital can make their living (and not much unoccupied land on which men with capital can either). Where would 209 million putatively justice-loving, non-Indian Americans go? Most of them—in the persons of their ancestors—came from Europe, but they wouldn't be welcomed back there. Anyway, Europeans have no better title to their land than we to ours. They also would have to give up their homes. (But to whom? And where would *they* go?)

Clearly, the concept of pure justice produces an **infinite regress.** The law long ago invented statutes of limitations to justify the rejection of pure justice, in the interest of preventing massive disorder. The law zealously defends property rights—but only *recent* property rights. It is as though the physical principle of exponential decay applies to property rights. Drawing a line in time may be unjust, but any other action is practically worse.

We are all the descendants of thieves, and the world's resources are inequitably distributed, but we must begin the journey to tomorrow from the point where we are today. We cannot remake the past. We cannot, without violent disorder and suffering, give land and resources back to the "original" owners—who are dead anyway.

We cannot safely divide the wealth equitably among all present peoples, so long as people reproduce at different rates, because to do so would guarantee that our grandchildren—everyone's grandchildren—would have only a ruined world to inhabit.

Must Exclusion be Absolute?

To show the logical structure of the immigration problem I have ignored many factors that would enter into real decisions made in a real world. No matter how convincing the logic may be, it is probable that we would want, from time to time, to admit a few people from the outside to our lifeboat. Political refugees in particular are likely to cause us to make exceptions: We remember the Jewish refugees from Germany after 1933, and the Hungarian refugees after 1956. Moreover, the interests of national defense, broadly conceived, could justify admitting many men and women of unusual talents, whether refugees or not. (This raises the quality issue, which is not the subject of this essay.)

Such exceptions threaten to create runaway population growth inside the lifeboat, i.e., the receiving country. However, the threat can be neutralized by a population policy that includes immigration. An effective policy is one of flexible control.

Suppose, for example, that the nation has achieved a stable condition of ZPG, which (say) permits 1.5 million births yearly. We must suppose that an acceptable system of allocating birth-rights to potential parents is in effect. Now suppose that an inhumane regime in some other part of the world creates a horde of refugees, and that there is a wide-spread desire to admit some to our country. At the same time, we do not want to sabotage our population control system. Clearly, the rational path to pursue is the following. If we decide to admit 100,000 refugees this year we should compensate for this by reducing the allocation of birth-rights in the following year by a similar amount, that is, downward to a total of 1.4 million. In that way we could achieve both humanitarian and population control goals. (And the refugees would have to accept the population controls of the society that admits them. It is not inconceivable that they might be given proportionately fewer rights than the native population.)

In a democracy, the admission of immigrants should properly be voted on. But by whom? It is not obvious. The usual rule of a democracy is votes for all. But it can be questioned whether a universal franchise is the most just one in a case of this sort. Whatever benefits there are in the admission of immigrants presumably accrue to everyone. But the costs would be seen as falling most heavily on potential parents, some of whom would have to postpone or forego having their (next) child because of the influx of immigrants. The double question *Who benefits? Who pays?* suggests that a restriction of the usual democratic franchise would be appropriate and just in this case. Would our particular quasi-democratic form of government be flexible enough to institute such a novelty? If not, the majority might, out of humanitarian motives, impose an unacceptable burden (the foregoing of parenthood) on a minority, thus producing political instability.

Plainly many new problems will arise when we consciously face the immigration question and seek rational answers. No workable answers can be found if we ignore population problems. And—if the argument of this essay is correct—so long as there is no true world government to control reproduction everywhere it is impossible to survive in dignity if we are to be guided by spaceship ethics. Without a world government that is sovereign in reproductive matters mankind lives, in fact, on a number of sovereign lifeboats. For the foreseeable future survival demands that we govern our actions by the ethics of a lifeboat. Posterity will be ill served if we do not.

Reference Notes

Anonymous. 1974. *Wall Street Journal* 19 Feb.

Borlaug, N. 1973. Civilization's future: a call for international granaries. *Bull. At. Sci.* 29: 7-15.

Boulding, K. 1966. The economists of the coming Spaceship Earth. *In* H. Jarrett, ed. Environmental Quality in a Growing Economy. Baltimore: John Hopkins Press.

Buchanan, W. 1973. Immigration statistics. *Equilibrium* 1(3): 16-19.

Davis, K. 1963. Population. *Sci. Amer.* 209(3): 62-71.

Farvar, M. T., and J. P. Milton. 1972. The Careless Technology. Garden City, NY: Natural History Press.

Gregg, A. 1955. A medical aspect of the population problem. *Science* 121:681-682.

Hardin, G. 1966. Chap. 9 *in* Biology: Its Principles and Implications, 2nd ed. San Francisco: Freeman.

________. 1968. The tragedy of the commons. *Science* 162: 1243-1248.

________. 1969a Page 18 *in* Population, Evolution, and Birth Control, 2nd ed. San Francisco: Freeman.

________. 1969b. The economics of wilderness. *Nat. Hist.* 78(6): 20-27.

________. 1972a. Pages 81-82 *in* Exploring New Ethics for Survival: The Voyage of the Spaceship *Beagle*. New York: Viking. ________. 1972b. Preserving quality on Spaceship Earth. *In* J. B. Trefethen, ed. Transactions of the Thirty-Seventh North American Wildlife and Natural Resources Conference. Wildlife Management Institute, Washington, D.C.

________. 1973. Chap. 23 *in* Stalking the Wild Taboo. Los Altos, CA: Kaufmann.

Harris, M. 1972. How green the revolution. *Nat. Hist.* 81(3):28-30.

Langer, S. K. 1942. Philosophy in a New Key. Cambridge, MA: Harvard University Press.

Lansner, K. 1974. Should foreign aid begin at home? *Newsweek*, 11 Feb., p. 32.

Marx, K. 1875. Critique of the Gotha program. Page 388 *in* R. C. Tucker, ed. The Marx-Engels Reader. New York: Norton, 1972.

Ophuls, W. 1974. The scarcity society. *Harpers* 248 (1487): 47-52.

Paddock, W. C. 1970. How green is the green revolution? *BioScience* 20: 897-902.

Paddock, W., and E. Paddock. 1973. We Don't Know How. Ames, IA: Iowa State University Press.

Paddock, W., and P. Paddock. 1967. Famine—1975! Boston: Little, Brown.

Wilkes, H. G. 1972. The green revolution. *Environment* 14(8): 32-39.

Review Questions

1. What is wrong with the spaceship metaphor according to Hardin?
2. Explain Hardin's lifeboat metaphor.
3. According to Hardin, why can't we live by the Christian or the Marxian ideal?
4. Explain what Hardin calls the tragedy of the commons. How is this supposed to apply to rich and poor nations?
5. Explain the ratchet effect and a pejoristic system.
6. Why isn't benign demographic transition possible according to Hardin?
7. Why doesn't Hardin think that the Green Revolution will solve the problem of world hunger?
8. Explain Hardin's opposition to present immigration policies.

Discussion Questions

1. Are there any respects in which the United States is not a lifeboat?
2. Is there any solution to the problem of overpopulation in poor countries that does not involve letting people die? What is it?

3. Is there any way to avoid the tragedy of the commons that does not involve private ownership? Explain.
4. Is there any way to avoid the ratchet effect? Explain.
5. Should we allow more people to immigrate into the United States? Why or why not?

Robert N. Van Wyk

Perspectives on World Hunger and the Extent of Our Positive Duties

Robert N. Van Wyk is Associate Professor of Philosophy at the University of Pittsburgh.

Van Wyk attacks both Singer's and Hardin's utilitarian approach to the problem of world hunger and suggests an alternative Kantian ethic. In the Kantian view, individuals have a strict duty to give a fair share and a duty of reparation to needy people in other countries because of past harms done to them in violation of the duty not to harm others.

I Introduction to the Issue

A moral problem that faces institutions—especially governments, as well as individuals, is the question of the extent of the duty to prevent harm to other people, and/or benefit them. This is not an academic problem but one that stares us in the face through the eyes of starving and malnourished people, and in particular, children. . . .

II Utilitarian/Consequentialist Approaches

A The Views of Peter Singer and Garrett Hardin

According to some moral theories the very fact of widespread hunger imposes a duty on each person to do whatever he or she is capable of doing to accomplish whatever is necessary to see to it that all people have enough to eat. Peter Singer, a utilitarian, writes:

> I begin with the assumption that suffering and death from lack of food, shelter, and medical care are bad . . . My next point is this: if it is in our power to prevent something bad from happening without thereby sacrificing anything of comparable moral importance, we ought, morally, to do it.[1]

Does this mean that governments of prosperous countries ought to call upon their citizens to sacrifice enough of the luxuries of life to pay taxes that will be used to see to it that everyone in the world has the basic necessities of life? Suppose that governments do not do this. Suppose I give a considerable amount of famine relief but the need remains great because many others have not given. Is this case parallel to the following one to which Singer compares it? I have saved the life of one drowning person. There is still another person who needs to be saved. Other people could have saved the second person while I was saving the first but no one did. Even though I have saved one, and even though other people have failed in their duty to try to save the other, it would seem reasonable to claim that I have a duty to try to do so. Would I similarly have a duty to keep on giving more to aid the hungry regardless of the personal sacrifice involved? Many objections raised against giving sacrificially have to do with whether certain kinds of assistance really do

From Robert N. Van Wyk, "Perspectives on World Hunger and the Extent of Our Positive Duties," *Public Affairs Quarterly*, Vol. 2 (April 1988).

much good. But such objections do not really affect the question of how much one should sacrifice to help others, but only to have to do with the best way of using what is given (for example, for food assistance, development assistance, family planning, encouraging political change, supporting education, and so on). But if we reach the conclusion that we have a duty to do all we can, just as in the case of the drowning people, we are faced with the problem that James Fishkin has written about, of being overwhelmed with obligations in a way that expands the area of moral duty to the point of obliterating both the area of the morally indifferent and the area of the morally supererogatory.[2]

There are, however, other considerations. What are the long range consequences of keeping people alive? 'Neo-malthusians" and "crisis environmentalists" argue that population growth is outstripping food production and also leading both to the depletion of the world's natural resources and the pollution of the environment, so that the more people who are saved the more misery there will be in the long run. Garrett Hardlin compares rich nations to lifeboats and the poor of the world to drowning people trying to get into the lifeboats. To allow them in would be to risk sinking the lifeboats and so to risk bringing disaster on everyone. The high rate of population growth among the poor nations insures that even if there is enough room at the moment, eventually the lifeboats will be swamped.[3] The lifeboat ethic is an application of what Hardin calls the logic of the commons. If a pasture is held as common property each herdsman is tempted to overgraze it for the sake of short-term profits. Even the individual who wants to preserve the land for the future has no reason to stop as long as there are others who will continue to overgraze it. Similarly, if we regard the food production of the world as a "commons" to which everyone is entitled we undermine any incentive among the poor of the world to increase production and limit population growth. The increasing population will continually reduce the amount available for each individual while at the same time increasing pollution and putting other strains on the environment.[4] So Hardin writes that "for posterity's sake we should never send food to any population that is beyond the realistic carrying capacity of its land." [5] This view that certain countries should be left to have "massive diebacks of population," [6] while others should perhaps be helped, has been called "triage."

B Questions about These Approaches

One way of responding to Hardin's argument is to raise questions about the choice of metaphors and their applicability.[7] Why speak of lifeboats rather than of luxury liners? Why should the Asian or African people be compared to the "sheep" who are the greatest threat to the commons when the average American uses up thirty times the amount of the earth's resources as does the average Asian or African, and when the developed nations import more protein from the developing nations than they export to them? How are the lifeboat metaphors applicable when apart from special famine conditions almost every country in the world has the resources necessary to feed its people if they were used primarily for that purpose?

The focus here, however, will be on moral theory. In spite of their very different conclusions, Singer and Hardin both presuppose a utilitarian position that says that what we ought to do depends completely on the anticipated consequences of our choices. A defender of Singer might say that all Hardin's observations do is to impose on all people a duty to redouble their efforts to find and support solutions that avoid both short range hunger and long range disaster. But that answer only increases the problem of overload that Fishkin is concerned with.

III Hunger, Respect for Persons and Negative Duties

Many philosophers, especially those emphasizing the stringency of negative duties, subscribe to Kant's principle of respect for persons, whether or not they are supporters of Kant's moral philosophy taken as a whole. Robert Nozick uses the principle of respect for persons to defend absolute duties to do no harm while at the same time denying the existence of any duties to benefit others.[8] Kant himself, however, maintained that we have **imperfect duties** to help others. One might still claim that government may not collect taxes for the sake of aiding others, since one ought not to force people (taxpayers) to fulfill imperfect duties when doing so violates the **perfect duty** to respect the right of citizens to use their resources as they themselves choose to do so. Kant himself did not reach such a conclusion,[9] but Nozick does, arguing that since "individuals are ends and not merely means; they may not be sacrificed, or used for the achieving of other ends without their consent." [10]

Nozick's views can be attacked at many points. Even if they were correct, however, it would not follow that governments would have no right to tax citizens to aid people in distress. This is because individuals, corporations (to which individuals are related as stockholders and employees), and governments would still have duties not to harm, and thus also duties to take corrective action in response to past harms. So wealthy countries and their citizens could still have many responsibilities of compensatory justice with respect to the world's poor. Some countries face poverty because their economies are heavily dependent on a single export material or crop (for example, copper in Chile), the prices of which are subject to great fluctuations, were brought about by policies of wealthy nations or their corporations, then suffering does not just happen but is caused by the actions of people in developed nations. If corporations can strangle economies of developing nations and choose to do so if they do not get special tax advantages, or unfairly advantageous contracts, then poverty and hunger are harms caused by the decisions of the wealthy. If, furthermore, government officials are bribed to keep taxes down, as was done in Honduras by the banana companies, then poverty is directly caused by human actions. If a developed nation overthrows the government of a poor nation which tries to correct some past injustice (as was done when the C.I.A. helped overthrow the democratically elected government of Guatamala in 1954 in order to protect the interests of the United Fruit Company), then poverty is a harm caused by human actions. The decisions of the Soviet Union to import large amounts of grain from the United States during the Nixon administration led to a dramatic and unexpected rise in the price of grain on the world market, which in turn caused hunger. Americans' use of energy at twice the rate of Western Europeans must raise energy prices for the poor. Dramatic price increases by oil exporting nations no doubt meant that people went without petroleum-based fertilizers, or energy to transport food or pump water for irrigation, and so led to additional people dying of hunger. When petroleum prices fall the poverty of people in some oil-exporting countries is aggravated because of the difficulty their governments have financing their debts—debts which were acquired partially due to the encouragement of the banks in the wealthy countries.

What duties do the wealthy countries have to the poor and hungry of the world? The first duty is not to harm them. While seldom are the hungry intentionally killed, they are often killed in the same way that someone is killed by a reckless driver who just does not take into consideration what his actions might do to other vulnerable human beings, and there is no doubt that reckless drivers are to be held accountable for what they do. In some cases it may be morally justifiable to endanger the lives of people in order to work toward some desirable goal, as it may be morally justifiable to risk people's lives in order to rush a critically ill person to the hospital. But a person who is speeding for good reason, or who benefits from that speeding, is not thereby relieved of responsibility for someone who is thereby injured, for otherwise the endangered or harmed would be treated only as means to the ends of others. Similarly, those who make or benefit from economic and political decisions are not relieved of responsibility for those who are thereby harmed or endangered. So even if we were to accept the view that no individual or government has any duty to aid those in distress simply because they are in distress, there would still be a few people of more than adequate means in the real world who would not have an obligation to aid those in need. As Onora Nell writes:

> Only if we knew that we were not part of any system of activities causing unjustifiable deaths could we have no duties to support policies which seek to avoid such deaths. Modern economic causal chains are so complex that it is likely that only those who are economically isolated and self-sufficient could know that they are part of no such system of activities.[11]

With respect to compensating those who have been harmed we do not have to be part of the causal chain that causes harm in order to have an obligation to those who still bear the effects of past harm. If *A* stole *B*'s money yesterday and gave the money to *C* today, *C* obviously has a duty to return it. While in some cases mentioned above decisions were made by companies, individuals and governments still were beneficiaries of such decisions through lower prices and increased tax revenue. Furthermore, it would not make any difference if *A* stole *B*'s money before *C* was born. Consider the following case:

> Bengal (today's Bangledesh and the West Bengal state of India), the first territory the British conquered in Asia, was a prosperous province with highly developed centers of manufacturing and trade, and an economy as advanced as any prior to the industrial revolution. The British reduced Bengal to poverty through plunder, heavy land taxes and trade restrictions that barred competitive Indian goods from England, but gave British goods free entry into India. India's late Prime Minister Nehru commented bitterly, "Bengal can take pride in the fact that she helped greatly in giving birth to the Industrial Revolution in England." [12]

Those who benefited from the Industrial Revolution in England, including those alive today, would still have duties to aid Bengal, just as those who inherited a fortune partially based on stolen money have a duty to return what was stolen, with interest, even though they themselves are in no way guilty of the theft. So it is with most citizens of the industiralized West with respect to the poor of some parts of the world. However, in the light of the complexity of both the causal chains of harm and the causal chains of benefit, we are again faced with a great deal of uncertainty as to the allocation of responsibility for correcting for past injustices.[13]

IV Hunger, Positive Duties, and the Idea of a Fair Share

So there is no doubt that a Kantian ethic would include duties of reparation for harms done to people in the past and that this would be a basis of obligations to aid many of the underdeveloped countries in the world today, even though it would be difficult to specify the extent of obligation. But is there a duty to help those in severe need even if the causes of the need are not due to any past injustice or are unknown, as may also be true about parts of the world today? Kant does not always treat duties to aid others as fully binding, but whether or not, as one Kantian argues, "it is impermissible not to promote the well-being of others,"[14] it can be argued that it is impermissible not to relieve others in distress and provide them with the basic necessities of life, for this is to fail to treat them as having any value as ends in themselves. To put it another way, failing to help is to violate subsistence rights, and, as Henry Shue argues, whatever sorts of reasons can be given in favor of regarding human beings as having security rights can also be given in favor of regarding them as having subsistence rights.[15] Or, to put it another way, it is to fail to take into account the vulnerability of the world's poor toward the affluent (taken collectively), and it is the vulnerability of people to others (individually or collectively) that is the foundation of most (or all) of both our **positive and negative duties** to others.[16]

To what extent do individuals and nations have a duty to relieve those in distress? Is there a middle way between Singer and Nozick? Perhaps the following line of reasoning would provide a guideline. An estimate can be made of what resources would be needed to feed the hungry, bring about political and economic change, promote development, limit population growth, and to do whatever is necessary to see that all people have a minimally decent standard of living (or that their basic rights are met).

Some formula based on ability to help could determine what a fair share would be for each citizen of a developed country to contribute to the needs of those in distress in that country and to that country's share of helping the people of other nations. To the extent that nations adopt this procedure and make it part of their tax structure a person could fulfill the duty of doing her share by paying her taxes. The ideal would be for nations to do this so that the responsibilities would be carried out and the burden would be distributed fairly. To the extent that nations have not done this (and it is unlikely that any have) what duties do citizens have to contribute through private or religious agencies? Henry Shue correctly observes that "How much sacrifice can reasonably be expected from one person for the sake of another, even for the sake of honoring the other's rights, is one of the most fundamental questions in morality." [17] Nozick, as we have seen, answers with "None." Many answer with "Some" without going on to give a more precise answer. In the absence of adequate government action each individual could still make some sort of estimate of what a fair share would be and give that amount (or what remains of that amount after taking into consideration that part of her taxes that are used for appropriate purposes) through private or religious agencies. I am claiming that it is a strict duty or duty of perfect obligation for an individual to give at least her fair share, according to some plausible formula, toward seeing that all human beings are treated as ends in themselves, which involves seeing that they have the basic necessities of life in so far as that can depend on the actions of others. This conclusion can also be supported by a generalization argument. If everyone contributed at least a fair share the subsistence rights of human beings would cease to be violated (since that would be one of the criteria for deciding on a fair share). There is a problem about the applicability of generalization arguments where the efforts of one individual accomplishes nothing if most other people do not also do their fair share. (It is, for example, probably pointless to be the only person who refrains from taking a short cut across the grass; the grass will not grow.) In such cases the failure of some to fulfill their duties may relieve others of theirs. The duty to contribute to the cause of combatting hunger, however, is not of this sort, since one individual's contributions still accomplish some good whether or not other people are giving their fair share.

On the other hand there is the problem of whether the failure of some people to fulfill their duties increases the duties of others. If many are not giving a fair share, does the individual who is already giving a fair share have a duty to give more? The example of the two drowning people suggests that the individual who has done his fair share does have a duty to do more. But there is a major difference between the two cases. Saving people from drowning, in so far as the chances of losing one's own life are not great, is something that takes a minimal amount of time out of the rescuer's life and does not threaten his ability to live a life of pursuing goals he sets for himself. A similar duty to keep on giving of one's resources, even after one has done his fair share, would threaten to eclipse everything else a person might choose to do with his life, for example, develop his talents, raise a family, send his children to college, and so on, so that that person would become nothing but a means to meeting the needs of others. The idea of a strict duty to do at least one's fair share seems to avoid the problem of overload (unless the total need is overwhelming) and draws a line at a plausible point somewhere between doing nothing and sacrificing one's whole life to the cause of relieving the distress of others. This approach does make one's duty to those in need agent-specific, since one's duty does depend on one's past history, on what sacrifices one has already made, but it is not clear to me why this is a defect. Of course a person might choose to make the rescuing of those in distress her special vocation, and it may be noble for her to do so, but to claim that if the needs of others are great enough she has a duty to surrender any choice about the direction of her own life is to claim that a person has a duty to be purely the means to meeting the needs of others, and so in fact a duty to love others not as oneself, but instead of oneself. On the other hand, not to recognize a duty to give a fair share is to indicate that one believes either that it is not important that the needs of those in distress should be met (perhaps because they do not have subsistence rights) or that others should do more than their fair share.[18] It might be said that the first is at least a sin against compassion (if not also against justice) and the second is a sin against fairness or justice. In either case one is treating the ends and purposes of others as having less validity than one's own, or, from another point of view, one is not loving others as oneself.

V Considerations Beyond a Fair Share

If redistribution of wealth were in fact the major need of the most vulnerable in the world, and if in fact government foreign aid programs could be modified so that they could be trusted to meet that need, then, in agreement with Shue and Goodin, I would claim that for the sake of fairness both to those in need and those willing to help, it would be better if everyone did his or her fair share and it would be legitimate to coerce people through the tax system to do so.[19] In the absence of such taxation and in the absence of any official calculation of such a share, individuals generally do not have the information on which to assess their own fair share, and if they did they would probably tend to underestimate it. What most people tend to think of as their fair share depends much less on any informed calculation than on what they think their neighbors, fellow citizens, or fellow church members, are contributing,[20] consoling themselves with the thought that it cannot really be their duty to do more than others. But since most people who do something probably tend to think that they are doing more with respect to their resources than others, the idea of a duty to do a fair share is in danger of succumbing to a downward pressure to require less and less. If the vulnerable are to be protected, then perhaps doing one's fair share to meet their needs is not the only duty. Rather there must also be a duty to put upward pressure on the prevailing idea of a fair share. This can be done only by those who do considerably more than what is perceived of as a fair share, and often more than an actual fair share. This is embodied in Christian ethics in the ideal of being a light to witness to a higher and more demanding way of life and in the ideal of being the salt of the earth that preserves it from decay, perhaps primarily the decay brought about by downward pressure on prevailing standards. Probably a secular counterpart to these ideals would be accepted by others.

There are doubts about whether redistribution of wealth is the major need, as opposed to various changes in policies, including trade policies. There are also grave doubts concerning the degree to which government aid in the past has really benefited the most vulnerable and about its prospects of doing so in the future. That raises the possibility that the major duty individuals have is that of exerting pressure on government to make sure that policies do protect the vulnerable. (In American society people are not quick to recognize this as a moral duty. Churches have much more success in getting their members to contribute to "One Great Hour of Sharing" and "Hunger Fund" offerings than they do in getting them to write letters to their Senators and Congressmen about hunger issues.) Donald Regan writes that our duty is "to cooperate with whoever else is cooperating, in the production of the best consequences possible given the behaviour of non-cooperators."[21] There is an organization, Bread for the World, which analyzes policy, supports legislation on hunger issues, and conducts coordinated letter-writing drives through its members and its affiliated churches. Those who would write letters to their representatives in conjunction with such an effort would be acting in accordance with Regan's principle. But the principle does not say how much time, effort, and money an individual has a duty to devote to cooperating with others to bring it about that governments act in ways that protect the vulnerable.[22] Giving one's fair share to help those in need accomplishes some good whether or not others are cooperating by doing their share. In the matter of influencing legislation an insufficient number of people doing their fair share (with respect to all who might participate in the effort) may accomplish nothing. Does the failure of enough others to do their fair share release one from one's duty to work for change (as it may release one from the duty not to walk on the grass)? If so, the vulnerable are left without protection. Or does such a failure impose a duty on others to do as much as possible (as in the case of saving drowning people), so that we could again be faced with the problem of overload? In this case, however, one sort of fair share is so minimal there is no problem in doing much more. If an individual wrote at least one letter a year to her Senators and Congressman on one piece of legislation critical to meeting the needs of the hungry in the world, that individual would on this matter be doing perhaps 50 times a fair share, in that letters from two percent of the electorate would be regarded by those legislators as an overwhelming mandate on the issue. But an individual could write many such letters a year, and encourage others to do likewise, without sacrificing anything significant. Perhaps there is no precise answer to the question of just how much more money or effort than prevailing standards require one "ought" to devote to the cause here being considered, since this may be a matter of living up to an ideal rather than fulfilling a perfect duty to a specific individual, or a perfect duty of doing a fair share. Even in the absence of any way of determining what a fair share might be one can attempt to live by this ideal by doing significantly more than the society as a whole generally thinks is required.

Furthermore, may not some people have an agent-specific duty to do more than a fair share (perhaps much more) about some specific matter because of their peculiar awareness of the problem, knowledge of what needs to be done, and sensitivity to it? Religious people might say that all people have a duty to ask themselves whether they may have been "called" to a special vocation of taking on this cause, with the assurance that some people are called to this vocation and all people are called to some such vocation(s). In addition, a religious ethic generally emphasizes the faithfulness of one's witness more than the extent of one's accomplishments, and so may succeed in sustaining an individual's effort to bring about change when the prospects of succeeding seem slight. Perhaps some would argue for secular equivalents to these emphases.

VI Postscript: Additional Kantian Reflections on Duties of Others

There are still a number of things to be taken into consideration. Kant says that a person should "not push the expenditure of his means in beneficence . . . to the point where he would finally need the beneficence of others." [23] That could be regarded as treating others as a means to one's own end of trying to achieve some kind of sainthood. Secondly, help should not be given in a manner or to an extent that reduces the ability of the person (or group) that is helped to be self-reliant and self-determining. It is doubtful whether the wealthy have ever given too much help to the poor, but they have sometimes (perhaps frequently) given in a manner which made the recipients more dependent in the long run, for example, in a way that reduced the incentives of local farmers to increase production. Thirdly, according to Kant, every effort must be made to "carefully avoid any appearance of intending to obligate the other person, lest he (the giver) not render a true benefit, inasmuch as by his act he expresses that he wants to lay an obligation upon the receiver." [24] Presumably nations such as the United States can and do give aid for ulterior purposes, such as to get rid of agricultural surpluses, help farm prices, gain political influence, or to stimulate markets and/or a favorable climate of investment for U.S. companies, but then citizens of these nations ought not congratulate themselves on their generosity (as Americans often do). Such acts are not acts of beneficence and from Kant's point of view they have no moral worth since they are not done for the sake of duty, nor are they done from other motives that might be regarded as being other than morally neutral.

Fourthly, there are conditions under which it could be argued that a wealthy country has the right to refuse to give aid, other than emergency disaster aid, if it is not something that is owed as reparations. Suppose that achieving the goal of advancing the self-sufficiency and self-determination of a nation depends in part on the receiving nation's own effort to make necessary changes such as redistributing land, bringing population growth under control, and so on. It could be argued that if the receiving nation fails to make a good-faith effort to bring about these changes, and if it then asks for additional aid, the developed country may legitimately claim that it is being used, and its people are being used, solely as means to the ends of the under developed country or its people. The major problem with using this line of argument is that the people who are facing hunger may have little to say about the decisions of their government. That problem, however, does not prevent the aid-giving country from legitimately making demands for reform in advance, from doing what it can to see to it that they are carried out, and from threatening sanctions other than those that would increase the deprivation of hungry people.[25] Perhaps it has seldom, if ever, happened that a developed nation has given enough non-military aid to an underdeveloped nation to be in a position to dictate what steps the receiving nation should take to improve the ability of its people to be self-sufficient; or perhaps it has been in the interest of the political strategy, military effort, or business investment of the developed nations not to demand that specific remedial steps be taken on the part of the receiving country; but it would seem to be legitimate to make such demands.

Endnotes

1. Peter Singer, "Famine, Affluence, and Morality," *Philosophy and Public Affairs,* vol. 1 (1972), p. 231.
2. James Fishkin, *The Limits of Obligation* (New Haven: Yale University Press, 1982), especially chapters 1-7, 9 and 18.
3. Garrett Hardin, "Lifeboat Ethics: "The Case Against Helping the Poor," *Psychology Today,* vol. 8 (1974), pp. 38-43, 123-126.
4. Garrett Hardin, "The Tragedy of the Commons," *Science,* vol. 102 (1968), pp. 1243-1248.
5. Garrett Hardin, "Carrying Capacity as an Ethical Concept," in George R. Lucas and Thomas W. Ogletree (eds.), *Lifeboat Ethics: The Moral Dilemmas of World Hunger,* (New York: Harper and Row, 1976), p. 131.
6. Part of the title of an article by Garrett Hardin, "Another Face of Bioethics: The Case for Massive 'Diebacks' of Population," *Modern Medicine,* vol. 65 (March 1, 1975).
7. Paul Verghese, "Muddled Metaphors," in Lucas and Ogletree, *op. cit.*, p. 152.
8. Robert Nozick, *Anarchy, State and Utopia* (New York: Basic Books, Inc., 1974), pp. 30-35.
9. Immanuel Kant, *The Metaphysical Elements of Justice* (Part 1 of the *Metaphysics of Morals*), tr. by John Ladd (Indianapolis: Bobbs-Merrill Co., 1965), p. 93 (326).
10. Nozick, *op. cit.*, p. 31.
11. Onora Nell, "Lifeboat Earth," *Philosophy and Public Affairs,* vol. 4 (1975), p. 286.
12. Arthur Simon, *Bread for the World,* (New York: Paulist Press, 1975), p. 41.
13. For some of these problems see Goodin, *Protecting the Vulnerable* (Chicago: University of Chicago Press, 1986), pp. 159-160.
14. Alan Donagan, *Theory of Morality* (Chicago: University of Chicago Press, 1977), p. 85.
15. Henry Shue, *Basic Rights* (Princeton: Princeton University Press, 1980), Chapters 1 & 2.
16. This is the thesis of Goodin's book (*op. cit.*) with which I am in general agreement.
17. Shue, *op. cit.*, p. 114.
18. See also Goodin, *op. cit.*, p. 165.
19. *Ibid.*, p. 164; Shue, *op. cit.*, p. 118.
20. See Singer, "Famine, Affluence, and Morality," *op. cit.*, p. 30.
21. Donald Regan, *Utilitarianism and Cooperation* (Oxford: Clarendon Press, 1980), p. 124; also cited by Goodin as expressing his own view (*op., cit.*, p. 164).
22. For some suggestions concerning such ways, see Frances Moore Lappé and Joseph Collins, *World Hunger: 10 Myths,* (San Francisco: Institute for Food and Development Policy, 4th ed., 1982), pp. 49-50.
23. *Metaphysical Principles of Virtue, op. cit.*, p. 118 (454).
24. *Ibid.* (453).
25. See Shue, *Basic Rights,* Part III, "Policy Implications," *op. cit.*, pp. 155-174.

Review Questions

1. What criticisms does Van Wyk make of Singer and Hardin?
2. How does a Kantian ethic view obligations to others according to Van Wyk?
3. What is Van Wyk's proposal for helping the hungry?

Discussion Questions

1. Is Van Wyk's proposal for aid acceptable?
2. Do individuals have a strict duty to help others or is this optional? If there is such a strict duty, just what does it require us to do?

Peter Marin

Helping and Hating the Homeless

Peter Marin is a contributing editor of Harper's Magazine.

Marin divides the homeless into two main categories: those who are involuntarily homeless, such as the mentally or physically ill, and those who choose to be homeless. With respect to the first category, Marlin believes that society owes them aid; people in this category have earned a right to aid if they have contributed to society. As for those who choose to be homeless, Marin thinks that at least they should be given a place to exist. This is not a moral obligation, but what he calls an existential obligation that recognizes the importance of freedom.

The trouble begins with the word "homeless." It has become such an abstraction, and is applied to so many different kinds of people, with so many different histories and problems, that it is almost meaningless.

Homelessness, in itself, is nothing more than a condition visited upon men and women (and, increasingly, children) as the final stage of a variety of problems about which the word "homelessness" tells us almost nothing. Or, to put it another way, it is a catch basin into which pour all of the people disenfranchised or marginalized or scared off by processes beyond their control, those which lie close to the heart of American life. Here are the groups packed into the single category of "the homeless":

Veterans, mainly from the war in Vietnam. In many American cities, vets make up close to 50 percent of all homeless males.

The mentally ill. In some parts of the country, roughly a quarter of the homeless would, a couple of decades ago, have been institutionalized.

The physically disabled or chronically ill, who do not receive any benefits or whose benefits do not enable them to afford permanent shelter.

The elderly on fixed incomes whose funds are no longer sufficient for their needs.

Men, women, and whole families pauperized by the loss of a job.

Single parents, usually women, without the resources or skills to establish new lives.

Runaway children, many of whom have been abused.

Alcoholics and those in trouble with drugs (whose troubles often begin with one of the other conditions listed here).

Immigrants, both legal and illegal, who often are not counted among the homeless because they constitute a "problem" in their own right.

Traditional tramps, hobos, and transients, who have taken to the road or the streets for a variety of reasons and who prefer to be there.

You can quickly learn two things about the homeless from this list. First, you can learn that many of the homeless, before they were homeless, were people more or less like ourselves: members of the working or middle class. And you can learn that the world of the homeless has its roots in various policies, events, and ways of life for which some of us are responsible and from which some of us actually prosper.

We decide, as a people, to go to war, we ask our children to kill and to die, and the result, years later, is grown men homeless on the street.

We change, with the best intentions, the laws pertaining to the mentally ill and then, without intention, neglect to provide them with services;

From Peter Marin, "Helping and Hating the Homeless." Reprinted from the January 1987 issue by special permission.

and the result, in our streets, drives some of us crazy with rage.

We cut taxes and prune budgets, we modernize industry and shift the balance of trade, and the result of all these actions and errors can be read, sleeping form by sleeping form, on our city streets.

The liberals cannot blame the conservatives. The conservatives cannot blame the liberals. Homelessness is the *sum total* of our dreams, policies, intentions, errors, omissions, cruelties, kindnesses, all of it recorded, in flesh, in the life of the streets.

You can also learn from this list one of the most important things there is to know about the homeless—that they can be roughly divided into two groups: those who have had homelessness forced upon them and want nothing more than to escape it; and those who have at least in part *chosen* it for themselves, and now accept, or in some cases, embrace it.

I understand how dangerous it is to introduce the idea of choice into a discussion of homelessness. It can all too easily be used to justify indifference or brutality toward the homeless, or to argue that they are only getting what they "deserve." And yet it seems to me that it is only by taking choice into account, in all of the intricacies of its various forms and expressions, that one can really understand certain kinds of homelessness.

The fact is, many of the homeless are not only hapless victims but voluntary exiles, "domestic refugees," people who have turned not against life itself but against *us*, our life, American life. Look for a moment at the vets. The price of returning to America was to forget what they had seen or learned in Vietnam, to "put it behind them." But some could not do that, and the stress of trying showed up as alcoholism, broken marriages, drug addiction, crime. And it showed up too as life on the street, which was for some vets a desperate choice made in the name of life—the best they could manage. It was a way of avoiding what might have occurred had they stayed where they were: suicide, or violence done to others.

We must learn to accept that there may indeed be people, and not only vets, who have seen so much of our world, or seen it so clearly, that to live in it becomes impossible. Here, for example, is the story of Alice, a homeless middle-aged woman in Los Angeles, where there are, perhaps, 50,000 homeless people. It was set down a few months ago by one of my students at the University of California, Santa Barbara, where I taught for a semester. I had encouraged them to go find the homeless and listen to their stories. And so, one day, when this student saw Alice foraging in a dumpster outside a McDonald's, he stopped and talked to her:

> She told me she had led a pretty normal life as she grew up and eventually went to college. From there she went on to Chicago to teach school. She was single and lived in a small apartment.
>
> One night, after she got off the train after school, a man began to follow her to her apartment building. When she got to her door she saw a knife and the man hovering behind her. She had no choice but to let him in. The man raped her.
>
> After that, things got steadily worse. She had a nervous breakdown. She went to a mental institution for three months, and when she went back to her apartment she found her belongings gone. The landlord had sold them to cover the rent she hadn't paid.
>
> She had no place to go and no job because the school had terminated her employment. She slipped into depression. She lived with friends until she could muster enough money for a ticket to Los Angeles. She said she no longer wanted to burden her friends, and that if she had to live outside, at least Los Angeles was warmer than Chicago.
>
> It is as if she began back then to take on the mentality of a street person. She resolved herself to homelessness. She's been out West since 1980, without a home or job. She seems happy, with her best friend being her cat. But the scars of memories still haunt her, and she is running from them, or should I say *him*.

This is, in essence, the same story one hears over and over again on the street. You begin with an ordinary life; then an event occurs—traumatic, catastrophic; smaller events follow, each one deepening the original wound; finally, homelessness becomes inevitable, or begins to *seem* inevitable to the person involved—the only way out of an intolerable situation. You are struck continually, hearing these stories, by something seemingly unique in American life, the absolute isolation involved. In what other culture would there be such an absence or failure of support from familial, social, or institutional sources? Even more disturbing is the fact that it is often our supposed sources of support—family, friends, government organizations—that have caused the problem in the first place.

Everything that happened to Alice—the rape, the loss of job and apartment, the breakdown—was part and parcel of a world gone radically wrong, a world, for Alice, no longer to be counted on, no longer worth living in. Her homelessness can be seen as flight, as failure of will or nerve, even, perhaps, as *disease.* But it can also be seen as a mute, furious refusal, a self-imposed exile far less appealing to the rest of us than ordinary life, but *better,* in Alice's terms.

We like to think, in America, that everything is redeemable, that everything broken can be magically made whole again, and that what has been "dirtied" can be cleansed. Recently I saw on television that one of the soaps had introduced the character of a homeless old woman. A woman in her thirties discovers that her long-lost mother has appeared in town, on the streets. After much searching the mother is located and identified and embraced; and then she is scrubbed and dressed in style, restored in a matter of days to her former upper-class habits and role.

A triumph—but one more likely to occur on television than in real life. Yes, many of those on the streets could be transformed, rehabilitated. But there are others whose lives have been irrevocably changed, damaged beyond repair, and who no longer want help, who no longer recognize the *need* for help, and whose experience in our world has made them want only to be left alone. How, for instance, would one restore Alice's life, or reshape it in a way that would satisfy *our* notion of what a life should be? What would it take to return her to the fold? How to erase the four years of homelessness, which have become as familiar to her, and as much a home, as her "normal" life once was? Whatever we think of the way in which she has resolved her difficulties, it constitutes a sad peace made with the world. Intruding ourselves upon it in the name of redemption is by no means as simple a task—or as justifiable a task—as one might think.

It is important to understand too that however disorderly and dirty and unmanageable the world of homeless men and women like Alice appears to us, it is not without its significance, and its rules and rituals. The homeless in our cities mark out for themselves particular neighborhoods, blocks, buildings, doorways. They impose on themselves often obsessively strict routines. They reduce their world to a small area, and thereby protect themselves from a world that might otherwise be too much to bear. . . .

It is important to recognize the immensity of the changes that have occurred in the marginal world in the past twenty years. Whole sections of many cities—the Bowery in New York, the Tenderloin in San Francisco—were once ceded to the transient. In every skid-row area in America you could find what you needed to survive: hash houses, saloons offering free lunches, pawnshops, surplus-clothing stores, and, most important of all, cheap hotels and flophouses and two-bit employment agencies specializing in the kinds of labor (seasonal, shape-up) transients have always done.

It was by no means a wonderful world. But it *was* a world. Its rituals were spelled out in ways most of the participants understood. In hobo jungles up and down the tracks, whatever there was to eat went into a common pot and was divided equally. Late at night, in empties crisscrossing the country, men would speak with a certain anonymous openness, as if the shared condition of transience created among them a kind of civility.

What most people in that world wanted was simply to be left alone. Some of them had been on the road for years, itinerant workers. Others were recuperating from wounds they could never quite explain. There were young men and a few women with nothing better to do, and older men who had no families or had lost their jobs or wives, or for whom the rigor and pressure of life had proved too demanding. The marginal world offered them a respite from the other world, a world grown too much for them.

But things have changed. There began to pour into the marginal world—slowly in the sixties, a bit faster in the seventies, and then faster still in the eighties—more and more people who neither belonged nor knew how to survive there. The sixties brought the counterculture and drugs; the streets filled with young dropouts. Changes in the law loosed upon the streets mentally ill men and women. Inflation took its toll, then recession. Working-class and even middle-class men and women—entire families—began to fall into a world they did not understand.

At the same time the transient world was being inundated by new inhabitants, its landscape, its economy, was shrinking radically. Jobs became harder to find. Modernization had something to do with it; machines took the place of men and women. And the influx of workers from Mexico and points farther south created a class of semipermanent workers who took the place of casual transient labor. More important, perhaps, was the fact that the forgotten parts of many cities began to attract attention. Downtown areas were redeveloped, reclaimed. The skid-row sections of smaller cities were turned into "old townes." The old hotels that once catered to transients were upgraded or torn down or became warehouses for welfare families—an arrangement far more profitable to the owners. The price of housing increased; evictions increased. The mentally ill, who once could afford to house themselves in cheap rooms, the alcoholics, who once would drink themselves to sleep at night in their cheap hotels, were on the street—exposed to the weather and to danger, and also in plain and public view: "problems" to be dealt with.

Nor was it only cheap shelter that disappeared. It was also those "open" spaces that had once been available to those without other shelter. As property rose in value, the nooks and crannies in which the homeless had been able to hide became more visible. Doorways, alleys, abandoned buildings, vacant lots—these "holes" in the cityscape, these gaps in public consciousness, became *real estate*. The homeless, who had been there all the time, were overtaken by economic progress, and they became intruders.

You cannot help thinking, as you watch the process, of what happened in parts of Europe in the eighteenth and nineteenth centuries: the effects of the enclosure laws, which eliminated the "commons" in the countryside and drove the rural poor, now homeless, into the cities. The centuries-old tradition of common access and usage was swept away by the beginnings of industrialism; land became *privatized*, a commodity. At the same time something occurred in the cultural psyche. The world itself, space itself, was subtly altered. It was no longer merely to be lived in; it was now to be owned. What was enclosed was not only the land. It was also *the flesh itself*; it was cut off from, denied access to, the physical world.

And one thinks too, when thinking of the homeless, of the American past, the settlement of the "new" world which occurred at precisely the same time that the commons disappeared. The dream of freedom and equality that brought men and women here had something to do with *space*, as if the wilderness itself conferred upon those arriving here a new beginning: the Eden that had been lost. Once God had sent Christ to redeem men; now he provided a new world. Men discovered, or believed, that this world, and perhaps time itself, had no edge, no limit. Space was a sign of God's magnanimity. It was a kind of grace.

Somehow, it is all this that is folded into the sad shapes of the homeless. In their mute presence one can sense, however faintly, the dreams of a world gone aglimmering, and the presence of our failed hopes. A kind of claim is made, silently, an ethic is proffered, or, if you will, a whole cosmology, one older than our own ideas of privilege and property. It is as if flesh itself were seeking, this one last time, the home in the world it has been denied.

Daily the city eddies around the homeless. The crowds flowing past leave a few feet, a gap. We do not touch the homeless world. Perhaps we cannot touch it. It remains separate even as the city surrounds it.

The homeless, simply because they are homeless, are strangers, alien—and therefore a threat.

Their presence, in itself, comes to constitute a kind of violence; it deprives us of our sense of safety. Let me use myself as an example. I know, and respect, many of those now homeless on the streets of Santa Barbara. Twenty years ago, some of them would have been my companions and friends. And yet, these days, if I walk through the park near my home and see strangers bedding down for the night, my first reaction, if not fear, is a sense of annoyance and intrusion, of worry and alarm. I think of my teenage daughter, who often walks through the park, and then of my house, a hundred yards away, and I am tempted—only tempted, but tempted, still—to call the "proper" authorities to have the strangers moved on. Out of sight, out of mind.

Notice: I do not bring them food. I do not offer them shelter or a shower in the morning. I do not even stop to talk. Instead, I think: my daughter, my house, my privacy. What moves me is not the threat of *danger*—nothing as animal as that. Instead there pops up inside of me, neatly in a row, a set of anxieties, ones you might arrange in a dollhouse living room and label: Family of bourgeois fears. The point is this: our response to the homeless is fed by a complex set of cultural attitudes, habits of thought, and fantasies and fears so familiar to us, so common, that they have become a *second* nature and might as well be instinctive, for all the control we have over them. And it is by no means easy to untangle this snarl of responses. What does seem clear is that the homeless embody all that bourgeois culture has for centuries tried to eradicate and destroy.

If you look to the history of Europe you find that homelessness first appears (or is first acknowledged) at the very same moment that bourgeois culture begins to appear. The same processes produced them both: the breakup of feudalism, the rise of commerce and cities, the combined triumphs of capitalism, industrialism, and individualism. The historian Fernand Braudel, in *The Wheels of Commerce,* describes, for instance, the armies of impoverished men and women who began to haunt Europe as far back as the eleventh century. And the makeup of these masses? Essentially the same then as it is now: the unfortunates, the throwaways, the misfits, the deviants. . . .

It is in the nineteenth century, in the Victorian era, that you can find the beginnings of our modern strategies for dealing with the homeless: the notion that they should be controlled and perhaps eliminated through "help." With the Victorians we begin to see the entangling of self-protection with social obligation, the strategy of masking self-interest and the urge to control as *moral duty.* Michel Foucault has spelled out this in his books on madness and punishment: the zeal with which the overseers of early bourgeois culture tried to purge, improve, and purify all of urban civilization—whether through schools and prisons, or, quite literally, with public baths and massive new water and sewage systems. Order, ordure—this is, in essence, the tension at the heart of bourgeois culture, and it was the singular genius of the Victorians to make it the main component of their medical, aesthetic, *and* moral systems. It was not a sense of justice or even empathy which called for charity or new attitudes toward the poor; it was *hygiene.* The very same attitudes appear in nineteenth-century America. Charles Loring Brace, in an essay on homeless and vagrant children written in 1876, described the treatment of delinquents in this way: "Many of their vices drop from them like the old and verminous clothing they left behind. . . . The entire change of circumstances seems to cleanse them of bad habits." Here you have it all: *vices, verminous clothing, cleansing them of bad habits*—the triple association of poverty with vice with dirt, an equation in which each term comes to stand for all of them. . . .

What I am getting at here is the *nature* of the desire to help the homeless—what is hidden behind it and why it so often does harm. Every government program, almost every private project, is geared as much to the needs of those giving help as it is to the needs of the homeless. Go to any government agency, or, for that matter, to most private charities, and you will find yourself enmeshed, at once, in a bureaucracy so tangled and oppressive, or confronted with so much moral arrogance and contempt, that you will be driven back out into the streets for relief.

Santa Barbara, where I live, is as good an example as any. There are three main shelters in the city—all of them private. Between them they provide fewer than a hundred beds a night for the homeless. Two of the three shelters are religious in nature: the Rescue Mission and the Salvation Army. In the mission, as in most places in the country, there are elaborate and stringent rules. Beds go first to those who have not been there for two months, and you can stay for only two nights in any two-month period. No shelter is given to those who are not sober. Even if you go to the mission only for a meal, you are required to listen to sermons and participate in prayer, and you are regularly proselytized—sometimes overtly, sometimes subtly. There are obligatory, regimented showers. You go to bed precisely at ten: lights out, no reading, no talking. After the lights go out you will find fifteen men in a room with double-decker bunks. As the night progresses the room grows stuffier and hotter. Men toss, turn, cough, and moan. In the morning you are awakened precisely at five forty-five. Then breakfast. At seven-thirty you are back on the street.

The town's newest shelter was opened almost a year ago by a consortium of local churches. Families and those who are employed have first call on the beds—a policy which excludes the congenitally homeless. Alcohol is not simply forbidden *in* the shelter; those with a history of alcoholism must sign a "contract" pledging to remain sober and chemical-free. Finally, in a paroxysm of therapeutic bullying, the shelter has added a new wrinkle: if you stay more than two days you are required to fill out and then discuss with a social worker a complex form listing what you perceive as your personal failings, goals, and strategies—all of this for men and women who simply want a place to lie down out of the rain!

It is these attitudes, in various forms and permutations, that you find repeated endlessly in America. We are moved either to "redeem" the homeless or to punish them. Perhaps there is nothing consciously hostile about it. Perhaps it is simply that as the machinery of bureaucracy cranks itself up to deal with these problems, attitudes assert themselves automatically. But whatever the case, the fact remains that almost every one of our strategies for helping the homeless is simply an attempt to rearrange the world *cosmetically,* in terms of how it looks and smells to *us*. Compassion is little more than the passion for control.

The central question emerging from all this is, What does a society owe to its members in trouble, and *how* is that debt to be paid? It is a question which must be answered in two parts: first, in relation to the men and women who have been marginalized against their will, and then, in a slightly different way, in relation to those who have chosen (or accept or even prize) their marginality.

As for those who have been marginalized against their wills, I think the general answer is obvious: A society owes its members whatever it takes for them to regain their places in the social order. And when it comes to specific remedies, one need only read backward the various processes which have created homelessness and then figure out where help is likely to do the most good. But the real point here is not the specific remedies required—affordable housing, say—but the basis upon which they must be offered, the necessary underlying ethical notion we seem in this nation unable to grasp that those who are the inevitable casualties of modern industrial capitalism and the free-market system are entitled, *by right,* and by the simple virtue of their participation in that system, to whatever help they need. They are entitled to help to find and hold their places in the society whose social contract they have, in effect, signed and observed.

Look at that for just a moment: the notion of a contract. The majority of homeless Americans have kept, insofar as they could, to the terms of that contract. In any shelter these days you can find men and women who have worked ten, twenty, forty years, and whose lives have nonetheless come to nothing. These are people who cannot afford a place in the world they helped create. And in return? Is it life on the street they have earned? Or the cruel charity we so grudgingly grant them?

But those marginalized against their will are only half the problem. There remains, still, the question of whether we owe anything to those who are voluntarily marginal. What about them: the street people, the rebels, and the recalcitrants, those who have torn up their social contracts or returned them unsigned?

I was in Las Vegas last fall, and I went out to the Rescue Mission at the lower end of town, on the edge of the black ghetto, where I first stayed years ago on my way west. It was twilight, still hot; in the vacant lot next door to the mission 200 men were lining up for supper. A warm wind blew along the street lined with small houses and salvage yards, and in the distance I could see the desert's edge and the smudge of the low hills in the fading light. There were elderly alcoholics in line, and derelicts, but mainly the men were the same sort I had seen here years ago: youngish, out of work, restless and talkative, the drifters and wanderers for whom the word "wanderlust" was invented.

At supper—long communal tables, thin gruel, stale sweet rolls, ice water—a huge black man in his twenties, fierce and muscular, sat across from me. "I'm from the Coast, man," he said. "Never been away from home before. Ain't sure I like it. Sure don't like *this* place. But I lost my job back home a couple of weeks ago and figured, why wait around for another. I thought I'd come out here, see me something of the world."

After supper, a squat Portuguese man in his mid-thirties, hunkered down against the mission wall, offered me a smoke and told me: "Been sleeping in my car, up the street, for a week. Had my own business back in Omaha. But I got bored, man. Sold everything, got a little dough, came out here. Thought I'd work construction. Let me tell you, this is one tough town."

In a world better than ours, I suppose, men (or women) like this might not exist. Conservatives seem to have no trouble imagining a society so well disciplined and moral that deviance of this kind would disappear. And leftists envision a world so just, so generous, that deviance would vanish along with inequity. But I suspect that there will always be something at work in some men and women to make them restless with the systems others devise for them, and to move them outward toward the edges of the world, where life is always riskier, less organized, and easier going.

Do we owe anything to these men and women, who reject our company and what we offer and yet nonetheless seem to demand *something* from us?

We owe them, I think, at least a place to exist, a way to exist. That may not be a *moral* obligation, in the sense that our obligation to the involuntarily marginal is clearly a moral one, but it is an obligation nevertheless, one you might call an existential obligation.

Of course, it may be that I think we owe these men something because I have liked men like them, and because I want their world to be there always, as a place to hide or rest. But there is more to it than that. I think we as a society need men like these. A society needs its margins as much as it needs art and literature. It needs holes and gaps, *breathing spaces,* let us say, into which men and women can escape and live, when necessary, in ways otherwise denied them. Margins guarantee to society a flexibility, an elasticity, and allow it to accommodate itself to the natures and needs of its members. When margins vanish, society becomes too rigid, too oppressive by far, and therefore inimical to life.

It is for such reasons that, in cultures like our own, marginal men and women take on a special significance. They are all we have left to remind us of the narrowness of the received truths we take for granted. "Beyond the pale," they somehow redefine the pale, or remind us, at least, that *something* is still out there, beyond the pale. They preserve, perhaps unconsciously, a dream that would otherwise cease to exist, the dream of having a place in the world, and of being *left alone.*

Quixotic? Infantile? Perhaps. But remember Pavlov and his reflexes coded in the flesh: animal, and therefore as if given by God. What we are talking about here is *freedom,* and with it, perhaps, an echo of the dream men brought long ago, to wilderness America. I use the word "freedom" gingerly, in relation to lives like these: skewed, crippled, emptied of everything we associate with a full, or realized, freedom. But perhaps this is the condition into which freedom has fallen among us. Art has been "appreciated" out of existence; literature has become an extension of the university, replete with tenure and pensions; and as for politics, the ideologies which ring us round seem too silly or shrill by far to speak for life. What is left, then, is this mute and intransigent independence, this "waste" of life which refuses even interpretation, and which cannot be assimilated to any ideology, and which therefore can be put to no one's use. In its crippled innocence and the perfection of its superfluity it amounts, almost, to a rebellion against history, and that is no small thing.

Let me put it as simply as I can: what we see on the streets of our cities are two dramas, both of which cut to the troubled heart of the culture and demand from us a response we may not be able to make. There is the drama of those struggling to survive by regaining their place in the social order. And there is the drama of those struggling to survive outside of it.

The resolution of both struggles depends on a third drama occurring at the heart of the culture: the tension and contention between the magnanimity we owe to life and the darker tendings of the human psyche: our fear of strangeness, our hatred of defiance, our love of order and control. How we mediate by default or design between those contrary forces will determine not only the destinies of the homeless but also something crucial about the nation, and perhaps—let me say it—about our own souls.

Review Questions

1. Who are the homeless?
2. Why are people homeless according to Marin?
3. Why do the affluent want to help the homeless in Marin's view?

Discussion Questions

1. "Compassion is little more than the passion for control." Is this true?
2. Does society owe anything to those who choose to be homeless and not work?

Trudy Govier

The Right to Eat and the Duty to Work

Trudy Govier has taught philosophy at Trent University in Ontario and has written several articles on moral philosophy.

Govier discusses three different positions on the welfare question: Do needy people in an affluent society have a legal right to welfare benefits? First, there is the individualist position (called libertarianism by Hospers) that no one has a legal right to welfare benefits, not even in an affluent society. Second, there is the permissive position that in an affluent society, everyone has an unconditional legal right to welfare benefits. Third, there is the puritan position that everyone has a legal right to welfare, but this right ought to be conditional on one's willingness to work. After evaluating these three positions in terms of their social consequences (the "teleological appraisal") and social justice, Govier concludes that the permissive position is superior.

Although the topic of welfare is not one with which philosophers have often concerned themselves, it is a topic which gives rise to many complex and fascinating questions—some in the area of political philosophy, some in the area of ethics, and some of a more practical kind. The variety of issues related to the subject of welfare

From Trudy Govier, "The Right to Eat and the Duty to Work," *Philosophy of the Social Sciences*, Vol. 5 (1975), pp. 125-143. Reprinted with permission of the author and *Philosophy of the Social Sciences*.

makes it particularly necessary to be clear just which issue one is examining in a discussion of welfare. In a recent book on the subject, Nicholas Rescher asks:

> In what respects and to what extent is society, working through the instrumentality of the state, responsible for the welfare of its members? What demands for the promotion of his welfare can an individual reasonably make upon his society? These are questions to which no answer can be given in terms of some ***a priori*** approach with reference to universal ultimates. Whatever answer can appropriately be given will depend, in the final analysis, on what the society decides it should be.[1]

Rescher raises this question only to avoid it. His response to his own question is that a society has all and only those responsibilities for its members that it thinks it has. Although this claim is trivially true as regards legal responsibilities, it is inadequate from a moral perspective. If one imagines the case of an affluent society which leaves the blind, the disabled, and the needy to die of starvation, the incompleteness of Rescher's account becomes obvious. In this imagined case one is naturally led to raise the question as to whether those in power ought to supply those in need with the necessities of life. Though the needy have no legal right to welfare benefits of any kind, one might very well say that they ought to have such a right. It is this claim which I propose to discuss here.[2]

I shall approach this issue by examining three positions which may be adopted in response to it. These are:

1. *The Individualist Position:* Even in an affluent society, one ought not to have any legal right to state-supplied welfare benefits.
2. *The Permissive Position:* In a society with sufficient resources, one ought to have an unconditional legal right to receive state supplied welfare benefits. (That is, one's right to receive such benefits ought not to depend on one's behavior, it should be guaranteed).
3. *The Puritan Position:* In a society with sufficient resources one ought to have a legal right to state-supplied welfare benefits; this right ought to be conditional, however, on one's willingness to work.

But before we examine these positions, some preliminary clarification must be attempted. . . .

Welfare systems are state-supported systems which supply benefits, usually in the form of cash income, to those who are in need. Welfare systems thus exist in the sort of social context where there is some private ownership of property. If no one owned anything individually (except possibly his own body), and all goods were considered to be the joint property of everyone, then this type of welfare system could not exist. A state might take on the responsibility for the welfare of its citizens, but it could not meet this responsibility by distributing a level of cash income which such citizens would spend to purchase the goods essential for life. The welfare systems which exist in the western world do exist against the background of extensive private ownership of property. It is in this context that I propose to discuss moral questions about having a right to welfare benefits. By setting out my questions in this way, I do not intend to endorse the institution of private property, but only to discuss questions which many people find real and difficult in the context of the social organization which they actually do experience. The present analysis of welfare is intended to apply to societies which (*a*) have the institution of private property, if not for means of production, at least for some basic good; and (*b*) possess sufficient resources so that it is at least possible for every member of the society to be supplied with the necessities of life.

The Individualist View

It might be maintained that a person in need has no legitimate moral claim on those around him and that the hypothetical inattentive society which left its blind citizens to beg or starve cannot rightly be censured for doing so. This view, which is dramatically at odds with most of contemporary social thinking, lives on in the writings of Ayn Rand and her followers.[3] The Individualist sets a high value on uncoerced personal choice. He sees each person as a responsible agent who is able to make his own decisions and to plan his own life. He insists that with the freedom to make decisions goes responsibility for the consequences of those decisions. A person has every right, for example, to spend ten years of his life studying Sanskrit—but, if as a result of this choice, he is unemployable, he ought not to expect others to labour on his behalf. No one has a proper claim on the labour of another, or on the income ensuing from that labour, unless he can repay the labourer in a way acceptable to that labourer himself. Government welfare schemes provide benefits from funds gained largely by taxing earned income. One cannot "opt out" of such schemes. To the Individualist, this means that a person is forced to work part of his time for others.

Suppose that a man works forty hours and earns two hundred dollars. Under modern-day taxation, it may well be that he can spend only two-thirds of that money the way he chooses. The rest is taken by government and goes to support programmes which the working individual may not himself endorse. The beneficiaries of such programmes—those beneficiaries who do not work themselves—are as though they have slaves working for them. Backed by the force which government authorities can command, they are able to exist on the earnings of others. Those who support them do not do so voluntarily, out of charity; they do so on government command.

Someone across the street is unemployed. Should you be taxed extra to pay for his expenses? Not at all. You have not injured him, you are not responsible for the fact that he is unemployed (unless you are a senator or bureaucrat who agitated for further curtailing of business which legislation passed, with the result that your neighbor was laid off by the curtailed business). You may voluntarily wish to help him out, or better still, try to get him a job to put him on his feet again; but since you have initiated no aggressive act against him, and neither purposefully nor accidentally injured him in any way, you should not be legally penalized for the fact of his unemployment.[4]

The Individualist need not lack concern for those in need. He may give generously to charity; he might give more generously still, if his whole income were his to use, as he would like it to be. He may also believe, that, as a matter of empirical fact, existing government programmes do not actually help the poor. They support a cumbersome bureaucracy and they use financial resources which, if untaxed, might be used by those with initiative to pursue job-creating endeavors. The thrust of the Individualist's position is that each person owns his own body and his own labour; thus each person is taken to have a virtually unconditional right to the income which that labour can earn him in a free market place.[5] For anyone to pre-empt part of a worker's earnings without the worker's voluntary consent is tantamount to robbery. And the fact that the government is the intermediary through which this deed is committed does not change its moral status one iota.

On an Individualist's view, those in need should be cared for by charities or through other schemes to which contributions are voluntary. Many people may wish to insure themselves against unforeseen calamities and they should be free to do so. But there is no justification for non-optional government schemes financed by taxpayers' money. . . .

The Permissive View

Directly contrary to the Individualist view of welfare is what I have termed the Permissive view. According to this view, in a society which has sufficient resources so that everyone could be supplied with the necessities of life, every individual ought to be given the legal right to social security, and this right ought not to be conditional in any way upon an individual's behavior. *Ex hypothesi* the society which we are discussing has sufficient goods to provide everyone with food, clothing, shelter and other necessities. Someone who does without these basic goods is scarcely living at all, and a society which takes no steps to change this state of affairs implies by its inaction that the life of such a person is without value. It does not execute him; but it may allow him to die. It does not put him in prison; but it may leave him with a life of lower quality than that of some prison inmates. A society which can rectify these circumstances and does not can justly be accused of imposing upon the needy either death or lifelong deprivation. And those characteristics which make a person needy—whether they be illness, old age, insanity, feeblemindedness, inability to find paid work, or even poor moral character—are insufficient to make him deserve the fate to which an inactive society would in effect condemn him. One would not be executed for inability or failure to find paid work; neither should one be allowed to die for this misfortune or failing.

A person who cannot or does not find his own means of social security does not therefore forfeit his status as a human being. If other human beings, with physical, mental and moral qualities different from his, are regarded as having the right to life and to the means of life, then so too should he be regarded. A society which does not accept the responsibility for supplying such a person with the basic necessities of life is, in effect, endorsing a difference between its members which is without moral justification. . . .

The adoption of a Permissive view of welfare would have significant practical implications. If there were a legal right, unconditional upon behaviour, to a specified level of state-supplied benefits, then state investigation of the prospective welfare recipient could be kept to a minimum. Why he is in need, whether he can work, whether he is willing to work, and what he does while receiving welfare benefits are on this view quite irrelevant to his right to receive those benefits. A welfare recipient is a person who claims from his society that to which he is legally entitled under a morally based welfare scheme. The fact that he makes this claim licenses no special state or societal interference with his behaviour. If the Permissive view of welfare were widely believed, then there would be no social stigma attached to being on welfare. There is such a stigma, and many long-term welfare recipients are considerably demoralized by their dependent status.[6] These facts suggest that the Permissive view of welfare is not widely held in our society.

The Puritan View

This view of welfare rather naturally emerges when we consider that no one can have a right to something without someone else's, or some group of other persons', having responsibilities correlative to this right. In the case in which the right in question is a legal right to social security, the correlative responsibilities may be rather extensive. They have been deemed responsibilities of "the state." The state will require resources and funds to meet these responsibilities, and these do not emerge from the sky miraculously, or zip into existence as a consequence of virtually effortless acts of will. They are taken by the state from its citizens, often in the form of taxation on earned income. The funds given to the welfare recipient and many of the goods which he purchases with these funds are produced by other members of society, many of whom give a considerable portion of their time and their energy to this end. If a state has the moral responsibility to ensure the social security of its citizens then all the citizens of that state have the responsibility to provide state agencies with the means to carry out their duties. This responsibility, in our present contingent circumstances, seems to generate an obligation to *work*.

A person who works helps to produce the goods which all use in daily living and, when paid, contributes through taxation to government endeavours. The person who does not work, even though able to work, does not make his contribution to social efforts towards obtaining the means of life. He is not entitled to a share of the goods produced by others if he chooses not to take part in their labours. Unless he can show that there is a moral justification for his not making the sacrifice of time and energy which others make, he has no legitimate claim to welfare benefits. If he is disabled or unable to obtain work, he cannot work; hence he has no need to justify his failure to work. But if he does choose not to work, he would have to justify his choice by saying "others should sacrifice their time and energy for me; I have no need to sacrifice time and energy for them." This principle, a version of what Rawls refers to as a **free-rider's principle**, simply will not stand up to criticism.[7] To deliberately avoid working and benefit from the labours of others is morally indefensible.

Within a welfare system erected on these principles, the right to welfare is conditional upon one's satisfactorily accounting for his failure to obtain the necessities of life by his own efforts. Someone who is severely disabled mentally or physically, or who for some other reason cannot work, is morally entitled to receive welfare benefits. Someone who chooses not to work is not. The Puritan view of welfare is a kind of compromise between the Individualist view and the Permissive view. . . .

The Puritan view of welfare, based as it is on the inter-relation between welfare and work, provides a rationale for two connected principles which those establishing welfare schemes in Canada and in the United States seem to endorse. First of all, those on welfare should never receive a higher income than the working poor. Secondly, a welfare scheme should, in some way or other, incorporate incentives to work. These principles, which presuppose that it is better to work than not to work, emerge rather naturally from the contingency which is at the basis of the Puritan view: the goods essential for social security are products of the labour of some members of society. If we wish to have a continued supply of such goods, we must encourage those who work to produce them. . . .

Appraisal of Policies: Social Consequences and Social Justice

In approaching the appraisal of prospective welfare policies under these two aspects I am, of course, making some assumptions about the moral appraisal of suggested social policies. Although these cannot possibly be justified here, it may be helpful to articulate them, at least in a rough way.

Appraisal of social policies is in part teleological. To the extent that a policy, P, increases the total human welfare more than does an alternate policy, P′, P is a better social policy than P′. Or, if P leaves the total human welfare as it is, while P′ diminishes it, then to that extent, P is a better social policy than P′. Even this skeletal formulation of the teleological aspect of appraisal reveals why appraisal cannot be entirely teleological. We consider total consequences—effects upon the total of "human well-being in a society. But this total is a summation of consequences on different individuals. It includes no judgments as to how far we allow one individual's well-being to decrease while another's increases, under the same policy. Judgements relating to the latter problems are judgements about social justice.

In appraising social policies we have to weigh up considerations of total well-being against considerations of justice. Just how this is to be done, precisely, I would not pretend to know. However, the absence of precise methods does not mean that we should relinquish attempts at appraisal: some problems are already with us, and thought which is necessarily tentative and imprecise is still preferable to no thought at all.

Consequences of Welfare Schemes

First, let us consider the consequences of the non-scheme advocated by the Individualist. He would have to abolish all non-optional government programmes which have as their goal the improvement of anyone's personal welfare. This rejection extends to health schemes, pension plans and education, as well as to welfare and unemployment insurance. So following the Individualist would lead to very sweeping changes.

The Individualist will claim (as do Hospers and Ayn Rand) that on the whole his non-scheme will bring beneficial consequences. He will admit, as he must, that there are people who would suffer tremendously if welfare and other social security programmes were simply terminated. Some would even die as a result. We cannot assume that spontaneously developing charities would cover every case of dire need. Nevertheless the Individualist wants to point to benefits which would accrue to businessmen and to working people and their families if taxation were drastically cut. It is his claim that consumption would rise, hence production would rise, job opportunities would be extended, and there would be an economic boom, if people could only spend all their earned income as they wished. This boom would benefit both rich and poor.

There are significant omissions which are necessary in order to render the Individualist's optimism plausible. Either workers and businessmen would have insurance of various kinds, or they would be insecure in their prosperity. If they did have insurance to cover health problems, old age and possible job loss, then they would pay for it; hence they would not be spending their whole earned income on consumer goods. Those who run the insurance schemes could, of course, put this money back into the economy—but government schemes already do this. The economic boom under Individualism would not be as loud as originally expected. Furthermore the goal of increased consumption-increased productivity must be questioned from an ecological viewpoint: many necessary materials are available only in limited quantities.

Finally, a word about charity. It is not to be expected that those who are at the mercy of charities will benefit from this state, either materially or psychologically. Those who prosper will be able to choose between giving a great deal to charity and suffering from the very real insecurity and guilt which would accompany the existence of starvation and grim poverty outside their padlocked doors. It is to be hoped that they would opt for the first alternative. But, if they did, this might be every bit as expensive for them as government-supported benefit schemes are now. If they did not give generously to charity, violence might result. However one looks at it, the consequences of Individualism are unlikely to be good.

Welfare schemes operating in Canada today are almost without exception based upon the principles of the Puritan view. To see the consequences of that type of welfare scheme we have only to look at the results of our own welfare programmes. Taxation to support such schemes is high, though not so intolerably so as to have led to widescale resentment among taxpayers. Canadian welfare programmes are attended by complicated and often cumbersome bureaucracy, some of which results for the interlocking of municipal, provincial and federal governments in the administration and financing of welfare programmes. The cost of the programmes is no doubt increased by this bureaucracy; not all the tax money directed to welfare programmes goes to those in need. Puritan welfare schemes do not result in social catastrophe or in significant business stagnation—this much we know, because we already live with such schemes. Their adverse consequences, if any, are felt primarily not by society generally nor by businessmen and the working segment of the public, but rather by recipients of welfare.

Both the Special Senate Committee Report on Poverty and the Real Poverty Report criticize our present system of welfare for its demoralization of recipients, who often must deal with several levels of government and are vulnerable to arbitrary interference on the part of administering officials. Welfare officials have the power to check on welfare recipients and cut off or limit their benefits under a large number of circumstances. The dangers to welfare recipients in terms of anxiety, threats to privacy and loss of dignity are obvious. According to the Senate Report, the single aspect shared by all Canada's welfare system is "a record of failure and insufficiency, of bureaucratic rigidities that often result in the degradation, humiliation and alienation of recipients." [8] The writers of this report cite many instances of humiliation, leaving the impression that these are too easily found to be "incidental aberrations." [9] Concern that a welfare recipient either be unable to work or be willing to work (if unemployed) can easily turn into concern about how he spends the income supplied him, what his plans for the future are, where he lives, how many children he has. And the rationale underlying the Puritan scheme makes the degradation of welfare recipients a natural consequence of welfare institutions. Work is valued and only he who works is thought to contribute to society. Welfare recipients are regarded as parasites and spongers—so when they are treated as such, this is only what we should have expected. Being on welfare in a society which thinks and acts in this fashion can be psychologically debilitating. Welfare recipients who are demoralized by their downgraded status and relative lack of personal freedom can be expected to be made less capable of self-sufficiency. To the extent that this is so, welfare systems erected on Puritan principles may defeat their own purposes.

In fairness, it must be noted here that bureaucratic checks and controls are not a feature only of Puritan welfare systems. To a limited extent, Permissive systems would have to incorporate them too. Within those systems, welfare benefits would be given only to those whose income was inadequate to meet basic needs. However, there would be no checks on "willingness to work," and there would be no need for welfare workers to evaluate the merits of the daily activities of recipients. If a Permissive guaranteed income system were administered through income tax returns, everyone receiving the basic income and those not needing it paying it back in taxes, then the special status of welfare recipients would fade. They would no longer be singled out as a special group within the population. It is to be expected that living solely on government-supplied benefits would be psychologically easier in that type of situation.

Thus it can be argued that for the recipients of welfare, a Permissive scheme has more advantages that a Puritan one. This is not a very surprising conclusion. The Puritan scheme is relatively disadvantageous to recipients, and Puritans would acknowledge this point; they will argue that the overall consequences of Permissive schemes are negative in that these schemes benefit some at too great a cost to others. (Remember, we are not yet concerned with the *justice* of welfare policies, but solely with their consequences as regards *total* human well-being within the society in question.) The concern which most people have regarding the Permissive scheme relates to its costs and its dangers to the "work ethic." It is commonly thought that people work only because they have to work to survive in a tolerable style. If a guaranteed income scheme were adopted by the government, this incentive to work would disappear. No one would be faced with the choice between a nasty and boring job and starvation. Who would do the nasty and boring jobs then? Many of them are not eliminable and they have to be done somehow, by someone. Puritans fear that a great many people—even some with relatively pleasant jobs—might simply cease to work if they could receive non-stigmatized government money to live on. If this were to happen, the permissive society would simply grind to a halt.

In addressing these anxieties about the consequences of Permissive welfare schemes, we must recall that welfare benefits are set to ensure only that those who do not work have a bearable existence, with an income sufficient for basic needs, and that they have this income regardless of why they fail to work. Welfare benefits will not finance luxury living for a family of five! If jobs are adequately paid so that workers receive more than the minimum welfare income in an earned salary, then there will still be a financial incentive to take jobs. What guaranteed income schemes will do is to raise the salary floor. This change will benefit the many non-unionized workers in service and clerical occupations.

Furthermore it is unlikely that people work solely due to (i) the desire for money and the things it can buy and (ii) belief in the Puritan work ethic. There are many other reasons for working, some of which would persist in a society which had adopted a Permissive welfare system. Most people are happier when their time is structured in some way, when they are active outside their own homes, when they feel themselves part of an endeavour whose purposes transcend their particular egoistic ones. Women often choose to work outside the home for these reasons as much as for financial ones. With these and other factors operating I cannot see that the adoption of a Permissive welfare scheme would be followed by a level of slothfulness which would jeopardize human well-being.

Another worry about the Permissive scheme concerns cost. It is difficult to comment on this in a general way, since it would vary so much from case to case. Of Canada at the present it has been said that a guaranteed income scheme administered through income tax would cost less than social security payments administered through the present bureaucracies. It is thought that this saving would result from a drastic cut in administrative costs. The matter of the work ethic is also relevant to the question of costs. Within a Puritan framework it is very important to have a high level of employment and there is a tendency to resist any reorganization which results in there being fewer jobs available. Some of these proposed reorganizations would save money; strictly speaking we should count the cost of keeping jobs which are objectively unnecessary as part of the cost of Puritanism regarding welfare.

In summary, we can appraise Individualism, Puritanism and Permissivism with respect to their anticipated consequences, as follows: Individualism is unacceptable; Puritanism is tolerable, but has some undesirable consequences for welfare recipients; Permissivism appears to be the winner. Worries about bad effects which Permissive welfare schemes might have due to high costs and (alleged) reduced work-incentives appear to be without solid basis.

Social Justice Under Proposed Welfare Schemes

We must now try to consider the merits of Individualism, Puritanism and Permissivism with regard to their impact on the distribution of the goods necessary for well-being. [Robert] Nozick has argued against the whole conception of a distributive justice on the grounds that it presupposes that goods are like manna from heaven: we simply get them and then have a problem—to whom to give them. According to Nozick we know where things come from and we do not have the problem of to whom to give them. There is not really a problem of distributive justice, for there is no central distributor giving out manna from heaven! It is necessary to counter Nozick on this point since his reaction to the (purported) problems of distributive justice would undercut much of what follows.[10]

There is a level at which Nozick's point is obviously valid. If A discovers a cure for cancer, then it is A and not B or C who is responsible for this discovery. On Nozick's view this is taken to imply that A should reap any monetary profits which are forthcoming; other people will benefit from the cure itself. Now although it cannot be doubted that A is a bright and hard-working person, neither can it be denied that A and his circumstances are the product of many co-operative endeavours: schools and laboratories, for instance. Because this is so, I find Nozick's claim that "we know where things come from" unconvincing at a deeper level. Since achievements like A's presuppose extensive social co-operation, it is morally permissible to regard even the monetary profits accruing from them as shareable by the "owner" and society at large.

Laws support existing income levels in many ways. Governments specify taxation so as to further determine net income. Property ownership is a legal matter. In all these ways people's incomes and possibilities for obtaining income are affected by deliberate state action. It is always possible to raise questions about the moral desirability of actual conventional arrangements. Should university professors earn less than lawyers? More than waitresses? Why? Why not? Anyone who gives an account of distributive justice is trying to specify principles which will make it possible to answer questions such as these, and nothing in Nozick's argument suffices to show that the questions are meaningless or unimportant.

Any human distribution of anything is unjust insofar as differences exist for no good reason. If goods did come like manna from heaven and the Central Distributor gave A ten times more than B, we should want to know why. The skewed distribution might be deemed a just one if A's needs were objectively ten times greater than B's, or if B refused to accept more than his small portion of goods. But is no reason at all could be given for it, or if only an irrelevant reason could be given (e.g., A is blue-eyed and B is not), then it is an unjust distribution. All the views we have expounded concerning welfare permit differences in income level. Some philosophers would say that such differences are never just, although they may be necessary, for historical or utilitarian reasons. Whether or not this is so, it is admittedly very difficult to say just what would constitute a good reason for giving A a higher income than B. Level of need, degree of responsibility, amount of training, unpleasantness of work—all these have been proposed and all have some plausibility. We do not need to tackle all this larger problem in order to consider justice under proposed welfare systems. For we can deal here solely with the question of whether everyone should receive a floor level of income; decisions on this matter are independent of decisions on overall equality or principles of variation among incomes above the floor. The Permissivist contends that all should receive at least the floor income; the Individualist and the Puritan deny this. All would claim justice for their side.

The Individualist attempts to justify extreme variations in income, with some people below the level where they can fulfill their basic needs, with reference to the fact of people's actual accomplishments. This approach to the question is open to the same objections as those which have already been raised against Nozick's non-manna-from-heaven argument, and I shall not repeat them here. Let us move on to the Puritan account. It is because goods emerge from human efforts that the Puritan advances his view of welfare. He stresses the unfairness of a system which would permit some people to take advantage of others. A Permissive welfare system would do this, as it makes no attempt to distinguish between those who choose not to work and those who cannot work. No one should be able to take advantage of another under the auspices of a government institution. The Puritan scheme seeks to eliminate this possibility, and for that reason, Puritans would allege, it is a more just scheme than the Permissive one.

Permissivists can best reply to this contention by acknowledging that any instance of free-riding would be an instance where those working were done an injustice, but by showing that any justice which the Puritan preserves by eliminating free-riding is outweighed by *injustice* perpetrated elsewhere. Consider the children of the Puritan's free-riders. They will suffer greatly for the "sins" of their parents. Within the institution of the family, the Puritan cannot suitably hurt the guilty without cruelly depriving the innocent. There is a sense, too, in which Puritanism does injustice to the many people on welfare who are not free-riders. It perpetuates the opinion that they are non-contributors to society and this doctrine, which is over-simplified if not downright false, has a harmful effect upon welfare recipients.

Social justice is not simply a matter of the distribution of goods, or the income with which goods are to be purchased. It is also a matter of the protection of rights. Western societies claim to give their citizens equal rights in political and legal contexts; they also claim to endorse the larger conception of a right to life. Now it is possible to interpret these rights in a limited and formalistic way, so that the duties correlative to them are minimal. On the limited, or negative, interpretation, to say that A has a right to life is simply to say that others have a duty not to interfere with A's attempts to keep himself alive. This interpretation of the right to life is compatible with Individualism as well as with Puritanism. But it is an inadequate interpretation of the right to life and of other rights. A right to vote is meaningless if one is starving and unable to get to the polls; a right to equality before the law is meaningless if one cannot afford to hire a lawyer. And so on.

Even a Permissive welfare scheme will go only a very small way towards protecting people's rights. It will amount to a meaningful acknowledgment of a right to life, by ensuring income adequate to purchase food, clothing and shelter—at the very least. These minimum necessities are presupposed by all other rights a society may endorse in that their possession is a precondition of being able to exercise these other rights. Because it protects the rights of all within a society better than do Puritanism and Individualism, the Permissive view can rightly claim superiority over the others with regard to justice.

Endnotes

1. Nichols Rescher, *Welfare: Social Issues in Philosophical Perspective,* p. 114.
2. One might wish to discuss moral questions concerning welfare in the context of **natural rights** doctrines. Indeed, Article 22 of the United Nations Declaration of Human Rights states, "Everyone, as a member of society, has the right to social security and is entitled, through a national effort and international cooperation and in accordance with the organization and resources of each State, to the economic, social, and cultural

rights indispensable for his dignity and the free development of his personality." I make no attempt to defend the right to welfare as a natural right. Granting that rights imply responsibilities or duties and that "ought" implies "can," it would only be intelligible to regard the right to social security as a natural right if all states were able to ensure the minimum well-being of their citizens. This is not the case. And a natural right is one which is by definition supposed to belong to all human beings simply in virtue of their status as human beings. The analysis given here in the permissive view is compatible with the claim that all human beings have a *prima facie* natural right to social security. It is not, however, compatible with the claim that all human beings have a natural right to social security if this right is regarded as one which is so absolute as to be inviolable under any and all conditions.

3. See, for example, Ayn Rand's *Atlas Shrugged, The Virtue of Selfishness, and Capitalism: the Unknown Ideal.*
4. John Hospers, *Libertarianism: A Political Philosophy for Tomorrow,* p. 67.
5. I say virtually unconditional, because an Individualist such as John Hospers sees a legitimate moral role for government in preventing the use of force by some citizens against others. Since this is the case, I presume that he would also regard as legitimate such taxation as was necessary to support this function. Presumably that taxation would be seen as consented to by all, on the grounds that all "really want" government protection.
6. Ian Adams, William Cameron, Brian Hill, and Peter Penz, *The Real Poverty Report,* pp. 167-187.
7. See *A Theory of Justice,* pp. 124, 136. Rawls defines the free-rider as one who relies on the principle "everyone is to act justly except for myself, if I choose not to," and says that his position is a version of egoism which is eliminated as a morally acceptable principle by formal constraints. This conclusion regarding the tenability of egoism is one which I accept and which is taken for granted in the present context.
8. *Senate Report on Poverty,* p. 73.
9. The Hamilton Public Welfare Department takes automobile license plates from recipients, making them available again only to those whose needs meet with the Department's approval. (*Real Poverty Report,* p. 186.) The *Globe and Mail* for 12 January 1974 reported that welfare recipients in the city of Toronto are to be subjected to computerized budgeting. In the summer of 1973, the two young daughters of an Alabama man on welfare were sterilized against their own wishes and without their parents' informed consent. (See *Time,* 23 July 1973.)
10. Robert Nozick, "Distributive Justice," *Philosophy and Public Affairs,* Fall 1973.

Review Questions

1. Distinguish between the individualist view, the permissive view, and the puritan view (as Govier explains them).
2. State the free-rider principle. Why does Govier reject it?
3. Compare the consequences of the three views as Govier describes them.
4. What is Govier's conclusion with respect to the consequences of the three positions?
5. What is Govier's objection to the individualist's view with respect to justice?
6. How does Govier characterize social justice?
7. Which of the three positions is superior according to Govier and why?

Discussion Questions

1. Does everyone in a rich society such as the United States have a right to welfare? Explain your answer.
2. Does everyone in a society who is able to work have a right to work? Why or why not?
3. Is a person who is able to work, but who chooses not to work entitled to welfare? What is your position on this free-rider problem?
4. Some women with dependent children receive more money from welfare than they could make working at low-paying jobs. This gives them an incentive not to work. Is this acceptable? What is your view?
5. Is a guaranteed income administered through the income tax a good idea? What do you think of Govier's suggestion?

Charles Murray

A Proposal for Public Welfare

Charles Murray is a Bradley Fellow at the Manhattan Institute for Policy Research. The reading is taken from his book Losing Ground: American Social Policy 1950-1980 (1984).

Murray advocates a radical conservative solution to the welfare problem: Eliminate all federal welfare for working-aged persons except unemployment insurance. He argues that most of the population will be unaffected, and those who are affected will be strongly encouraged to support themselves. The hard-core welfare-dependents who can't or won't find jobs can turn to their families, or local or private services.

I begin with the proposition that it is within our resources to do enormous good for some people quickly. We have available to us a program that would convert a large proportion of the younger generation of hardcore unemployed into steady workers making a living wage. The same program would drastically reduce births to single teenage girls. It would reverse the trendline in the breakup of poor families. It would measurably increase the upward socioeconomic mobility of poor families. These improvements would affect some millions of persons.

All these are results that have eluded the efforts of the social programs installed since 1965, yet, from everything we know, there is no real question about whether they would occur under the program I propose. A wide variety of persuasive evidence from our own culture and around the world, from experimental data and longitudinal studies, from theory and practice, suggests that the program would achieve such results.

The proposed program, our final and most ambitious thought experiment, consists of scrapping the entire federal welfare and income-support structure for working-aged persons, including AFDC, Medicaid, Food Stamps, Unemployment Insurance, Worker's Compensation, subsidized housing, disability insurance, and the rest. It would leave the working-aged person with no recourse whatsoever except the job market, family members, friends, and public or private locally funded services. It is the Alexandrian solution: cut the knot, for there is no way to untie it.

It is difficult to examine such a proposal dispassionately. Those who dislike paying for welfare are for it without thinking. Others reflexively imagine bread lines and people starving in the streets. But as a means of gaining fresh perspective on the problem of effective reform, let us consider what this hypothetical society might look like.

A large majority of the population is unaffected. A surprising number of the huge American middle and working classes go from birth to grave without using any social welfare benefits until they receive their first Social Security check. Another portion of the population is technically affected, but the change in income is so small or so sporadic that it makes no difference in quality of life. A third group comprises persons who have to make new arrangements and behave in different ways. Sons and daughters who fail to find work continue to live with their parents or relatives or friends. Teenage mothers have to rely on support from their parents or the father of the child and perhaps work as well. People laid off from work have to use their own savings or borrow from others to make do until the next job is found. All these changes involve great disruption in expectations and accustomed roles.

From Charles Murray, *Losing Ground: American Social Policy,1950-1980. Copyright © 1984 by Charles Murray. Reprinted by permission of Basic Books, a division of HarperCollins Publishers, Inc.*

Along with the disruptions go other changes in behavior. Some parents do not want their young adult children continuing to live off their income, and become quite insistent about their children learning skills and getting jobs. This attitude is most prevalent among single mothers who have to depend most critically on the earning power of their offspring.

Parents tend to become upset at the prospect of a daughter's bringing home a baby that must be entirely supported on an already inadequate income. Some become so upset that they spend considerable parental energy avoiding such an eventuality. Potential fathers of such babies find themselves under more pressure not to cause such a problem, or to help with its solution if it occurs.

Adolescents who are not job-ready find they are job-ready after all. It turns out that they can work for low wages and accept the discipline of the workplace if the alternative is grim enough. After a few years, many—not all, but many—find that they have acquired salable skills, or that they are at the right place at the right time, or otherwise find that the original entry-level job has gradually been transformed into a secure job paying a decent wage. A few—not a lot, but a few—find that the process leads to affluence.

Perhaps the most rightful, deserved benefit goes to the much larger population of low-income families who have been doing things right all along and have been punished for it: the young man who has taken responsibility for his wife and child even though his friends with the same choice have called him a fool; the single mother who has worked full time and forfeited her right to welfare for very little extra money; the parents who have set an example for their children even as the rules of the game have taught their children that the example is outmoded. For these millions of people the instantaneous result is that no one makes fun of them any longer. The longer-term result will be that they regain the status that is properly theirs. They will not only be the bedrock upon which the community is founded (which they always have been), they will be recognized as such. The process whereby they regain their position is not magical, but a matter of logic. When it becomes highly dysfunctional for a person to be dependent, status will accrue to being independent, and in fairly short order. Noneconomic rewards will once again reinforce the economic rewards of being a good parent and provider.

The prospective advantages are real and extremely plausible. In fact, if a government program of the traditional sort (one that would "do" something rather than simply get out of the way) could *as plausibly* promise these advantages, its passage would be a foregone conclusion. Congress, yearning for programs that are not retreads of failures, would be prepared to spend billions. Negative side-effects (as long as they were the traditionally acceptable negative side-effects) would be brushed aside as trivial in return for the benefits. For let me be quite clear: I am not suggesting that we dismantle income support for the working-aged to balance the budget or punish welfare cheats. I am hypothesizing, with the advantage of powerful collateral evidence, that the lives of large numbers of poor people would be radically changed for the better.

There is, however, a fourth segment of the population yet to be considered, those who are pauperized by the withdrawal of government supports and unable to make alternate arrangements: the teenaged mother who has no one to turn to; the incapacitated or the inept who are thrown out of the house; those to whom economic conditions have brought long periods in which there is no work to be had; those with illnesses not covered by insurance. What of these situations?

The first resort is the network of local services. Poor communities in our hypothetical society are still dotted with storefront health clinics, emergency relief agencies, employment services, legal services. They depend for support on local taxes or local philanthropy, and the local taxpayers and philanthropists tend to scrutinize them rather closely. But, by the same token, they also receive considerably more resources than they formerly did. The dismantling of the federal services has poured tens of billions of dollars back into the private economy. Some of that money no doubt has been spent on Mercedes and summer homes on the Cape. But some has been spent on capital investments that generate new jobs. And some has been spent on increased local services to the poor, voluntarily or as decreed by this municipality. In many cities, the coverage provided by this network of agencies is more generous, more humane, more wisely distributed, and more effective in its results than the services formerly subsidized by the federal government.

But we must expect that a large number of people will fall between the cracks. How might we go about trying to retain the advantages of a zero-level welfare system and still address the residual needs?

As we think about the nature of the population still in need, it becomes apparent that their basic problem in the vast majority of the cases is the lack of a job, and this problem is temporary. What they need is something to tide them over while finding a new place in the economy. So our first step is to reinstall the Unemployment Insurance program in more or less its previous form. Properly administered, unemployment insurance makes sense. Even if it is restored with all the defects of current practice, the negative effects of Unemployment Insurance *alone* are relatively minor. Our objective is not to wipe out chicanery or to construct a theoretically unblemished system, but to meet legitimate human needs without doing more harm than good. Unemployment Insurance is one of the least harmful ways of contributing to such ends., Thus the system has been amended to take care of the victims of short-term swings in the economy.

Who is left? We are now down to the hardest of the hard core of the welfare-dependent. They have no jobs. They have been unable to find jobs (or have not tried to find jobs) for a longer period of time than the unemployment benefits cover. They have no families who will help. For some reason, they cannot get help from local services or private charities except for the soup kitchen and a bed in the Salvation Army hall.

What will be the size of this population? We have never tried a zero-level federal welfare system under conditions of late-twentieth-century national wealth, so we cannot do more than speculate. But we may speculate. Let us ask of whom the population might consist and how they might fare.

For any category of "needy" we may name, we find ourselves driven to one of two lines of thought. Either the person is in a category that is going to be at the top of the list of services that localities vote for themselves, and at the top of the list of private services, or the person is in a category where help really is not all that essential or desirable. The burden of the conclusion is that every single person will be taken care of, but that the extent of resources to deal with needs is likely to be very great—not based on wishful thinking, but on extrapolations from reality.

To illustrate, let us consider the plight of the stereotypical welfare mother—never married, no skills, small children, no steady help from a man. It is safe to say that, now as in the 1950s, there is no one who has less sympathy from the white middle class, which is to be the source of most of the money for the private and local services we envision. Yet this same white middle class is a soft touch for people trying to make it on their own, and a soft touch for "deserving" needy mothers—AFDC was one of the most widely popular of the New Deal welfare measures, intended as it was for widows with small children. Thus we may envision two quite different scenarios.

In one scenario, the woman is presenting the local or private service with this proposition: "Help me find a job and day-care for my children, and I will take care of the rest." In effect, she puts herself into the same category as the widow and the deserted wife—identifies herself as one of the most obviously deserving of the deserving poor. Welfare mothers who want to get into the labor force are likely to find a wide range of help. In the other scenario, she asks for an outright and indefinite cash grant—in effect, a private or local version of AFDC—so that she can stay with the children and not hold a job. In the latter case, it is very easy to imagine situations in which she will not be able to find a local service or a private philanthropy to provide the help she seeks. The question we must now ask is: What's so bad about that? If children were always better off being with their mother all day and if, by the act of giving birth, a mother acquired the inalienable right to be with the child, then her situation would be unjust to her and injurious to her children. Neither assertion can be defended, however—especially not in the 1980s, when more mothers of all classes work away from the home than ever before, and even more especially not in view of the empirical record for the children growing up under the current welfare system. Why should the mother be exempted by the system from the pressures that must affect everyone else's decision to work?

As we survey these prospects, important questions remain unresolved. The first of these is why, if federal social transfers are treacherous, should locally mandated transfers be less so? Why should a municipality be permitted to legislate its own AFDC or Food Stamp program if their results are so inherently bad?

Part of the answer lies in conceptions of freedom. I have deliberately avoided raising them—the discussion is about how to help the disadvantaged, not about how to help the advantaged cut their taxes, to which arguments for personal freedom somehow always get diverted. Nonetheless, the point is valid: Local or even state systems leave much more room than a federal system for everyone, donors and recipients alike, to exercise freedom of choice about the kind of system they live under. Laws are more easily made and changed, and people who find them unacceptable have much more latitude in going somewhere more to their liking.

But the freedom of choice argument, while legitimate, is not necessary: We may put the advantages of local systems in terms of the **Law of Imperfect Selection**. A federal system must inherently employ very crude, inaccurate rules for deciding who gets what kind of help, . . . At the opposite extreme—a neighbor helping a neighbor, a family member helping another family member—the law loses its validity nearly altogether. Very fine-grained judgments based on personal knowledge are being made about specific people and changing situations. In neighborhoods and small cities, the procedures can still bring much individualized information to bear on decisions. Even systems in large cities and states can do much better than a national system; a decaying industrial city in the Northeast and a booming sunbelt city of the same size can and probably should adopt much different rules about who gets what and how much.

A final and equally powerful argument for not impeding local systems is diversity. We know much more in the 1980s than we knew in the 1960s about what does not work. We have a lot to learn about what *does* work. Localities have been a rich source of experiments. Localities have been a rich source of experiments. Marva Collins in Chicago gives us an example of how a school can bring inner-city students up to national norms. Sister Falaka Fattah in Philadelphia shows us how homeless youths can be rescued from the streets. There are numberless such lessons waiting to be learned from the diversity of local efforts. By all means, let a hundred flowers bloom, and if the federal government can play a useful role in lending a hand and spreading the word of success, so much the better.

The ultimate unresolved question about our proposal to abolish income maintenance for the working-aged is how many people will fall through the cracks. In whatever detail we try to foresee the consequences, the objection may always be raised: We cannot be *sure* that everyone will be taken care of in the degree to which we would wish. But this observation by no means settles the question. If one may point in objection to the child now fed by Food Stamps who would go hungry, one may also point with satisfaction to the child who would have an entirely different and better future. Hungry children should be fed; there is no argument about that. It is no less urgent that children be allowed to grow up in a system free of the forces that encourage them to remain poor and dependent. If a strategy reasonably promises to remove those forces, after so many attempts to "help the poor" have failed, it is worth thinking about.

But the rationale is too vague. Let me step outside the persona I have employed and put the issue in terms of one last intensely personal hypothetical example. Let us suppose that you, a parent, could know that tomorrow your own child would be made an orphan. You have a choice. You may put your child with an extremely poor family, so poor that you child will be badly clothed and will indeed sometimes be hungry. But you also know that the parents have worked hard all their lives, will make sure your child goes to school and studies, and will teach your child that independence is a primary value. Or you may put your child with a family with parents who have never worked, who will be incapable of overseeing your child's education—but who have plenty of food and good clothes, provided by others. If the choice about where one would put one's own child is as clear to you as it is to me, on what grounds does one justify support of a system that, indirectly but without doubt, makes the other choice for other children? The answer that "What we really want is a world where that choice is not forced upon us" is no answer. We have tried to have it that way. We failed. Everything we know about why we failed tells us that more of the same will not make the dilemma go away.

The Ideal of Opportunity

Billions for equal opportunity, not one cent for equal outcome—such is the slogan to inscribe on the banner of whatever cause my proposals constitute. Their common theme is to make it possible to get as far as one can go on one's merit, hardly a new ideal in American thought.

The ideal itself has never lapsed. What did lapse was the recognition that practical merit exists. Some people are better than others. They deserve more of society's rewards, of which money is only one small part. A principal function of social policy is to make sure they have the opportunity to reap those rewards. Government cannot identify the worthy, but it can protect a society in which the worthy can identify themselves.

I am proposing a triage of a sort, triage by self-selection. In triage on the battlefield, the doctor makes the decision—this one gets treatment, that one waits, the other one is made comfortable while waiting to die. In our social triage, the decision is left up to the patient. The patient always has the right to say "I can do X" and get a chance to prove it. Society always has the right to hold him to that pledge. The patient always has the right to fail. Society always has the right to let him in.

There is in this stance no lack of compassion but a presumption of respect. People—all people, black or white, rich or poor—may be unequally responsible for what has happened to them in the past, but all are equally responsible for what they do next. Just as in our idealized educational system a student can come back a third, fourth or fifth time to a course, in our idealized society a person can fail repeatedly and always be qualified for another chance—to try again, to try something easier, to try something different. The options are always open. Opportunity is endless. There is no punishment for failure, only a total absence of rewards. Society—or our idealized society—should be preoccupied with making sure that achievement is rewarded.

There is no shortage of people to be rewarded. Go into any inner-city school and you will find students of extraordinary talent, kept from knowing how good they are by rules we imposed in the name of fairness. Go into any poor community, and you will find people of extraordinary imagination and perseverance, energy and pride, making tortured accommodations to the strange world we created in the name of generosity. The success stories of past generations of poor in this country are waiting to be repeated.

There is no shortage of institutions to provide the rewards. Our schools know how to educate students who want to be educated. Our industries know how to find productive people and reward them. Our police know how to protect people who are ready to cooperate in their own protection. Our system of justice knows how to protect the rights of individuals who know how to protect the rights of individuals who know what their rights are. Our philanthropic institutions know how to multiply the effectiveness of people who are already trying to help themselves. In short, American society is very good at reinforcing the investment of an individual in himself. For the affluent and for the middle-class, these mechanisms continue to work about as well as they ever have, and we enjoy their benefits. Not so for the poor. American government, in its recent social policy, has been ineffectual in trying to stage-manage the decision to invest, and it has been unintentionally punitive toward those who make the decision on their own. It is time to get out of the way.

Review Question

1. Explain Murray's proposal for eliminating the welfare system. What are the advantages? What are the disadvantages?

Discussion Question

1. All things considered, would Murray's proposal have good consequences in our society or not? What do you think?

Nancy Fraser

Women, Welfare, and the Politics of Need Interpretation

Nancy Fraser teaches philosophy and women's studies at Northwestern University. The reading is taken from her book Unruly Practices: Power, Discourse, and Gender in Contemporary Social Theory *(1989).*

Fraser gives a feminist analysis of the U.S. social-welfare system. She claims the system reflects patriarchal gender norms that relegate women to the role of care-giver and unpaid domestic worker while assigning men the role of breadwinner. The system also defines women as dependent clients and men as rights-bearing beneficiaries. So political issues about the interpretation of people's needs have been translated into legal, administrative, and/or therapeutic matters.

What some writers are calling "the coming welfare wars" will be largely wars about, even against, women. Because women comprise the overwhelming majority of social-welfare program recipients and employees, women and women's needs will be the principal stakes in the battles over social spending likely to dominate national politics in the coming period. Moreover, the welfare wars will not be limited to the tenure of Reagan or even of Reaganism. On the contrary, they will be protracted wars both in time and in space. What James O'Connor (1973) theorized nearly fifteen years ago as "the fiscal crisis of the state" is a long-term, structural phenomenon of international proportions. Not just the U.S., but every late-capitalist welfare state in Western Europe and North America is facing some version of it. And the fiscal crisis of the welfare state coincides everywhere with a second long-term, structural tendency: the feminization of poverty. This is Diana Pearce's (1979) term for the rapidly increasing proportion of women in the adult poverty population, an increase tied to, *inter alia*, the rise in "female-headed households." In the U.S., this trend is so pronounced and so steep that analysts project that, should it continue, the poverty population will consist entirely of women and their children before the year 2000 (Ehrenreich and Piven 1984).

This conjunction of the fiscal crisis of the state and the feminization of poverty suggests that struggles around social-welfare will and should become increasingly focal for feminists. But such struggles raise a great many problems. Some of these, like the following, can be thought of as structural: On the one hand, in-

From Nancy Fraser, *Unruly Practices: Power, Discourse, and Gender in Contemporary Social Theory* (Mpls, MN: Univ. of Minnesota Press, 1989).

creasing numbers of women depend directly for their livelihoods on social-welfare programs; and many others benefit indirectly, since the existence of even a minimal and inadequate "safety net" increases the leverage of women who are economically dependent on individual men. Thus, feminists have no choice but to oppose social-welfare cuts. On the other hand, economists like Pearce (1979), Nancy Barrett (1984) and Steven Erie, Martin Rein, and Barbara Wiget (1983) have shown that programs like Aid to Families with Dependent Children actually institutionalize the feminization of poverty. The benefits they provide are system-conforming ones which reinforce rather than challenge basic structural inequalities. Thus, feminists cannot simply support existing social-welfare programs. To use the suggestive but ultimately too simple terms popularized by Carol Brown (1981): If to eliminate or to reduce welfare is to bolster "private patriarchy," then simply to defend it is to consolidate "public patriarchy." [1]

Feminists also face a second set of problems in the coming welfare wars. These problems, seemingly more ideological and less structural than the first set, arise from the typical way in which issues get framed as a result of the institutional dynamics of the political system.[2] Typically, social-welfare issues are posed as follows: Shall the state undertake to satisfy the social needs of a given constituency and to what degree? Now, this way of framing issues permits only a relatively small number of answers; and it tends to cast debates in quantitative terms. More importantly, it takes for granted the definition of the needs in question, as if that were self-evident and beyond dispute. It therefore occludes the fact that the interpretation of people's needs is itself a political stake, indeed sometimes *the* political stake. Clearly, this way of framing issues poses obstacles for feminist politics, since at the heart of such politics lie questions like, what do various groups of women really need, and whose interpretations of women's needs should be authoritative. Only in terms of a discourse oriented to the *politics of need interpretation* [3] can feminists meaningfully intervene in the coming welfare wars. But this requires a challenge to the dominant policy framework.

Both sets of problems, the structural and the ideological, are extremely important and difficult. In what follows, I shall not offer solutions to either of them. Rather, I want to attempt the much more modest and preliminary task of exploring how they might be thought about in relation to one another. Specifically, I want to propose a framework for inquiry which can shed light on both of them simultaneously.

Consider that, in order to address the structural problem, it will be necessary to clarify the phenomenon of "public patriarchy." One type of inquiry which is useful here is the familiar sort of economic analysis alluded to earlier, analysis which shows, for example, that "workfare" programs function to subsidize employers of low-wage, "women's work" in the service sector and thus to reproduce the sex-segmented, dual-labor market. Now, important as such inquiry is, it does not tell the whole story, since it leaves out of focus the discursive or ideological dimension of social-welfare programs. By the discursive or ideological dimension, I do not mean anything distinct from or epiphenomenal with respect to welfare practices; I mean, rather, the tacit norms and implicit assumptions which are constitutive of those practices. To get at this dimension requires a meaning-oriented sort of inquiry, one which considers welfare programs as, among other things, institutionalized patterns of interpretation.[4] Such inquiry would make explicit the social meanings embedded within welfare programs, meanings which tend otherwise simply to go without saying.

In spelling out such meanings, the inquiry I am proposing could do two things simultaneously. First, it could tell us something important about the structure of the U.S. welfare system, since it might identify some underlying norms and assumptions which lend a measure of coherence to diverse programs and practices. Second, it could illuminate what I called "the politics of need interpretation," since it could expose the processes by which welfare practices construct women and women's needs according to certain specific and in principle contestable interpretations, even as they lend those interpretations an aura of facticity which discourages contestation. Thus, this inquiry could shed light on both the structural and ideological problems identified earlier.

The principal aim of this paper is to provide an account of this sort for the present U.S. social-welfare system. The account is intended to help clarify some key structural aspects of male dominance in welfare-capitalists societies. At the same time, it is meant to point the way to a broader, discourse-oriented focus which can address political conflicts over the interpretation of women's needs.

The paper proceeds from some relatively "hard," uncontroversial facts about the U.S. social-welfare system (section I) through a series of increasingly interpreted accounts of the system (sections II and III). These culminate (in section IV) in a highly theorized characterization of the welfare system as a "juridical-administrative-therapeutic state apparatus" (JAT). Finally (in section V), the paper situates that apparatus as one actor among others in a larger and highly contested political field of discourse about needs which also includes the feminist movement.

I

Long before the emergence of welfare states, governments have defined legally secured arenas of social action. In so doing, they have at the same time codified corresponding patterns of agency or social roles. Thus, early modern states defined an economic arena and the corresponding role of an economic person capable of entering into contracts. More or less at the same time, they codified the "private sphere" of the household and the role of household head with dependents. Somewhat later, governments were led to secure a sphere of political participation and the corresponding role of citizen with (limited) political rights. In each of these cases, the original and paradigmatic subject of the newly codified social role was made. Only secondarily and much later was it conceded that women, too, could occupy these subject-positions, without however entirely dispelling the association with masculinity.

Matters are different, however, with the contemporary welfare state. When this type of government defined a new arena of activity—call it "the social"—and a new social role, the welfare client, it included women among its original and paradigmatic subjects. Today, in fact, women have become the principal subjects of the welfare state. On the one hand, they comprise the overwhelming majority both of program recipients and of paid social service workers. On the other hand, they are the wives, mothers and daughters whose unpaid activities and obligations are redefined as the welfare state increasingly oversees forms of caregiving. Since this beneficiary-social worker-caregiver nexus of roles is constitutive of the social-welfare arena, one might even call the latter as feminized terrain.

A brief statistical overview confirms women's greater involvement with and dependence on the U.S. social-welfare system. Consider first women's greater dependence as program clients and beneficiaries. In each of the major "means-tested" programs in the U.S., women and the children for whom they are responsible now comprise the overwhelming majority of clients. For example, more than 81% of households receiving Aid to Families with Dependent Children (AFDC) are headed by women; more than 60% of families receiving food stamps or Medicaid are headed by women; and 70% of all households in publicly owned or subsidized housing are headed by women (Erie, Rein, Wiget 1983; Nelson 1984). High as they are, these figures actually underestimate the representation of women. As Barbara Nelson (1984) notes, in the androcentric reporting system, households counted as male-headed by definition contain no healthy adult men. But healthy adult women live in most households counted as male-headed. Such women may directly or indirectly receive benefits going to "male-headed" households, but they are invisible in the statistics, even though they usually do the work of securing and maintaining program eligibility.

Women also predominate in the major U.S. "age-tested" programs. For example, 61.6% of all adult beneficiaries of Social Security are women; and 64% of those covered by Medicare are women (Eric, Rein, Wiget 1983; Nelson 1984). In sum, because women as a group are significantly poorer than men—indeed they now comprise nearly two-thirds of all U.S. adults below the official poverty line—and because women tend to live longer than men, women depend more on the social-welfare system as clients and beneficiaries.

But this is not the whole story. Women also depend more on the social-welfare system as paid human service workers—a category of employment which includes education and health, as well as social work and services administration. In 1980, 70% of the 17.3 million paid jobs in this sector in the U.S. were held by women. This accounts for one-third of U.S. women's total paid employment and a full 80% of all professional jobs held by women. The figures for women of color are even higher than this average, since 37% of their total paid employment and 82.4% of their professional employment is in this sector (Erie, Rein, Wiget 1983). It is a distinctive feature of the U.S. social-welfare system, as opposed to, say, the British and Scandinavian systems, that only 3% of these jobs are in the form of direct federal government employment. The rest are in state and local government, in the "private non-profit" sector and in the "private" sector. But the more decentralized and privatized character of the U.S. system does not make paid welfare workers any less vulnerable in the face of federal program cuts. On the contrary, the level of federal social-welfare spending affects the level of human service employment in *all* sectors. State and local government jobs depend on federal and federally-financed state and local government contracts; and private profit and non-profit jobs depend on federally financed transfer payments to the individuals and households for the purchase of services like health care in the market (Erie, Rein, Wiget 1983). Thus, reductions in social spending mean the loss of jobs for women. Moreover, as Barbara Ehrenreich and Frances Fox Piven (1984) note, this loss is not compensated when spending is shifted to the military, since only 0.5% of the entire female paid workforce is employed in work on military contracts. In fact, one study they cite estimates that with each one billion dollar increase in military spending, 9500 jobs are lost to women.

Finally, women are subjects of and to the social-welfare system in their traditional capacity as unpaid caregivers. It is well known that the sexual division of labor assigns women primary responsibility for the care of those who cannot care for themselves. (I leave aside women's traditional obligations to provide personal services to adult males—husbands, fathers, grown sons, lovers—who can very well care for themselves.) Such responsibility includes child care, of course, but also care for sick and/or elderly relatives, often parents. For example, a 1975 British study cited by Hilary Land (1978) found that three times as many elderly people live with married daughters as with married sons, and that those without a close female relative were more likely to be institutionalized, irrespective of degree of infirmity. As unpaid caregivers, then, women are more directly affected than men by the level and character of government social services for children, the sick and the elderly.

As clients, paid human service workers and unpaid caregivers, then, women are the principal subjects of the social-welfare system. It is as if this branch of the state were in effect a "Bureau of Women's Affairs."

II

Of course, the welfare system does not deal with women on women's terms. On the contrary, it has its own characteristic ways of interpreting women's needs and positioning women as subjects. In order to understand these, we need to examine how gender norms and meanings are reflected in the structure of the U.S. social-welfare system.

This issue is quite complicated. On the one hand, nearly all U.S. social-welfare programs are officially gender neutral. Yet the system as a whole is a dual or two-tiered one; and it has an unmistakable gender subtext.[5] There is one set of programs oriented to *individuals* and tied to participation in the paid workforce, for example, unemployment insurance and Social Security. These programs are designed to supplement and compensate for the primary market in paid labor power. There is a second set of programs oriented to *households* and tied to combined household income, for example, AFDC, food stamps and Medicaid. These programs are designed to compensate for what are considered to be family failures, generally the absence of a male breadwinner.

What integrates the two sets of programs is a common core of assumptions, underlying both, concerning the sexual division of labor, domestic and non-domestic. It is assumed that families do or should contain one primary breadwinner who is male and one unpaid domestic worker (homemaker and mother) who is female. It is further assumed that when a woman undertakes paid work outside the home this is or should be in order to supplement the male breadwinner's wage and so it neither does nor ought override her primary housewifely and maternal responsibilities. It is assumed, in other words, that society is divided into two separate spheres of home and outside work and that these are women's and men's spheres respectively.[8]

These assumptions are increasingly counterfactual. At present, fewer than 15% of U.S. families conform to the normative ideal of a domicile shared by a husband who is the sole breadwinner, a wife who is a full-time homemaker and their offspring.

Nonetheless, the separate spheres norms determine the structure of the social-welfare system. They determine that it contain a primary labor market-related subsystem and a family or household-related subsystem. Moreover, they determine that these subsystems be gender-linked, that the labor market-related system be implicitly "masculine" and the family-related system be implicitly "feminine." Consequently, the normative, ideal-typical recipient of primary labor market-oriented programs is a (white) male, while the normative, ideal-typical client of household-based programs is a female.

This gender subtext of the U.S. welfare system is confirmed when we take a second look at participation figures. Consider again the figures just cited for the "feminine" or family-based programs, which I earlier referred to as "means-tested" programs: more than 81% of households receiving AFDC are female-headed, as are more than 70% of those receiving housing assistance and more than 60% of those receiving Medicaid and food stamps. Now recall that these figures do not compare female vs. male individuals, but rather female vs. male headed-*households*. They therefore confirm four things: 1) these programs have a distinctive administrative identity in that their recipients are not individualized but *familialized;* 2) they serve what are considered to be defective families, overwhelmingly families without a male breadwinner; 3) the ideal-typical (adult) client is female; and 4) she makes her claim for benefits on the basis of her status as an unpaid domestic worker, a homemaker and mother, not as a paid worker based in the labor market.

Now contrast this with the case of a typical labor market-based and thus "masculine" program, namely, unemployment insurance. Here the percentage of female claimants drops to 38%, a figure which contrasts female vs. male *individuals,* as opposed to households. As Diana Pearce (1979) notes, this drop reflects at least two different circumstances. First, and most straightforwardly, it reflects women's lower rate of participation in the paid workforce. Second, it reflects the fact that many women wage-workers are not eligible to participate in this program, for example, paid household service workers, part-time workers, pregnant workers and workers in the "irregular economy" such as prostitutes, baby-sitters and home typists. The exclusion of these predominantly female wage-workers testifies to the existence of a gender segmented labor market, divided into "primary" and "secondary" employment. It reflects the more general assumption that women's earnings are "merely supplementary," not on a par with those of the primary (male) breadwinner. Altogether, then, the figures tell us four things about programs like unemployment insurance: 1) they are administered in a way which *individualizes* rather than familializes recipients; 2) they are designed to compensate primary labor market effects, such as the temporary displacement of a primary breadwinner; 3) the ideal-typical recipient is male; and 4) he makes his claim on the basis of his identity as a paid worker, not as an unpaid domestic worker or parent. . . .

III

So far, we have established the dualistic structure of the U.S. social-welfare system and the gender subtext of the dualism. Now, we can better tease out the system's implicit norms and tacit assumptions by examining its mode of operation. To see how welfare programs interpret women's needs, we should consider what benefits consist in. To see how programs position women as subjects, we should examine administrative practices. In general, we shall see that the "masculine" and "feminine" subsystems are not only separate but also unequal.

Consider that the "masculine" social-welfare programs are social insurance schemes. They include unemployment insurance, Social Security (retirement insurance), Medicare (age-tested health insurance) and Supplemental Social Security Insurance (disability insurance for those with paid work records). These programs are contributory; wage-workers and their employers pay into trust funds. They are administered on a national basis and benefit levels are uniform across the country. Though bureaucratically organized and administered, they require less, and less demeaning effort on the part of beneficiaries in qualifying and maintaining eligibility than do "feminine" programs. They are far less subject to intrusive controls and in most cases lack the dimension of surveillance. They also tend to require less of beneficiaries in the way of benefit-collection efforts, with the notable exception of unemployment insurance.

In sum, "masculine" social insurance schemes position recipients primarily as *rights-bearers*. The beneficiaries of these programs are in the main not stigmatized. Neither administrative practice nor popular discourse constitutes them as "on the dole." They are constituted rather as receiving what they deserve, what they, in "partnership" with their employers, have already paid in for, what they, therefore, have a *right* to. Moreover, these beneficiaries are also positioned as *purchasing consumers*. They receive cash as opposed to "in kind" benefits and so are positioned as having "the liberty to strike the best bargain they can in purchasing services of their choice on the open market." In sum, these beneficiaries are what C. B. MacPherson (1964) calls "possessive individuals." Proprietors of their own persons who have freely contracted to sell their labor-power, they become participants in social insurance schemes and, thence, paying consumers of human services. They therefore qualify as *social citizens* in virtually the fullest sense that term can acquire within the framework of a male-dominated capitalist society.

All this stands in stark contrast to the "feminine" sector of the U.S. social-welfare system. This sector consists in relief programs, such as AFDC, food stamps, Medicaid and public housing assistance. These programs are not contributory, but are financed out of general tax revenues, usually with one-third of the funds coming from the federal government and two-thirds coming from the states. They are not administered nationally but rather by the states. As a result, benefit levels vary dramatically, though they are everywhere inadequate, deliberately pegged below the official poverty line. The relief programs are notorious for the varieties of administrative humiliation they inflict upon clients. They require considerable work in qualifying and maintaining eligibility; and they have a heavy component of surveillance.

These programs do not in any meaningful sense position their subjects as rights-bearers. Far from being considered as having a right to what they receive, recipients are defined as "beneficiaries of governmental largesse" or "clients of public charity." [7] In the androcentric-administrative framework, "welfare mothers" are considered not to work and so are sometimes required, that is to say coerced, to work off their benefits via "workfare." They thus become inmates of what Diana Pearce (1979) calls a "workhouse without walls." Indeed, the only sense in which the category of rights is relevant to these clients' situation is the somewhat dubious one according to which they are entitled to treatment governed by the standards of formal-bureaucratic procedural rationality. But if that right is construed as protection from administrative caprice, then even it is widely and routinely disregarded. Moreover, recipients of public relief are generally not positioned as purchasing consumers. A significant portion of their benefits is "in kind" and what cash they get comes already carved up and ear-marked for specific, administratively designated purposes. These recipients are therefore essentially *clients*, a subject-position which carries far less power and dignity in capitalist societies than does the alternative position of purchaser. In these societies, to be a client in the sense relevant to relief recipients is to be an abject dependent. Indeed, this sense of the term carries connotations of a fall from autonomy, as when we speak, for example, of "the client-states of empires or superpowers." As clients, then, recipients of relief are *the negatives of possessive individuals.* Largely excluded from the market, both as workers and as consumers, claiming benefits not as individuals but as members of "failed" families, these recipients are effectively denied the trappings of social-citizenship as the latter are defined within male-dominated capitalist societies.[8]

Clearly, this system creates a double-bind for women raising children without a male breadwinner. By failing to offer them day care, job training, a job that pays a "family wage" or some combination of these, it constructs them exclusively as mothers. As a consequence, it interprets their needs as maternal needs and their sphere of activity as that of "the family." Now, according to the ideology of separate spheres, this should be an honorific social identity. Yet the system does not honor these women. On the contrary, instead of providing them with a guaranteed income equivalent to a family wage as a matter of right, it stigmatizes, humiliates and harasses them. In effect, it decrees that these women must be, yet cannot be, normative mothers.

Moreover, the way in which the U.S. social-welfare system interprets "maternity" and "the family" is race- and culture-specific. The bias is made plain by Carol Stack's (1974) study, *All Our Kin.* Stack analyzes domestic arrangements of very poor Black welfare recipients in a midwestern city. Where ideologues see "the disorganization of *the* [sic] black family," she finds complex, highly organized kinship structures. These include kin-based networks of resource pooling and exchange which enable those in direct poverty to survive economically and communally. The networks organize delayed exchanges or "gifts," in Mauss' (1967) sense, of prepared meals, food stamps, cooking, shopping, groceries, furniture, sleeping space, cash (including wages and AFDC allowances), transportation, clothing, child care, even children. They span several physically distinct households and so transcend the principal administrative category which organizes relief programs. It is significant that Stack took great pains to conceal the identities of her subjects, even going so far as to disguise the identity of their city. The reason, though unstated, is obvious: these people would lose their benefits if program administrators learned that they did not utilize them within the confines and boundaries of a "household."

We can summarize the separate and unequal character of the two-tiered, gender-linked, race- and culture-biased U.S. social-welfare system in the following formulae: Participants in the "masculine" subsystem are positioned as *rights-bearing beneficiaries and purchasing consumers of services.* Participants in the "feminine" subsystem, on the other hand, are positioned as *dependent clients.*

IV

Clearly, the identities and needs which the social-welfare system fashions for its recipients are *interpreted* identities and needs. Moreover, they are highly political interpretations which are in principle subject to dispute. Yet these needs and identities are not always recognized as interpretations. Too often, they simply go without saying and are rendered immune from analysis and critique.

Doubtless one reason for this "reification effect" is the depth at which gender meanings and norms are embedded in our general culture. But there may also be another reason more specific to the welfare system.

Let me suggest yet another way of analyzing the U.S. social-welfare system, this time as a "juridical-administrative-therapeutic state apparatus" (JAT).[9] The point is to emphasize a distinctive style of operation. *Qua* JAT, the welfare system works by linking together a series of juridical, administrative and therapeutic procedures. As a consequence, it tends to translate political issues concerning the interpretation of people's needs into legal, administrative and/or therapeutic matters. Thus, the system executes political policy in a way which appears nonpolitical and tends to be depoliticizing.

Consider that, at an abstract level, the subject-positions constructed for beneficiaries of *both* the "masculine" and the "feminine" components of the system can be analyzed as combinations of three distinct elements. The first element is a *juridical* one which positions recipients vis-a-vis the legal system by according or denying them various *rights*. Thus, the subject of the "masculine" subsystem has a right to benefits and is protected from some legally sanctioned forms of administrative caprice, while the subject of the "feminine" subsystem largely lacks rights.

This juridical element is then linked with a second one, an *administrative* element. For in order to qualify to receive benefits, subjects must assume the stance of petitioners with respect to an administrative body; they must petition a bureaucratic institution empowered to decide their claims on the basis of administratively defined criteria. In the "masculine" subsystem, for example, claimants must prove their "cases" meet administratively defined criteria of entitlement; in the "feminine" subsystem, on the other hand, they must prove conformity to administratively defined criteria of need. The enormous qualitative differences between the two sets of procedures notwithstanding, both are variations on the same administrative moment. Both require claimants to translate their experienced situations and life-problems into administerable needs, to present the former as bonafide instances of specified generalized states of affairs which could in principle befall anyone (Habermas 1981).

If and when they qualify, social-welfare claimants get positioned either as purchasing consumers or dependent clients. In either case, their needs are redefined as correlates of bureaucratically administered satisfactions. This means they are quantified, rendered as equivalents of a sum of money (Habermas 1981). Thus, in the "feminine" subsystem, clients are positioned passively to receive monetarily measured, predefined and prepackaged services; in the "masculine" subsystem, on the other hand, they receive a specified, predetermined amount of cash.

In both subsystems, then, people's needs are subject to a sort of rewriting operation. Experienced situations and life-problems are translated into administerable needs. And since the latter are not necessarily isomorphic to the former, the possibility of a gap between them arises. This possibility is especially likely in the "feminine" subsystem. For there, as we saw, clients are constructed as deviant and service provision has the character of normalization—albeit normalization designed more to stigmatize than to "reform."

Here, then is the opening for the third, *therapeutic* moment of the JAT's *modus operandi*. Especially in the "feminine" subsystem, service provision often includes an implicit or explicit therapeutic or quasi-therapeutic dimension. In AFDC, for example, social workers concern themselves with the "mental health" aspects of their clients lives, often construing these in terms of "character problems." More explicitly and less moralistically, municipal programs for poor, unmarried, pregnant teenage women include not only pre-natal care, mothering instruction and tutoring or schooling, but also counseling sessions with psychiatric social workers. As observed by Prudence Rains (1971), such sessions are intended to bring girls to acknowledge what are considered to be their true, deep, latent, emotional problems on the assumption that this will enable them to avoid future pregnancies. Ludicrous as this sounds, it is only an extreme example of a more pervasive phenomenon, namely, the tendency of especially "feminine" social-welfare programs to construct gender-political and political-economic issues as individual, psychological problems. In fact, some therapeutic or quasi-therapeutic welfare services can be regarded as second-order services. In any case, the therapeutic dimension of the U.S. social-welfare encourages clients to close gaps between their culturally shaped lived experience and their administratively defined situation by bringing the former into line with the latter.

Clearly, this analysis of the U.S. welfare system as a "juridical-administrative-therapeutic state apparatus" lets us see both subsystems more critically. It suggests that the problem is not only that women are disempowered by the *denial* of social citizenship in the "feminine" subsystem, although they are. It is also that women and men are disempowered by the *realization* of an androcentric, possessive individualist form of social citizenship in the "masculine" subsystem. In *both* subsystems, including the "masculine" one, the JAT positions its subjects in ways which do not empower them. It individualizes them as "cases" and so militates against collective identification. It imposes monological, administrative definitions of situation and need and so preempts dialogically achieved self-definition and self-determination. It positions its subjects as passive client or consumer recipients and not as active co-participants involved in shaping their life-conditions. Lastly, it construes experienced discontent with these arrangements as material for adjustment-oriented, usually sexist therapy and not as material for empowering processes of consciousness-raising.

All told, then, the form of social citizenship constructed even in the *best* part of the U.S. social-welfare system is a degraded and depoliticized one. It is a form of passive citizenship in which the state preempts the power to define and satisfy people's needs.

This form of passive citizenship arises in part as a result of the JAT's distinctive style of operation. The JAT treats the interpretation of people's needs as pregiven and unproblematic, while itself redefining them as amenable to system-conforming satisfactions. Thus, the JAT shifts attention away from the question: Who interprets social needs and how? It tends to substitute the *juridicial, administrative and therapeutic management of need satisfaction* for the *politics of need interpretation*. That is, it tends to substitute *monological, administrative processes of need definition* for *dialogical, participatory processes of need interpretation*.[10]. . .

Endnotes

1. I believe that Brown's terms are too simple on two counts. First, for reasons elaborated by Gayle Rubin (1975), I prefer not to use 'patriarchy' as a generic term for male dominance but rather as the destination of a specific historical social formation. Second, Brown's public/private contrast oversimplifies the structure of both laissez-faire and welfare capitalism, since it posits two major societal zones where there are actually four (family, official-economy, state, and sphere of public political discourse) and conflates two distinct public-private divisions. (For a discussion of this second problem, see Fraser 1985b.) These problems notwithstanding, it remains the case that Brown's terms are immensely suggestive and that we currently have no better terminology. Thus, in what follows I occasionally use 'public patriarchy' for want of an alternative.
2. For an analysis of the dynamics whereby late-capitalist political systems tend to select certain types of interests while excluding others, see Claus Offe (1972, 1974, 1980). For a feminist application of Offe's approach, see Drude Dahlerup (1984).
3. This phrase owes it inspiration to Jürgen Habermas (1975).
4. I owe this phrase to Thomas McCarthy (personal communication).
5. I owe the phrase 'gender subtext' to Dorothy Smith (1984). A number of writers have noticed the two-tiered character of the U.S. social-welfare system. Andrew Hacker (1985) correlates the dualism with class but not with gender. Diana Pearce (1979) and Erie, Rein and Wiget (1983) correlate the dualism with gender and with the dual labor market, itself gender-correlated. Barbara Nelşon (1984) correlates the dualism with gender, the dual labor market and the sexual division of paid *and unpaid* labor. My account owes a great deal to all of these writers, especially Barbara Nelson.
6. Hilary Land (1978) identifies similar assumptions at work in the British social-welfare system. My formulation of them is much indebted to her.
7. I owe these formulations to Virginia Held (personal communication).
8. It should be noted that I am here taking issue with the view of some left theorists that "decommodification" in the form of in kind social-welfare benefits represents an emancipatory or progressive development. In the context of a two-tiered welfare system like the one described here, this assumption is clearly false, since in kind benefits are qualitatively and quantitatively inferior to the corresponding commodities and since they function to stigmatize those who receive them.
9. This term echoes Louis Althusser's (1984) term, "ideological state apparatus." Certainly, the U.S. social-welfare system as described in the present section of this paper counts as an "ISA" in Althusser's sense. However, I prefer the term "juridical-administrative-therapeutic state apparatus" as more concrete and descriptive of the specific ways in which welfare programs produce and reproduce ideology. In general, then, a JAT can be understood as a subclass of an ISA. On the other hand, Althusserian-like terminology aside, readers will find that the account in this section owes more to Michael Foucault (1979) and Jürgen Habermas (1981) than to Althusser. Of course, neither Habermas nor Foucault is sensitive to the gendered character of social-welfare programs. For a critique of Habermas in this respect, see Fraser (1985b). For my views about Foucault, see Fraser (1981, 1983 and 1985a).
10. These formulations owe much to Jürgen Habermas (1975, 1981). . . .

Reference Notes

Althusser, Louis. 1984. Ideology and ideological state apparatuses: Notes towards an investigation. In *Essays on ideology*, ed. Althusser. London: Verso.

Arendt, Hannah. 1958. *The human condition.* Chicago and London: The University of Chicago Press.

Barrett, Nancy S. 1984. Mothers, fathers, and children: From private to public patriarchy. In *Women and revolution*, ed. Lydia Sargent. Boston: South End Press.

Dahlerup, Drude. 1984. Overcoming the barriers: An approach to the study of how women's issues are kept from the political agenda. In *Women's views of the political world of men*, ed. Judith H. Stiehm. Dobbs Ferry, NY: Transnational Publishers.

Ehrenreich, Barbara and Frances Fox Piven, 1984. The feminization of poverty. *Dissent*, Spring: 162-170.

Erie, Steven P., Martin Rein, and Barbara Wiget. 1983. Women and the Reagan's revolution: Thermidor for the social welfare economy. In *Families, politics, and public policies: A feminist dialogue on women and the state*, ed. Irene Diamond. New York and London.: Longman.

Foucault, Michel. 1979. *Discipline and punish: The birth of the prison.* Trans. Alan Sheridan. New York: Vintage.

Fraser, Nancy. 1981. Foucault on modern power: Empirical insights and normative confusions, *Praxis International* 1:272-87.

________. 1983. Foucault's body-language: A posthumanist political rhetoric? *Salmagundi* 61:55-70.

________. 1985a. Michel Foucault: A "Young Conservative"? The case of Habermas and Gender. *New German Critique* 35:97-131.

Habermas, Jürgen. 1975. *Legitimation crisis.* Boston: Beacon.

________. 1981. *Theorie des kommunikativen Handelns, Band II, Zur Kritik der funktionalistischen Vernunft.* Frankfurt am Main: Suhrkamp Verlag.

Hacker, Andrew. 1985. 'Welfare': The future of an illusion. *New York Review of Books* February 28:37-43.

Land, Hilary. 1978. Who cares for the family? *Journey of Social Policy* 7:257-284.

MacPherson, C. B. 1964. *The political theory of possessive individualism: Hobbs to Locke.* New York and London: Oxford University Press.

Mauss, Marcel. 1967. *The gift: Forms and functions of exchange in archaic societies.* Trans. Ian Cunnison. New York and London: W. W. Norton & Company.

Nelson, Barbara J. 1984. Women's poverty and women's citizenship: Some political consequences of economic marginality. *Signs: Journal of Women in Culture and Society* 10:209-231.

O'Connor, James. 1973. *The fiscal crisis of the state.* New York: St. Martin's Press.

Offe, Claus. 1972. Political authority and class structure: An analysis of late capitalist societies. *International Journal of Sociology* 2:73-108.

________. 1974. Structural problems of the capitalist state: Class rule and the political system. On the selectiveness of political institutions. In *German Political Studies*, ed., Klaus von Beyme. London: Sage Publications.

________. 1980. The separation of form and content in liberal democratic politics. *Studies in Political Economy* 3:5-16.

Pearce, Diana. 1979. Women, work, and welfare: The feminization of poverty. In *Working Women and Families*, ed. Karen Wolk Feinstein. Beverly Hills, CA: Sage Publications.

Rains, Prudence Mors. 1971. *Becoming an unwed mother: A sociological account.* Chicago: Aldine Atherton, Inc.

Rubin, Gayle. 1975. The traffic in women: Notes on the "Political Economy" of sex. In *Towards an Anthropology of Women*, ed. Rayna R. Reiter. New York: Monthly Review Press.

Skocpol, Theda. 1980. Political response to capitalist crisis: Neo-Marxist theories of the state and the case of the new Deal. *Politics and Society* 10:155-201.

Smith, Dorothy. 1984. The gender subtext of power. Unpublished manuscript.

Stack, Carol B. 1974. *All our kin: Strategies for survival in a black community.* New York, Evanston, San Francisco, London: Harper & Row.

REVIEW QUESTIONS

1. In Fraser's analysis, why are women the principal subjects and workers in the welfare system?
2. How do welfare programs interpret women and their needs? How are men treated?
3. Explain Fraser's interpretation of the U.S. welfare system as a juridical-administrative-therapeutic state apparatus.

DISCUSSION QUESTIONS

1. Why shouldn't men be breadwinners and women wives and mothers? What is wrong with these gender roles?
2. Do women have real needs that are different from the ones constructed in a male-dominated capitalistic society? If so, what are they?

PROBLEM CASES

1. ***Periodic Famines and Somalia.*** (This topic is discussed by Sylvia Nassar in an article in The *New York Times*, January 17, 1993.) The view of Malthus and his followers, like Hardin in the read-

ings, is that famines are caused by food shortages which are in turn caused by drought or other natural disasters. There is a long history of periodic famines which seems to bear this out: Potato famines in Ireland in 1846-1851, China's famine in 1928 after a drought, Ethiopia's famine in 1973 after a drought, Bangladesh's famine in 1974 after floods, and the ongoing problems in sub-Saharan Africa (including Ethiopia, Sudan, and Somalia) after a prolonged drought in the area.

The view that famines and food shortages are caused by natural disasters has been challenged by Amartya Sen and others (See the Suggested Readings.) Sen argues that world food production has kept ahead of population growth, and that famines are not caused by drought, flood, or other natural disaster. Typically a country that has people dying of starvation has enough food to go around. The problem is that the starving people cannot get the food because of high prices, unemployment, distribution problems, civil war, or other human factors.

Consider the recent and continuing starvation of hundreds of thousands of people in Somalia and Sudan. The United States and other countries have contributed a massive amount of aid, probably enough aid to prevent starvation, but the relief efforts have been frustrated by the continuing fighting between various rival political factions. Many foreign-aid workers have been killed in the fighting. The United States led a military intervention in Somalia in December, 1992, but the coalition force failed to ensure peace. Bandits continued to rob or extort money from relief groups, and rioting and clan fighting continued to interrupt food deliveries. The situation seems to be even worse in Sudan where there is enough food to feed the people, but difficulties in delivering it to remote villages.

The pessimistic view of Sen is that military intervention will not solve the problems of countries like Somalia and Sudan. The only lasting solution is a stable democratic government that protects the poor and lets farmers grow.

Do you agree with Sen? If so, how can we bring about stable democratic governments in countries like Somalia and Sudan?

2. *Eritrea.* (Reported in the *Star Tribune* newspaper of Minneapolis, Oct. 29, 1989.) Eritrea is a province of Ethiopia that has been plagued by war, drought, and famine for many years. A rebel group, the Eritrean People Liberation Front has been fighting for twenty-eight years to become independent of the Soviet-supported Ethiopian government. The land is rocky, mountainous, and subject to droughts. A drought occurs roughly every eleven years, and crops have failed in four of the last six years. In 1989, the rains failed again and the harvest was poor. International agencies estimate that more than a million people in this area will need emergency food aid to avert starvation. Should any aid be given to these people? Why or why not?

3. ***The Poor in Brazil.*** The population of Brazil is growing rapidly. If its present rate of growth of 2.8 percent continues, it will soon become the most populous country in the Western Hemisphere. Although Brazil is rich in natural resources and has significant economic growth, most of the benefits have gone to the rich. Forty percent of the population is under fifteen years of age, and unemployment is high. Population growth in the cities has made it difficult for the government to provide education, health care, water, sanitation, food, and housing for the poor. What steps, if any, should be taken to provide for the poor and needy people in this country? Explain your proposals.

4. ***The Boarder Baby Scandal.*** (As reported by Andrew Stein, president of the New York City Council in The *New York Times*, Saturday, Jan. 17, 1987.) New York City is the most prosperous city in the world with a 21-billion-dollar budget and immense private and community wealth. Yet it has a very serious problem—abandoned and homeless children. At the end of 1986, the city officially counted 11,000 such children and babies living in municipal shelters, decrepit welfare hotels, and hospitals. Many have been living this way for years. They are known as boarder babies because their parents abandoned them in hospitals. Due to a lack of certified foster parents or couples willing to adopt them, they are likely to remain there. Others have been removed from their homes for their own protection; reports of child abuse and neglect (including a 250 percent increase in cases of drug-addicted babies) have risen so dramatically that welfare offices are overwhelmed with children, often keeping them overnight in the offices or placing them illegally in group foster homes.

What, if anything, should be done about these babies and children? Explain your recommendations carefully.

5. ***A Case of Unemployment.*** John Smith and his wife Jane have three small children. Until recently, John had a good job in a factory in Dallas, Texas, and a good life: house, car, T.V., new furniture, and so on. Unfortunately, he lost his job when the

factory closed. He has sold all his possessions, exhausted his unemployment compensation and cannot collect AFDC. (Married men and women do not qualify for Aid to Families with Dependent Children (AFDC); in fact, no welfare at all is available for him in Dallas.) Jane tried working as a waitress, leaving John to care for the children, but she did not make enough money to pay the bills. Now they are living on the street and getting one free meal a day at the Salvation Army. The children are suffering from exposure and malnutrition; John and Jane are tired, hungry, dirty, and depressed.

Should such a family receive welfare benefits? Explain your answer.

*6. **A Homeless Person.*** (Reported in the *St. Cloud* (Minnesota) *Times*, Oct. 6, 1989.) Sharon Lenger, forty-eight, has a bachelor's degree in psychology and an associate of arts degree in drug counseling. She worked as a residential counselor in a home for abused and molested adolescents in California until she was severely assaulted by one of the residents. As a result of the injuries sustained in the attack, she was unable to work in the home and moved out. She received worker's compensation, but this was not enough to live on in California since it was based on her low salary and did not take into account the free room and board provided at the home where she had worked. She moved to Minnesota to live near her sick and elderly parents. Then the state of California stopped her worker's compensation payments. She needed further surgery because of the assault injuries, so she applied for medical assistance and general assistance. Now she receives $203 a month in general assistance payments, not enough to pay for food and a place to live. Currently she is staying at an emergency shelter run by Catholic Charities, and describes herself as one step away from the street. In other words, she is a homeless person.

Does Sharon Lenger have a right to adequate shelter? If so, how should this be provided?

SUGGESTED READINGS

1. Peter G. Brown, Conrad Johnson, and Paul Vernier, eds., *Income Support: Conceptual and Policy Issues* (Totowa, NJ: Rowman and Littlefield, 1981). This anthology contains articles on the moral and conceptual issues involved in the income-support policies of the United States.

2. Nick Eberstadt, "Myths of the Food Crisis," *The New York Review of Books* (February 19, 1976), pp. 32-37, argues that the cause of starvation today is not overpopulation but inequalities in food distribution. Welfare-style transfers of income cannot eliminate this inequality. The world's poor must improve their productivity.

3. Milton Friedman, *Capitalism and Freedom* (Chicago: University of Chicago Press, 1962, is an economist who espouses the principle of distributing income in a free society according to what one produces or what one's instruments produce.

4. Michael Harrington, *Socialism* (New York: Saturday Review Press, 1970), presents a version of socialism that is different from both communism and the welfare state.

5. John Hospers, "What Libertarianism Is," in *The Libertarian Alternative,* Tibor R. Machan, ed. (Chicago: Nelson-Hall Co., 1974), pp. 3-20. Hospers defends the libertarian position that everyone has an equal right to liberty, life, and property, where these rights are interpreted negatively in terms of noninterference. The only proper role of the government is to protect these negative rights; the government is not obligated to help the needy or protect people from themselves.

6. Frances Moore Lappe, *World Hunger: Twelve Myths* (New York: Grove Press, 1986). This is an informed look at various aspects of the problem of world hunger by a liberal who thinks that people in rich countries should change their diet.

7. William W. Murdoch and Allen Oaten, "Population and Food: Metaphors and the Reality," *Bioscience,* September 9, 1975, pp. 561-567. Murdoch and Oaten attack Hardin's lifeboat ethics; they argue that factors other than food supply affect population growth.

8. Robert Nozick, *Anarchy, State, and Utopia* (New York: Basic Books, 1974). Nozick defends a libertarian conception of justice. This book has produced a great deal of discussion (some of it very hostile) among philosophers concerned with distributive justice.

9. Ernest Patridge, ed., *Responsibilities to Future Generations* (Buffalo, NY: Prometheus, 1981). This is a collection of readings on whether or not we have any obligations to people who will live in the future.

10. Onora O'Neill, "Lifeboat Earth," *Philosophy & Public Affairs,* vol. 4 no. 3 (Spring, 1975), assumes that people on the lifeboat Earth have a right not to be killed (except in cases of unavoidable killing and self-defense), and a corollary duty not to kill others. It follows from this, she argues, that we ought to adopt policies to prevent others from dying of starvation.

11. ———, "The Moral Perplexities of Famine and World Hunger," in *Matters of Life and Death,* 3rd ed., Tom Regan, ed. (New York: Random House, 1993), pp. 235-279. After covering some facts about famine, O'Neill compares the utilitarian and Kantian approaches to famine problems.

12. James Rachels, "Killing and Starving to Death," *Philosophy* 54, no. 208, (April 1979), pp.159-171. Rachels argues that our duty not to let people die of starvation is just as strong as our duty not to kill them. He defends this Equivalence Thesis against various attempts to show that there is a moral difference between killing and letting die.

13. Amartya Sen, *Poverty and Famines* (Oxford: Oxford University Press, 1981), argues that famines are not caused by natural disasters such as droughts and floods but by various human problems including widespread unemployment, high prices, civil unrest, and war.

14. Henry Shue, *Basic Rights* (Princeton, NJ: Princeton University Press, 1980). Shue defends the view that everyone has a right to subsistence, and that this economic right is as important as political rights such as the right to liberty. It follows, Shue argues, that rich nations (those with a gross domestic product per capita of U.S. $400 or more) should make welfare-style transfers of food or money to poor nations. He claims that they could do this without impoverishing themselves or even causing a decline in their growth rate.

15. Charles B. Shuman, "Food aid and the free market," in *Food Policy,* Peter G. Brown and Henry Shue, eds. (New York: The Free Press), pp. 145-163. In opposition to Shue, Shuman advocates a free-market approach to the problem of hunger and starvation.

16. Julian L. Simon, *The Ultimate Resource* (Princeton, NJ: Princeton University Press, 1981) argues for a position directly opposed to Hardin.

17. Peter Singer, *Practical Ethics* (Cambridge, MA: Cambridge University Press, 1979), pp. 158-181. Singer argues that rich nations have a moral obligation to help poor ones.

18. James P. Sterba, "Human Rights: A Social Contract Perspective," *American Catholic Philosophical Association Proceedings,* Vol. 55 (1981), pp. 268-275. Sterba develops a conception of human rights based on Rawls' social contract theory. Based on this conception, the right to life has priority over the right to property—the right to life interpreted mean noninterference with a person's attempts to acquire the goods and resources necessary for satisfying basic needs.

Chapter Six

WOMEN'S ISSUES

Introduction

In this chapter we turn to some problems of special concern to women. It is an unfortunate fact that in our society women are much more likely to be victims of assault and abuse than men. Women are raped, beaten, and abused every day, and clearly this is wrong. However, three forms of alleged harm to women have generated controversy: date rape, sexual harassment, and pornography. We will consider each of these in turn.

Date Rape. In the readings, Lois Pineau and Camille Paglia agree that rape is wrong and that rapists should be punished. Their disagreement is about the nature and cause of date rape and what should be done about it.

Pineau defines date rape as nonconsensual sex that does not involve physical injury. One practical problem with this definition is that the courts have traditionally accepted only physical injury as evidence that consent was not given, and in the absence of such injury, it is not clear what should count as evidence for nonconsent.

Understanding what constitutes a woman's consent is problematic, since some men believe that a woman may say no when she means yes. Or a woman may say nothing at the time and only later express her lack of consent. In such a case, Pineau would call it rape, but Paglia would not. Paglia rejects the view that a woman's consent must be as explicit as a legal contract, and if it isn't, then she is a victim of rape.

Pineau complains that discussions of rape are vexed by myths that confuse sexual assault with seduction, and submission with enjoyment. Even worse are myths about the natural aggression of men which describe men as incapable of restraint after they are provoked or aroused. Pineau argues that these myths need to be dispelled, and the contractual model of sex replaced with a communicative model.

Paglia has a different view of rape and sex. She defends the so-called myth that men are naturally aggressive. She claims that young men pumped up with testosterone are dangerous sexual animals who are programmed for sex—to hunt, pursue, and capture. The woman who is not careful and provokes or arouses such men is very foolish. As Paglia puts it in the SPIN magazine interview (see the Suggested Readings), such a woman is acting like a woman who leaves her purse on a park bench in Central Park in New York and walks away. Maybe she has a right to complain when her purse is stolen, but leaving it unattended was a dumb thing to do. Instead of claiming victim status, then, women should be careful and responsible; this, says Paglia, is the price women pay for freedom in our society.

Sexual Harassment. Similar issues about definitions arise in discussions of sexual harassment. Again, the issue is not whether sexual harassment is wrong—in the readings both Tong and Paul agree that it is; rather the disagreement is about what counts as sexual harassment and what should be done about it.

Legal treatments of sexual harassment usually begin with the definition given by the United States government. The Equal Employment Opportunity Commission guidelines (which are part of Title VII of the amended Civil Rights Act of 1964) give the following definition:

> Unwelcome sexual advances, requests for sexual favors, and other verbal or physical conduct of a sexual nature constitute sexual harassment when (1) submission to such conduct is made either explicitly or implicitly a term or condition of an individual's employment; (2) submission to or rejection of such conduct by an individual is used as the basis for employment decisions affecting such individual; or (3) such conduct has the purpose or effect of unreasonably interfering with an individual's work performance or creating an intimidating, hostile, or offensive working environment. (Federal Register 45 November 10, 1980: 74675-74677)

In the courts, the type of harassment described in the first two parts of the definition is called **quid pro quo** harassment. This seems to be what Tong has in mind when she talks about coercive sexual harassment which threatens or offers a reward to the victim—although perhaps Tong's category is meant to be more inclusive than quid pro quo harassment.

One of the features of quid pro quo harassment or what Tong calls coercive harassment is that the intentions or beliefs of the accused harasser are not considered. What if the alleged harasser merely intends to be friendly or is flirting? An overly sensitive individual might mistakenly interpret such behavior as sexual harassment. To deal with this problem, the courts have ruled that it must be conduct which a reasonable person (or reasonable woman in the case of *Ellison* v. *Brady,* 1991) would accept as sexual harassment. Of course, this leaves room for disagreement about who is reasonable and what reasonable people would say.

In the readings, Paul mentions another problem with the prosecution of quid pro quo harassment. As she puts it, Title VII is too blunt an instrument. Victims of serious injury who only get back pay are not adequately compensated, and the target of litigation is the employer rather than the harasser. Paul suggests that it would be better if the courts treated sexual harassment as a private injury (a tort in law) and not as a violation of the Civil Rights Act of 1964.

The third part of the sexual harassment definition under Title VII refers to "a hostile environment." This seems to be what Tong has in mind when she talks about noncoercive sexual harassment which aims to annoy or offend the woman rather than obtain sexual favors.

Paul objects that the category of hostile environment is too elastic. On the one hand, it includes trivial offenses such as looks and off-color jokes; and on the other hand, it includes outrageous acts such as repeated obscene gestures and behavior. She suggests that we make a distinction between offensive behavior and serious harm, and only make the latter a criminal offense.

Pornography. As with sexual harassment, discussions of pornography are plagued with definition problems. What is pornography? In the law, pornography has been equated with obscenity. But then the problem is to define obscenity. In the case of *Roth* (1957), the Supreme Court held that the test for obscenity is whether the material taken as a whole appeals to the prurient interest of the average person. The Court ruled that such material is not protected by the First Amendment which guarantees free speech. But who is the average person? If it is a heterosexual person, then materials which appeal to homosexuals but not heterosexuals would not count as obscene. To avoid this problem, and related problems, the Court in *Miller* (1973) modified its position by formulating a threefold test for obscenity: A work is obscene if (1) the average person applying community standards finds that it appeals to prurient interest, (2) the work depicts or describes sexual conduct defined by the law in a patently offensive way, and (3) the work lacks serious literary, artistic, political, or scientific value. Given this definition, what is called hard-core pornography is obscene and may be censored.

But there are still problems. The *Miller* test requires states banning obscenity to formulate standards. These standards can vary from one state to another; what is seen as obscene in Topeka, Kansas, may be viewed as only erotic in New York City. Another objection is that it still allows what is called soft-core pornography, which some people believe should be censored too. Finally, the concept of obscene is still vague. In his dissenting opinion in *Paris Adult Theatre* (1973), Justice Brennan argued that the concept of obscene is so vague that any attempt to censor pornography would necessarily infringe on the right to free speech.

A broader attempt at legally censoring pornography was made by Andrea Dworkin and Catharine MacKinnon in an ordinance for the city of Minneapolis. (See the suggested Readings for books by Dworkin and MacKinnon.) They define pornography as a practice of sex discrimination, and therefore a violation of women's civil rights. It subordinates women and depicts them as abused and dehumanized sex objects. Furthermore, MacKinnon thinks that there is a well-established causal connection between pornography and harm to women: it causes men to rape, batter, prostitute, molest, and sexually harass women.

In the last reading for the chapter, Mark Wicclair agrees that pornography is morally offensive but argues that this by itself does not justify its censorship. He maintains that the causal connection between pornography and harm to women has not been established and offers some reasons for holding that pornography actually reduces harm to women rather than increases it. He provides several more reasons for doubting that the offensive nature of pornography justifies its censorship. Among other things, he suggests, it is doubtful that censorship would do much to help women achieve equality, that there are other better things to do (like passing and enforcing the Equal Rights Amendment), and that the negative side effects of censorship are substantial.

Lois Pineau

Date Rape: A Feminist Analysis

Lois Pineau is Professor of Philosophy at Kansas State University.

Pineau defines date rape as nonaggravated and nonconsensual sex that does not involve physical injury. She maintains that, given this definition, date rape is difficult to prove in court because the prevailing criterion for consent is that consent is implied unless there is active resistance. Underlying this criterion are a number of myths about sex, e.g., that women who are sexually provocative are asking for it, that the male sex drive cannot be controlled, and that women want to be raped. Pineau believes that these myths, and the prevailing contractual model of sex, should be rejected and replaced by a communicative model of sex.

Date rape is nonaggravated sexual assault, nonconsensual sex that does not involve physical injury, or the explicit threat of physical injury. But because it does not involve physical injury, and because physical injury is often the only criterion that is accepted as evidence that the ***actus reas*** is nonconsensual, what is really sexual assault is often mistaken for seduction. The replacement of the old rape laws with the new laws on sexual assault has done nothing to resolve this problem. The question of whether someone has consented to a sexual encounter is still important, and the criteria for consent continue to be the central concern of discourse on sexual assault.

However, if a man is to be convicted, it does not suffice to establish that the *actus reas* was nonconsensual. In order to be guilty of sexual assault a man must have the requisite ***mens rea,*** i.e., he must either have believed that his victim did not consent or that she was probably not consenting. . . .

The criteria for *mens rea,* for the reasonableness of belief, an for consent are closely related. For although a man's sincere belief in the consent of his victim may be sufficient to defeat *mens rea,* the court is less likely to believe his belief is sincere if his belief is unreasonable. If his belief is reasonable, they are more likely to believe in the sincerity of his belief. But evidence of the reasonableness of his belief is also evidence that consent really did take place. For the very things that make it reasonable for *him* to believe that the defendant consented are often the very things that incline the court to believe that she consented. What is often missing is the voice of the woman herself, an account of what it would be reasonable for *her* to agree to, that is to say, an account of what is reasonable from *her* standpoint. . . .

The following statements by self-confessed date rapists reveal how our lack of a solution for dealing with date rape protects rapists by failing to provide their victims with legal recourse:

> All of my rapes have been involved in a dating situation where I've been out with a woman I know. . . . I wouldn't take no for an answer. I think it had something to do with my acceptance of rejection. I had low self-esteem and not much self-confidence and when I was rejected for something which I considered to be rightly mine, I became angry and I went ahead anyway. And this was the same in any situation, whether it was rape or it was something else.[1]

There is, at this time, nothing to protect women from this kind of unscrupulous victimization. A woman on a casual date with a virtual stranger has almost no chance of bringing a complaint of sexual assault before the courts. One reason for this is the prevailing criterion for consent. According to this criterion, consent is implied unless some emphatic episodic sign of resistance occurred, and its occurrence can be established. But if no episodic act occurred, or if it did occur, and the defendant claims that it didn't, or if the defendant threatened the plaintiff but won't admit it in court, it is almost impossible to find any evidence that would support the plaintiff's word against the defendant. This difficulty is exacerbated by suspicion on the part of the courts, police, and legal educators that even where an act of resistance occurs, this act should not be interpreted as a withholding of consent, and this suspicion is especially upheld where the accused is a man who is known to the female plaintiff.

In Glanville Williams's classic textbook on criminal law we are warned that where a man is unknown to a woman, she does not consent if she expresses her rejection in the form of an episodic and vigorous act at the "vital moment." But if the man is known to the woman she must, according to Williams, make use of "all means available to her to repel the man." [2] Williams warns that women often welcome a "mastery advance" and present a token resistance. He quotes Byron's couplet,

> A little still she strove, and much repented
> And whispering "I will ne'er consent"—
> consented

by way of altering law students to the difficulty of distinguishing real protest from pretence.[3] Thus, while in principle, a firm unambiguous stand, or a healthy show of temper ought to be sufficient, if established, to show nonconsent, in practice the forceful overriding of such a stance is apt to be taken as an indication that the resistance was not seriously intended, and that the seduction had succeeded. The consequence of this is that it is almost impossible to establish the defendant's guilt beyond a reasonable doubt.

Thus, on the one hand, we have a situation in which women are vulnerable to the most exploitive tactics at the hands of men who are known to them. On the other hand, almost nothing will count as evidence of their being assaulted, including their having taken an emphatic stance in withholding their consent. The new laws have done almost nothing to change this situation. Yet clearly, some solutions must be sought. Moreover, the road to that solution presents itself clearly enough as a need for a reformulation of the criterion of consent. It is patent that a criterion that collapses whenever the crime itself succeeds will not suffice. . . .

The Problem of the Criterion

The reasoning that underlies the present criterion of consent is entangled in a number of mutually supportive mythologies which see sexual assault as masterful seduction, and silent submission as sexual enjoyment. Because the prevailing ideology has so much informed our conceptualization of sexual interaction, it is extraordinarily difficult for us to distinguish between assault and seduction, submission and enjoyment, or so we imagine. At the same time, this failure to distinguish has given rise to a network of rationalizations that support the conflation of assault with seduction, submission with enjoyment. I therefore want to begin my argument by providing an example which shows both why it is so difficult to make this distinction, and that it exists. Later, I will identify and attempt to unravel the lines of reasoning that reinforce this difficulty.

The woman I have in mind agrees to see someone because she feels an intimate attraction to him and believes that he feels the same way about her. She goes out with him in the hope that there will be mutual enjoyment and in the course of the day or evening an increase of mutual interest. Unfortunately, these hopes of *mutual* and *reciprocal* interest are not realized. We do not know how much interest she has in him by the end of their time together, but whatever her feelings she comes under pressure to have sex with him, and she does not want to have the kind of sex he wants. She may desire to hold hands and kiss, to engage in more intense caresses or in some form of foreplay, or she may not want to be touched. She may have reasons unrelated to desire for not wanting to engage in the kind of sex he is demanding. She may have religious reservations, concerns about pregnancy or disease, a disinclination to be just another conquest. She may be engaged in a seduction program of her own which sees abstaining from sexual activity as a means of building an important emotional bond. She feels she is desirable to him, and she knows, and he knows that he will have sex with her if he can. And while she feels she doesn't owe him anything, and that it is her prerogative to refuse him, this feeling is partly a defensive reaction against a deeply held belief that if he is in need, she should provide. If she buys into the myth of insistent male sexuality she may feel he is suffering from sexual frustration and that she is largely to blame.

We do not know how much he desires her, but we do know that his desire for erotic satisfaction can hardly be separated from his desire for conquest. He feels no dating obligation, but has a strong commitment to scoring. He uses the myth of "so hard to control" male desire as a rhetorical tactic, telling her how frustrated she will leave him. He becomes overbearing. She resists, voicing her disinclination. He alternates between telling her how desirable she is and taking a hostile stance, charging her with misleading him, accusing her of wanting him, and being coy, in short of being deceitful, all the time engaging in rather aggressive body contact. It is late at night, she is tired and a bit queasy from too many drinks, and he is reaffirming her suspicion that perhaps she has misled him. She is having trouble disengaging his body from hers, and wishes he would just go away. She does not adopt a strident angry stance, partly because she feels she thinks he is acting normally and does not deserve it, partly because she feels she is partly to blame, and partly because there is always the danger that her anger will make him angry, possibly violent. It seems that the only thing to do, given his aggression, and her queasy fatigue, is to go along with him and get it over with, but this decision is so entangled with the events in process it is hard to know if it is not simply a recognition of what is actually happening. She finds the whole encounter a thoroughly disagreeable experience, but he does not take any notice, and wouldn't have changed course if he had. He congratulates himself on his sexual prowess and is confirmed in his opinion that aggressive tactics pay off. Later she feels that she has been raped, but paradoxically tells herself that she let herself be raped.

The paradoxical feelings of the woman in our example indicate her awareness that what she feels about the incident stands in contradiction to the prevailing cultural assessment of it. She knows that she did not want to have sex with her date. She is not so sure, however, about how much her own desires count, and she is uncertain that she has made her desires clear. Her uncertainty is reinforced by the cultural reading of this incident as an ordinary seduction.

As for us, we assume that the woman did not want to have sex, but just like her, we are unsure whether her mere reluctance, in the presence of high-pressure tactics, constitutes nonconsent. We suspect that submission to an overbearing and insensitive lout is no way to go about attaining sexual enjoyment, and we further suspect that he felt no compunction about providing it, so that on the face of it, from the outside looking in, it looks like a pretty unreasonable proposition for her.

Let us look at this reasoning more closely. Assume that she was not attracted to the kind of sex offered by the sort of person offering it. Then it would be *prima facie* unreasonable for her to agree to have sex, unreasonable, that is, unless she were offered some pay-off of her stoic endurance, money perhaps, or tickets to the opera. The reason is that in sexual matters, agreement is closely connected to attraction. Thus, where the presumption is that she was not attracted, we should at the same time presume that she did not consent. Hence, the burden of proof should be on her alleged assailant to show that she had good reasons for consenting to an unattractive proposition.

This is not, however, the way such situations are interpreted. In the unlikely event that the example I have described should come before the courts, there is little doubt that the law would interpret the woman's eventual acquiescence or "going along with" the sexual encounter as consent. But along with this interpretation would go the implicit understanding that she had consented because when all was said and done, when the "token" resistances to the "masterful advances" had been made, she had wanted to after all. Once the courts have constructed this interpretation, they are then forced to conjure up some horror story of feminine revenge in order to explain why she should bring charges against her "seducer."

In the even more unlikely event that the courts agreed that the woman had not consented to the above encounter, there is little chance that her assailant would be convicted of sexual assault.[4] The belief that the man's aggressive tactics are a normal part of seduction means that *mens rea* cannot be established. Her eventual "going along" with his advances constitutes reasonable grounds for his believing in her consent. These "reasonable" grounds attest to the sincerity of his belief in her consent. This reasonableness means that *mens rea* would be defeated even in jurisdictions which make *mens rea* a function of objective standards of reasonableness. Moreover, the sympathy of the court is more likely to lie with the rapist than with his victim, since, if the court is typical, it will be strongly inclined to believe that the victim had in some way "asked for it."

The position of the courts is supported by the widespread belief that male aggression and female reluctance are normal parts of seduction. Given their appearance of this model, the logic of their response must be respected. For if sexual aggression is a part of ordinary seduction, then it cannot be inconsistent with the legitimate consent of the person allegedly seduced by this means. And if it is normal for a woman to be reluctant, then this reluctance must be consistent with her consent as well. The position of the courts is not inconsistent just so long as they allow that some sort of protest on the part of a woman counts as a refusal. As we have seen, however, it frequently happens that no sort of a protest would count as a refusal. Moreover, if no sort of protest, or at least if precious few count, then the failure to register these protests will amount to "asking for it," it will amount, in other words, to agreeing.

The court's belief in "natural" male aggression and "natural" female reluctance has increasingly come under attack by feminist critics who see quite correctly that the entire legal position would collapse if, for example, it were shown empirically that men were not aggressive, and that women, at least when they wanted sex, were. This strategy is of little help, however, so long as aggressive men can still be found, and relics of reluctant women continue to surface. Fortunately, there is another strategy. The position collapses through the weakness of its internal logic. The next section traces several lines of this logic.

Rape Myths

The belief that the natural aggression of men and the natural reluctance of women somehow makes date rape understandable underlies a number of prevalent myths about rape and human sexuality. These beliefs maintain their force partly on account of a logical compulsion exercised by them at an unconscious level. The only way of refuting them effectively is to excavate the logical propositions involved, and to expose their misapplication to the situations to which they have been applied. In what follows, I propose to excavate the logical support for popular attitudes that are tolerant of date rape. These myths are not just popular, however, but often emerge in the arguments of judges who acquit date rapists, and policemen who refuse to lay charges.

The claim that the victim provoked a sexual incident, that "she asked for it," is by far the most common defense given by men who are accused of sexual assault. . . .

The least sophisticated of the "she asked for it" rationales, and in a sense, the easiest to deal with, appeals to an injunction against sexually provocative behaviour on the part of women. If women should not be sexually provocative, then, from this standpoint, a woman who is sexually provocative deserves to suffer the consequences. Now it will not do to respond that women get raped even when they are not sexually provocative, or that it is men who get to interpret (unfairly) what counts as sexually provocative. The question should be: Why shouldn't a woman be sexually provocative? Why should this behaviour warrant any kind of aggressive response whatsoever?

Attempts to explain that women have a right to behave in sexually provocative ways without suffering dire consequences still meet with surprisingly tough resistance. Even people who find nothing wrong or sinful with sex itself, in any of its forms, tend to suppose that women must not behave sexually unless they are prepared to carry through on some fuller course of sexual interaction. The logic of this response seems to be that at some point a woman's behavior commits her to following through on the full course of a sexual encounter as it is defined by her assailant. At some point she has made an agreement, or formed a contract, and once that is done, her contractor is entitled to demand that she satisfy the terms of that contract. Thus, this view about sexual responsibility and desert is supported by other assumptions about contracts and agreement. But we do not normally suppose that casual nonverbal behavior generates agreements. Nor do we normally grant private persons the right to enforce contracts. What rationale would support our conclusion in this case?

The rationale, I believe, comes in the form of a belief in the especially insistent nature of male sexuality, an insistence which lies at the root of natural male aggression, and which is extremely difficult, perhaps impossible, to contain. At a certain point in the arousal process, it is thought, a man's rational will gives way to the perogatives of nature. His sexual need can and does reach a point where it is uncontrollable, and his natural masculine aggression kicks in to assure that this need is met. Women, however, are naturally more contained, and so it is their responsibility not to provoke the irrational in the male. If they do go so far as that, they have both failed in their responsibilities, and subjected themselves to the inevitable. One does not go into the lion's cage and expect not to be eaten. Natural feminine reluctance, it is thought, is no protection against a sexually aroused male.

The belief about the normal aggressiveness of male sexuality is complemented by common knowledge about female gender development. Once, women were taught to deny their sexuality and to aspire to ideals of chastity. Things have not changed so much. Women still tend to eschew conquest mentalities in favor of a combination of sex and affection. Insofar as this is thought to be merely a cultural requirement, however, there is an expectation that women will be coy about their sexual desire. The assumption that women both want to indulge sexually, and are inclined to sacrifice this desire for higher ends, gives rise to the myth that they want to be raped. After all, doesn't rape give them the sexual enjoyment they *really* want, at the same time that it relieves them of the responsibility for admitting to and acting upon what they want? And how then can we blame men, who have been socialized to be aggressively seductive precisely for the purpose of overriding female reserve? If we find fault at all, we are inclined to cast our suspicions on the motives of the woman. For it is on her that the contradictory roles of sexual desirer and sexual denier have been placed. Our awareness of the contradiction expected of her makes us suspect her honesty. In the past, she was expected to deny her complicity because of the shame and guilt she felt at having submitted. This expectation persists in many quarters today, and is carried over into a general suspicion about her character, and the fear that she might make a false accusation out of revenge, or some other low motive. . . .

Dispelling the Myths

The "she asked for it" justification for sexual assault incorporates a conception of a contract that would be difficult to defend in any other context and the presumptions about human sexuality which function to reinforce sympathies rooted in the contractual notion of just deserts are not supported by empirical research.

The belief that a woman generates some sort of contractual obligation whenever her behavior is interpreted as seductive is the most indefensible part of the mythology of rape. In law, contracts are not legitimate just because a promise has been made. In particular, the use of pressure tactics to extract agreement is frowned upon. . . .

Even if we assume that a woman has initially agreed to an encounter, her agreement does not automatically make all subsequent sexual activity to which she submits legitimate. If during coitus a woman should experience pain, be suddenly overcome with guilt or fear of pregnancy, or simply lose her initial desire, those are good reasons for her to change her mind. Having changed her mind, neither her partner nor the state has any right to force her to continue. But then if she is forced to continue she is assaulted. Thus, establishing that consent occurred at a particular point during a sexual encounter should not conclusively establish the legitimacy of the encounter. What is needed is a reading of whether she agreed throughout the encounter.

If the "she asked for it" contractual view of sexual interchange has any validity, it is because there is a point at which there is no stopping a sexual encounter, a point at which that encounter becomes the inexorable outcome of the unfolding of natural events. If a sexual encounter is like a slide on which I cannot stop halfway down, it will be relevant whether I enter the slide of my own free will, or am pushed.

But there is no evidence that the entire sexual act is like a slide. While there may be a few seconds in the "plateau" period just prior to orgasm in which people are "swept" away by sexual feelings to the point where we could justifiably understand their lack of heed for the comfort of their partner, the greater part of a sexual encounter comes well within the bounds of morally responsible control of our own actions. Indeed, the available evidence shows that most of the activity involved in sex has to do with building the requisite level of desire, a task that involves the proper use of foreplay, the possibility of which implies control over the form that foreplay will take. Modern sexual therapy assumes that such control is universally accessible, and so far there has been no reason to question that assumption. Sexologists are unanimous, moreover, in holding that mutual sexual enjoyment requires an atmosphere of comfort and communication, a minimum of pressure, and an ongoing check-up on one's partner's state. They maintain that different people have different predilections, and that what is pleasurable for one person is very often anathema to another. These findings show that the way to achieve sexual pleasure, at any time at all, let alone with a casual acquaintance, decidedly does not involve overriding the other person's express reservations and providing them with just any kind of sexual stimulus. . . . In this case science seems to concur with women's perception that aggressive incommunicative sex is not what they want. But if science and the voice of women concur, if aggressive seduction does not lead to good sex, if women do not like it or want it, then it is not rational to think that they would agree to it. Where such sex takes place, it is therefore rational to presume that the sex was not consensual. . . .

In conclusion, there are no grounds for the "she asked for it" defence. Sexually provocative behaviour does not generate sexual contracts. Even where there are sexual agreements, they cannot be legitimately enforced either by the State, or by private right, or by natural prerogative. Secondly, all the evidence suggests that neither women nor men find sexual enjoyment in rape or in any form of non-communicative sexuality. Thirdly, male sexual desire is containable, and can be subjected to moral and rational control. Fourthly, since there is no reason why women should not be sexually provocative, they do not "deserve" any sex they do not want. This last is a welcome discovery. The taboo on sexual provocativeness in women is a taboo both on sensuality and on teasing. But sensuality is a source of delight, and teasing is playful and inspires wit. What a relief to learn that it is not sexual provocativeness, but its enemies, that constitutes a danger to the world.

Communicative Sexuality: Reinterpreting the Kantian Imperative

The present criterion of consent sets up sexual encounters as contractual events in which sexual aggression is presumed to be consented to unless there is some vigorous act of refusal. As long as we view sexual interaction on a contractual model, the only possibility for finding fault is to point to the presence of such an act. But it is clear that whether or not we can determine such a presence, there is something strongly disagreeable about the sexual aggression described above.

In thinking about sex we must keep in mind its sensual ends, and the facts show that aggressive high-pressure sex contradicts those ends. Consensual sex in dating situations is presumed to aim at mutual enjoyment. It may not always do this, and when it does, it might not always succeed. There is no logical incompatibility between wanting to continue a sexual encounter, and failing to derive sexual pleasure from it.

But it seems to me that there is a presumption in favour of the connection between sex and sexual enjoyment, and that if a man wants to be sure that he is not forcing himself on a woman, he has an obligation either to ensure that the encounter really is mutually enjoyable, or to know the reasons why she would want to continue the encounter in spite of her lack of enjoyment. A closer investigation of the nature of this obligation will enable us to construct a more rational and a more plausible norm of sexual conduct. . . .

The obligation to promote the sexual ends of one's partner implies the obligation to know what those ends are, and also the obligation to know how those ends are attained. Thus, the problem comes down to a problem of epistemic responsibility, the responsibility to know. The solution, in my view, lies in the practice of a communicative sexuality, one which combines the appropriate knowledge of the other with respect for the dialectics of desire.

So let us, for a moment, conceive of sexual interaction on a communicative other than a contractual model. Let us look at it the way I think it should be looked at, as if it were a proper conversation rather than an offer from the Mafia. . . .

The communicative interaction involved in conversation is concerned with a good deal more than didactic content and argument. Good conversationalists are intuitive, sympathetic, and charitable. Intuition and charity aid the conversationalist in her effort to interpret the words of the other correctly and sympathy enables her to enter into the other's point of view. Her sensitivity alerts her to the tone of the exchange. Has her point been taken good-humouredly or resentfully? Aggressively delivered responses are taken as a sign that ***ad hominems*** are at work, and that the respondent's self-worth has been called into question. Good conversationalists will know to suspend further discussion until this sense of self-worth has been reestablished. Angry responses, resentful responses, bored responses, even over-enthusiastic responses require that the emotional ground be cleared before the discussion be continued. Often it is better to change the topic, or to come back to it on another day under different circumstances. Good conversationalists do not overwhelm their respondents with a barrage of their own opinions. While they may be persuasive, the forcefulness of their persuasion does not lie in their being overbearing, but rather in their capacity to see the other's point of view, to understand what it depends on, and so to address the essential point, but with tact and clarity.

Just as communicative conversationalists are concerned with more than didactic content, persons engaged in communicative sexuality will be concerned with more than achieving coitus. They will be sensitive to the responses of their partners. They will, like good conversationalists, be intuitive, sympathetic, and charitable. Intuition will help them to interpret their partner's responses; sympathy will enable them to share what their partner is feeling; charity will enable them to care. Communicative sexual partners will not overwhelm each other with the barrage of their own desires. They will treat negative, bored, or angry responses as a sign that the erotic ground needs to be either cleared or abandoned. Their concern with fostering the desire of the other must involve an ongoing state of alertness in interpreting her responses.

Just as a conversationalist's prime concern is for the mutuality of the discussion, a person engaged in communicative sexuality will be most concerned with the mutuality of desire. As such, both will put into practice a regard for their respondent that is guaranteed no place in the contractual language of rights, duties, and consent. The **dialectics** of both activities reflect the dialectics of desire insofar as each person's interest in continuing is contingent upon the other person wishing to do so too, and each person's interest is as much fueled by the other's interest as it is by her own. . . .

Cultural Presumptions

. . . Traditionally, the decision to date indicates that two people have an initial attraction to each other, that they are disposed to like each other, and look forward to enjoying each other's company. Dating derives its implicit meaning from this tradition. It retains this meaning unless other aims are explicitly stated, and even then it may not be possible to alienate this meaning. It is a rare woman who will not spurn a man who states explicitly, right at the onset, that he wants to go out with her solely on the condition that he have sexual intercourse with her at the end of the evening, and that he has no interest in her company apart from gaining that end, and no concern for mutual satisfaction.

Explicit protest to the contrary aside, the conventions of dating confer on it its social meaning, and this social meaning implies a relationship which is more like friendship than the cutthroat competition of opposing teams. As such, it requires that we do more than stand on our rights with regard to each other. As long as we are operating under the auspices of a dating relationship, it requires that we behave in the mode of friendship and trust. But if a date is more like friendship than a business contract, then clearly respect for the dialectics of desire is incompatible with the sort of sexual pressure that is inclined to end in date rape. And clearly, also, a conquest mentality which exploits a situation of trust and respect for purely selfish ends is morally pernicious. Failure to respect the dialectics of desire when operating under the auspices of friendship and trust is to act in flagrant disregard of the moral requirement to avoid manipulative, coercive, and exploitive behaviour. Respect for the dialectics of desire is *prima facie* inconsistent with the satisfaction of one person at the expense of the other. The proper end of friendship relations is mutual satisfaction. But the requirement of mutuality means that we must take a communicative approach to discovering the ends of the other, and this entails that we respect the dialectics of desire.

But now that we know what communicative sexuality is, and that it is morally required, and that it is the only feasible means to mutual sexual enjoyment, why not take this model as the norm of what is reasonable in sexual interaction? The evidence of sexologists strongly indicates that women whose partners are aggressively uncommunicative have little chance of experiencing sexual pleasure. But it is not reasonable for women to consent to what they have little chance of enjoying. Hence it is not reasonable for women to consent to aggressive noncommunicative sex. Nor can we reasonably suppose that women have consented to sexual encounters which we know and they know they do not find enjoyable. With the communicative model as the norm, the aggressive contractual model should strike us as a model of deviant sexuality, and sexual encounters patterned on that model should strike us as encounters to which *prima facie* no one would reasonably agree. But if acquiescence to an encounter counts as consent only if the acquiescence is reasonable, something to which a reasonable person, in full possession of knowledge relevant to the encounter, would agree, then acquiescence to aggressive noncommunicative sex is not reasonable. Hence, acquiescence under such conditions should not count as consent.

Thus, where communicative sexuality does not occur, we lack the main ground for believing that the sex involved was consensual. Moreover, where a man does not engage in communicative sexuality, he acts either out of reckless disregard, or out of willful ignorance. For he cannot know, except through the practice of communicative sexuality, whether his partner has any sexual reason for continuing the encounter. And where she does not, he runs the risk of imposing on her what she is not willing to have. All that is needed then, in order to provide women with legal protection from "date rape," is to make both reckless indifference and willful ignorance a sufficient condition of *mens rea* and to make communicative sexuality the accepted norm of sex to which a reasonable woman would agree. Thus, the appeal to communicative sexuality as a norm for sexual encounters accomplishes two things. It brings the aggressive sex involved in "date rape" well within the realm of sexual assault, and it locates the guilt of date rapists in the failure to approach sexual relations on a communicative basis. . . .

Endnotes

1. *Why Men Rape,* Sylvia Levine and Joseph Loenig, eds. (Toronto: Macmillan, 1980), p. 83.
2. Williams, *Textbook of Criminal Law* (1983), p. 238.
3. Ibid.
4. See Jeanne C. Marsh, Allison Geist, and Nathan Caplan, *Rape and the Limits of Law Reform* (Boston: Auburn House, 1982), p. 32. According to Marsh's study on the impact on the Michigan reform of rape laws, convictions were increased for traditional conceptions of rape, i.e., aggravated assault. However date rape, which has a much higher incidence than aggravated assault, has a very low rate of arrest and an even lower one of conviction.

Review Questions

1. How does Pineau define date rape?
2. Why is it difficult to prove in court that date rape has occurred?
3. Pineau gives a hypothetical example of date rape. Why would the man be found not guilty of rape in a court of law?
4. According to Pineau, there are several myths about rape and sex in our culture. What are they and why should they be dispelled?
5. Explain Pineau's communicative model of sex, as distinguished from the contractual model.

Discussion Questions

1. Is the hypothetical example Pineau describes really a case of rape? Why or why not?
2. Pinaeu argues that women have a right to be sexually provocative without suffering any dire consequences. Do you agree?
3. Is seduction even possible on Pineau's communicative model? Explain your view.

Camille Paglia

Rape and Modern Sex War

Camille Paglia is Professor of Humanities at the University of the Arts in Philadelphia. She is the author of Sexual Personnae: Art and Decadence from Nefertiti to Emily Dickinson *(1990), and* Sex, Art, and American Culture *(1992).*

Paglia expresses a theory of sex that is different from Pinea's view. Paglia denies that the male sex drive can be controlled or is formed by the environment; instead, she claims, a strong and uncontrollable sex drive is biologically programmed into males. The male sex drive is deeply intertwined with aggression, hunting, pursuit, and capture. Given these facts about males, women who provoke or arouse men are not just putting themselves at risk—they are fools. Instead of whining about being victims, women should deal with problems about sex and rape with self-awareness, self-control, and acceptance of personal responsibility.

Rape is an outrage that cannot be tolerated in civilized society. Yet feminism, which has waged a crusade for rape to be taken more seriously, has put young women in danger by hiding the truth about sex from them.

In dramatizing the pervasiveness of rape, feminists have told young women that before they have sex with a man, they must give consent as explicit as a legal contract's. In this way, young women have been convinced that they have been the victims of rape. On elite campuses in the Northeast and on the West Coast, they have held consciousness-raising sessions, petitioned administrations, demanded inquests. At Brown University, outraged, panicky "victims" have scrawled the names of alleged attackers on the walls of women's rest rooms. What marital rape was to the Seventies, "date rape" is to the Nineties.

The incidence and seriousness of rape do not require this kind of exaggeration. Real acquaintance rape is nothing new. It has been a horrible problem for women for all of recorded history. Once fathers and brothers protected women from rape. Once the penalty for rape was death. I come from a fierce Italian tradition where, not so long ago in the motherland, a rapist would end up knifed, castrated, and hung out to dry.

But the old clans and small rural communities have broken down. In our cities, on our campuses far from home, young women are vulnerable and defenseless. Feminism has not prepared them for this. Feminism keeps saying the sexes are the same. It keeps telling women they can do anything, go anywhere, say anything, wear anything. No, they can't. Women will always be in sexual danger.

One of my male students recently slept overnight with a friend in a passageway of the Great Pyramid in Egypt. He described the moon and sand, the ancient silence and eerie echoes. I will never experience that. I am a woman. I am not stupid enough to believe I could ever be safe there. There is a world of solitary adventure I will never have. Women have always known these somber truths. But feminism, with its pie-in-the-sky fantasies about the perfect world, keeps young women from seeing life as it is.

We must remedy social injustice wherever we can. But there are some things we cannot change. There are sexual differences that are based in biology. Academic feminism is lost in a fog of **social constructionism**. It believes we are totally the product of our environment. This idea was invented by Rousseau. He was wrong. Emboldened by dumb French language theory, academic feminists repeat the same hollow slogans over and over to each other. Their view of sex is naïve and prudish. Leaving sex to the feminists is like letting your dog vacation at the taxidermist's.

From Camille Paglia, *New York Newsday*, January 27, 1991. Reprinted in Camille Paglia, *Sex, Art, and American Culture* (New York: Vintage Books, 1992).

The sexes are at war. Men must struggle for identity against the overwhelming power of their mothers. Women have menstruation to tell them they are women. Men must do or risk something to be men. Men become masculine only when other men say they are. Having sex with a woman is one way a boy becomes a man.

College men are at their hormonal peak. They have just left their mothers and are questing for their male identity. In groups, they are dangerous. A woman going to a fraternity party is walking into Testosterone Flats, full of prickly cacti and blazing guns. If she goes, she should be armed with resolute alertness. She should arrive with girlfriends and leave with them. A girl who lets herself get dead drunk at a fraternity party is a fool. A girl who goes upstairs alone with a brother at a fraternity party is an idiot. Feminists call this "blaming the victim." I call it common sense.

For a decade, feminists have drilled their disciples to say, "Rape is a crime of violence but not of sex." This sugar-coated Shirley Temple nonsense has exposed young women to disaster. Misled by feminism, they do not expect rape from the nice boys from good homes who sit next to them in class.

Aggression and eroticism are deeply intertwined. Hunt, pursuit, and capture are biologically programmed into male sexuality. Generation after generation, men must be educated, refined, and ethically persuaded away from their tendency toward anarchy and brutishness. Society is not the enemy, as feminism ignorantly claims. Society is woman's protection against rape. Feminism, with its solemn Carry Nation repressiveness, does not see what is for men the eroticism or fun element in rape, especially the wild, infectious delirium of gang rape. Women who do not understand rape cannot defend themselves against it.

The date-rape controversy shows feminism hitting the wall of its own broken promises. The women of my Sixties generation were the first respectable girls in history to swear like sailors, get drunk, stay out all night—in short, to act like men. We sought total sexual freedom and equality. But as time passed, we woke up to cold reality. The old double standard protected women. When anything goes, it's women who lose.

Today's young women don't know what they want. They see that feminism has not brought sexual happiness. The theatrics of public rage over date rape are their way of restoring the old sexual rules that were shattered by my generation. Because nothing about the sexes has really changed. The comic film *Where the Boys Are* (1960), the ultimate expression of Fifties man-chasing, still speaks directly to our time. It shows smart, lively women skillfully anticipating and fending off the dozens of strategies with which horny men try to get them into bed. The agonizing date-rape subplot and climax are brilliantly done. The victim, Yvette Mimieux, makes mistake after mistake, obvious to the other girls. She allows herself to be lured away from her girlfriends and into isolation with boys whose character and intentions she misreads. *Where the Boys Are* tells the truth. It shows courtship as a dangerous game in which the signals are not verbal but subliminal.

Neither militant feminism, which is obsessed with politically correct language, nor academic feminism, which believes that knowledge and experience are "constituted by" language, can understand preverbal or nonverbal communication. Feminism, focusing on sexual politics, cannot see that sex exists in and through the body. Sexual desire and arousal cannot be fully translated into verbal terms. This is why men and women misunderstand each other.

Trying to remake the future, feminism cut itself off from sexual history. It discarded and suppressed the sexual myths of literature, art, and religion. Those myths show us the turbulence, the mysteries and passions of sex. In mythology we see men's sexual anxiety, their fear of woman's dominance. Much sexual violence is rooted in men's sense of psychological weakness toward women. It takes many men to deal with one woman. Woman's voracity is a persistent motif. Clara Bow, it was rumored, took on the USC football team on weekends. Marilyn Monroe, singing "Diamonds Are a Girl's Best Friend," rules a conga line of men in tuxes. Half-clad Cher, in the video for "If I Could Turn Back Time," deranges a battleship of screaming sailors and straddles a pink-lit cannon. Feminism, coveting social power, is blind to woman's cosmic sexual power.

To understand rape, you must study the past. There never was and never will be sexual harmony. Every woman must take personal responsibility for her sexuality, which is nature's red flame. She must be prudent and cautious about where she goes and with whom. When she makes a mistake, she must accept the consequences and, through self-criticism, resolve never to make that mistake again. Running to Mommy and Daddy on the campus grievance committee is unworthy of strong women. Posting lists of guilty men in the toilet is cowardly, infantile stuff.

The Italian philosophy of life espouses high-energy confrontation. A male student makes a vulgar remark about your breasts? Don't slink off to whimper and simper with the campus shrinking violets. Deal with it. On the spot. Say, "Shut up, you jerk! And crawl back to the barnyard where you belong!" In general, women who project this take-charge attitude toward life get harassed less often. I see too many dopey, immature, self-pitying women walking around like melting sticks of butter. It's the Yvette Mimieux syndrome: make me happy. And listen to me weep when I'm not.

The date-rape debate is already smothering in propaganda churned out by the expensive Northeastern colleges and universities, with their overconcentration of boring, uptight academic feminists and spoiled, affluent students. Beware of the deep manipulativeness of rich students who were neglected by their parents. They love to turn the campus into hysterical psychodramas of sexual transgression, followed by assertions of parental authority and concern. And don't look for sexual enlightenment from academe, which spews out mountains of books but never looks at life directly.

As a fan of football and rock music, I see in the simple, swaggering masculinity of the jock and in the noisy posturing of the heavy-metal guitarist certain fundamental, unchanging truths about sex. Masculinity is aggressive, unstable, combustible. It is also the most creative cultural force in history. Women must reorient themselves toward the elemental powers of sex, which can strengthen or destroy.

The only solution to date rape is female self-awareness and self-control. A woman's number one line of defense is herself. When a real rape occurs, she should report it to the police. Complaining to college committees because the courts "take too long" is ridiculous. College administrations are not a branch of the judiciary. They are not equipped or trained for legal inquiry. Colleges must alert incoming students to the problems and dangers of adulthood. Then colleges must stand back and get out of the sex game.

Review Questions

1. Compare Paglia's view of sex with that of Pineau.
2. Paglia makes a number of criticisms of academic feminism and militant feminism. What are they?
3. What is Paglia's view of rape, as distinguished from that of Pineau?

Discussion Questions

1. What do you think Paglia would say about Pineau's example?
2. Who has a more accurate view of sex and rape—Pineau or Paglia?

Rosemarie Tong

Sexual Harassment

Rosmarie Tong teaches philosophy at Davidson College in Davidson, North Carolina. Our reading is taken from her book Women, Sex, and the Law *(1984).*

Tong distinguishes between three different kinds of harassment in the workplace. Coercive sexual harassment is sexual misconduct that offers a benefit or threatens some harm to the person to whom it is directed. Noncoercive sexual harassment is sexual misconduct that is intended to annoy or offend the victim. Gender harassment is a more general category of sexual harassment whose intent is to dominate women or keep them subordinate to men.

Although definitions of sexual harassment are by no means uniform, many feminist antiharassers agree that sexual harassment involves four conditions: (1) an annoying or unwelcome sexual advance or imposition; (2) a negative response to this sexual advance/imposition; (3) the presence of intimidation or coercion when the sexual harasser holds more power than the person sexually harassed and, frequently, (4) the suggestion that institutionally inappropriate rewards or penalties will result from compliance or refusal to comply.

This preliminary definition, critics point out, leaves much to be desired. First, it fails to illuminate the connection between the sexual advance/imposition, the negative response, and the institutional consequences. For instance, how forceful must the response be? How serious must the consequences be? Second, the definition fails to make clear who this society's powerholders are. Must one be an employer or a professor in order to have power over a woman employee or a woman student? Or does the mere fact that a person is male give him an automatic power over a female's fate? Third, it fails to distinguish between the kind of coercion that consists of a threatened penalty and the kind that consists of a promised reward. Properly speaking, is not the latter form of coercion more aptly described as a pressure tactic or an incentive technique? Fourth, and most important, the definition fails to indicate which of the four conditions are necessary for sexual harassment and which are sufficient.

In response to these criticisms, but especially the last one, feminists have refined their definition of sexual harassment. As they see it, there are two types of sexual harassment: coercive and noncoercive. Coercive sexual harassment includes (1) sexual misconduct that offers a benefit or reward to the person to whom it is directed, as well as (2) sexual misconduct that threatens some harm to the person to whom it is directed. An example of the first instance would be offering someone a promotion only if she provides a sexual favor. An example of the second instance would be stating that one will assign a student a failing grade unless she performs a sexual favor. In contrast, noncoercive sexual harassment denotes sexual misconduct that merely annoys or offends the person to whom it is directed. Examples of noncoercive sexual misconduct are repeatedly using a lewd nickname ("Boobs") to refer to an attractive coworker, or prowling around the women's dormitory after midnight. What coercive and noncoercive modes of sexual harassment have in common, of course, is that they are unsolicited, unwelcome, and generally unwanted by the women to whom they are directed.[1]

Coercive Sexual Harassment

According to feminists, a coercive act is "one where the person coerced is made to feel com-

---

"Sexual Harassment" from "Black Perspectives on Sex and the Law," in *Women, Sex, and the Law* by Rosemarie Tong (Totowa, NJ: Rowman and Littlefield, 1984).

pelled to do something he or she would not normally do.[2] This compulsion is accomplished by the coercer's "adversely changing the options available for the victim's choosing."[3] The paradigm case of coercion is, of course, the use of physical or psychological restraint, but *threats* of physical or psychological restraint/reprisal are also coercive to a lesser degree. Although it is difficult to determine whether a sexual harasser has in fact narrowed for the worse the options available for a woman's choosing, John Hughes and Larry May provide two tests to facilitate such determinations: would the woman have "freely chosen" to change her situation before the alleged threat was made for her situation after the broaching of the alleged threat; and, would the woman be made "worse off" than she otherwise would be by not complying with the offer?[4]

Relying on Hughes and May's twofold test, feminists maintain that sexual advances/impositions that threaten some harm to the person to whom they are directed are clearly coercive. "If you don't go to bed with me, Suzy, I'll fail you in this course." Assuming that Suzy has not been secretly longing to sleep with her professor or to flunk her course, she would not freely choose to change her situation to one in which the only way she can attain a passing grade is by sleeping with him. Therefore, because Suzy's professor has adversely altered her options, he has coerced her into a very tight corner; and since a coercive sexual advance is by definition an instance of sexual harassment, Suzy's professor is guilty of sexual harassment.

In contrast to sexual advances backed by threats, feminists admit that sexual advances backed by offers do not constitute clear cases of sexual harassment. Nonetheless, like sexual threats, sexual offers are coercive. It is just that the bitter pill of coercion is coated with a sugary promise: "If you go to bed with me, Suzy, I'll give you an 'A' in this course." According to critics, however, feminists confuse seduction with sexual harassment when they conflate sexual offers with sexual threats—when they insist that every time a man pressures a woman for a sexual favor by promising her a reward, he coerces her into saying an unwilling yes to his request. In this connection, Michael Bayles asks feminists to ponder the following hypothetical case:

> Assume there is a mediocre woman graduate student who would not receive an assistantship. Suppose the department chairman offers her one if she goes to bed with him, and she does so. In what sense has the graduate student acted against her will? She apparently preferred having the assistantship and sleeping with the chairman to not sleeping with the chairman and not having the assistantship . . . the fact that choice has undesirable consequences does not make it against one's will. One may prefer having clean teeth without having to brush them; nonetheless, one is not acting against one's will when one brushes them.[5]

As Bayles sees it, the department chairman has not coerced the graduate student to sleep with him. Rather he has seduced her to sleep with him. Consequently, whatever the chairman is guilty of, it is not sexual harassment. Bayles's reasons for insisting that the graduate student has not been coerced are two. First, she would have freely chosen to move from the preoffer stage (no chance of an assistantship) to the postoffer stage (a chance of an assistantship). Second, her options after the sexual offer are not worse than before. If she refuses the sexual offer, she will not lose a chance for an assistantship because she was never in the running; and if she accepts the sexual offer, she will have not only a chance for an assistantship, but an assistantship. Despite the superficial plausibility of Bayles's analysis, feminists (once again following Hughes and May) insist that a deeper reading of the graduate student's dilemma indicates that she has in fact been coerced by her department chairman. In the first place, assuming the graduate student has not been dying to go to bed with her chairman, and that she is not a calculating mercenary who has been hoping for a sexual offer to bail her out of a dead-end career trajectory, it is not clear that she would have freely chosen to move from the preoffer stage to the postoffer stage. The best reason for her not wishing to move to the post-offer stage is that it places her in a "damned if you do, damned if you don't" predicament.

On the one hand, if the graduate student refuses to sleep with her chairman, she will of course *not* receive an undeserved assistantship. In addition, she will place herself at considerable risk. Perhaps the chairman is talking sweetly today only because he thinks the graduate student will be in his bed tomorrow. Should she disappoiont him, he may turn against her. This is a real possibility, given the unpredictable character of sexual feelings and the history of reprisals against women who turn down sexual offers. On the other hand, if the graduate student agrees to sleep with the chairman—either because she wants an assistantship or because she fears angering him (a possibility that Bayles overlooks)—she increases her vulnerability to other professors as well as to the chairman. Other professors might imitate their chairman's behavior—after all, he got away with it—adding a degree of instability and potential for arbitrary treatment not only to this particular student's future, but to all female graduate student's futures. Once such considerations are factored in, feminists observe that the chairman has in fact boxed his graduate student into a corner from which she cannot emerge unscathed. Consequently, whatever else the chairman is guilty of (such as depriving a worthy candidate of an assistantship), he is also guilty of sexual harassment.[6]

Noncoercive Sexual Harassment

Clear cases of coercive sexual harassment affect a woman's options so adversely that she gives in to her harasser's threats or offers simply because her other options seem so much worse. Unlike the sexual seducer who showers a woman with gifts so that she will at long last *willingly* leap into his arms, the coercive sexual harasser waves his stick or carrot in front of woman, not caring how *unwilling* she is when she jumps into his bed. Significantly, what distinguishes the noncoercive sexual harasser from both the sexual seducer and the coercive sexual harasser is that his primary aim is not to get a woman to perform sexually for him, but simply to annoy or offend her.

Although it is possible to argue that the ogler's, pincher's, or squeezer's sexual misconduct is coercive, it is difficult. Many women fear calling attention not only to the sexual misconduct of their employers and professors, who can cost them their jobs or academic standing, but also to the sexual misconduct of strangers—strangers who have no long-term economic or intellectual power over them, but who nonetheless have the short-term power of physical strength over them. For example, in a recent *New York Times* article, Victoria Balfour reported that although women are frequently sexually harassed at movie theaters, they very rarely complain to theater managers. One highly educated woman who had been afraid to report an incident of sexual harassment to the theater manager commented: "He might think that somehow I had done something that made the man want to bother me, that I had provoked him. To me, harassment has its implications, like rape." [7] Two other women silently endured a harasser for the duration of another film. Although their harasser's behavior was extremely offensive, they did not report the incident: "He was staring heavily, breathing heavily and making strange noises. We didn't move because we were afraid if we got somebody to deal with him, he'd be waiting outside afterward with a knife." [8] All three of these women kept silent because they feared provoking their harassers to some heinous deed.

To claim that these theatergoers were *coerced* into silence is, according to feminists, to accomplish some good at the risk of effecting considerable harm. On the one hand, the public ought to realize that, for women, being bothered at the movies, in the subways, and on the streets by youthful girl-watchers, middle-aged creeps, and dirty old men is a routine occurrence. On the other hand, women ought not to think of themselves as helpless victims who dare not confront their harassers for fear of retaliatory violence. Therefore, on balance, feminists are of the opinion that it is best to reserve the term *coercive* for cases of sexual harassment that involve specific threats or offers, especially if these threats or offers are made in the context of the workplace or academy. This is not to suggest, however, that feminists think that cases of noncoercive sexual harassment are always less serious than cases of coercive sexual harassment. No woman wants to be coerced into a man's bed; but neither does a woman want to be hounded by a man who takes delight in insulting, belittling, or demeaning her, and who may even find satisfaction in driving her to distraction. This being the case, feminists insist that the law attend to cases of unwanted *noncoercive* as well as unwanted *coercive* sexual harassment. But this is no light request to make of a law that, like some Freudians, is still wondering what women really want. . . .

Gender harassment is related to sexual harassment as genus is to species: Sexual harassment is a form of gender harassment. Catherine MacKinnon comments "Gender *is* a power division and sexuality is one sphere of its expression. One thing wrong with sexual harassment. . . . is that it eroticizes women's subordination. It acts out and deepens the powerlessness of women as a gender, *as women*." [9] Whereas gender harassment is a relatively abstract way to remind women that their gender role is one of subordination, sexual harassment is an extremely concrete way to remind women that their subordination as a gender is intimately tied to their sexuality, in particular to their reproductive capacities and in general to their bodily contours.

Examples of verbal sexual harassment include those comments (in this case, written comments) to which female coal miners were subjected at the Shoemaker Mine in the late 1970s. Because women had never worked in the mine before, they were, from the moment they appeared on the scene, scrutinized by male eyes. Although the tension between the female and male coal miners was considerable, it was bearable until a rash of graffiti appeared on the mine walls. The graffiti focused on the women's physical characteristics. For example, one woman who had small breasts was called "inverted nipples," and another woman who supposedly had protruding lower vaginal lips was called the "low-lip express." [10] Subjected to such offensive social commentary on this and other occasions, the female miners found it increasingly difficult to maintain their sense of self-respect, and their personal and professional lives began to deteriorate.[11]

In contrast to these examples of verbal sexual harassment stand more sanitized but not necessarily less devastating examples of verbal gender harassment. Unlike instances of verbal sexual harassment that focus on women's bodies, these latter comments, illustrations, and jokes call attention to women's gender traits and roles. It is interesting that a gender harasser may describe female gender traits and roles either in negative terms (women are irrational, hysterical, defective) or in seemingly positive terms (women are nurturing, self-sacrificing, closer to nature). In both cases, however, the gender harassers will add credence to the "**kinder, kirche, kuche**" theory of womanhood, according to which women's biology and psychology naturally suit them for bearing and raising children, praying in church, and cooking.[12]

Although women are routinely subjected to gender harassment, society as a whole remains unconvinced that female students, for example, should take umbrage when their professors gender harass them. Nonetheless, given the educational mission of academic institutions, and the fact that women students may be more vulnerable to their professors' sexist remarks ("Women can't do math") than their professors' sexual innuendos ("It's a joy having your body—oops! your *person*—in this class, Miss Jones"), Title IX should, and probably does, cover cases of gender harassment.

In this connection, it is important to note that Title VII has already covered several gender-harassment cases. Recently, for example, a woman named Ms. Bay, who was employed by EFCS (Executive Financial Counseling Service) in Philadelphia, won a successful sex-discrimination suit against her boss, Gordon Campbell. Although Mr. Campbell never sexually harassed Ms. Bay by calling attention to or touching her body in any way, he did gender-harass her. On one occasion Mr. Campbell asked Ms. Bay whether her husband would "suffer for food and clean clothes while she was away on business trips." On other occasions he contacted clients, on his own initiative, to inquire whether they objected to dealing with a woman and to see what they though of Ms. Bay, "although such evaluations had never been requested for a male member of the EFCS staff." On still another occasion he arranged a seminar training program for a male employee while providing no such training program for Ms. Bay, despite her requests and despite Mr. Campbell's private comments to his superiors that her seminar performance was weak and in need of improvement. After listening to the recounting of these and other incidents, the judge ruled that, although Ms. Bay quit, she was really fired because "any reasonable person would have reacted to the situation at EFCS much as she did." [13]

Realizing that liability for sexual harassment and gender harassment belong to them as well as to authorities in the workplace, academic deans and other college personnel have tried to handle student harassment complaints informally. Their attempts have not always been successful. Not wanting to make mountains out of molehills, and arguing that young women frequently "imagine" things, some college officials have downplayed student reports of gender and sexual harassment. Even where they have taken such reports seriously and acted upon them, they have tended to keep them quiet in the name of discretion, preferring to let things "cool off" or "work themselves out." As a result of the students' rights movement, students have pressed their respective colleges and universities to handle such matters in a more formal and public manner. Students have also become much more concerned about student-on-student sexual harassment, which is a very pervasive fact of campus life. Understandably, deans and professors, who have by and large abandoned their *in loco parentis* roles, fear to invade their students' privacy. Realizing that students who come from diverse backgrounds will, as a matter of course, experience some difficulty in adjusting to one another's sexual mores, they fear making an issue out of what may be nothing more than normal social adjustment. And even when college officials discern a problem on campus, they resist setting up quasi-legal procedures to handle it. Predictably, deans and professors tend to argue that the way to handle sensitive problems such as sexual harassment is through educational forums rather than litigation.

Indeed, education is needed. Despite the breakdown of many sexual stereotypes, the macho ideal of the strong man lives on, as does the ideal of the vulnerable female. In large measure, this fact explains the growing incidence of "date-rape" on campuses. Crossed signals and mixed messages characterize many student sexual relations. Says one man:

> I get told "no," . . . and I keep going. I guess if someone said, "Look, sorry, I thought I wanted to, but I changed my mind, no way!" I'd listen, but if we're lying on the bed and she puts here little hands up in front of her chest and says, "Oh, please, no, I'm not sure about this," I ignore it. Nobody complains afterward." [14]

Women have to learn to say no, and men have to learn to take a *no* at face value. Moreover, women have to stop blaming themselves when men sexually harass them. This may be particularly difficult for a young woman to do. She may not have met enough different types of men to realize that it's not always something about her or her body that turns a man on, but something about his need to assert himself. Arguably, the more secure a man is about his masculinity, the less need he will have to harass women sexually or otherwise. Failing to understand this, a young woman may berate herself for her harasser's conduct. She may punish herself for being sexed by starving or neglecting her body. The epidemic of anorexia on many campuses is not unrelated to young women's fear of their own sexuality; and the unkempt appearance of some young women is often evidence of their attempt to kill the "temptress" in themselves.

Endnotes

1. John C. Hughes and Larry May, "Sexual Harassment," *Social Theory and Practice* 6 (Fall 1980): 251.
2. Ibid., p. 252.
3. Ibid.
4. Ibid.

5. Ibid., p. 249; cf. Michael Bayles, "Coercive Offers and Public Benefits," *The Personalist* 55 (Spring 1974): 142–43.
6. For a detailed version of this argument, see Hughes and May, "Sexual Harassment," pp. 255–56.
7. Victoria Balfour, "Harassment at Movies: Complaints Rare," *New York Times*, November 17, 1982, p. C24.
8. Ibid.
9. MacKinnon, *Sexual Harassment of Working Women*, pp. 220–21.
10. Raymond M. Lane, "A Man's World: An Update on Sexual Harassment," *The Village Voice*, December 16, 1981, p. 20.
11. As in the case with many women who are sexually harassed, these women coal miners suffered physical and psychological problems, such as loss of appetite, insomnia, and a feeling of guilt and self-loathing. See ibid.
12. Women as well as men may of course be guilty of gender, or even sexual, harassment of women. For example, some female opponents of the Equal Rights Amendment gender-harassed their feminist sisters, arguing that woman's role was to defer to man. And conceivably, a lesbian could sexually harass a female employee or student whom she found attractive, a particularly awkward and distressing situation in the event that the latter woman proves to be heterosexual. Likewise, women as well as men may also be guilty of gender and sexual harassment of men. A female English professor may repeatedly remind her male students that "Men are incapable of understanding poetry," or she may sexually harass one of her less able but more handsome male students. In practice, however, the harassment of men is not likely to be effective in a society such as ours, where men are socialized not to take abuse. Consequently, gender harassment will remain largely a woman's problem for some time, whether or not it manifests itself as sexual harassment.
13. *Philadelphia Inquirer*, September 9, 1982, p. 1A.
14. Karen Barret, "Sex on a Saturday Night," *Ms.*, September 1982, p. 50.

Review Questions

1. What is coercive sexual harassment according to Tong? What are the two tests for coercion provided by Hughes and May?
2. What is noncoercive sexual harassment?
3. How does Tong explain gender harassment?

Discussion Questions

1. Is the hypothetical case of Michael Bayles that Tong cites a case of seduction or sexual harassment?
2. Is unwanted flirting or asking for dates a form of harassment? What do you think?

Ellen Frankel Paul

Bared Buttocks and Federal Cases

Ellen Frankel Paul is affiliated with the Social Philosophy and Policy Center, Bowling Green State University, Ohio.

Although Paul agrees with feminists that there are obvious cases of wrongful sexual harassment, she expresses some reservations about the definition of sexual harassment and the way it is treated in the law. A distinction should be drawn between rape and sexual harassment. Quid pro quo sexual harassment should not be prosecuted under Title VII (of the Civil Rights Act of 1964), and the harasser should be prosecuted, not the employer. Hostile environment sexual harassment should be redefined to cover outrageous sexual behavior (such as bared buttocks), but not trivial offenses (such as off-color jokes).

Women in American society are victims of sexual harassment in alarming proportions. Sexual harassment is an inevitable corollary to class exploitation; as capitalists exploit workers, so do males in positions of authority exploit their female subordinates. Male professors, supervisors, and apartment managers in ever increasing

---

From Ellen Frankel Paul, "Bared Buttocks and Federal Cases," *Society*, No. 4 (1991).

numbers take advantage of the financial dependence and vulnerability of women to extract sexual concessions.

These are the assertions that commonly begin discussions of sexual harassment. For reasons that will be adumbrated below, dissent from the prevailing view is long overdue. Three recent episodes will serve to frame this disagreement.

Valerie Craig, an employee of Y & Y Snacks, Inc., joined several co-workers and her supervisor for drinks after work one day in July of 1978. Her supervisor drove her home and proposed that they become more intimately acquainted. She refused his invitation for sexual relations, whereupon he said that he would "get even" with her. Ten days after the incident she was fired from her job. She soon filed a complaint of sexual harassment with the Equal Employment Opportunity Commission (EEOC), and the case wound its way through the courts. Craig prevailed, the company was held liable for damages, and she received back pay, reinstatement, and an order prohibiting Y & Y from taking reprisals against her in the future.

Carol Zabowicz, one of only two female forklift operators in a West Bend Co. warehouse, charged that her co-workers over a four year period from 1978–1982 sexually harassed her by such acts as: asking her whether she was wearing a bra; two of the men exposing their buttocks between ten and twenty times; a male co-worker grabbing his crotch and making obscene suggestions of growling; subjecting her to offensive and abusive language; and exhibiting obscene drawings with her initials on them. Zabowicz began to show symptoms of physical and psychological stress, necessitating several medical leaves, and she filed a sexual harassment complaint with the EEOC. The district court judge remarked that "The sustained, malicious, and brutal harassment meted out . . . was more than merely unreasonable; it was malevolent and outrageous." The company knew of the harassment and took corrective actions only after the employee filed a complaint with the EEOC. The company was, therefore, held liable, and Zabowicz was awarded back pay for the period of her medical absence, and a judgment that her rights were violated under the Civil Rights Act of 1964.

On September 17, 1990, Lisa Olson, a sports reporter for the *Boston Herald,* charged five football players of the just-defeated New England Patriots with sexual harassment for making sexually suggestive and offensive remarks to her when she entered their locker room to conduct a post-game interview. The incident amounted to nothing short of "mind rape," according to Olson. After vociferous lamentations in the media, the National Football League fined the team and its players $25,000 each. The National Organization of Women called for a boycott of Remington electric shavers because the owner of the company, Victor Kiam, also owns the Patriots and allegedly displayed insufficient sensitivity at the time when the episode occurred.

All these incidents are indisputably disturbing. In an ideal world—one needless to say far different from the one that we inhabit or are ever likely to inhabit—women would not be subjected to such treatment in the course of their work. Women, and men as well, would be accorded respect by co-workers and supervisors, their feelings would be taken into account, and their dignity would be left intact. For women to expect reverential treatment in the workplace is utopian, yet they should not have to tolerate outrageous, offensive sexual overtures and threats as they go about earning a living.

One question that needs to be pondered is: What kinds of undesired sexual behavior should women be protected against by law? That is, what kind of actions are deemed so outrageous and violate a woman's rights to such [an] extent that the law should intervene, and what actions should be considered inconveniences of life, to be morally condemned but not adjudicated? A subsidiary question concerns the type of legal remedy appropriate for the wrongs that do require redress. Before directly addressing these questions, it might be useful to diffuse some of the hyperbole adhering to the sexual harassment issue.

Surveys are one source of this hyperbole. If their results are accepted at face value, they lead to the conclusion that women are disproportionately victims of legions of sexual harassers. A poll by the Albuquerque *Tribune* found that nearly 80 percent of the respondents reported that they or someone they knew had been victims of sexual harassment. The Merit Systems Protection Board determined that 42 percent of the women (and 14 percent of men) working for the federal government had experienced some form of unwanted sexual attention between 1985 and 1987, with unwanted "sexual teasing" identified as the most prevalent form. A Defense Department survey found that 64 percent of the women in the military (and 17 percent of the men) suffered "uninvited and unwanted sexual attention" within the previous year. The United Methodist Church established that 7 percent of its clergywomen experienced incidents of sexual harassment, with 41 percent of these naming a pastor or colleague as the perpetrator, and 31 percent mentioning church social functions as the setting.

A few caveats concerning polls in general, and these sorts of polls in particular, are worth considering. Pollsters looking for a particular social ill tend to find it, usually in gargantuan proportions. (What fate would lie in store for a pollster who concluded that child abuse, or wife beating, or mistreatment of the elderly had dwindled to the point of negligibility!) Sexual harassment is a notoriously ill-defined and almost infinitely expandable concept, including everything from rape to unwelcome neck massaging, discomfiture upon witnessing sexual overtures directed at others, yelling at and blowing smoke in the ears of female subordinates, and displays of poronographic pictures in the workplace. Defining sexual harassment, as the United Methodists did, as "any sexually related behavior that is unwelcome, offensive or which fails to respect the rights of others," the concept is broad enough to include everything from "unsolicited suggestive looks or leers [or] pressures for "dates" to "actual sexual assaults or rapes." Categorizing everything from rape to "looks" as sexual harassment makes us all victims, a state of affairs satisfying to radical feminists, but not very useful for distinguishing serious injuries from the merely trivial.

Yet, even if the surveys exaggerate the extent of sexual harassment, however defined, what they do reflect is a great deal of tension between the sexes. As women in ever increasing numbers entered the workplace in the last two decades, as the women's movement challenged alleged male hegemony and exploitation with ever greater intemperance, and as women entered previously all-male preserves from the board rooms to the coal pits, it is lamentable, but should not be surprising, that this tension sometimes takes sexual form. Not that sexual harassment on the job, in the university, and in other settings is a trivial or insignificant matter, but a sense of proportion needs to be restored and, even more importantly, distinctions need to be made. In other words, sexual harassment must be de-ideologized. Statements that paint nearly all women as victims and all men and their patriarchal, capitalist system as perpetrators, are ideological fantasy. Ideology blurs the distinction between being injured—being a genuine victim—and merely being offended. An example is this statement by Catharine A. MacKinnon, a law professor and feminist activist:

> Sexual harassment perpetuates the interlocked structure by which women have been kept sexually in thrall to men and at the bottom of the labor market. Two forces of American society converge: men's control over women's sexuality and capital control over employees' work lives. Women historically have been required to exchange sexual services for material survival, in one form or another. Prostitution and marriage as well as sexual harassment in different ways institutionalize this arrangement.

Such hyperbole needs to be diffused and distinctions need to be drawn. Rape, a nonconsensual invasion of a person's body, is a crime clear and simple. It is a violation of the right to the physical integrity of the body (the right to life, as John Locke or Thomas Jefferson would have put it). Criminal law should and does prohibit rape. Whether it is useful to call rape "sexual harassment" is doubtful, for it makes the latter concept overly broad while trivializing the former.

Intimidation in the workplace of the kind that befell Valerie Craig—that is, extortion of sexual favors by a supervisor from a subordinate by threatening to penalize, fire, or fail to reward—is what the courts term *quid pro quo* sexual harassment. Since the mid-1970s, the federal courts have treated this type of sexual harassment as a form of sex discrimination in employment proscribed under Title VII of the Civil Rights Act of 1964. A plaintiff who prevails against an employer may receive such equitable remedies as reinstatement and back pay, and the court can order the company to prepare and disseminate a policy against sexual harassment. Current law places principal liability on the company, not the harassing supervisor, even when higher management is unaware of the harassment and, thus, cannot take any steps to prevent it.

Quid pro quo sexual harassment is morally objectionable and analogous to extortion: the harasser extorts property (i.e., use of the woman's body) through the leverage of fear for her job. The victim of such behavior should have legal recourse, but serious reservations can be held about rectifying these injustices through the blunt instrument of Title VII. In [outrageous] cases the victim is left less than whole (for back pay will not compensate for her ancillary losses), and no prospect for punitive damages are offered to deter would-be harassers. Even more distressing about Title VII is the fact that the primary target of litigation is not the actual harasser, but rather the employer. This places a double burden on a company. The employer is swindled by the supervisor because he spent his time pursuing sexual gratification and thereby impairing the efficiency of the workplace by mismanaging his subordinates, and the employer must endure lengthy and expensive litigation, pay damages, and suffer loss to its reputation. It would be fairer to both the company and the victim to treat sexual harassment as a tort—that is, as a private wrong or injury for which the court can assess damages. Employers should be held vicariously liable only when they know of an employee's behavior and do not try to redress it.

As for the workplace harassment endured by Carole Zabowicz—the bared buttocks, obscene portraits, etc.—that too should be legally redressable. Presently, such incidents also fall under the umbrella of Title VII, and are termed hostile environment sexual harassment, a category accepted later than *quid pro quo* and with some judicial reluctance. The main problem with this category is that it has proven too elastic: cases have reached the courts based on everything from off-color jokes to unwanted, persistant sexual advances by co-workers. A new tort of sexual harassment would handle these cases better. Only instances above a certain threshold of egregiousness or outrageousness would be actionable. In other words, the behavior that the plaintiff found offensive would also have to be offensive to the proverbial "reasonable man" of the tort law. That is, the behavior would have to be objectively injurious rather than merely subjectively offensive. The defendant would be the actual harasser not the company, unless it knew about the problem and failed to act. Victims of scatological jokes, leers, unwanted offers of dates, and other sexual annoyances would no longer have their day in court.

A distinction must be restored between morally offensive behavior and behavior that causes serious harm. Only the latter should fall under the jurisdiction of criminal or tort law. Do we really want legislators and judges delving into our most intimate private lives, deciding when a look is a leer, and when a leer is a Civil Rights Act offense? Do we really want courts deciding, as one recently did, whether a school principal's disparaging remarks about a female school district administrator was sexual harassment and, hence, a breach of Title VII, or merely the act of spurned and vengeful lover? Do we want judges settling disputes such as the one that arose at a car dealership after a female employee turned down a male co-worker's offer of a date and his colleagues retaliated by calling her offensive names and embarrassing her in front of customers? Or another case in which a female shipyard worker complained of an "offensive working environment" because of the prevalence of pornographic material on the docks? Do we want the state to prevent or compensate us for any behavior that someone might find offensive? Should people have a legally enforceable right not to be offended by others? At some point, the price for such protection is the loss of both liberty and privacy rights.

Workplaces are breeding grounds of envy, personal grudges, infatuation, and jilted loves, and beneath a fairly high threshold of outrageousness, these travails should be either suffered in silence, complained of to higher management, or left behind as one seeks other employment. No one, female or male, can expect to enjoy a working environment that is perfectly stress-free, or to be treated always and by everyone with kindness and respect. To the extent that sympathetic judges have encouraged women to seek monetary compensation for slights and annoyances, they have not done them a great service. Women need to develop a thick skin in order to survive and prosper in the work force. It is patronizing to think that they need to be recompensed by male judges for seeing a few pornographic pictures on a wall. By their efforts to extend sexual harassment charges to even the most trivial behavior, the radical feminists send a message that women are not resilient enough to ignore the run-of-the-mill, churlish provocation from male co-workers. It is difficult to imagine a suit by a longshoreman complaining of mental stress due to the display of nude male centerfolds by female co-workers. Women cannot expect to have it both ways: equality where convenient, but special dispensations when the going gets rough. Equality has its price and that price may include unwelcome sexual advances, irritating and even intimidating sexual jests, and lewd and obnoxious colleagues.

[Outrageous] acts—sexual harassment per se—must be legally redressable. Lesser but not trivial offenses, whether at the workplace or in other more social settings, should be considered moral lapses for which the offending party receives opprobrium, disciplinary warnings, or penalties, depending on the setting and the severity. Trivial offenses, dirty jokes, sexual overtures, and sexual innuendoes do make many women feel intensely discomfited, but, unless they become outrageous through persistence or content, these too should be taken as part of life's annoyances. The perpetrators should be either endured, ignored, rebuked, or avoided, as circumstances and personal inclination dictate. Whether Lisa Olson's experience in the locker room of the Boston Patriots falls into the second or third category is debatable. The media circus triggered by the incident was certainly out of proportion to the event.

As the presence of women on road gangs, construction crews, and oil rigs become a fact of life, the animosities and tensions of this transition period are likely to abate gradually. Meanwhile, women should "lighten up," and even dispense a few risqué barbs of their own, a sure way of taking the fun out of it for offensive male bores.

Review Questions

1. Why does Paul have reservations about surveys?
2. What objections does Paul raise to using Title VII law to prosecute quid pro quo harassment?
3. What is wrong with the definition of hostile-environment sexual harassment?

Discussion Questions

1. Paul thinks that we should restore a distinction between morally offensive behavior and behavior that causes serious harm. Do you agree? If so, just how would you draw this distinction?
2. Do you agree that behavior such as looks and jokes do not cause serious harm?

Mark R. Wicclair

Feminism, Pornography, and Censorship

Mark R. Wicclair is Professor of Philosophy at West Virginia University and an associate at the Center for Medical Ethics, University of Pittsburgh. He is the author of Ethics and the Elderly *(forthcoming).*

Wicclair accepts the definition of pornography given by feminists such as MacKinnon and Longino; he agrees that pornography is morally repugnant. But he argues that the sexist and misogynistic nature of pornography does not justify its censorship, given the importance of freedom of expression in our society. According to Wicclair, the causal connection between pornography and harm to women has not been established, and indeed pornography may reduce harm to women. In any event, he claims the censorship of pornography is not likely to help women achieve equality in our society; there are better things to do to improve the status of women that do not have the substantial negative side effects of censorship.

It is sometimes claimed that pornography is objectionable because it violates conventional standards of sexual morality. Although feminists tend to agree that pornography is objectionable, they reject this particular argument against it.[1] This argument is unacceptable to feminists because it is associated with an oppressive Puritanical sexual ethic that inhibits the sexual fulfillment of all people, but especially women. In order to understand why feminists find pornography objectionable, one has to keep in mind that they do not equate the terms "pornographic" and "sexually explicit." Rather, sexually explicit material is said to be "pornographic" only if it depicts and condones the exploitation, dehumanization, subordination, abuse, or denigration of women. By definition, then, all pornography is sexist and misogynistic. Some pornographic material has the additional feature of depicting and condoning acts of *violence* against women (e.g., rape, brutality, torture, sadism). Thus there is a world of difference between harmless "erotica" and pornography. Whereas erotica depicts sexual activity in a manner which is designed to produce sexual arousal and is therefore likely to be objectionable only to those who subscribe to a Puritanical sexual ethic, pornography is "material that explicitly represents or describes degrading and abusive sexual behavior so as to endorse and/or recommend the behavior as described." [2]

Despite the general agreement among feminists that pornography, understood in the way just described, is objectionable, they are sharply divided over the question of its *censorship*. Whereas some feminists find pornography to be so objectionable that they call for its censorship, others oppose this proposal.[3] I will argue that anyone who supports the aims of feminism and who seeks the liberation of all people should reject the censorship of pornography.[4]

When discussing censorship, it is important to keep in mind that there are very strong reasons to be wary of its use. In our society, the importance of the principle of freedom of expression—an anticensorship principle—is widely recognized. The ability to speak one's mind and to express ideas and feelings without the threat of legal penalties or government control is rightly perceived as an essential feature of a truly free society. Moreover, an environment that tolerates the expression of differing views about politics, art, lifestyles, etc., encourages progress and aids in the search for truth and justice. In addition to the many important

Mark R. Wicclair, "Feminism, Pornography, and Censorship," from *Social Ethics, Fourth Edition*, Thomas A. Mappes and Jane S. Zembaty, eds. (New York: McGraw-Hill, 1992).

values associated with the principle of freedom of expression, it is also necessary to consider likely negative side effects of censorship. There is a serious risk that once any censorship is allowed, the power to censor will, over time, expand in unintended and undesirable directions (the "slippery slope"). This is not mere speculation, for such an expansion of the power to censor is to be expected in view of the fact that it is extremely difficult, if not impossible, to formulate unequivocal and unambiguous criteria of censorship. Then, too, the power to censor can all too easily be abused or misused. Even though it may arise in a genuine effort to promote the general welfare and to protect certain rights, officials and groups might use the power to censor as a means to advance their own interests and values and to suppress the rights, interests, and values of others. Thus, given the value of freedom of expression and the many dangers associated with censorship, there is a strong *prima facie* case against censorship. In other words, advocates of censorship have the burden of showing that there are sufficiently strong overriding reasons which would justify it in a specific area.

Like racist and antisemitic material, sexist, and misogynistic films, books, and magazines surely deserve condemnation. But censorship is another matter. In view of the strength of the case against censorship in general, it is unwise to advocate it merely to prevent depicting morally objectionable practices in a favorable light. Fortunately, proponents of the censorship of pornography tend to recognize this, for they usually base their call for censorship on a claim about the *effects* of pornography. Pornography, it is held, is *injurious* or *harmful* to women because it fosters the objectionable practices that it depicts. Pornography generally is said to promote the exploitation, humiliation, denigration, subordination, etc., of women; and pornography that depicts acts of violence against women is said to cause murder, rape, assault, and other acts of violence. On the basis of the "harm principle"—a widely accepted principle that allows us to restrict someone's freedom in order to prevent harm to others—it would appear to be justified to override the principle of freedom of expression and to restrict the freedom of would-be producers, distributors, sellers, exhibitors, and consumers of pornography. In short it seems that censorship of pornography is a legitimate means of preventing harm to women.

However, there are a number of problems associated with this attempt to justify censorship. To begin with, it is essential to recognize the important difference between words and images, on the one hand, and actions, on the other hand. A would-be rapist poses a *direct* threat to his intended victim, and by stopping him, we prevent an act of violence. But if there is a connection between the depiction of a rape—even one which appears to condone it—and someone's committing an act of violence against a woman, the connection is relatively *indirect;* and stopping the production, distribution, sale, and exhibition of depictions of rape does not directly restrict the freedom of would-be rapists to commit acts of violence against women. In recognition of the important difference between restricting words and images and preventing harmful behavior, exceptions to the principle of freedom of expression are generally thought to be justified only if words or images present a "clear and present danger" of harm or injury. Thus, to cite a standard example, it is justified to stop someone from falsely shouting "Fire!" in a crowded theater, for this exclamation is likely to cause a panic that would result in serious injury and even death.

It is doubtful that pornography satisfies the "clear and present danger" condition. for there does not seem to be conclusive evidence that establishes its *causal* significance. Most studies are limited to violent pornography. And even though some of these studies do suggest a *temporary* impact on *attitudes* (e.g., those who view violent pornography may be more likely to express the view that women seek and "enjoy" violence), this does not show that viewing violent pornography causes violent *behavior*. Moreover, there is some evidence suggesting that the effect on attitudes is only temporary and that it can be effectively counteracted by additional information.[5]

But even if there is no conclusive evidence that pornography causes harm, is it not reasonable to "play it safe," and does this not require censorship? Unfortunately, the situation is not as simple as this question appears to suggest. For one thing, it is sometimes claimed that exposure to pornography has a "cathartic" effect and that it therefore produces a net *reduction* in harm to women. This claim is based upon two assumptions, neither of which has been proven to be false: (1) Men who are not already violence-prone are more likely to be "turned off" than to be "turned on" by depictions of rape, brutality, dismemberment, etc. (2) For men in the latter category, exposure to pornography can function as a substitute for actually causing harm. It is also necessary to recall that there are significant values associated with the principle of freedom of expression, and that a failure to observe it involves a number of serious dangers. Since censorship has costs which are substantial and not merely speculative, the more speculative the connection between pornography and harm to women, the less basis there is for incurring the costs associated with censorship.

Just as it is easy to overlook the negative side of censorship, it is also common to overplay its positive effects. Surely it would be foolish to think that outlawing antisemitism in sexually explicit material would have halted the slaughter of Jews in Hitler Germany or that prohibiting racism in sexually explicit material would reduce the suffering of Blacks in South Africa. Similarily, in view of the violent nature of American society generally and the degree to which sexism persists to this day, it is unlikely that censorship of pornography by itself would produce any significant improvement in the condition of women in the United States. Fortunately, there are other, more effective and direct means of eliminating sexism than by censoring pornography. Passage and strict enforcement of the Equal Rights Amendment, electing feminists to local, state, and national political office, achieving genuine economic justice for women, and securing their reproductive freedom will do considerably more to foster the genuine liberation of women in the United States than will the censorship of pornography. With respect to rape and other acts of violence, it has often been noted that American society is extremely violent, and sadly, there are no magic solutions to the problems of rape and violence. But the magnitude of the problem suggests that censoring pornography only addresses a symptom and not the underlying disease. Although there is still much dispute about the causes of violence generally and rape in particular, it is unlikely that there will be a serious reduction in acts of violence against women until there are rather drastic changes in the socioeconomic environment and in the criminal justice system.

Those who remain concerned about the possible contribution of pornography to violence and sexism should keep in mind that it can be "neutralized" in ways that avoid the dangers of censorship. One important alternative to government censorship is to help people understand why pornography is objectionable and why it and its message should be rejected. This can be accomplished by means of educational campaigns, discussions of pornography on radio and television and at public forums, letter writing, and educational picketing. In addition, attempts might be made to prevent or restrict the production, distribution, display, sale, and consumption of pornographic material by means of organized pickets, boycotts, and the like. Such direct measures by private citizens raise some troubling questions, but the dangers and risks which they pose are considerably less than those associated with government censorship.

There are several other reasons for questioning the view that the sexist and misogynistic nature of pornography justifies its censorship. Some of the more important of these include the following:

1 Although pornography depicts some practices that are both morally objectionable and illegal (e.g., rape, assault, torture), many of the practices depicted are morally repugnant *but do not break any law*. Thus, for example, our legal system does not explicitly prohibit men from treating women in a degrading or humiliating manner; and with some exceptions, it is not a crime to treat women exclusively as sex objects or to use them exclusively as means and not ends. But is it not odd to recommend making illegal the production, distribution, sale, and exhibition of materials that depict practices that are not themselves illegal?

2 It is essential that laws be clearly formulated and that vagueness be avoided. Vague laws can have a "chilling effect" on unobjectionable

activities, and they tend to undermine the fair and effective enforcement of the law by giving police, prosecutors, and judges too much discretionary power. But those who call for the censorship of pornography on the grounds that it is sexist and misogynistic fail to recognize the difficulty of formulating laws which wold have an acceptable degree of clarity and specificity. Proponents of censorship use terms like "degrading," "humiliating," "debasing," "exploitative," and "subordination of women." But these terms are far from unambiguous. In fact, they are highly subjective in the sense that different people have different criteria for deciding when something is degrading, humilitating, etc. For example, someone might think that the depiction of an unmarried female or a lesbian couple having and enjoying sex is "demeaning" or "debasing." Thus, in order to prevent censorship from being applied in unintended and undesirable ways, it is necessary to offer clear and unambiguous operational criteria for terms like "demeaning," "humiliating," etc. But the feasibility of articulating generally acceptable criteria of this sort remains highly doubtful.

3 Sexually explicit material that depicts violence against women or that depicts sexist practices is said to be subject to censorship only if it *condones* the objectionable practices. Thus, for example, news films, documentaries, and works which take a critical stance toward those practices are not to be censored. But it is exceedingly difficult in many cases to determine the "point of view" of films, books, photographs, etc.[6] If scholars who have advanced degrees in film, literature, and art can come to no general consensus about the "meaning" or "message" of certain works, is it plausible to think that prosecutors, judges, and juries are likely to fare any better?

4 Why call for the censorship of sexist and misogynistic books, magazines, films, and photographs only if they include an explicit depiction of *sexual activity?* There is no conclusive evidence showing that material that includes a depiction of sexual activity has a greater causal impact on attitudes and behavior.[7] Moreover, it will not do to claim that such material is not worthy of protection under the principle of freedom of expression. Surely, many works which include explicit depictions of sex are not totally devoid of significant and challenging ideas. Consequently, advocates of censorship are faced with a dilemma: Either they can call for the censorship of *all* material that contains objectionable images of women; or they can call for censorship only in the case of sexually explicit materials of that nature. If the first alternative is chosen, then given the pervasiveness of objectionable portrayals of women in art, literature, and the mass media, very little would be immune from censorship. But in view of the strong *prima facie* case against censorship, this seems unacceptable. On the other hand, if the second alternative is chosen, this invites the suspicion that the restriction to sexual material is based upon the very same Puritanical sexual ethic which feminists rightly tend to reject. I am not suggesting that feminists who call for censorship wish to champion sexual oppression. But it is noteworthy that many conservatives who generally do not support the aims of feminism align themselves with feminists who advocate censoring pornography.

5 Why call for censorship of materials only if they depict violence or other objectionable practices in relation to *women?* Wouldn't consistency require censoring *all* violence and material that portrays *anyone* in a derogatory light? But this is clearly unacceptable. For so much of our culture is permeated with images of violence and morally distasteful treatment of people that it is hard to think of many films, television programs, books, or magazines which would be totally immune from censorship. Censorship would be the rule rather than an exception, and such pervasive censorship is incompatible with a truly free society. It also won't do to limit censorship to members of historically oppressed groups (e.g., women, Blacks, Jews). First, it is very unlikely that such "preferential censorship" would be accepted by the majority for too long. Sooner or later others would object and/or press for protection too. Second, in view of the significant costs of censorship, even if it were limited to the protection of historically oppressed groups, it would not be justified unless there were a demonstrable "clear and present danger; " and this remains doubtful. But what

about the view that only pornography should be subject to censorship because *women need special protection?* This position is also unacceptable. For since men are victimized by acts of racism, antisemitism, and violence, and since there is no evidence to prove that depictions of objectionable practices have a greater effect on behavior in pornographic material than they do in nonpornographic material, this position seems to be based on the sexist assumption that women need greater protection than men because they are "naturally" more fragile and vulnerable.

I have tried to show that censorship of pornography is neither the most effective nor a legitimate means to achieve the aims of feminism. Much pornographic material is morally repugnant, but there are less costly ways to express one's moral outrage and to attempt to "neutralize" pornography than by censorship. Moreover, pornography is only a relatively minor manifestation of the sexist practices and institutions that still pervade our society. Hence, the genuine liberation of women—and men—is best served by directly attacking those oppressive practices and institutions. It may be easier to identify and attack pornography—and to win some battles—but the payoff would be slight, and the negative side effects would be substantial.

Endnotes

1. Just as the civil rights movement in the United States in the 1950's and 1960's included many people who were not black, so one does not have to be a woman to be a feminist. As I am using the term, a feminist is any person who supports the fundamental goal of feminism: the liberation of women.
2. Helen E. Longino, "Pornography, Oppression, and Freedom: A Closer Look," in Laura Lederer, ed., *Take Back the Night* (New York: William Morrow and Company, Inc., 1980), p. 44. Longino also stipulates that the sexual activities depicted in pornography are degrading or abusive *to women.*
3. In response to the generally pro-censorship Women Against Violence in Pornography and Media, other feminists have organized the Feminist Anti-Censorship Taskforce.
4. Until recently, advocates of censorship have pressed for laws which prohibit or restrict the production, distribution, sale, and exhibition of pornographic material. However, pro-censorship feminists have hit upon a new strategy: Ordinances which stipulate that pornography is *sex discrimination,* enabling women to file sex discrimination lawsuits against producers, distributors, sellers, and exhibitors of pornography. Most of the criticisms of censorship which I discuss in this paper apply to both strategies.
5. For a discussion of research on the effects of pornography, see Edward Donnerstein and Neil Malamuth, eds., *Pornography and Sexual Aggression* (New York: Academic Press, 1984).
6. An informative illustration of how a film can resist unambiguous classification as either progressive or retrograde from a feminist perspective is provided in Lucy Fischer and Marcia Landy, "*The Eyes of Laura Mars:* A Binocular Critique," *Screen,* Vol. 23, Nos. 3–4 (September-October 1982).
7. In fact some researchers claim that the impact of depictions of violence is *greater* in material which is *not* pornographic. See, for example, the contribution of Edward Donnerstein and Daniel Linz to a section on pornography, "Pornography: Love or Death?" in *Film Comment,* vol. 20, No. 6 (December 1984), pp. 34–35.

Review Questions

1. According to Wicclair, why should we be wary of censorship?
2. What is the harm principle? How is it applied? Give some examples.
3. In Wicclair's view, what is the connection between pornography and acts of violence against women?
4. How does pornography reduce harm to women according to Wicclair? Why would censorship fail to reduce this harm?
5. Wicclair gives five additional reasons for denying that censorship of pornography is justified. What are they?

Discussion Questions

1. Is Wicclair a feminist? Why or why not?
2. Wicclair doubts that pornography presents a clear and present danger to women. What would MacKinnon say? What do you think?
3. Wicclair claims that the passage and enforcement of the Equal Rights Amendment (which says that people's rights cannot be denied or abridged on account of sex) would do more to secure women's liberation in our society than the censorship of pornography. What is your view about this?

Problem Cases

1. ***Fraternities and Rape.*** (This problem is discussed by Patricia Yancey Martin and Robert A. Hummer, "Fraternities and Rape on Campus, *Gender and Society* 3, December 1989, pp. 457–473.) According to Martin and Hummer, many unreported rapes including date rapes and gang rapes occur in fraternity houses on college and university campuses. Their research on the problem shows that the social conditions of fraternities encourage the sexual abuse of women. Fraternities are vitally concerned with creating a macho image that stresses competition, winning, dominance, alcohol consumption, and the sexual possession of women. (They avoid recruiting so-called geeks and nerds, that is, men who are interested in academic, intellectual, or artistic activities.) The preoccupation with loyalty, group protection, and secrecy requires the brothers to shield the fraternity from any criticism. They use alcohol as a ploy to obtain sex from women and sanction the use of violence and physical force against them if they resist. Women are treated as bait and sexual prey to attract new members.

Given these facts about fraternities, what should be done? At some universities, women have listed the names of alleged rapists and fraternities on walls in public places. "Apple Pi Rapes Women—Stay Away!" read recent graffiti in a women's restroom at Drexel University in Philadelphia. Is this a good idea? How about closing offending fraternities? Do they really belong on college campuses?

At St. Cloud State University, students are required to attend an information session where date rape is portrayed and explained by actors. At Brown University, the campus police offers women's self-defense classes at the student union. If this is not enough, what else should be done?

2. ***Ellison* v. *Brady*.** (924 F.2d. 872, 1991) In this case, Kerry Ellison, an employee of the Internal Revenue Service, charged her employer with sexual harassment due to a hostile working environment. Although the federal district court found that she had failed to prove her case, the circuit appeals court ruled in her favor.

During her initial training, Ellison met Sterling Gray, another trainee. Both obtained a job in the same office in San Mateo, California, with Gray's desk only twenty feet from Ellison's. Gray asked Ellison out to lunch, and she accepted. After lunch, Gray took Ellison to his house and gave her a tour. Ellison alleged that after this lunch date, Gray pestered her with questions and asked her out again. Ellison declined, but he suggested that they have lunch the following week. She did not want to have any more dates with Gray and continued to decline his invitations. Gray then began to write notes and letters to Ellison which upset her. She complained to her supervisor, who arranged Gray's transfer to a different office in San Francisco. Then Gray filed union grievances requesting a return to the San Mateo office. His request was granted, provided he promise not to bother Ellison. At this point, Ellison filed a formal complaint alleging hostile environment sexual harassment.

In its decision, the court ruled that in deciding what counts as sexual harassment, the perspective of the victim should be used and not that of the harasser or the employer. In order to avoid frivolous complaints by hyper-sensitive women, the court held that hostile environment sexual harassment occurs only if the conduct at issue is that which a reasonable woman would consider to be severe enough to alter the conditions of employment.

Is this reasonable woman standard more appropriate than a sex-neutral reasonable person standard?

Assuming the reasonable woman standard, was Ellison really a victim of hostile environment sexual harassment or was this merely a failed relationship? What do you think?

3. ***Senator Bob Packwood.*** (This story has been widely reported in the newspapers.) Bob Packwood is a Republican senator from Oregon. His supporters claim that he has been a friend of women's causes; he hired a majority of women for his staff long before others became sensitive to the issue of sex discrimination, and he has been a longtime and unwavering advocate of abortion rights. Yet he seems to have a problem with women. He is charged with grabbing and kissing several women against their will. The most prominent example is a female reporter he kissed after a routine interview in his office. The reporter was shocked and offended. Packwood has publically apologized, blaming his behavior on alcoholism. Furthermore Packwood was not in a position of power or authority over the reporter; she was not hired, promoted, or fired because of her reaction to Packwood's kiss. Nevertheless, the Senate Ethics Committee is charging him with sexual harassment.

Packwood admits that his behavior was rude and offensive. But does it constitute real sexual harassment?

4. ***American Booksellers*** **v.** ***Hudnutt.*** In this much publicized case, the issue before the federal court (that is, the U.S. District Court and Court of Appeals) was whether an Indianapolis ordinance that prohibited pornography as a violation of women's civil rights was restricting speech rather than conduct; and if it was restricting speech, whether it was unconstitutional under the First Amendment.

The Indianapolis ordinance defined pornography as the graphic, sexually explicit subordination of women, whether in pictures or in words, that presents women as sex objects who enjoy pain and humiliation, or who want to be raped.

The court ruled that the ordinance sought to restrict speech rather than conduct and that such speech was protected by the First Amendment. In the decision, the court argued that the definition of pornography proposed in the ordinance was not the ordinary one accepted in law. The legal definition provided in the Introduction to the chapter is the three-fold *Miller* test which defines pornography in terms of obscenity, and not in terms of women's subordination. Adult women are able to protect themselves from participating in and being personally victimized by pornography, and there is insufficient evidence for the claim that pornography harms all women or society as a whole.

This case raises some basic questions about pornography.

What is an acceptable definition of pornography? Should we use the ordinary, the legal, or the feminist definition?

Once we have defined pornography, we need to determine if it is harmful or not. How should this be done?

If it is harmful, does this justify its censorship? If so, why not censor other materials that may be harmful, such as graphic depictions of violence?

5. ***Mapplethorpe and 2 Live Crew.*** (Discussed in *Newsweek,* Oct. 15, 1990, p. 74). In Cincinnati, a judge acquitted Dennis Barrie, the director of the Contemporary Arts Center, of obscenity charges for displaying the controversial photographs of the late Robert Mapplethorpe. These photographs graphically and explicitly show homosexual acts and nude depictions of children. When surveyed, most people in politically conservative Cincinnati thought the photographs were obscene (although it was not clear how many had actually been to the exhibit). One woman who saw the show reported that the flower photographs were offensive; she was not bothered by penises. The jury viewed only seven photographs out of the exhibition's one hundred seventy-five. Five of them showed homosexual and sadomasochistic acts, and two depicted children with exposed genitals. After hearing testimony by various art experts, the jury was not convinced that they were obscene according to the *Miller* test. Apparently the jury thought that they did not appeal to the prurient interests of the average person, that they did not depict sexual conduct in a patently offensive way, and that they did not lack serious artistic value.

About the same time, in Florida, an all-white jury decided that 2 Live Crew's album "As Nasty As They Wanna Be" was obscene because it described sexual violence against women. Charles Freeman, the Ft. Lauderdale record store owner who sold the album to an undercover policeman, was found guilty of violating the law prohibiting the sale of pornography. He faces a maximum sentence of a year in jail, and a $1,000 fine. He complained that the jury knew nothing about the ghetto, and they did not reflect his community standards as a black man in Broward County, Florida. He plans to appeal the decision.

What definitions of pornography did the juries use in their respective decisions? Are these definitions appropriate?

Suppose you had been on the two juries. How would you have decided these two cases?

Suggested Readings

1. Robin Warshaw, *I Never Called It Rape: The Ms. Report on Recognizing, Fighting and Surviving Date and Acquaintance Rape* (New York: Harper and Row, 1988) discusses the nature of date rape and the factors that make it widespread such as the role of alcohol and drugs, myths about rape, and the macho attitudes of men. Also included are a number of personal cases by women who have been raped by men they knew.

2. Tim Beneke, *Men on Rape* (New York: St. Martin's Press, 1982) explains how the threat of rape affects the lives of women, and discusses some of the ways in which men blame women for rape. The book features interviews with men on sexual violence.

3. Diana E. H. Russell, *Rape in Marriage* (Bloomington, IN: Indiana University Press, Expanded Edition, 1990) covers the phenomenon of marital rape. She claims that one out of seven married women is raped by her husband.

4. Susan Brownmiller, *Against Our Will: Men, Women, and Rape* (New York: Simon and Schuster, 1975). This is a classical feminist work which argues that rape is a crime of violence (rather than sex) that threatens all women.

5. Sylvia Levine and Joseph Loenig, eds., *Why Men Rape* (Toronto: Macmillan, 1980). This book has shocking interviews with rapists; it is based on the National Film Board of Canada's film *Why Men Rape*. Pineau quotes from the book in her reading.

6. Billie Wright Dziech and Linda Weiner, *The Lecherous Professor: Sexual Harassment on Campus* (Boston: Beacon Press, 1984) gives an analysis of a common form of quid pro quo sexual harassment. The focus is on male professors suffering from midlife crisis.

7. Catharine A. MacKinnon, *Sexual Harassment of Working Women: A Case of Sex Discrimination* (New Haven, CT: Yale University Press, 1979). MacKinnon gives a feminist analysis of sexual harassment. Like pornography, it is a form of sex discrimination where men try to dominate women.

8. Catharine MacKinnon, *Feminism Unmodified* (Cambridge: Harvard University Press, 1987). In the Chapter titled "Francis Biddle's Sister," MacKinnon defines pornography as a form of sex discrimination that depicts through pictures and words the subordination of women as dehumanized, abused, and degraded sexual objects. According to MacKinnon, pornography violates women's civil rights and should be illegal. Furthermore, MacKinnon claims that pornography, as distinguished from erotica which depicts sex between equals, is a major cause of harm to women. It causes men to rape, batter, prostitute, molest, and sexually harass women.

9. Alan Soble, *Pornography* (New Haven: Yale University Press, 1986). Soble claims pornography is not objectionable in a society that does not exploit women, but in a society that does, it is wrong.

10. Andrea Dworkin, *Pornography: Men Possessing Women* (New York: Perigee, 1981). Dworkin is a feminist who holds that in a patriarchal society pornography depicting women necessarily degrades and subordinates them.

11. Camille Paglia, *Sexual Personae* (New York: Vintage Books, 1990). This book has generated much discussion, not all of it favorable. Paglia presents her controversial views about sex and violence, along with occasional jabs at feminism, in the first chapter, titled "Sex and Violence, or Nature and Art."

12. Camille Paglia, *Sex, Art, and American Culture* (New York: Vintage Books, 1992). This is a collection of essays on topics ranging from Madonna to Zen Buddhism. In "The Strange Case of Clarence Thomas and Anita Hill," Paglia argues that Hill was not a victim of sexual harassment even if she was telling the truth in the Senate confirmation hearings. "The Rape Debate, Continued" has various interviews of Paglia on date rape including the interview that appeared in *Spin* magazine where she gives a further explanation and defense of her position.

13. Edmund Wall, ed., *Sexual Harassment* (Buffalo, NY: Prometheus Books, 1992). This is a useful collection of articles on sexual harassment. It is divided into three parts: definition and policy descriptions of sexual harassment in the university and the workplace, explanations and causes, and the treatment of sexual harassment in the law.

14. Rosemarie Tong, *Women, Sex, and the Law* (Totowa, NJ: Rowman & Allanheld, 1984) covers several different women's issues as they relate to the law. Chapter 1 is on pornography, Chapter 3 is on sexual harassment, and Chapter 4 discusses rape.

15. John Arthur, *The Unfinished Constitution* (Belmont, CA: Wadsworth, 1989) discusses the constitutional issues raised by pornography including the proposed feminist ordinances in Minneapolis and Indianapolis that attempted to outlaw pornography.

16. David Copp and Susan Wendell, eds., *Pornography and Censorship* (Buffalo, NY: Prometheus Books, 1983). This collection contains philosophical essays, articles by social scientists on the effects of pornography, and essays on pornography and the law.

17. Laura Lederer, ed., *Take Back the Night: Women on Pornography* (New York: Morrow, 1980). This anthology states the feminist view of pornography as degrading and harmful to women.

Chapter Seven

SEX, TESTING, AND AIDS

Introduction

A traditional view of sex. The Jewish-Christian tradition maintains the position that the main purpose of sex is the procreation of children within the context of marriage. Nonmarital sex—adultery, premarital sex, fornication, prostitution, masturbation, and homosexuality—is morally wrong. In the first reading, the Vatican Declaration on Sexual Ethics presents an influential statement of this Christian view of sex.

The Vatican position has been attacked by those both inside and outside the Church. One prominent Catholic critic of the Church's position on sexuality is Father Curran, former Professor of Theology at the Catholic University of America. In his book *Issues in Sexual and Medical Ethics* (1978), Father Curran argues that it is an error to reject all nonreproductive sex as wrong without taking into account the person and the person's relationship with others. The Church responded by suspending Father Curran from his teaching duties and issuing a statement reaffirming its condemnation of homosexuality. Nevertheless, homosexual priests and others continue to challenge the Church's position. For example, some homosexual priests have argued that while homosexual practices may be wrong for priests who have vowed to be celibate, their is nothing intrinsically wrong with being homosexual in orientation.

Controversy also surrounds the use of contraceptives. The official teaching of the Church, stated in the 1968 papal encyclical *Humane Vitae,* rejects artificial birth control as immoral, even for those who are married. Recently, a committee of bishops issued a statement strongly rejecting the use of condoms to prevent the spread of sexually transmitted diseases (including AIDS) and urging schools to teach chastity as the only acceptable approach to sex for adolescents and others who are unmarried. Surveys have shown, however, that the majority of Catholics in the United States and Canada do not agree that artificial birth control is always immoral.

Natural Law Theory. To understand the traditional Christian view of sex, it is essential to know something about the natural law theory used to support it. Natural law is a set of prescriptive rules of conduct binding on all human beings because of their human nature. In natural law theory, human action is naturally directed towards certain goals and purposes such as life and procreation. These natural goals and purposes are good, and to interfere with them is morally wrong. Accordingly, if the natural goal or purpose of sexual activity is reproduction within the context of marriage, then interfering with this natural goal is morally wrong.

The Vatican Declaration espouses this natural law theory. According to this declaration, homosexuality is seriously disordered because it contradicts its so-called finality, that is, it opposes the natural end of sex, which is procreation. Masturbation is also a serious disorder for the same reason. Premarital sexual relations are condemned because they often exclude the prospect of children, and even if children are produced, they will be deprived of a proper and stable environment.

It is hard to find anyone who seriously defends the condemnation of masturbation; this is not a serious issue for most people. Premarital sex involving engaged couples does not seem to be much of an issue either, although some writers hold it is immoral. (See the book by Vincent C. Punzo listed in the Suggested Readings.) Most of the current debate focuses on homosexuality. In the second reading, Paul Cameron attacks homosexuality, but from a different point of view than the Vatican Declaration. Instead of saying that homosexuality is unnatural, he contends that there are a number of natural factors which favor the adaptation of homosexuality by young people. These factors include the extreme homosociality of children, the superiority of homosexual sex, and the egocentric or self-oriented personality of the young. Cameron argues that despite the natural predisposition to homosexuality, discrimination against homosexuality is justified because homosexuality leads to unstable relationships, selfishness, suicide, homicide, and unhappiness.

In the next reading, Richard D. Mohr replies to various claims made about homosexuality including those made by the Vatican and Cameron. Homosexuality is not the result of a deliberate choice, nor is it unnatural or immoral. Homosexuals are not self-centered. They desire permanent relationships, and many would like to raise foster children. Discrimination against people because of their sexual orientation is no more justified than discrimination based on race. Like race and ethnic background, homosexuality is something that is not within a person's control. Society would be improved (not worse off as Cameron would have it) if gays were socially accepted.

AIDS. In the 1980s, AIDS (acquired immune deficiency syndrome) commanded widespread public attention and fear. Initially, it was thought to be a disease found only in gay men, but as it spread to drug users and heterosexuals, it was perceived as a threat to everyone. In the reading, Dr. Theresa L. Crenshaw states that the disease is now an epidemic with more than 1.5 million people infected with the HIV virus thought to cause AIDS. The fear of heterosexual transmission dramatically increased when Magic Johnson, the famous basketball player, tested positive for the HIV virus. In public appearances and interviews on television, Magic insisted that he was infected by a woman, and that his wife and child were not infected. Within a year of that announcement, the well-known tennis player Arthur Ashe died of AIDS. He said he contracted the virus as a result of blood transfusions following open heart surgery.

Not all the facts about AIDS are known. Although some AIDS researchers remain doubtful, most attribute the cause of AIDS to a virus called HIV, which is transmitted by sexual intercourse, sharing infected needles, transfusions with infected blood or blood products, and pregnancy (mother to fetus). It is possible to transmit the HIV virus in other ways, such as accidents where one's blood comes in contact with an infected person's blood, but these incidents are very rare. Blood tests can detect antibodies, indicating exposure to the virus, but at the present state of development, these tests are inconclusive.

Dr. Crenshaw discusses the problem of false negative readings in HIV tests. The virus apparently hides and reproduces in cells of the immune system for a year or more before it is detected by the blood tests currently used. There can also be false positive tests. Dr. Crenshaw notes that the **ELISA test**, the standard test for the HIV virus, does have a high percentage of false positives. Her solution to the problem is to repeat the test along with other tests. If all these are positive, then the chance of a false positive approaches zero.

But there are still uncertainties. Not everyone who tests HIV positive develops full-blown AIDS which leads to illness and death. Some HIV-positive people develop less serious symptoms—AIDS-related complex (ARC)—and do not get AIDS itself. The picture is further complicated by the fact that the time from exposure to the virus until the appearance of the full-blown AIDS symptoms can be unusually long (in some cases up to seven years), and no upper limit is known.

Another confusing development was reported at the Eighth International Conference on AIDS, which took place in Amsterdam, July 20–24, 1992, and was given prominent coverage in the media (see the *SPIN* article mentioned in the Suggested Readings.) There are a significant number of cases of AIDS with no trace of HIV present, but all of the other classical symptoms—various opportunistic infections and low **T4 cell** counts. In these cases, there seems to be some cause other than the HIV virus. (At least continual tests with the latest detection technologies have been negative for the HIV virus.) One doctor, Dr. Sudhir Gupta, said he found a new retrovirus (HICRV) in nine patients who have clinical AIDS but not HIV. So there may be more than one virus that causes AIDS, and perhaps there are other undiscovered factors that contribute to the development of AIDS.

Testing for AIDS. How should the AIDS epidemic be controlled, particularly when 90 percent of those infected with the HIV virus do not know it? In the reading, Dr. Crenshaw recommends required HIV testing for hospital admission, certain jobs, and other relevant situations. Most of her reading is devoted to replying to various objections to required testing: the problem of false positive and false negative tests, the violation of confidentiality and privacy, and other adverse consequences.

In the next reading, Richard D. Mohr claims that the appeal to public health benefits does not justify mandatory HIV testing in the military, prisons, and other institutions. He makes some of the same objections that Dr. Crenshaw discusses; that mandatory HIV testing would drive AIDS underground and that false test results would produce tragic results. He argues that the real point of such testing is the degradation of gays and the reconsecration of heterosexuality as a sacred value in our society.

In the final reading for the chapter, Grant Gillett focuses on the problem of confidentiality, a problem that might arise frequently if required testing were to be implemented. Suppose a patient who tests positive for the HIV virus refuses to inform his wife or allow others to inform her. Does the doctor have an obligation to inform the wife, or does he have a duty to the patient to keep this information confidential?

The Vatican

Declaration on Sexual Ethics

The Declaration on Sexual Ethics was issued in Rome by the Sacred Congregation for the Doctrine of the Faith on December 29, 1975.

The authors defend the Christian doctrine that "every genital act must be within the framework of marriage." Premarital sex, masturbation, and homosexuality are specifically condemned, and chastity is recommended as a virtue.

1. According to contemporary scientific research, the human person is so profoundly affected by sexuality that it must be considered as one of the factors which give to each individual's life the principal traits that distinguish it. In fact it is from sex that the human person receives the characteristics which, on the biological, psychological and spiritual levels, make that person a man or a woman, and thereby largely condition his or her progress towards maturity and insertion into society. Hence sexual matters, as is obvious to everyone, today constitute a theme frequently and openly dealt with in books, reviews, magazines, and other means of social communication.

In the present period, the corruption of morals has increased, and one of the most serious indications of this corruption is the unbridled exaltation of sex. Moreover, through the means of social communication and through public entertainment this corruption has reached the point of invading the field of education and of infecting the general mentality.

In this context certain educators, teachers, and moralists have been able to contribute to a better understanding and integration into life of the values proper to each of the sexes; on the other hand there are those who have put forward concepts and modes of behavior which are contrary to the true moral exigencies of the human person. Some members of the latter group have even gone so far as to favor a licentious hedonism.

As a result, in the course of a few years, teachings, moral criteria, and modes of living hitherto faithfully preserved have been very much unsettled, even among Christians. There are many people today who, being confronted with so many widespread opinions opposed to the teachings which they received from the Church, have come to wonder what they must still hold as true.

2. The Church cannot remain indifferent to this confusion of minds and relaxation of morals. It is a question, in fact, of a matter which is of the utmost importance both for the personal lives of Christians and for the social life of our time.[1]

The Bishops are daily led to note the growing difficulties experienced by the faithful in obtaining knowledge of wholesome moral teaching, especially in sexual matters, and of the growing difficulties experienced by pastors in expounding this teaching effectively. The Bishops know that by their pastoral charge they are called upon to meet the needs of their faithful in this very serious matter, and important documents dealing with it have already been published by some of them or by Episcopal Conferences. Nevertheless, since the erroneous opinions and resulting deviations are continuing to spread everywhere, the Sacred Congregation for the Doctrine of the Faith, by virtue of its function in the universal Church[2] and by a mandate of the Supreme Pontiff, has judged it necessary to publish the present Declaration.

3. The people of our time are more and more convinced that the human person's dignity and vocation demand that they should discover, by the light of their own intelligence, the values innate in their nature, that they should ceaselessly develop these values and realize them in their lives, in order to achieve an ever greater development.

In moral matters man cannot make value judgments according to his personal whim: "In the depths of his conscience, man detects a law which he does not impose on himself, but which holds him to obedience. . . . For man has in his heart a law written by God. To obey it is the very dignity of man; according to it he will be judged." [3]

Moreover, through his revelation God has made known to us Christians his plan of salvation, and he has held up to us Christ, the Saviour and Sanctifier, in his teaching and example, as the supreme and immutable law of life: "I am the light of the world; anyone who follows me will not be walking in the dark, he will have the light of life." [4]

Therefore there can be no true promotion of man's dignity unless the essential order of his nature is respected. Of course, in the history of civilization many of the concrete conditions and needs of human life have changed and will continue to change. But all evolution of morals and every type of life must be kept within the limits imposed by the immutable principles based upon every human person's constitutive elements and essential relations—elements and relations which transcend historical contingency.

These fundamental principles, which can be grasped by reason, are contained in "the divine law—eternal, objective, and universal—whereby God orders, directs, and governs the entire universe and all the ways of the human community, by a plan conceived in wisdom and love. Man has been made by God to participate in this law, with the result that, under the gentle disposition of divine Providence, he can come to perceive ever increasingly the unchanging truth." [5] This divine law is accessible to our minds.

4. Hence, those many people are in error who today assert that one can find neither in human nature nor in the revealed law any absolute and immutable norm to serve for particular actions other than the one which expresses itself in the general law of charity and respect for human dignity. As a proof of their assertion they put forward the view that so-called norms of the natural law or precepts of Sacred Scripture are to be regarded only as given expressions of a form of particular culture at a certain moment of history.

But in fact, divine Revelation and, in its own proper order, philosophical wisdom, emphasize the authentic exigencies of human nature. They thereby necessarily manifest the existence of immutable laws inscribed in the constitutive elements of human nature and which are revealed to be identical in all beings endowed with reason.

Furthermore, Christ instituted his Church as "the pillar and bulwark of truth." [6] With the Holy Spirit's assistance, she ceaselessly preserves and transmits without error the truths of the moral order, and she authentically interprets not only the revealed positive law but "also . . . those principles of the moral order which have their origin in human nature itself" [7] and which concern man's full development and sanctification. Now in fact the Church throughout her history has always considered a certain number of precepts of the natural law as having an absolute and immutable value, and in their transgression she has seen a contradiction of the teaching and spirit of the Gospel.

5. Since sexual ethics concern certain fundamental values of human and Christian life, this general teaching equally applies to sexual ethics. In this domain there exist principles and norms which the Church has always unhesitatingly transmitted as part of her teaching, however much the opinions and morals of the world may have been opposed to them. These principles and norms in no way owe their origin to a certain type of culture, but rather to knowledge of the divine law and of humane nature. They therefore cannot be considered as having become out of date or doubtful under the pretext that a new cultural situation has arisen.

It is these principles which inspired the exhortations and directives given by the Second Vatican Council for an education and an organization of social life taking account of the equal dignity of man and woman while respecting their difference.[8]

Speaking of "the sexual nature of man and the human faculty of procreation," the Council noted that they "wonderfully exceed the dispositions of lower forms of life." [9] It then took particular care to expound the principles and criteria which concern human sexuality in marriage, and which are based upon the finality of the specific function of sexuality.

In this regard the Council declares that the moral goodness of the acts proper to conjugal life, acts which are ordered according to true human dignity, "does not depend solely on sincere intentions or on an evaluation of motives. It must be determined by objective standards. These, based on the nature of the human person and his acts, preserve the full sense of mutual self-giving and human procreation in the context of true love." [10]

These final words briefly sum up the Council's teaching—more fully expounded in an earlier part of the same Constitution[11]—on the finality of the sexual act and on the principal criterion of its morality: it is respect for its finality that ensures the moral goodness of this act.

This same principle, which the Church holds from divine Revelation and from her authentic interpretation of the natural law, is also the basis of her traditional doctrine, which states that the use of the sexual function has its true meaning and moral rectitude only in true marriage.[12]

6. It is not the purpose of the present declaration to deal with all the abuses of the sexual faculty, nor with all the elements involved in the practice of chastity. Its object is rather to repeat the Church's doctrine on certain particular points, in view of the urgent need to oppose serious errors and widespread aberrant modes of behavior.

7. Today there are many who vindicate the right to sexual union before marriage, at least in those cases where a firm intention to marry and an affection which is already in some way conjugal in the psychology of the subjects require this completion, which they judge to be connatural. This is especially the case when the celebration of the marriage is impeded by circumstances or when this intimate relationship seems necessary in order for love to be preserved.

This opinion is contrary to Christian doctrine, which states that every genital act must be within the framework of marriage. However firm the intention of those who practice such premature sexual relations may be, the fact remains that these relations cannot ensure, in sincerity and fidelity, the interpersonal relationship between a man and a woman, nor especially can they protect this relationship from whims and caprices. Now it is a stable union that Jesus willed, and he restored its original requirement, beginning with the sexual difference. "Have you not read that the creator from the beginning made them male and female and that he said: This is why a man must leave father and mother, and cling to his wife, and the two become one body? They are no longer two, therefore, but one body. So then, what God has united, man must not divide." [13] Saint Paul will be even more explicit when he shows that if unmarried people or widows cannot live chastely they have no other alternative than the stable union of marriage: ". . . it is better to marry than to be aflame with passion." [14] Through marriage, in fact, the love of married people is taken up into that love which Christ irrevocably has for the Church,[15] while dissolute sexual union[16] defiles the temple of the Holy Spirit which the Christian has become. Sexual union therefore is only legitimate if a definitive community of life has been established between the man and the woman.

This is what the Church has always understood and taught,[17] and she finds a profound agreement with her doctrine in men's reflection and in the lessons of history.

Experience teaches us that love must find its safeguard in the stability of marriage, if sexual intercourse is truly to respond to the requirements of its own finality and to those of human dignity. These requirements call for a conjugal contract sanctioned and guaranteed by society—a contract which establishes a state of life of capital importance both for the exclusive union of the man and the woman and for the good of their family and of the human community. Most often, in fact, premarital relations exclude the possibility of children. What is represented to be conjugal love is not able, as it absolutely should be, to develop into paternal and maternal love. Or, if it does happen to do so, this will be to the detriment of the children, who will be deprived of the stable environment in which they ought to develop in order to find in it the way and the means of their insertion into society as a whole.

The consent given by people who wish to be united in marriage must therefore be manifested externally and in a manner which makes it valid in the eyes of society. As far as the faithful are concerned, their consent to the setting up of a community of conjugal life must be expressed according to the laws of the Church. It is a consent which makes their marriage a Sacrament of Christ.

8. At the present time there are those who, basing themselves on observations in the psychological order, have begun to judge indulgently, and even to excuse completely, homosexual relations between certain people. This they do in opposition to the constant teaching of the Magisterium and to the moral sense of the Christian people.

A distinction is drawn, and it seems with some reason, between homosexuals whose tendency comes from a false education, from a lack of normal sexual development, from habit, from bad example, or from other similar causes, and is transitory or at least not incurable; and homosexuals who are definitively such because of some kind of innate instinct or a pathological constitution judged to be incurable.

In regard to this second category of subjects, some people conclude that their tendency is so natural that it justifies in their case homosexual relations within a sincere communion of life and love analogous to marriage insofar as such homosexuals feel incapable of enduring a solitary life.

In the pastoral field, these homosexuals must certainly be treated with understanding and sustained in the hope of overcoming their personal difficulties and their inability to fit into society. Their culpability will be judged with prudence. But no pastoral method can be employed which would give moral justification to these acts on the grounds that they would be consonant with the condition of such people. For according to the objective moral order, homosexual relations are acts which lack an essential and indispensable finality. In Sacred Scripture they are condemned as a serious depravity and even presented as the sad consequence of rejecting God.[18] This judgment of Scripture does not of course permit us to conclude that all those who suffer from this anomaly are personally responsible for it, but it does attest to the fact that homosexual acts are intrinsically disordered and can in no case be approved.

9. The traditional Catholic doctrine that masturbation constitutes a grave moral disorder is often called into doubt or expressly denied today. It is said that psychology and sociology show that it is a normal phenomenon of sexual development, especially among the young. It is stated that there is real and serious fault only in the measure that the subject deliberately indulges in solitary pleasure closed in on self ("ipsation"), because in this case the act would indeed be radically opposed to the loving communion between persons of different sex which some hold is what is principally sought in the use of the sexual faculty.

This opinion is contradictory to the teaching and pastoral practice of the Catholic Church. Whatever the force of certain arguments of a biological and philosophical nature, which have sometimes been used by theologians, in fact both the Magisterium of the Church—in the course of a constant tradition—and the moral sense of the faithful have declared without hesitation that masturbation is an intrinsically and seriously disordered act.[19] The main reason is that, whatever the motive for acting in this way, the deliberate use of the sexual faculty outside normal conjugal relations essentially contradicts the finality of the faculty. For it lacks the sexual relationship called for by the moral order, namely the relationship which realizes "the full sense of mutual self-giving and human procreation in the context of true love." [20] All deliberate exercise of sexuality must be reserved to this regular relationship. Even if it cannot be proved that Scripture condemns this sin by name, the tradition of the Church has rightly understood it to be condemned in the New Testament when the latter speaks of "impurity," "unchasteness," and other vices contrary to chastity and continence.

Sociological surveys are able to show the frequency of this disorder according to the places, populations, or circumstances studied. In this way facts are discovered, but facts do not constitute a criterion for judging the moral value of human acts.[21] The frequency of the phenomenon in question is certainly to be linked with man's innate weakness following original sin; but it is also to be linked with the loss of a sense of God, with the corruption of morals engendered by the commercialization of vice, with the unrestrained licentiousness of so many public entertainments and publications, as well as with the neglect of modesty, which is the guardian of chastity.

On the subject of masturbation modern psychology provides much valid and useful information for formulating a more equitable judgment on moral responsibility and for orienting pastoral action. Psychology helps one to see how the immaturity of adolescence (which can sometimes persist after that age), psychological imbalance, or habit can influence behavior, diminishing the deliberate character of the act and bringing about a situation whereby subjectively there may not always be serious fault. But in general, the absence of serious responsibility must not be presumed; this would be to misunderstand people's moral capacity.

In the pastoral ministry, in order to form an adequate judgment in concrete cases, the habitual behavior of people will be considered in its totality, not only with regard to the individual's practice of charity and of justice but also with regard to the individual's care in observing the particular precepts of chastity. In particular, one will have to examine whether the individual is using the necessary means, both natural and supernatural, which Christian asceticism from its long experience recommends for overcoming the passions and progressing in virtue. . . .

Endnotes

1. See Vatican II, *Pastoral Constitution on the Church in the World of Today*, no. 47: *Acta Apostolicae Sedis* 58 (1966) 1067 [*The Pope Speaks* XI, 289–290].
2. See the Apostolic Constitution *Regimini Ecclesiae Universae* (August 15, 1967), no. 29: *AAS* 59 (1967) 897 [*TPS* XII, 401–402].
3. *Pastoral Constitution on the Church in the World of Today*, no. 16: *AAS* 58 (1966) 1037 [*TPS* XI, 268].
4. *Jn* 8, 12.
5. *Declaration on Religious Freedom*, no. 3: *AAS* 58 (1966) 931 [*TPS* XI, 86].
6. 1 *Tm* 3, 15.
7. *Declaration on Religious Freedom*, no. 14: *AAS* 58 (1966) 940 [*TPS* XI, 93]. See also Pius XI, Encyclical *Casti Connubii* (December 31, 1930): *AAS* 22 (1930) 579–580; Pius XII, Address of November 2, 1954 *AAS* 46 (1954) 671–672 [*TPS* I 380–381]; John XXIII, Encyclical *Mater et Magistra* (May 25, 1961), no. 239: *AAS* 53 (1961) 457 [*TPS* VII, 388]; Paul VI, Encyclical *Humanae Vitae* (July 25, 1968), no. 4: *AAS* 60 (1968) 483 [*TPS* XIII, 331–332].
8. See Vatican II, *Declaration on Christian Education*, nos. 1 and 8: *AAS* 58 (1966) 729–730, 734–736 [*TPS* XI, 201–202, 206–207]; *Pastoral Constitution on the Church in the World of Today*, nos. 29, 60, 67: *AAS* 58 (1966) 1048–1049, 1080–181, 1088–1089 [*TPS* XI, 276–277, 299–300, 304–305].
9. *Pastoral Constitution on the Church in the World of Today*, no. 51: *AAS* 58 (1966) 1072 [*TPS* XI, 293].
10. *Loc. cit.*; see also no. 49: *AAS* 58 (1966) 1069–1070 [*TPS* XI, 291–292].
11. See *Pastoral Constitution on the Church in the World of Today*, nos. 49–50: *AAS* 58 (1966) 1069–1072 [*TPS* XI, 291–293].
12. The present Declaration does not review all the moral norms for the use of sex, since they have already been set forth in the encyclicals *Casti Connubii* and *Humanae Vitae*.
13. *Mt* 19, 4–6.
14. 1 *Cor* 7, 9.
15. See *Eph* 5, 25–32.
16. Extramarital intercourse is expressly condemned in *1 Cor* 5, 1; 6, 9; 7, 2; 10, 8; *Eph* 5, 5–7; 1 *Tm* 1, 10; *Heb* 13, 4; there are explicit arguments given in 1 *Cor* 6, 12–20.
17. See Innocent IV, Letter *Sub Catholicae professione* (March 6, 1254) (*DS* 835); Pius II, Letter *Cum sicut accepimus* (November 14, 1459) (*DS* 1367); Decrees of the Holy Office on September 24, 1665 (*DS* 2045) and March 2, 1679 (*DS* 2148); Pius XI, Encyclical *Casti Conubii* (December 31, 1930): *AAS* 22 (1930) 538–539.
18. *Rom* 1:24–27: "In consequence, God delivered them up in their lusts to unclean practices; they engaged in the mutual degradation of their bodies, these men who exchanged the truth of God for a lie and worshipped and served the creature rather than the Creator—blessed be he forever, amen! God therefore delivered them to disgraceful passions. Their women exchanged natural intercourse for unnatural, and the men gave up natural intercourse with women and burned with lust for one another. Men did shameful things with men, and thus received in their own persons the penalty for their perversity." See also what St. Paul says of sodomy in 1 *Cor* 6, 9; 1 *Tm* 1, 10.
19. See Leo IX, Letter *Ad splendidum nitentes* (1054) (*DS* 687–688); Decree of the Holy Office on March 2, 1679 (*DS* 2149); Pius XII, Addresses of October 8, 1953: *AAS* 45 (1953) 677–678, and May 19, 1956: *AAS* 48 (1956) 472–473.

20. *Pastoral Constitution on the Church in the World of Today,* no. 51: *AAS* 58 (1966) 1072 [*TPS* XI, 293].
21. See Paul VI, Apostolic Exhortation *Quinque iam anni* (December 8, 1970): *AAS* 63 (1971) 102 [*TPS* XV, 329]: "If sociological surveys are useful for better discovering the thought patterns of the people of a particular place, the anxieties and needs of those to whom we proclaim the word of God, and also the oppositions made to it by modern reasoning through the widespread notion that outside science there exists no legitimate form of knowledge, still the conclusions drawn from such surveys could not of themselves constitute a determining criterion of truth."

Review Questions

1. What is the traditional Christian doctrine about sex, according to the declaration?
2. Why does the declaration find premarital sexual relations to be immoral?
3. What is the declaration's objection to homosexuality?
4. What is wrong with masturbation, according to the declaration?

Discussion Questions

1. Is celibacy a violation of natural law? Explain your view.
2. Is contraception wrong too? Defend your answer.
3. Is procreation the only natural purpose of sex? Defend your position.

Paul Cameron

A Case Against Homosexuality

Paul Cameron is a psychologist who has published articles on homosexuality and a book, The Life Cycle: Perspectives and Commentary *(1977).*

Cameron believes that human sexuality is learned and that the developmental process is tilted toward the adoption of homosexuality rather than heterosexuality or bisexuality. The factors producing the homosexual tilt are the extreme homosociality of children, the fact that males are more interested in sex than females, the fact that homosexual sex is more satisfying than heterosexual sex, and the egocentricity of the young. Nevertheless, Cameron argues that homosexuality should be discriminated against as an undesirable lifestyle because it produces undesirable personality traits—a self-centered orientation, irresponsibility, and a tendency towards suicide and homicide. Heterosexuality should be encouraged because it produces more desirable personality traits and more happiness than homosexuality.

Paul Cameron, Chairman, Family Research Institute, P.O. Box 2091, Washington, D.C. 20013.

In some segments of the mass media, the homosexuality issue takes on the appearance of a struggle between orange juice peddlers and bathhouse owners. At a different level individual rights vs. the interests of society provide the conflict. Some argue that adult homosexuals ought to be allowed to do what they want behind closed doors. Others, often seeing the issue in terms of rights, honesty, and overpopulation, seek to grant homosexuality equal status with heterosexuality. The school system of San Francisco, apparently resonating with the latter tack, is offering a course including "homosexual lifestyles." Liberals attempt to shame as unenlightened all who oppose complete equality as vigorously as conservative Bible-thumpers threaten wrath from above.

No known human society has ever granted equal status to homo and heterosexuality. What information do those who desire social equivalence for these two sexual orientations possess that assures them that this new venture in human social organization is called for at this time? Have the cultures of the past practiced discrimination against homosexuality out of a mere prejudice, or was there substance to their bias? At the risk of seeming rather out of step with the academic community, no new information has surfaced that would lead me to discount the social policies of the past. On the contrary, the policies of the past in regard to homosexuality appear generally wise, and considerable discrimination against homosexuality and for heterosexuality, marriage and parenthood appears needful for the social good.

Discrimination

Discrimination is something all humans and all human communities do. Individually we discriminate for certain things and against others, e.g., movies over T.V. Collectively we discriminate for and against selected: 1) acts (pleasantries, sharing vs. murder, robbery), 2) traits (generous, kind vs. whiny, hostile) and 3) life-styles (independent, productive vs. gambling, indolent). Prejudice is unwarranted discrimination. The issue is not whether discrimination should exist—for human society to exist, it must. The issues are always: 1) is discrimination called for? and 2) how much is necessary? Reasonable people can and do disagree on what ought to be discriminated for and against, to what degree, and even if discrimination is prejudicial rather than called for. But reasoned opinion *can* hold that homosexuality and homosexuals ought to be discriminated against. . . .

The Case Against Homosexuality/ Wisdom of the Ages

No contemporary society accords homosexuality equivalent status with heterosexuality. No known society has accorded equivalent status in the past (Karlen, 1971). No current or ancient religion of any consequence has failed to teach discrimination against homosexuality. The Judeo-Christian tradition is no exception to this rule. The Old Testament made homosexuality a capital offense, and while the New Testament writers failed to invoke capital punishment for any offense, they did manage to consign homosexuals to eternal hell for the practice. Church fathers and traditions have stayed in line with this position until recently. To the degree that tradition and agreed-upon social policy ought to carry weight in our thinking about issues, the weight of tradition is preponderately on the side of discrimination. The same is true if we "poll" famous thinkers of the past: Plato, for instance, who at one time of his life provided some endorsement of homosexuality, but switched to a strongly negative vote by the end of his career. Aristotle simply considered homosexuality a depravity and Plutarch noted that "no wise father would permit a notable Greek philosopher near his sons." St. Augustine condemned homosexuality and St. Thomas Aquinas ranked homosexuality just a rung above bestiality.

While it is somewhat fashionable to claim that the ancient Greeks legalized and practiced homosexuality, it rather appears that this was, at most, true for only a short time, and only for the leisure class (Karlen, 1971). Similarly, while a number of American Indian societies had a place for the homosexual, it was, all in all, a rather unpleasant one (the Mohave interchanged the word for "coward" and "queer"). Most of the anthropological information that alludes to common practicing of homosexuality among males of various tribes neglects to note that the members of the tribe didn't consider what they were doing sexual, much less homosexual (various touching customs among males featured no erections, etc.) Further, the common anti-female bias of the Greeks and other philosophic systems is not fairly construed as homosexuality. Aristotle claimed that the best forms of friendship and love were found "between men," but condemned homosexuality. One can be pro-male without necessitating elimination of copulation between the sexes. It is quite possible to keep love and sex, or friendship and sex, almost completely separate.

While one cannot carry the "wisdom of the ages" argument too far—just because all peoples up to a certain point in time believed something does not necessarily mean that it was so—yet it appears more than a little injudicious to cast it aside as merely "quaint." Probably no issue has occupied man's collective attentions more than successful living together. That such unanimity of opinion and practice should exist must give one pause. Certainly such congruence "puts the ball in the changer's court." As in so many spheres of human endeavor, when we know that we can get on in a particular way, the burden of proof that we can get on as well or better by following a different custom falls upon those seeking the change. The "fallacy of the ages" is that we "got here because we did X" (we might have gotten here just as well, thank you, by doing K) but that we are regarding fallacy rather than wisdom must still be *proven* by those seeking change.

To date, those seeking change have not been flush with scientific evidence that homosexuality is not socially disruptive. On the contrary, the arguments that have been advanced have been little more than "people ought not to be discriminated against; homosexuals are people; ergo homosexuals ought not to be discriminated against" shouted larger and louder. No one to my knowledge has ever claimed that homosexuals were not people, and one would have to be a dunce to believe that being a person qualifies one, *ipso facto,* for nondiscrimination. Aside from this argument repeated in endless variations and *ad nauseam,* the evidence is simply not there. I'll admit to a charm in residing in a society undergoing dramatic change. You get to stand at the end of the tunnel of history and help dig a new hole (something that particularly excites the modern scholar and local news team). But let us be sure we are not digging new holes just for our amusement. Meddling with procreation and heterosexuality is considerably more than a parlor game in which the stakes are but a trifle. Because what we are about is so very serious, if anything, an even better set of evidence needs to be produced by those seeking change, not, as is the case today, mere syllogistic flatus.

Homosociality Coupled with Increasing Self-Centeredness Could Lead to Widespread Homosexuality

. . . Jimmy Carter said: "I don't see homosexuality as a threat to the family." . . . His sentiments probably echo those of the educated class of our society. They trust that "only deviants" are really into homosexuality anyway, and, more importantly, that "mother nature" will come through in the last analysis. Biology, they assume, has a great deal to do with sexuality and sexual attraction, and millions of years of heterosexuality has firmly engraved itself on the genetic code.

Such thinking betrays a lack of appreciation of the enormous component of learning that goes into human sexuality. The point that anthropology has made over the past hundred years is the *tremendous diversity of human social organization.* Marvelously varied are the ways man rears his young, honors his dead, plays the game of procreation, or practices dental hygiene. While the onset of the events of puberty vary relatively little from one society to another, the onset of copulation varies over a full quarter of the life-span—from 5 or 6 years of age to mid-20s. While three-spine stickle-backs predictably go into paroxysms of delight over a given colored shape, the object of man's sexual desires varies from car mufflers, to animals, to various ages, and sexes of his own kind. Many mammals practice sex for only a few days or weeks in the year, but man varies from untrammeled lust to studied virginity. While I have enumerated my reasons more fully elsewhere (Cameron, 1977), I believe that the most reasonable construal of the evidence to date suggests that *human sexuality is totally learned.*

There are really only three ways for human sexuality to develop. Humans are among, if not *the,* most gregarious creatures. We are reared by our kind, schooled with and by our kind, and just generally like to be around other humans (my research into the contents of consciousness suggests that, world-wide, *the* most frequent topic of thought is other humans). We prefer to do just about anything with one or more other humans. We prefer to eat with another human, we would rather go to the movies, picnic, take walks with another, etc. We are firmly gregarious. The same is true for sexuality. For all but the kinkiest of us, we would rather "do it" with another human. Bestiality, necrophilia, vacuum cleaners, dolls, you name it, none of these sexual aberrations will ever become modal sex—they will always appeal to only a few. Since modal human sexuality must needs be confined to other humans, the three ways to "fly" are obvious modes: heterosexuality, homosexuality, or bisexualty. Because human sexuality is totally learned, humans must be pointed in the "right" direction, and taught how and with whom to perform. And there's the rub. Homosexuality and heterosexuality do not start off on the same footing. *Au contraire,* one gets a number of important boosts in the scheme of things. In our society the developmental process is decidedly *tilted toward the adoption of homosexuality!*

Part of the homosexual tilt is the extreme homosociality of children starting around the age of 5. As everyone is aware, boys want to play with boys and girls with girls, and they do so with a vengeance. It's quite reasonable, on their part. First, boys' and girls' bodies are different and they are aware that their bodies-to-be will differ still more. In part because of this the games, sports and skills they practice differ. As if in anticipation of the differing roles they will have, their interests and proclivities differ. Even if they try, few girls can do as well as most boys at "boy things" and few boys can do as well as girls at "girl things." They almost inhabit different worlds. Not surprisingly for members of two different "races," poles apart psychologically, socially, and physically, they "stick to their own kind." . . .

There are three other components that contribute to the homosexual tilt. First, on the average in our society, males are considerably more taken with sex than females are. In my 1975 survey of 818 persons on the east coast of the U.S., respondents were asked to rate the degree of pleasure they obtained from 22 activities including "being with one's family," "listening to music," "being out in nature," "housework," and "sexual activity." Between the late teens through middle age, sexual activity topped the male list as the "most pleasurable activity." It did manage to rank as high as fifth place for young adult women (aged 18 to 25), but, overall for the female life span, was outscored by almost everything including "housework" (which, incidentally ranked dead last among males). . . .

How well suited are "hot" males to "cool" females? Not very. One of (if not *the*) most common problems in marital counseling is sexual incompatibility. *Females pay sex as the price of love/companionship and males pay love for sex.* While this is rather too aphoristic to capture all that goes on in the male-female struggle, there is a great deal of truth to it. Even among homosexuals, the males probably out sex lesbians by a factor of 5 to 1 (see Tripp's sympathetic treatment for elaboration on this theme). Where is a male most apt to find his counterpart, among maledom or femaledom? If he wants hot, dripping sex, what better place to find it than with another of similar bent? If she wants tender companionship, which sex is most apt to provide the partner? The answers are obvious.

The second part of the homosexual tilt derives from the fact that *homosexual encounter offers better sex,* on the average, *than heterosexual sex.* If pleasure is what you are after, who better to fulfill you than a partner who has a body and predilections like yours? One of the things that both the male homosexual and lesbian societies advertise is that "they satisfy." The Greek literature of yore also contains the "better sex" claim of homosexuals. And why not? A male, who has the same basic equipment and rhythms is most able to satisfy—particularly initially (heterosexual "one nite stands" are frequently exciting, but just as frequently lacking in sexual satisfaction for both participants—not so homosexual "one niters"). Who better to understand "what you need" than someone whose needs are as your own? From a sexual standpoint, a female can offer little extra orifice as compensation for her: ignorance, timidity, desire for companionship first, etc. Further, sex between members of a sex assures that there will be no pregnancy problems further on down the line.

Another developmental boost for homosexuality comes from the self-servingness/egocentricity of the young. Humans are born with, at best, rudimentary consciousness. Then, over time and experience, they learn to differentiate themselves from the environment. From about the age of 5 or 6 onward for the next decade or so of life, they are engrossed in themselves, in the service of themselves, their pleasures, their interests, their ways. Reciprocity of interaction is rendered begrudgingly, certainly far from spontaneously. My research, involving the interviewing of over 8,000 respondents from the U.S. and five other nations, in which we asked persons to tell us: 1) whose interests they had just been thinking about serving—their own or another's or others' and 2) whether they had just been thinking about themselves, things, or other people, indicated that younger persons more frequently reported themselves in a self-serving attitude and thinking about themselves than adults did. In the U.S., adults of both sexes typically reported themselves in an other-serving attitude. But U.S. males "switched" from self-servingness to other-servingness around age 26 while for females the switch occurred in the middle teens. If one is after self-fulfillment, pleasure for self, which sexual orientation "fits" better? Homosexuality, obviously. One can have his homosociality and sex too. One can comfortably neglect the painful transformation from self-interest to other-interest. Me and mine to the fore.

Which kind of sexuality is the more compelling? The one that can say "come, sex my way and I will show you a life of complexity. Of children and responsibility. Of getting on with 'that other kind.' I will offer you poorer sex initially, and, who knows, perhaps you will just have to satisfy yourself with poorer sex permanently. But you will be able to 'glimpse immortality in your children' (Plato)." Or "come, sex my way and I will give it to you straight and hot. Pleasures of the best quality, almost on demand, with persons with whom you already share a great deal, and I will enable you to share more. It will not be difficult, in fact, it will be fun. You will not have to change or adapt your personality style or your egocentric orientation. You'll fit right in immediately. None of this hemming and hawing—you'll get what you want when you want it. Motto? Pleasure—now. The future? Who knows, but the present is going to be a dilly." Which kind of sexuality is the more compelling? Does anyone doubt which way most youth would turn if equivalent social status attended homosexuality and heterosexuality? . . .

The myths about love and romance that grace our society have been almost 100% heterosexual. From children's readers to tube fare, heterosexuality has been the "only game in town." Tom and Jane live with their parents Dick and Sue, *not* Tim and Jim. Dagwood has Blondie, and the odd couple is squarely heterosexual. Yet even in the glare of the massive efforts of religions, customs, laws, and example, about 2% of the citizenry fail to accomplish the mental gymnastic of separating sexual object from social object. They go the developmentally "easy way," and add sexuality to homosociality. What if society offered an honest to goodness *choice* between the two sexual orientations? The current lock on the myth-making, image-providing process by heterosexuality may be an instance of overkill. Perhaps an 80/20 hetero-homosexuality split would still result in 96% heterosexuality. Maybe even a 60/40 split would. But we've got 2% now with something like a 99/1 split, and somewhere up the line, growth in homosexual mythology and literature *has* to have an effect (unless one can seriously believe that to which people are exposed does not influence them).

It appears that once a solid choice for either homo or heterosexuality is made, the "other way" becomes unlikely, and, in fact, disgusting. True, with the current pro-heterosexual bias in the psychiatric community, about a third of homosexuals in treatment can, with considerable effort, be "switched." But as "even-steven" literature grows and becomes incorporated into the psychiatric community's consciousness, the attempt to convert will be made less frequently. Tripp's *The Homosexual Matrix* is a well-received work that melds the myths of love, sex, homo and heterosexuality. It certainly constitutes a solid start toward "even-steven" in myth-making. The resolutions of the American Psychiatric and American Psychological Associations calling for equality or near equality of treatment of professionals and clients with either homo or hetero orientations demonstrate a further movement toward equality of the sexual orientations. Pre-teens and teens are the battle ground. With the exception of the San Francisco school system, students' official fare is still 100% heterosexual. In my opinion, heterosexuality "needs all the help it can get," and these current developments portend a much more homosexual future. . . .

A Cluster of Undesirable Traits Is Disproportionately Associated with Homosexuality

Though some may shriek that "my personality traits are my business," let us acknowledge that some traits are society's business. A person's traits can lead to actions which affect the collectivity. Megalomania often proves socially disruptive, and sometimes, as in the case of Hitler, leads to incredible human destruction. It is obviously in society's interest to encourage those social roles and traits that tend to social cohesion and betterment. Similarly, it is in the social interest to discourage those that tend to produce disruption and harm. Any life-style that leads to, or is more frequently associated with, undesirable personality traits suitably receives discouragement. Most traits, e.g. intelligence, appear unsystematically related to either homo or heterosexuality, but those that are systematically related are socially important.

It would be as silly to contend that each of the following traits is associated with each homosexual as to argue that none of these appear in heterosexuals (or even worse, that the obverse of these traits always accompanies heterosexuality). However, for social policy formulation, it is enough to demonstrate disproportionate "loading" of undesirable traits within a given subgroup or subculture to justify social discrimination.

The Egocentric/Supercilious/Narcissistic/Self-Oriented/Hostile Complex

This cluster of traits appears to "go together" with homosexuality. . . . A person who, in part, seeks more of himself in his lover, is more apt to remain in the egocentric/self-centered orientation of youth. Such a person is more apt to gravitate toward those kinds of professions in which he can be a "star" and be noticed. . . .

The "star" lives for gratification of self. *My way* is his motto. . . . The star need not accommodate himself to the needs of others to the same degree as most folk. If a current love is "not working out" he can be discarded and a more suitable one found. . . .

Superciliousness—an attitude of aloof, hostile disdain—is also consonant with the egocentric person. If you will not realize his marvelous qualities and pay homage, he still has you one down. After all he treated you with contempt *first*. Even if you become hostile, his preceded yours. I am well aware that much of what I have written frequently applies to notable Hollywood and Broadway actors. Adoration-seekers disproportionately frequently make poor models for marriages. As the columnists often put it, "there was too much ego to go around." . . .

The greater component of the childish "I want it my way" associated with homosexuality stems, in part, from the greater ease connected with homosexual attachments. Developmentally, both hetero and homosexuals want things "their way." But the kinds of accommodations and adjustment necessary for successful heterosexuality assure participants that it won't be all their way. Just because so much of the time things don't work out perfectly in the face of such effort helps wean one from the coddled security of childhood. Parents and the rest of society work to "make the world nice" for children. Every childhood painting is worthy of note, as is every musical note. But adulthood is strewn with disappointments. Heterosexuality is a "maturing" sexual orientation. . . .

. . . It appears to me that homosexuality leads to a shallower commitment to society and its betterment. Such shallowness comes about both because of a lack of children and the ease of sexual gratification. The *effort* involved in being heterosexual, the *effort* expended in being a parent—these are denied the homosexual. As he *has* less responsibility and commitment, so he *is* or becomes less responsible and committed. It is difficult to develop personality characteristics that fail to resonate with one's environment. While we are not totally creatures of our environment, it is far easier to "swim with the tide."

It is difficult to find anything like "hard" scientific evidence to substantiate the notion that homosexuals are on the average, less responsible/trustworthy than heterosexuals. The Weinberg and Williams sample of homosexuals was asked a question that bears upon the issue. Do you agree or disagree with the statement "most people can be trusted?" To a degree, since a person cannot know "most people" it appears reasonable to assume that he might project his own personality onto "most people" and/or assume that those people with whom he comes in contact are like "most people." While 77% of a reasonably representative sample of the U.S. population chose "agree," only 47% of the homosexuals picked the same response. Because of the ambiguity of such items, I would not make too much of the difference. But it could suggest that homosexuals are less trustworthy.

Homosexuality Is Associated with Personal Lethality

One of the more troubling traits associated with homosexuality is personal lethality. Extending back in time to classical Greece, a lethal theme shines through. In Greece, if historical sources are to be believed, companies of homosexual warriors were assembled because it was believed that they made better killers.

. . . In our society the childless are more apt to suicide and childless couples are more apt to be involved in homicide.

Heterosexuality Provides the Most Desirable Model of Love

Myths are created not only by storytellers but by people living within the myth. Almost all (95% or so) heterosexuals get married, and 75%–80% stay married to their original partner till death. To be sure, there are marriage "hogs" within the heterosexual camp who play serial monogamy and assure that a third of all marriages end in divorce. Further, about half of all married men and about a third of all married women admit to one or more infidelities over the duration of their marriage (probably the greater bulk of the "cheaters" come from the serial monogamy camp). While heterosexuality's colors are far from simon pure, the relationship heterosexuality spawns is among, if not *the,* most enduring of human bonds. . . .

Homosexuality offers no comparison in durability. While "slam, bam, thank you ma'am" occurs in heterosexuality, few heterosexuals could more than fantasize about what occurs in homosexual bathhouses or tearooms. As Weinberg and Williams note, the homosexual community typically features "sex for sex's sake." Their survey in which two thirds of their respondents chose to respond "no" to whether they had limited their ". . . sexual relationships primarily to (another)" is telling. Names and banter are typically neglected in bathhouses. . . .

When people are merely "getting their jollies," and fantasizing perfection while doing so, reduced communication is an asset. If you discover that your beautiful lover holds political views antithetical to your own, how can you really enjoy him/her? The "less known the better" is fantasy sex. Communicating, mutually knowledgeable people often have to "work it out" before attempts at sex can even occur. But while typically short on durability, some homosexual relationships are more lasting. The quality of even these is often questionably desirable. Part of the problem lies in the lack of commitment that follows lower effort in the homosexual pairing. Tripp, for instance, opines that part ". . . of the reason many homosexual relationships do not survive the first serious quarrel is that one or both partners simply find it much easier to remarket themselves than work out conflicts (p. 155)." In heterosexuality, no matter how similar the participants, there is always a considerable gap between them. To stay together takes great effort, and the expenditure of this effort prompts both personal and social commitment to the partner.

. . . Because the heterosexual partners are so dissimilar, accommodation and adjustment are their key strategies. Because mutually satisfying heterosexual sexing takes so long and so much effort, both participants have to "hang in there" long after "sane people" would have toddled off in frustration. *We become the way we act. The heterosexual relationship places a premium on "getting on" and thus provides a model to smooth countless other human interactions.* The homosexual model is a considerably less satisfactory one upon which to build a civilization. Note Tripp again (p. 167): ". . . the problems encountered in balancing heterosexual and homosexual relationships are strikingly different. The *heterosexual blend tends to be rich in stimulating contrasts and short on rapport*—so much so that popular marriage counseling literature incessantly hammers home the advice that couples should develop common interests and dissolve their conflicts by increasing their 'communication.' By comparison, homosexual relationships are overclose, fatigue-prone, and are often adjusted to such narrow, trigger-sensitive tolerances that a mere whisper of disrapport can jolt the partners into making repairs, or into conflict." . . .

Our social system also features large components of delay of gratification. The heterosexual "carrot" is hard to get and requires a lot of input before successful outcome is achieved. The homosexual model is too immediate and influences people to expect instant results. . . .

In short, heterosexuality is effortful, durable, and demands delay of gratification. While any human relationship takes effort, homosexuality pales in comparison to heterosexuality on each count. . . .

No one is rich enough, powerful enough, or attractive enough to guarantee himself personal happiness. Incredibly wealthy, fabulously beautiful people have taken their lives in despair. *Nothing* guarantees happiness. On the other hand, extremely poor, grotesquely ugly people have achieved personal life-satisfaction. So it can likewise be said that nothing guarantees misery. More than any other single factor, happiness or life-satisfaction is an *achievement*. (The greatest "secret" to happiness is a dogged determination to wrest happiness from the cards life deals.)

Both degree of determination to be happy and the stage upon which happiness is pursued are influential in life-satisfaction. Since the stage is important, the prudent person attempts to include "props" that aid rather than hinder his pursuit of happiness. From the prudent perspective, it is foolish to neglect one's body or engage in needlessly hazardous pursuits. Similarly, it is wise to seek sufficient wherewithal to be free of nagging financial concern. From the prudent standpoint, homosexuality is an obstacle in the pursuit of happiness.

The best evidence on the question of homosexuals' happiness is, like most of what is known about homosexuality, not the best. But it is "fair" evidence from a social science standpoint. In their survey of 1,117 homosexuals, Weinberg & Williams asked respondents to answer "yes" or "no" to "I am a happy person." In an earlier poll of over 3,000 citizens, 92.8% had chosen "yes" to this question, but only 68.8% of the homosexuals did the same. Now I would not argue that 92.8% of Americans are "happy persons" because they chose "yes" rather than "no" to this kind of item—such questions probably can be used to suggest differences between groups of persons, but hardly deserve to be considered precise. Answering such questions is rather like being asked "do you like ice cream, yes or no?" Both the person who LOVES ice cream and those who merely think its "OK" probably check "yes" rather than "no." And those who HATE ice cream check "no" along with those who just feel indifferent to it. But even with this caveat, and it's an important one, the way the responses fell suggests that homosexuals *are* less happy, on-the-average, than heterosexuals are. My educated guess is that most homosexuals are "happy" with life, just as most heterosexuals are. It probably works both ways—that is, unhappy people may be attracted to homosexuality and/or homosexuality may be a "negative prop" on the "life-satisfaction stage." But, either way, evidence such as Weinberg and Williams report cannot just be tossed aside. Even if their findings only mean that homosexuality attracts unhappy, less cheery sorts of people, a person "buying into" homosexuality is going to have to run his "happiness play" on a stage disproportionately filled with "unhappy props."

Does homosexuality make being happy more difficult? In the Weinberg and Williams study, homosexuals were asked to respond "yes" or "no" to the statement "no one cares what happens to you." While a general population sample had chosen "yes" 23% of the time, 34% of homosexuals chose "yes." . . . Heterosexuality helps generate the very kinds of props and reasons that contribute toward making life-satisfaction more possible. *In the long run,* heterosexuality has a lot more to offer as a life-style than homosexuality. . . .

Summary

In sum, there are a number of reasons why homosexuality is best treated as a deviant sexual mode. I do not believe that homosexuality ought to be placed on an even-keel with heterosexuality. Further, homosexuals ought not, in my opinion, to be permitted to openly ply their sexual orientation and retain influential positions in the social system. Thus teachers, or pastors who "come out," ought, in my opinion, to lose their claim to the roles they occupy.

Reasonable people can and do differ on the degree and kind of discrimination that is to be laid against undesirable life-styles. There are a number of issues that appear substantive and weigh against the liberalization of social policy toward homosexuality. The burden of proof always justly falls upon those who would change the social system. If the homosexual community and/or those who endorse the liberalization of social policy toward homosexuality have evidence that bears upon these points, by all means bring it forward and let us reason together. But mere cries of "we are being discriminated against" are not evidence. The collection of decent evidence takes organized time and effort. I am weary of those who feel that a case has been made just because they have gotten blisters on the streets or their voices are louder.

Reference Notes

Allport, G. W. *The Person in Psychology.* NY: Beacon, 1961.

Atkins, J. *Sex in Literature.* NY: Grove Press, 1970.

Bergler, E. *Homosexuality: Disease or Way of Life?* NY: Macmillan, 1956.

Bieber, I. *Homosexuality: A Psychoanalytic Study.* NY: Basic Books, 1962.

Cameron, P. "Immolations to the Juggernaut," *Linacre Quarterly,* 1977, 44, 64–74.

Cameron, P. *The Life-Cycle: Perspectives and Commentary.* NY: General Health, 1977.

Cameron, P. & Oeschger, D. "Homosexuality in the Mass Media as Indexed by Magazine Literature over the Past Half Century in the U.S." Paper presented at Eastern Psychological Association Convention, New York, April 4, 1975.

Davis, N. & Graubert, J. *Heterosexual.* NY: Vantage Press, 1975.

Freud, S. "Three Contributions to Sexual Theory," *Nervous and Mental Disease Monograph Series,* 1925, 7.

Gubrium, J. F. "Being Single in Old Age," *International Journal of Aging and Human Development,* 1975, 6, 29–41.

Hunt, M. *Sexual Behavior in the 1970s.* Chicago: Playboy Press, 1974.

Karlen, A. *Sexuality and Homosexuality.* NY: Norton, 1971.

Kastenbaum, R. J. & Costa, P. T. "Psychological Perspectives on Death," *Annual Review of Psychology,* 1977, 28, 225–49.

Maugham, S. *El Greco.* NY: Doubleday, 1950.

Sears, R. R. "Sources of Life Satisfactions of the Terman Gifted Man," *American Psychologist,* 1977, 32, 119–128.

Tripp, C. A. *The Homosexual Matrix.* NY: McGraw-Hill, 1975.

Weinberg, M. S. & Williams, C. J. *Male Homosexuals: Their Problems and Adaptations.* NY: Oxford University Press, 1974.

Review Questions

1. According to Cameron, what is the so-called wisdom of the ages about homosexuality?
2. Why does Cameron think that social development favors homosexuality?
3. What personality traits go with homosexuality according to Cameron?
4. In Cameron's view, why is heterosexuality more desirable than homosexuality?

Discussion Questions

1. Cameron asserts that human sexuality is learned. Is this true? What about the evidence that it is genetically determined?
2. Cameron does not discuss bisexuality, but how do you think he would explain it?
3. Does Cameron convince you that homosexuality should be discriminated against? Why or why not?

Richard D. Mohr

Gay Basics: Some Questions, Facts, and Values

Richard D. Mohr teaches philosophy at the University of Illinois. He is the author of Gays/Justice: A Study of Ethics, Society, and Law *(1988) and of several articles on gay rights.*

After examining some facts about gays including stereotypes and discrimination in our society, Mohr replies to the charge that homosexuality is immoral. He argues that condemning homosexuality on religious grounds violates the Constitution, and that appeals to nature or natural law are unconvincing. He claims that our society would be improved if gays were given the rights and benefits of the heterosexual majority.

I. Who Are Gays Anyway?

A recent Gallup poll found that only one in five Americans reports having a gay or lesbian acquaintance.[1] This finding is extraordinary given the number of practicing homosexuals in America. Alfred Kinsey's 1948 study of the sex lives of 12,000 white males shocked the nation: 37 percent had at least one homosexual experience to orgasm in their adult lives; an additional 13 percent had homosexual fantasies to orgasm; 4 percent were exclusively homosexual in their practices; another 5 percent had virtually no heterosexual experience; and nearly 20 percent had at least as many homosexual as heterosexual experiences.[2]

Two out of five men one passes on the street have had orgasmic sex with men. Every second family in the country has a member who is essentially homosexual and many more people regularly have homosexual experiences. Who are homosexuals? They are your friends, your minister, your teacher, your bank teller, your doctor, your mail carrier, your officemate, your roommate, your congressional representative, your sibling, parent, and spouse. They are everywhere, virtually all ordinary, virtually all unknown.

Several important consequences follow. First, the country is profoundly ignorant of the actual experience of gay people. Second social attitudes and practices that are harmful to gays have a much greater overall harmful impact on society than is usually realized. Third, most gay people live in hiding—in the closet—making the "coming out" experience the central fixture of gay consciousness and invisibility the chief characteristic of the gay community.

II. Ignorance, Stereotype, and Morality

Ignorance about gays, however, has not stopped people from having strong opinions about them. The void which ignorance leaves has been filled with stereotypes. Society holds chiefly two groups of anti-gay stereotypes; the two are an oddly contradictory lot. One set of stereotypes revolves around alleged mistakes in an individual's gender identity: lesbians are women that want to be, or at least look and act like, men—bull dykes, diesel dykes; while gay men are those who want to be, or at least look and act like, women—queens, fairies, limp-wrists, nellies. These stereotypes of mismatched genders provide the materials through which gays and lesbians become the butts of ethniclike jokes. These stereotypes and jokes, though derisive, basically view gays and lesbians as ridiculous.

Another set of stereotypes revolves around gays as a pervasive, sinister, conspiratorial threat. The core stereotype here is the gay person as child molester, and more generally as sex-crazed maniac. These stereotypes carry with them fears of the very destruction of family and civilization itself. Now, that which is essentially ridiculous can hardly have such a staggering effect. Something must be afoot in this incoherent amalgam.

Sense can be made of this incoherence if the nature of stereotypes is clarified. Stereotypes are not *simply* false generalizations from a skewed sample of cases examined. Admittedly, false generalizing plays some part in the stereotypes a society holds. If, for instance, one takes as one's sample homosexuals who are in psychiatric hospitals or prisons, as was done in nearly all early investigations, not surprisingly one will probably find homosexuals to be of a crazed and criminal cast. Such false generalizations, though, simply confirm beliefs already held on independent grounds, ones that likely led the investigator to the prison and psychiatric ward to begin with. Evelyn Hooker, who in the late fifties carried out the first rigorous studies to use nonclinical gays, found that psychiatrists, when presented with case files including all the standard diagnostic psychological profiles—but omitting indications of sexual orientation—were unable to distinguish files of gays from those of straights, even though they believed gays to be crazy and supposed themselves to be experts in detecting craziness.[3] These studies proved a profound embarrassment to the psychiatric establishment, the financial well-being of which has been substantially enhanced by "curing" allegedly insane gays. The studies led the way to the American Psychiatric Association finally in 1973 dropping homosexuality from its registry of mental illnesses.[4] Nevertheless, the stereotype of gays as sick continues apace in the mind of America.

False generalizations *help maintain* stereotypes; they do not *form* them. As the history of Hooker's discoveries shows, stereotypes have a life beyond facts; their origin lies in a culture's ideology—the general system of beliefs by which it lives—and they are sustained across generations by diverse cultural transmissions, hardly any of which, including slang and jokes, even purport to have a scientific basis. Stereotypes, then, are not the products of bad science but are social constructions that perform central functions in maintaining society's conception of itself.

On this understanding, it is easy to see that the anti-gay stereotypes surrounding gender identification and chiefly means of reinforcing still powerful gender roles in society. If, as this stereotype presumes and condemns, one is free to choose one's social roles independently of gender, many guiding social divisions, both domestic and commercial, might be threatened. The socially gender-linked distinctions between breadwinner and homemaker, boss and secretary, doctor and nurse, protector and protected would blur. The accusations "dyke" and "fag" exist in significant part to keep women in their place and to prevent men from breaking ranks and ceding away theirs.

The stereotypes of gays as child molesters, sex-crazed maniacs, and civilization destroyers function to displace (socially irresolvable) problems from their actual source to a foreign (and so, it is thought, manageable) one. Thus the stereotype of child molester functions to give the family unit a false sheen of absolute innocence. It keeps the unit from being examined too closely for incest, child abuse, wife-battering, and the terrorism of constant threats. The stereotype teaches that the problems of the family are not internal to it, but external.[5]

One can see these cultural forces at work in society's and the media's treatment of current reports of violence, especially domestic violence. When a mother kills her child or a father rapes his daughter—regular Section B fare even in major urban papers—this is never taken by reporters, columnists, or pundits as evidence that there is something wrong with heterosexuality or with traditional families. These issues are not even raised. But when a homosexual child molestation is reported it is taken as confirming evidence of the way homosexuals are. One never hears of heterosexual murders, but one regularly hears of "homosexual" ones. Compare the social treatment of Richard Speck's sexually motivated mass murder of Chicago nurses with that of John Wayne Gacy's murders of Chicago youths. Gacy was in the culture's mind taken as symbolic of gay men in general. To prevent the possibility that The Family was viewed as anything but an innocent victim in this affair, the mainstream press knowingly failed to mention that most of Gacy's adolescent victims were homeless hustlers. That knowledge would be too much for the six o'clock news and for cherished beliefs.

Because "the facts" largely don't matter when it comes to the generation and maintenance of stereotypes, the effects of scientific and academic research and of enlightenment generally will be, at best, slight and gradual in the changing fortunes of lesbians and gay men. If this account of stereotypes holds, society has been profoundly immoral. For its treatment of gays is a grand scale rationalization, a moral sleight-of-hand. The problem is not the society's usual standards of evidence and procedure in coming to judgments of social policy have been misapplied to gays; rather when it comes to gays, the standards themselves have simply been ruled out of court and disregarded in favor of mechanisms that encourage unexamined fear and hatred.

III. Are Gays Discriminated Against? Does it Matter?

Partly because lots of people suppose they don't know any gay people and partly through willful ignorance of its own workings, society at large is unaware of the many ways in which gays are subject to discrimination in consequence of widespread fear and hatred. Contributing to this social ignorance of discrimination is the difficulty for gay people, as an invisible minority, even to complain of discrimination. For if one is gay, to register a complaint would suddenly target one as a stigmatized person, and so in the absence of any protections against discrimination, would simply invite additional discrimination. Further, many people, especially those who are persistently downtrodden and so lack a firm sense of self to begin with, tend either to blame themselves for their troubles or to view injustice as a matter of bad luck rather than as indicating something wrong with society. The latter recognition would require doing something to rectify wrong and most people, especially the already beleaguered, simply aren't up to that. So for a number of reasons discrimination against gays, like rape, goes seriously underreported.

First, gays are subject to violence and harassment based simply on their perceived status rather than because of any actions they have performed. A recent extensive study by the National Gay Task Force found that over 90 percent of gays and lesbians had been victimized in some form on the basis of their sexual orientation.[6] Greater than one in five gay men and nearly one in ten lesbians had been punched, hit, or kicked; a quarter of all gays had objects thrown at them; a third had been chased; a third had been sexually harassed; and 14 percent had been spit on—all just for being perceived as gay.

The most extreme form of anti-gay violence is "queerbashing"—where groups of young men target a person who they suppose is a gay man and beat and kick him unconscious and sometimes to death amid a torrent of taunts and slurs. Such seemingly random but in reality socially encouraged violence has the same social origin and function as lynchings of blacks—to keep a whole stigmatized group in line. As with lynchings in the recent past, the police and courts have routinely averted their eyes, giving their implicit approval to the practice.

Few such cases with gay victims reach the courts. Those that do are marked by inequitable procedures and results. Frequently judges will describe "queerbashers" as "just all-American boys." Recently a District of Columbia judge handed suspended sentences to queerbashers whose victim had been stalked, beaten, stripped at knife point, slashed, kicked, threatened with castration, and pissed on, because the judge thought the bashers were good boys at heart—after all, they went to a religious prep school.[7]

Police and juries will simply discount testimony from gays; they typically construe assaults on and murders of gays as "justified" self-defense—the killer need only claim his act was a panicked response to a sexual overture. Alternatively, when guilt seems patent, juries will accept highly implausible "diminished capacity" defenses, as in the case of Dan White's 1978 assassination of openly gay San Francisco city councilman Harvey Milk: Hostess Twinkies made him do it.[8]

These inequitable procedures and results collectively show that the life and liberty of gays, like those of blacks, simply count for less than the life and liberty of members of the dominant culture.

The equitable rule of law is the heart of an orderly society. The collapse of the rule of law for gays shows that society is willing to perpetrate the worst possible injustices against them. Conceptually there is only a difference in degree between the collapse of the rule of law and systematic extermination of members of a population simply for having some group status independent of any act an individual has performed. In the Nazi concentration camps, gays were forced to wear pink triangles as identifying badges, just as Jews were forced to wear yellow stars. In remembrance of that collapse of the rule of law, the pink triangle has become the chief symbol of the gay rights movement.[9]

Gays are subject to widespread discrimination in employment—the very means by which one puts bread on one's table and one of the chief means by which individuals identify themselves to themselves and achieve personal dignity. Governments are leading offenders here. They do a lot of discriminating themselves, require that others do it (e.g., government contractors), and set precedents favoring discrimination in the private sector. The federal government explicitly discriminates against gays in the armed forces, the CIA, FBI, National Security Agency, and the state department. The federal government refuses to give security clearances to gays and so forces the country's considerable private sector military and aerospace contractors to fire known gay employees. State and local governments regularly fire gay teachers, policemen, firemen, social workers, and anyone who has contact with the public. Further, through licensing laws states officially bar gays from a vast array of occupations and professions—everything from doctors, lawyers, accountants, and nurses to hairdressers, morticians, and used car dealers. The American Civil Liberties Union's handbook *The Rights of Gay People* lists 307 such prohibited occupations.[10]

Gays are subject to discrimination in a wide variety of other ways, including private-sector employment, public accommodations, housing, immigration and naturalization, insurance of all types, custody and adoption, and zoning regulations that bar "singles" or "nonrelated" couples. All of these discriminations affect central components of a meaningful life; some even reach to the means by which life itself is sustained. In half the states, where gay sex is illegal, the central role of sex to meaningful life is officially denied to gays.

All these sorts of discriminations also affect the ability of people to have significant intimate relations. It is difficult for people to live together as couples without having their sexual orientation perceived in the public realm and so becoming targets for discrimination. Illegality, discrimination, and the absorption by gays of society's hatred of them all interact to impede or block altogether the ability of gays and lesbians to create and maintain significant personal relations with loved ones. So every facet of life is affected by discrimination. Only the most compelling reasons could justify it.

IV. But Aren't They Immoral?

Many people think society's treatment of gays is justified because they think gays are extremely immoral. To evaluate this claim, different senses of "moral" must be distinguished. Sometimes by "morality" is meant the overall beliefs affecting behavior in a society—its mores, norms, and customs. On this understanding, gays certainly are not moral: lots of people hate them and social customs are designed to register widespread disapproval of gays. The problem here is that this sense of morality is merely a *descriptive* one. On this understanding *every* society has a morality—even Nazi society, which had racism and mob rule as central features of its "morality," understood in this sense. What is needed in order to use the notion of morality to praise or condemn behavior is a sense of morality that is *prescriptive* or *normative*—a sense of morality whereby, for instance, the descriptive morality of the Nazis is found wanting.

As the Nazi example makes clear, that something is descriptively moral is nowhere near enough to make it normatively moral. A lot of people in a society saying something is good, even over eons, does not make it so. Our rejection of the long history of socially approved and state-enforced slavery is another good example of this principle at work. Slavery would be wrong even if nearly everyone liked it. So consistency and fairness require that we abandon the belief that gays are immoral simply because most people dislike or disapprove of gays or gay acts, or even because gay sex acts are illegal.

Furthermore, recent historical and anthropological research has shown that opinion about gays has been by no means universally negative. Historically, it has varied widely even within the larger part of the Christian era and even within the church itself.[11] There are even societies—current ones—where homosexuality is not only tolerated but a universal compulsory part of social maturation.[12] Within the last thirty years, American society has undergone a grand turnabout from deeply ingrained, near total condemnation to near total acceptance on two emotionally charged "moral" or "family" issues: contraception and divorce. Society holds its current descriptive morality of gays not because it has to, but because it chooses to.

If popular opinion and custom are not enough to ground moral condemnation of homosexuality, perhaps religion can. Such argument proceeds along two lines. One claims that the condemnation is a direct revelation of God, usually through the Bible; the other claims to be able to detect condemnation in God's plan as manifested in nature.

One of the more remarkable discoveries of recent gay research is that the Bible may not be as univocal in its condemnation of homosexuality as has been usually believed.[13] Christ never mentions homosexuality. Recent interpreters of the Old Testament have pointed out that the story of Lot at Sodom is probably intended to condemn inhospitality rather than homosexuality. Further, some of the Old Testament condemnations of homosexuality seem simply to be ways of tarring those of the Israelites' opponents who happened to accept homosexual practices when the Israelites themselves did not. If so, the condemnation is merely a quirk of history and rhetoric rather than a moral precept.

What does seem clear is that those who regularly cite the Bible to condemn an activity like homosexuality do so by reading it selectively. Do ministers who cite what they take to be condemnations of homosexuality in Leviticus maintain in their lives all the hygienic and dietary laws of Leviticus? If they cite the story of Lot at Sodom to condemn homosexuality, do they also cite the story of Lot in the cave to praise incestuous rape? It seems then not that the Bible is being used to ground condemnations of homosexuality as much as society's dislike of homosexuality is being used to interpret the Bible.[14]

Even if a consistent portrait of condemnation could be gleaned from the Bible, what social significance should it be given? One of the guiding principles of society, enshrined in the Constitution as a check against the government, is that decisions affecting social policy are not made on religious grounds. If the real ground of the alleged immorality invoked by governments to discriminate against gays in religious (as it has explicitly been even in some recent court cases involving teachers and guardians), then one of the major commitments of our nation is violated.

V. But Aren't They Unnatural?

The most noteworthy feature of the accusation of something being unnatural (where a moral rather than an advertising point is being made) is that the plaint is so infrequently made. One used to hear the charge leveled against abortion, but that has pretty much faded as anti-abortionists have come to lay all their chips on the hope that people will come to view abortion as murder. Incest used to be considered unnatural but discourse now usually assimilates it to the moral machinery of rape and violated trust. The charge comes up now in ordinary discourse only against homosexuality. This suggests that the charge is highly idiosyncratic and has little, if any, explanatory force. It fails to put homosexuality in a class with anything else so that one can learn by comparison with clear cases of the class just exactly what it is that is allegedly wrong with it.

Though the accusation of unnaturalness looks whimsical, in actual ordinary discourse when applied to homosexuality, it is usually delivered with venom aforethought. It carries a high emotional charge, usually expressing disgust and evincing queasiness. Probably it is nothing but an emotional charge. For people get equally disgusted and queasy at all sorts of things that are perfectly natural—to be expected in nature apart from artifice—and that could hardly be fit subjects for moral condemnation. Two typical examples in current American culture are some people's responses to mothers' suckling in public and to women who do not shave body hair. When people have strong emotional reactions, as they do in these cases, without being able to give good reasons for them, we think of them not as operating morally, but rather as being obsessed and manic. So the feelings of disgust that some people have to gays will hardly ground a charge of immorality. People fling the term "unnatural" against gays in the same breath and with the same force as when they call gays "sick" and "gross." When they do this, they give every appearance of being neurotically fearful and incapable of reasoned discourse.

When "nature" is taken in *technical* rather than ordinary usages, it looks like the notion also will not ground a charge of homosexual immorality. When unnatural means "by artifice" or "made by humans," it need only be pointed out that virtually everything that is good about life is unnatural in this sense, that the chief feature that distinguishes people from other animals is their very ability to make over the world to meet their needs and desires, and that their well-being depends upon these departures from nature. On this understanding of human nature and the natural, homosexuality is perfectly unobjectionable.

Another technical sense of natural is that something is natural and so, good, if it fulfills some function in nature. Homosexuality on this view is unnatural because it allegedly violates the function of genitals, which is to produce babies. One problem with this view is that lots of bodily parts have lots of functions and just because some one activity can be fulfilled by only one organ (say, the mouth for eating) this activity does not condemn other functions of the organ to immorality (say, the mouth for talking, licking stamps, blowing bubbles, or having sex). So the possible use of the genitals to produce children does not, without more, condemn the use of the genitals for other purposes, say, achieving ecstasy and intimacy.

The functional view of nature will only provide a morally condemnatory sense to the unnatural if a thing which might have many uses has but one proper function to the exclusion of other possible functions. But whether this is so cannot be established simply by looking at the thing. For what is seen is all its possible functions. The notion of function seemed like it might ground moral authority, but instead it turns out that moral authority is needed to define proper function. Some people try to fill in this moral authority by appeal to the "design" or "order" of an organ, saying, for instance, that the genitals are designed for the purpose of procreation. But these people cheat intellectually if they do not make explicit *who* the designer and orderer is. If it is God, we are back to square one—holding others accountable for religious beliefs.

Further, ordinary moral attitudes about childbearing will not provide the needed supplement which in conjunction with the natural function view of bodily parts would produce a positive obligation to use the genitals for procreation. Society's attitude toward a childless couple is that of pity, not censure—even if the couple could have children. This pity may be an unsympathetic one, that is, not registering a course one would choose *for oneself,* but this does not make it a course one would *require* of others. The couple who discovers they cannot have children are viewed not as having thereby had a debt canceled, but rather as having to forgo some of the richness of life, just as a quadriplegic is viewed not as absolved from some moral obligation to hop, skip, and jump, but as missing some of the richness of life. Consistency requires then that, at most, gays who do not or cannot have children are to be pitied rather than condemned. What *is* immoral is the willful preventing of people from achieving the richness of life. Immorality in this regard lies with those social customs, regulations, and statutes that prevent lesbians and gay men from establishing blood or adoptive families, not with gays themselves.

Sometimes people attempt to establish authority for a moral obligation to use bodily parts in a certain fashion simply by claiming that moral laws are natural laws and vice versa. On this account, inanimate objects and plants are good in that they follow natural laws by necessity, animals by instinct, and persons by a rational will. People are special in that they must first discover the laws that govern them. Now, even if one believes the view—dubious in the post-Newtonian, post-Darwinian world—that natural laws in the usual sense ($E = mc^2$, for instance) have some moral content, it is not at all clear how one is to discover the laws in nature that apply to people.

On the one hand, if one looks to people themselves for a model—and looks hard enough—one finds amazing variety, including homosexuality as a social ideal (upper-class fifth-century Athens) and even as socially mandatory (Melanesia today). When one looks to people, one is simply unable to strip away the layers of social custom, history, and taboo in order to see what's really there to any degree more specific than that people are the creatures that make over their world and are capable of abstract thought. That this is so should raise doubts that neutral principles are to be found in human nature that will condemn homosexuality.

On the other hand, if one looks to nature apart from people for models, the possibilities are staggering. There are fish that change gender over their lifetimes: should we "follow nature" and be operative transsexuals? Orangutans, genetically our next of kin, live completely solitary lives without social organization of any kind: ought we to "follow nature" and be hermits? There are many species where only two members per generation reproduce: should we be bees? The search in nature for people's purpose, far from finding sure models for action, is likely to leave one morally rudderless.

VI. But Aren't Gays Willfully the Way They Are?

It is generally conceded that if sexual orientation is something over which an individual—for whatever reason—has virtually no control, then discrimination against gays is especially deplorable, as it is against racial and ethnic classes, because it holds people accountable without regard for anything they themselves have done. And to hold a person accountable for that over which the person has no control is a central form of prejudice.

Attempts to answer the question whether or not sexual orientation is something that is reasonably thought to be within one's own control usually appeal simply to various claims of the biological or "mental" sciences. But the ensuing debate over genes, hormones, twins, early childhood development, and the like, is as unnecessary as it is currently inconclusive.[15] All that is needed to answer the question is to look at the actual experience of gays in current society and it becomes fairly clear that sexual orientation is not likely a matter of choice. For coming to have a homosexual identity simply does not have the same sort of structure that decision making has.

On the one hand, the "choice" of the gender of a sexual partner does not seem to express a trivial desire that might be as easily well fulfilled by a simple substitution of the desired object. Picking the gender of a sex partner is decidedly dissimilar, that is, to such activities as picking a flavor of ice cream. If an ice-cream parlor is out of one's flavor, one simply picks another. And if people were persecuted, threatened with jail terms, shattered careers, loss of family and housing, and the like, for eating, say, rocky road ice cream, no one would ever eat it; everyone would pick another easily available flavor. That gay people abide in being gay even in the face of persecution shows that being gay is not a matter of easy choice.

On the other hand, even if establishing a sexual orientation is not like making a relatively trivial choice, perhaps it is nevertheless relevantly like making the central and serious life choices by which individuals try to establish themselves as being of some type. Again, if one examines gay experience, this seems not to be the case. For one never sees anyone setting out to become a homosexual, in the way one does see people setting out to become doctors, lawyers, and bricklayers. One does not find "gays-to-be" picking some end—"At some point in the future, I want to become a homosexual"—and then setting about planning and acquiring the ways and means to that end, in the way one does see people deciding that they want to become lawyers, and then sees them plan what courses to take and what sort of temperaments, habits, and skills to develop in order to become lawyers. Typically gays-to-be simply find themselves having homosexual encounters and yet at least initially resisting quite strongly the identification of being homosexual. Such a person even very likely resists having such encounters, but ends up having them anyway. Only with time, luck, and great personal effort, but sometimes never, does the person gradually come to accept her or his orientation, to view it as a given material condition of life, coming as materials do with certain capacities and limitations. The person begins to act in accordance with his or her orientation and its capacities, seeing its actualization as a requisite for an integrated personality and as a central component of personal well-being. As a result, the experience of coming out to oneself has for gays the basic structure of a discovery, not the structure of a choice. And far from signaling immorality, coming out to others affords one of the few remainingopportunities in ever more bureaucratic, mechanistic, and socialistic societies to manifest courage.

VII. How Would Society at Large be Changed if Gays Were Socially Accepted?

Suggestions to change social policy with regard to gays are invariably met with claims that to do so would invite the destruction of civilization itself: after all, isn't that what did Rome in? Actually Rome's decay paralleled not the flourishing of homosexuality but its repression under the later Christianized emperors.[16] Predictions of American civilization's imminent demise have been as premature as they have been frequent. Civilization has shown itself rather resilient here, in large part because of the country's traditional commitments to a respect for privacy, to individual liberties, and especially to people minding their own business. These all give society an open texture and the flexibility to try out things to see what works. And because of this one now need not speculate about what changes reforms in gay social policy might bring to society at large. For many reforms have already been tried.

Half the states have decriminalized homosexual acts. Can you guess which of the following states still have sodomy laws: Wisconsin, Minnesota; New Mexico, Arizona; Vermont, New Hampshire; Nebraska, Kansas. One from each pair does and one does not have sodomy laws. And yet one would be hard pressed to point out any substantial difference between the members of each pair. (If you're interested, it is the second of each pair with them.) Empirical studies have shown that there is no increase in other crimes in states that have decriminalized.[17] Further, sodomy laws are virtually never enforced. They remain on the books not to "protect society" but to insult gays, and for that reason need to be removed.

Neither has the passage of legislation barring discrimination against gays ushered in the end of civilization. Some 50 counties and municipalities, including some of the country's largest cities (like Los Angeles and Boston), have passed such statutes and among the states and colonies Wisconsin and the District of Columbia have model protective codes. Again, no more brimstone has fallen in these places than elsewhere. Staunchly anti-gay cities, like Miami and Houston, have not been spared the AIDS crisis.

Berkeley, California, has even passed domestic partner legislation giving gay couples the same rights to city benefits as married couples, and yet Berkeley has not become more weird than it already was.

Seemingly hysterical predictions that the American family would collapse if such reforms would pass proved false, just as the same dire predictions that the availability of divorce would lessen the ideal and desirability of marriage proved completely unfounded. Indeed if current discriminations, which drive gays into hiding and into anonymous relations, were lifted, far from seeing gays raze American families, one would see gays forming them.

Virtually all gays express a desire to have a permanent lover. Many would like to raise or foster children—perhaps those alarming numbers of gay kids who have been beaten up and thrown out of their "families" for being gay. But currently society makes gay coupling very difficult. A life of hiding is a pressure-cooker existence not easily shared with another. Members of non-gay couples are here asked to imagine what it would take to erase every trace of their own sexual orientation for even just a week.

Even against oppressive odds, gays have shown an amazing tendency to nest. And those gay couples who have survived the odds show that the structure of more usual couplings is not a matter of destiny but of personal responsibility. The so-called basic unit of society turns out not to be a unique immutable atom, but can adopt different parts, be adapted to different needs, and even be improved. Gays might even have a thing or two to teach others about division of labor, the relation of sensuality and intimacy, and stages of development in such relations.

If discrimination ceased, gay men and lesbians would enter the mainstream of the human community openly and with self-respect. The energies that the typical gay person wastes in the anxiety of leading a day-to-day existence of systematic disguise would be released for use in personal flourishing. From this release would be generated the many spinoff benefits that accrue to a society when its individual members thrive.

Society would be richer for acknowledging another aspect of human richness and diversity. Families with gay members would develop relations based on truth and trust rather than lies and fear. And the heterosexual majority would be better off for knowing that they are no longer trampling their gay friends and neighbors.

Finally and perhaps paradoxically, in extending to gays the rights and benefits it has reserved for its dominant culture, America would confirm its deeply held vision of itself as a morally progressing nation, a nation itself advancing and serving as a beacon for others—especially with regard to human rights. The words with which our national pledge ends—"with liberty and justice for all"—are not a description of the present but a call for the future. Ours is a nation given to a prophetic political rhetoric which acknowledges that morality is not arbitrary and that justice is not merely the expression of the current collective will. It is this vision that led the black civil rights movement to its successes. Those congressmen who opposed that movement and its centerpiece, the 1964 Civil Rights Act, on obscurantist grounds, but who lived long enough and were noble enough, came in time to express their heartfelt regret and shame at what they had done. It is to be hoped and someday to be expected that those who now grasp at anything to oppose the extension of that which is best about America to gays will one day feel the same.

Endnotes

1. "Public Fears—And Sympathies," *Newsweek,* August 12, 1985, p. 23.
2. Alfred C. Kinsey, *Sexual Behavior in the Human Male* (Philadelphia: Saunders, 1948), pp. 650–651. On the somewhat lower incidences of lesbianism, see Alfred C. Kinsey, *Sexual Behavior in the Human Female* (Philadelphia: Saunders, 1953), pp. 472–475.
3. Evelyn Hooker, "The Adjustment of the Male Overt Homosexual," *Journal of Projective Techniques* 21 (1957): 18–31, reprinted in Hendrik M. Ruitenbeek, ed., *The Problem of Homosexuality* (New York: Dutton, 1963), pp. 141–161.
4. See Ronald Bayer, *Homosexuality and American Psychiatry* (New York: Basic Books, 1981).
5. For studies showing that gay men are no more likely—indeed, are less likely—than heterosexuals to be child molesters and that the largest groups of sexual abusers of children and the people most persistent in their molestation of children are the children's fathers or stepfathers or mother's boyfriends, see Vincent DeFrancis, *Protecting the Child Victim of Sex Crimes Committed by Adults* (Denver: The American Humane Association, 1969), pp. vii, 38, 69–70; A. Nicholas Groth, "Adult Sexual Orientation and Attraction to Underage Per-

sons," *Archives of Sexual Behavior* 7 (1978): 175–181; Mary J. Spencer, "Sexual Abuse of Boys," *Pediatrics* 78, no. 1 (July 1986): 133–138.

6. See National Gay Task Force, *Anti-Gay/Lesbian Victimization* (New York: NGTF, 1984).
7. "2 St. John's Students Given Probation in Assault on Gay," *The Washington Post*, May 15, 1984, p. 1.
8. See Randy Shilts, *The Mayor of Castro Street: The Life and Times of Harvey Milk* (New York: St. Martin's, 1982), pp. 308–325.
9. See Richard Plant, *The Pink Triangle: The Nazi War Against Homosexuals* (New York: Holt, 1986).
10. E. Carrington Boggan, *The Rights of Gay People: The Basic ACLU Guide to a Gay Person's Rights* (New York: Avon, 1975), pp. 211–235.
11. John Boswell, *Christianity, Social Tolerance and Homosexuality: Gay People in Western Europe from the Beginning of the Christian Era to the Fourteenth Century* (Chicago: University of Chicago Press, 1980).
12. See Gilbert Herdt, *Guardians of the Flute: Idioms of Masculinity* (New York: McGraw-Hill, 1981), pp. 232—239, 284–288; and see generally Gilbert Herdt, ed., *Ritualized Homosexuality in Melanesia* (Berkeley: University of California Press, 1984). For another eye-opener, see Walter L. Williams, *The Spirit and the Flesh: Sexual Diversity in American Indian Culture* (Boston: Beacon, 1986).
13. See especially Boswell, *Christianity*, ch. 4.
14. For Old Testament condemnations of homosexual acts, see Leviticus 18:22, 21:3. For hygienic and dietary codes, see, for example, Leviticus 15:19–27 (on the uncleanliness of women) and Leviticus 11:1–47 (on not eating rabbits, pigs, bats, finless water creatures, legless creeping creatures, etc.). For Lot at Sodom, see Genesis 19:1–25. For Lot in the cave, see Genesis 19:30–38.
15. The preponderance of the scientific evidence supports the view that homosexuality is either genetically determined or a permanent result of early childhood development. See the Kinsey Institute's study by Alan Bell, Martin Weinberg, and Sue Hammersmith, *Sexual Preference: Its Development in Men and Women* (Bloomington: Indiana University Press, 1981); Frederick Whitam and Robin Mathy, *Male Homosexuality in Four Societies* (New York: Praeger, 1986), ch. 7.
16. See Boswell, *Christianity*, ch. 3.
17. See Gilbert Geis, "Reported Consequences of Decriminalization of Consensual Adult Homosexuality in Seven American States," *Journal of Homosexuality* 1, no. 4 (1976): 419–426; Ken Sinclair and Michael Ross, "Consequences of Decriminalization of Homosexuality: A Study of Two Australian States," *Journal of Homosexuality* 12, no. 1 (1985): 119–127.

Review Questions

1. How does Mohr explain the stereotypes about gays?
2. According to Mohr, how are gays discriminated against?
3. Does the Bible condemn homosexuality? What is Mohr's view?
4. How does Mohr respond to the charge that homosexuality is unnatural?
5. According to Mohr, why isn't homosexuality a matter of choice?
6. What would happen if gays were socially accepted in our society according to Mohr?

Discussion Questions

1. Does the Bible condemn homosexuality? If it does, is this a good reason for saying that it is immoral? Is this a good reason for making it illegal?
2. Is being gay a matter of choice? What is your view?
3. Is homosexuality immoral? Why or why not?
4. Should homosexuality be illegal? What is your position?

Richard D. Mohr

Mandatory AIDS Testing

For biographical information on Richard D. Mohr, see the preceding reading.

Mohr claims that the appeal to public health benefits does not justify mandatory AIDS testing (testing for the HIV virus). Mohr insists the real reason for this testing is not public health or social benefits but the degradation of gays and the reconsecration of heterosexuality as a sacred value. He argues that this is the motivation behind the proposal for mandatory AIDS testing of marriage license applicants, military recruits, and prison inmates.

Six years into the AIDS crisis the nation's civic leader and moral paterfamilias gave his first speech on AIDS. Without ever mentioning gays, he entrusted the moral evaluation of the disease's possessors to the future estate and its judgment of God, while resting present judgment in an awkwardness-dodging silence.[1]

In marked contrast, the speech carefully attended to recommended statute, administrative policy, and government practice, which he announced ought chiefly to take the form of mandatory testing for AIDS antibodies among certain segments of society: marriage license applicants, prisoners, and immigrants applying for permanent U.S. residency.[2] Subsequently, the latter two forms of testing were formally instituted at the national level through administrative rule[3] and the Illinois legislature has passed mandatory marital testing—the first state legislature to do so.[4] Other groups already subject to mandatory federal AIDS testing are military recruits and active duty personnel, Foreign Service officers, and employees of the Job Corps.[5]

Doctors, social workers, government health agencies, medical ethics thinktanks, AIDS support groups, gay and other civil rights groups and the like have done a passable, if mixed and modest, job—sometimes marred by phony patriotism[6]—in showing that mandatory testing policies are not justified on traditional public health grounds. They have shown in particular that coerced testing is unlikely to do much to stop the spread of the disease but is likely to drive the disease underground. They have also shown it to be a very poor investment of social dollars, incapable of justification on a cost-benefit analysis, and having consequences that are tragic when producing false test results and absurd considering that the funds for the tests' administration could be going into desperately needed research and patient care.[7]

However, this public health community, in showing that mandatory testing is nonsensical from the point of view of social utility and in opposing it on that ground, has completely missed the social point of the statutes and rules mandating antibody testing; indeed in its very claims (though true) that the laws are inefficient, it actually sustains the evil of the laws' real purposes. For legislative and administrative actions mandating AIDS testing are not miscalculations, merely misdirected attempts to maximize utility, nor are they failed attempts to provide the things that everyone wants but can only get through the intervention and coercive coordinations of the state—the admitted aims of most legitimate legislation. Rather they are social rituals through which the nation expresses and strengthens its highest values, its sacred values—the values, that is, for which it will pay any price.[8]

Such rituals and their values are the means by which and the forms in which the nation identifies itself to itself, and through which it maintains, largely unconsciously, its group solidarity. But group solidarity comes with a price—or as the anthropologist and social theorist Mary Douglas has summarized the main finding of her lifework: "Solidarity is only gesturing when it involves no sacrifice."[9] The social inefficiency of AIDS testing demonstrated by the public health community is the sacrifice that society has accepted to express and reconfigure its solidarity around its central sacred value. An examination of cases—especially that of marital testing—will show that the chief sacred value wrought by various AIDS testing laws is what Adrienne Rich has called compulsory heterosexuality.[10]

Mandatory AIDS antibody testing laws are social purification rituals through which, by calling for sacrifices of and by the dominant culture, that culture reaffirms the sanctity of compulsory heterosexuality and rededicates heterosexuality's central and controlling place in society. The imprecatory counterpoint of such sanctification is the degradation of gays, even though in part for social convenience and moral salve the laws make no mention of them.

But even setting aside attempts to skirt possible political ugliness and taboos on speaking of sex, it is still probable that gays would not be mentioned in AIDS legislation—at least for now. For typically, especially when all goes passably well, a society does not have a foreground cognition of what its highest values are. They are not the object of its active concern but a filter through which all social structures are projected and, in turn, through which social behavior is perceived.[11] The latter filtering explains, for instance, the leaden density of most people's inability to see even openly gay people.

Paradoxically, then, in the case at hand, that which is most degraded—the gay person—goes entirely unmentioned, while the most carefully articulated values and best justified actions—those of the public health community—actually contribute to overall social evil.

If I am anywhere near the mark, then we shall unhappily have broached a justifiable skepticism about the nature and existence of human goodness and the worth of democracies, even constitutionally restrained ones.

A. Marital Testing

The most obvious case for my general thesis is mandatory testing as a condition for getting a marriage licence—remember gays need not apply.

Courts have done backflips in order to uphold cases of the legal existence of marriages even when the formal requirements (like age) and procedural requirements (like solemnization) for entry into marriage have been wholly absent or blatantly violated.[12] They have done so to such an extent as to draw into doubt the rule of law in this area. The one spot, though, where they have balked at allowing access to marriage is access for gays. The courts have used every legal contrivance to block the recognition of gay marriages.[13] These paired legal patterns showing a systematic and uniform warping of supposedly impartial and rational judicial judgment clearly suggest that here we have reached the bedrock and fundamental stuff of society—the thing that will not be budged, the thing that cannot be remade.

Now, when absolutes are challenged, beware. And that is what is happening in the AIDS crisis, in part because it has thrown gays more prominently and more threateningly into social consciousness than ever before and in part because of the transfiguration of sexual values wrought by it, a change that would be comical if it were not so scary in what it tells us about people's ability to distinguish means and ends.

AIDS has caused people to confuse the merely instrumental virtue of prudence with the final goods for the acquisition of which one would want to be prudent. AIDS has certainly upped the ante on the means to a robust sex life; promiscuity unguarded is not now prudent. But rather than seeing AIDS as merely raising prudential concerns, weak minds, including most gay ones, have looked for deeper meanings and unwittingly transferred the badness of means—high costs—to sex as an end. Sex is now a final bad, to be tolerated and redeemed, if at all, only within an abiding relation for which it serves as a token or symbol—a relation not merely of monogamy (for one can, after all, be monogamous with a stranger) but a relation of exclusive marriage. Those who have bought into this romantic reformation, though using a somewhat different rhetoric, are conceptually indistinguishable from those who believe that AIDS is the judgment of God. For all the wrong reasons, AIDS has applied practical pressures to the heterosexual purchase on marriage.

Now, marriage is the central institution of heterosexuality. In a culture where religion, sports, and political affiliation have become a matter of personal taste, heterosexuality is the standard form and standard bearer of social cohesion. If, under pressures exterior to the institution of marriage but interior to the society which it is supposed to epitomize and valorize, the institution is to be maintained in its traditional form, it must be purified and reanointed. Simply perpetuating the old bar to gay legal marriages is not sufficient to new circumstances. A new ritual is called for and it is handily supplied by the AIDS crisis itself, since there is a virtual identification in the mind of America between AIDS and gays, as revealed most clearly in acronymic jokes and AIDS graffiti, those distillates of popular morality. The new ritual that, within the configuration of marriage, will do the requisite work is to test those who are to be married to make sure that they are not polluted with the very stigma that challenges the institution itself. Here a social policy, perfectly absurd when viewed in terms of social utility, makes perfect sense when viewed as a social purification ritual.

The cost of the policy is the social sacrifice the dominant culture is willing to make in order to worship fully its final values, just as Abraham is willing to sacrifice his own son to show his praise of and obedience to God. A willingness to sacrifice someone else's child, as in Aztec blood sacrifices, will not do the same moral work. That is merely negotiating with the gods. It does not express or generate sacred values. Similarly poisoning one's enemies' wells with the corpses of their dead degrades the enemy not so much as when oneself is there wanting for water. So too, degrading gays by purifying marriage of their taint does not count as much, does not register and express value as much, unless some sacrifice is incurred by those who do the degrading.

The practical or policy-oriented rationalizations that have been tendered for marital testing are quite bad. The President's rationale is that such testing would help in tracking the natural history of the disease: "AIDS is surreptitiously spreading throughout our population, and yet we have no accurate measure of its scope. . . . And that is why I support . . . testing." [14] Now, this research agenda is very bad science, for it appeals even on its face directly to a self-selecting sample, the members of which, moreover, may have some doubts about or inklings of how the results may eventually be put to use. But even this rationale is perhaps not so crazy after all, if again viewed not as public policy but as part of social ritual. For such selective testing might approximate a showing of the incidence of AIDS exposure among those who *really* count, if to "really count" means to participate in the institution by which society defines itself. The real people are those who are allowed to marry and indeed usually do.

More sophisticated arguments for marital testing are based on paternalism, but also fall stillborn from the mind. They are concocted out of the materials mined from the quarry of public health and so lack even the hidden ritualistic value of the President's rationale. A pragmatic paternalism compares AIDS testing to testing for syphilis. But this is a misguided analogy. For, unlike syphilis, AIDS currently has no cure. Jack can't go off and get cured before he marries Jill. Note that on the syphilis-based testing model, the one partner need never know the other's test results; they must each simply come up clean to the state before the license is issued.

Some feminists, focusing on Jill, have advanced as a ground for mandatory marital testing a paternalism of enforced shared knowledge: the test gives a woman knowledge that is relevant for making a rational decision on whether to go ahead and get married.[15] But this argument comes too late in the day. The legal institution of marriage is shot through with regulations, legal commitments, binding obligations, and risks affecting major life components about which the partners typically know nothing and about which indeed they are socially and legally encouraged to stay in ignorance.[16] This paternalistic argument played out consistently then draws into doubt the whole institution of marriage as a legal entity.

Standard public policy gambits directed at social efficiency make no sense as explanations of AIDS marital testing. An interpretation of the phenomenon as social purification ritual makes much better sense.

It should not be surprising that Illinois—Northern in gesture and form, Southern in substance and sincerity—should be the first state to pass marital testing. AIDS has replaced abortion as the issue of choice on the state assembly's social agenda. Illinois has done for abortion litigation what New York has done for the Interstate Commerce Clause and Georgia for obscenity law. Session after session, the Illinois legislature has passed abortion restrictions, even though they have already been struck down as unconstitutional and even though it costs the state a great deal of money to see them so declared. In 1987, however, no coercive abortion legislation was passed. Instead, the legislature enacted a host of coercive AIDS measures. This transfer of attention, though, should not come as a surprise, for the passing of abortion bars too should be viewed not as standard public policy making but essentially as rituals of sanctification. And the value these rituals develop and express is the same value as the AIDS testing rituals—compulsory heterosexuality. . . .

B. Immigration and the Military

Other categories and forms of mandatory AIDS antibody testing can be treated in shorter compass. Immigration policy and military policy are nominally designed to defend the nation but the history of both institutions, their racial histories, for instance,[17] shows that their chief function is not so much defending what the nation is but determining what the nation is. This is the real reason that mandatory AIDS testing has been instituted in these two areas.

The military's own rationales are two. One is paternalistic: knowing a soldier's antibody status will allow the army to better take care of him. This paternalistic argument is wholly bogus. In no other area is the army suddenly concerned with the better care of its personnel. Indeed it has recently fought to the mat for—and won—an uncontestable right to feed soldiers LSD under false pretenses.[18] The other Army rationale is nominally strategic: soldiers are supposed to be walking bloodbanks, but this rationale is simply so statistically overinclusive as to be an intellectual ruse. The National Academy of Science study of the AIDS crisis showed that such battlefield transfusions virtually never occur, thanks to the extensive use of much safer blood-volume expanders.[19] One normally does not, and indeed the armed forces do not, make policy based on the oddball case. Rationally self-interested people do not spend huge sums to increase their safety only marginally, and the armed forces certainly do not spend large sums to guard against every eventuality to personnel who after all are not even there, in the army's eyes, for their own good. Yet an oddly wide spectrum of people including some nominally activist gays have bought this military argument for testing simply in order not to appear unpatriotic.

What tips the military's hand to reveal its true motives is its actual practice. Even though Congress has barred the armed forces from using a soldier's antibody status as a reason for demobbing him, in practice the military simply badgers the antibody positive soldier until he admits he's queer and then discharges him on that ground—so much for care and concern.[20] Antibody testing is the physical correlate for heterosexuality that the military has long been seeking in order to purge itself of pogues. Recent empirical studies have shown that the military's past record of discovering even its sexually active gay males has been very poor indeed.[21] In the World War II era, it used a tongue depressor test to discern queers. If a recruit failed to gag on the depressor when it was stuck suddenly to the back of the throat, then in the army's mind that meant that other things less savory had likely been there and the recruit would be rejected.[22] With AIDS testing the army now thinks it has found the tool for which it has long hankered. The purpose of AIDS antibody testing in the army and its twin, immigration policy, is the purge of gay people in order to keep pure the institutions by which the nation defines itself.

C. Of Walls and Vampires

Prison testing is a convoluted yet particularly telling case. Here the nominal public health rationale for such testing, pushed for instance by the American Medical Association, is that sex in prison will spread the disease, so that body-positives have to be segregated from the general population to prevent its spread. This argument shows a certain forgetfulness about the mode of the disease's transmission and an ignorance of prison life. Given that in men's prisons no one is transmitting the virus perinatally, a prisoner, unless coerced, has to expose himself to the virus in order to get it. Nonviolent positives are being put in "protective custody"—basically, solitary confinement, something than which nothing greater can be conceived—because *other people* may be violent toward them or coerce them into having sex. Here the health rationale makes sense only if one accepts as sound the heckler's veto argument—and in a form elevated to a level that permits the utter crushing of human dignity, a commodity already rare in gang-run U.S. prisons. Is America in the AIDS crisis suddenly so concerned about the health and well-being of its prison populations? If you are naïve enough to believe that one, you are naïve enough to believe that when prison guards use with the press the studied ambiguity "homosexual rape," it is the homosexuals that are doing the raping.[23]

The Justice Department spokesman who announced the beginning of mandatory testing in federal prisons gave two rationales for it: "the testing [is] designed to gauge the extent of AIDS infection among prisoners and the department's ability to conduct routine testing." [24] Note that neither of these rationales has anything specifically to do with prisons and prisoners; they might as well have been claimed on behalf of Boy Scouts or blondes or indeed any group. The second rationale ought to have sounded alarms, but has not: why learn how to do routine testing on a large scale unless one has big plans for its use. In any case, the rationales offered for prison testing fail to justify the vigor with which the policy is being pursued nationally and locally.

No, the real reason for prison testing is provided by a remark, cryptic on its surface, made by the U.S. Attorney General, the man to whom America has entrusted the realization of justice. He claimed that prison testing is necessary because when prisoners are released many of them gravitate toward jobs in daycare centers.[25] I take it that this dense remark, when unfolded, entails something like the following concatenation of ideas: one, gays should be in prison and some actually are put there; two, homosexuality is a corruptive contagion, so that even if one was not queer going into prison, one likely is when coming out; three, all gays are child molesters, who, if unchecked, will destroy civilization through the corruptive contagion of its most tender link, its children, its future.

A corruptive contagion is a disease that reproduces itself from one person to the next simply and sufficiently through its symptoms. The myth that homosexuality is a corruptive contagion—that one gets it from someone performing homosexual acts upon or near one—runs very deep in our culture. In 1978, Associate Justice, now Chief Justice, Rehnquist, while protesting the Supreme Court's declining to hear a successful gay student case, went out of his way to hold that a gay student organization's claim to campus recognition is "akin to . . . those suffering from measles [claiming they] have a constitutional right, in violation of quarantine regulations, to associate together and with others who do not presently have measles, in order to urge repeal of state law providing that measles sufferers be quarantined." [26]

AIDS too is mistakenly thought by America to be a corruptive contagion: irrational fears of casual contagion and the mistaken but popular comparison of it to airborne diseases, like influenza,[27] suggest that it is a disease the symptoms of which are the proximate cause of its transmission, where in fact, since it is a bloodborne disease, the actions of the person who gets the disease are the proximate cause of its transmission. It is the clustering of these two errors of taking gays and AIDS as each a vampire-like corruptive contagion, together with a statistical overlap between the two on a par with that of poverty and color, that has led to the virtual identification of AIDS and gays in the mind of America: they are taken as a tandem of invisible lurking evils, lying in wait to get you.

Gays then would do well to remember that in 1987 the Supreme Court first upheld the preventive detention of those who are innocent yet deemed by the courts a danger to society[28] and then the very next week punted on an opportunity to overturn the World War II Japanese internment case.[29] *Korematsu* is still good law: all U.S. citizens of Japanese descent can be indefinitely interned because the government cannot determine who, if any, of them might actually be dangerous.[30]

The social thinking revealed in the real rationales for antibody testing in prisons, with its companion concentrations, applies just as well to gays who are not in prison, whether testing positive or not. The ritualistic purpose of prison testing is to assert the social validity of the purging of gays from the general population. Gays might well remember here too that the 1942 immurement of the Warsaw ghetto was promulgated as a public health measure—to stop the spread of typhus. It made no reference to Jews. And gays would do well to remember that FDR's executive order 9066, which set up America's concentration camps, made no mention of Japanese-Americans; rather it authorized the military to exclude "any and all persons" from designated areas to protect national security.

Antibody testing of hospital personnel and patients appeals so obviously to the blood stigmas which in the past have been hurled against blacks and Jews that their resurrection in time of "the gay plague" to help search out invisible lurking evils perhaps needs no comment to be seen for what it is. Note that the policy's marginal health utility comes into play only when health care personnel are doing their jobs poorly, so any public health rationale for it is in fact immoral: the bad, in this case the incompetent, are the prompt for imposing coercive policy upon the innocent.[37] Again we have not public policy but purification ritual at work.

Prognosis

Testing discovers and divides. Testing discovers the invisible and mysterious and it divides "us" from "them." It is the perfect vehicle for a civilization in need of reasserting its most basic values under challenge. It casts lurking threats into the light so that they may be exiled or committed to the flames. At the same time, testing regroups the dominant culture by showing that it is willing not only to sacrifice others *to* its values but sacrifice itself *for the sake of* them as well.

This sacrifice by and of the dominant culture may be understood on an analogy to civil disobedience in which an individual sacrifices his interests or at least puts them imminently at risk for the sake of his central values, his personal integrity. With AIDS testing and other purification rituals the body politic sacrifices its interests for the sake of a higher goal, that of preserving and solidifying its identity and integrity. The difference between civil disobedience and social purification rituals of course is that in civil disobedience the state is resisted, while in purification rituals the state is blindly affirmed and strengthened as the instrument and vehicle of the purification.

When a government uses coercion to express a society's deepest values and establish or rededicate them as sacred, there will be no stopping it however odious and immoral its acts, for these values are already or come to be embedded in a pre-institutional social knowledge which serves as a lens through which all else is judged. The pairing of coercion and sacred values will simply short circuit the usual procedures that put limits on tyranny. Through the filter of sacred values, what is zany as social policy and might be discovered as such through, say, careful legislative hearings, will be seen rather as natural, necessary, and good—not in need of any articulated or particularized justification. And any hint of attack on the values themselves must and will be dealt with as through expiation—prayer in action, holy war—a cleansing of taint and a rededication through self-sacrifice of purity restored.

If we now ask what is to be done and what is to become of things, I fear my social interpretation of AIDS testing counsels little, if any, hope—and perhaps it will be resisted for that very reason. As we have seen in the transfiguration of sexual values worked by the AIDS crisis, people yearn for purpose in their lives to such an extent that they will even scan the universe looking for it when they fail to find it in themselves or hereabout. This tendency of the human mind, while in a way admirable—for it shows a certain intrepidness of the human spirit even among human weaklings—is nevertheless scary—for it means that people will try anything and they rarely, especially if weak, just stop at trying it on and for themselves. One sees this in people who have voluntarily taken the antibody test, come up negative, and then mount a pretty high horse calling for coerced testing of others. The political right is counting on the large number of recently married body-negatives to serve as the advance troops for universal mandatory testing.

Even if mandatory testing were to take its most severe forms, the Supreme Court, which Martin Luther King Jr. always paired with God and which in our society is structurally the chief dispenser of rights, will be of no help in blunting the coercive state.[32] Compulsory heterosexuality need not have been mentioned in the nation's constitution, for all that is in it would be interpreted through that filter. Thus the Supreme Court could rule that gays have no privacy right to have sex, without even discussing gays or privacy or sex.[33] Under the filter of heterosexuality, the configuration of gays, sex, and privacy was completely invisible, not even a mote on the field of rights. Yet when glitches in custom have legally burdened traditional family structures, the Court has come to the rescue with the constitutional magic of Substantive Due Process—voiding laws in order to assert and restore familial sanctity is beyond calculations of social utility.[34] The Courts will be no help in addressing mandatory AIDS testing for similar reasons. The legislation in its social function—as the expression of sacred values—asserts the very values that make up the Court's interpretative lens.

The picture is gloomier still. If the courts will not work, what of trying to educate society? If my interpretation is anywhere near the mark, then many liberals (and I include myself here) have been mistaken to suppose that society's response to the AIDS crisis is a panicked response caused largely by ignorance. Rather the coercive legislation which society is now enacting in response to AIDS is simply the expected working out of the country's governing social knowledge as it has become aware of new facts. Mary Douglas might as well have had the AIDS crisis specifically in mind when she wrote quite generally:

> The conclusion [is] that individuals in crises do not make life and death decisions on their own. Who shall be saved and who shall die is settled by institutions. Putting it even more strongly, individual ratiocination cannot solve such problems. An answer is only seen to be the right one if it sustains the institutional thinking that is already in the minds of individuals as they try to decide.[35]

Society's response to the AIDS crisis could be changed only if the culture itself were changed, and that is not going to occur, if ever, twixt now and Vaccine Day, should it come. Societies are even less likely than individuals to change behavior through education and we have seen that traditional educational efforts have had no significant effect in stopping the spread of AIDS among gays; urban centers where educational efforts were most intense now have AIDS-saturated gay male populations.[36] Such change as has occurred in gay male behavior patterns is not the result of safe-sex pamphlets broadcasting, as they do, mixed and confusing messages about sex and sexuality. No, the educator was death. And we know from the history of war that death wins no teaching awards. And we should remember too that when death is the social educator, society responds not with new ideas and liberality but with fear and retrenchment.

Still less likely are educational efforts going to be effective because AIDS social coercion has become a body accelerated under the gravitational pull of our anxieties over nuclear destruction. Doing anything significant to alleviate the prospects of the collective death of everything that can die is effectively out of the reach of any ordinary individual and indeed of any political group now in existence. So individuals transfer the focus of their anxieties from nuclear omnicide to AIDS, by which they feel equally and similarly threatened, but about which they think they can do something—at least through government. AIDS coercion is doing double duty as a source of sacred values and as a vent for universal anxieties over universal destruction. Against this daunting combination, no educational efforts will have any significant effects.

What of the public health community? Here the paradox is that the more the public health community points up the irrationality of mandatory testing by its own criteria, the more it underscores and contributes to the true public function of the testing, which is the assertion of group solidarity through self-sacrifice. In this crisis, the good intentions, good will, sometimes good arguments, and even some good actions of the public health community all inadvertently contribute to evil. Theodicy is here inverted. The public health community in the crisis is the lone lit candle in Kafka's cathedral: its singular flame simply makes the darkness darker.

Well-intended gay leaders and theorists, particularly of a socialist stripe,[37] have, I fear, also inadvertently contributed to this evil. Gays—for reasons as diverse as self-hatred and hoped-for social collegiality—have played a shell game of statistics in order to claim that AIDS is not a gay disease. In doing so, they simply misunderstand the operative social dynamics of the crisis and reinforce irrelevant public health thinking on AIDS. As gays indulge the discomforts of nongays in the crisis by denying these dynamics, they act as abused children do who try to comfort their parent even while he is beating them. When gays fail to oppose marital testing, because they think it does not affect them, and hope thereby to score a few social points by appearing patriotic, they are as aware of social realities as European Jewry of the 1930s allowed itself to be when it failed to opposed antimiscegenation laws on the ground that Jews were supposed to marry Jews anyway.

When gays are not busy indulging worldly heterosexuals, they are scampering off to God, the big heterosexual in the sky. Instead of thus shooting into the void their ability to generate value through reverence, gays should begin to establish rituals by which they value and honor themselves. Some recent gay AIDS burial rituals, though marred by religiosity, have been a step in the right direction.[38] The ritualistic dimensions of old-fashioned consciousness-raising groups are another. Finally, by laying hearthstones together, gays would help return sacred values to their most proper place, the sanctities of the home and the privacies of life.[39] And instead of pinning their hopes on answered prayer from Masses or on compassion from the masses, gays should prepare to resist. Now when The Good is receding from gays with all the speed and brilliance of quasars, it is time to stop looking for silver linings.

I fully expect though that gay self-hatred, exacerbated as it has been by the AIDS crisis and its concomitant transvaluation of sex and sexuality, will defeat both efforts—not a promising picture, but then it should be beginning to become clear that we have grossly underestimated the evil of men and the cussedness of things.

Endnotes

1. *The Advocate* [Los Angeles], July 7, 1987, no. 476, p. 11.
2. "President Calls for Widespread Testing," *The New York Times,* June 1, 1987, p. 1.
3. "AIDS Test Ordered for U.S. Prisoners and Immigration," *The New York Times,* June 9, 1987, p. 1.
4. "Illinois Backs AIDS Tracing," *The New York Times,* July 1, 1987, p. Y9; "Veto of AIDS Bills Urged in Illinois," *The New York Times,* July 7, 1987, p. Y11. Illinois was the first state to have its legislature pass mandatory marital AIDS-antibody testing. Between the passage of the bill and its signing by Illinois' governor several months later, Louisiana's legislature passed and its governor signed such legislation; the bills in both states went into effect on January 1, 1988. "Broad Laws on AIDS Signed in Illinois," *The New York Times,* September 22, 1987, p. Y15; "AIDS Bills Focus on Education," *Chicago Tribune,* September 22 1987, p. 1.

   When the implementation of the Illinois testing law proved socially unwieldy, its senate sponsor claimed that "the cost of implementing the law was not a consideration in creating it." "Prenuptial AIDS Screening a Strain in Illinois," *The New York Times,* January 26, 1988, p. 1.
5. "AIDS Test Ordered for U.S. Prisoners and Immigration," *The New York Times,* June 9, 1987, p. 1. Popular support for all forms of testing is overwhelming. A Gallup poll shows that 90 percent of people favor testing immigrants, 88 percent federal prisoners, 83 percent military personnel, 80 percent marriage license applicants and 52 percent all Americans. "Widespread Tests for AIDS Virus Favored by Most, Gallup Reports," *The New York Times,* July 13, 1987, p. Y11.
6. The American Medical Association, for example, is on record as supporting testing of prisoners and immigrants. "Doctors' Panel Suggests Limited AIDS Testing," *The New York Times,* June 21, 1987, p. Y19.

7. "Need to Widen [Voluntary] AIDS Testing Seen as Health Forum Ends" and "Homosexuals Applaud Rejection of Mandatory Test for AIDS: Advocates Express Relief over Consensus," *The New York Times*, February 26, 1987, p. Y13.
8. For an analysis of sacred or priceless values in government deliberations, see Douglas MacLean "Social Values and the Distribution of Risk" in Douglas MacLean, ed., *Values at Risk*, pp. 85–93 (Totowa, N.J.: Rowman and Allanheld, 1986).
9. Mary Douglas, *How Institutions Think* (Syracuse: Syracuse University Press, 1986), p. 4.
10. Adrienne Rich, "Compulsory Heterosexuality and Lesbian Existence," *Signs: Journal of Women in Culture and Society* (Summer 1980) 5(4):631–60.
11. Mary Douglas explains:

    For Fleck, the thought style [of society] sets the preconditions of any cognition, and determines what can be counted as a reasonable question and a true or false answer. It provides the context and sets the limits for any judgment about objective reality. Its essential feature is to be hidden from the members of the thought collective.
12. For cases and discussion, see Harry D. Krause, *Family Law*, 2d ed. (St. Paul: West, 1983), pp. 31–74.
13. See, for example, *Singer* v. *Hara*, 522 P.2d 1187, 1194–95 (1974), in which Washington's supreme court held that the requirement that men marry one but not the other gender was not a requirement that triggered a state constitutional bar on distinctions made with respect to gender. See also *Adams* v. *Howerton*, 486 F.Supp. 1119, 1124–25 (C.D. Cal. 1980) in which the court claimed that even if gays did have a fundamental right to marry, a bar on gays marrying would still be upheld because necessary to a compelling state interest.
14. "President Calls for Widespread Testing," *The New York Times*, June 1, 1987, p. 1.
15. Julien S. Murphy, "Women with AIDS: Sexual Ethics in an Epidemic," in Inge Corless and Mary Pittman-Lineman, eds., *AIDS: Principles, Practices and Politics*, pp. 67–71 (New York: Harper and Row, 1988).
16. On formal and substantive failings of marriage as a contract, see Sara Ann Ketchum, "Liberalism and Marriage Law" in Mary Vetterling-Braggin, et al., eds., *Feminism and Philosophy*, pp. 247–76 (Totowa, N.J.: Littlefield Adams, 1977).
17. See Bernard C. Nalty, *Strength for the Fight: A History of Black Americans in the Military* (New York: The Free Press, 1986) and Elizabeth Hull, *Without Justice for All: The Constitutional Rights of Aliens* (Westport, Conn.: Greenwood Press, 1985), chapter 1.
18. *United States* v. *James B. Stanley*, 107 S.Ct.. 3054 (1987).
19. Institute of Medicine, National Academy of Science, *Confronting AIDS: Directions for Public Health, Health Care and Research* (Washington: National Academy Press, 1986), p. 122. The Army's own study and account of blood transfusions in the Vietnam War makes no mention at all of any battlefield transfusions other than the extensive use of plasma expanders. The study concludes that "from the standpoint of methods used to wound—mines, high-velocity missiles, and booby-traps—as well as the locale in which many were injured—in paddyfields or along waterways where human and animal excreta were common—Vietnam was quite a 'dirty' war." Nevertheless "the availability of whole blood, which had been a problem early in each major war to date, was not a problem in Vietnam. An efficient distribution system kept pace with the increasing requirements for whole blood; in no instance was blood unavailable when, where and in the types and amounts needed." Major General Spurgeon Neel, *Medical Support of the U.S. Army in Vietnam*, 1965–1970 (Washington, D.C.: Department of the Army [Vietnam Studies], 1973), pp. 49–50, 55–56, 66, 114–26, 172–73, quotes from pp. 49, 172–73.
20. See Rhonda R. Rivera, "The Military," in Harlon Dalton, Scott Burris, and the Yale AIDS Law Project, eds., *AIDS and the Law: A Guide for the Public*, pp. 221–34 (New Haven: Yale University Press, 1987).
21. See Joseph Harry, "Homosexual Men and Women Who Served Their Country," *Journal of Homosexuality* (1984) 10(1–2: 117–25.
22. See Allan Bérubé, "Gays at War," *Mother Jones* (February–March 1983) 8(11):23–29, 45, and "Marching to a Different Drummer," *The Advocate*, October 15, 1981, no. 328, pp. 20–25, reprinted in Ann Snitnow, et al., eds., *Powers of Desire: The Politics of Sexuality*, pp. 88–99 (New York: Monthly Review Press, 1983).
23. See Wayne Wooden and Jay Parker, *Men Behind Bars: Sexual Exploitation in Prison* (New York: Plenum, 1982).
24. "AIDS Test Ordered for U.S. Prisons and Immigration," *The New York Times*, June 9, 1987, p. Y22.
25. *Ibid.*
26. *Ratchford* v. *Gay Lib*, 434 U.S. 1080, 1082 (1978). Though the genre of dissent from a denial of certiorari requires Rehnquist to have stated the position as a hypothetical, his immediately preceding discussion of the facts of the case make it clear that he does indeed accept the hypothesis as true.
27. For a mainstream piece of influential hysteria, see Dr. Richard Restak's widely reprinted op-ed piece, "Worry About Survival of Society First; Then AIDS Victims' Rights," *The Washington Post*, September 8, 1985, p. C1.
28. *United States* v. *Salerno*, 107 S.Ct. 2095 (1987).
29. *United States* v. *Hohri*, 107 S.Ct. 2246 (1987).
30. *Korematsu* v. *United States*, 323 U.S. 214 (1944). Justice Jackson warned in dissent that "the principle [that the innocent, the merely potentially dangerous, may be put in concentration camps] . . . lies about like a loaded weapon ready for the hand of any authority that can bring forward a plausible claim of an urgent need." *Ibid.* at 246. Gays ought to be more than a little leery

of the war metaphors that have been circulating amongst governmental officials addressing the AIDS crisis and surely ought themselves to cease using as names for their own efforts such violence-evoking metaphors as "The New Manhattan Project" and "Stamp Out AIDS"—especially given the social mind's perception of a virtual identity between gays and AIDS.

31. See "Three Health Workers Found Infected by Blood of Patients with AIDS," *The New York Times,* May 20, 1987, p. Y1.
32. See Deborah Jones Meritt, "Communicable Disease and Constitutional Law: Controlling AIDS," *New York University Law Review* (1986) 61:739–99.
33. *Bowers* v. *Hardwick,* 106 S.Ct. 2841 (1986).
34. See, for example, *Meyer* v. *Nebraska,* 262 U.S. 390, 399–401 (1923) (giving parents a constitutional right of Substantive Due Process to have their children taught German), *Pierce* v. *Society of Sisters,* 268 U.S. 510, 534–35 (1925) (Substantive Due Process used to strike down a Ku Klux Klan inspired Oregon law requiring parents to send their children to public schools), and *Moore* v. *City of East Cleveland,* 431 U.S. 494 (1977) (Substantive Due Process used to void a zoning ordinance barring grandchildren from living with their grandparents). Moore provided the constitutional standard that was used in *Bowers,* 106 S.Ct. at 2844, to claim basically that gays have no place in the constitutional scheme of the United States: "Our decisions establish that the Constitution protects the sanctity of the family precisely because the institution of the family is deeply rooted in this Nation's history and tradition. It is through the family that we inculcate and pass down many of our most cherished values, moral and cultural." *Moore,* at 503–4, footnotes omitted.
35. Douglas, *How Institutions Think,* p. 4.
36. "Five-Year Plan to Fight AIDS Drafted by New York," *The New York Times,* May 25, 1987, p. Y11.
37. See, for example, Dennis Altman, *AIDS in the Mind of America* (Garden City, N.Y.: Doubleday, 1986), chapter 3.
38. "New Rituals Ease Grief as AIDS Tool Increases," *The New York Times,* May 11, 1987, p. C11.
39. I do not think that rituals and sacred values have no role in public life or even government actions. The use of public funds for government-sponsored voluntary initiatives that enhance the value which people in general place on the particularized lifeplans of individuals is quite unobjectionable and actually will tend to put breaks on governmental tyranny, by asserting the value of the right of individuals to live out their own distinctive lives and not to be viewed socially and legally as merely filling socially assigned functions. Rescue missions are clear cases of such admirable social ritual:

    Startling examples of ritualized behavior are common in our dealings with hazard and risks. We need only to consider our willingness to engage in rescue missions when identified individuals are involved: saving crash victims, fliers lost at sea, or an astronaut; retrieving the wounded or dead in battle; diverting resources from making mines safer in order to mount rescue missions for trapped miners; or even supporting individual medical treatment rather than more public health research. These actions and policies defy economic or even risk-minimizing sense.

    MacLean, "Social Values," p. 87.

Review Questions

1. Why does Mohr think that mandatory HIV testing is not justified on traditional public health grounds?
2. What is behind the proposal for compulsory testing according to Mohr?
3. What is Mohr's view of marital testing for AIDS?
4. What is the military's rationale for mandatory AIDS testing? What is Mohr's reply?
5. According to Mohr, what is the real reason for mandatory AIDS testing in prison?

Discussion Questions

1. Is mandatory HIV testing degrading to gays? Why or why not?
2. Does mandatory AIDS testing violate the right to privacy? What do you think?

Theresa L. Crenshaw

HIV Testing: Voluntary, Mandatory, or Routine?

Dr. Theresa L. Crenshaw is a physician and member of the President's Commission on the HIV Epidemic.

Dr. Crenshaw argues that we should require HIV testing for hospital admission and certain jobs like pilots and air traffic controllers. Such testing might also be appropriate for other occupations and situations. She replies to various objections to required HIV testing. One of the most important objections is that the ELISA test produces many false positive and false negative test results. Other objections focus on possible bad results of required testing, e.g., the invasion of privacy, suicide, and the use of quarantines.

The AIDS virus is formidable. For a preventable disease, it continues to spread at an alarming rate. As long as 90 percent of those who are infected—1.5 million people or more in the United States—don't know it and continue to spread it to others, we have little hope of controlling this epidemic.

Yet, there are many dilemmas and questions that face us as individuals and as a society. Isn't it better for a person who is infected not to know? How can one expect an infected person to stop having sex when he or she is already suffering more than a human being can bear? Are condoms sufficient protection? Is testing dependable? How can we protect the civil rights of the ill and the civil rights of the healthy?

There is no simple solution. Testing alone is not enough. We need all of our resources: common sense, sexual integrity, compassion, love, exclusivity, education, discipline, testing, condoms, and spermicides—to name just a few. We also need an emphatic, positive message that promotes *quality* sex rather than *quantity* sex. Multiple partners and casual sex are not in the best interest of health, but within an exclusive relationship quality sex can thrive.

In this context, perhaps we could take an in-depth look at the controversial issue of HIV-testing. Widespread voluntary testing, if encouraged by health officials and physicians, will most probably be successful, making widespread mandatory testing unnecessary. The general population will cooperate. However, under certain circumstances, required or routine testing might be considered and could be implemented whenever common sense dictates without the feared repercussions of quarantine and discrimination. Regardless of whether testing is voluntary, required, or routine, maintaining confidentiality is critical. It is vitally important to understand that public health officials are trained to maintain confidentiality in all cases; they do not put advertisements in the newspaper or call a person's employer.

Confidentiality is nonetheless a genuine concern. Lists of infected persons have been stolen. There is probably no way humanly possible to ensure against any and all breaches of confidentiality throughout the United States and the world. It would be unrealistic to falsely assure individuals that confidentiality would be 100 percent secure. On the other hand, we must do everything within our power to come as close as possible to 100 percent confidentiality and to assure those who are concerned that these efforts are being made. There are many things we can do to improve our recording and to improve confidentiality systems. These aspects are being investigated and will hopefully be implemented by federal, state, and local authorities.

An encouraging point is that in Colorado, where HIV-positive status is reportable and contact tracing is routine, *there has not been one episode of breach of confidentiality*, demonstrat-

"HIV Testing: Voluntary, Mandatory, or Routine?" by Dr. Theresa L. Crenshaw first appeared in the Jan/Feb 1988 issue of *The Humanist* and is reprinted with permission.

ing that when extra care is taken there can be great success. Often forgotten is the fact that confidentiality is equally important for voluntary, required, and routine testing. It must be applied to *all* forms of testing, and it must not be used to distinguish between them.

Mandatory testing brings to mind visions of concentration camps and human beings subjected to arbitrary and insensitive public health tactics. In practice, however, nothing could be further from the truth. Urine tests and blood counts are routinely required upon hospital admission. If a patient refuses, he or she will generally not be accepted by the hospital and certainly won't be allowed to undergo surgery. That's mandatory testing, but we take it in stride. And it has no hint of repressiveness; it is simply a reasonable measure for the protection and well-being of both the patient and the hospital.

Likewise, tests for syphilis are mandatory in many states. In many countries, certain tests and inoculations are required before one can travel. In the not-so-distant past, health cards had to be carried by travelers along with their passports, proving that they had had certain immunizations. There is also required testing of school children for childhood diseases, which includes the tuberculin skin test, and various inoculations, without which they are not permitted to enter school. These are just a few examples of mandatory testing or treatments that are routine in our everyday lives—and that do not compromise our civil rights. However, since the term *mandatory* is emotionally charged, substituting the term *required* might more accurately reflect the intent.

Our society takes in stride sensible, necessary tests and treatments which in many circumstances are required in order to travel abroad or to perform certain jobs. However, strenuous arguments against any form of required testing for AIDS persist. The following are some of the issues most commonly raised by opponents of mandatory testing. I have attempted to analyze each argument.

Mandatory testing will drive infected individuals underground. They will hide out and refuse to be tested. Since 90 percent of the 1.5 million or more individuals who are infected within the United States don't even know it, *they are already underground.* While certain numbers of people may use creative methods to avoid testing procedures, we would be able to reduce that percentage of people who do not know their HIV status to 10 percent instead of 90 percent, because most people would cooperate voluntarily.

Testing would cause more problems than it solves because huge numbers of people would receive false positive test results. Their lives would be destroyed by such test results. The enzyme linked immunosorbent assay, or ELISA test, does have a high percentage of false positives, just as the tuberculin skin test has a high percentage of false positives. *That does not mean it is without value.* Whenever a test such as this is performed, a physician never stops at screening tests. Follow-up studies are required to confirm a positive test result. For example, with tuberculosis, chest X-rays and sputum cultures are performed until a positive diagnosis of tuberculosis can be made. The tuberculin skin test is used to determine whether there are indications for further studies. The AIDS antibody test is used in the same fashion. If the ELISA is positive, it should be repeated again and the **Western Blot test** performed. If these are all positive, the likelihood of the result being a false positive approaches zero (per 400,000, according to Dr. James Curran of the Centers for Disease Control). Immune system studies can then be done and, although it is expensive and somewhat logistically difficult, a patient who wants additional proof of infection can request actual viral cultures. Since recent research demonstrates that there can be a year or more during which the virus is present but antibodies have not yet developed—the so-called window in time—the far greater problem with testing is the high number of false negatives that still will be missed. Another study by A. Ranki et al., in the September 12, 1987, issue of *Lancet,* indicates that up to 36 percent of ELISAs are false negatives in those individuals who have had sex with an infected person. As you see, the screening test is not perfect. There will be false negatives that escape detection, so the test should be repeated periodically. All false positives would be followed up with additional tests until a confirmed positive result can be established. In the near future, we will have a test for the virus itself, solving some of the problems we now face, especially the "window in time" between infection and antibody development.

There is no point in having yourself tested because there is no cure. Although there is no cure, and indeed *because* there is no cure, it is even more essential to be tested and to know what your antibody status is, because, if you test positive, you must take every precaution not to infect another person. If this disease were curable, perhaps we could be more cavalier. But since we must protect individuals in society from it, we must motivate those who are already infected not to infect anyone else. To assume that everyone should and will behave as though they were infected is optimistic and unreasonable, although I think many can achieve this end. It is unlikely, however, for an individual to take complete responsibility for his or her actions without definitive knowledge of infection. Even then it is a challenge.

There are other reasons for being tested. Someone who tests positive will live longer if counseled not to become exposed unnecessarily to other infections by visiting sick friends at home or in the hospital or by traveling extensively to countries where foreign organisms can cause unusual infections. Additional health counseling can lead to a healthier lifestyle, the avoidance of other opportunistic infections or cofactors, improved nutrition, and planning for the future—which includes estate planning, a will, and making other practical arrangements as indicated.

Perhaps the most important reason for being tested early is that many of the treatments becoming available are more effective the earlier they are instituted. If you know you are HIV-positive, you can apply for research projects for experimental protocols or arrange to take AZT (which is now available) or other similar drugs when they become approved for clinical use. In short, the reasons for being tested far outweigh the reasons for not being tested.

Testing is undesirable for many individuals who are unable to cope with the knowledge that they are infected. These people are better off not being tested. Anyone who is asked whether or not they think they will be able to cope with the news of an HIV-positive test result would ordinarily say no. It is normal not to be able to cope well with a deadly, incurable disease. Most people who are tested receive pretest counseling. Often pretest counseling, advertently or inadvertently, dissuades individuals from being tested. At a recent conference in New York cosponsored by the American Medical Association and the Centers for Disease Control, one physician said that, with just three minutes on the telephone with someone inquiring about being tested, he succeeds in talking 57 percent of potential patients out of being tested. In the anonymous testing centers, we need only look at the numbers of people who show up for testing compared to those who leave without being tested to assess the effectiveness of some counseling in discouraging testing.

Yet, imagine an analogous situation for a woman needing a breast biopsy. If the physician asked, "Are you sure you want this biopsy? Do you realize that the results could show that you have cancer? Are you prepared to live with that? If the biopsy is positive, you'll need to have your breast removed. Do you think you can cope? How do you think your husband will feel about you sexually? What if the cancer is incurable and you're given a short time to live? Do you think you can handle that?" Of course, the answer to most of these questions would be "no," and many women needing breast biopsies would not pursue them. Instead, doctors help a woman confront the need for the biopsy. They support her in helping her to deal with the natural reluctance and fear involved and help her to find the courage and determination to proceed.

We must do the same with AIDS testing. Instead of asking, "Are you sure you want this test?" and "Do you think you can cope?" the physician, psychologist, or therapist must take the same kind of approach they do with other necessary or valuable medical procedures. Assume it is a good idea to be tested. Compliment the person for his or her courage and self-responsibility in pursing the test. Let each person know that you intend to help him or her get through some of the difficulties and will be there to talk in detail about the issues should that person's test turn out to be positive. Let patients know that you appreciate the courage it takes for them to proceed with the test. Emphasize that the test will be of value to them whether it turns out to be negative or positive. By taking the approach that it is valuable and worthwhile to be tested, counselors can help patients deal with their fear and discomfort rather than contribute to it. Many counseling centers are beginning to change to this approach, but too many still follow the one that effectively discourages testing.

Testing isn't cost effective except in high-risk populations. Required testing will simply waste a lot of money getting nothing but negative results. A negative result is exceedingly valuable and can be utilized to maintain health. Any individual who tests negative should be given written, taped, or individual information on how to remain uninfected so that they are motivated to protect that fortunate status. Some studies have found that an HIV-negative result alone is sometimes not sufficient to motivate a change in sexual behavior. It is exceedingly worthwhile to test negative, especially if it can be combined with some information or counseling so that the individual can be given an opportunity to remain HIV-negative for life.

The cost of testing the entire population and counseling those who are HIV-positive on how not to spread the disease is a fraction of the cost that would be required to care for those who would otherwise become infected.

Testing is no good. The day after someone has the test they could become infected. That's why safe sex cards don't work. It is true that moments after blood has been drawn for an AIDS test the person could have sex and become infected. There is no question that the test is only as good as the behavior that follows it. On the other hand, if a person gets tested fairly regularly (every six months or once a year) and you meet that person five years after their first test and learn that that person has had the discipline and the concern about his or her health to remain negative for that period of time, it tells you something about that person's judgment and health status. One test may not carry a great deal of meaning, except to the individual who knows whether or not his or her behavior has been risky since the last test. On the other hand, a series of tests that are negative makes a statement of great importance.

It is also important to emphasize that testing is not enough. I do not support safe sex cards if they are used in singles clubs with the recommendation that anyone who tests negative and carries a card can have sex with anyone else holding a similar card. Multiple partners multiplies the possible error. On the other hand, I think that one or more tests are very valuable if used as a prerequisite to a monogamous relationship and if condoms and spermicide are also used until at least a year has passed to protect against the window in time mentioned earlier.

If you institute mandatory testing, what are you going to do with the individuals who test positive? Isolate them? Quarantine them? Society will do the same thing with individuals who test HIV-positive on mandatory testing that they will do with any individuals who test HIV-positive on widespread voluntary testing. Most people who are fighting mandatory testing are actually fighting quarantine, afraid that one will lead to the other. I would much prefer that they support the valuable and meaningful step of testing and fight the issue of quarantine, rather than fight step two to avoid step three.

You should not test because some people will panic when they are told of a positive result and commit suicide. This is one of the most worrisome consequences of testing. It is understandable that someone who tests positive would fleetingly consider taking his or her own life, and some individuals might progress to actually doing so. This is one of the reasons a positive test result should never be given by phone. A patient should be called to see his or her physician or counselor or to the anonymous testing center so that he or she can be counseled extensively at that moment.

There are no guarantees that will ensure that someone would not commit suicide, but we must do everything humanly possible to prevent it—short of not testing. The reason for this is simple: if that person were not tested and did not know that he or she were HIV-positive, the odds are good that that person would take someone else's life unknowingly through continued sexual activity. So, even in this case, informing and counseling the individual are preferable to allowing that person to remain ignorant and perhaps infect not one but many others, thereby sentencing them to death.

Contact tracing is of no value, requires too much manpower, and violates privacy. Contact tracing is *always* voluntary. A patient must be willing to identify sexual partners for it to be successful. When the public health department performs contact tracing, it contacts the sexual partner without giving him or her the name of the person involved. Instead, health officials say, "It has come to our attention that you have been exposed to the AIDS virus and it is important that you be tested in order to determine whether you have become infected." It is true that if the individual has had only one sexual partner in his or her entire life he or she will be able to deduce who the person was. Since this is the exception rather than the general rule, and since the incubation period of this disease might go back a decade or more, in most cases it would be very difficult to identify the other individual involved.

Under what circumstances could required testing be instituted, and what rationale would justify implementing this system? Hospital admission is an important opportunity for mandatory or required testing. In order to give the best care to a patient who is HIV-positive, a physician must know the patient's antibody status. A physician would treat a post-operative infection or any other infection far more aggressively with antibiotics in a patient that the physician knew to be HIV-positive than in one who did not have the potential for immune system compromise. Anyone admitted with an infection would be watched more closely if HIV-positive and would probably be treated earlier than someone whose immune system was more dependable.

Many argue that the doctor should use his or her discretion on whom to test. I argue that that feeds into a discriminatory bias suggesting that one can prejudge who might be suspiciously gay. There are no indicators in the healthy HIV-positive person to cause a physician to suspect which person needs testing.

One case history was particularly convincing that physicians need the test to help make a proper diagnosis. A woman called a television program in San Francisco. She said that she had AIDS. Several months before, she had flown to San Diego to donate blood for her mother's elective surgery. Subsequently, she returned to San Francisco, had several additional sexual partners, and eventually was admitted to San Francisco General Hospital for acute respiratory distress. She was treated for allergies and asthma but almost died. During the time that she was in the hospital, she received a letter from the blood bank informing her that her blood had tested HIV-positive. She asked her roommate to open the letter. The doctors then made the diagnosis of **Pneumocystis pneumonia**, treated her, and she was discharged from the hospital a few days later.

San Francisco General is one of the hospitals that has the most experience in diagnosing and dealing with the AIDS virus. They missed this diagnosis and might not have made it without the aid of the mandatory AIDS test performed by the blood bank. The patient would have died without a change in treatment approach. It seems to me that if such a sophisticated treatment center can miss the diagnosis it would be common in less experienced hospitals. Physicians need the assistance of this kind of testing to guide them.

This also pertains to mental hospital admissions. AIDS dementia and central nervous system infection are proving to be more common than uncommon. Some researchers believe that over 90 percent of those infected manifest some degree of central nervous system involvement.

Most psychologists and psychiatrists would still not suspect organic disease due to AIDS when a patient manifests acute or chronic depression, psychoses, schizophrenia, sociopathy, or aggressive or violent behavior. The virus can infect any part of the brain and, depending upon the location of infection, the resultant behavioral changes can be quite varied.

Should HIV testing be required for any special jobs? Another challenging aspect of HIV infection not yet confronted by our society is the otherwise asymptomatic individual who has extensive central nervous system or brain infection causing impaired judgment and interference with fine motor coordination. Pilots, air traffic controllers, and those in similar professions could be affected. Testing for the AIDS virus under these circumstances is common sense, not discrimination.

Mandatory or routine testing has been suggested for many other situations and occupations. Testing is already common in the military, prisons, and during immigration. Other situations becoming more common opportunities for testing are during prenatal examinations and in substance abuse programs. Other situations being heatedly debated are premarital testing and testing for food handlers, teachers, health care workers, and business travelers. . . .

Having reviewed the common arguments against mandatory or required testing, we have only to devise methods that will alleviate the concerns of those who oppose mandatory testing. The two greatest obstacles are concerns about confidentiality and fear of quarantine. Everything possible must be done to improve the security of our record-keeping systems. Simultaneously, society must be taught that everyone who is ill deserves our compassion, care, and respect, regardless of the source of infection.

The issue of testing must be separated from the issue of quarantine. We have tested and reported people with AIDS to the public health department for many years, and there has been no hint of quarantining unless violent or aggressive behavior put others in danger. The issue of quarantining is independent, but related, and should be fought on a different front.

Mandatory, or preferably "required," testing under certain circumstances incorporates all the virtues of voluntary testing without the drawbacks. We do not now have widespread compliance with voluntary testing. Many individuals still prefer not to know. If only one person's health were at stake, this privilege could persist. However, the ostrich approach has never demonstrated itself to be of much value. In order to deal with reality, one must face it. Self-responsibility and responsibility to others require it.

There would be widespread voluntary compliance with required testing just as there is for blood counts and tuberculin tests once it becomes widely recognized as a matter of common sense for health—for the benefit of every individual—and not an issue of coercion.

Voluntary testing is ideal but unrealistic in many situations. Required testing under certain circumstances is best for all concerned if handled with confidentiality and consideration. Routine testing in other circumstances will naturally evolve out of the preceding two. Should these trends materialize, being tested for AIDS will become a way of life. The challenge then becomes how to preserve the quality of life for everyone—the healthy and the ill.

Review Questions

1. Why does Dr. Crenshaw think that confidentiality is a real concern?
2. In what cases is mandatory testing already practiced according to Dr. Crenshaw?
3. Dr. Crenshaw discusses numerous objections to required testing for the HIV virus. What are they? How does she respond to these objections?

Discussion Questions

1. Dr. Crenshaw argues that HIV testing should be required for hospital admission. Does she convince you? Explain your answer.
2. Would you be willing to be tested for the HIV virus? If not, why not?

Grant Gillett

AIDS and Confidentiality

Dr. Grant Gillett is Senior Lecturer in Medical Ethics, University of Otago Medical School, New Zealand.

Gillett discusses a case in which a man infected with the AIDS virus insists that his condition be kept confidential, even from his wife. After considering a deontological and a rule-utilitarian defense of confidentiality, Gillett argues that the doctor's moral duty does not require that the patient's request for confidentiality be honored. The duty to do this is only a prima facie *duty that can be overridden by stronger moral duties such as the duty not to harm others.*

Does a doctor confronted by a patient with AIDS have a duty to maintain absolute confidentiality or could that doctor be considered to have some overriding duty to the sexual contacts of the AIDS sufferer? AIDS or Acquired Immune Deficiency Syndrome is a viral disease transmitted for the most part by sexual contact. It is fatal in the short or long term (i.e. nine months to six years) in those infected people who go on to develop the full-blown form of the disease.

Let us say that a 39-year-old man goes to his family doctor with a dry persistent cough which has lasted three or four weeks and a 10 day history of night sweats. He admits that he is bisexually active. He is tested and found to have antibodies to HIV virus (indicating that he is infected with the virus that causes AIDS). In the setting of this clinical picture he must be considered to have the disease. He is told of his condition and also, in the course of a prolonged interview, of the risk to his wife and of the distinct possibility of his children aged one and three years old being left without parents should she contract the disease. He refuses to allow her to be told of his condition. The doctor finally accedes to his demand for absolute confidentiality. After one or two initial illnesses which are successfully combatted he dies some 18 months later. Over the last few weeks of his life he relents on his former demands and allows his wife to be informed of his problem. She is tested and, though asymptomatic, is found to be antibody positive. A year later she goes to the doctor with fever, dry cough and loss of appetite. Distraught on behalf of her children, she bitterly accuses the doctor of having failed her and them by allowing her husband to infect her when steps could have been taken to diminish the risk had she only known the truth.

In this case there is a powerful inclination to say that the wife is justified in her grievance. It seems just plain wrong for her doctor to sit back and allow her to fall victim to a fatal disease because of the wish of her husband. Against this intuition we can mobilise two powerful arguments—one deontological and the other utilitarian (of a rule or restricted utilitarian type).[1]

(i) On a deontological view the practice of medicine will be guided by certain inviolate or absolute rules (not to harm, not to neglect the welfare of one's patients, etc.). Among these will be respect for confidentiality. Faced with this inviolable principle the deontologically inclined physician will not disclose what he has been told in confidence—he will regard the tacit agreement not to disclose his patient's affairs to others as tantamount to a substantive promise which he cannot break. Against this, in the present case, we might urge his *prima facie* duty not to neglect the welfare of his other patient, the young man's wife. His inaction has contributed to her death. In response to this he could both defend the absolute duty to respect confiden-

From Grant Gillett, "AIDS and Confidentiality," *Journal of Applied Philosophy*, Vol. 4, No. 1 (1987), pp.15–20. Reprinted by permission of the editor and the author, Grant Gillett, University of Otago Medical School.

tiality in general and urge some version of the doctrine of double effect,[2] claiming that his clear duty was to honour his implicit vow of confidentiality but it had the unfortunate effect, which he had foreseen as possible but not intended, that it caused the death of his other patient. One is inclined to offer an intuitive response such as 'No moral duty is so binding that you can hazard another person's life in this manner'. It is a notorious feature of deontological systems that they involve conflicts of duties for which there exists no principled method of resolution.

(ii) A rule-utilitarian doctor can mount a more convincing case. He can observe that confidentiality is a cornerstone of a successful AIDS practice. Lack of confidentiality can cause the irrational victimisation of sufferers by a poorly educated public who are prone to witch-hunts of all kinds. The detection and treatment of AIDS, and the consequent protection of that large group of people who have contacts with the patients being treated depends on the patients who seek medical advice believing that medical confidentiality is inviolate. If confidentiality were seen as a relative duty only, suspended or breached at the discretion of the doctor, then far fewer cases would present for detection and crucial guidance about diminishing risks of spread would not be obtained. This would lead to more people suffering and dying. It may be hard on a few, unfortunate enough to be involved with people like the recalcitrant young husband, but the general welfare can only be served by a compassionate but resolute refusal to abandon sound principles in the face of such cases. Many find this a convincing argument but I will argue that it is superficial in the understanding of moral issues that it espouses.

Imagine, in order to soften the way for a rather less neatly argued position, a doctor confronted by a young man who has a scratched face and blood on his shirt and who wants to be checked for VD. In the course of the doctor's taking his history it emerges that he has forcibly raped two women and is worried that the second was a prostitute. He says to the doctor "Of course, I am telling you this in confidence, doc, because I know that you won't rat on me". Producing a knife, he then says, "See, this is the blade that I get them going with". Rather troubled, the doctor takes samples and tells the young man that there is no evidence of VD. He tries to talk his patient into giving himself up for some kind of psychiatric treatment but the young man is adamant. It becomes clear that he has certain delusional and persecutional ideas. Two days later the doctor reads that his patient has been arrested because after leaving the surgery he raped and savagely mutilated a young woman who, as a result, required emergency surgery for multiple wounds and remains in a critical condition.

Here we might well feel that any principle which dictates that it is the moral duty of the doctor to keep silent is wrong—but as yet no principles conflicting with or supplementing those above have been introduced. A possible loophole is introduced by the rapist's sadomasochism and probable psychosis but we need to spell out why this is relevant. In such a case we suspend our normal moral obligations to respect the avowed interests of the patient and claim that he is incompetent to make a responsible and informed assessment of his own interests and so we assume the right to make certain decisions on his behalf. In this case it would probably mean arranging for him to be given psychiatric help and society to be protected from him in the meantime. Notice that he may have demonstrated a 'lucid' and 'intelligent' grasp of his predicament, *vis-á-vis* his own wish to avoid detection but we discern that his instrumental rationality is deployed in service of a deep or moral insanity. His lack of awareness of the enormity of what he is doing to others counts as a sufficient basis to diagnose madness even in the face of astute inferential thought. He is insane because a normal person would never begin from the moral position he occupies and so his rights, including that to medical confidentiality, are suspended. He has moved outside the community of trust, mutual concern and nonmalificence in which moral considerations for the preferences of others have their proper place. It is not that one 'contracts in' to such a community,[3] nor that one in any sense volunteers,[4] but rather one is a *de facto* member of it by virtue of possessing those human sensitivities and vulnerabilities which give moral predicates their meaning and importance.[5] Such weight as one claims for one's own personal privileges and moral principles—such as the demand for confidentiality—is derived from a 'form of life' where the interpersonal transactions which define trust, respect, harm, and so on, are in play (it is important that no particular ideological overlay has been grafted onto these). Of the insane rapist we can say that he has excluded himself from that moral community by the very fact of his violation of certain of its most basic tenets and assumptions. He has no right to demand a full place in that structure where morally significant human exchanges are operative because his behavior and attitudes do not fit the place to which he pretends. We are, of course, not released from a *prima facie* duty to try and help him in his odious predicament but we cannot be expected to accord him the full privileges of a member of the moral community as he persists, for whatever reason, in callously turning his back on the constraints normally operative there (albeit, perhaps, without reflective malevolence in its more usual forms). So, in this case, confidentiality can be suspended for legitimate moral reasons. The mad rapist has moved beyond the pale in terms of normal moral interactions and though we may have a duty to try and restore him to full participation within that order we are also entitled to protect ourselves in the interim at the expense of those considerations that would apply to a normal person. Notice again that the boundaries of our attitudes are not arbitrary or merely conventional but involve our most basic human feelings and reactions to one another.[6]

We can now move from a case where insanity weights the decision in a certain direction to a case where the issues are more purely moral. Imagine that a 45-year-old man goes to see his family doctor and is also worried about a sexually transmitted disease. On being questioned he admits, in confidence, not only to intercourse with a series of prostitutes but also to forced sexual intercourse with his daughter. He is confident that she will not tell anyone what is happening because she is too ashamed and scared. After counseling he gives no sign of a wish to change his ways but rather continues to justify himself because of his wife's behaviour. The doctor later hears from the school psychological service that the daughter is showing some potentially serious emotional problems.

Here, it seems to me, we have few compunctions about setting in motion that machinery to deal with child abuse, even though the sole source of our information is what was said, in medical confidence, by the father. The justification we might give for the doctor's actions is illuminating. We are concerned for the actual harm being done to the child, both physical and psychological, and we overturn the father's injunction to confidence in order to prevent further harm being done. In so doing we class the situation as one in which a *prima facie* moral claim can be suspended because of the actions and attitudes involved. I believe that we do so because we implicitly realise that here also the agent has acted in such a way as to put himself beyond the full play of moral consideration and to justify our withholding certain of his moral 'dues'. Confidentiality functions to allow the patient to be honest with the doctor and to put trust in him. Trust is (at least in part) a two-way thing and can only exist between morally sensitive human beings (this, of course, blurs a vast range of distinctions between degrees of sensitivity). A basic element of such moral attitudes is the responsiveness of the agents concerned to the moral features of human interactions. The legitimate expectation that a doctor be trustworthy and faithful to his patient's wishes regardless of the behaviour of that patient is undermined when the patient abuses the relationship so formed in ways which show a lack of these basic human reactions because it is just these reactions which ground the importance of confidentiality in general. Therefore, if the father in this example refuses to accept the enormity of what he is doing to his daughter, he thereby casts doubt upon his standing as a moral agent. Stated baldly, that sounds like an open warrant for moralistic medical paternalism, but I do not think it need be. In asking that his affairs be concealed from others, a person is demanding *either* the right to preserve himself from the harms that might befall him if the facts about his life were generally known, *or* that his sensitivity as an individual be respected and protected. On either count it is inconsistent for him to claim some moral justification for that demand when it is made solely with the aim of allowing him to inflict comparable disregard or harm upon another. By his implicit intention to use a position, which only remains tenable with the collusion of the doctor, callously to harm another individual, the father undermines the moral force of his own appeal. His case is only worsened by the fact that from any moral perspective he would be considered to have a special and protective obligation toward his own offspring.

Implicit within what I have said is a reappraisal of the nature of medical confidentiality. I have argued that it is not to be treated as an absolute duty but is rather to rank among other *prima facie* duties and responsibilities of the doctor-patient relationship. Just as the performance of a life-saving procedure can be vetoed by the patient's choice to forego treatment, even though it is a doctor's duty to strive for his patient's life, so each of these duties can be negated by certain considerations. One generally attempts to prevent a fatal illness overtaking a patient but in the case of a deformed neonate or an elderly and demented patient often the attempt is not made. In the case of confidentiality, I have claimed that we recognise the right of a patient to preserve his own personal life as inviolate. We accept that patients can and should share with a doctor details which it would not be right to disclose to other people. But we must also recognise that implicit within this recognition is the assumption that the patient is one of us, morally speaking. Our attitude to him and his rights assumes that he is one of or a participant in a community of beings who matter (or are morally interacting individuals like himself to whom the same considerations apply). We could offer a superficial and rather gross systematisation of this assumption in the universalisability test.[7] The patient in the last two cases applies a standard to his own human concerns which he is not prepared to extend to others involved with him in relevant situations. We must therefore regard his moral demands as spurious; we are not at liberty to harm him but we are bound to see that his cynical abuse of the moral code within which he lives does not harm others. At this point it might be objected that we are on a 'slippery slope'. Will any moral transgression suffice to undermine the moral privileges of the patient? I do not think that this extreme conclusion can be supported from what I have said. Williams, remarking on the tendency to slide down 'slippery slopes', observes, "that requires that there should be some motive to move from one step to the next" and "Possible cases are not enough, and the situation must have some other feature which means that those cases have to be confronted."[8] Here we are not in such a position. Doctors in general have a strong tendency to protect their patients and keep their confidences. They require strong moral pressures to contemplate doing otherwise. All I have sought to do is to make explicit the moral justification upon which these exceptions can be seen to rest. I have not spelled out any formal decision-making procedure whereby the right answer will be yielded in each case. Indeed it is possible that whereas grounds and reasons recommending a certain course of action are the lifeblood of moral philosophy, such clearcut principles and derivations are a 'will o' the wisp'.

Now we can return to the AIDS patient. From what I have said it becomes clear that it is only the moral intransigent who forces us to breach confidentiality. In most cases it will be possible to guide the patient into telling those who need to know or allowing them to be told (and where it is possible to so guide him it will be mandatory to involve him in an informed way). In the face of an expressed disregard for the harm being caused to those others concerned, we will be morally correct in abandoning what would otherwise be a binding obligation. We should and do feel the need to preserve and protect the already affected life of the potential victim of his deception and in this feeling we exhibit a sensitivity to moral rectitude. Of course, it is only the active sexual partners of the patient who are at risk and thus it is only to them that we and the patient have a moral duty (in this respect talk of 'society at large' is just rhetoric). If it is the case that sexual activity, as Nagel claims, involves a mutual openness in those who have intercourse,[9] one could plausibly argue that the cynical moral and interpersonal attitudes here evinced undermined the patient's sexual rights (assuming that people have such). The sexual activity of this individual is aberrant or perverted in the important respect that it involves a harmful duplicity toward or deception of his sexual partner. Whereas people may have a right to sexual fulfillment in general, they can hardly be said to have a right to perverted sexual fulfillment; but both Nagel's contentions and this talk of rights are contentious and it is outside my present brief to discuss them.

The doctor's obligation to inform, in the face of an enjoinder to keep his confidence, can, even if I am right, be seen to be restricted to those in actual danger and would in no wise extend to employers, friends or non-sexually interacting relatives of the patient or any other person with an even more peripheral interest. His duty extends only so far as to avert the actual harm that he can reasonably expect to arise from his keeping confidence.

Given the intransigent case, one further desideratum presents itself. I believe that doctors should be open with their patients and that therefore the doctor is bound to share his moral dilemma with the patient and inform him of his intention to breach confidentiality. I think he can legitimately claim a pre-emptive duty to prevent harm befalling his patients and should do so in the case of the abuse of others which the patient intends. It may be the case, with the insane rapist for instance, that the doctor will need to deceive in order to carry out his prevailing duty but this will hardly ever be so, and should, I believe, be regarded as unacceptable in general.

One thorny problem remains—the possible deleterious effect on the detection and treatment of AIDS if confidentiality is seen as only a relative principle in medical practice. Clearly, if the attitude were ever to take root that the medical profession could not be trusted to 'keep their mouths shut' then the feared effect would occur. I believe that where agencies and informal groups were told of the *only* grounds on which confidentiality would be breached and the *only* people who would be informed then this effect would not occur.

It seems to me that the remarkable intensification of one's sensitivity to personal and ethical values that is produced by contact with life-threatening or 'abyss' situations means that the cynical abuse of confidentiality by the patient which I have sought to address is likely to be both rare and transient. The greatest resource available to any of us in 'the valley of the shadow' is the closeness of those who will walk alongside us, and for many that will be a close spiritual and sexual partner. Confidentiality within the mutuality of that relationship rather than interpersonal dishonesty would thus seem to be vital to the welfare not only of the co-respondent but also of the patient himself as he struggles to cope with the disease that has him in its grip. To foster that welfare seems to me to be as close as a doctor can ever come to an absolute duty.

Endnotes

1. John Rawls, "Two Concepts of Rules," *Philosophical Review* 64 (1955): 3–32.
2. Jonathan Glover, *Causing Death and Saving Lives* (London: Penguin, 1977).
3. As is suggested by John Rawls in *A Theory of Justice* (Cambridge, Mass.: Harvard University Press, 1971).
4. Philippa Foot, "Morality As a System of Hypothetical Imperatives," in *Virtues and Vices* (Berkeley: University of California Press, 1978).
5. John McDowell suggests that one imbibes the capacities for such judgments as part of the rule-following in which one acquires language, in "Virtue and Reason," *Monist* 62 (1978): 331–350.
6. I stress this point in order to distance the considerations that are guiding our judgment in this case from those situations in which an ideological framework has been used to override these very natural human reactions and provide a 'justification' for an inhuman moral code.
7. R. M. Hare, *Freedom and Reason* (New York: Oxford University Press, 1965).
8. Bernard Williams, "Which Slopes are Slippery?" in M. Lockwood, ed., *Moral Dilemma in Modern Medicine* (Oxford: Oxford University Press, 1986).
9. Thomas Nagel, "Sexual Perversion," in *Mortal Questions* (London: Cambridge University Press, 1979).

Review Questions

1. What is the moral dilemma raised by the case of the man who tests positive for the AIDS virus?

2. Gillett discusses two arguments supporting confidentiality. What are they, and why doesn't Gillett accept them?
3. What is the point of the cases about the mad rapist and the child abuser?
4. How does Gillett view the nature of medical confidentiality?

DISCUSSION QUESTIONS

1. Is the man who tests positive for the AIDS virus comparable to the mad rapist and the child abuser or not? Why or why not?
2. Suppose that certain people are, as Gillett says, beyond the pale of normal moral interaction. Does this mean that we have no moral duties or obligations towards these people? What do you think?
3. Gillett admits that his position "sounds like an open warrant for moralistic medical paternalism." Does his view amount to this or not? Explain your answer.
4. Does a person with multiple sexual partners have a moral obligation to be routinely tested for the AIDS virus?

PROBLEM CASES

*1. **Gays in the Military.*** (This issue has received a great deal of attention in the press.) The official policy of the Pentagon is to prohibit homosexuals and lesbians from serving in the military. The Pentagon stated its rationale for banning gays in the military in a policy statement issued in 1982. The statement claims that men or women who engage in homosexual (or lesbian) conduct undermine discipline, good order, and morale. The military has maintained this policy despite evidence that a large number of gays and lesbians now serve in the military and openly admit their sexual orientation.

Not long after he took office, President Bill Clinton ordered the Pentagon to review its policy on gays and to report on the implications of lifting the current ban. President Clinton has stated that he wants to lift the ban on gays.

The military is strongly opposed. A representative argument against lifting the ban appears in an article on the Op-Ed page of the *New York Times*, March 29, 1993 by Bernard E. Trainor, a retired Marine lieutenant, and Eric L. Chase, a colonel in the Marine Corps Reserve. These marines deny that they are bigots and reject the charge that discrimination against gays is analogous to racial discrimination (which they condemn). They give two reasons for banning gays from the military. The first one has to do with male bonding. To be effective in combat, men must bond together. But heterosexual men, they say, could never bond in the right way with homosexual men. (Male bonding must never be sexual.) The second reason is that homosexuals in the military would produce unacceptable sexual tension.

This argument raises some interesting questions. What is male bonding, and why is it necessary for combat? Why can't heterosexual men nonsexually bond with homosexual men? Why is sexual tension unacceptable?

Suppose we accept these as good reasons for banning gays from the military. Don't they apply equally well to women? Should women be banned too?

If we allow women in the military, but exclude them from combat, then should we have the same policy for gays?

*2. **Gay Partnerships.*** (Reported in *The New York Times*, October 2, 1989.) In the reading, Mohr notes that gay men cannot get married in the United States. But Denmark has recently legalized gay unions or partnerships after a forty-year campaign by gay rights advocates. Gay men and women can be legally joined in registered partnerships that provide most of the same rights as marriage. The partners are liable for each other's maintenance; they have the automatic right to inherit each other's property; they must undergo legal proceedings to dissolve the partnership; and if separated, they may have to pay alimony. The gay partners, however, are not allowed to adopt or obtain joint custody of a child.

Are these partnerships morally acceptable? If not, then why not? Are there any reasons why gay couples should not be allowed to adopt or have custody of children? Why are they?

*3. **Premarital AIDS Tests.*** (Reported in *The New York Times*, September 25, 1989.) Since 1938, couples in Illinois have been required to take premarital blood tests to get a marriage license. Originally, the test was for syphilis. But in June 1987, Illinois added a required test for the HIV virus at a cost of $20 to $150 per person. The test has been blamed for a sharp drop in the number of marriage licenses issued in Illinois, from nearly 100,000 in 1987 to fewer than 80,000 in 1988. In the first one and a half years that the test was used, there were fifty-two HIV-positive tests among the 240,000 tests.

Should a premarital HIV test be required? What is your position?

4. ***An HIV Test Without Consent.*** (This case is described and discussed by Joel D. Howell and Carl Cohen in *The Hastings Center Report*, August/September, 1988, pp. 18–20. Howell is opposed to the test, and Cohen is in favor of it.) A sixty-seven-year-old woman is admitted to the hospital with a recent onset of jaundice. She has a two-year history of pancytopenia, or aplastic anemia, a blood disease in which the red cells, white cells, and platelet cells in the blood are reduced in number. It is caused by a failure to produce stem cells, the earliest form of all blood cells in the bone marrow. She is weak and has an abnormal chest X-ray. After several days of intense investigation, the primary care physician and consulting doctors remain uncertain about the underlying disease and how to treat it.

While reviewing her chart, the attending physician notes the order for an HIV antibody test. (The woman received blood transfusions five years earlier, before blood supplies were routinely screened for the presence of antibodies to the HIV virus.) No one has told the woman about the test, despite the fact that she is mentally competent. When asked about the test, the hospital staff replies that the HIV test is medically indicated and that blood samples are routinely drawn without obtaining specific consent.

Should hospital patients be told and give their consent before an HIV test is conducted?

5. ***AIDS and Insurance.*** As Dr. Crenshaw said in the reading, there are about 1.5 million Americans infected with the AIDS virus. Let us conservatively estimate that the cost of care per AIDS patient is $100,000. This figure covers only hospital care and not outpatient care, counseling, or other expenses. That brings the total cost of hospital treatment for the 1.5 million HIV-positive people to approximately 150 billion dollars. This assumes that the number of HIV-positive people remains constant, which, of course, is unlikely. The other variable is the number of HIV-positive patients who actually receive care in a hospital. Now the problem is obvious: Who is going to pay?

No doubt, insurance companies will be paying billions of dollars for AIDS-related claims in the next few years as they fulfill their obligations to current policyholders. But should insurance companies continue to do this? If they do, they will have to raise their rates to cover the increased cost, and HIV-negative people will have to subsidize the care of HIV-positive people. Is this fair? Why not charge more for those who test positive for HIV? To do this, insurance companies would have to screen insurance applicants for the AIDS virus; they would have to require HIV testing.

Should HIV testing be required in order to obtain medical insurance? If not, then who should pay for AIDS treatment?

Suggested Readings

1. Robert Baker and Frederick Elliston, eds., *Philosophy and Sex,* new revised edition (Buffalo, NY: Prometheus Books, 1984). This anthology contains a number of useful articles relevant to sexual morality.

2. Peter A. Bertocci, *Sex, Love, and the Person* (New York: Sheed & Ward, 1967). Bertocci defends conventional morality.

3. Andrea Dworkin, *Intercourse* (New York: Macmillan, The Free Press, 1987). Dworkin is a radical feminist who argues that heterosexual intercourse is a patriarchal institution that degrades and enslaves women.

4. Burton Leiser, *Liberty, Justice and Morals,* 2nd Edition (New York: Macmillan, 1979). In Chapter 2, Leiser attacks arguments for saying that homosexuality is immoral.

5. Michael Ruse, *Homosexuality: A Philosophical Inquiry* (Cambridge, MA: Basil Blackwell, 1990). Ruse gives a careful and detailed discussion of various issues related to homosexuality. He argues that homosexuality is not unnatural, not immoral, and not a sexual perversion.

6. Michael Levin, "Why Homosexuality is Abnormal," *The Monist,* vol. 67, no. 2 (1984), pp. 260–276. Levin argues that homosexuality is inherently abnormal and immoral because it is a misuse of body parts.

7. Vincent C. Punzo, *Reflective Naturalism* (New York: Macmillan, 1969). Punzo argues against premarital sex. In his view, marriage is constituted by mutual and total commitment, and absent commitment, sexual unions are morally deficient.

8. Richard Taylor, *Having Love Affairs* (Buffalo, NY: Prometheus Books, 1982). Taylor claims that people have a right to love affairs even if they are married. He also thinks there is nothing wrong with people living together without being legally married.

9. Carl Wellman, *Morals and Ethics* (Glenview, IL: Scott, Foresman, 1975). In Chapter 5, Wellman examines arguments for and against the morality of premarital sex.

10. Jeffner Allen, ed., *Lesbian Philosophies* (Albany, NY: State University of New York Press, 1990). This is a collection of articles on lesbianism by lesbians. It includes a candid account of lesbian sex by Marilyn Frye; one of the important features is the lack of phallocentricity (to use her term).

11. Nora Kizer Bell, "Women and AIDS: Too Little, Too Late," *Hypatia,* Vol. 4, No. 3 (Fall, 1989), pp. 3–22. Bell discusses the risk of women contracting the AIDS virus through sexual contact. she reports an increase in the number of women getting AIDS from heterosexual sex. One reason for this, she says, is that it is easier for the HIV virus to be transmitted from a man to a woman than vice versa.

12. Carol Levine and Joyce Bermel, eds. "AIDS: The Emerging Ethical Dilemmas," *Hasting Center Report, A Special Supplement* (August 1985), pp. 1–31. This report covers various issues arising from the AIDS epidemic.

13. Gerald M. Oppenheimer and Robert A. Padgag, "AIDS: The Risks to Insurers, The Threat to Equity," *Hastings Center Report* (October 1986), pp. 18–22. The authors discuss the problems the AIDS crisis poses for the insurance industry.

14. Lawrence O. Gostin, William J. Curran, and Mary E. Clark, "The Case against Compulsory Casefinding in Controlling AIDS—Testing, Screening, and Reporting," *American Journal of Law and Medicine* 12 (1987), pp. 7–53. The authors argue against HIV testing and screening because the human and economic costs outweigh the benefits for public health.

15. Christine Pierce and Donald VanDeVeer, eds., *AIDS: Ethics and Public Policy* (Belmont, CA: Wadsworth, 1987). This collection of readings includes David Mayo, "AIDS, Quarantines, and Non-Compliant Positives"; Donald Chambers, "AIDS Testing: An Insurer's Viewpoint"; Kenneth R. Howe, "Why Mandatory Screening for AIDS Is a Very Bad Idea"; and other interesting articles on AIDS and its implications.

16. *SPIN* Magazine has an article on AIDS in every issue. In the January 1993, issue Celia Farber discusses cases of clinical AIDS without the HIV virus. These cases raise troubling questions about the cause of AIDS: Is the HIV virus really the cause? Are there other causes? In the October 1992, and April 1993, issues, Farber covers the AIDS crisis in Africa. Again, there are questions about what counts as AIDS and what causes AIDS. Farber claims that the AIDS epidemic in Africa is not as extensive as in the U.S.

Chapter Eight

ANIMALS AND THE ENVIRONMENT

Introduction

Humans cause a great deal of animal suffering. Consider this example of animal experimentation taken from Peter Singer's book *Animal Liberation*. At the Lovelace Foundation in New Mexico, experimenters forced sixty-four beagles to inhale radioactive strontium 90. Twenty-five of the dogs died; initially most of them were feverish and anemic, suffering from hemorrhages and bloody diarrhea. One of the deaths occurred during an epileptic seizure, and another resulted from a brain hemorrhage. In a similar experiment, beagles were injected with enough strontium 90 to produce early death in fifty percent of the group. Are experiments such as these really necessary? It was already known that strontium 90 was unhealthy and that the dogs would suffer and die. Furthermore, these experiments did not save any human lives or have any important benefits for humans. So why were they done?

Another common human practice that produces considerable animal suffering is factory farming. Take the treatment of veal calves for example. In order to make their flesh pale and tender, these calves are given special treatment. They are put in narrow stalls and tethered with a chain so that they cannot turn around, lie down comfortably, or groom themselves. They are fed a totally liquid diet to promote rapid weight gain. This diet is deficient in iron, and, as a result, the calves lick the sides of the stall, which are impregnated with urine containing iron. They are given no water because thirsty animals eat more than those who drink water. Is this cruel treatment morally justified? Should we do this to animals just because we enjoy eating their flesh?

Speciesism. In the first reading for the chapter, Peter Singer introduces the term speciesism. As he defines it, speciesism is "a prejudice or attitude of bias toward the interests of members of one's own species and against those of members of other species." Singer goes on to argue that speciesism is analogous to racism and sexism. It is unjust to discriminate against blacks because of their color or against women because of their sex. Their interests, e.g., their interest in voting, have to be considered equally to those of whites and men. Similarly, it is unjust to discriminate against nonhuman animals because of their species. Their interests, and particularly their interest in not suffering, have to be considered too.

But how do we go about reducing animal suffering? Does this mean that we should become vegetarians and eat no meat? Singer thinks so, but of course this is very controversial in our meat-eating society. In Singer's view, we should stop eating meat in order to eliminate factory farming or at least to protest against it; we should not treat animals as means to our end (to use Kant's phrase).

Singer's position is attacked by Bonnie Steinbock in our readings. Steinbock thinks that Singer's view has counter-intuitive results. It implies, for example, that it is unfair to feed starving children before feeding starving dogs. But it seems intuitively obvious that the interests of humans are more important than those of animals. Why is this? According to Steinbock, humans have a higher moral status than animals because humans have certain morally relevant capacities that animals do not have—for example, the capacity to be morally responsible for actions, to have altruistic or moral reasons, and to desire self-respect.

Tom Regan takes a different position on the moral status of nonhuman animals. Unlike Singer, he does not want to appeal to any form of utilitarianism. According to Regan, utilitarianism is not an acceptable moral theory because it incorrectly makes the morality of individual acts dependent on how others behave. Nevertheless, Regan does think that we ought to be vegetarians and oppose commercial animal agriculture. We should do this not simply because of the good consequences, but because some animals are persons who have moral rights, and commercial animal agriculture violates these rights.

Rights Theory. In his defense of vegetarianism, Regan relies heavily on the concept of a moral right, but there is controversy about the concept of a right and how it should be applied.

According to Joel Feinberg, to have a right is to have a claim *to* something and *against* someone. In his view, only beings who are capable of having interests are capable of having these claim-rights. But animals do have interests, and so they can have rights.

H. J. McCloskey has a different theory of rights. (His view is discussed in the Feinberg reading.) In McCloskey's analysis, a right is an entitlement to something and not a claim against someone. A person could have a right and not have a claim against someone else, for example, if he or she were the last person on earth. Nevertheless, McCloskey holds that being able to make a claim, either directly or through a representative, is essential to the possession of rights. Since animals cannot do this (or so McCloskey says), they cannot be possessors of rights.

Regan agrees with Feinberg that in order for an individual to have a right, there must be other people; it would not make sense to say that the last person on earth has any rights. In Regan's account, if an individual has a moral right, then there must be other moral agents who have a duty to respect it. But who possesses rights? Regan's answer is different from that of Feinberg or McCloskey. Regan's position is that only individuals who have inherent value have rights, where inherent value is a value that does not depend on utility. Those who have this inherent value are persons, and according to Regan, some animals are persons who have rights.

Mary Anne Warren rejects Regan's strong animal rights position, the view that some nonhuman mammals have the same basic moral rights as humans. She complains that Regan's notion of inherent value is a mysterious non-natural property that is not adequately explained. As a result, it fails to produce any clear distinction between those who have rights and those who don't. She calls her own alternative view a weak animal rights theory. On this theory, animals have rights, but they are weaker than human rights. Still these weak animal rights require us not to make animals suffer and not to kill them without a good reason.

Sentientism. Singer, Regan, and Feinberg all seem to assume that only conscious or sentient beings can have rights or be of moral concern. Trees and other natural objects are not conscious, so, in their view, they cannot have rights. But isn't this sentientism (to put a label on it) just another kind of prejudice? They have escaped one prejudice, speciesism, only to embrace another, namely sentientism. Why not say that nonsentient things such as forests have rights too?

This is the approach of Christopher D. Stone in the reading. Stone argues that in order to protect and preserve the environment, we should extend legal rights to trees, forests, rivers, and other natural objects. Even though this may seem absurd at first, Stone maintains that natural objects should have the same legal status as other things that cannot speak for themselves such as infants, estates, corporations, or universities. Lawyers could act as friends of natural objects and protect their interests. This would make it easier to preserve the natural environment, and it would result in a different perspective on nature—where nature is not just something to be used up.

Anthropocentrism. The view rejected by Stone is sometimes called anthropocentrism; this is the view that the natural environment has value only as means of producing human benefits. Although he does not use the term, Baxter seems to adopt and defend anthropocentrism in the reading. He claims that the natural environment (including penguins) counts only as a means of producing various human benefits; it is not an end in itself, and has no value apart from humans.

Holism. William Godfrey-Smith rejects the anthropocentric view that the environment has only instrumental value for humans. He thinks that instrumental justifications for environmental conservation—saving the wilderness because it is a cathedral, a laboratory, a silor, or a gymnasium—all fail to provide a satisfactory rationale. Not only are there conflicts between the activities that can be justified, there is also the feeling that the wilderness has more than **instrumental value**, that is has an **intrinsic value.** Instead of sentientism or an anthropocentric view, Godfrey-Smith suggests that we adopt a holistic concept of nature where we think of humans and nature together forming a moral community, and where we must engage in cooperative (not exploitive) behavior for the sake of the health of the whole community. This means that we should have empathy for nature and not think of ourselves as separate from it or superior to it.

Peter Singer

All Animals Are Equal

For biographical information on Singer, see his reading in Chapter 3.

Singer defines speciesism as a prejudice towards the interests of members of one's own species and against those of members of other species. He argues that speciesism is analogous to racism and sexism. If it is unjust to discriminate against women and blacks by not considering their interests, it is also unfair to ignore the interests of animals, particularly their interest in not suffering.

From Peter Singer, *Animal Liberation* (The New York Review, 1975). Reprinted by permission of the author.

"Animal Liberation" may sound more like a parody of other liberation movements than a serious objective. The idea of "The Rights of Animals" actually was once used to parody the case for women's rights. When Mary Wollstonecraft, a forerunner of today's feminists, published her *Vindication of the Rights of Women* in 1792, her views were widely regarded as absurd, and before long an anonymous publication appeared entitled *A Vindication of the Rights of Brutes*. The author of this satirical work (now known to have been Thomas Taylor, a distinguished Cambridge philosopher) tried to refute Mary Wollstonecraft's arguments by showing that they could be carried one stage further. If the argument for equality was sound when applied to women, why should it not be applied to dogs, cats, and horses? The reasoning seemed to hold for these "brutes" too, yet to hold that brutes had rights was manifestly absurd; therefore the reasoning by which this conclusion had been reached must be unsound, and if unsound when applied to brutes, it must also be unsound when applied to women, since the very same arguments had been used in each case.

In order to explain the basis of the case for the equality of animals, it will be helpful to start with an examination of the case for the equality of women. Let us assume that we wish to defend the case for women's rights against the attack by Thomas Taylor. How should we reply?

One way in which we might reply is by saying that the case for equality between men and women cannot validly be extended to nonhuman animals. Women have a right to vote, for instance, because they are just as capable of making rational decisions about the future as men are; dogs, on the other hand, are incapable of understanding the significance of voting, so they cannot have the right to vote. There are many other obvious ways in which men and women resemble each other closely, while humans and animals differ greatly. So, it might be said, men and women are similar beings and should have similar rights, while humans and nonhumans are different and should not have equal rights.

The reasoning behind this reply to Taylor's analogy is correct up to a point, but it does not go far enough. There *are* important differences between humans and other animals, and these differences must give rise to *some* differences in the rights that each have. Recognizing this obvious fact, however, is no barrier to the case for extending the basic principle of equality to nonhuman animals. The differences that exist between men and women are equally undeniable, and the supporters of Women's Liberation are aware that these differences may give rise to different rights. Many feminists hold that women have the right to an abortion on request. It does not follow that since these same feminists are campaigning for equality between men and women they must support the right of men to have abortions too. Since a man cannot have an abortion, it is meaningless to talk of his right to have one. Since a dog can't vote, it is meaningless to talk of its right to vote. There is no reason why either Women's Liberation or Animal Liberation should get involved in such nonsense. The extension of the basic principle of equality from one group to another does not imply that we must treat both groups in exactly the same way, or grant exactly the same rights to both groups. Whether we should do so will depend on the nature of the members of the two groups. The basic principle of equality does not require equal or identical *treatment;* it requires equal *consideration*. Equal consideration for different beings may lead to different treatment and different rights.

So there is a different way of replying to Taylor's attempt to parody the case for women's rights, a way that does not deny the obvious differences between humans and nonhumans but goes more deeply into the question of equality and concludes by finding nothing absurd in the idea that the basic principle of equality applies to so-called brutes. At this point such a conclusion may appear odd; but if we examine more deeply the basis on which our opposition to discrimination on grounds of race or sex ultimately rests, we will see that we would be on shaky ground if we were to demand equality for blacks, women, and other groups of oppressed humans while denying equal consideration to nonhumans. To make this clear we need to see first, exactly why racism and sexism are wrong.

When we say that all human beings, whatever their race, creed, or sex, are equal, what is it that we are asserting? Those who wish to defend hierarchical, inegalitarian societies have often pointed out that by whatever test we choose it simply is not true that all humans are equal. Like it or not we must face the fact that humans come in different shapes and sizes; they come with different moral capacities, different intellectual abilities, different amounts of benevolent feeling and sensitivity to the needs of others, different abilities to communicate effectively, and different capacities to experience pleasure and pain. In short, if the demand for equality were based on the actual equality of all human beings, we would have to stop demanding equality.

Still, one might cling to the view that the demand for equality among human beings is based on the actual equality of the different races and sexes. Although, it may be said, humans differ as individuals there are no differences between the races and sexes *as such*. From the mere fact that a person is black or a woman we cannot infer anything about that person's intellectual or moral capacities. This, it may be said, is why racism and sexism are wrong. The white racist claims that whites are superior to blacks, but this is false—although there are differences among individuals, some blacks are superior to some whites in all of the capacities and abilities that could conceivably be relevant. The opponent of sexism would say the same: a person's sex is no guide to his or her abilities, and this is why it is unjustifiable to discriminate on the basis of sex.

The existence of individual variations that cut across the lines of race or sex, however, provides us with no defense at all against a more sophisticated opponent of equality, one who proposes that, say, the interests of all those with IQ scores below 100 be given less consideration than the interests of those with ratings over 100. Perhaps those scoring below the mark, would, in this society, be made the slaves of those scoring higher. Would a hierarchical society of this sort really be so much better than one based on race of sex? I think not. But if we tie the moral principle of equality to the factual equality of the different races or sexes, taken as a whole, our opposition to racism and sexism does not provide us with any basis for objecting to this kind of inegalitarianism.

There is a second important reason why we ought not to base our opposition to racism and sexism on any kind of actual equality, even the limited kind that asserts that variations in capacities and abilities are spread evenly between the different races and sexes: we can have no absolute guarantee that these capacities and abilities really are distributed evenly, without regard to race or sex, among human beings. So far as actual abilities are concerned there do seem to be certain measurable differences between both races and sexes. These differences do not, of course, appear in each case, but only when averages are taken. More important still, we do not yet know how much of these differences is really due to the different genetic endowments of the different races and sexes, and how much is due to poor schools, poor housing, and other factors that are the result of past and continuing discrimination. Perhaps all the important differences will eventually prove to be environmental rather than genetic. Anyone opposed to racism and sexism will certainly hope that this will be so, for it will make the task of ending discrimination a lot easier; nevertheless it would be dangerous to rest the case against racism and sexism on the belief that all significant differences are environmental in origin. The opponent of, say, racism who takes this line will be unable to avoid conceding that *if* differences in ability do after all prove to have some genetic connection with race, racism would in some way be defensible.

Fortunately there is no need to pin the case for equality to one particular outcome of a scientific investigation. The appropriate response to those who claim to have found evidence of genetically based differences in ability between the races or sexes is not to stick to the belief that the genetic explanation must be wrong, whatever evidence to the contrary may turn up: instead we should make it quite clear that the claim to equality does not depend on intelligence, moral capacity, physical strength, or similar matters of fact. Equality is a moral idea, not an assertion of fact. There is no logically compelling reason for assuming that a factual difference in ability between two people justifies any difference in the amount of consideration we give to their needs and interests. *The principle of the equality of human beings is not a description of an alleged actual equality among humans; it is a prescription of how we should treat humans.*

Jeremy Bentham, the founder of the reforming utilitarian school of moral philosophy, incorporated the essential basis of moral equality into his system of ethics by means of the formula: "Each to count for one and none for more than one." In other words, the interests of every being affected by an action are to be taken into account and given the same weight as the like interests of any other being. A later utilitarian, Henry Sidgwick, put the point in this way: "The good of any one individual is of no more importance, from the point of view (if I may say so) of the Universe, than the good of any other." More recently the leading figures in contemporary moral philosophy have shown a great deal of agreement in specifying as a fundamental presupposition of their moral theories some similar requirement that operates so as to give everyone's interests equal consideration—although these writers generally cannot agree on how this requirement is best formulated.[1]

It is an implication of this principle of equality that our concern for others and our readiness to consider their interests ought not to depend on what they are like or on what abilities they may possess. Precisely what this concern or consideration requires us to do may vary according to the characteristics of those affected by what we do: concern for the well-being of a child growing up in America would require that we teach him to read; concern for the well-being of a pig may require no more than that we leave him alone with other pigs in a place where there is adequate food and room to run freely. But the basic element—the taking into account of the interests of the being, whatever those interests may be—must, according to the principle of equality, be extended to all beings, black or white, masculine or feminine, human or nonhuman.

Thomas Jefferson, who was responsible for writing the principle of the equality of men into the American Declaration of Independence, saw this point. It led him to oppose slavery even though he was unable to free himself fully from his slaveholding background. He wrote in a letter to the author of a book that emphasized the notable intellectual achievements of Negroes in order to refute the then common view that they had limited intellectual capacities:

> Be assured that no person living wishes more sincerely than I do, to see a complete refutation of the doubts I have myself entertained and expressed on the grade of understanding allotted to them by nature, and to find that they are on a par with ourselves . . . but whatever be their degree of talent it is no measure of their rights. Because Sir Isaac Newton was superior to others in understanding, he was not therefore lord of the property or person of others.[2]

Similarly when in the 1850s the call for women's rights was raised in the United States a remarkable black feminist named Sojourner Truth made the same point in more robust terms at a feminist convention:

> . . . they talk about this thing in the head; what do they call it? ["Intellect," whispered someone near by.] That's it. What's that got to do with women's rights or Negroes' rights? If my cup won't hold but a pint and yours holds a quart, wouldn't you be mean not to let me have my little half-measure full?[3]

It is on this basis that the case against racism and the case against sexism must both ultimately rest; and it is in accordance with this principle that the attitude that we may call "speciesism," by analogy with racism, must also be condemned. Speciesism—the word is not an attractive one, but I can think of no better term—is a prejudice or attitude of bias toward the interests of members of one's own species and against those of members of other species. It should be obvious that the fundamental objections to racism and sexism made by Thomas Jefferson and Sojourner Truth apply equally to speciesism. If possessing a higher degree of intelligence does not entitle one human to use another for his own ends, how can it entitle humans to exploit nonhumans for the same purpose?[4]

Many philosophers and other writers have proposed the principle of equal consideration of interests, in some form or other, as a basic moral principle, but not many of them have recognized that this principle applies to members of other species as well as to our own. Jeremy Bentham was one of the few who did realize this. In a forward-looking passage written at a time when black slaves had been freed by the French but the British dominions were still being treated in the way we now treat animals, Bentham wrote:

> The day may come when the rest of the animal creation may acquire those rights which never could have been withholden from them but by the hand of tyranny. The French have already discovered that the blackness of the skin is no reason why a human being should be abandoned without redress to the caprice of a tormentor. It may one day come to be recognized that the number of the legs, the villosity of the skin, or the termination of the os sacrum are reasons equally insufficient for abandoning a sensitive being to the same fate. What else is it that should trace the insuperable line? Is it the faculty of reason, or perhaps the faculty of discourse? But a full-grown horse or dog is beyond comparison a more rational, as well as a more conversable animal, than an infant of day or a week or even a month old. But suppose they were otherwise, what would it avail? The question is not, Can they reason? nor Can they talk? but, Can they suffer? [5]

In this passage Bentham points to the capacity for suffering as the vital characteristic that gives a being the right to equal consideration. The capacity for suffering—or more strictly, for suffering and/or enjoyment or happiness—is not just another characteristic like the capacity for language or higher mathematics. Bentham is not saying that those who try to mark "the insuperable line" that determines whether the interests of a being should be considered happen to have chosen the wrong characteristic. By saying that we must consider the interests of all beings with the capacity for suffering or enjoyment Bentham does not arbitrarily exclude from consideration any interests at all—as those who draw the line with reference to the possession of reason or language do. The capacity for suffering and enjoyment is a *prerequisite for having interests at all*, a condition that must be satisfied before we can speak of interests in a meaningful way. It would be nonsense to say that it was not in the interests of a stone to be kicked along the road by a schoolboy. A stone does not have interests because it cannot suffer. Nothing that we can do to it could possibly make any difference to its welfare. A mouse, on the other hand, does have an interest in not being kicked along the road, because it will suffer if it is.

If a being suffers there can be no moral justification for refusing to take that suffering into consideration. No matter what the nature of the being, the principle of equality requires that its suffering be counted equally with the like suffering—insofar as rough comparisons can be made—of any other being. If a being is not capable of suffering, or of experiencing enjoyment or happiness, there is nothing to be taken into account. So the limit of sentience (using the term as a convenient if not strictly accurate shorthand for the capacity to suffer and/or experience enjoyment) is the only defensible boundary of concern for the interests of others. To mark this boundary by some other characteristic like intelligence or rationality would be to mark it in an arbitrary manner. Why not choose some other characteristic, like skin color?

The racist violates the principle of equality by giving greater weight to the interests of members of his own race when there is a clash between their interests and the interests of those of another race. The sexist violates the principle of equality by favoring the interests of his own sex. Similarly the speciesist allows the interests of his own species to override the greater interests of members of other species. The pattern is identical in each case.

Most human beings are speciesists. Ordinary human beings—not a few exceptionally cruel or heartless humans, but the overwhelming majority of humans—take an active part in, acquiesce in, and allow their taxes to pay for practices that require the sacrifice of the most important interests of members of other species in order to promote the most trivial interests of our own species. . . .

Animals can feel pain. As we saw earlier, there can be no moral justification for regarding the pain (or pleasure) that animals feel as less important than the same amount of pain (or pleasure) felt by humans. But what exactly does this mean, in practical terms? To prevent misunderstanding I shall spell out what I mean a little more fully.

If I give a horse a hard slap across its rump with my open hand, the horse may start, but it presumably feels little pain. Its skin is thick enough to protect it against a mere slap. If I slap a baby in the same way, however, the baby will cry and presumably does feel pain, for its skin is more sensitive. So it is worse to slap a baby than a horse, if both slaps are administered with equal force. But there must be some kind of blow—I don't know exactly what it would be, but perhaps a blow with a heavy stick—that would cause the horse as much pain as we cause a baby by slapping it with our hand. That is what I mean by "the same amount of pain" and if we consider it wrong to inflict that much pain on a baby for no good reason then we must, unless we are speciesists, consider it equally wrong to inflict the same amount of pain on a horse for no good reason.

There are other differences between humans and animals that cause other complications. Normal adult human beings have mental capacities that will, in certain circumstances, lead them to suffer more than animals would in the same circumstances. If, for instance, we decided to perform extremely painful or lethal scientific experiments on normal adult humans, kidnapped at random from public parks for this purpose, every adult who entered a park would become fearful that he would be kidnapped. The resultant terror would be a form of suffering additional to the pain of the experiment. The same experiments performed on nonhuman animals would cause less suffering since the animals would not have the anticipatory dread of being kidnapped and experimented upon. This does not mean, of course, that it would be right to perform the experiment on animals, but only that there is a reason, which is *not* speciesist, for preferring to use animals rather than normal adult humans, if the experiment is to be done at all. It should be noted, however, that this same argument gives us a reason for preferring to use human infants—orphans perhaps—or retarded humans for experiments, rather than adults, since infants and retarded humans would also have no idea of what was going to happen to them. So far as this argument is concerned nonhuman animals and infants and retarded humans are in the same category; and if we use this argument to justify experiments on nonhuman animals we have to ask ourselves whether we are also prepared to allow experiments on humans, on what basis can we do it, other than a barefaced—and morally indefensible—preference for members of our own species?

There are many areas in which the superior mental powers of normal adult humans make a difference: anticipation, more detailed memory, greater knowledge of what is happening, and so on. Yet these differences do not all point to greater suffering on the part of the normal human being. Sometimes an animal may suffer more because of his more limited understanding. If, for instance, we are taking prisoners in wartime we can explain to them that while they must submit to capture, search, and confinement they will not otherwise be harmed and will be set free at the conclusion of hostilities. If we capture a wild animal, however, we cannot explain that we are not threatening its life. A wild animal cannot distinguish an attempt to overpower and confine from an attempt to kill; the one causes as much terror as the other.

It may be objected that comparisons of the sufferings of different species are impossible to make, and that for this reason when the interests of animals and humans clash the principle of equality gives no guidance. It is probably true that comparisons of suffering between members of different species cannot be made precisely, but precision is not essential. Even if we were to prevent the infliction of suffering on animals only when it is quite certain that the interests of humans will not be affected to anything like the extent that animals are affected, we would be forced to make radical changes in our treatment of animals that would involve our diet, the farming methods we use, experimental procedures in many fields of science, our approach to wildlife and to hunting, trapping and the wearing of furs, and areas of entertainment like circuses, rodeos, and zoos. As a result, a vast amount of suffering would be avoided.

So far I have said a lot about the infliction of suffering on animals, but nothing about killing them. This omission has been deliberate. The application of the principle of equality to the infliction of suffering is, in theory at least, fairly straightforward. Pain and suffering are bad and should be prevented or minimized, irrespective of the race, sex, or species of the being that suffers. How bad a pain is depends on how intense it is and how long it lasts, but pains of the same intensity and duration are equally bad, whether felt by humans or animals.

The wrongness of killing a being is more complicated. I have kept, and shall continue to keep, the question of killing in the background because in the present state of human tyranny over other species the more simple, straightforward principle of equal consideration of pain or pleasure is a sufficient basis for identifying and protesting against all the major abuses of animals that humans practice. Nevertheless, it is necessary to say something about killing.

Just as most humans are speciesists in their readiness to cause pain to animals when they would not cause a similar pain to humans for the same reason, so most humans are speciesists in their readiness to kill other animals when they would not kill humans. We need to proceed more cautiously here, however, because people hold widely differing views about when it is legitimate to kill humans, as the continuing debates over abortion and euthanasia attest. Nor have moral philosophers been able to agree on exactly what it is that makes it wrong to kill humans, and under what circumstances killing a human being may be justifiable.

Let us consider first the view that it is always wrong to take an innocent human life. We may call this the "sanctity of life" view. People who take this view oppose abortion and euthanasia. They do not usually, however, oppose the killing of nonhumans—so perhaps it would be more accurate to describe this view as the "sanctity of *human* life" view.

The belief that human life, and only human life, is sacrosanct is a form of speciesism. To see this, consider the following example.

Assume that, as sometimes happens, an infant has been born with massive and irreparable brain damage. The damage is so severe that the infant can never be any more than a "human vegetable," unable to talk, recognize other people, act independently of others, or develop a sense of self-awareness. The parents of the infant, realizing that they cannot hope for any improvement in their child's condition and being in any case unwilling to spend, or ask the state to spend, the thousands of dollars that would be needed annually for proper care of the infant, ask the doctor to kill the infant painlessly.

Should the doctor do what the parents ask? Legally, he should not, and in this respect the law reflects the sanctity of life view. The life of every human being is sacred. Yet people who would say this about the infant do not object to the killing of nonhuman animals. How can they justify their different judgments? Adult chimpanzees, dogs, pigs, and many other species far surpass the brain-damaged infant in their ability to relate to others, act independently, be self-aware, and any other capacity that could reasonably be said to give value to life. With the most intensive care possible, there are retarded infants who can never achieve the intelligence level of a dog. Nor can we appeal to the concern of the infant's parents, since they themselves, in this imaginary example (and in some actual cases), do not want the infant kept alive.

The only thing that distinguishes the infant from the animal, in the eyes of those who claim it has a "right to life," is that it is, biologically, a member of the species Homo Sapiens, whereas chimpanzees, dogs, and pigs are not. But to use *this* difference as the basis for granting a right to life to the infant and not to the other animals is, of course, pure speciesism.[6] It is exactly the kind of arbitrary difference that the most crude and overt kind of racist uses in attempting to justify racial discrimination.

This does not mean that to avoid speciesism we must hold that it is as wrong to kill a dog as it is to kill a normal human being. The only position that is irredeemably speciesist is the one that tries to make the boundary of the right to life run exactly parallel to the boundary of our own species. Those who hold the sanctity of life view do this because while distinguishing sharply between humans and other animals they allow no distinctions to be made within our own species, objecting to the killing of the severely retarded and the hopelessly senile as strongly as they object to the killing of normal adults.

To avoid speciesism we must allow that beings that are similar in all relevant respects have a similar right to life—and mere membership in our own biological species cannot be a morally relevant criterion for this right. Within these limits we could still hold that, for instance, it is worse to kill a normal adult human, with a capacity for self-awareness, and the ability to plan for the future and have meaningful relations with others, than it is to kill a mouse, which presumably does not share all of these characteristics; or we might appeal to the close family and other personal ties that humans have but mice do not have to the same degree; or we might think that it is the consequences for other humans, who will be put in fear of their own lives, that makes the crucial difference; or we might think it is some combination of these factors, or other factors altogether.

Whatever criteria we choose, however, we will have to admit that they do not follow precisely the boundary of our own species. We may legitimately hold that there are some features of certain beings which make their lives more valuable than those of other beings; but there will surely be some nonhuman animals whose lives, by any standards, are more valuable than the lives of some humans. A chimpanzee, dog, or pig, for instance, will have a higher degree of self-awareness and a greater capacity for meaningful relations with others than a severely retarded infant or someone in a state of advanced senility. So if we base the right to life on these characteristics we must grant these animals a right to life as good as, or better than, such retarded or senile humans.

Now this argument cuts both ways. It could be taken as showing that chimpanzees, dogs, and pigs, along with some other species, have a right to life and we commit a grave moral offense whenever we kill them, even when they are old and suffering and our intention is to put them out of their misery. Alternatively one could take the argument as showing that the severely retarded and hopelessly senile have no right to life and may be killed for quite trivial reasons, as we now kill animals.

Since the focus here is on ethical questions concerning animals and not on the morality of euthanasia I shall not attempt to settle this issue finally. I think it is reasonably clear, though, that while both of the positions just described avoid speciesism, neither is entirely satisfactory. What we need is some middle position that would avoid speciesism but would not make the lives of the retarded and senile as cheap as the lives of pigs and dogs now are, nor make the lives of pigs and dogs so sacrosanct that we think it wrong to put them out of hopeless misery. What we must do is bring nonhuman animals within our sphere of moral concern and cease to treat their lives as expendable for whatever trivial purposes we may have. At the same time, once we realize that the fact that a being is a member of our own species is not in itself enough to make it always wrong to kill that being, we may come to reconsider our policy of preserving human lives at all costs, even when there is no prospect of a meaningful life or of existence without terrible pain.

I conclude, then, that a rejection of speciesism does not imply that all lives are of equal worth. While self-awareness, intelligence, the capacity for meaningful relations with others, and so on are not relevant to the question of inflicting pain—since pain is pain, whatever other capacities, beyond the capacity to feel pain, the being may have—these capacities may be relevant to the question of taking life. It is not arbitrary to hold that the life of a self-aware being, capable of abstract thought, of planning for the future, of complex acts of communication, and so on, is more valuable than the life of a being without these capacities. To see the difference between the issues of inflicting pain and taking life, consider how we would choose within our own species. If we had to choose to save the life of a normal human or a mentally defective human, we would probably choose to save the life of the normal human; but if we had to choose between preventing pain in the normal human or the mental defective—imagine that both have received painful but superficial injuries, and we only have enough painkiller for one of them—it is not nearly so clear how we ought to choose. The same is true when we consider other species. The evil of pain is, in itself, unaffected by the other characteristics of the being that feels the pain; the value of life is affected by these other characteristics.

Normally this will mean that if we have to choose between the life of a human being and the life of another animal we should choose to save the life of the human, but there may be special cases in which the reverse holds true, because the human being in question does not have the capacities of a normal human being. So this view is not speciesist, although it may appear to be at first glance. The preference, in normal cases, for saving a human life over the life of an animal when a choice *has* to be made is a preference based on the characteristics that normal humans have, and not on the mere fact that they are members of our own species. This is why when we consider members of our own species who lack the characteristics of normal humans we can no longer say that their lives are always to be preferred to those of other animals. In general, the question of when it is wrong to kill (painlessly) an animal is one to which we need give no precise answer. As long as we remember that we should give the same respect to the lives of animals as we give to the lives of those humans at a similar mental level, we shall not go far wrong.

In any case, the conclusions that are argued for here flow from the principle of minimizing suffering alone. The idea that it is also wrong to kill animals painlessly gives some of these conclusions additional support that is welcome, but strictly unnecessary. Interestingly enough, this is true even of the conclusion that we ought to become vegetarians, a conclusion that in the popular mind is generally based on some kind of absolute prohibition on killing.

Endnotes

1. For Bentham's moral philosophy, see his *Introduction to the Principles of Morals and Legislation,* and for Sidgwick's see *The Methods of Ethics* (the passage quoted is from the seventh edition, p. 382). As examples of leading contemporary moral philosophers who incorporate a requirement of equal consideration of interests, see R. M. Hare, *Freedom and Reason* (New York, Oxford University Press, 1963) and John Rawls, *A Theory of Justice* (Cambridge: Harvard University Press, Belknap Press, 1972). For a brief account of the essential agreement on this issue between these and other positions, see R. M. Hare, "Rules of War and Moral Reasoning," *Philosophy and Public Affairs* 1 (1972).
2. Letter to Henri Gregoire, February 25, 1809.
3. Reminiscences by Francis D. Gage, from Susan B. Anthony, *The History of Woman Suffrage,* vol. 1; the passage is to be found in the extract in Leslie Tanner, ed., *Voices from Women's Liberation* (New York: Signet, 1970).
4. I owe the term "speciesism" to Richard Ryder.
5. *Introduction to the Principles of Morals and Legislation,* chapter 17.
6. I am here putting aside religious views, for example the doctrine that all and only humans have immortal souls, or are made in the image of God. Historically these views have been very important, and no doubt are partly responsible for the idea that human life has a special sanctity. Logically, however, these religious views are unsatisfactory, since a reasoned explanation of why it should be that all humans and no nonhumans have immortal souls is not offered. This belief too, therefore, comes under suspicion as a form of speciesism. In any case, defenders of the "sanctity of life" view are generally reluctant to base their position on purely religious doctrines, since these doctrines are no longer as widely accepted as they once were.

Review Questions

1. Explain the principle of equality that Singer adopts.
2. How does Singer define speciesism?
3. What is the sanctity of life view? Why does Singer reject this view?

Discussion Questions

1. Is speciesism analogous to racism and sexism? Why, or why not?
2. Is there anything wrong with killing animals painlessly? Defend your view.
3. Do human interests outweigh animal interests? Explain your position.

Bonnie Steinbock

Speciesism and the Idea of Equality

Bonnie Steinbock teaches philosophy at the State University of New York at Albany.

Steinbock presents a defense of speciesism, the practice of weighing human interests more heavily than those of animals. While she agrees with Singer that nonhuman pain and suffering deserve some moral consideration, she denies that this consideration should be equal to that given to humans. She claims that humans have morally relevant capacities that nonhuman animals do not have, and this entitles humans to greater moral consideration. These capacities include the ability to be morally responsible, to reciprocate in ways that animals cannot, and to desire self-respect.

Most of us believe that we are entitled to treat members of other species in ways which would be considered wrong if inflicted on members of our own species. We kill them for food, keep them confined, use them in painful experiments. The moral philosopher has to ask what relevant difference justifies this difference in treatment. A look at this question will lead us to re-examine the distinctions which we have assumed make a moral difference.

It has been suggested by Peter Singer[1] that our current attitudes are 'speciesist', a word intended to make one think of 'racist' or 'sexist'. The idea is that membership in a species is in itself not relevant to moral treatment, and that much of our behaviour and attitudes towards non-human animals is based simply on this irrelevant fact.

From Bonnie Steinbock, "Speciesism and the Idea of Equality," *Philosophy* 53, No. 204 (April 1978).

There is, however, an important difference between racism or sexism and 'speciesism'. We do not subject animals to different moral treatment simply because they have fur and feathers, but because they are in fact different from human beings in ways that could be morally relevant. It is false that women are incapable of being benefited by education, and therefore that claim cannot serve to justify preventing them from attending school. But this is not false of cows and dogs, even chimpanzees. Intelligence is thought to be a morally relevant capacity because of its relation to the capacity for moral responsibility.

What is Singer's response? He agrees that non-human animals lack certain capacities that human animals possess, and that this may justify different *treatment*. But it does not justify giving less consideration to their needs and interests. According to Singer, the moral mistake which the racist or sexist makes is not essentially the factual error of thinking that blacks or women are inferior to white men. For even if there were no factual error, even if it were true that blacks and women are less intelligent and responsible than whites and men, this would not justify giving less consideration to their needs and interests. It is important to note that the term 'speciesism' is in one way like, and in another way unlike, the terms 'racism' and 'sexism'. What the term 'speciesism' has in common with these terms is the reference to focusing on a characteristic which is, in itself, irrelevant to moral treatment. And it is worth reminding us of this. But Singer's real aim is to bring us to a new understanding of the idea of equality. The question is, on what do claims to equality rest? The demand for *human* equality is a demand that the interests of all human beings be considered equally, unless there is a moral justification for not doing so. But why should the interests of all human beings be considered equally? In order to answer this question, we have to give some sense to the phrase, 'All men (human beings) are created equal'. Human beings are manifestly *not* equal, differing greatly in intelligence, virtue and capacities. In virtue of what can the claim to equality be made?

It is Singer's contention that claims to equality do not rest on factual equality. Not only do human beings differ in their capacities, but it might even turn out that intelligence, the capacity for virtue, etc., are not distributed evenly among the races and sexes:

> The appropriate response to those who claim to have found evidence of genetically based differences in ability between the races or sexes is not to stick to the belief that the genetic explanation must be wrong, whatever evidence to the contrary may turn up; instead we should make it quite clear that the claim to equality does not depend on intelligence, moral capacity, physical strength, or similar matters of fact. Equality is a moral ideal, not a simple assertion of fact. There is no logically compelling reason for assuming that a factual difference in ability between two people justifies any difference in the amount of consideration we give to satisfying their needs and interests. The principle of equality of human beings is not a description of an alleged actual equality among humans: it is a prescription of how we should treat humans.[2]

In so far as the subject is human equality, Singer's view is supported by other philosophers. Bernard Williams, for example, is concerned to show that demands for equality cannot rest on factual equality among people, for no such equality exists.[3] The only respect in which all men are equal, according to Williams, is that they are all equally men. This seems to be a platitude, but Williams denies that it is trivial. Membership in the species *homo sapiens* in itself has no special moral significance, but rather the fact that all men are human serves as a *reminder* that being human involves the possession of characteristics that are morally relevant. But on what characteristics does Williams focus? Aside from the desire for self-respect (which I will discuss later), Williams is not concerned with uniquely human capacities. Rather, he focuses on the capacity to feel pain and the capacity to feel affection. It is in virtue of these capacities, it seems, that the idea of equality is to be justified.

Apparently Richard Wasserstrom has the same idea as he sets out the racist's 'logical and moral mistakes' in 'Rights, Human Rights and Racial Discrimination'.[4] The racist fails to acknowledge that the black person is as capable of suffering as the white person. According to Wasserstrom, the reason why a person is said to have a right not to be made to suffer acute physical pain is that we all do in fact value freedom from such pain. Therefore, if anyone has a right to be free from suffering acute physical pain, *everyone* has this right, for there is no possible basis of discrimination. Wasserstrom says, 'For, if all persons do have equal capacities of these sorts and if the existence of these capacities is the reason for ascribing these rights to anyone, then all persons ought to have the right to claim equality of treatment in respect to the possession and exercise of these rights'.[5] The basis of equality, for Wasserstrom as for Williams, lies not in some uniquely human capacity, but rather in the fact that all human beings are alike in their capacity to suffer. Writers on equality have focused on this capacity, I think, because it functions as some sort of lowest common denominator, so that whatever the other capacities of a human being, he is entitled to equal consideration because, like everyone else, he is capable of suffering.

If the capacity to suffer is the reason for ascribing a right to freedom from acute pain, or a right to well being, then it certainly looks as though these rights must be extended to animals as well. This is the conclusion Singer arrives at. The demand for human equality rests on the equal capacity of all human beings to suffer and to enjoy well being. But if this is the basis of the demand for equality, then this demand must include all beings which have an equal capacity to suffer and enjoy well being. That is why Singer places at the basis of the demand for equality, not intelligence or reason, but sentience. And equality will mean, not equality of treatment, but 'equal consideration of interests'. The equal consideration of interests will often mean quite different treatment, depending on the nature of the entity being considered. (It would be as absurd to talk of a dog's right to vote, Singer says, as to talk of a man's right to have an abortion.)

It might be thought that the issue of equality depends on a discussion of rights. According to this line of thought, animals do not merit equal consideration of interests because, unlike human beings, they do not, or cannot, have rights. But I am not going to discuss rights, important as the issue is. The fact that an entity does not have rights does not necessarily imply that its interests are going to count for less than the interests of entities which are right-bearers. According to the view of rights held by H.L.A. Hart and S. I. Benn, infants do not have rights, nor do the mentally defective, nor do the insane, in so far as they all lack certain minimal conceptual capabilities for having rights.[6] Yet is certainly does not seem that either Hart or Benn would agree that *therefore* their interests are to be counted for less, or that it is morally permissible to treat them in ways in which it would not be permissible to treat right-bearers. It seems to mean only that we must give different sorts of reasons for our obligations to take into consideration the interests of those who do not have rights.

We have reasons concerning the treatment of other people which are clearly independent of the notion of rights. We would say that it is wrong to punch someone because doing that infringes his rights. But we could also say that it is wrong because doing that hurts him, and that is, ordinarily, enough of a reason not to do it. Now this particular reason extends not only to human beings, but to all sentient creatures. One has a *prima facie* reason not to pull the cat's tail (whether or not the cat has rights) because it hurts the cat. And this is the only thing, normally, which is relevant in this case. The fact that the cat is not a 'rational being', that it is not capable of moral responsibility, that it cannot make free choices or shape its life—all of these differences from us have nothing to do with the justifiability of pulling its tail. Does this show that rationality and the rest of it are irrelevant to moral treatment?

I hope to show that this is not the case. But first I want to point out that the issue is not one of cruelty to animals. We all agree that cruelty is wrong, whether perpetrated on a moral or non-moral, rational or non-rational agent. Cruelty is defined as the infliction of unnecessary pain or suffering. What is to count as necessary or unnecessary is determined, in part, by the nature of the end pursued. Torturing an animal is cruel, because although the pain is logically necessary for the action to be torture, the end (deriving enjoyment from seeing the animal suffer) is monstrous. Allowing animals to suffer from neglect or for the sake of large profits may also be thought to be unnecessary and therefore cruel. But there may be some ends, which are very good (such as the advancement of medical knowledge), which can be accomplished by subjecting animals to pain in experiments. Although most people would agree that the pain inflicted on animals used in medical research ought to be kept to a minimum, they would consider pain that cannot be eliminated 'necessary' and therefore not cruel. It would probably not be so regarded if the subjects were non-voluntary human beings. Necessity, then, is defined in terms of human benefit, but this is just what is being called into question. The topic of cruelty to animals, while important from a practical viewpoint, because much of our present treatment of animals involves the infliction of suffering for no good reason, is not very interesting philosophically. What is philosophically interesting is whether we are justified in having different standards of necessity for human suffering and for animal suffering.

Singer says, quite rightly I think, 'If a being suffers, there can be no moral justification for refusing to take that suffering into consideration'.[7] But he thinks that the principle of equality requires that, no matter what the nature of the being, its suffering be counted equally with the like suffering of any other being. In other words sentience does not simply provide us with reasons for acting; it is the *only* relevant consideration for equal consideration of interests. It is this view that I wish to challenge.

I want to challenge it partly because it has such counter-intuitive results. It means, for example, that feeding starving children before feeding starving dogs is just like a Catholic charity's feeding hungry Catholics before feeding hungry non-Catholics. It is simply a matter of taking care of one's own, something which is usually morally permissible. But whereas we would admire the Catholic agency which did not discriminate, but fed all children, first come, first served, we would feel quite differently about someone who had this policy for dogs and children. Nor is this, it seems to me, simply a matter of a sentimental preference for our own species. I might feel much more love for my dog than for a strange child—and yet I might feel morally obliged to feed the child before I fed my dog. If I gave in to the feelings of love and fed my dog and let the child go hungry, I would probably feel guilty. This is not to say that we can simply rely on such feelings. Huck Finn felt guilty at helping Jim escape, which he viewed as stealing from a woman who had never done him any harm. But while the existence of such feelings does not settle the morality of an issue, it is not clear to me that they can be explained away. In any event, their existence can serve as a motivation for trying to find a rational justification for considering human interests above non-human ones.

However, it does seem to me that this *requires* a justification. Until now, common sense (and academic philosophy) have seen no such need. Benn says, 'No one claims equal consideration for all mammals—human beings count, mice do not, though it would not be easy to say *why* not. . . . Although we hesitate to inflict unnecessary pain on sentient creatures, such as mice or dogs, we are quite sure that we do not need to show good reasons for putting human interests before theirs.' [8]

I think we do have to justify counting our interests more heavily than those of animals. But how? Singer is right, I think, to point out that it will not do to refer vaguely to the greater value of human life, to human worth and dignity:

> Faced with a situation in which they see a need for some basis for the moral gulf that is commonly thought to separate humans and animals, but can find no concrete difference that will do this without undermining the equality of humans, philosophers tend to waffle. They resort to high-sounding phrases like 'the intrinsic dignity of the human individual'. They talk of 'the intrinsic worth of all men' as if men had some worth that other beings do not have or they say that human beings, and only human beings, are 'ends in themselves', while 'everything other than a person can only have value for a person'. . . . Why should we not attribute 'intrinsic dignity' or 'intrinsic worth' to ourselves? Why should we not say that we are the only things in the universe that have intrinsic value? Our fellow human beings are unlikely to reject the accolades we so generously bestow upon them and those to whom we deny the honour are unable to object.[9]

Singer is right to be sceptical of terms like 'intrinsic dignity' and 'intrinsic worth'. These phrases are no substitute for a moral argument. But they may point to one. In trying to understand what is meant by these phrases, we may find a difference or differences between human beings and non-human animals that will justify different treatment while not undermining claims for human equality. While we are not compelled to discriminate among people because of different capacities, if we can find a significant difference in capacities between human and non-human animals, this could serve to justify regarding human interests as primary. It is not arbitrary or smug, I think, to maintain that human beings have a different moral status from members of other species because of certain capacities which are characteristic of being human. We may not all be equal in these capacities, but all human beings possess them to some measure, and non-human animals do not. For example, human beings are normally held to be responsible for what they do. In recognizing that someone is responsible for his or her actions, you accord that person a respect which is reserved for those possessed of moral autonomy, or capable of achieving such autonomy. Secondly, human beings can be expected to reciprocate in a way that nonhuman animals cannot. Non-human animals cannot be motivated by altruistic or moral reasons; they cannot treat you fairly or unfairly. This does not rule out the possibility of an animal being motivated by sympathy or pity. It does rule out altruistic motivation in the sense of motivation due to the recognition that the needs and interests of others provide one with certain reasons for acting.[10] Human beings are capable of altruistic motivation in this sense. We are sometimes motivated simply by the recognition that someone else is in pain, and that pain is a bad thing, no matter who suffers it. It is this sort of reason that I claim cannot motivate an animal or any entity not possessed of fairly abstract concepts. (If some non-human animals do possess the requisite concepts—perhaps chimpanzees who have learned a language—they might well be capable of altruistic motivation.) This means that our moral dealings with animals are necessarily much more limited than our dealings with other human beings. If rats invade our houses, carrying disease and biting our children, we cannot reason with them, hoping to persuade them of the injustice they do us. We can only attempt to get rid of them. And it is this that makes it reasonable for us to accord them a separate and not equal moral status, even though their capacity to suffer provides us with some reason to kill them painlessly, if this can be done without too much sacrifice of human interests. Thirdly, as Williams points out, there is the 'desire for self-respect': 'a certain human desire to be identified with what one is doing, to be able to realize purposes of one's own, and not to be the instrument of another's will unless one has willingly accepted such a role'.[11] Some animals may have some form of this desire, and to the extent that they do, we ought to consider their interest in freedom and self-determination. (Such considerations might affect our attitudes toward zoos and circuses.) But the desire for self-respect *per se* requires the intellectual capacities of human beings, and this desire provides us with special reasons not to treat human beings in certain ways. It is an affront to the dignity of a human being to be a slave (even if a well-treated one); this cannot be true for a horse or a cow. To point this out is of course only to say that the justification for the treatment of an entity will depend on the sort of entity in question. In our treatment of other entities, we must consider the desire for autonomy, dignity and respect, but only where such a desire exists. Recognition of different desires and interests will often require different treatment, a point Singer himself makes.

But is the issue simply one of different desires and interests justifying and requiring different treatment? I would like to make a stronger claim, namely, that certain capacities, which seem to be unique to human beings, entitle their possessors to a privileged position in the moral community. Both rats and human beings dislike pain, and so we have a *prima facie* reason not to inflict pain on either. But if we can free human beings from crippling diseases, pain and death through experimentation which involves making animals suffer, and if this is the only way to achieve such results, then I think that such experimentation is justified because human lives are more valuable than animals lives. And this is because of certain capacities and abilities that normal human beings have which animals apparently do not, and which human beings cannot exercise if they are devastated by pain or disease.

My point is not that the lack of the sorts of capacities I have been discussing gives us a justification for treating animals just as we like, but rather that it is these differences between human beings and non-human animals which provide a rational basis for different moral treatment and consideration. Singer focuses on sentience alone as the basis of equality, but we can justify the belief that human beings have a moral worth that nonhuman animals do not, in virtue of specific capacities, and without resorting to 'highsounding phrases'.

Singer thinks that intelligence, the capacity for moral responsibility, for virtue, etc., are irrelevant to equality, because we would not accept a hierarchy based on intelligence any more than one based on race. We do not think that those with greater capacities ought to have their interests weighed more heavily than those with lesser capacities, and this, he thinks, shows that differences is such capacities are irrelevant to equality. But it does not show this at all. Kevin Donaghy argues (rightly, I think) that what entitles us human beings to a privileged position in the moral community is a certain minimal level of intelligence, which is a prerequisite for morally relevant capacities.[12] The fact that we would reject a hierarchical society based on degree of intelligence does not show that a minimal level of intelligence cannot be used as a cutoff point, justifying giving greater consideration to the interests of those entities which meet this standard.

Interestingly enough, Singer concedes the rationality of valuing the lives of normal human beings over the lives of non-human animals.[13] We are not required to value equally the life of a normal human being and the life of an animal, he thinks, but only their suffering. But I doubt that the value of an entity's life can be separated from the value of its suffering in this way. If we value the lives of human beings more than the lives of animals, this is because we value certain capacities that human beings have and animals do not. But freedom from suffering is, in general, a minimal condition for exercising these capacities, for living a fully human life. So, valuing human life more involves regarding human interests as counting for more. That is why we regard human suffering as more deplorable than comparable animal suffering.

But there is one point of Singer's which I have not yet met. Some human beings (if only a very few) are less intelligent than some nonhuman animals. Some have less capacity for moral choice and responsibility. What status in the moral community are these members of our species to occupy? Are their interests to be considered equally with ours? Is experimenting on them permissible where such experiments are painful or injurious, but somehow necessary for human well being? If it is certain of our capacities which entitle us to a privileged position, it looks as if those lacking those capacities are not entitled to a privileged position. To think it is justifiable to experiment on an adult chimpanzee but not on a severely mentally incapacitated human being seems to be focusing on membership in a species where that has no moral relevance. (It is being 'speciesist' in a perfectly reasonable use of the word.) How are we to meet this challenge?

Donaghy is untroubled by this objection. He says that it is fully in accord with his intuitions, that he regards the killing of a normally intelligent human being as far more serious than the killing of a person so severely limited that he lacked the intellectual capacities of an adult pig. But this parry really misses the point. The question is whether Donaghy thinks that the killing of a human being so severely limited that he lacked the intellectual capacities of an adult pig would be less serious than the killing of that pig. If superior intelligence is what justifies privileged status in the moral community, then the pig who is smarter than a human being ought to have superior moral status. And I doubt that this is fully in accord with Donaghy's intuitions.

I doubt that anyone will be able to come up with a concrete and morally relevant difference that would justify, say, using a chimpanzee in an experiment rather than a human being with less capacity for reasoning, moral responsibility, etc. Should we then experiment on the severely retarded? Utilitarian considerations aside (the difficulty of comparing intelligence between species, for example), we feel a special obligation to care for the handicapped members of our own species, who cannot survive in this world without such care. Non-human animals manage very well, despite their 'lower intelligence' and lesser capacities; most of them do not require special care from us. This does not, of course, justify experimenting on them. However, to subject to experimentation those people who depend on us seems even worse than subjecting members of other species to it. In addition, when we consider the severely retarded, we think, 'That could be me'. It makes sense to think that one might have been born retarded, but not to think that one might have been born a monkey. And so, although one can imagine oneself in the monkey's place, one feels a closer identification with the severely retarded human being. Here we are getting away from such things as 'morally relevant differences' and are talking about something much more difficult to articulate, namely, the role of feeling and sentiment in moral thinking. We would be *horrified* by the use of the retarded in medical research. But what are we to make of this horror? Has it moral significance or is it 'mere' sentiment, of no more importance than the sentiment of whites against blacks? It is terribly difficult to know how to evaluate such feelings.[14] I am not going to say more about this, because I think that the treatment of severely incapacitated human beings does not pose an insurmountable objection to the privileged status principle. I am willing to admit that my horror at the thought of experiments being performed on severely mentally incapacitated human beings in cases in which I would find it justifiable and preferable to perform the same experiments on nonhuman animals (capable of similar suffering) may not be a moral emotion. But it is certainly not wrong of us to extend special care to members of our own species, motivated by feelings of sympathy, protectiveness, etc. If this is speciesism, it is stripped of its tone of moral condemnation. It is not racist to provide special care to members of your own race; it is racist to fall below your moral obligation to a person because of his or her race. I have been arguing that we are morally obliged to consider the interests of all sentient creatures, but not to consider those interests equally with human interests. Nevertheless, even this recognition will mean some radical changes in our attitude toward and treatment of other species.[15]

Endnotes

1. Peter Singer, *Animal Liberation* (A New York Review Book, 1975).
2. Singer, 5.
3. Bernard Williams, 'The Idea of Equality', *Philosophy, Politics and Society* (Second Series), Laslett and Runciman (eds.) (Blackwell, 1962), 110–113, reprinted in *Moral Concepts,* Feinberg (ed.) (Oxford, 1970), 153–171.
4. Richard Wasserstrom, 'Rights, Human Rights, and Racial Discrimination', *Journal of Philosophy* 61, No. 20 (1964), reprinted in *Human Rights,* A. I. Melden (ed.) (Wadsworth, 1970), 96–110.
5. Ibid., 106.
6. H.L.A. Hart, 'Are There Any Natural Rights?', *Philosophical Review* 64 (1955), and S. I. Benn, 'Abortion, Infanticide, and Respect for Persons', *The Problem of Abortion,* Feinberg (ed.) (Wadsworth, 1973), 92–104.
7. Singer, 9.
8. Benn 'Equality, Moral and Social', *The Encyclopedia of Philosophy* 3, 40.
9. Singer, 266–267.
10. This conception of altruistic motivation comes from Thomas Nagel's *The Possibility of Altruism* (Oxford, 1970).
11. Williams, op. cit., 157.
12. Kevin Donaghy, 'Singer on Speciesism', *Philosophic Exchange* (Summer 1974).
13. Singer, 22.
14. We run into the same problem when discussing abortion. Of what significance are our feelings toward the unborn when discussing its status? Is it relevant or irrelevant that it looks like a human being?
15. I would like to acknowledge the help of, and offer thanks to, Professor Richard Arneson of the University of California, San Diego; Professor Sidney Gendin of Eastern Michigan University; and Professor Peter Singer of Monash University, all of whom read and commented on earlier drafts of this paper.

Review Questions

1. According to Steinbock, what is the important difference between racism or sexism and speciesism?
2. What is the basis for equality according to Singer, Williams, Wasserstrom, and Steinbock?
3. Steinbock claims that Singer's view has counterintuitive results. What are they?
4. According to Steinbock, why are we justified in counting human interests more heavily than those of animals?

Discussion Questions

1. Steinbock maintains that we should give greater moral consideration to severely mentally incapacitated humans than to animals who may have a greater mental capacity. Does she give good reasons for this? How would Singer reply?
2. Do Steinbock's criticisms of Singer also apply to Regan? Explain your answer.
3. Suppose that alien beings settle on the earth. They are superior to humans in intelligence, moral virtue, desire for self-respect, and so on. What is their moral status? Are they equal to humans? Do they have a higher moral status, just as humans have a higher moral status than animals? What would Steinbock say? What do you think?

Tom Regan

Ethical Vegetarianism and Commercial Animal Farming

Tom Regan teaches philosophy at North Carolina State University. He has written numerous books and articles, and he has edited many textbooks. His most recent books on the subject of animal rights are All That Dwell Therein: Essays on Animal Rights and Environmental Ethics *(1982) and* The Case for Animal Rights *(1984).*

Regan begins with a discussion of moral anthropocentrism, the view of Kant and others that only human interest should be morally considered. This view is rejected by utilitarianism and by some proponents of moral rights including Regan. Regan does not find the utilitarianism of Bentham and Singer to be morally acceptable. Instead he defends a rights theory. On this theory, moral rights imply a duty to respect the rights. Persons with "inherent value" possess rights, and some animals are persons. So we have a duty to respect animal rights by abolishing commercial animal farming and becoming vegetarians.

INTRODUCTION

Time was when a few words in passing usually were enough to exhaust the philosophical interest in the moral status of animals other than human beings. "Lawless beasts," writes Plato. "Of the order of sticks and stones," opines the nineteenth-century Jesuit W. D. Ritchie. True, there are notable exceptions, at least as far back as Pythagoras, who advocated vegetarianism on ethical grounds—Cicero, Epicurus, Herodotus, Horace, Ovid, Plutarch, Seneca, Virgil: hardly a group of "animal crazies"! By and large, however, a few words would do nicely, thank you, or, when one's corpus took on grave proportions, a few paragraphs or pages. Thus we find Kant, for example, by all accounts one of the most influential philosophers in the history of ideas, devoting almost two full pages to the question of our duties to animals, while St. Thomas Aquinas, easily the most important philosopher-theologian in the Catholic tradition, bequeaths perhaps ten pages to the topic at hand.

Times change. Today an even modest bibliography listing titles of the past decade's work on the moral status of animals would easily equal the length of Kant's and Aquinas' treatments combined, a quantitative symbol of the changes that have taken place, and continue to take place, in philosophy's attempts to rouse slumbering prejudices lodged in the anthropocentrism of western thought.

With relatively few speaking to the contrary (St. Francis always comes to mind in this context), theists and humanists, rowdy bedfellows in most quarters, have gotten along amicably when questions were raised about the moral center of the terrestrial universe: *Human* interests form the center of that universe. Let the theist look hopefully beyond the harsh edge of bodily death, let the humanist denounce, in Freud's terms, this "infantile view of the world," at least the two could agree that the moral universe revolves around us humans—our desires, our needs, our goals, our preferences, our love for one another. The intense dialectic now characterizing philosophy's assaults on the traditions of humanism and theism, assaults aimed not only at the traditional account of the moral status of animals but at the foundation of our moral dealings with the natural environment, with Nature generally—these assaults should not be viewed as local skirmishes between obscure academicians each bent on occupying a

From R. Haynes and R. Lanier, eds., *Agriculture, Change, and Human Values: Proceedings of a Multi-Disciplinary Conference*, October 1982. Humanities and Agriculture Program, Gainesville, Florida, 1984.

deserted fortress. At issue are the validity of alternative visions of the scheme of things and our place in it. The growing philosophical debate over our treatment of animals and the environment is both a symptom and a cause of a culture's attempt to come to critical terms with its past as it attempts to shape its future.

At present there are three major challenges being raised against moral anthropocentrism. The first is the one issued by *utilitarians;* the second, by proponents of *moral rights;* and the third emanates from the camp of those who advocate what we shall term a *holistic ethic.* This essay offers brief summaries of each position with special reference to how their advocates answer two questions: (a) Is vegetarianism required on ethical grounds? and (b) Judged ethically, what should we say, and what should we do, about commercial animal agriculture? To ask whether vegetarianism is required on ethical grounds is to ask whether there are reasons other than those that relate to one's own welfare (for example, other than those that relate to one's own health or financial well-being) that call for leading a vegetarian way of life. As for the expression "commercial animal agriculture," that should be taken to apply to the practice of raising animals to be sold for food. The ethics of other practices that involve killing animals (for example, hunting, the use of animals in science, "the family farm" where the animals raised are killed and eaten by the people who raise them, etc.) will not be considered, except in passing, not because the ethics of these practices should not demand our close attention but because space and time preclude our giving them this attention here. Time and space also preclude anything approaching "complete" assessments of the three views to be discussed. None can be proven right or wrong in a few swift strokes. Even so, it will be clear where my own sympathies lie.

Traditional Moral Anthropocentrism

Aquinas and Kant speak for the anthropocentric tradition. That tradition does not issue a blank check when it comes to the treatment of animals. Morally, we are enjoined to be kind to animals and, on the other side of the coin, not to be cruel to them. But we are not enjoined to be the one and prohibited from being the other because we owe such treatment to *animals themselves*—not, that is, because we have any duties *directly* to nonhumans; rather, it is because of *human* interests that we have these duties regarding animals. "So far as animals are concerned," writes Kant, "we have no direct duties. . . . Our duties to animals are merely indirect duties to mankind." In the case of cruelty, we are not to be cruel to animals because treating them cruelly will develop a habit of cruelty, and a habit of cruelty, once it has taken up lodging in our breast, will in time include human beings among its victims. "(H)e who is cruel to animals becomes hard also in his dealings with men." And *that* is why cruelty to animals is wrong. As for kindness, "(t)ender feelings towards dumb animals develop humane feelings toward mankind." [1] And *that* is why we have a duty to be kind to animals.

So reasons Kant. Aquinas, predictably, adds theistic considerations, but the main storyline is the same, as witness the following passage from his *Summa Contra Gentiles.*

> Hereby is refuted the error of those who said it is sinful for a man to kill dumb animals: for by divine providence they are intended for man's use in the natural order. Hence it is not wrong for man to make use of them, either by killing, or in any other way whatever. . . . And if any passages of Holy Writ seem to forbid us to be cruel to dumb animals, for instance to kill a bird with its young: this is either to remove men's thoughts from being cruel to other men, and lest through being cruel to animals one becomes cruel to human beings: or because injury to an animal leads to the temporal hurt of man, either of the doer of the deed, or of another: or on account of some (religious) signification: thus the Apostle expounds the prohibition against muzzling the ox that treadeth the corn.[2]

To borrow a phase from the twentieth-century English philosopher Sir W. D. Ross, our treatment of animals, both for Kant and Aquinas, is "a practice ground for moral virtue." The *moral game* is played between human players or, on the theistic view, human players plus God. The way we treat animals is a sort of moral warmup, character calisthenics, as it were, for the moral game in which animals themselves play no part.

The Utilitarian Challenge

The first fairly recent spark of revolt against moral anthropocentrism comes, as do other recent protests against institutionalized prejudice, from the pens of the nineteenth-century utilitarians, most notably Jeremy Bentham and John Stuart Mill. These utilitarians—who count the balance of pleasure over pain for all sentient creatures as the yardstick of moral right and wrong, and who reject out of hand Descartes' famous teaching that animals are "nature's machines," lacking any trace of conscious awareness—recognize the direct moral significance of the pleasures and pains of animals. In an oft-quoted passage, Bentham enfranchises animals within the utilitarian moral community by declaring that "(t)he question is not, Can they talk?, or Can they reason?, but, Can they suffer?" [3] And Mill stakes the credibility of utilitarianism itself on its implications for the moral status and treatment of animals, writing that "(w)e (that is, those who subscribe to utilitarianism) are perfectly willing to stake the whole question on this one issue. Granted that any practice causes more pain to animals than it gives pleasure to man: is that practice moral or immoral? And if, exactly in proportion as human beings raise their heads out of the slough of selfishness, they do not with one voice answer 'immoral' let the morality of the principle of utility be forever condemned." [4] The duties we have regarding animals, then, are duties we have *directly to them,* not indirect duties to humanity. For utilitarians, animals are themselves involved in the moral game.

Viewed against this historical backdrop, the position of the contemporary Australian moral philosopher Peter Singer can be seen to be an extension of the attack on the tradition of moral anthropocentrism initiated by his utilitarian forebears. For though this sometimes goes unnoticed by friend and foe alike, Singer, whose book *Animal Liberation* is unquestionably the most influential work published in the 1970s on the topic of the ethics of our treatment of animals, is a utilitarian.[5] That view requires, he believes, observance of the equality of interests principle. This principle requires that, before we decide what to do, we consider the interests (that is, the preferences) of all those who are likely to be affected by what we do *and* weigh equal interests equally. We must not, that is, refuse to consider the interests of some of those who will be affected by what we do because, say, they are Catholic, or female, or black. *Everyone's* interests must be considered. And we must not discount the importance of comparable interests because they are the interests of, say, a Catholic, woman, or black. Everyone's interests must be weighed *equitably*. Of course, to ignore or discount the importance of a woman's interests *because she is a woman* is the very **paradigm** of the moral prejudice we call sexism, just as to ignore or discount the importance of the interests of blacks (or Native Americans, Chicanos, etc.) are paradigmatic forms of racism. It remained for Singer to argue, which he does with great vigor, passion, and skill, that a similar moral prejudice lies at the heart of moral anthropocentrism, a prejudice that Singer, borrowing a term first coined by the English author and animal activist Richard Ryder, denominates *speciesism.*[6] *Like Bentham and Mill before him, Singer, the utilitarian, denies* that we are to treat animals well in the name of the betterment of humanity, *denies* that we are to do this because this will help us discharge our duties to our fellow humans, *denies* that acting dutifully toward animals is a moral warmup for the real moral game played between humans, or, as theists would add, between humans-and-humans-and-God. *We owe it to those animals who have interests to take their interests into account, just as we also owe it to them to count their interests equitably*. Our duties regarding animals are, in these respects, *direct* duties we have to them, not indirect duties to humanity. To think otherwise is to give sorry testimony to the prejudice of speciesism Singer is intent upon unmasking.

Farming Today

Singer believes that the utilitarian case for ethical vegetarianism is strengthened when we inform ourselves of the changes taking place in commercial animal farming today. In increasing numbers, animals are being brought in off the land and raised indoors, in unnatural, crowded conditions—raised "intensively," to use the jargon of the animal industry, in structures that look for all the world like factories. Indeed, it is now common practice to refer to such commercial ventures as *factory farms*. The inhabitants of these "farms" are kept in cages, or stalls, or pens, or closely-confined in other ways, living out their abbreviated lives in a technologically created and sustained environment: automated feeding, automated watering, automated light cycles, automated waste removal, automated what-not. And the crowding: as many as nine hens in cages that measure eighteen by twenty-four inches; veal calves confined to twenty-two inch wide stalls; hogs similarly confined, sometimes in tiers of cages—two, three, four rows high. Could any impartial, morally sensitive person view what goes on in a factory farm with benign approval? Certainly many of the basic interests of the animals are simply ignored or undervalued, Singer claims, because they do not compute economically. Their interest in physical freedom or in associating with members of their own species, these interests routinely go by the board. And for what? So that we humans can dine on steaks and chops, drumsticks and roasts, food that is simply inessential for our own physical well-being. Add to this sorry tale of speciesism on today's farm the enormous waste that characterizes animal industry, waste to the tune of six or seven pounds of vegetable protein to produce a pound of animal protein in the case of beef cattle, for example, and add to the accumulated waste of nutritious food the chronic need for just such food throughout the countries of the Third World, whose populations characteristically are malnourished at best and literally starving to death at worst—add all these factors together and we have, Singer believes, the basis for the utilitarian's answers to our two questions. In response to the question, "Is vegetarianism required on ethical grounds?" the Singer-type utilitarian replies affirmatively. For it is not for self-interested reasons that Singer calls us to vegetarianism (though such reasons, including a concern for one's health, are not irrelevant). It is for ethical reasons that we are to take up a vegetarian way of life. And as for our second question, the one that asks what we should think and do about commercial animal farming, Singer's utilitarian argument prescribes, he thinks, that we should think ill of today's factory farms and act to bring about significant humane improvements by refusing to purchase their products. Ethically considered, we ought to become vegetarians.

The Challenge to Utilitarianism

Singer, then, is the leading contemporary representative of the utilitarian critique of the anthropocentric heritage bequeathed to us by humanism and theism. How should we assess his critique? Our answer requires answering two related questions. First, How adequate is the general utilitarian position Singer advocates? Second, How adequate is Singer's application of this general position to the particular case of commercial animal agriculture and, allied with this, the case for ethical vegetarianism? A brief response to each question, beginning with the second, will have to suffice. Consider Singer's claim that each of us has a duty to become a vegetarian. How can this alleged duty be defended on *utilitarian* grounds? Well, on this view, we know, the act I *ought* to perform, the act I have a *duty* to do, is the one that will bring about the best consequences for all those affected by the outcome, which, for Singer, means the act that will bring about the optimal balance of preference satisfaction over preference frustration. But it is naive in the extreme to suppose that, were I individually henceforth to abstain from eating meat and assiduously lead a vegetarian existence, this will improve the lot of a single animal. Commercial animal farming simply does not work in this way. It does not, that is, fine-tune its production to such a high degree that it responds to the decisions of each individual consumer. So, no, the individual's abstention from meat will not make the slightest dent, will not effect the smallest change, in commercial animal agriculture. No one, therefore, Singer included, can ground *the individual's* ethical obligation to be vegetarian on the effects *the individual's* acts will have on the welfare of animals.

Similar remarks apply to the other presumed beneficiaries of the individual's conversion to vegetarianism. The starving, malnourished masses of the Third World will not receive the food they need if I would but stop eating animals. For it is, again, naive in the extreme to suppose that the dietary decisions and acts of any given *individual* will make the slightest difference to the quality of life for any inhabitant in the Third World. Even were it true, which it is not (and it is not true because commercial animal agriculture is not so fine-tuned in this respect either), that a given amount of protein-rich grain *would not be fed to animals* if I abstained from eating meat, it simply would not follow that this grain *would find its way to any needy human being.* To suppose otherwise is to credit one's individual acts and decisions with a kind of godlike omnipotence a robust sense of reality cannot tolerate. Thus, since the type of utilitarianism Singer advocates prescribes that we decide what our ethical duties are by asking what will be the consequences of our acts, and since there is no realistic reason to believe that the consequences of my abstaining from meat will make any difference whatever to the quality of life of commercially raised farm animals or the needy people of the Third World, the alleged duties to become a vegetarian and to oppose commercial animal agriculture lack the kind of backing a utilitarian like Singer requires.

Here one might attempt to defend Singer by arguing that it is the total or sum of the consequences of *many* people becoming vegetarians, not just the results of each individual's decisions, that will spare some animals the rigors of factory farms and save some humans from malnutrition or starvation. Two replies to this attempted defense may be briefly noted. First, this defense almost gives *a sketch of a possible* reply; it does not give a finished one. As a utilitarian, Singer must show that the consequences for everyone involved would be better if a number of people became vegetarians than if they did not. But to show this, Singer must provide a thorough rundown of what the consequences would be, or would be in all probability, if we abstained from eating meat, *or* ate less of it, *or* ate none at all. and this is no easy task. Would the grains not fed to animals even be grown if the animal industry's requirements for them were reduced or eliminated? Would there be an economically viable market for corn, oats, and other grains if we became vegetarians? Would farmers have the necessary economic incentive to produce enough grain to feed the world's hungry human beings? Who knows? In particular, does Singer know? One looks in vain to find the necessary empirical backing for an answer here. Or consider: Suppose the grain is available. From a utilitarian point of view, would it be best (that is, would we be acting to produce the best consequences) if we made this grain available to the present generation of the world's malnourished? Or would it be better in the long run to refuse to aid these people at this point in time? After all, if we assist them now, will they not simply reproduce? And won't their additional numbers make the problem of famine for the next generation even more tragic? Who knows what the correct answers to these questions are? Who knows what is even "most likely" to be true? It is not unfair to a utilitarian such as Singer to mark the depths of our ignorance in these matters. And neither is it unfair to emphasize how our ignorance stands in the way of his attempt to ground the obligatoriness of vegetarianism on utilitarian considerations. If we simply do not know what the consequences of our becoming vegetarians would be, or are most likely to be, and if we simply do not know whether the consequences that would result would be, or are most likely to be, better than those that would obtain if we did not become vegetarians, then we simply lack any semblance of a utilitarian justification for the obligation to become vegetarians or for amounting a frontal assault on commercial animal agriculture. The decision to lead a vegetarian way of life and, by doing so, to lodge a moral complaint against commercial animal agriculture, viewed from the perspective of Singer's utilitarianism, must be diagnosed as at best symbolic gestures.

Aside from these matters, what can be said about the adequacy of utilitarianism in general? That is a question raised earlier to which we must now direct our attention. There is a vast literature critical of utilitarian theory, and it will obviously not be possible to survey it here. Here let us note just one difficulty. Utilitarianism, at least as understood by Singer, implies that whether *I* am doing what I ought to do is crucially dependent on what *other* people do. For example, although the consequences of *my* abstaining from eating meat are too modest to make any difference to how animals are raised or whether grains are made available to needy people, if enough *other* people join me in a vegetarian way of life we could collectively bring about changes in the number of animals raised, how they are raised, what use is made of grain, etc. The situation, in other words, is as follows: If enough people join me so that the consequences of what we do *collectively* makes some impact, then what I do might be right, whereas if too few people join me, with the result that the consequences of what we do fails to make any difference to how animals are raised, etc., then I am *not* doing what is right.

To make the morality of an individual's acts depend on how others behave is a highly unsatisfactory consequence for any moral theory. When people refuse to support racist or sexist practices (for example, in employment or education), they do what is right, but their doing what is right does not depend on how many *other* people join them. The number of people who join them determines how many people do or support what is right, *not* what is right in the first place. Utilitarianism, because it makes *what is right* dependent in many cases on how many people act in a certain way, puts the moral cart before the horse. What we want is a theory that illuminates moral right and wrong independently of how many people act in this or that way. And that is precisely what utilitarianism, at least in the form advocated by Singer, fails to give us. For all its promise as an attack on the anthropocentric traditions of humanism and theism, for all its insistence on the direct relevance of the interests of animals, and despite the radical sounding claims made by utilitarians in criticism of current practices on the farm and in the laboratory, utilitarianism proves to be more ethical shadow than substance. If we look beyond the rhetoric and examine the arguments, utilitarianism might not change these practices as much as it would fortify them.[7]

The Rights View

An alternative to the utilitarian attack on anthropocentrism is what we shall call "the rights view."[8] Those who accept this view hold that (1) certain individuals have certain moral rights, (2) these individuals have these rights independently of considerations about the value of the consequences of treating them in one way or another, and (3) the duty the individual has to respect the rights of others does not depend on how many other people act in ways that respect these rights. The first point distinguishes proponents of the rights view from, among others, those utilitarians like Bentham and Singer who deny that individuals have moral rights; the second distinguishes advocates of the rights view from, among others, those utilitarians such as Mill who hold that individuals have moral rights if, and only if, the general welfare would be promoted by saying and acting as if they do; and the third point distinguishes those who champion the rights view from, among others, any advocate of utilitarianism who holds that my duty to act in certain ways depends on how many other people act in these ways. According to the rights view, certain individuals have moral rights, and my duty to act in ways that respect such an individual's (A's) rights is a duty I have directly to A, a duty I have to A that is not grounded in considerations about the value of consequences for all those affected by the outcome, and a duty I have to A whatever else others might do to A. *Those who advocate animal rights, understanding this idea after the fashion of the rights view, believe that some of those individuals who have moral rights, and thus some of those to whom we have duties of the type just described, are animals.*

Grounds for the Rights View

To proclaim "the moral rights of Man" sounds good but is notoriously difficult to defend. Bentham, who writes more forcefully to support what he rejects than to establish what he accepts, dismisses rights other than legal rights as "nonsense upon stilts." So we will not settle the thorny question about human rights of an essay's reading or writing. And, it goes without saying, the moral rights of animals must remain even less established. Were Betham in his grave (in fact he remains above ground, encased in glass in an anteroom in University College, London, where he is dutifully brought to dinner each year on the occasion of his birthday) he would most certainly roll over at the mere mention of *animal* rights! Still, something needs to be said about the rational grounds for the rightsview.

An important (but not the only possible) argument in this regard takes the following form: Unless we recognize that certain individuals have moral rights, we will be left holding moral principles that sanction morally reprehensible conduct. Thus, in order to avoid holding principles that allow such conduct, we must recognize that certain individuals have moral rights. The following discussion of utilitarianism is an example of this general line of argument.

Utilitarians cut from the same cloth as Bentham would have us judge moral right and wrong by appeal to the consequences of what we do. Well, suppose aged Aunt Bertha's heirs could have a lot more pleasure than she is likely to have in her declining years if she were to die. But suppose that neither nature nor Aunt Bertha will cooperate: She simply refuses to die as expeditiously as, gauged by the interest of her heirs, is desirable. Why not speed up the tempo of her demise? The reply given by Bentham-type utilitarians show how far they are willing to twist our moral intuitions to save their theory. If we were to kill Aunt Bertha, especially if we took care to do so painlessly, then, these utilitarians submit, we would do no wrong to Aunt Bertha. However, if *other* people found out about what we did, they would quite naturally grow more anxious, more insecure about their own safety and mortality, and these mental states (anxiety, insecurity, and the like) are painful. Thus, so we are told, killing Aunt Bertha is wrong (if it is) because of the painful consequences for others!

Except for those already committed to a Bentham-style utilitarianism, few are likely to find this account satisfactory. Its shortcomings are all the more evident when we note that *if* others did not find out about our dastardly deed (and so were not made more anxious and insecure by their knowledge of what we did), and *if* we have a sufficiently undeveloped conscience not to be terribly troubled by what we did, and *if* we do not get caught, and *if* we have a jolly good time with Aunt Bertha's inheritance, a much better time, in fact, than we would have had if we had waited for nature to run its course, then Bentham-style utilitarianism implies that we did nothing wrong in killing Aunt Bertha and, indeed, acted as we morally ought to have acted. People who, in the face of this kind of objection, remain Bentham-type utilitarians, may hold a consistent position. But one pays a price for a "foolish consistency." The spectacle of people "defending their theory to the last" in spite of its grave implications must, to put it mildly, take one's moral breath away.

There are, of course, many ethical theories in addition to utilitarianism, and many versions of utilitarianism in addition to the one associated with Bentham. So even if the sketch of an argument against Bentham's utilitarianism proves successful, the rights view would not thereby "win" in its competition with other theories. But the foregoing does succeed in giving a representative sample of one argument deployed by those who accept the rights view: If you deny moral rights, as Bentham does, then the principles you put in their place, which, in Bentham's case, is the principle of utility, will sanction morally reprehensible conduct (for example, the murder of Aunt Bertha). If those who affirm and defend the rights view could show this given *any* initially plausible theory that denies moral rights, and if they could crystallize and defend the methodology on which this argument depends, then they would have a powerful reason for their position.

The Value of the Individual

The rights view aspires to satisfy our intellect, not merely our appetite for rhetoric, and so it is obliged to provide a theoretical home for moral rights. Part, but by no means not the whole, of this home is furnished by the rights views' theory of value. Unlike utilitarian theories (for example, value hedonism), the rights view recognizes *the value of individuals,* not just the value of their mental states (for example, their pleasures). Following custom, let us call these latter sorts of value "intrinsic values" and let us introduce the term "inherent value" for the type of value attributed to individuals. Then the notion of inherent value can be explained as follows. First, the inherent value of an individual who has such value is not the same as, is not reducible to, and is incommensurate with the intrinsic value of that individual's, or of any combination of individuals', mental states. The inherent value of an individual, in other words, is not equal to any sum of intrinsic values (for example, any sum of pleasures). Second, all individuals who have inherent value have it equally. Inherent value, that is, does not come in degrees; some who have it do not have it more or less than others. One either has it or one does not, and all who have it have it to the same extent. It is, one might say, a categorical concept. Third, the possession of inherent value by individuals does not depend on their utility relative to the interests of others, which, if it were true, would imply that some individuals have such value to a greater degree than do others, because some (for example, surgeons) have greater utility than do others (for example, bank thieves). Fourth, and relatedly, individuals cannot acquire or lose such value by anything they do. And fifth, and finally, the inherent value of individuals does not depend on what or how others think or feel about them. The loved and admired are neither more nor less inherently valuable than the despised and forsaken.

Now, the rights view claims that any individual who has inherent value is due treatment that respects this value (has, that is, a *moral right* to such treatment), and though not everything can be said here about what such respect comes to, at least this much should be clear: We fail to treat individuals with the respect they are due whenever we assume that how we treat them can be defended *merely* by asking about the value of the mental states such treatment produces for those affected by the outcome. This must fail to show appropriate respect since it is tantamount to treating these individuals as if they lacked inherent value—as if, that is, we treat them as we ought whenever we can justify our treatment of them *merely* on the grounds that it promotes the interests other individuals have in obtaining preferred mental states (for example, pleasure). Since individuals who have inherent value have a kind of value that is not reducible to their utility relative to the interests of others, we are not to treat them merely as a means to bringing about the best consequences. We ought not, then, kill Aunt Bertha, given the rights view, even if doing so brought about "the best" consequences. That would be to treat her with a lack of appropriate respect, something she has a moral right to. To kill her for these reasons would be to violate her rights.

Which Individuals Have Inherent Value?

Even assuming the rights view could succeed in providing a coherent, rationally persuasive theoretical framework for "the rights of Man," further argument would be necessary to illuminate and justify the rights of animals. That argument, not surprisingly, will be long and torturous. At least we can be certain of two things, however. First, it must include considerations about the criteria of right possession; and, second, it will have to include an explanation and defense of how animals meet these criteria. A few remarks about each of these two points will have to suffice.

Persons[9] are the possessors of moral rights, and though most human beings are persons, not all are. And some persons are not human beings. Persons are individuals who have a cluster of actual (not merely potential or former) abilities. These include awareness of their environment, desires and preferences, goals and purposes, feelings and emotions, beliefs and memories, a sense of the future and of their own identity. Most adult humans have these abilities and so are persons. But some (the irreversibly comatose, for example) lack them and so are not persons. Human fetuses and infants also are not persons, given this analysis, and so have no moral rights (which is not to say that we may therefore do anything to them that we have a mind to; there are moral constraints on what we may do in addition to those constraints that involve respect for the moral rights of others—but this is a long story . . . !).

As for nonhumans who are persons, the most famous candidate is God as conceived, for example, by Christians. When believers speak of "the blessed Trinity, three persons in one," they don't mean "three human beings in one." Extraterrestrials are another obvious candidate, at least as they crop up in standard science fiction. The extraterrestrials in Ray Bradbury's *Martian Chronicals,* for example, are persons, in the sense explained, but they assuredly are not human beings. But of course, the most important candidates for our purposes are animals. And they are successful candidates if they perceive and remember, believe and desire, have feelings and emotions, and, in general, actually possess the other abilities mentioned earlier.

Those who affirm and defend the rights of animals believe that some animals actually possess these abilities. Of course, there are some who will deny this. All animals, they will say, lack all, or most, or at least some of the abilities that make an individual a person. In a fuller discussion of the rights view, these worries would receive the respectful airing they deserve. It must suffice here to say that the case for animal rights involves the two matters mentioned and explained—first, considerations about the criteria of right possession (or, alternatively, personhood), and, second, considerations that show that some animals satisfy these criteria. Those who would squelch the undertaking before it gets started by claiming that "it's *obvious* that animals cannot be persons!" offer no serious objection; instead, they give sorry expression to the very speciesist prejudice those who affirm and defend the rights of animals seek to overcome.

LINE DRAWING

To concede that some animals are persons and so have moral rights is not to settle the question, *Which* animals are persons? "Where do we draw the line?" it will be asked; indeed, it must be asked. The correct answer seems to be: We do not know with certainty. Perhaps there is no exact line to be drawn in this case, any more than there is an exact line to be drawn in other cases (for example, "Exactly how tall do you have to be to be tall?" "Exactly how old must you be before you are old?"). What we must ask is where in the animal kingdom we find individuals who are *most like* paradigmatic persons—that is, most like us, both behaviorally and physiologically. The greater the similarity in these respects, the stronger the case for believing that these animals have a *mental life similar to our own* (including memory and emotion, for example), a case that is strengthened given the major thrust of evolutionary theory. So, while it remains a matter of uncertainty *exactly* where we are to draw this line, it is implausible to deny that adult mammalian animals have the abilities in question (just as, analogously, it would be implausible to deny that eighty-eight-year-old Aunt Bertha is old because we don't know exactly how old someone must be before they are old). To get this far in the argument for animal rights is not to finish the story, but it is to give a rough outline of a major chapter in it.

THE INHERENT VALUE OF ANIMALS

Moral rights, as explained earlier, need a theoretical home, and the rights view provides this by its use of the notion of inherent value. Not surprisingly, therefore, the rights view affirms this value in the case of those animals who are persons; not to do so would be to slide back into the prejudice of speciesism. Moreover, because all who possess this value possess it equally, the rights view makes no distinction between the inherent value human persons possess as distinct from that possessed by those persons who are animals. And just as *our* inherent value, as persons, does not depend on our utility relative to the interests of others, or on how much we are liked or admired, or on anything we do or fail to do, the same must be true in the case of animals who, as persons, have the same inherent value we do.

To regard animals in the way advocated by the rights view makes a truly profound difference to our understanding of what, morally speaking, we may do to them, as well as how, morally speaking, we can defend what we do. Those animals who have inherent value have a moral right to respectful treatment, a right we fail to respect whenever we attempt to justify what we do to them by appeal to "the best consequences." What these animals are due, in other words, is the same respectful treatment we are. We must never treat them in this or that way merely because, we claim, doing so is necessary to bring about "the best consequences" for all affected by the outcome.

The rights view therefore calls for the total dissolution of commercial animal agriculture as we know it. Not merely "modern" intensive rearing methods must cease. For though the harm visited upon animals raised in these circumstances is real enough and is morally to be condemned, its removal would not eliminate the basic wrong its presence compounds. The *basic* wrong is that animals raised for commercial profit are viewed and treated in ways that fail to show respect for their moral right to respectful treatment. *They* are not (though of course they may be treated as if they are), "commodities," "economic units," "investments," "a renewable resource," etc. They are, like us, persons and so, like us, are owed treatment that accords with their right to be treated with respect, a respect we fail to show when we end their life before doing so can be defended on the grounds of mercy. Since animals are routinely killed on grounds other than mercy in the course of commercial animal agriculture, that human enterprise violates the rights of animals.

Unlike the utilitarian approach to ethical vegetarianism, the rights view basis does not require that we know what the consequences of our individual or collective abstention from meat will be. The moral imperatives to treat farm animals with respect and to refuse to support those who fail to do so do not rest on calculations about consequences. And unlike a Singer-type utilitarianism, the rights view does not imply that the individual's duty to become a vegetarian depends on how many other people join the ranks. *Each individual* has the duty to treat others with the respect they are due independently of how many others do so, and each has a similar duty to refrain in principle from supporting practices that fail to show proper respect. Of course, anyone who accepts the rights view must profoundly wish that others *will* act similarly, with the result that commercial animal agriculture, from vast agribusiness operations to the traditional family farm, will go the way of the slave trade—will, that is, cease to exist. But the *individual's* duty to cease to support those who violate the rights of animals does not depend on humanity in general doing so as well.

The rights view is, one might say, a "radical" position, calling, as it does, for the total abolition of a culturally accepted institution to wit, commercial animal farming. The way to "clean up" this institution is not by giving animals bigger cages, cleaner stalls, a place to roost, thus and so much hay, etc. When an institution is grounded in injustice, because it fails to respect the rights of those involved, there is no room for internal house cleaning. Morality will not be satisfied with anything less than its total abolition. And that, for the reasons given, is the rights view's verdict regarding commercial animal agriculture.

Holism

The "radical" implications of the rights view suggest how far some philosophers have moved from the anthropocentric traditions of theism and humanism. But, like the utilitarian attacks on this tradition, one should note that the rights view seeks to make its case by working within the major ethical categories of this tradition. For example, hedonistic utilitarians do not deny the moral relevance of human pleasures and pain, so important to our humanist forebears; rather, they accept this and seek to extend our moral horizons to include the moral relevance of the pleasures and pains of animals. And the rights view does not deny the distinctive moral importance of the individual, a central article of belief in theistic thought; rather, it accepts this moral datum and seeks to widen the class of individuals who are to be thought of in this way to include many animals.

Because both the positions discussed in the preceding work with major ethical categories handed down to us by our predecessors, some influential thinkers argue that these positions are, despite all appearances, in the hip pocket, so to speak, of the *Weltanschauung* they aspire to overturn. What is needed, these thinkers contend or imply, is not a broader interpretation of traditional categories (for example, the category of "the rights of the individual"); rather, what is required is the overthrow of these categories. Only then will we have a new vision, one that liberates us from the last vestiges of anthropocentrism.

"The Land Ethic"

Among those whose thought moves in this direction, none is more influential than Aldo Leopold.[10] *Very* roughly, Leopold can be seen as rejecting the "atomism" dear to the hearts of those who build their moral thinking on "the value (or rights) of the individual." What has ultimate value is not the individual but the collective, not the "part" but the "whole," whereby "the whole" is meant the entire biosphere: the *totality* of the things and systems in the natural order. Acts are right, Leopold claims, if they tend to promote the integrity, beauty, diversity, and harmony of the biosphere; they are wrong if they tend contrariwise. As for individuals, be they humans or animals, they are merely "members of the biotic team," having neither more nor less value in themselves than any other member—having, that is, *no* value "in themselves." What good individuals have, so far as this is computable at all, is instrumental only: They are good to the extent that they promote the "welfare," so to speak, of the biosphere. For a Leopoldian, the rights view rests on the fictional view that individuals have a kind of value they in fact lack.

Traditional utilitarianism, not just the rights view, goes by the board, given Leopold's vision. To extend our moral concern to the experiences of animals (for example, their pleasures and pains) is not to overcome the prejudices indigenous to anthropocentrism. One who does this is still in the grip of these prejudices, supposing that mental states that matter to humans must be the yardstick of what matters morally. Utilitarians are people who escape from one prejudice (speciesism) only to embrace another (what we might call "sentientism," the view that mental states allied with or reducible to pleasure and pain are what matter morally). "Animal liberation" is not "nature liberation." In order to forge an ethic that liberates us from our anthropocentric tradition, we must develop a holistic understanding of things, a molecular, rather than an atomistic, vision of the scheme of things and our place in it. "The land" must be viewed as meriting our moral concern. Water, soil, plants, rocks—inanimate, not just animate, existence must be seen to be morally considerable. All are "members" of the same team—the "biotic team."

Holism and Ethical Vegetarianism

The holism Leopold advocates has interesting implications regarding how we should approach the issue of ethical vegetarianism. Appeals to the rights of animals, of course, are ruled out from the start. Based, as they are, on ideas about the independent value of the individual, such appeals are the voice of anthropocentrism past. That ghost can be exorcised once and for all only if we see the illusoriness of the atomistic view of the individual, *any* individual, as having an independent value, dignity, sanctity, etc. Standard versions of utilitarianism, restricted, as they are, to sentient creation, are similarly out of place. The "moral community" is comprised of all that inhabits the biosphere, not just some select portion of it, and there is no guarantee that what optimizes the balance of, say, pleasure over pain for sentient creation would be the right thing to do, when gauged by what promotes the "welfare" of the biosphere as a whole. If we are to approach the question of ethical vegetarianism with a clear head, therefore, we should refuse the guidance of both the rights view and utilitarianism.

Holism implies that the case for or against ethical vegetarianism must be decided by asking how certain practices involving animals promote or diminish the integrity, diversity, beauty, and harmony of the biosphere. This will be no easy task. Utilitarianism, as was noted earlier, encounters a very serious problem, when it faces the difficulty of saying what the consequences will be, or are most likely to be, if we do one thing rather than another. And this problem arises for utilitarians despite the fact that they restrict their calculations just to the effects on sentient creation. How much more difficult it must be, then, to calculate the consequences for *the biosphere*! There is some danger that "the Land Ethic" will not be able to get off the ground.

Let us assume, however, that this challenge could be met. Then it seems quite likely that the land ethic might judge some practices involving animals morally right, others wrong. For example, raising cattle on nonarable pastures might promote the biosphere's "welfare," whereas destroying a delicately balanced ecosystem in order to construct a factory farm, or allowing chemicals used in animal agriculture to pollute a stream or pond, might be roundly condemned as "unhealthy" for the biosphere. Holism, in short, presumably would decide the ethics of animal agriculture on a case by case basis. When a given commercial undertaking meets the principles of the land ethic, it is right, and we are free to support it by purchasing its wares. When a given commercial undertaking fails to meet the appropriate principles, it is wrong, and we ought not to help it along by buying its products. So far as the matter of the pain, stress, and deprivations that might be caused farm animals in a commercial endeavor that promotes the "welfare" of the biosphere, these "mental states" simply do not compute, and to be morally troubled by such concerns in unwittingly to slip back into the misplaced atomistic concern for the individual holism aspires to redirect.

Holism as Environmental Fascism

Few will be easily won over to this "new vision" of things. Like political fascism, where "the good of the State" supercedes "the good of the individual," what holism gives us is a fascist understanding of the environment. Rare species of wild grasses doubtless contribute more to the diversity of the biosphere than do the citizens of Cleveland. But are we therefore morally obliged to "save the wild grasses" at the expense of the life or welfare of these people? If holism is to hold its ground, it must acknowledge that it has this implication, and, in acknowledging this it must acknowledge further that its theoretical boat will come to grief on the shoals of our considered moral beliefs. Of course, those who are determined to awaken us to holism's virtues may be expected to reply that they are out to *reform* our moral vision, to *change* it, and so should not be expected to provide us with a theory that conforms with our "moral intuitions"—intuitions that, they are likely to add, are but another layer of our uncritical acceptance of our anthropocentric traditions and the ethnocentrism with which they are so intimately allied.

Well, perhaps this is so. Everything depends on the arguments given to support these bold pronouncements. What those arguments come to, or even if they come, must be considered elsewhere.[11] Here it must suffice to note that people who remain sympathetic to notions like "the rights of Man" and "the value of the individual" will not find environmental fascism congenial. And that is a crucial point, given the debate over ethical vegetarianism and commercial animal agriculture. For one cannot consistently defend meat-eating or commercial animal agriculture by appeal to the principles of "the Land Ethic," on the one hand, and, on the other, appeal to principles involving human rights and the value of the individual to defend one's convictions about how human beings should be treated. Environmental fascism and *any* form of a rights theory are like oil and water; they don't mix.

SUMMARY

Two related questions have occupied our attention throughout: (1) Is vegetarianism required on moral grounds? and (2) Judged ethically, what should we say, and what should we do, about commercial animal agriculture? Three different ways to approach these questions have been characterized: utilitarianism, the rights view, and holism. Of the three, the rights view is the most "radical"; it calls for the total abolition of commercial animal agriculture and argues that, as individuals, we have an obligation to cease eating meat, including the meat produced by the animal industry, independently of how many other people do so and independently of the actual consequences our individual abstention have on this industry. Since this industry routinely violates the rights of farm animals, those who support it, not just those who run and profit from it, have "dirty hands."

Some utilitarians evidently seek the same answers offered by the rights view, but their arguments are radically different. Since what we ought to do depends on the consequences, and since our individual abstention from meat eating would not make a whit of difference to any individual animal, it seems we cannot have an obligation to be vegetarians, judged on utilitarian grounds. If, in reply, we are told that it is the consequences of *many* people becoming vegetarians, not just those that flow from the individual's abstention, that grounds the obligation to be vegetarian, utilitarians are, so to speak, out of the frying pan but into the fire. First, we do not know what the consequences will be (for example, for the economy, the starving masses of the Third World, or even farm animals) if many people became vegetarians, and, second, it distorts our very notion of the duties of the individual to suppose that these duties depend on how many other people act in similar ways. So, no, these utilitarians do not succeed in showing *either* that we have an obligation to be vegetarians *or* that commercial animal agriculture is morally to be condemned. These utilitarians may want the conclusions the rights view reaches, but, paradoxically, their utilitarianism stands in the way of getting them.

Holism (the kind of theory we find in Aldo Leopold's work, for example) was the third view considered. So long as we have reason to believe that this or that commercial endeavor in farm animals is not contrary to the beauty, harmony, diversity, and integrity of the biosphere, we have no reason to condemn its operation nor any reason to refuse to consume its products. If, however, particular commercial ventures are destructive of these qualities of the biosphere, we ought to bring them to a halt, and one way of helping to do this is to cease to buy their products. Holism, in short, answers our two questions, one might say, with an unequivocal "Yes and no." Very serious questions remain, however, concerning how we can know what, according to holism, we must know, before we can say that a given act or practice is right or wrong. Can we really presume to know the consequences of our acts "for the biosphere?" Moreover, holism implies that individuals are of no consequence apart from their role as "members of the biotic team," a fascist view of the individual that would in principle allow mass destruction of the members of a plentiful species (for example, Homo sapiens) in order to preserve the last remaining members of another (for example, a rare wild flower), all in the name of preserving "the diversity" of the biosphere. Few will find holism intuitively congenial, and none can rely on it to answer our two questions and, in mid-stride, invoke "the rights of man" to defend a privileged moral status for human beings. At least none can consistently do this.

Despite their noteworthy differences, the three views we have examined speak with one voice on the matter of the tradition of anthropocentrism bequeathed to us by humanism and theism. That tradition is morally bankrupt. On that the three are agreed. And on this, it seems, we may all agree as well. That being so, and while conceding that the foregoing does not "prove" its merits, it can be no objection to the rights view's answers to our two questions to protest that they are at odds with our moral traditions. To be at odds with these traditions is devoutly to be wished.

Nor is it an objection to the rights view to claim that because it proclaims the rights of animals, it must be unmindful of "the rights of Man" or insensitive to the beauty or integrity of the environment. The rights view does not deny "the rights of Man"; it only refuses to be species-bound in its vision of inherent value and moral rights. No principle it upholds opposes making grains not fed to animals available to needy humans, as commercial animal agriculture winds down. It simply insists that *these* (real or imaginary) consequences of the dissolution of commercial animal agriculture are not the reason why we ought to seek to dissolve it. As for the natural environment, one can only wonder what more one could do to ensure that its integrity and beauty are promoted or retained, than to act in ways that show respect to animals, including wild animals. In respecting the rights of this "part" of the biosphere, will not the "welfare of the whole" be promoted?

CONCLUSION

Theories are one thing; our practice quite another. And so it may seem that all this talk about rights and duties, utility and preferences, the biosphere and anthropocentrism comes to naught. People are people, and they will do what they are used to doing, what they like to do. History gives the lie to this lazy acquiescence in the face of custom and convenience. Were it true, whites would still own blacks, women would still lack the vote, and people could still be put to death for sodomy. Times and customs change, and one (but by no means not the only) force for change are the ideas that trickle down over time into the language and thought of a culture. The language of "animal rights" is in the air, and the thought behind those words is taking root. What not too long ago could be laughed out of court now elicits serious concern. Mill says it well: "All great movements go through three stages: ridicule, discussion, adoption." The movement for animal rights is beyond the stage of ridicule. For those persuaded of its truth, it is an irresistible force. Commercial animal agriculture is the movable object.

Endnotes

1. Immanuel Kant, "Duties to Animals and Spirits," *Lectures on Ethics,* trans. Louis Infield (New York: Harper and Row, 1963), pp. 239–41. Collected in *Animal Rights and Human Obligations,* Tom Regan and Peter Singer, eds. (Englewood Cliffs, NJ: Prentice-Hall Inc., 1976), pp. 122–23.
2. St. Thomas Aquinas, *Summa Contra Gentiles,* literally translated by the English Dominican Fathers (Benzinger Books, 1928), Third Book, Part II, Chap. C XII. Collected in *Animal Rights and Human Obligations,* op. cit., pp. 58–59.
3. Jeremy Bentham, *The Principles of Morals and Legislation* (1789: many editions), Chapter XVII, Section 1. Collected in *Animal Rights and Human Obligations,* op. cit., pp. 129–30.
4. John Stuart Mill, "Whewell on Moral Philosophy," *Collected Works,* Vol. X, pp. 185–87. Collected in *Animal Rights and Human Obligations,* op. cit., pp. 131–32.
5. Peter Singer, *Animal Liberation* (New York: Avon Books, 1975). By far the best factual account of factory farming is J. Mason and Peter Singer, *Animal Factories* (New York: Collier Books, 1982).
6. Richard Ryder, "Experiments on Animals," in *Animals, Men and Morals,* ed. S. and R. Godlovitch and J. Harris (New York: Taplinger, 1972). Collected in *Animal Rights and Human Obligations,* op. cit., pp. 33-47.
7. These criticisms of utilitarianism are developed at greater length in my *The Case For Animal Rights* (Berkeley: University of California Press. London: Routledge and Kegan Paul, 1983).
8. The rights view is developed at length in *The Case For Animal Rights,* ibid.
9. I use the familiar idea of "person" here because it is helpful. I do not use it in *The Case For Animal Rights.* I do not believe anything of substance turns on its use or nonuse.
10. Aldo Leopold, *A Sand County Almanac* (New York: Oxford University Press, 1949). For additional criticism and suggested readings, see William Aiken, "Ethical Issues in Agriculture," in Tom Regan, ed., *Earthbound:*

New Introductory Essays in Environmental Ethics (New York: Random House (paper); Philadelphia: Temple University Press (cloth), 1983), pp. 268–70.
11. See *The Case For Animal Rights,* op. cit., ch. 5.

REVIEW QUESTIONS

1. Explain Regan's account of traditional moral anthropocentrism.
2. What is the utilitarian objection to this view according to Regan?
3. What objections does Regan make to Singer's position?
4. What is the rights view as Regan expounds it?
5. What is inherent value in Regan's view?
6. Who has rights according to Regan?
7. Why does Regan think that commercial animal agriculture violates the rights of animals?
8. What is the holistic view advocated by Leopold (according to Regan)?
9. Why doesn't Regan accept this view?

DISCUSSION QUESTIONS

1. Does Regan refute utilitarianism or not? Explain your answer.
2. Is Regan's notion of inherent value coherent?
3. Do you agree that some animals are persons? Defend your answer.
4. Do you eat meat? If so, do you think that there is anything morally wrong with this practice? Defend your position.

Mary Anne Warren

Difficulties with the Strong Animal Rights Position

For biographical information on Warren, see her reading in Chapter 2.

Warren explains and then attacks Regan's strong animal rights position, the view that non-human animals have the same basic moral rights as humans. She makes two criticisms of Regan's position: It rests on an obscure concept of inherent value, and it fails to draw a sharp line between living things which have inherent value and moral rights and other living things which don't have such value or rights. Warren concludes with a defense of the weak animal rights position—that animal rights are weaker than human rights because humans are rational and animals are not.

From Mary Anne Warren, "Difficulties with the Strong Animal Rights Position," *Between the Species,* Vol. 2, No. 4 (Fall, 1987). Reprinted by permission.

Tom Regan has produced what is perhaps the definitive defense of the view that the basic moral rights of at least some non-human animals are in no way inferior to our own. In *The Case for Animal Rights,* he argues that all normal mammals over a year of age have the same basic moral rights.[1] Non-human mammals have essentially the same right not to be harmed or killed as we do. I shall call this "the strong animal rights position," although it is weaker than the claims made by some animal liberationists in that it ascribes rights to only some sentient animals.[2]

I will argue that Regan's case for the strong animal rights position is unpersuasive and that this position entails consequences which a reasonable person cannot accept. I do not deny that some non-human animals have moral rights; indeed, I would extend the scope of the rights claim to include all sentient animals, that is, all those capable of having experiences, including experiences of pleasure or satisfaction and pain, suffering, or frustration.[3] However, I do not think that the moral rights of most non-human animals are identical in strength to those of persons.[4] The rights of most non-human animals may be overridden in circumstances which would not justify overriding the rights of persons. There are, for instance, compelling realities which sometimes require that we kill animals for reasons which could not justify the killing of persons. I will call this view "the weak animal rights" position, even though it ascribes rights to a wider range of animals than does the strong animal rights position.

I will begin by summarizing Regan's case for the strong animal rights position and noting two problems with it. Next, I will explore some consequences of the strong animal rights position which I think are unacceptable. Finally, I will outline the case for the weak animal rights position.

Regan's Case

Regan's argument moves through three stages. First, he argues that normal, mature mammals are not only sentient but have other mental capacities as well. These include the capacities for emotion, memory, belief, desire, the use of general concepts, intentional action, a sense of the future, and some degree of self-awareness. Creatures with such capacities are said to be subjects-of-a-life. They are not only alive in the biological sense but have a psychological identity over time and an existence which can go better or worse for them. Thus, they can be harmed or benefited. These are plausible claims, and well defended. One of the strongest parts of the book is the rebuttal of philosophers, such as R. G. Frey, who object to the application of such mentalistic terms to creatures that do not use a human-style language.[5] The second and third stages of the argument are more problematic.

In the second stage, Regan argues that subjects-of-a-life have inherent value. His concept of inherent value grows out of his opposition to utilitarianism. Utilitarian moral theory, he says, treats individuals as "mere receptacles" for morally significant value, in that harm to one individual may be justified by the production of a greater net benefit to other individuals. In opposition to this, he holds that subjects-of-a-life have a value independent of both the value they may place upon their lives or experiences and the value others may place upon them.

Inherent value, Regan argues, does not come in degrees. To hold that some individuals have more inherent value than others is to adopt a "perfectionist" theory, i.e., one which assigns different moral worth to individuals according to how well they are thought to exemplify some virtue(s), such as intelligence or moral autonomy. Perfectionist theories have been used, at least since the time of Aristotle, to rationalize such injustices as slavery and male domination, as well as the unrestrained exploitation of animals. Regan argues that if we reject these injustices, then we must also reject perfectionism and conclude that all subjects-of-a-life have equal inherent value. Moral agents have no more inherent value than moral patients, i.e., subjects-of-a-life who are not morally responsible for their actions.

In the third phase of the argument, Regan uses the thesis of equal inherent value to derive strong moral rights for all subjects-of-a-life. This thesis underlies the Respect Principle, which forbids us to treat beings who have inherent value as mere receptacles, i.e., mere means to the production of the greatest overall good. This principle, in turn, underlies the Harm Principle, which says that we have a direct *prima facie* duty not to harm beings who have inherent value. Together, these principles give rise to moral rights. Rights are defined as valid claims, claims to certain goods and against certain beings, i.e., moral agents. Moral rights generate duties not only to refrain from inflicting harm upon beings with inherent value but also to come to their aid when they are threatened by other moral agents. Rights are not absolute but may be overridden in certain circumstances. Just what these circumstances are we will consider later. But first, let's look at some difficulties in the theory as thus far presented.

The Mystery of Inherent Value

Inherent value is a key concept in Regan's theory. It is the bridge between the plausible claim that all normal, mature mammals—human or otherwise—are subjects-of-a-life and the more debatable claim that they all have basic moral rights of the same strength. But it is a highly obscure concept, and its obscurity makes it ill-suited to play this crucial role.

Inherent value is defined almost entirely in negative terms. It is not dependent upon the value which either the inherently valuable individual or anyone else may place upon that individual's life or experiences. It is not (necessarily) a function of sentience or any other mental capacity, because, Regan says, some entities which are not sentient (e.g., trees, rivers, or rocks) may, nevertheless, have inherent value (p. 246). It cannot attach to anything other than an individual; species, eco-systems, and the like cannot have inherent value.

These are some of the things which inherent value is not. But what is it? Unfortunately, we are not told. Inherent value appears as a mysterious non-natural property which we must take on faith. Regan says that it is a *postulate* that subjects-of-a-life have inherent value, a postulate justified by the fact that it avoids certain absurdities which he thinks follow from a purely utilitarian theory (p. 247). But why is the postulate that *subjects-of-a-life* have inherent value? If the inherent value of a being is completely independent of the value that it or anyone else places upon its experiences, then why does the fact that it has certain sorts of experiences constitute evidence that it has inherent value? If the reason is that subjects-of-a-life have an existence which can go better or worse for them, then why isn't the appropriate conclusion that all sentient beings have inherent value, since they would all seem to meet that condition? Sentient but mentally unsophisticated beings may have a less extensive range of possible satisfactions and frustrations, but why should it follow that they have—or may have—no inherent value at all?

In the absence of a positive account of inherent value, it is also difficult to grasp the connection between being inherently valuable and having moral rights. Intuitively, it seems that value is one thing, and rights are another. It does not seem incoherent to say that some things (e.g., mountains, rivers, redwood trees) are inherently valuable and yet are not the sorts of things which can have moral rights. Nor does it seem incoherent to ascribe inherent value to some things which are not individuals, e.g., plant or animal species, though it may well be incoherent to ascribe moral rights to such things.

In short, the concept of inherent value seems to create at least as many problems as it solves. If inherent value is based on some natural property, then why not try to identify that property and explain its moral significance, without appealing to inherent value? And if it is not based on any natural property, then why should we believe in it? That it may enable us to avoid some of the problems faced by the utilitarian is not a sufficient reason, if it creates other problems which are just as serious.

Is There a Sharp Line?

Perhaps the most serious problems are those that arise when we try to apply the strong animal rights position to animals other than normal, mature mammals. Regan's theory requires us to divide all living things into two categories: those which have the same inherent value and the same basic moral rights that we do, and those which have no inherent value and presumably no moral rights. But wherever we try to draw the line, such a sharp division is implausible.

It would surely be arbitrary to draw such a sharp line between normal, mature mammals and all other living things. Some birds (e.g., crows, magpies, parrots, mynahs) appear to be just as mentally sophisticated as most mammals and thus are equally strong candidates for inclusion under the subject-of-a-life criterion. Regan is not in fact advocating that we draw the line here. His claim is only that normal mature mammals are clear cases, while other cases are less clear. Yet, on his theory, there must be such a sharp line *somewhere,* since there are no degrees of inherent value. But why should we believe that there is a sharp line between creatures that are subjects-of-a-life and creatures that are not? Isn't it more likely that "subjecthood" comes in degrees, that some creatures have only a little self-awareness, and only a little capacity to anticipate the future, while some have a little more, and some a good deal more?

Should we, for instance, regard fish, amphibians, and reptiles as subjects-of-a-life? A simple yes-or-no answer seems inadequate. On the one hand, some of their behavior is difficult to explain without the assumption that they have sensations, beliefs, desires, emotions, and memories; on the other hand, they do not seem to exhibit very much self-awareness or very much conscious anticipation of future events. Do they have enough mental sophistication to count as subjects-of-a-life? Exactly how much is enough?

It is still more unclear what we should say about insects, spiders, octopi, and other invertebrate animals which have brains and sensory organs but whose minds (if they have minds) are even more alien to us than those of fish or reptiles. Such creatures are probably sentient. Some people doubt that they can feel pain, since they lack certain neurological structures which are crucial to the processing of pain impulses in vertebrate animals. But this argument is inconclusive, since their nervous systems might process pain in ways different from ours. When injured, they sometimes act as if they are in pain. On evolutionary grounds, it seems unlikely that highly mobile creatures with complex sensory systems would not have developed a capacity for pain (and pleasure), since such a capacity has obvious survival value. It must, however, be admitted that we do not *know* whether spiders can feel pain (or something very like it), let alone whether they have emotions, memories, beliefs, desires, self-awareness, or a sense of the future.

Even more mysterious are the mental capacities (if any) of mobile microfauna. The brisk and efficient way that paramecia move about in their incessant search for food *might* indicate some kind of sentience, in spite of their lack of eyes, ears, brains, and other organs associated with sentience in more complex organisms. It is conceivable—though not very probable—that they, too, are subjects-of-a-life.

The existence of a few unclear cases need not pose a serious problem for a moral theory, but in this case, the unclear cases constitute most of those with which an adequate theory of animal rights would need to deal. The subject-of-a-life criterion can provide us with little or no moral guidance in our interactions with the vast majority of animals. That might be acceptable if it could be supplemented with additional principles which would provide such guidance. However, the radical dualism of the theory precludes supplementing it in this way. We are forced to say that either a spider has the same right to life as you and I do, or it has no right to life whatever—and that only the gods know which of these alternatives is true.

Regan's suggestion for dealing with such unclear cases is to apply the "benefit of the doubt" principle. That is, when dealing with beings that may or may not be subjects-of-a-life, we should act as if they are.[6] But if we try to apply this principle to the entire range of doubtful cases, we will find ourselves with moral obligations which we cannot possibly fulfill. In many climates, it is virtually impossible to live without swatting mosquitoes and exterminating cockroaches, and not all of us can afford to hire someone to sweep the path before we walk, in order to make sure that we do not step on ants. Thus, we are still faced with the daunting task of drawing a sharp line somewhere on the continuum of life forms—this time, a line demarcating the limits of the benefit of the doubt principle.

The weak animal rights theory provides a more plausible way of dealing with this range of cases, in that it allows the rights of animals of different kinds to vary in strength. . . .

Why Are Animal Rights Weaker Than Human Rights?

How can we justify regarding the rights of persons as generally stronger than those of sentient beings which are not persons? There are a plethora of bad justifications, based on religious premises or false or unprovable claims about the differences between human and non-human nature. But there is one difference which has a clear moral relevance: people are at least sometimes capable of being moved to action or inaction by the force of reasoned argument. Rationality rests upon other mental capacities, notably those which Regan cites as criteria for being a subject-of-a-life. We share these capacities with many other animals. But it is not just because we are subjects-of-a-life that we are both able and morally compelled to recognize one another as beings with equal basic moral rights. It is also because we are able to "listen to reason" in order to settle our conflicts and cooperate in shared projects. This capacity, unlike the others, may require something like a human language.

Why is rationality morally relevant? It does not make us "better" than other animals or more "perfect." It does not even automatically make us more intelligent. (Bad reasoning reduces our effective intelligence rather than increasing it.) But it is morally relevant insofar as it provides greater possibilities for cooperation and for the nonviolent resolution of problems. It also makes us more dangerous than non-rational beings can ever be. Because we are potentially more dangerous and less predictable than wolves, we need an articulated system of morality to regulate our conduct. Any human morality, to be workable in the long run, must recognize the equal moral status of all persons, whether through the postulate of equal basic moral rights or in some other way. The recognition of the moral equality of other persons is the price we must each pay for their recognition of our moral equality. Without this mutual recognition of moral equality, human society can exist only in a state of chronic and bitter conflict. The war between the sexes will persist so long as there is sexism and male domination; racial conflict will never be eliminated so long as there are racist laws and practices. But, to the extent that we achieve a mutual recognition of equality, we can hope to live together, perhaps as peacefully as wolves, achieving (in part) through explicit moral principles what they do not seem to need explicit moral principles to achieve.

Why not extend this recognition of moral equality to other creatures, even though they cannot do the same for us? The answer is that we cannot. Because we cannot reason with most non-human animals, we cannot always solve the problems which they may cause without harming them—although we are always obligated to try. We cannot negotiate a treaty with the feral cats and foxes, requiring them to stop preying on endangered native species in return for suitable concessions on our part.

> If rats invade our houses . . . we cannot reason with them, hoping to persuade them of the injustice they do us. We can only attempt to get rid of them.[7]

Aristotle was not wrong in claiming that the capacity to alter one's behavior on the basis of reasoned argument is relevant to the full moral status which he accorded to free men. Of course, he was wrong in his other premise, that women and slaves by their nature cannot reason well enough to function as autonomous moral agents. Had that premise been true, so would his conclusion that women and slaves are not quite the moral equals of free men. In the case of most non-human animals, the corresponding premise is true. If, on the other hand, there are animals with whom we can (learn to) reason, then we are obligated to do this and to regard them as our moral equals.

Thus, to distinguish between the rights of persons and those of most other animals on the grounds that only people can alter their behavior on the basis of reasoned argument does not commit us to a perfectionist theory of the sort Aristotle endorsed. There is no excuse for refusing to recognize the moral equality of some people on the grounds that we don't regard them as quite as rational as we are, since it is perfectly clear that most people can reason well enough to determine how to act so as to respect the basic rights of others (if they choose to), and that is enough for moral equality.

But what about people who are clearly not rational? It is often argued that sophisticated mental capacities such as rationality cannot be essential for the possession of equal basic moral rights, since nearly everyone agrees that human infants and mentally incompetent persons have such rights, even though they may lack those sophisticated mental capacities. But this argument is inconclusive, because there are powerful practical and emotional reasons for protecting non-rational human beings, reasons which are absent in the case of most non-human animals. Infancy and mental incompetence are human conditions which all of us either have experienced or are likely to experience at some time. We also protect babies and mentally incompetent people because we care for them. We don't normally care for animals in the same way, and when we do—e.g., in the case of much-loved pets—we may regard them as having special rights by virtue of their relationship to us. We protect them not only for their sake but also for our own, lest we be hurt by harm done to them. Regan holds that such "side-effects" are irrelevant to moral rights, and perhaps they are. But in ordinary usage, there is no sharp line between moral rights and those moral protections which are not rights. The extension of strong moral protections to infants and the mentally impaired in no way proves that nonhuman animals have the same basic moral rights as people.

Why Speak of "Animal Rights" At All?

If, as I have argued, reality precludes our treating all animals as our moral equals, then why should we still ascribe rights to them? Everyone agrees that animals are entitled to some protection against human abuse, but why speak of animal *rights* if we are not prepared to accept most animals as our moral equals? The weak animal rights position may seem an unstable compromise between the bold claim that animals have the same basic moral rights that we do and the more common view that animals have no rights at all.

It is probably impossible to either prove or disprove the thesis that animals have moral rights by producing an analysis of the concept of a moral right and checking to see if some or all animals satisfy the conditions for having rights. The concept of a moral right is complex, and it is not clear which of its strands are essential. Paradigm rights holders, i.e., mature and mentally competent persons, are *both* rational and morally autonomous beings and sentient subjects-of-a-life. Opponents of animal rights claim that rationality and moral autonomy are essential for the possession of rights, while defenders of animal rights claim that they are not. The ordinary concept of a moral right is probably not precise enough to enable us to determine who is right on purely definitional grounds.

If logical analysis will not answer the question of whether animals have moral rights, practical considerations may, nevertheless, incline us to say that they do. The most plausible alternative to the view that animals have moral rights is that, while they do not have *rights,* we are, nevertheless, obligated not to be cruel to them. Regan argues persuasively that the injunction to avoid being cruel to animals is inadequate to express our obligations towards animals, because it focuses on the mental states of those who cause animal suffering, rather than on the harm done to the animals themselves (p. 158). Cruelty is inflicting pain or suffering and either taking pleasure in that pain or suffering or being more or less indifferent to it. Thus, to express the demand for the decent treatment of animals in terms of the rejection of cruelty is to invite the too easy response that those who subject animals to suffering are not being cruel because they regret the suffering they cause but sincerely believe that what they do is justified. The injunction to avoid cruelty is also inadequate in that it does not preclude the killing of animals—for any reason, however trivial—so long as it is done relatively painlessly.

The inadequacy of the anti-cruelty view provides one practical reason for speaking of animal rights. Another practical reason is that this is an age in which nearly all significant moral claims tend to be expressed in terms of rights. Thus, the denial that animals have rights, however carefully qualified, is likely to be taken to mean that we may do whatever we like to them, provided that we do not violate any human rights. In such a context, speaking of the rights of animals may be the only way to persuade many people to take seriously protests against the abuse of animals.

Why not extend this line of argument and speak of the rights of trees, mountains, oceans, or anything else which we may wish to see protected from destruction? Some environmentalists have not hesitated to speak in this way, and, given the importance of protecting such elements of the natural world, they cannot be blamed for using this rhetorical device. But, I would argue that moral rights can meaningfully be ascribed only to entities which have some capacity for sentience. This is because moral rights are protections designed to protect rights holders from harms or to provide them with benefits which matter *to them*. Only beings capable of sentience can be harmed or benefited in ways which matter to them, for only such beings can like or dislike what happens to them or prefer some conditions to others. Thus, sentient animals, unlike mountains, rivers, or species, are at least logically possible candidates for moral rights. This fact, together with the need to end current abuses of animals—e.g., in scientific research . . .—provides a plausible case for speaking of animal rights.

Conclusion

I have argued that Regan's case for ascribing strong moral rights to all normal, mature mammals is unpersuasive because (1) it rests upon the obscure concept of inherent value, which is defined only in negative terms, and (2) it seems to preclude any plausible answer to questions about the moral status of the vast majority of sentient animals. . . .

The weak animal rights theory asserts that (1) any creature whose natural mode of life includes the pursuit of certain satisfactions has the right not to be forced to exist without the opportunity to pursue those satisfactions; (2) that any creature which is capable of pain, suffering, or frustration has the right that such experiences not be deliberately inflicted upon it without some compelling reason; and (3) that no sentient being should be killed without good reason. However, moral rights are not an all-or-nothing affair. The strength of the reasons required to override the rights of a non-human organism varies, depending upon—among other things—the probability that it is sentient and (if it is clearly sentient) its probable degree of mental sophistication. . . .

Endnotes

1. Tom Regan, *The Case for Animal Rights* (Berkeley: University of California Press, 1983). All page references are to this edition.
2. For instance, Peter Singer, although he does not like to speak of rights, includes all sentient beings under the protection of his basic utilitarian principle of equal respect for like interests. (Animal Liberation [New York: Avon Books, 1975], p. 3.)
3. The capacity for sentience, like all of the mental capacities mentioned in what follows, is a disposition. Dispositions do not disappear whenever they are not currently manifested. Thus, sleeping or temporarily unconscious persons or non-human animals are still sentient in the relevant sense (i.e., still capable of sentience), so long as they still have the neurological mechanisms necessary for the occurrence of experiences.
4. It is possible, perhaps probable that some non-human animals—such as cetaceans and anthropoid apes—should be regarded as persons. If so, then the weak animal rights position holds that these animals have the same basic moral rights as human persons.
5. See R. G. Frey, *Interests and Rights: The Case Against Animals* (Oxford: Oxford University Press, 1980).
6. See, for instance, p. 319, where Regan appeals to the benefit of the doubt principle when dealing with infanticide and late-term abortion.
7. Bonnie Steinbock, "Speciesism and the Idea of Equality," *Philosophy* 53 (1978):253.

Review Questions

1. Distinguish between what Warren calls the strong animal rights position and the weak animal rights position.
2. What problems does Warren find in Regan's case for the strong animal rights position?
3. Explain Warren's defense of the weak animal rights position.

Discussion Questions

1. Has Warren refuted Regan's strong animal rights position? Does he have an adequate reply?
2. In Warren's view, rationality is essential for having equal basic moral rights. But infants and mentally incompetent humans are not rational; therefore, they do not have moral rights. Does Warren have an acceptable reply to this argument?

Joel Feinberg

The Rights of Animals and Unborn Generations

Joel Feinberg is Professor of Philosophy at the University of Arizona. He is the author of Doing and Deserving *(1970),* Social Philosophy *(1973), and* The Moral Limits of the Criminal Law *(1984-) (in four volumes), and editor of* Reason and Responsibility *(1965-) and* Moral Concepts *(1969).*

Feinberg begins with an analysis of the concept of a right: To have a right is to have a claim to something against *someone. But who has rights? Feinberg's answer is that any being who can have an interest can have a right. This interest principle (as Feinberg calls it) implies that humans and animals can have rights, but rocks, vegetables, and whole species cannot have rights. Future generations of people do have rights, but only contingent on their coming into existence; they do not have a right to existence.*

Every philosophical paper must begin with an unproved assumption. Mine is the assumption that there will still be a world five hundred years from now, and that it will contain human beings who are very much like us. We have it within our power now, clearly, to affect the lives of these creatures for better or worse by contributing to the conservation or corruption of the environment in which they must live. I shall assume furthermore that it is psychologically possible for us to care about our remote descendants, that many of us in fact do care, and indeed that we ought to care. My main concern then will be to show that it makes sense to speak of the rights of unborn generations against us, and that given the moral judgment that we ought to conserve our environmental inheritance for them, and its grounds, we might well say that future generations *do* have rights correlative to our present duties toward them. Protecting our environment now is also a matter of elementary prudence, and insofar as we do it for the next generation already here in the persons of our children, it is a matter of love. But from the perspective of our remote descendants it is basically a matter of justice, of respect for their rights. My main concern here will be to examine the concept of a right to better understand how that can be.

The Problem

To have a right is a have a claim[1] *to* something and *against* someone, the recognition of which is called for by legal rules or, in the case of moral rights, by the principles of an enlightened conscience. In the familiar cases of rights, the claimant is a competent adult human being, and the claimee is an officeholder in an institution or else a private individual, in either case, another competent adult human being. Normal adult human beings, then, are obviously the sorts of beings of whom rights can meaningfully be predicated. Everyone would agree to that, even extreme misanthropes who deny that anyone in fact has rights. On the other hand, it is absurd to say that rocks can have rights, not because rocks are morally inferior things unworthy of rights (that statement makes no sense either), but because rocks belong to a category of entities of whom rights cannot be meaningfully predicated. That is not to say that there are no circumstances in which we ought to treat rocks carefully, but only that the rocks themselves cannot validly claim good treatment from us. In between the clear cases of rocks and normal human beings, however, is a spectrum of less obvious cases, including some bewildering borderline ones. Is it meaningful or concep-

From Joel Feinberg, "The Rights of Animals and Unborn Generations" in William T. Blackstone, ed., *Philosophy and Environmental Crisis*.

tually possible to ascribe rights to our dead ancestors? to individual animals? to whole species of animals? to plants? to idiots and madmen? to fetuses? to generations yet unborn? Until we know how to settle these puzzling cases, we cannot claim fully to grasp the concept of a right, or to know the shape of its logical boundaries.

One way to approach these riddles is to turn one's attention first to the most familiar and unproblematic instances of rights, note their most salient characteristics, and then compare the borderline cases with them, measuring as closely as possible the points of similarity and difference. In the end, the way we classify the borderline cases may depend on whether we are more impressed with the similarities or the differences between them and the cases in which we have the most confidence.

It will be useful to consider the problem of individual animals first because their case is the one that has already been debated with the most thoroughness by philosophers so that the dialectic of claim and rejoinder has now unfolded to the point where disputants can get to the end game quickly and isolate the crucial point at issue. When we understand precisely what *is* at issue in the debate over animal rights, I think we will have the key to the solution of all the other riddles about rights.

Individual Animals

Almost all modern writers agree that we ought to be kind to animals, but that is quite another thing from holding that animals can claim kind treatment from us as their due. Statutes making cruelty to animals a crime are now very common, and these, of course, impose legal duties on people not to mistreat animals; but that still leaves open the question whether the animals, as beneficiaries of those duties, possess rights correlative to them. We may very well have duties *regarding* animals that are not at the same time duties *to* animals, just as we may have duties regarding rocks, or buildings, or lawns, that are not duties *to* the rocks, buildings, or lawns. Some legal writers have taken the still more extreme position that animals themselves are not even the directly intended beneficiaries of statutes prohibiting cruelty to animals. During the nineteenth century, for example, it was commonly said that such statutes were designed to protect human beings by preventing the growth of cruel habits that could later threaten human beings with harm too. Prof. Louis B. Schwartz finds the rationale of the cruelty-to-animals prohibition in its protection of animal lovers from affronts to their sensibilities. "It is not the mistreated dog who is the ultimate object of concern," he writes. "Our concern is for the feelings of other human beings, a large proportion of whom, although accustomed to the slaughter of animals for food, readily identify themselves with a tortured dog or horse and respond with great sensitivity to its sufferings." [2] This seems to me to be factitious. How much more natural it is to say with John Chipman Gray that the true purpose of cruelty-to-animals statutes is "to preserve the dumb brutes from suffering." [3] The very people whose sensibilities are invoked in the alternative explanation, a group that no doubt now includes most of us, are precisely those who would insist that the protection belongs primarily to the animals themselves, not merely to their own tender feelings. Indeed, it would be difficult even to account for the existence of such feelings in the absence of a belief that the animals deserve the protection in their own right and for their own sakes.

Even if we allow, as I think we must, that animals are the intended direct beneficiaries of legislation forbidding cruelty to animals, it does not follow directly that animals have legal rights, and Gray himself, for one,[4] refused to draw this further inference. Animals cannot have rights, he thought, for the same reason they cannot have duties, namely, that they are not genuine "moral agents." Now, it is relatively easy to see why animals cannot have duties, and this matter is largely beyond controversy. Animals cannot be "reasoned with" or instructed in their responsibilities; they are inflexible and unadaptable to future contingencies; they are subject to fits of instinctive passion which they are incapable of repressing or controlling, postponing or sublimating. Hence, they cannot enter into contractual agreements, or make promises; they cannot be trusted; and they cannot (except within very narrow limits and for purposes of conditioning) be blamed for what would be called "moral failures" in a human being. They are therefore incapable of being moral subjects, of acting rightly or wrongly in the moral sense, of having, discharging, or breaching duties and obligations.

But what is there about the intellectual incompetence of animals (which admittedly disqualifies them for duties) that makes them logically unsuitable for rights? The most common reply to this question is that animals are incapable of *claiming* rights on their own. They cannot make motion, on their own, to courts to have their claims recognized or enforced; they cannot initiate, on their own, to courts to have their claims recognized or enforced; they cannot initiate, on their own, any kind of legal proceedings; nor are they capable of even understanding when their rights are being violated, of distinguishing harm from wrongful injury, and responding with indignation and an outraged sense of justice instead of mere anger or fear.

No one can deny any of these allegations, but to the claim that they are the grounds for disqualification of rights of animals, philosophers on the other side of this controversy have made convincing rejoinders. It is simply not true, says W. D. Lamont,[5] that the ability to understand what a right is and the ability to set legal machinery in motion by one's own initiative are necessary for the possession of rights. If that were the case, then neither human idiots nor wee babies would have any legal rights at all. Yet it is manifest that both of these classes of intellectual incompetents have legal rights recognized and easily enforced by the courts. Children and idiots start legal proceedings, not on their own direct initiative, but rather through the actions of proxies or attorneys who are empowered to speak in their names. If there is no conceptual absurdity in this situation, why should there be in the case where a proxy makes a claim on behalf of an animal? People commonly enough make wills leaving money to trustees for the care of animals. Is it not natural to speak of the animal's right to his inheritance in cases of this kind? If a trustee embezzles money from the animal's account,[6] and a proxy speaking in the dumb brute's behalf presses the animal's claim, can he not be described as asserting the animal's *rights*? More exactly, the animal itself claims its rights through the vicarious actions of a human proxy speaking in its name and in its behalf. There appears to be no reason why we should require the animal to understand what is going on (so the argument concludes) as a condition for regarding it as a possessor of rights.

Some writers protest at this point that the legal relation between a principal and an agent cannot hold between animals and human beings. Between humans, the relation of agency can take two very different forms, depending upon the degree of discretion granted to the agent, and there is a continuum of combinations between the extremes. On the one hand, there is the agent who is the mere "mouthpiece" of this principal. He is a "tool" in much the same sense as is a typewriter or telephone; he simply transmits the instructions of his principal. Human beings could hardly be the agents or representatives of animals in this sense, since the dumb brutes could no more use human "tools" than mechanical ones. On the other hand, an agent may be some sort of expert hired to exercise his professional judgment on behalf of, and in the name of, the principal. He may be given, within some limited area of expertise, complete independence to act as he deems best, binding his principal to all the beneficial or detrimental consequences. This is the role played by trustees, lawyers, and ghost-writers. This type of representation requires that the agent have great skill, but makes little or no demand upon the principal, who may leave everything to the judgment of his agent. Hence, there appears, at first, to be no reason why an animal cannot be a totally passive principal in this second kind of agency relationship.

There are still some important dissimilarities, however. In the typical instance of representation by an agent, even of the second, highly discretionary kind, the agent is hired by a principal who enters into an agreement or contract with him; the principal tells his agent that within certain carefully specified boundaries "You may speak for me," subject always to the principal's approval, his right to give new directions, or to cancel the whole arrangement. No dog or cat could possibly do any of those things. Moreover, if it is the assigned task of the agent to defend the principal's rights, the principal may often decide to release his claimee, or to waive his own rights, and instruct his agent accordingly. Again, no mute cow or horse can do that. But although the possibility of hiring, agreeing, contracting, approving, directing, canceling, releasing, waiving, and instructing is present in the typical (all-human) case of agency representation, there appears to be no reason of a logical or conceptual kind why that *must* be so, and indeed there are some special examples involving human principals where it is not in fact so. I have in mind legal rules, for example, that require that a defendant be represented at his trial by an attorney, and impose a state-appointed attorney upon reluctant defendants, or upon those tried *in absentia,* whether they like it or not. Moreover, small children and mentally deficient and deranged adults are commonly represented by trustees and attorneys, even though they are incapable of granting their own consent to the representation, or of entering into contracts, of giving directions, or waiving their rights. It may be that it is unwise to permit agents to represent principals without the latters' knowledge or consent. If so, then no one should ever be permitted to speak for an animal, at least in a legally binding way. But that is quite another thing than saying that such representation is logically incoherent or conceptually incongruous—the contention that is at issue.

H. J. McCloskey,[7] I believe, accepts the argument up to this point, but he presents a new and different reason for denying that animals can have legal rights. The ability to make claims, whether directly or through a representative, he implies, is essential to the possession of rights. Animals obviously cannot press their claims on their own, and so if they have rights, these rights must be assertable by agents. Animals, however, cannot be represented, McCloskey contends, and not for any of the reasons already discussed, but rather because representation, in the requisite sense, is always of interests, and animals (he says) are incapable of having interests.

Now, there is a very important insight expressed in the requirement that a being have interests if he is to be a logically proper subject of rights. This can be appreciated if we consider just why it is that mere things cannot have rights. Consider a very precious "mere thing"—a beautiful natural wilderness, or a complex and ornamental artifact, like the Taj Mahal. Such things ought to be cared for, because they would sink into decay if neglected, depriving some human beings, or perhaps even all human beings, of something of great value. Certain persons may even have as their own special job the care and protection of these valuable objects. But we are not tempted in these cases to speak of "thing-rights" correlative to custodial duties, because, try as we might, we cannot think of mere things as possessing interests of their own. Some people may have a duty to preserve, maintain, or improve the Taj Mahal, but they can hardly have a duty to help or hurt it, benefit or aid it, succor or relieve it. Custodians may protect it for the sake of a nation's pride and art lovers' fancy; but they don't keep it in good repair for "its own sake," or for "its own true welfare," or "well-being." A mere thing, however valuable to others, has no good of its own. The explanation of that fact, I suspect, consists in the fact that mere things have no conative life: no conscious wishes, desires, and hopes; or urges and impulses; or unconscious drives, aims, and goals; or latent tendencies, direction of growth, and natural fulfillments. Interests must be compounded somehow out of conations; hence mere things have no interests. *A fortiori,* they have no interests to be protected by legal or moral rules. Without interests a creature can have no "good" of its own, the achievement of which can be its due. Mere things are not loci of value in their own right, but rather their value consists entirely in their being objects of other beings' interests.

So far McCloskey is on solid ground, but one can quarrel with his denial that any animals but humans have interests. I should think that the trustee of funds willed to a dog or cat is more than a mere custodian of the animal he protects. Rather his job is to look our for the interests of the animal and make sure no one denies it its due. The animal itself is the beneficiary of his dutiful services. Many of the higher animals at least have appetites, conative urges, and rudimentary purposes, the integrated satisfaction of which constitutes their welfare or good. We can, of course, with consistency treat animals as mere pests and deny that they have any rights; for most animals, especially those of the lower orders, we have no choice but to do so. But it seems to me, nevertheless, that in general, animals *are* among the sorts of beings of whom rights can meaningfully be predicated and denied.

Now, if a person agrees with the conclusion of the argument thus far, that animals are the sorts of beings that *can* have rights, and further, if he accepts the moral judgment that we ought to be kind to animals, only one further premise is needed to yield the conclusion that some animals do in fact have rights. We must now ask ourselves for whose sake ought we to treat (some) animals with consideration and humaneness? If we conceive our duty to be one of obedience to authority, or to one's own conscience merely, or one of consideration for tender human sensibilities only, then we might still deny that animals have rights, even though we admit that they are the kinds of beings that *can* have rights. But if we hold not only that we ought to treat animals humanely but also that we should do so for the animals' own sake, that such treatment is something we owe animals as their due, something that can be claimed for them, something the withholding of which would be an injustice and a wrong, and not merely a harm, then it follows that we do ascribe rights to animals. I suspect that the moral judgments most of us make about animals do pass these phenomenological tests, so that most of us do believe that animals have rights, but are reluctant to say so because of the conceptual confusions about the notion of a right that I have attempted to dispel above.

Now we can extract from our discussion of animal rights a crucial principle for tentative use in the resolution of the other riddles about the applicability of the concept of a right, namely, that the sorts of beings who *can* have rights are precisely those who have (or can have) interests. I have come to this tentative conclusion for two reasons: (1) because a right holder must be capable of being represented and it is impossible to represent a being that has no interests, and (2) because a right holder must be capable of being a beneficiary in his own person, and a being without interests is a being that is incapable of being harmed or benefitted, having no good or "sake" of its own. Thus, a being without interests has no "behalf" to act in, and no "sake" to act for. My strategy now will be to apply the "interest principle," as we can call it, to the other puzzles about rights, while being prepared to modify it where necessary (but as little as possible), in the hope of separating in a consistent and intuitively satisfactory fashion the beings who can have rights from those which cannot.

Vegetables

It is clear that we ought not to mistreat certain plants, and indeed there are rules and regulations imposing duties on persons not to misbehave in respect to certain members of the vegetable kingdom. It is forbidden, for example, to pick wildflowers in the mountainous tundra areas of national parks, or to endanger trees by starting fires in dry forest areas. Members of Congress introduce bills designed, as they say, to "protect" rare redwood trees from commercial pillage. Given this background, it is surprising that no one[8] speaks of plants as having rights. Plants, after all, are not "mere things"; they are vital objects with inherited biological propensities determining their natural growth. Moreover, we do say that certain conditions are "good" or "bad" for plants, thereby suggesting that plants, unlike rocks, are capable of having a "good." (This is a case, however, where "what we say" should not be taken seriously: we also say that certain kinds of paint are good or bad for the internal walls of a house, and this does not commit us to a conception of walls as being possessed of a good or welfare of their own.)

Finally, we are capable of feeling a kind of affection for particular plants, though we rarely personalize them, as we do in the case of animals, by giving them proper names.

Still, all are agreed that plants are not the kinds of beings that can have rights. Plants are never plausibly understood to be the direct intended beneficiaries of rules designed to "protect" them. We wish to keep redwood groves in existence for the sake of human beings who can enjoy their serene beauty, and for the sake of generations of human beings yet unborn. Trees are not the sorts of beings who have their "own sakes," despite the fact that they have biological propensities. Having no conscious wants or goals of their own, trees cannot know satisfaction or frustration, pleasure or pain. Hence, there is no possibility of kind or cruel treatment of trees. In these morally crucial respects, trees differ from the higher species of animals.

Yet trees are not mere things like rocks. They grow and develop according to the laws of their own nature. Aristotle and Aquinas both took trees to have their own "natural ends." Why then do I deny them the status of beings with interests of their own? The reason is that an interest, however the concept is finally to be analyzed, presupposes at least rudimentary cognitive equipment. Interests are compounded out of *desires* and *aims,* both of which presuppose something like *belief,* or cognitive awareness. . . .

Whole Species

The topic of whole species, whether of plants or animals, can be treated in much the same way as that of individual plants. A whole collection, as such, cannot have beliefs, expectations, wants, or desires, and can flourish or languish only in the human interest-related sense in which individual plants thrive and decay. Individual elephants can have interests, but the species elephant cannot. Even where individual elephants are not granted rights, human beings may have an interest—economic, scientific, or sentimental—in keeping the species from dying out, and *that* interest may be protected in various ways by law. But that is quite another matter from recognizing a right to survival belonging to the species itself. Still, the preservation of a whole species may quite properly seem to be a morally more important matter than the preservation of an individual animal. Individual animals can have rights but it is implausible to ascribe to them a right to life on the human model. Nor do we normally have duties to keep individual animals alive or even to abstain from killing them provided we do it humanely and nonwantonly in the promotion of legitimate human interests. On the other hand, we do have duties to protect threatened species, not duties to the species themselves as such, but rather duties to future human beings, duties derived from our housekeeping role as temporary inhabitants of this planet.

We commonly and very naturally speak of corporate entities, such as institutions, churches, and national states as having rights and duties, and an adequate analysis of the conditions for ownership of rights should account for that fact. A corporate entity, of course, is more than a mere collection of things that have some important traits in common. Unlike a biological species, an institution has a charter, or constitution, or bylaws, with rules defining offices and procedures, and it has human beings whose function it is to administer the rules and apply the procedures. When the institution has a duty to an outsider, there is always some determinant human being whose duty it is to do something for the outsider, and when the state, for example, has a right to collect taxes, there are always certain definite flesh and blood persons who have rights to demand tax money from other citizens. We have no reluctance to use the language of corporate rights and duties because we know that in the last analysis these are rights or duties of individual persons, acting in their "official capacities." And when individuals act in their official roles in accordance with valid empowering rules, their acts are imputable to the organization itself and become "acts of state." Thus, there is no need to posit any individual superperson named by the expression "the State" (or for that matter, "the company," "the club," or "the church.") Nor is there any reason to take the rights of corporate entities to be exceptions to the interest principle. The United States is not a superperson with wants and beliefs of its own, but it is a corporate entity with corporate interests that are, in turn, analyzable into the interests of its numerous flesh and blood members.

Dead Persons

So far we have refined the interest principle but we have not had occasion to modify it. Applied to dead persons, however, it will have to be stretched to near the breaking point if it is to explain how our duty to honor commitments to the dead can be thought to be linked to the rights of the dead against us. The case against ascribing rights to dead men can be made very simply: a dead man is a mere corpse, a piece of decaying organic matter. Mere inanimate things can have no interests, and what is incapable of having interests is incapable of having rights. If, nevertheless, we grant dead men rights against us, we would seem to be treating the interests they had while alive as somehow surviving their deaths. There is the sound of paradox in this way of talking, but it may be the least paradoxical way of describing our moral relations to our predecessors. And if the idea of an interest's surviving its possessor's death is a kind of fiction, it is a fiction that most living have a real interest in preserving.

Most persons while still alive have certain desires about what is to happen to their bodies, their property, or their reputations after they are dead. For that reason, our legal system has developed procedures to enable persons while still alive to determine whether their bodies will be used for purposes of medical research or organic transplantation, and to whom their wealth (after taxes) is to be transferred. Living men also take out life insurance policies guaranteeing that the accumulated benefits be conferred upon beneficiaries of their own choice. They also make private agreements, both contractual and informal, in which they receive promises that certain things will be done after their deaths in exchange for some present service or consideration. In all these cases promises are made to living persons that their wishes will be honored after they are dead. Like all other valid promises, they impose duties on the promisor and confer correlative rights on the promisee.

How does the situation change after the promisee has died? Surely the duties of the promisor do not suddenly become null and void. If that were the case, and known to be the case, there could be no confidence in promises regarding posthumous arrangements; no one would bother with wills or life insurance companies to pay benefits to survivors, which are, in a sense, only conditional duties before a man dies. They come into existence as categorical demands for immediate action only upon the promisee's death. So the view that death renders them null and void has the truth exactly upside down.

The survival of the promisor's duty after the promisee's death does not prove that the promisee retains a right even after death, for we might prefer to conclude that there is one class of cases where duties to keep promises are not logically correlated with a promisee's right, namely, cases where the promisee has died. Still, a morally sensitive promisor is likely to think of his promised performance not only as a duty (i.e., a morally required action) but also as something owed to the deceased promisee as his due. Honoring such promises is a way of keeping faith with the dead. To be sure, the promisor will not think of his duty as something to be done for the promisee's "good," since the promisee, being dead, has no "good" of his own. We can think of certain of the deceased's interests, however, (including especially those enshrined in wills and protected by contracts and promises) as surviving their owner's death, and constituting claims against us that persist beyond the life of the claimant. Such claims can be represented by proxies just like the claims of animals. This way of speaking, I believe, reflects more accurately than any other an important fact about the human condition: we have an interest while alive that other interests of ours will continue to be recognized and served after we are dead. The whole practice of honoring wills and testaments, and the like, is thus for the sake of the living, just as a particular instance of it may be thought to be for the sake of one who is dead.

Conceptual sense, then, can be made of talk about dead men's rights; but it is still a wide open moral question whether dead men in fact have rights, and if so, what those rights are. In particular, commentators have disagreed over whether a man's interest in his reputation deserves to be protected from defamation even after his death. With only a few prominent exceptions, legal systems punish a libel on a dead man "only when its publication is in truth an attack upon the interests of living persons."[9] A widow or a son may be wounded, or embarrassed, or even injured economically, by a defamatory attack on the memory of their dead husband or father. In Utah defamation of the dead is a misdemeanor, and in Sweden a cause of action in tort. The law rarely presumes, however, that a dead man himself has any interests, representable by proxy, that can be injured by defamation, apparently because of the maxim that what a dead man doesn't know can't hurt him.

This presupposes, however, that the whole point of guarding the reputations even of living men, is to protect them from hurt feelings, or to protect some other interests, for example, economic ones, that do not survive death. A moment's thought, I think, will show that our interests are more complicated than that. If someone spreads a libelous description of me, without my knowledge, among hundreds of persons in a remote part of the country, so that I am, still without my knowledge, an object of general scorn and mockery in that group, I have been injured, even though I never learn what has happened. That is because I have an interest, so I believe, in having a good reputation *simpliciter,* in addition to my interest in avoiding hurt feelings, embarrassment, and economic injury. In the example, I do not know what is being said and believed about me, so my feelings are not hurt; but clearly if I did know, I would be enormously distressed. The distress would be the natural consequence of my belief that an interest other than my interest in avoiding distress had been damaged. How else can I account for the distress? If I had no interest in a good reputation as such, I would respond to news of harm to my reputation with indifference.

While it is true that a dead man cannot have his feelings hurt, it does not follow, therefore, that his claim to be thought of no worse than he deserves cannot survive his death. Almost every living person, I should think, would wish to have this interest protected after his death, at least during the lifetimes of those persons who were his contemporaries. We can hardly expect the law to protect Julius Caesar from defamation in the history books. This might hamper historical research and restrict socially valuable forms of expression. Even interests that survive their owner's death are not immortal. Anyone should be permitted to say anything he wishes about George Washington or Abraham Lincoln, though perhaps not everything is morally permissible. Everyone ought to refrain from malicious lies even about Nero or King Tut, though not so much for those ancients' own sakes as for the sake of those who would now know the truth about the past. We owe it to the brothers Kennedy, however, as their due, not to tell damaging lies about them to those who were once their contemporaries. If the reader would deny that judgment, I can only urge him to ask himself whether he now wishes his own interest in reputation to be respected, along with his interest in determining the distribution of his wealth, after his death.

Human Vegetables

Mentally deficient and deranged human beings are hardly ever so handicapped intellectually that they do not compare favorably with even the highest of the lower animals, though they are commonly so incompetent that they cannot be assigned duties or be held responsible for what they do. Since animals can have rights, then, it follows that human idiots and madmen can too. It would make good sense, for example, to ascribe to them a right to be cured whenever effective therapy is available at reasonable cost, and even those incurables who have been consigned to a sanatorium for permanent "warehousing" can claim (through a proxy) their right to decent treatment.

Human beings suffering extreme cases of mental illness, however, may be so utterly disoriented or insensitive as to compare quite unfavorably with the brightest cats and dogs. Those suffering from catatonic schizophrenia may be barely distinguishable in respect to those traits presupposed by the possession of interests from the lowliest vegetables. So long as we regard these patients as potentially curable, we may think of them as human beings with interests in their own restoration and treat them as possessors of rights. We may think of the patient as a genuine human person inside the vegetable casing struggling to get out, just as in the old fairy tales a pumpkin could be thought of as a beautiful maiden under a magic spell waiting only the proper words to be restored to her true self. Perhaps it is reasonable never to lose hope that a patient can be cured, and therefore to regard him always as a person "under a spell" with a permanent interest in his own recovery that is entitled to recognition and protection.

What if, nevertheless, we think of the catatonic schizophrenic and the vegetating patient with irreversible brain damage as absolutely incurable? Can we think of them at the same time as possessed of interests and rights too, or is this combination of traits a conceptual impossibility? Shocking as it may at first seem, I am driven unavoidably to the latter view. If redwood trees and rosebushes cannot have rights, neither can incorrigible human vegetables.[10] The trustees who are designated to administer funds for the care of these unfortunates are better understood as mere custodians than as representatives of their interests since these patients no longer have interests. It does not follow that they should not be kept alive as long as possible: that is an open moral question not foreclosed by conceptual analysis. Even if we have duties to keep human vegetables alive, however, they cannot be duties *to* them. We may be obliged to keep them alive to protect the sensibilities of others, or to foster humanitarian tendencies in ourselves, but we cannot keep them alive for their own good, for they are no longer capable of having a "good" of their own. Without awareness, expectation, belief, desire, aim, and purpose, a being can have no interests; without interests, he cannot be benefited; without the capacity to be a beneficiary, he can have no rights. But there may nevertheless be a dozen other reasons to treat him as if he did.

Fetuses

If the interest principle is to permit us to ascribe rights to infants, fetuses, and generations yet unborn, it can only be on the grounds that interests can exert a claim upon us even before their possessors actually come into being, just the reverse of the situation respecting dead men where interests are respected even after their possessors have ceased to be. Newly born infants are surely noisier than mere vegetables, but they are just barely brighter. They come into existence, as Aristotle said, with the capacity to acquire concepts and dispositions, but in the beginning we suppose that their consciousness of the world is a "blooming, buzzing confusion." They do have a capacity, no doubt from the very beginning, to feel pain, and this alone may be sufficient ground for ascribing both an interest and a right to them. Apart from that, however, during the first few hours of their lives, at least, they may well lack even the rudimentary intellectual equipment necessary to the possession of interests. Of course, this induces no moral reservations whatever in adults. Children grow and mature almost visibly in the first few months so that those future interests that are so rapidly emerging from the unformed chaos of their earliest days seem unquestionably to be the basis of their present rights. Thus, we say of a newborn infant that he has a right now to live and grow into his adulthood, even though he lacks the conceptual equipment at this very moment to have this or any other desire. A new infant, in short, lacks the traits necessary for the possession of interests, but he has the capacity to acquire those traits, and his inherited potentialities are moving quickly toward actualization even as we watch him. Those proxies who make claims in behalf of infants, then, are more than mere custodians: they are (or can be) genuine representatives of the child's emerging interests, which may need protection even now if they are to be allowed to come into existence at all.

The same principle may be extended to "unborn persons." After all, the situation of fetuses one day before birth is not strikingly different from that a few hours after birth. The rights our law confers on the unborn child, both proprietary and personal, are for the most part, placeholders or reservations for the rights he shall inherit when he becomes a full-fledged interested being. The law protects a potential interest in these cases before it has even grown into actuality, as a garden fence protects newly seeded flower beds long before blooming flowers have emerged from them. The unborn child's present right to property, for example, is a legal protection offered now to his future interest, contingent upon his birth, and instantly voidable if he dies before birth. As Coke put it: "The law in many cases hath consideration of him in respect of the apparent expectation of his birth";[11] but this is quite another thing than recognizing a right actually to be born. Assuming that the child will be born, the law seems to say, various interests that he will come to have after birth must be protected from damage that they can incur even before birth. Thus prenatal injuries of a negligently inflicted kind can give the newly born child a right to sue for damages which he can exercise through a proxy-attorney and in his own name any time *after* he is born.

There are numerous other places, however, where our law seems to imply an unconditional right to be born, and surprisingly no one seems ever to have found that idea conceptually absurd. One interesting example comes from an article given the following headline by the *New York Times:* "Unborn Child's Right Upheld Over Religion." [12] A hospital patient in her eighth month of pregnancy refused to take a blood transfusion even though warned by her physician that "she might die at any minute and take the life of her child as well." The ground of her refusal was that blood transfusions are repugnant to the principles of her religion (Jehovah's Witnesses). The Supreme Court of New Jersey expressed uncertainty over the constitutional question of whether a non-pregnant adult might refuse on religious grounds a blood transfusion pronounced necessary to her own survival, but the court nevertheless ordered the patient in the present case to receive the transfusion on the grounds that "the unborn child is entitled to the law's protection."

It is important to reemphasize here that the questions of whether fetuses do or ought to have rights are substantive questions of law and morals open to argument and decision. The prior question of whether fetuses are the kind of beings that can have rights, however, is a conceptual, not a moral, question, amenable only to what is called "logical analysis," and irrelevant to moral judgment. The correct answer to the conceptual question, I believe, is that unborn children are among the sorts of beings of whom possession of rights can meaningfully be predicated, even though they are (temporarily) incapable of having interests, because their future interests can be protected now, and it does make sense to protect a potential interest even before it has grown into actuality. The interest principle, however, makes perplexing, at best, talk of a noncontingent fetal right to be born; for fetuses, lacking actual wants and beliefs, have no actual interests in being born, and it is difficult to think of any other reason for ascribing any rights to them other than on the assumption that they will in fact be born.[13]

Future Generations

We have it in our power now to make the world a much less pleasant place for our descendants than the world we inherited from our ancestors. We can continue to proliferate in ever greater numbers, using up fertile soil at an even greater rate, dumping our wastes into rivers, lakes, and oceans, cutting down our forests, and polluting the atmosphere with noxious gases. All thoughtful people agree that we ought not to do these things. Most would say that we have a duty not to do these things, meaning not merely that conservation is morally required (as opposed to merely desirable) but also that it is something due our descendants, something to be done for their sakes. Surely we owe it to future generations to pass on a world that is not a used up garbage heap. Our remote descendants are not yet present to claim a livable world as their right, but there are plenty of proxies to speak now in their behalf. These spokesmen, far from being mere custodians, are genuine representatives of future interests.

Why then deny that the human beings of the future have rights which can be claimed against us now in their behalf? Some are inclined to deny them present rights out of a fear of falling into obscure metaphysics, by granting rights to remote and unidentifiable beings who are not yet even in existence. Our unborn great-great-grandchildren are in some sense "potential" persons, but they are far more remotely potential, it may seem, than fetuses. This, however, is not the real difficulty. Unborn generations are more remotely potential than fetuses in one sense, but not in another. A much greater period of time with a far greater number of causally necessary and important events must pass before their potentiality can be actualized, it is true; but our collective posterity is just as certain to come into existence "in the normal course of events" as is any given fetus now in its mother's womb. In that sense the existence of the distant human future is no more remotely potential than that of a particular child already on its way.

The real difficulty is not that we doubt whether our descendants will ever be actual, but rather that we don't know who they will be. It is not their temporal remoteness that troubles us so much as their indeterminacy—their present facelessness and namelessness. Five centuries from now men and women will be living where we live now. Any given one of them will have an interest in living space, fertile soil, fresh air, and the like, but that arbitrarily selected one has no other qualities we can presently envision very clearly. We don't even know who his parents, grandparents, or great-grandparents are, or even whether he is related to us. Still, whoever these human beings may turn out to be, and whatever they might reasonably be expected to be like, they will have interests that we can affect, for better or worse, right now. That much we can and do know about them. The identity of the owners of these interests is now necessarily obscure, but the fact of their interest-ownership is crystal clear, and that is all that is necessary to certify the coherence of present talk about their rights. We can tell, sometimes, that shadowy forms in the spatial distance belong to human beings, though we know not who or how many they are; and this imposes a duty on us not to throw bombs, for example, in their direction. In like manner, the vagueness of the human future does not weaken its claim on us in light of the nearly certain knowledge that it will, after all, be human.

Doubts about the existence of a right to be born transfer neatly to the question of a similar right to come into existence ascribed to future generations. The rights that future generations certainly have against us are contingent rights: the interests they are sure to have when they come into being (assuming of course that they will come into being) cry out for protection from invasions that can take place now. Yet there are no actual interests, presently existent, that future generations, presently nonexistent, have now. Hence, there is no actual interest that they have in simply coming into being, and I am at a loss to think of any other reason for claiming that they have a right to come into existence (though there may well be such a reason). Suppose then that all human beings at a given time voluntarily form a compact never again to produce children, thus leading within a few decades to the end of our species. This of course is a wildly improbable hypothetical example but a rather crucial one for the position I have been tentatively considering. And we can imagine, say, that the whole world is converted to a strange ascetic religion which absolutely requires sexual abstinence for everyone. Would this arrangement violate the rights of anyone? No one can complain on behalf of presently nonexistent future generations that their future interests which give them a contingent right of protection have been violated since they will never come into existence to be wronged. My inclination then is to conclude that the suicide of our species would be deplorable, lamentable, and a deeply moving tragedy, but that it would violate no one's rights. Indeed if, contrary to fact, all human beings could ever agree to such a thing, that very agreement would be a symptom of our species' biological unsuitability for survival anyway.

Conclusion

For several centuries now human beings have run roughshod over the lands of our planet, just as if the animals who do live there and the generations on humans who will live there had no claims on them whatever. Philosophers have not helped matters by arguing that animals and future generations are not the kinds of beings who can have rights now, that they don't presently qualify for membership, even "auxiliary membership," in our moral community. I have tried in this essay to dispel the conceptual confusions that make such conclusions possible. To acknowledge their rights is the very least we can do for members of endangered species (including our own). But that is something.

Appendix

The Paradoxes of Potentiality

Having conceded that rights can belong to beings in virtue of their merely potential interests, we find ourselves on a slippery slope; for it may seem at first sight that anything at all can have potential interests, or much more generally, that anything at all can be potentially almost anything else at all! Dehydrated orange powder is potentially orange juice, since if we add water to it, it will be orange juice. More remotely, however, it is also potentially lemonade, since it will become lemonade if we add a large quantity of lemon juice, sugar, and water. It is also a potentially poisonous brew (add water and arsenic), a potential orange cake (add flour, etc., and bake), a potential orange-colored building block (add cement and harden), and so on, *ad infinitum*. Similarly a two-celled embryo, too small to be seen by the unaided eye, is a potential human being; and so is an unfertilized ovum; and so is even an "uncapacitated" spermatozoan. Add the proper nutrition to an implanted embryo (under the same conditions) and it becomes a fetus and then a child. Looked at another way, however, the implanted embryo has been combined (under the same conditions) with the nutritive elements, which themselves are converted into a growing fetus and child. Is it then just as proper to say that food is a "potential child" as that an embryo is a potential child? If so, then what isn't a "potential child?" (Organic elements in the air and soil are "potentially food," and hence potentially people!)

Clearly, some sort of line will have to be drawn between direct or proximate potentialities and indirect or remote ones; and however we draw this line, there will be borderline cases whose classification will seem uncertain or even arbitrary. Even though any *X* can become a *Y* provided only that it is combined with the necessary additional elements, *a, b, c, d,* and so forth, we cannot say of any given *X* that it is a "potential *Y*" unless certain further—rather strict—conditions are met. (Otherwise the concept of potentiality, being universally and promiscuously applicable, will have no utility.) A number of possible criteria of proximate potentiality suggest themselves. The first is the criterion of causal importance. Orange powder is not properly called a potential building block because of those elements needed to transform it into a building block, the cement (as opposed to any of the qualities of the orange powder) is the causally crucial one. Similarly, any pauper might (misleadingly) be called a "potential millionaire" in the sense that all that need be added to any man to transform him into a millionaire is a great amount of money. The absolutely crucial element in the change, of course, is not quality of the man himself but rather the million dollars "added" to him.

What is causally "important" depends upon our purposes and interests and is therefore to some degree a relativistic matter. If we seek a standard, in turn, of "importance," we may posit such a criterion, for example, as that of the ease or difficulty (to some persons or other) of providing those missing elements which, when combined with the thing at hand, convert it into something else. It does seem quite natural, for example, to say that the orange powder is potentially orange juice, and that is because the missing element is merely common tap water, a substance conveniently near at hand to everyone; whereas it is less plausible to characterize the powder as potential cake since a variety of further elements, and not just one, are required, and some of these are not conveniently near at hand to many. Moreover, the process of combining the missing elements into a cake is rather more complicated than mere "addition." It is less plausible still to call orange powder a potential curbstone for the same kind of reason. The criterion of ease or difficulty of the acquisition and combination of additional elements explains all these variations.

Still another criterion of proximate potentiality closely related to the others is that of degree of deviation required from "the normal course of events." Given the intentions of its producers, distributors, sellers, and consumers, dehydrated orange juice will, in the normal course of events, become orange juice. Similarly, a human embryo securely imbedded in the wall of its mother's uterus will in the normal course of events become a human child. That is to say that if no one deliberately intervenes to prevent it happening, it will, in the vast majority of cases, happen. On the other hand, an unfertilized ovum will not become an embryo unless someone intervenes deliberately to make it happen. Without such intervention in the "normal" course of events, an ovum is a mere bit of protoplasm of very brief life expectancy. If we lived in a world in which virtually every biologically capable human female became pregnant once a year throughout her entire fertile period of life, then we would regard fertilization as something that happens to every ovum in "the natural course of events." Perhaps we would regard every unfertilized ovum, in such a world, as a potential person even possessed of rights corresponding to its future interests. It would perhaps make conceptual if not moral sense in such a world to regard deliberate nonfertilization as a kind of homicide.

It is important to notice, in summary, that words like *important, easy,* and *normal* have sense only in relation to human experiences, purposes, and techniques. As the latter change, so will our notions of what is important, difficult, and usual, and so will the concept of potentiality, or our application of it. If our purposes, understanding, and techniques continue to change in indicated directions, we may even one day come to think of inanimate things as possessed of "potential interests." In any case, we can expect the concept of a right to shift its logical boundaries with changes in our practical experience.

Endnotes

1. I shall leave the concept of a claim unanalyzed here, but for a detailed discussion, see my "The Nature and Value of Rights," *Journal of Value Inquiry* 4 (Winter 1971): 263–277.
2. Louis B. Schwartz, "Morals, Offenses and the Model Penal Code," *Columbia Law Review* 63 (1963): 673.
3. John Chipman Gray, *The Nature and Sources of the Law,* 2d ed. (Boston: Beacon Press, 1963), p. 43.
4. And W. D. Ross for another. See *The Right and the Good* (Oxford: Clarendon Press, 1930), app. I, pp. 48–56.
5. W. D. Lamont, *Principles of Moral Judgment* (Oxford: Clarendon Press, 1946), pp. 83–85.
6. Cf. H. J. McCloskey, "Rights," *Philosophical Quarterly* 15 (1965): 121, 124.
7. Ibid.
8. Outside of Samuel Butler's *Erewbon.*
9. William Salmond, *Jurisprudence,* 12th ed., ed. P. J. Fitzgerald (London: Sweet and Maxwell, 1966), p. 304.
10. Unless, of course, the person in question, before he became a "vegetable," left testamentary directions about what was to be done with his body just in case he should ever become an incurable vegetable. He may have directed either that he be preserved alive as long as possible, or else that he be destroyed, whichever he preferred. There may, of course, be sound reasons of public policy why we should not honor such directions, but if we did promise to give legal effect to such wishes, we would have an example of a man's earlier interest in what is to happen to his body surviving his very competence as a person, in quite the same manner as that in which the express interest of a man now dead may continue to exert a claim on us.
11. As quoted by Salmond, *Jurisprudence,* p. 303. Simply as a matter of policy the potentiality of some future interests may be so remote as to make them seem unworthy of present support. A testator may leave property to his unborn child, for example, but not to his unborn grandchildren. To say of the potential person presently in his mother's womb that he owns property now is to say that certain property must be held for him until he is "real" or "mature" enough to possess it. "Yet the law is careful lest property should be too long withdrawn in this way from the uses of living men in

favor of generations yet to come; and various restrictive rules have been established to this end. No testator could now direct his fortune to be accumulated for a hundred years and then distributed among his descendants"—Salmond, ibid.

12. *The New York Times*, 17 June 1966, p. I.
13. In an essay entitled "Is There a Right to be Born?" I defend a negative answer to the question posed, but I allow that under certain very special conditions, there can be a "right *not* to be born." See *Abortion*, ed. J. Feinberg (Belmont, Calif.: Wadsworth, 1973).

Review Questions

1. Explain Feinberg's analysis of the concept of a right.
2. Do animals have rights? What is Gray's view? What is McCloskey's view? What position does Feinberg take?
3. According to Feinberg, what sorts of beings can have rights? Give examples of beings that do and do not have rights according to Feinberg.
4. On Feinberg's view, what sorts of rights do future generations have?

Discussion Questions

1. Suppose we grant that animals have rights. Exactly what rights do they have? For example, do they have a right to life?
2. Do dead people have rights? What would Feinberg say? What do you think?
3. Do human vegetables (as Feinberg calls them) have rights? What is Feinberg's answer? Do you agree or not?
4. What is Feinberg's position on fetuses and infants? Is it acceptable to you or not? Why or why not?
5. At the end of his article, Feinberg claims that the suicide of our species would violate no one's rights. Do you agree? Why or why not?

Christopher D. Stone

Should Trees Have Standing? Toward Legal Rights for Natural Objects

Christopher D. Stone is Professor of Law at the University of Southern California. He is the author of Where the Law Ends: The Social Control of Corporate Behavior *(1975), and* Earth and Other Ethics: The Case for Moral Pluralism *(1987).*

Christopher D. Stone, "Should Trees Have Standing? Toward Legal Rights for Natural Objects." Printed with permission of Christopher D. Stone and the U.S.C. Law Review

Stone argues that natural objects such as trees should be given legal rights and represented by legal friends who protect their interests. He admits that this is a radical idea, but he thinks it is no more radical than was the idea of women's rights in the past. The practical benefit would be that environmentalists could more easily protect the environment. Also it could produce a revolutionary way of viewing humans' relation to nature. Instead of seeing nature as something separate to be used, humans would see themselves as part of nature.

Throughout legal history, each successive extension of rights to some new entity has been, theretofore, a bit unthinkable. We are inclined to suppose the rightlessness of rightless "things" to be a decree of Nature, not a legal convention acting in support of some status quo. It is thus that we defer considering the choices involved in all their moral, social, and economic dimensions. And so the United States Supreme Court could straightfacedly tell us in *Dred Scott* that Blacks had been denied the rights of citizenship "as a subordinate and inferior class of beings, who had been subjugated by the dominant race. . . ."[1] In the nineteenth century, the highest court in California explained that Chinese had not the right to testify against white men in criminal matters because they were "a race of people whom nature has marked as inferior, and who are incapable of progress or intellectual development beyond a certain point . . . between whom and ourselves nature has placed an impassable difference."[2] The popular conception of the Jew in the thirteenth century contributed to a law which treated them as "men *ferae naturae,* protected by a quasi-forest law. Like the roe and the deer, they form an order apart."[3] Recall, too, that it was not so long ago that the foetus was "like the roe and the deer." In an early suit attempting to establish a wrongful death action on behalf of a negligently killed foetus (now widely accepted practice), Holmes, then on the Massachusetts Supreme Court, seems to have thought it simply inconceivable "that a man might owe a civil duty and incur a conditional prospective liability in tort to one not yet in being."[4] The first woman in Wisconsin who thought she might have a right to practice law was told that she did not, in the following terms:

> The law of nature destines and qualifies the female sex for the bearing and nurture of the children of our race and for the custody of the homes of the world. . . . [A]ll life-long callings of women, inconsistent with these radical and sacred duties of their sex, as is the profession of the law, are departures from the order of nature; and when voluntary, treason against it. . . . The peculiar qualities of womanhood, its gentle graces, its quick sensibility, its tender susceptibility, its purity, its delicacy, its emotional impulses, its subordination of hard reason to sympathetic feeling, are surely not qualifications for forensic strife. Nature has tempered woman as little for the juridical conflicts of the court room, as for the physical conflicts of the battle field. . . .[5]

The fact is, that each time there is a movement to confer rights onto some new "entity," the proposal is bound to sound odd or frightening or laughable. This is partly because until the rightless thing receives its rights, we cannot see it as anything but a *thing* for the use of "us"—those who are holding rights at the time. In this vein, what is striking about the Wisconsin case above is that the court, for all its talk about women, so clearly was never able to see women as they are (and might become). All it could see was the popular "idealized" version of *an object it needed.* Such is the way the slave South looked upon the Black. There is something of a seamless web involved; there will be resistance to giving the thing "rights" until it can be seen and valued for itself; yet, it is hard to see it and value it for itself until we can bring ourselves to give it "rights"—which is almost inevitably going to sound inconceivable to a large group of people.

The reason for this little discourse on the unthinkable, the reader must know by now, if only from the title of the paper. I am quite seriously proposing that we give legal rights to forests, oceans, rivers, and other so-called "natural objects" in the environment—indeed, to the natural environment as a whole. . . .

Toward Rights for the Environment

Now, to say that the natural environment should have rights is not to say anything as silly as that no one should be allowed to cut down a tree. We say human beings have rights, but—at least as of the time of this writing—they can be executed. Corporations have rights, but they cannot plead the fifth amendment; *In re Gault* gave fifteen-year-olds certain rights in juvenile proceedings, but it did not give them the right to vote. Thus, to say that the environment should have rights is not to say that it should have every right we can imagine, or even the same body of rights as human beings have. Nor is it to say that everything in the environment should have the same rights as every other thing in the environment. . . .

For a thing to be *a holder of legal rights* something more is needed than that some authoritative body will review the actions and processes of those who threaten it. As I shall use the term, "holder of legal rights," each of three additional criteria must be satisfied. All three, one will observe, go towards making a thing *count* jurally—to have a legally recognized worth and dignity in its own right, and not merely to serve as a means to benefit "us" (whoever the contemporary group of rights-holders may be). They are, first, that the thing can institute legal actions *at its behest;* second, that in determining the granting of legal relief, the court must take *injury to it* into account; and, third, that relief must run to the *benefit of it*. . . .

The Rightlessness of Natural Objects at Common Law

Consider, for example, the common law's posture toward the pollution of a stream. True, courts have always been able, in some circumstances, to issue orders that will stop the pollution. . . . But the stream itself is fundamentally rightless, with implications that deserve careful reconsideration.

The first sense in which the stream is not a rights-holder has to do with standing. The stream itself has none. So far as the common law is concerned, there is in general no way to challenge the polluter's actions save at the behest of a lower riparian—another human being—able to show an invasion of *his* rights. . . .

The second sense in which the common law denies "rights" to natural objects has to do with the way in which the merits are decided in those cases in which someone is competent and willing to establish standing. At its more primitive levels, the system protected the "rights" of the property owning human with minimal weighting of any values. . . . Today we have come more and more to make balances—but only such as will adjust the economic best interests of identifiable humans. . . .

Thus, we find the highest court of Pennsylvania refusing to stop a coal company from discharging polluted mine water into a tributary of the Lackawana River because a plaintiff's "grievance is for a mere personal inconvenience; and . . . mere private personal inconveniences . . . must yield to the necessities of a great public industry, which although in the hands of a private corporation, subserves a great public interest." [6] The stream itself is lost sight of in "a quantitative compromise between *two* conflicting interests." [7]

The third way in which the common law makes natural objects rightless has to do with who is regarded as the beneficiary of a favorable judgment. Here, too, it makes a considerable difference that it is not the natural object that counts in its own right. To illustrate this point let me begin by observing that it makes perfectly good sense to speak of, and ascertain, the legal damage to a natural object, if only in the sense of "making it whole" with respect to the most obvious factors. The costs of making a forest whole, for example, would include the costs of reseeding, repairing watersheds, restocking wildlife—the sorts of costs the Forest Service undergoes after a fire. Making a polluted stream whole would include the costs of restocking with fish, water-fowl, and other animal and vegetable life, dredging, washing out impurities, establishing natural and/or artificial aerating agents, and so forth. Now, what is important to note is that, under our present system, even if a plaintiff riparian wins a water pollution suit for damages, no money goes to the benefit of the stream itself to repair *its* damages. . . .

None of the natural objects, whether held in common or situated on private land, has any of the three criteria of a rights-holder. They have no standing in their own right; their unique damages do not count in determining outcome; and they are not the beneficiaries of awards. In such a fashion, these objects have traditionally been regarded by the common law, and even by all but the most recent legislation, as objects for man to conquer and master and use—in such a way as the law once looked upon "man's" relationships to African Negroes. Even where special measures have been taken to conserve them, as by seasons on game and limits on timber cutting, the dominant motive has been to conserve them *for us*—for the greatest good of the greatest number of human beings. Conservationists, so far as I am aware, are generally reluctant to maintain otherwise. As the name implies, they want to conserve and guarantee *our* consumption and *our* enjoyment of these other living things. In their own right, natural objects have counted for little, in law as in popular movements.

As I mentioned at the outset, however, the rightlessness of the natural environment can and should change; it already shows some signs of doing so.

Toward Having Standing in Its Own Right

It is not inevitable, nor is it wise, that natural objects should have no rights to seek redress in their own behalf. It is no answer to say that streams and forests cannot have standing because streams and forests cannot speak. Corporations cannot speak either; nor can states, estates, infants, incompetents, municipalities, or universities. Lawyers speak for them, as they customarily do for the ordinary citizen with legal problems. One ought, I think, to handle the legal problems of natural objects as one does the problems of legal incompetents—human beings who have become vegetable. If a human being shows signs of becoming senile and has affairs that he is de jure incompetent to manage, those concerned with his well being make such a showing to the court, and someone is designated by the court with the authority to manage the incompetent's affairs. . . .

On a parity of reasoning we should have a system in which, when a friend of a natural object perceives it to be endangered, he can apply to a court for the creation of a guardianship. . . .

The potential "friends" that such a statutory scheme would require will hardly be lacking. The Sierra Club, Environmental Defense Fund, Friends of the Earth, Natural Resources Defense Counsel, and the Izaak Walton League are just some of the many groups which have manifested unflagging dedication to the environment and which are becoming increasingly capable of marshalling the requisite technical experts and lawyers. If, for example, the Environmental Defense Fund should have reason to believe that some company's strip mining operations might be irreparably destroying the ecological balance of large tracts of land, it could, under this procedure, apply to the court in which the lands were situated to be appointed guardian. As guardian, it might be given rights of inspection (or visitation) to determine and bring to the court's attention a fuller finding on the land's condition. If there were indications that under the substantive law some redress might be available on the land's behalf, then the guardian would be entitled to raise the land's rights in the land's name, *i.e.*, without having to make the roundabout and often unavailing demonstration . . . that the "rights" of the club's members were being invaded. . . .

One reason for making the environment itself the beneficiary of a judgment is to prevent it from being "sold out" in a negotiation among private litigants who agree not to enforce rights that have been established among themselves. Protection from this will be advanced by making the natural object a party to an injunctive settlement. Even more importantly, we should make it a beneficiary of money awards. . . .

The idea of assessing damages as best we can and placing them in a trust fund is far more realistic than a hope that a total "freeze" can be put on the environmental status quo. Nature is a continuous theatre in which things and species (eventually man) are destined to enter and exit. In the meantime, co-existence of man and his environment means that *each* is going to have to compromise for the better of both. Some pollution of streams, for example, will probably be inevitable for some time. Instead of setting an unrealizable goal of enjoining absolutely the discharge of all such pollutants, the trust fund concept would (a) help assure that pollution would occur only in those instances where the social need for the pollutant's product (via his present method of production) was so high as to enable the polluter to cover *all* homocentric costs, plus some estimated costs to the environment *per se,* and (b) would be a corpus for preserving monies, if necessary, while the technology developed to a point where repairing the damaged portion of the environment was feasible. Such a fund might even finance the requisite research and development. . . .

A radical new conception of man's relationship to the rest of nature would not only be a step towards solving the material planetary problems; there are strong reasons for such a changed consciousness from the point of making us far better humans. If we only stop for a moment and look at the underlying human qualities that our present attitudes toward property and nature draw upon and reinforce, we have to be struck by how stultifying of our own personal growth and satisfaction they can become when they take rein of us. Hegel, in "justifying" private property, unwittingly reflects the tone and quality of some of the needs that are played upon:

> A person has as his substantive end the right of putting his will into any and every thing and thereby making it his, because it has no such end in itself and derives its destiny and soul from his will. This is the absolute right of appropriation which man has over all "things." [8]

What is it within us that gives us this need not just to satisfy basic biological wants, but to extend our wills over things, to object-ify them, to make them ours, to manipulate them, to keep them at a psychic distance? Can it all be explained on "rational" bases? Should we not be suspect of such needs within us, cautious as to why we wish to gratify them? When I first read that passage of Hegel, I immediately thought not only of the emotional contrast with Spinoza, but of the passage in Carson McCullers' "A Tree, a Rock, a Cloud," in which an old derelict has collared a twelve-year-old boy in a streetcar cafe. The old man asks whether the boy knows "how love should be begun."

> The old man leaned closer and whispered:
> "A tree. A rock. A cloud."
> "The weather was like this in Portland," he said. "At the time my science was begun. I meditated and I started very cautious. I would pick up something from the street and take it home with me. I bought a goldfish and I concentrated on the goldfish and I loved it. I graduated from one thing to another. Day by day I was getting this technique.
> . . . "For six years now I have gone around by myself and built up my science. And now I am a master. Son. I can love anything. No longer do I have to think about it even. I see a street full of people and a beautiful light comes in me. I watch a bird in the sky. Or I meet a traveler on the road. Everything, Son. And anybody. All stranger and all loved! Do you realize what a science like mine can mean?" [9]

To be able to get away from the view that Nature is a collection of useful senseless objects is, as McCullers' "madman" suggests, deeply involved in the development of our abilities to love—or, if that is putting it too strongly, to be able to reach a heightened awareness of our own, and others' capacities in their mutual interplay. To do so, we have to give up some psychic investment in our sense of separateness and specialness in the universe. And this, in turn, is hard giving indeed, because it involves us in a fight backwards, into earlier stages of civilization and childhood in which we had to trust (and perhaps fear) our environment, for we had not then the power to master it. Yet, in doing so, we—as persons—gradually free ourselves of needs for supportive illusions. Is not this one of the triumphs for "us" of our giving legal rights to (or acknowledging the legal rights of) the Blacks and women? . . .

The time may be on hand when these sentiments, and the early stirrings of the law, can be coalesced into a radical new theory or myth—felt as well as intellectualized—of man's relationships to the rest of nature. I do not mean "myth" in a demeaning sense of the term, but in the sense in which, at different times in history, our social "facts" and relationships have been comprehended and integrated by reference to the "myths" that we are co-signers of a social contract, that the Pope is God's agent, and that all men are created equal. Patheism, Shinto, and Tao all have myths to offer. But they are all, each in its own fashion, quaint, primitive, and archaic. What is needed is a myth that can fit our growing body of knowledge of geophysics, biology, and the cosmos. In this vein, I do not think it too remote that we may come to regard the Earth, as some have suggested, as one organism, of which Mankind is a functional part—the mind, perhaps: different from the rest of nature, but different as a man's brain is from his lungs.

Endnotes

1. *Dred Scott* v. *Sanford,* 60 U.S. (19 How.) 390, 404–05 (1856).
2. *People* v. *Hall,* 4 Cal. 399, 405 (1954).
3. Schechter, "The Rightlessness of Mediaeval English Jewry," 45 *Jewish Q. Rev.* 121, 135 (1954) quoting from M. Bateson, *Medieval England* 139 (1904).
4. *Dietrich* v. *Inhabitants of Northampton* 138 Mass. 14, 16 (1884).
5. *In re Goddell,* 39 Wisc. 232, 245 (1875).
6. *Pennsylvania Coal Co.* v. *Sanderson,* 113 Pa. 126, 149, 6 A. 453, 459 (1886).
7. Hand, J., in *Smith* v. *Staso Milling Co.,* 18 F.2d 736, 738 (2d Cir. 1927) (emphasis added).
8. G. Hegel, *Hegel's Philosophy of Right,* 41 (T. Knox transl. 1945).
9. C. McCullers, *The Ballad of the Sad Cafe and Other Stories,* 150–51 (1958).

REVIEW QUESTIONS

1. In Stone's analysis, what is required for something to be a holder of legal rights?
2. Stone says that common law makes natural objects rightless in three ways. What are they?
3. How should the law treat natural objects in Stone's view?
4. According to Stone, how should humans relate to nature?

DISCUSSION QUESTIONS

1. Should trees have legal rights? What do you think? Should they also have moral rights?
2. Stone compares the present status of natural objects to the past status of women and blacks. Is this an acceptable comparison? Why or why not?

William F. Baxter

People or Penguins: The Case for Optimal Pollution

William F. Baxter is William Benjamin Scott and Luna M. Scott Professor of Law at Stanford University. The reading is taken from his book People or Penguins: The Case for Optimal Pollution *(1974).*

Baxter formulates four goals that he thinks should be used as criteria for testing any position on pollution and the treatment of animals. All these goals relate to human benefits such as freedom, satisfaction, dignity, and equal treatment. In Baxter's anthropocentric view, the natural environment, including animals, counts only as a means of producing human benefits; it is not an end in itself and has no value apart from humans.

A "Good" Environment: Just One of the Set of Human Objectives

I start with the modest proposition that, in dealing with pollution, or indeed with any problem, it is helpful to know what one is attempting to accomplish. Agreement on how and whether to pursue a particular objective, such as pollution control, is not possible unless some more general objective has been identified and stated with reasonable precision. We talk loosely of having clean air and clean water, of preserving our wilderness areas, and so forth. But none of these is a sufficiently general objective: each is more accurately viewed as a means rather than as an end.

With regard to clean air, for example, one may ask, "how clean?" and "what does clean mean?" It is even reasonable to ask, "why have clean air?" Each of these questions is an implicit demand that a more general community goal be stated—a goal sufficiently general in its scope and enjoying sufficiently general assent among the community of actors that such "why" questions no longer seem admissible with respect to that goal.

If, for example, one states as a goal the proposition that "every person should be free to do whatever he wishes in contexts where his actions do not interfere with the interests of other human beings," the speaker is unlikely to be met with a response of "why." The goal may be criticized as uncertain in its implications or difficult to implement, but it is so basic a tenet of our civilization—it reflects a cultural value so broadly shared, at least in the abstract—that the question "why" is seen as impertinent or imponderable or both.

I do not mean to suggest that everyone would agree with the "spheres of freedom" objective just stated. Still less do I mean to suggest that a society could subscribe to four or five such general objectives that would be adequate in their coverage to serve as testing criteria by which all other disagreements might be measured. One difficulty in the attempt to construct such a list is that each new goal added will conflict, in certain applications, with each prior goal listed; and thus each goal serves as a limited qualification on prior goals.

Without any expectation of obtaining unanimous consent to them, let me set forth four goals that I generally use as ultimate testing criteria in attempting to frame solutions to problems of human organization. My position regarding pollution stems from these four criteria. If the criteria appeal to you and any part of what appears hereafter does not, our disagreement will have a helpful focus: which of us is correct, analytically, in supposing that his position on pollution would better serve these general goals. If the criteria do not seem acceptable to you, then it is to be expected that our more particular judgments will differ, and the task will then be yours to identify the basic set of criteria upon which your particular judgments rest.

My criteria are as follows:

1. The spheres of freedom criterion stated above.
2. Waste is a bad thing. The dominant feature of human existence is scarcity—our available resources, our aggregate labors, and our skill in employing both have always been, and will continue for some time to be, inadequate to yield to every man all the tangible and intangible satisfactions he would like to have. Hence, none of those resources, or labors, or skills, should be wasted—that is, employed so as to yield less than they might yield in human satisfactions.
3. Every human being should be regarded as an end rather than as a means to be used for the betterment of another. Each should be afforded dignity and regarded as having an absolute claim to an evenhanded application of such rules as the community may adopt for its governance.
4. Both the incentive and the opportunity to improve his share of satisfactions should be preserved to every individual. Preservation of incentive is dictated by the "no-waste" criterion and enjoins against the continuous, totally egalitarian redistribution of satisfactions, or wealth; but subject to that constraint, everyone should receive, by continuous redistribution if necessary, some minimal share of aggregate wealth so as to avoid a level of privation from which the opportunity to improve his situation becomes illusory.

The relationship of these highly general goals to the more specific environmental issues at hand may not be readily apparent, and I am not yet ready to demonstrate their pervasive implications. But let me give one indication of their implications. Recently scientists have informed us that use of DDT in food production is causing damage to the penguin population. For the present purposes let us accept that assertion as an indisputable scientific fact. The scientific fact is often asserted as if the correct implication—that we must stop agricultural use of DDT—followed from the mere statement of the fact of penguin damage. But plainly it does not follow if my criteria are employed.

My criteria are oriented to people, not penguins. Damage to penguins, or sugar pines, or geological marvels is, without more, simply irrelevant. One must go further, by my criteria, and say: Penguins are important because people enjoy seeing them walk about rocks; and furthermore, the well-being of people would be less impaired by halting use of DDT than by giving up penguins. In short, my observations about environmental problems will be people-oriented, as are my criteria. I have no interest in preserving penguins for their own sake.

It may be said by way of objection to this position, that it is very selfish of people to act as if each person represented one unit of importance and nothing else was of any importance. It is undeniably selfish. Nevertheless I think it is the only tenable starting place for analysis for several reasons. First, no other position corresponds to the way most people really think and act—i.e., corresponds to reality.

Second, this attitude does not portend any massive destruction of nonhuman flora and fauna, for people depend on them in many obvious ways, and they will be preserved because and to the degree that humans do depend on them.

Third, what is good for humans is, in many respects, good for penguins and pine trees—clean air for example. So that humans are, in these respects, surrogates for plant and animal life.

Fourth, I do not know how we could administer any other system. Our decisions are either private or collective. Insofar as Mr. Jones is free to act privately, he may give such preferences as he wishes to other forms of life: he may feed birds in winter and do with less himself, and he may even decline to resist an advancing polar bear on the ground that the bear's appetite is more important than those portions of himself that the bear may choose to eat. In short my basic premise does not rule out private altruism to competing life-forms. It does rule out, however, Mr. Jones' inclination to feed Mr. Smith to the bear, however hungry the bear, however despicable Mr. Smith.

Insofar as we act collectively on the other hand, only humans can be afforded an opportunity to participate in the collective decisions. Penguins cannot vote now and are unlikely subjects for the franchise—pine trees more unlikely still. Again each individual is free to cast his vote so as to benefit sugar pines if that is his inclination. But many of the more extreme assertions that one hears from some conservationists amount to tacit assertions that they are specially appointed representatives of sugar pines, and hence that their preferences should be weighted more heavily than the preferences of other humans who do not enjoy equal rapport with "nature." The simplistic assertion that agricultural use of DDT must stop at once because it is harmful to penguins is of that type.

Fifth, if polar bears or pine trees or penguins, like men, are to be regarded as ends rather than means, if they are to count in our calculus of social organization, someone must tell me how much each one counts, and someone must tell me how these life-forms are to be permitted to express their preferences, for I do not know either answer. If the answer is that certain people are to hold their proxies, then I want to know how those proxy-holders are to be selected: self-appointment does not seem workable to me.

Sixth, and by way of summary of all the foregoing, let me point out that the set of environmental issues under discussion—although they raise very complex technical questions of how to achieve any objective—ultimately raise a normative question: what *ought* we to do. Questions of *ought* are unique to the human mind and world—they are meaningless as applied to a nonhuman situation.

I reject the proposition that we *ought* to respect the "balance of nature" or to "preserve the environment" unless the reason for doing so, express or implied, is the benefit of man.

I reject the idea that there is a "right" or "morally correct" state of nature to which we should return. The word "nature" has no normative connotation. Was it "right" or "wrong" for the earth's crust to heave in contortion and create mountains and seas? Was it "right" for the first amphibian to crawl up out of the primordial ooze? Was it "wrong" for plants to reproduce themselves and alter the atmospheric composition in favor of oxygen? For animals to alter the atmosphere in favor of carbon dioxide both by breathing oxygen and eating plants? No answers can be given to these questions because they are meaningless questions.

All this may seem obvious to the point of being tedious, but much of the present controversy over environment and pollution rests on tacit normative assumptions about just such nonnormative phenomena: that it is "wrong" to impair penguins with DDT, but not to slaughter cattle for prime rib roasts. That it is wrong to kill stands of sugar pines and build housing for the poor. Every man is entitled to his own preferred definition of Walden Pond, but there is no definition that has any moral superiority over another, except by reference to the selfish needs of the human race.

From the fact that there is no normative definition of the natural state, it follows that there is no normative definition of clean air or pure water—hence no definition of polluted air—or of pollution—except by reference to the needs of man. The "right" composition of the atmosphere is one which has some dust in it and some lead in it and some hydrogen sulfide in it—just those amounts that attend a sensibly organized society thoughtfully and knowledgeably pursuing the greatest possible satisfaction for its human members.

The first and most fundamental step toward solution of our environmental problems is a clear recognition that our objective is not pure air or water but rather some optimal state of pollution. That step immediately suggests the question: How do we define and attain the level of pollution that will yield the maximum possible amount of human satisfaction?

Low levels of pollution contribute to human satisfaction but so do food and shelter and education and music. To attain ever lower levels of pollution, we must pay the cost of having less of these other things. I contrast that view of the cost of pollution control with the more popular statement that pollution control will "cost" very large numbers of dollars. The popular statement is true in some senses, false in others; sorting out the true and false senses is of some importance. The first step in that sorting process is to achieve a clear understanding of the difference between dollars and resources. Resources are the wealth of our nation; dollars are merely claim checks upon those resources. Resources are of vital importance; dollars are comparatively trivial.

Four categories of resources are sufficient for our purposes: At any given time a nation, or a planet if you prefer, has a stock of labor, of technological skill, of capital goods, and of natural resources (such as mineral deposits, timber, water, land, etc.). These resources can be used in various combinations to yield goods and services of all kinds—in some limited quantity. The quantity will be larger if they are combined efficiently, smaller if combined inefficiently. But in either event the resource stock is limited, the goods and services that they can be made to yield are limited; even the most efficient use of them will yield less than our population, in the aggregate, would like to have.

If one considers building a new dam, it is appropriate to say that it will be costly in the sense that it will require x hours of labor, y tons of steel and concrete, and z amount of capital goods. If these resources are devoted to the dam, then they cannot be used to build hospitals, fishing rods, schools, or electric can openers. That is the meaningful sense in which the dam is costly.

Quite apart from the very important question of how wisely we can combine our resources to produce goods and services, is the very different question of how they get distributed—who gets how many goods? Dollars constitute the claim checks which are distributed among people and which control their share of national output. Dollars are nearly valueless pieces of paper except to the extent that they do represent claim checks to some fraction of the output of goods and services. Viewed as claim checks, all the dollars outstanding during any period of time are worth, in the aggregate, the goods and services that are available to be claimed with them during that period—neither more nor less.

It is far easier to increase the supply of dollars than to increase the production of goods and services—printing dollars is easy. But printing more dollars doesn't help because each dollar then simply becomes a claim to fewer goods, i.e., becomes worth less.

The point is this: many people fall into error upon hearing the statement that the decision to build a dam, or to clean up a river, will cost $X million. It is regrettably easy to say: "It's only money. This is a wealthy country, and we have lots of money." But you cannot build a dam or clean a river with $X million—unless you also have a match, you can't even make a fire. One builds a dam or cleans a river by diverting labor and steel and trucks and factories from making one kind of goods to making another. The cost in dollars is merely a shorthand way of describing the extent of the diversion necessary. If we build a dam for $X million, then we must recognize that we will have $X million less housing and food and medical care and electric can openers as a result.

Similarly, the costs of controlling pollution are best expressed in terms of the other goods we will have to give up to do the job. This is not to say the job should not be done. Badly as we need more housing, more medical care, and more can openers, and more symphony orchestras, we could do with somewhat less of them, in my judgment at least, in exchange for somewhat cleaner air and rivers. But that is the nature of the trade-off, and analysis of the problem is advanced if that unpleasant reality is kept in mind. Once the trade-off relationship is clearly perceived, it is possible to state in a very general way what the optimal level of pollution is. I would state it as follows:

People enjoy watching penguins. They enjoy relatively clean air and smog-free vistas. Their health is improved by relatively clean water and air. Each of these benefits is a type of good or service. As a society we would be well advised to give up one washing machine if the resources that would have gone into that washing machine can yield greater human satisfaction when diverted into pollution control. We should give up one hospital if the resources thereby freed would yield more human satisfaction when devoted to elimination of noise in our cities. And so on, trade-off by trade-off, we should divert our productive capacities from the production of existing goods and services to the production of a cleaner, quieter, more pastoral nation up to—and no further than—the point at which we value more highly the next washing machine or hospital that we would have to do without than we value the next unit of environmental improvement that the diverted resources would create.

Now this proposition seems to me unassailable but so general and abstract as to be unhelpful—at least unadministerable in the form stated. It assumes we can measure in some way the incremental units of human satisfaction yielded by very different types of goods. The proposition must remain a pious abstraction until I can explain how this measurement process can occur. But I insist that the proposition stated describes the result for which we should be striving—and again, that it is always useful to know what your target is even if your weapons are too crude to score a bull's eye.

Review Question

1. Baxter gives four goals to be used as criteria in testing any environmental position. What are they?
2. According to Baxter, what are the implications of these criteria for animals and the environment?
3. Why does he think that the natural environment (including animals) are only means and not ends?

Discussion Questions

1. Baxter says that penguins are important only because humans like to look at them. The implication is that if humans derived no benefit or satisfaction from them, penguins would not be worth preserving. Do you agree? Explain your position.
2. Is the production of human benefit the only relevant moral consideration? If not, then what else should be considered?

William Godfrey-Smith

The Value of Wilderness

William Godfrey-Smith teaches philosophy at Australian National University (Canberra, Australia).

Godfrey-Smith explores two kinds of justification for wilderness preservation, an instrumental justification and a holistic one based on the intrinsic value of the wilderness. He finds that the instrumental justifications for conservation—saving the wilderness because it is a cathedral, a laboratory, a silo, or a gymnasium—all fail to provide a satisfactory rationale. Instead he suggests a holistic conception of nature where we think of humans and nature together forming a moral community, and where we must engage in cooperative behavior for the sake of the whole community.

Wilderness is the raw material out of which man has hammered the artifact called civilization.[1]

Aldo Leopold

The framework that I examine is the framework of *Western* attitudes toward our natural environment, and wilderness in particular. The philosophical task to which I shall address myself is an exploration of attitudes toward wilderness, especially the sorts of justification to which we might legitimately appeal for the preservation of wilderness: what grounds can we advance in support of the claim that wilderness is something that we should *value*?

There are two different ways of appraising something as valuable. It may be that the thing in question is good or valuable *for the sake* of something that we hold to be valuable. In this case the thing is not considered to be good in itself; value in this sense is ascribed in virtue of the thing's being a *means* to some valued end, and not as an *end in itself*. Such values are standardly designated *instrumental* values. Not everything that we hold to be good or valuable can be good for the sake of something else; our values must ultimately be *grounded* in something that is held to be good or valuable in itself. Such things are said to be *intrinsically* valuable. As a matter of historical fact, those things that have been held to be intrinsically valuable, within our Western traditions of thought, have nearly always been taken to be states or conditions of *persons*, e.g., happiness, pleasure, knowledge, or self-realization, to name but a few.

It follows from this that a very central assumption of Western moral thought is that value can be ascribed to the nonhuman world only insofar as it is good for the sake of the well-being of human beings.[2] Our entire attitude toward the natural environment, therefore, has a decidedly anthropocentric bias, and this fact is reflected in the sorts of justification that are standardly provided for the preservation of the natural environment.

A number of thinkers, however, are becoming increasingly persuaded that our anthropocentric morality is in fact inadequate to provide a satisfactory basis for a moral philosophy of ecological obligation. It is for this reason that we hear not infrequently the claim that we need a "new morality." A new moral framework—that is, a network of recognized obligations and duties—is not, however, something that can be casually conjured up in order to satisfy some vaguely felt need. The task of developing a sound biologically based moral philosophy, a philosophy that is not anthropocentrically based, and that provides a satisfactory justification for ecological obligation and concern, is, I think, one of the most urgent tasks confronting moral philosophers at the present. It will entail a radical reworking of accepted attitudes—attitudes that

From William Godfrey-Smith, "The Value of Wilderness," *Environmental Ethics* (1979). Reprinted with permission of *Environmental Ethics* and the author.

we currently accept as "self-evident"—and this is not something that can emerge suddenly. Indeed, I think the seminal work remains largely to be done, though I suggest below the broad outline that an environmentally sound moral philosophy is likely to take.

In the absence of a comprehensive and convincing ecologically based morality we naturally fall back on *instrumental* justifications for concern for our natural surroundings, and for preserving wilderness areas and animal species. We can, I think, detect at least four main lines of instrumental justification for the preservation of wilderness. By *wilderness* I understand any reasonably large tract of the earth, together with its plant and animal communities, which is substantially unmodified by humans and in particular by human technology. The natural contrast to *wilderness* and *nature* is an *artificial* or *domesticated* environment. The fact that there are borderline cases that are difficult to classify does not, of course, vitiate this distinction.

The first attitude toward wilderness espoused by conservationists to which I wish to draw attention is what I shall call the "cathedral" view. This is the view that wilderness areas provide a vital opportunity for spiritual revival, moral regeneration, and aesthetic delight. The enjoyment of wilderness is often compared in this respect with religious or mystical experience. Preservation of magnificent wilderness areas for those who subscribe to this view is essential for human well-being, and its destruction is conceived as something akin to an act of vandalism, perhaps comparable to—some may regard it as more serious than[3]—the destruction of a magnificent and moving human edifice, such as the Parthenon, the Taj Mahal, or the Palace of Versailles.

Insofar as the "cathedral" view holds that value derives solely from human satisfactions gained from its contemplation it is clearly an instrumentalist attitude. It does, however, frequently approach an *intrinsic value* attitude, insofar as the feeling arises that there is importance in the fact that it is there to be contemplated, whether or not anyone actually takes advantage of this fact. Suppose for example, that some wilderness was so precariously balanced that *any* human intervention or contact would inevitably bring about its destruction. Those who maintained that the area should, nevertheless, be preserved, unexperienced and unenjoyed, would certainly be ascribing to it an intrinsic value.

The "cathedral" view with respect to wilderness in fact is a fairly recent innovation in Western thought. The predominant Greco-Christian attitude, which generally speaking was the predominant Western attitude prior to eighteenth- and nineteenth-century romanticism, had been to view wilderness as threatening or alarming, an attitude still reflected in the figurative uses of the expression *wilderness*, clearly connoting a degenerate state to be avoided. Christianity, in general, has enjoined "the transformation of wilderness, those dreaded haunts of demons, the ancient nature-gods, into farm and pasture,"[4] that is, to a domesticated environment.

The second instrumental justification of the value of wilderness is what we might call the "laboratory" argument. This is the argument that wilderness areas provide vital subject matter for scientific inquiry that provides us with an understanding of the intricate interdependencies of biological systems, their modes of change and development, their energy cycles, and the source of their stabilities. If we are to understand our own biological dependencies, we require natural systems as a norm, to inform us of the biological laws that we transgress at our peril.

The third instrumentalist justification is the "silo" argument, which points out that one excellent reason for preserving reasonable areas of the natural environment intact is that we thereby preserve a stockpile of genetic diversity, which it is certainly prudent to maintain as a backup in case something should suddenly go wrong with the simplified biological systems that, in general, constitute agriculture. Further, there is the related point that there is no way of anticipating our future needs, or the undiscovered applications of apparently useless plants, which might turn out to be, for example, the source of some pharmacologically valuable drug—a cure, say, for leukemia. This might be called, perhaps, the "rare herb" argument, and it provides another persuasive instrumental justification for the preservation of wilderness.

The final instrumental justification that I think should be mentioned is the "gymnasium" argument, which regards the preservation of wilderness as important for athletic or recreational activities.

An obvious problem that arises from these instrumental arguments is that the various activities that they seek to justify are not always reconcilable with those of the ordinary vacationist. Still more obvious is the conflict between the recreational use of wilderness and the interests of the miner, the farmer, and the timber merchant.

The conflict of interest that we encounter here is one that it is natural to try and settle through the economic calculus of cost-benefit considerations. So long as the worth of natural systems is believed to depend entirely on instrumental values, it is natural to suppose that we can sort out the conflict of interests within an objective frame of reference, by estimating the human satisfactions to be gained from the preservation of wilderness, and by weighing these against the satisfactions that are to be gained from those activities that may lead to its substantial modification, domestication, and possibly even destruction.

Many thinkers are liable to encounter here a feeling of resistance to the suggestion that we can apply purely economic considerations to settle such conflicts of interest. The assumption behind economic patterns of thought, which underline policy formulation and planning, is that the values that we attach to natural systems and to productive activities are commensurable; this is an assumption that may be called into question. It is not simply a question of the difficulty of quantifying what value should be attached to the preservation of the natural environment. The feeling is more that economic considerations are simply out of place. This feeling is one that is often too lightly dismissed by tough-minded economists as being obscurely mystical or superstitious; but it is a view worth examining. What it amounts to, I suggest, is the belief that there is something *morally* objectionable in the destruction of natural systems, or at least in their wholesale elimination, and this is precisely the belief that natural systems, or economically "useless" species do possess an *intrinsic* value. That is, it is an attempt to articulate the rejection of the anthropocentric view that all value, ultimately, resides in *human* interests and concerns. But it is a difficult matter to try to provide justification for such attitudes, and this is, for reasons that are deeply bound up with the problems of resolving basic value conflict, a problem that I have discussed elsewhere.[5]

The belief that all values are commensurable, so that there is no problem *in principle* in providing a satisfactory resolution of value conflict, involves the assumption that the quantitative social sciences, in particular economics, can provide an *objective* frame of reference within which all conflicts of interest can be satisfactorily resolved. We should, however, note that in the application of cost-benefit analyses there is an inevitable bias in the sorts of values that figure in the calculation, to wit, a bias toward those considerations that are readily quantifiable, and toward those interests that will be staunchly defended. This is a fairly trivial point, but it is one that has substantial consequences, for there are at least three categories of values and interests that are liable to be inadequately considered, or discounted altogether.[6] First, there are the interests of those who are too widely distributed spatially, or too incrementally affected over time, to be strongly supported by any single advocate. Second, there are the interests of persons not yet existing, to wit, future generations, who are clearly liable to be affected by present policy, but who are clearly not in a position to press any claims. Third, there are interests not associated with humans at all, such as the "rights" of wild animals.[7]

This last consideration, in particular, is apt to impress many as ludicrous, as quite simply "unthinkable." It is an unquestioned axiom of our present code of ethics that the class of individuals to which we have obligations is the class of humans. The whole apparatus of rights and duties is in fact based on an ideal of reciprocal contractual obligations, and in terms of this model the class of individuals to whom we may stand in moral relations—i.e., those with whom we recognize a network of rights, duties, and obligations—is the class of humans. A major aspect of a satisfactory ethic of ecological obligation and concern will be to challenge this central anthropocentric assumption. I return to this point below.

Even restricting our attention to the class of human preference havers, however, we should be wary of dismissing as simply inadmissible the interests of future generations. The claims of posterity tend to be excluded from our policy deliberations not, I suspect, because we believe that future generations will be unaffected by our policies, but because we lack any clear idea as to how to set about attaching weight to their interests. This is an instance of the familiar problem of "the dwarfing of soft variables." In settling conflicts of interest, any consideration that cannot be precisely quantified tends to be given little weight or, more likely, left out of the equation altogether: "If you can't measure it, it doesn't exist."[8] The result of ignoring soft variables is a spurious appearance of completeness and precision, but in eliminating all soft variables from our cost-benefit calculations, the conclusion is decidedly biased. If, as seems plausible, it is *in principle* impossible to do justice to soft variables, such as the interests of posterity, it may be that we have to abandon the idea that the economic models employed in cost-benefit calculations are universally applicable for sorting out all conflicts of interest. It may be necessary to abandon the economic calculus as the universal model for rational deliberation.[9]

Another category of soft variable that tends to be discounted from policy deliberations is that which concerns economically unimportant species of animals or plants. A familiar subterfuge that we frequently encounter is the attempt to invest such species with spurious economic value, as illustrated in the rare herb argument. A typical example of this, cited by Leopold, is the reaction of ornithologists to the threatened disappearance of certain species of songbirds: they at once came forward with some distinctly shaky evidence that they played an essential role in the control of insects.[10] The dominance of economic modes of thinking is again obvious: the evidence has to be economic in order to be acceptable. This exemplifies the way in which we turn to instrumentalist justifications for the maintenance of biotic diversity.

The alternative to such instrumentalist justifications, the alternative that Leopold advocated with great insight and eloquence, is to widen the boundary of the moral community to include animals, plants, the soil, or collectively *the land.*[11] This involves a radical shift in our conception of nature, so that land is recognized not simply as property, to be dealt with or disposed of as a matter of expediency; land in Leopold's view is not a commodity that belongs to us, but a community to which we belong. This change in conception is far-reaching and profound. It involves a shift in our metaphysical conception of nature—that is, a change in what sort of thing we take our natural surroundings to *be.* This is a point that I would like to elaborate, albeit sketchily.

The predominant Western conception of nature is exemplified in—and to no small extent is a consequence of—the philosophy of Descartes, in which nature is viewed as something separate and apart, to be transformed and controlled at will. Descartes divided the world into conscious thinking substances—minds—and extended, mechanically arranged substances—the rest of nature. It is true that we find in Western thought alternatives to the Cartesian metaphysical conception of nature—the views of Spinoza and Hegel might be mentioned in particular[12]—but the predominant spirit, especially among scientists, has been Cartesian. These metaphysical views have become deeply embedded in Western thought, which has induced us to view the world through Cartesian spectacles. One of the triumphs of Descartes' mechanistic view of nature has been the elimination of occult qualities and forces from the explanation of natural events. The natural world is to be understood, in the Cartesian model, in purely mechanistic terms. An unfortunate consequence of the triumph, nevertheless, has been a persistent fear among some thinkers that the rejection of Cartesian metaphysics may lead to the reinstatement of occult and mystical views of nature.

An important result of Descartes' sharp ontological division of the world into active mental substances and inert material substances, has been the alienation of man from the natural world. Although protests have been raised against Cartesian metaphysics ever since its inception, it has exercised a deep influence on our attitudes toward nature. Descartes' mechanistic conception of nature naturally leads to the view that it is possible in principle to obtain complete mastery and technical control over the natural world. It is significant to recall that for Descartes the paradigm instance of a natural object was a lump of wax, the perfect exemplification of malleability. This conception of natural objects as wholly pliable and passive is clearly one that leaves no room for anything like a network of obligations.

A natural corollary of the mechanistic conception of nature, and integral to the Cartesian method of inquiry, is the role played by reductive thinking. In order to understand a complex system one should, on this view, break it into its component parts and examine them. The Cartesian method of inquiry is a natural correlate of Cartesian metaphysics, and is a leitmotif of our science-based technology.

It should be stressed that a rejection of the Cartesian attitude and its method of inquiry need *not* involve a regression to occult and mystical views about the "sacredness" of the natural world, and the abandoning of systematic rational inquiry. It must be conceded, however, that the rejection of the view that nature is an exploitable commodity has, unfortunately, frequently taken this form. This sort of romantic nature mysticism *does* provide a powerful exhortation for exercising restraint in our behavior to the natural world, but it carries with it a very clear danger. This is that while prohibiting destructive acts toward the natural world, it equally prohibits constructive acts; we surely cannot rationally adopt a complete "hands off" policy with respect to nature, on the basis of what looks like the extremely implausible—and highly cynical—a priori assumption that *any* attempt to modify our surroundings is bound to be for the worse.

It may, however, be that advocates of the "sacredness" of nature are attempting to do no more than articulate the idea that natural systems have their own intrinsic value, and adopt this manner of speaking as a convenient way of rejecting the dominant anthropocentric morality. If *this* is all that is being claimed, then I have no quarrel with it. And it may be inevitable that this mode of expression is adopted in the absence of a developed ecologically sound alternative morality. But I think we should be wary of this style of justification; what is needed, as Passmore has nicely expressed it, is not the spiritualizing of nature, but the naturalizing of man.[13] This involves a shift from the piecemeal reductive conception of natural items to a *holistic* or systemic view in which we come to appreciate the symbiotic interdependencies of the natural world. On the holistic or total-field view, organisms—including man—are conceived as nodes in a biotic web of intrinsically related parts.[14] That is, our understanding of biological organisms requires more than just an understanding of their structure and properties; we also have to attend seriously to their interrelations. Holistic or systemic thinking does not deny that organisms are complex physicochemical systems, but it affirms that the methods employed in establishing the high level functional relationships expressed by physical laws are often of very limited importance in understanding the nature of biological systems. We may now be facing, in the terminology of Thomas Kuhn,[15] a shift from a physical to a biological paradigm in our understanding of nature. This seems to me to be an important aspect of the rejection of Cartesian metaphysics.

The limitations of the physical paradigm have long been accepted in the study of human society, but the tendency has been to treat social behavior and human action as quite distinct from the operations of our natural surroundings. The inappropriateness of the physical paradigm for understanding *human* society seems to me to be quite correct; what is comparatively new is the post-Cartesian realization that the physical paradigm is of more limited application for our understanding of *nature* than was previously supposed.

The holistic conception of the natural world

contains, in my view, the possibility of extending the idea of community beyond human society. And in this way biological wisdom does, I think, carry implications for ethics. Just as Copernicus showed us that man does not occupy the physical center of the universe, Darwin and his successors have shown us that man occupies no *biologically* privileged position. We still have to assimilate the implications that this biological knowledge has for morality.

Can we regard man and the natural environment as constituting a community in any morally significant sense? Passmore, in particular, has claimed that this extended sense of community is entirely spurious.[16] Leopold, on the other hand, found the biological extension of community entirely natural.[17] If we regard a community as a collection of individuals who engage in cooperative behavior, Leopold's extension seems to me entirely legitimate. An ethic is no more than a code of conduct designed to ensure cooperative behavior among the members of a community. Such cooperative behavior is required to underpin the health of the community, in this biologically extended sense, *health* being understood as the biological capacity for self-renewal,[18] and *ill-health* as the degeneration or loss of this capacity.

Man, of course, cannot be placed on "all fours" with his biologically fellow creatures in all respects. In particular, man is the only creature who can act as a full-fledged moral agent, i.e., an individual capable of exercising reflective rational choice on the basis of principles. What distinguishes man from his fellow creatures is not the capacity to *act,* but the fact that his actions are, to a great extent, free from programming. This capacity to modify our own behavior is closely bound up with the capacity to acquire knowledge of the natural world, a capacity that has enabled us, to an unprecedented extent, to manipulate the environment, and—especially in the recent past—to alter it rapidly, violently, and globally. Our hope must be that the capacity for knowledge, which has made ecologically hazardous activities possible, will lead to a more profound understanding of the delicate biological interdependencies that some of these actions now threaten, and thereby generate the wisdom for restraint.

To those who are skeptical of the possibility of extending moral principles in the manner of Leopold, to include items treated heretofore as matters of expediency, it can be pointed out that extensions have, to a limited extent, already taken place. One clear—if partial—instance, is in the treatment of animals. It is now generally accepted, and this is a comparatively recent innovation,[19] that we have at least a *prima facie* obligation not to treat animals cruelly or sadistically. And this certainly constitutes a shift in moral attitudes. If—as seems to be the case—cruelty to animals is accepted as intrinsically wrong, then there *is* at least one instance in which it is *not* a matter of moral indifference how we behave toward the nonhuman world.

More familiar perhaps are the moral revolutions that have occurred within the specific domain of human society—witness the progressive elimination of the "right" to racial, class, and sex exploitation. Each of these shifts involves the acceptance, on the part of some individuals, of new obligations, rights, and values that, to a previous generation, would have been considered unthinkable.[20] The essential step in recognizing an enlarged community involves coming to see, feel, and understand what was previously perceived as alien and part: it is the evolution of the capacity of *empathy.*

I have digressed a little into the history of ideas, stressing in particular the importance of the influence of Descartes.[21] My justification for this excursion is that our present attitudes toward nature, and toward wilderness, are very largely the result of Descartes' metaphysical conception of what nature is, and the concomitant conception that man has of himself. Our metaphysical assumptions are frequently extremely influential invisible persuaders; they determine the boundaries of what is thinkable. In rejecting the Cartesian conception the following related shifts in attitudes can, I think, be discerned.

1. A change from reductive convergent patterns of thought to divergent holistic patterns.
2. A shift from man's conception of himself as the center of the biological world, to one in which he is conceived of as a component in

a network of biological relations, a shift comparable to the Copernican discovery that man does not occupy the *physical* center of the universe.
3. An appreciation of the fact that in modifying biological systems we do not simply modify the properties of a substance, but alter a network of relations. This rejection of the Cartesian conception of nature as a collection of independent physical parts is summed up in the popular ecological maxim "it is impossible to do only one thing."
4. A recognition that the processes of nature are independent and indifferent to human interests and concerns.
5. A recognition that biological systems are items that possess intrinsic value, in Kant's terminology, that they are "ends in themselves."

We can, however, provide—and it is important that we can provide—an answer to the question: "What is the *use* of wilderness?" We certainly ought to preserve and protect wilderness areas as gymnasiums, as laboratories, as stockpiles of genetic diversity, and as cathedrals. Each of these reasons provides a powerful and sufficient instrumental justification for their preservation. But note how the very posing of this question about the *utility* of wilderness reflects an anthropocentric system of values. From a genuinely eccentric point of view the question "What is the *use* of wilderness?" would be as absurd as the question "What is the *use* of happiness?"

The philosophical task is to try to provide adequate justification, or at least clear the way for a scheme of values according to which concern and sympathy for our environment is immediate and natural, and the desirability of protecting and preserving wilderness self-evident. When once controversial propositions become platitudes, the philosophical task will have been successful.

I will conclude, nevertheless, on a deflationary note. It seems to me (at least much of the time) that the shift in attitudes that I think is required for promoting genuinely harmonious relations with nature is too drastic, too "unthinkable," to be very persuasive for most people. If this is so, then it will be more expedient to justify the preservation of wilderness in terms of instrumentalist considerations, and I have argued that there *are* powerful arguments for preservation that can be derived from the purely anthropocentric considerations of human self-interest. I hope, however, that there will be some who feel that such anthropocentric considerations are not wholly satisfying, i.e., that they do not really do justice to our intuitions. But at a time when *human* rights are being treated in some quarters with a great deal of skepticism it is perhaps unrealistic to expect the rights of nonhumans to receive sympathetic attention. Perhaps, though, we should not be too abashed by this; extensions in ethics have seldom followed the path of political expediency.

Endnotes

1. Aldo Leopold, *A Sand County Almanac* (New York: Oxford University Press, 1949), p. 188.
2. Other cultures have certainly included the idea that nature should be valued for its own sake in their moral codes, e.g., the American Indians (cf. Chief Seattle's letter to Present Franklin Pierce of 1854, reprinted in *The Canberra Times*, 5 July 1966, p. 9), the Chinese (cf. Joseph Needham, "History and Human Values," in H. and S. Rose, eds. *The Radicalization of Science* [London: Macmillan, 1976], pp. 90–117), and the Australian Aborigines (cf. W. E. H. Stanner, *Aboriginal Man in Australia* [Sydney: Angus and Robertson, 1965], pp. 207–237).
3. We can after all *replace* human artifacts such as buildings with something closely similar, but the destruction of a wilderness or a biological species is irreversible.
4. John Passmore, *Man's Responsibility for Nature* (London: Duckworth, 1974; New York: Charles Scribner's Sons, 1974), p. 17; cf. ch. 5.
5. In "The Rights of Non-humans and Intrinsic Values," in M. A. McRobbie, D. Mannison, and R. Routley, eds. *Environmental Philosophy* (Canberra: Australian National University Research School of Social Services, forthcoming).
6. Cf. Laurence H. Tribe, "Policy Science: Analysis or Ideology?" *Philosophy and Public Affairs* 2 (1972–3): 66–110.
7. I should mention that I am a skeptic about "rights"; it seems to me that talk about rights is always eliminable in favor of talk about legitimate claims for considerations, and obligations to respect those claims. Rights-talk does, however, have useful rhetorical effect in exhorting people to recognize claims. The reason for this is that claims pressed in these terms perform the crucial trick of shifting the onus of proof. This is accomplished by the fact that a *denial* of a right appears to

be a more positive and deliberate act than merely refusing to acknowledge an obligation.

8. Laurence H. Tribe, "Trial by Mathematics: Precision and Ritual in Legal Process," *Harvard Law Review* 84 (1971): 1361.
9. Of course, in practice cost-benefit considerations *do* operate within deontic constraints, and we do *not* accept economics unrestrictedly as providing the model for rational deliberation. We would not accept exploitative child labor, for example, as a legitimate mode of production, no matter how favorable the economics. This is not just because we attach too high a cost to this form of labor; it is just unthinkable.
10. Aldo Leopold, "The Land Ethic," in *A Sand County Almanac*, p. 210.
11. CF. Aldo Leopold, "The Conservation Ethic," *Journal of Forestry* 31 (1933): 634–43, and "The Land Ethic," *Sand County Almanac*.
12. Cf. John Passmore, "Attitudes to Nature," in R. S. Peters, ed., *Nature and Conduct* (London: Macmillan, 1975), pp. 251–64.
13. Ibid., p. 260.
14. Cf. Arne Naess, "The Shallow and the Deep, Long-Range Ecology Movement," *Inquiry* 16 (1973): 95–100.
15. T. S. Kuhn, *The Structure of Scientific Revolutions* (Chicago: University of Chicago Press, 1962).
16. Passmore, *Man's Responsibility for Nature*, ch. 6; "Attitudes to Nature," p. 262.
17. Leopold, "The Land Ethic."
18. Ibid., p. 221.
19. Cf. Pasmore, "The Treatment of Animals," *Journal of the History of Ideas* 36 (1975): 195–218.
20. Cf. Christopher D. Stone, "Should Trees Have Standing? Toward Legal Rights for Natural Objects," *Southern California Law Review* 45 (1972): 450–501.
21. Here I differ from the well-known claim of Lynn White ("The Historical Roots of Our Ecological Crisis," *Science* 155 [1967]: 1203–7) that the Judeo-Christian tradition is predominantly responsible for the development of Western attitudes toward nature.

Review Questions

1. Distinguish between instrumental value and intrinsic value.
2. How does Godfrey-Smith define wilderness?
3. What is the cathedral view?
4. Explain the laboratory argument.
5. What is the silo argument?
6. What is the gymnasium argument?
7. What problems arise for these instrumental justifications for preserving wilderness areas?
8. What is the dominant Western conception of nature?
9. Explain the holistic conception of the natural world.

Discussion Questions

1. Is the holistic conception of the natural world acceptable? Defend your position.
2. Should human beings frustrate important interests in order to preserve the natural environment? Defend your answer.

Problem Cases

1. Beyond Beef. (Reported in St. Cloud State University's *Chronicle* by Brian Perry, April 20, 1993.) Beyond Beef is a grassroots coalition formed to protest beef eating and production. The group has targeted over 3,000 McDonald's restaurants in the United States, Canada, and Mexico with its so-called Adopt-A-McDonald's Campaign. The goals of the campaign are to reach one million customers with their message about the evils of eating beef, to get McDonald's to offer a vegetarian burger as an alternative to the standard beef hamburger, to get McDonald's to devote 25 percent of its advertising budget to promoting the vegetarian burger, and to make McDonald's pledge to avoid dairy products and meat tainted with Bovine Growth Hormone.

The tactics of the campaign involve telephone calls to McDonald's management, standing in front of the restaurants with signs having slogans like "Red Meat-Early Death," and handing out informational leaflets and brochures. The brochures claim that the synthetic Bovine Growth Hormone injected into animals to stimulate growth is unnatural and likely to cause health problems apart from those associated with a diet high in saturated fat and cholesterol. They assert that beef production has bad consequences for the environment in the form of pollution, water depletion, and global warming. Latin American countries have cleared land to create pasture land for grazing cattle, destroying fifty-five square feet of rain forest for every quarter pound of beef they export. (For more on rain forest destruction see the Problem Case below.)

McDonald's asserts that their menu reflects consumer demand—market research shows the consumer wants beef hamburgers, not vegetarian burgers. Besides, they already offer their customers alternatives to beef such as salads, fish, and chicken.

For the sake of discussion, let's agree that beef eating is unhealthy and that beef production is bad for the environment. What should be done? Is the campaign against McDonald's justified? How about warning labels on beef and dairy products like those on cigarettes and beer?

2. ***The Draize Test.*** The Draize eye test is used by cosmetic companies such as Revlon and Procter and Gamble to test the eye irritancy of their products—cosmetics, hair shampoos, and so on. The substance to be tested is injected into the eyes of rabbits; more specifically, 0.1 milligrams (a large volume dose) is injected into the conjuctival sac of one eye of each of six rabbits with the other eye serving as a control. The lids are held together for one second and then the animal is released. The eyes are examined at 24, 48, and 72 hours to see if there is corneal damage. Although the test is very painful, as you can imagine, anesthetics are not used. The eyes are not washed. Very large doses are used (often resulting in permanent eye damage) to provide a large margin of safety in extrapolating for human response. Should companies continue to test their new products in this way or not? What is your view?

3. ***Mechanical Mothers.*** (These experiments were mentioned in *Newsweek,* December 26, 1988.) Researchers at the Primate Research Center in Madison, Wisconsin, have been conducting experiments to gauge the effects of child abuse on monkeys. One experiment involves putting baby monkeys with mechanical surrogate mothers who eject sharp brass spikes when the babies try to hug them. Another experiment consists of impregnating females who have been driven insane by social isolation. When given their babies, the mothers crush their skulls with their teeth. Are these experiments justified or not?

4. ***Guerrilla Warfare in Cathedral Forest.*** (Reported in *Esquire,* Feb., 1987). Cathedral Forest in Oregon is one of the last large stands of virgin forest remaining on the North American continent. The forest is called old growth because the trees (Douglas firs) are among the oldest and biggest on the planet. Old growth constitutes an almost infinitesimal percentage of forested lands in the United States. Even though there is no commercial demand for the timber, the United States Forest Service has made the harvesting of the last of the old trees a priority. The Forest Service has sold Cathedral Forest to Willamette Industries, a large wood-products company.

To prevent the forest from being cut down, radical environmentalist Mike Roselle has resorted to an illegal guerrilla action called tree spiking. He has driven long nails into trees in a spiral pattern. Chain saws and saw blades will shatter when they hit the buried nails. Mike hopes that the spiked trees will prevent Willamette from cutting down the forest. Is this tree spiking morally justified or not? What is your view?

5. ***The Burning of Amazon Rain Forests.*** (See the cover story in *Time,* September 18, 1989.) Farmers and cattle ranchers in Brazil are burning the rain forests of the Amazon river to clear the land for crops and livestock. According to the article in *Time,* an estimated 12,350 square miles have been destroyed so far, and the burning continues. Conservationists and leaders of rich industrial nations have asked Brazil to stop the destruction. They claim that if the Amazon rain forests are destroyed, more than one million species will vanish. This would be a significant loss of the earth's genetic and biological heritage. Furthermore, they are worried about changes in the climate. The Amazon system of forests plays an important role in the way the sun's heat is distributed around the earth because it stores more than seventy-five billion tons of carbon in its trees. Burning the trees of the Amazon forests will produce a dramatic increase in the amount of carbon dioxide in the atmosphere. The trapping of heat by this atmospheric carbon dioxide—the green house effect—will significantly increase the global warming trend.

Brazilians reply that they have a sovereign right to use their land as they see fit. They complain that the rich industrial nations are just trying to maintain their economic supremacy. Brazilian President José Sarney argues that the burning is necessary for Brazilian economic development, particularly when Brazil is struggling under an $111 billion foreign debt load.

Should Brazil continue burning the Amazon rain forests? If not, then what should rich industrial nations do to help Brazil?

SUGGESTED READINGS

1. *Environmental Ethics*. This journal is edited by Eugene C. Hargrove and dedicated to the philosophical aspects of environmental problems.

2. Leslie Pickering Francis and Richard Norman, "Some Animals Are More Equal Than Others," *Philosophy* 53 (October 1978), pp. 507–527. Francis and Norman agree with Singer and others that it is wrong to cause animal suffering, but unlike Singer, they do not think that this requires us to adopt vegetarianism or abandon animal experimentation.

3. R. G. Frey, *Interests and Rights: The Case Against Animals* (Oxford: The Clarendon Press, 1980.) Frey argues that animals have neither interests nor moral rights.

4. William K. Frankena, "Ethics and the Environment," in *Ethics and Problems of the 21st Century,* Kenneth Goodpaster and K. M. Sayre, eds. (Notre Dame, Indiana: University of Notre Dame Press, 1979), pp. 3–19. Frankena defends sentientism as an adequate basis for environmental ethics.

5. Alastair S. Gunn, "Why Should We Care about Rare Species?" *Environmental Ethics*, vol. 2, no. 1 (Spring 1989), pp. 17–37. Gunn analyzes the concept of rarity and its relation to value. He argues that the extermination of a rare species is wrong because each species (as well as the ecological whole) has intrinsic value.

6. Aldo Leopold, "The Land Ethic," in *A Sand County Almanac* (New York: Oxford University Press, 1966), pp. 217–241. This is the classic presentation of Leopold's Land Ethic. As he puts it, "The land ethic simply enlarges the boundaries of the community to include soils, waters, plants, and animals, or collectively, the land."

7. J. Baird Callicott, "The Search For An Environmental Ethic," in *Matters of Life and Death: New Introductory Essays in Moral Philosophy*, Third Edition, Tom Regan, ed., (New York: McGraw-Hill, 1993), pp. 322–381. Callicott argues that ecocentrism, a conceptually developed version of Leopold's land ethic, is the most satisfactory environmental ethic.

8. James Rachels, *Created from Animals: The Moral Implications of Darwinism* (Oxford: Oxford University Press, 1990). Rachels defends animal rights.

9. H. J. McCloskey, "Moral Rights and Animals," *Inquiry* 22 (Spring-Summer 1979), pp. 25–54. McCloskey attacks Feinberg's analysis of the concept of a right and presents his own account. According to McCloskey, a right is an entitlement to something and not a claim against someone. Beings who are able to make a claim, either directly or through a representative, can possess rights. But since animals cannot do this, they cannot be said to possess rights.

10. John Passmore, *Man's Responsibility for Nature* (New York: Charles Scribner's Sons, 1974). Passmore thinks that we should not sacrifice art, science, or other human interests for the sake of conservation.

11. Tom Regan, ed., *Earthbound: New Introductory Essays in Environmental Ethics* (New York: Random House, 1984). This is a collection of original essays on a variety of topics related to the environment including Alastair S. Gunn, "Preserving Rare Species;" Annette Baier, "For the Sake of Future Generations;" and Mark Sagoff, "Ethics and Economics in Environmental Law."

12. Tom Regan, *The Case for Animal Rights* (Berkeley: University of California Press, 1983). Regan argues that animals are not thoughtless brutes, but persons who have beliefs and desires, memories and expectations, and who feel pleasure and pain. As such they have a basic moral right to be treated with respect. To do this we must eliminate commercial animal agriculture, hunting and trapping, and animal experimentation.

13. Mark Sagoff, "On Preserving the Natural Environment," *Yale Law Journal* 84 (December 1974), pp. 167–205. Sagoff proposes a nonutilitarian rationale for preserving the natural environment.

14. Donald Scherer and Thomas Attig, eds., *Ethics and the Environment* (Englewood Cliffs, NJ: Prentice-Hall, 1983). This is a collection of readings on specific environmental problems and the general question of defining an environmental ethic.

15. Paul W. Taylor, *Respect for Nature: A Theory of Environment Ethics* (Princeton, NJ: Princeton University Press, 1986). Taylor develops a theory of respect for nature that is similar to the ethical theory based on respect for persons. It requires us to see other living things as having an inherent worth

that is equal to our own, and a denial that humans have a higher worth or value.

16. Peter C. List, ed., *Radical Environmentalism: Philosophy and Tactics* (Belmont, CA: Wadsworth Publishing Co., 1993). This is a collection of articles on radical environmentalism. Included are articles on ecofeminism (the application of feminist theory to the environment) and deep ecology. As it is explained by Arne Naess in two articles, deep ecology starts with the view called holism in the readings but goes on to recommend a mystical vision of the whole of nature as the Self. Students of Hinduism will recognize this as the teaching of the Upanishads. Also covered are the tactics of radical environmental groups like Earth First! which engage in nonviolent resistance (called monkey wrenching, a term from Edward Abbey's book *The Monkey Wrench Gang)* and the Sea Shepherd Society which takes action to save marine animals like whales.

17. J. Baird Callicott, "Animal Liberation: A Triangular Affair," *Environmental Ethics* 2 (Winter 1980), pp. 311–338. Callicott discusses the conflict between animal rights advocates and environmentalists. For example, Singer thinks that hunting and killing animals is wrong, but Aldo Leopold did not think that the land ethic forbids hunting, killing, and eating animals. In fact, Leopold was an enthusiastic hunter and meat-eater.

18. Mary Anne Warren, "The Rights of the Nonhuman World," in *Environmental Philosophy,* Robert Elliot and Arran Gare, eds., (Queensland: The University of Queensland Press, 1983), pp. 109–134. Despite conflicts between the animal liberation view and Leopold's land ethic, Warren thinks that a compromise can be reached provided certain concessions are made by each side. The result of this compromise is a more complete nonhomocentric moral theory that explains why we should protect both animals and the natural environment.

19. Karen J. Warren, "The Power and the Promise of Ecological Feminism," *Environmental Ethics* 12 (Summer 1990), pp. 125–145. In Warren's view, there are important connections between the domination of women and the domination of nature. An explanation of the male domination of women can help explain the domination of the environment. The resulting theory which combines both feminist theory of male domination and an environmental ethic is called ecofeminism.

20. Barry Commoner, "Economic Growth and Environmental Quality: How to Have Both," *Social Policy* (Summer 1985), pp. 18–26. Environmentalists sometimes claim that if we are going to preserve the environment, we must give up unrestrained economic growth. Commoner's thesis is that the economic growth with a higher standard of living and more jobs is possible while still preserving the environment. The way to do this is to increase efficiency with better technology.

Chapter Nine

WAR

Introduction

Conventional and nuclear war. In this chapter we concern ourselves with conventional war, as distinguished from nuclear war. Recent history provides us with many examples: the Korean War, the Vietnam War, the war of Soviet intervention in Afghanistan, the invasion of Grenada by American forces, the Gulf War, and most recently, the war in Bosnia. World War II started out as a conventional war, but ended as a nuclear war with the destruction of Hiroshima and Nagasaki in August of 1945. World War II was the first, and it is hoped, the last nuclear war.

Perhaps it is premature to say that we have seen the last nuclear war. But it has been nearly fifty years since two atomic bombs (the only such weapons in existence at the time) were dropped on two undefended cities in Japan. Now there are thousands of such weapons in many different countries. Yet nobody has ever used them. Why? There are different answers. One is that their use is irrational; the dangers of retaliation, escalation, and radioactive fallout are too great for it to be in any country's best interest to use them. Another answer concerns the morality of their use; too many innocent noncombatants are killed.

Of course, it is always possible that an accident, an act of terrorism, or some irrational dictator could touch off a nuclear war. But whatever the prospects for nuclear war, it seems clear that the more urgent concern today is conventional war. At the time of writing, there was a war going on in Bosnia. The war started in 1992 when Serbian nationalists and the Yugoslav Army attacked Muslims in Bosnia and Herzegovina in a campaign of so-called ethnic cleansing. Reports in the newspapers characterized the ethnic cleansing as genocide or even a holocaust with many innocent people being killed. The Serbs laid siege to Sarajevo, the capital, but the city's Muslim defenders have held out so far with food relief from the U.N. In January of 1993, the situation became even more complicated when the Croatian Army launched an assault to retake territory in southern Croatia. Violence escalated between Croats, Muslims, and Serbs, with each group fighting the other two. Over 100,000 people have been killed so far, and more than 3.6 million people have been displaced by the war.

Two Issues. The readings address two main issues raised by conventional wars like the one in Bosnia: when, if ever, is war justified? And what methods are legitimate in fighting a war? In the case of the war in Bosnia, the United States was asked to intervene militarily to save the Muslims, in effect, to enter the war on the side of the Muslims. Senator Paul Wellstone, one of the few United States Senators to oppose the Gulf War, called for strong military intervention. One option considered was bombing the Serbian positions and supplying arms to the Muslims. Is American participation in such a war justified? In the attack on Sarajevo, snipers randomly shot noncombatants such as women and children. Is killing innocent people allowed in war?

Pacifism. One important position on these issues is pacifism. In the first reading for the chapter, Jan Narveson distinguishes between several different versions of pacifism. One view holds that pacifism is a matter of tactics rather than moral principle. Other views maintain that only pacifists have a duty not to meet force with force. But Narveson is only interested in the *universal* moral principle that it is morally wrong for *anyone* to use force to resist, punish, or prevent violence. He argues that this universal pacifism is incoherent or inconsistent because it assumes that people have a right not to be attacked, while forbidding them to defend that right.

In the next reading, Cheyney Ryan responds to Narveson. The version of pacifism that Ryan defends against Narveson's attack is not the broad view that all violence is wrong, but the narrower view that killing people is wrong. This narrow view implies that people have a right not to be killed and that people have a corresponding right to defend themselves from being killed. But there is no inconsistency in the pacifist's granting a right of self-defense, provided the pacifist places limits on the actions one may take in self-defense. One of the limits for the pacifist holding the narrower view is the proscription against killing. But this limit does not rule out other actions in self-defense, even violent ones, provided that no one is killed.

Just War Theory. Another influential view on war is just war theory. Medieval Christian theologians called the Scholastics originally formulated the theory, and it has been discussed ever since. The theory distinguishes between the two questions about war mentioned above. First, there is the question of **jus ad bellum** or the right to go to war: when is a state justified in going to war? Second there is the question of **jus in bello** or just conduct of war: how should we conduct ourselves in a just war?

As William V. O'Brien explains in the next reading, the theory has two components, one concerned with the right to go to war and the other with the conduct of war. There are three conditions that have to be met in order to establish the right to go to war: 1) the war must be declared by a competent authority; 2) there must be a just cause; and 3) there must be a right intention which ultimately aims at peace. The principles governing the conduct of a just war concern proportion (which compares the good achieved by the war with the evil it produces) and discrimination (which prohibits direct, intentional attacks on noncombatants).

The principle of discrimination requires us to make a distinction between combatants and noncombatants. But how do we make this distinction? According to Jeffrie G. Murphy, this distinction cannot be drawn using the concepts of innocence and guilt. Instead, he suggests that combatants are those engaged in an attempt to destroy you, provided your belief is reasonable. Noncombatants are those for whom the belief is not reasonable.

The principle of proportion involves a comparison of means and ends; the good, or end, achieved by war must not be outweighed by the evil of the means. In other words, there are certain evil things one is not allowed to do, even in the pursuit of achieving victory in war. For example, most codified laws governing war prohibit the killing of prisoners. But what is the basis for such prohibitions? According to Anthony E. Hartle, there are two possible humanitarian principles that could justify these limitations on conduct in war: the utilitarian principle that human suffering ought to be minimized and the Kantian principle that individuals deserve respect as persons. But these two principles can come into conflict, as Hartle points out in his example about the wounded enemy soldiers who are taken prisoner. In such cases, Hartle argues that the Kantian principle takes precedence over the utilitarian principle, and therefore the Kantian principle is the most fundamental basis governing conduct of war.

Holy War. Just war theory and pacifism have dominated discussions of war in western thought. Both of these developed in the tradition of Christianity. There is, however, another important doctrine about war that comes from Islam. This is the Islamic doctrine of jihād or holy war. As Khadduri explains it, jihād literally means exertion in Allah's path. A believer may do this with the heart, the tongue, the hands, or the sword. It is only in the last case that jihād means holy war. Holy war is the only kind of war allowed, and no distinction is made between offensive and defensive war. A holy war must be commanded by the Imam, the religious head of state, and as such it is considered to be commanded by God who rewards those who participate with eternal life in paradise.

Jan Narveson

Pacifism: A Philosophical Analysis

Jan Narveson is Professor of Philosophy at the University of Waterloo in Ontario, Canada, and the author of Morality and Utility. *(1967) and* The Libertarian Idea *(1989).*

Narveson distinguishes between several different doctrines, attitudes, and tactics that are pacifist in nature. He targets for attack the version of pacifism which says that, as a matter of moral principle, no one should use force, not even when attacked. He finds this universal moral pacifism objectionable. It assumes a right not to be attacked, and then does not allow for the defense of the right. This is self-contradictory and incoherent.

From *Ethics*, Vol. 75, No. 4 (July, 1965). Reprinted with permission of the author and the University of Chicago Press.

Several different doctrines have been called "pacifism," and it is impossible to say anything cogent about it without saying which of them one has in mind. I must begin by making it clear, then, that I am limiting the discussion of pacifism to a rather narrow band of doctrines, further distinctions among which will be brought out below. By "pacifism," I do *not* mean the theory that violence is evil. With appropriate restrictions, this is a view that every person with any pretensions to morality doubtless holds: Nobody thinks that we have a right to inflict pain wantonly on other people. The pacifist goes a very long step further. *His* belief is not only that violence is evil but also that it is morally wrong to use force to resist, punish, or prevent violence. This further step makes pacifism a radical moral doctrine. What I shall try to establish below is that it is in fact, more than merely radical—it is actually incoherent because it is self-contradictory in its fundamental intent. I shall also suggest that several moral attitudes and psychological views which have tended to be associated with pacifism as I have defined it do not have any necessary connection with that doctrine. Most proponents of pacifism, I shall argue, have tended to confuse these different doctrines, and that conclusion is probably what accounts for such popularity as pacifism has had.

It is next in order to point out that the pacifistic attitude is a matter of degree, and this in two respects. In the first place, there is the question: How much violence should not be resisted, and what degree of force is one not entitled to use in resisting, punishing, or preventing it? Answers to this question will make a lot of difference. For example, everyone would agree that there are limits to the kind and degree of force with which a particular degree of violence is to be met: we do not have a right to kill someone for rapping us on the ribs, for example, and yet there is no tendency toward pacifism in this. We might go further and maintain, for example, that capital punishment, even for the crime of murder, is unjustified without doing so on pacifist grounds. Again, the pacifist should say just what sort of a reaction constitutes a forcible or violent one. If somebody attacks me with his fists and I pin his arms to his body with wrestling holds which restrict him but cause him no pain, is that all right in the pacifist's book? And again, many non-pacifists could consistently maintain that we should avoid, to the extent that it is possible, inflicting a like pain on those who attempt to inflict pain on us. It is unnecessary to be a pacifist merely in order to deny the moral soundness of the principle, "an eye for an eye and a tooth for a tooth." We need a clarification, then from the pacifist as to just how far he is and is not willing to go. But this need should already make us pause, for surely the pacifist cannot draw these lines in a merely arbitrary manner. It is his reasons for drawing the ones he does that count, and these are what I propose to discuss below.

The second matter of degree in respect of which the pacifist must specify his doctrine concerns the question: Who ought not to resist violence with force? For example, there are pacifists who would only claim that they themselves ought not to. Others would say that only pacifists ought not to, or that all persons of a certain type, where the type is not specified in terms of belief or non-belief in pacifism, ought not to resist violence with force. And, finally, there are those who hold that everyone ought not to do so. We shall see that consideration about this second variable doom some forms of pacifism to contradiction.

My general program will be to show that (1) only the doctrine that everyone ought not to resist violence with force is of philosophical interest among these doctrines known as "pacifism"; (2) that doctrine, if advanced as a moral doctrine, is logically untenable; and (3) the reasons for the popularity of pacifism rest on failure to see exactly what the doctrine is. The things which pacifism wishes to accomplish, insofar as they are worth accomplishing, can be managed on the basis of quite ordinary and conservative moral principles.

Let us begin by being precise about the kind of moral force the principle of pacifism is intended to have. One good way to do this is to consider what it is intended to deny. What would non-pacifists, which I suppose includes most people, say of a man who followed Christ's suggestion and, when unaccountably slapped, simply turned the other cheek? They might say that such a man is either a fool or a saint. Or they might say, "It's all very well for him to do that, but it's not for me"; or they might simply shrug their shoulders and say, "Well, it takes all kinds, doesn't it?" But they would *not* say that a man who did that ought to be punished in some way; they would not even say that he had done anything wrong. In fact, as I have mentioned, they would more likely than not find something admirable about it. The point, then, is this: The non-pacifist does *not* say that it is your *duty* to resist violence with force. The non-pacifist is merely saying that there's nothing wrong with doing so, that one has every right to do so if he is so inclined. Whether we wish to add that a person would be foolish or silly to do so is quite another question, one on which the non-pacifist does not *need* to take any particular position.

Consequently, a genuine pacifist cannot merely say that we may, if we wish, prefer not to resist violence with force. Nor can he merely say that there is something admirable or saintly about not doing so, for, as pointed out above, the non-pacifist could perfectly well agree with that. He must say, instead, that, for whatever class of people he thinks it applies to, there is something positively wrong about meeting violence with force. He must say that, insofar as the people to whom his principle applies resort to force, they are committing a breach of moral duty—a very serious thing to say. Just how serious, we shall ere long see.

Next, we must understand what the implications of holding pacifism as a moral principle are, and the first such implication requiring our attention concerns the matter of the size of the class of people to which it is supposed to apply. It will be of interest to discuss two of the four possibilities previously listed, I think. The first is that in which the pacifist says that only pacifists have the duty of pacifism. Let us see what this amounts to.

If we say that the principle of pacifism is the principle that all and only pacifists have a duty of not opposing violence with force, we get into a very odd situation. For suppose we ask ourselves, "Very well, which people are the pacifists then?" The answer will have to be "All those people who believe that pacifists have the duty not to meet violence with force." But surely one could believe that a certain class of people, whom we shall call "pacifists," have the duty not to meet violence with force without believing that one ought not, oneself, to meet violence with force. That is to say, the "principle" that pacifists ought to avoid meeting violence with force, is circular: It presupposes that one already knows who the pacifists are. Yet this is precisely what that statement of the principle is supposed to answer! We are supposed to be able to say that anybody who believes that principle is a pacifist; yet, as we have seen, a person could very well believe that a certain class of people called "pacifists" ought not to meet violence with force without believing that he himself ought not to meet violence with force. Thus everyone could be a "pacifist" in the sense of believing that statement and yet no one believe that he *himself* (or anyone in particular) ought to avoid meeting violence with force. Consequently, pacifism cannot be specified in that way. A pacifist must be a person who believes either that he himself (at least) ought not to meet force with force or that some larger class of persons, perhaps everyone, ought not to meet force with force. He would then be believing something definite, and we are then in a position to ask why.

Incidentally, it is worth mentioning that when people say things such as "Only pacifists have the duty of pacifism," "Only Catholics have the duties of Catholicism," and, in general, "Only *X*-ists have the duties of *X*-ism" they probably are falling into a trap which catches a good many people. It is, namely, the mistake of supposing that what it *is* to have a certain duty is to *believe* that you have a certain duty. The untenability of this is parallel to the untenability of the previously mentioned attempt to say what pacifism is. For, if having a duty is believing that you have a certain duty, the question arises, "*What* does such a person believe?" The answer that must be given if we follow this analysis would then be, "He believes that he believes that he has a certain duty"; and so on, ad infinitum.

On the other hand, one might believe that having a duty does not consist in believing that one has and yet believe that only those people really have the duty who believe that they have it. But in that case, we would, being conscientious, perhaps want to ask the question, "Well, *ought* I to believe that I have that duty, or oughtn't I?" If you say that the answer is "Yes," the reason cannot be that you already do believe it, for you are asking whether you *should*. On the other hand, the answer "No" or "It doesn't make any difference—it's up to you," implies that there is really no reason for doing the thing in question at all. In short, asking whether I ought to believe that I have a duty to do *x*, is equivalent to asking whether I should *do x*. A person might very well believe that he ought to do *x* but be wrong. It might be the case that he really ought *not* to do *x;* in that case the fact that he believes he ought to do *x,* far from being a reason why he ought to do it, is a reason for us to point out his error. It also, of course, presupposes that he has some reason other than his belief for thinking it is his duty to do *x*.

Having cleared this red herring out of the way, we must consider the view of those who believe that they themselves have a duty of pacifism and ask ourselves the question: What general kind of reason must a person have for supposing a certain type of act to be *his* duty, in a moral sense? Now, one answer he might give is that pacifism as such is a duty, that is, that meeting violence with force is, as such, wrong. In that case, however, what he thinks is not merely that *he* has this duty, but that *everyone* has this duty.

Now he might object, "Well, but no; I don't mean that everyone has it. For instance, if a man is defending, not himself, but *other* people, such as his wife and children, then he has a right to meet violence with force." Now this, of course, would be a very important qualification to his principle and one of a kind which we will be discussing in a moment. Meanwhile, however, we may point out that he evidently still thinks that, if it weren't for certain more important duties, everyone would have a duty to avoid meeting violence with force. In other words, he then believes that, other things being equal, one ought not to meet violence with force. He believes, to put it yet another way, that if one does meet violence with force, one must have a special excuse or justification of a moral kind; then he may want to give some account of just which excuses and justifications would do. Nevertheless, he is now holding a general principle.

Suppose, however, he holds that no one *else* has this duty of pacifism, that only he himself ought not to meet force with force, although it is quite all right for others to do so. Now if this is what our man feels, we may continue to call him a "pacifist," in a somewhat attenuated sense, but he is then no longer holding pacifism as a *moral* principle or, indeed, as a principle at all.[1] For now his disinclination for violence is essentially just a matter of taste. I like pistachio ice cream, but I wouldn't dream of saying that other people have a duty to eat it; similarly, this man just doesn't *like* to meet force with force, although he wouldn't dream of insisting that others act as he does. And this is a secondary sense of "pacifism," first, because pacifism has always been advocated on moral grounds and, second, because non-pacifists can easily have this same feeling. A person might very well feel squeamish, for example, about using force, even in self-defense, or he might not be able to bring himself to use it even if he wants to. But none of these has anything to do with asserting pacifism to be a duty. Moreover, a mere attitude could hardly license a man to refuse military service if it were required of him, or to join ban-the-bomb crusades, and so forth. (I fear, however, that such attitudes have sometimes caused people to do those things.)

And, in turn, it is similarly impossible to claim that your support of pacifism is a moral one if your position is that a certain selection of people, but no one else, ought not to meet force with force, even though you are unprepared to offer any reason whatever for this selection. Suppose, for example, that you hold that only the Arapahoes, or only the Chinese, or only people more than six feet high have this "duty." If such were the case, and no reasons offered at all, we could only conclude that you had a very peculiar attitude toward the Arapahoes, or whatever, but we would hardly want to say that you had a moral principle. Your "principle" amounts to saying that these particular individuals happen to have the duty of pacifism just because they are the individuals they are, and this, as Bentham would say, is the "negation of all principles." Of course, if you meant that somehow the property of being over six feet tall *makes* it your duty not to use violence, then you have a principle, all right, but a very queer one indeed unless you can give some further reasons. Again, it would not be possible to distinguish this from a sheer attitude.

Pacifism, then, must be the principle that the use of force to meet force is wrong *as such,* that is, that nobody may do so unless he has a special justification.

There is another way in which one might advocate a sort of "pacifism," however, which we must also dispose of before getting to the main point. One might argue that pacifism is desirable as a tactic: that, as a matter of fact, some good end, such as the reduction of violence itself, is to be achieved by "turning the other cheek." For example, if it were the case that turning the other cheek caused the offender to break down and repent, then that would be a very good reason for behaving "pacifistically." If unilateral disarmament causes the other side to disarm, then certainly unilateral disarmament would be a desirable policy. But note that its desirability, if this is the argument, is due to the fact that peace is desirable, a moral position which anybody can take, pacifist or no, plus the purely contingent fact that this policy causes the other side to disarm, that is, it brings about peace.

And, of course, that's the catch. If one attempts to support pacifism because of its probable effects, then one's position depends on what the effects are. Determining what they are is a purely empirical matter, and, consequently, one could not possibly be a pacifist as a matter of pure principle if his reasons for supporting pacifism are merely tactical. One must, in this case, submit one's opinions to the governance of fact.

It is not part of my intention to discuss matters of fact, as such, but it is worthwhile to point out that the general history of the human race certainly offers no support for the supposition that turning the other cheek always produces good effects on the aggressor. Some aggressors, such as the Nazis, were apparently just "egged on" by the "pacifist" attitude of their victims. Some of the S.S. men apparently became curious to see just how much torture the victim would put up with before he began to resist. Furthermore, there is the possibility that, while pacifism might work against some people (one might cite the British, against whom pacifism in India was apparently rather successful—but the British are comparatively nice people), it might fail against others (e.g., the Nazis).

A further point about holding pacifism to be desirable as a tactic is that this could not easily support the position that pacifism is a *duty*. The question whether we have no *right* to fight back can hardly be settled by noting that not to fight back might cause the aggressor to stop fighting. To prove that a policy is a desirable one because it works is not to prove that it is *obligatory* to follow it. We surely need considerations a good deal less tenuous than this to prove such a momentous contention as that we have no *right* to resist.

It appears, then, that to hold the pacifist position as a genuine, full-blooded moral principle is to hold that nobody has a right to fight back when attacked, that fighting back is inherently evil, as such. It means that we are all mistaken in supposing that we have a right of self-protection. And, of course, this is an extreme and extraordinary position in any case. It appears to mean, for instance, that we have no right to punish criminals, that all of our machinery of criminal justice is, in fact, unjust. Robbers, murderers, rapists, and miscellaneous delinquents ought, on this theory, to be let loose.

Now, the pacifist's first move, upon hearing this, will be to claim that he has been misrepresented. He might say that it is only one's *self* that one has no right to defend, and that one may legitimately fight in order to defend other people. This qualification cannot be made by those pacifists who qualify as conscientious objectors, however, for the latter are refusing to defend their fellow citizens and not merely themselves. But this is comparatively trivial when we contemplate the next objection to this amended version of the theory. Let us now ask ourselves what it is about attacks on *other* people which could possibly justify *us* in defending them, while we are not justified in defending ourselves? It cannot be the mere fact that they are other people than ourselves, for, of course, everyone is a different person from everyone else, and if such a consideration could ever of itself justify anything at all it could also justify anything whatever. That mere difference of person, as such, is of no moral importance, is a presupposition of anything that can possibly pretend to be a moral theory.

Instead of such idle nonsense, then, the pacifist would have to mention some specific characteristic which every *other* person has which we lack and which justifies us in defending them. But this, alas, is impossible, for, while there may be some interesting differences between *me*, on the one hand, and everyone else, on the other, the pacifist is not merely addressing himself to me. On the contrary, as we have seen, he has to address himself to everyone. He is claiming that each person has no right to defend himself, although he does have a right to defend other people. And, therefore, what is needed is a characteristic which distinguishes *each* person from everyone else, and not just *me* from everyone else—which is plainly self-contradictory.

If the reader does not yet see why the "characteristic" of being identical with oneself cannot be used to support a moral theory, let him reflect that the proposition "Everyone is identical with himself" is a trivial truth—as clear an example of an **analytic proposition** as there could possibly be. But a statement of moral principle is not a trivial truth; it is a substantive moral assertion. But non-tautologous statements, as everyone knows, cannot logically be derived from **tautologies**, and, consequently, the fact that everyone is identical with himself cannot possibly be used to prove a moral position.

Again, then, the pacifist must retreat in order to avoid talking idle nonsense. His next move, now, might be to say that we have a right to defend all those who are not able to defend themselves. Big, grown-up men who are able to defend themselves ought not to do so, but they ought to defend mere helpless children who are unable to defend themselves.

This last, very queer theory could give rise to some amusing logical gymnastics. For instance, what about groups of people? If a group of people who cannot defend themselves singly can defend themselves together, then when it has grown to that size ought it to stop defending itself? If so, then every time a person *can* defend someone else, he would form with the person being defended a "defensive unit" which was able to defend itself, and thus would by his very presence debar himself from making the defense. At this rate, no one will ever get defended, it seems: The defenseless people by definition cannot defend themselves, while those who can defend them would enable the group consisting of the defenders and the defended to defend themselves, and hence they would be obligated not to do so.

Such reflections, however, are merely curious shadows of a much more fundamental and serious logical problem. This arises when we begin to ask: But why should even defenseless people be defended? If resisting violence is inherently evil, then how can it suddenly become permissible when we use it on behalf of other people? The fact that they are defenseless cannot possibly account for this, for it follows from the theory in question, that everyone ought to put himself in the position of people who are defenseless by refusing to defend himself. This type of pacifist, in short, is using the very characteristic (namely, being in a state of not defending oneself) which he wishes to encourage in others as a reason for denying it in the case of those who already have it (namely, the defenseless). This is indeed self-contradictory.

To attempt to be consistent, at least, the pacifist is forced to accept the characterization of him at which we tentatively arrived. He must indeed say that no one ought ever to be defended against attack. The right of self-defense can be denied coherently only if the right of defense, in general, is denied. This in itself is an important conclusion.

It must be borne in mind, by the way, that I have not said anything to take exception to the man who simply does not wish to defend himself. So long as he does not attempt to make his pacifism into a principle, one cannot accuse him of any inconsistency, however much one might wish to say that he is foolish or eccentric. It is solely with moral principles that I am concerned here.

We now come to the last and most fundamental problem of all. If we ask ourselves what the point of pacifism is, what gets it going, so to speak, the answer is, of course, obvious enough: opposition to violence. The pacifist is generally thought of as the man who is so much opposed to violence that he will not even use it to defend himself or anyone else. And it is precisely this characterization which I wish to show is far from being plausible, morally inconsistent.

To begin with, we may note something which at first glance may seem merely to be a matter of fact, albeit one which should worry the pacifist, in our latest characterization of him. I refer to the commonplace observation that, generally speaking, we measure a man's degree of opposition to something by the amount of effort he is willing to put forth against it. A man could hardly be said to be dead set against something if he is not willing to lift a finger to keep it from going on. A person who claims to be completely opposed to something yet does nothing to prevent it would ordinarily be said to be a hypocrite.

As facts, however, we cannot make too much of these. The pacifist could claim to be willing to go to any length, short of violence, to prevent violence. He might, for instance, stand out in the cold all day long handing out leaflets (as I have known some to do), and this would surely argue for the sincerity of his beliefs.

But would it really?

Let us ask ourselves, one final time, what we are claiming when we claim that violence is morally wrong and unjust. We are, in the first place, claiming that a person *has no right* to indulge in it, as such (meaning that he has no right to indulge in it, *unless* he has an overriding justification). But what do we mean when we say that he has no right to indulge in it? Violence, of the type we are considering, is a two-termed affair: one does violence *to* somebody, one cannot simply "do violence." It might be oneself, of course, but we are not primarily interested in those cases, for what makes it wrong to commit violence is that it harms the people to whom it is done. To say that it is wrong is to say that those to whom it is done have a right *not* to have it done to them. (This must again be qualified by pointing out that this is so only if they have done nothing to merit having that right abridged.)

Yet what could that right to their own security, which people have, possibly consist in, if not a right at least to defend themselves from whatever violence might be offered them? But lest the reader think that this is a gratuitous assumption, note carefully the reason why having a right involves having a right to be defended from breaches of that right. It is because the prevention of infractions of that right is precisely what one has a right to when one has a right at all. A right just *is* a status justifying preventive action. To say that you have a right to *X* but that no one has any justification whatever for preventing people from depriving you of it, is self-contradictory. If you claim a right to *X*, then to describe some action as an act of depriving you of *X*, is logically to imply that its absence is one of the things that you have a right to.

Thus far it does not follow logically that we have a right to use force in our own or anyone's defense. What does follow logically is that one has a right to whatever may be necessary to prevent infringements of his right. One might at first suppose that the universe *could* be so constructed that it is never necessary to use force to prevent people who are bent on getting something from getting it.

Yet even this is not so, for when we speak of "force" in the sense in which pacifism is concerned with it, we do not mean merely physical "force." To call an action a use of force is not merely to make a reference to the laws of mechanics. On the contrary, it is to describe whatever is being done as being a means to the infliction on somebody of something (ordinarily physical) which he does not want done to him; and the same is true for "force" in the sense in which it applies to war, assault and battery, and the like.

The proper contrary of "force" in this connection is "rational persuasion." Naturally, one way there *might* be of getting somebody not to do something he has no right to do is to convince him he ought not to do it or that it is not in his interest to do it. But it is inconsistent, I suggest, to argue that rational persuasion is the only morally permissible method of preventing violence. A pragmatic reason for this is easy enough to point to: Violent people are too busy being violent to be reasonable. We cannot engage in rational persuasion unless the enemy is willing to sit down and talk; but what if he isn't? One cannot contend that every human being can be persuaded to sit down and talk before he strikes, for this is not something we can determine just by reasoning: it is a question of observation, certainly. But these points are not strictly relevant anyway, for our question is not the empirical question of whether there is some handy way which can always be used to get a person to sit down and discuss moral philosophy when he is about to murder you. Our question is: *If* force is the only way to prevent violence in a given case, is its use justified *in that case?* This is a purely moral question which we can discuss without any special reference to matters of fact. And, moreover, it is precisely this question which we should have to discuss with the would-be violator. The point is that if a person can be rationally persuaded that he ought not to engage in violence, then precisely what he would be rationally persuaded of if he were to succeed would be the proposition that the use of force is justifiable to prevent him from doing so. For note that if we were to argue that only rational persuasion is permissible as a means of preventing him, we would have to face the question: Do we mean *attempted* rational persuasion, or *successful* rational persuasion, that is, rational persuasion which really does succeed in preventing him from acting? Attempted rational persuasion might fail (if only because the opponent is unreasonable), and then what? To argue that we have a right to use rational persuasion which also succeeds (i.e., we have a right to its success as well as to its use) is to imply that we have a right to prevent him from performing the act. But this, in turn, means that, if attempts at rational persuasion fail, we have a right to the use of force. Thus what we have a right to, if we ever have a *right* to anything, is not merely the use of rational persuasion to keep people from depriving you of the thing to which you have the right. We do indeed have a right to do that, but we also have a right to anything else that might be necessary (other things being equal) to prevent the deprivation from occurring. And it is a logical truth, not merely a contingent one, that what *might* be necessary is *force.* (If merely saying something could miraculously deprive someone of the ability to carry through a course of action, then those speech-acts would be called a type of force, if a very mysterious one. And we could properly begin to oppose their use for precisely the same reasons as we now oppose violence.)

What this all adds up to, then, is that *if* we have any rights at all, we have a right to use force to prevent the deprivation of the thing to which we are said to have a right. But the pacifist, of *all* people, is the one most concerned to insist that we do have some rights, namely, the right not to have violence done to us. This is logically implied in asserting it to be a duty on everyone's part to avoid violence. And this is why the pacifist's position is self-contradictory. In saying that violence is wrong, one is at the same time saying that people have a right to its prevention, by force if necessary. Whether and to what extent it may be necessary is a question of fact, but, since it is a question of fact only, the *moral* right to use force on some possible occasions is established.

We now have an answer to the question. How much force does a given threat of violence justify for preventive purposes? The answer, in a word, is "Enough." That the answer is this simple may at first sight seem implausible. One might suppose that some elaborate equation between the aggressive and the preventive force is needed: the punishment be proportionate to the crime. But this is a misunderstanding. In the first place, prevention and punishment are not the same, even if punishment is thought to be directed mainly toward prevention. The punishment of a particular crime logically cannot prevent *that* instance of the crime, since it presupposes that it has already been performed; and punishment need not involve the use of any violence at all, although law-enforcement officers in some places have a nasty tendency to assume the contrary. But preventive force is another matter. If a man threatens to kill me, it is desirable, of course, for me to try to prevent this by the use of the least amount of force sufficient to do the job. But I am justified even in killing him *if* necessary. This much, I suppose, is obvious to most people. But suppose his threat is much smaller: suppose that he is merely pestering me, which is a very mild form of aggression indeed. Would I be justified in killing him to prevent this, under any circumstances whatever?

Suppose that I call the police and they take out a warrant against him, and suppose that when the police come, he puts up a struggle. He pulls a knife or a gun, let us say, and the police shoot him in the ensuing battle. Has my right to the prevention of his annoying me extended to killing him? Well, not exactly, since the immediate threat in response to which he is killed is a threat to the lives of the policemen. Yet my annoyer may never have contemplated real violence. It is an unfortunate case of unpremeditated escalation. But this is precisely what makes the contention that one is justified in using enough force to do the job, whatever amount that may be, to prevent action which violates a right less alarming than at first sight it seems. For it is difficult to envisage a reason why extreme force is needed to prevent mild threats from realization except by way of escalation, and escalation automatically justifies increased use of preventive force.

The existence of laws, police, courts, and more or less civilized modes of behavior on the part of most of the populace naturally affects the answer to the question of how much force is necessary. One of the purposes of a legal system of justice is surely to make the use of force by individuals very much less necessary than it would otherwise be. If we try to think back to a "state of nature" situation, we shall have much less difficulty envisaging the need for large amounts of force to prevent small threats of violence. Here Hobbes's contention that in such a state every man has a right to the life of every other becomes understandable. He was, I suggest, relying on the same principle as I have argued for here: that one has a right to use as much force as necessary to defend one's rights, which include the right of safety of person.

I have said that the duty to avoid violence is only a duty, other things being equal. We might arrive at the same conclusion as we have above by asking the question: Which "other things" might count as being *unequal?* The answer to this is that whatever else they may be, the purpose of preventing violence from being done is necessarily one of these justifying conditions. That the use of force is never justified to prevent initial violence being done to one logically implies that there is nothing wrong with this initial violence. We cannot characterize it as being wrong if preventive violence is not simultaneously being characterized as justifiable.

We often think of pacifists as being gentle and idealistic souls, which in its way is true enough. What I have been concerned to show is that they are also confused. If they attempt to formulate their position using our standard concepts of rights, their position involves a contradiction: Violence is wrong, *and* it is wrong to resist it. But the right to resist is precisely what having a right of safety of person is, if it is anything at all.

Could the position be reformulated with a less "committal" concept of rights? I do not think so. It has been suggested [2] that the pacifist need not talk in terms of this "kind" of rights. He can affirm, according to this suggestion, simply that neither the aggressors nor the defenders "have" rights to what they do, that to affirm their not having them is simply to be against the use of force, without this entailing the readiness to use force if necessary to protect the said rights. But this will not do, I believe. For I have not maintained that having a right, or believing that one has a right, entails a *readiness* to defend that right. One has a perfect right not to resist violence to oneself if one is so inclined. But our question has been whether self-defense is justifiable, and not whether one's belief that violence is wrong entails a willingness or readiness to use it. My contention has been that such a belief does entail the justifiability of using it. If one came upon a community in which no sort of violence was ever resisted and it was claimed in that community that the non-resistance was a matter of conscience, we should have to conclude, I think, not that this was a community of saints, but rather that this community lacked the concept of justice—or perhaps that their nervous systems were oddly different from ours.

The true test of the pacifist comes, of course, when he is called upon to assist in the protection of the safety of other persons and not just to himself. For while he is, as I have said, surely entitled to be pacific about his own person if he is so inclined, he is not entitled to be so about the safety of others. It is here that the test of principles comes out. People have a tendency to brand conscientious objectors as cowards or traitors, but this is not quite fair. They are acting as if they were cowards or traitors, but claiming to do so on principle. It is not surprising if a community should fail to understand such "principles," for the test of adherence to a principle is willingness to act on it, and the appropriate action, if one believes a certain thing to be grossly wrong, is to take steps to prevent or resist it. Thus people who assess conscientious objection as cowardice or worse are taking an understandable step: from an intuitive feeling that the pacifist does not really believe what he is saying they infer that his actions (or inaction) must be due to cowardice. What I am suggesting is that this is not correct: The actions are due, not to cowardice, but to confusion. . . .

Many questions remain to be discussed, but I hope to have exposed the most fundamental issues surrounding this question and to have shown that the pacifist's central position is untenable.

Endnotes

1. Compare, for example, K. Bair, *The Moral Point of View* (Cornell, 1958), p. 191.
2. I owe this suggestion to my colleague, Leslie Armour.

Review Questions

1. Narveson distinguishes between several different pacifist doctrines. What are they?
2. Which pacifist doctrine does Narveson attack?
3. What objections does Narveson make to pacifism as a universal moral principle?

Discussion Questions

1. Narveson attempts to show that the pacifist position is self-contradictory. Does he prove this? Can the pacifist avoid this difficulty? How?

Cheyney Ryan

The Morality of Pacifism

Cheyney Ryan teaches philosophy at the University of Oregon.

After summarizing Narveson's argument, Cheyney replies that there are limits to what actions one may take to defend a right. The pacifist position is not self-contradictory or incoherent because it does allow actions in defense of the right to life; it just doesn't allow killing. As Cheyney characterizes it, pacifism is not a matter of rights, but rather an attitude of respect for others which recognizes a personal relationship or bond between all humans.

Pacifism has been construed by some as the view that all violence or coercion is wrong. This seems to be too broad, though undoubtedly some pacifists have held to this position. I shall focus here on the pacifist's opposition to killing, which stands at the heart of his opposition to war in any form.

In recent years, prompted largely by an article of Jan Narveson's, there has been a good deal of clucking about the "inconsistency" and "incoherence" of the pacifist position. Narveson's argument, in a nutshell, is that, if the pacifist grants people the right not to be subjected to violence, or the right not to be killed, *then by logic he must accord them the right to engage in any actions (hence, those involving killing) to protect that right.* This argument fails for a number of reasons,[1] but the most interesting one involves the protective status of rights. *Possession*

From Cheyney C. Ryan, "Self-Defense, Pacifism, and the Possibility of Killing," *Ethics*, Vol. 93, No. 3 (April 1983). Reprinted with permission of the author and the University of Chicago Press. [This article has been substantially abridged—Ed.]

of a right generally entitles one to take some actions in defense of that right, but clearly there are limits to the actions one may take. To get back the washcloth which you have stolen from me, I cannot bludgeon you to death; even if this were the *only* way I had of securing my right to the washcloth, I could not do it. What the pacifist and the nonpacifist disagree about, then, are the limits to which one may go in defending one's right to life, or any other right. The "logic of rights" alone will not settle this disagreement, and such logic certainly does not render the pacifist's restrictions incoherent. That position might be incoherent, in Narveson's sense, if the pacifist allowed *no* actions in defense of the right to life, but this is not his position. The pacifist's position does seem to violate a fairly intuitive principle of proportionality, that in defense of one's rights one may take actions whose severity is equal to, though not greater than, the threat against one. This rules out the bludgeoning case but allows killing so as not to be killed. The pacifist can respond, though, that this principle becomes rather suspect as we move to more extreme actions. It is not *obviously* permissible to torture another so as not to be tortured or to rain nuclear holocaust on another country to prevent such a fate for oneself. Thus when the pacifist rejects the *proportionality* principle in cases of killing, insisting that such cases are themselves most extreme, the principle he thereby rejects hardly has the status of a self-evident truth.

I have touched on this issue not merely to point out the shallowness of some recent arguments against pacifism but because I believe that any argument pro or con which hinges on the issue of rights is likely to get us nowhere. . . .

George Orwell tells how early one morning [during the Spanish Civil War] he ventured out with another man to snipe at the fascists from the trenches outside their encampment. After having little success for several hours, they were suddenly alerted to the sound of Republican airplanes overhead. Orwell writes,

> At this moment a man, presumably carrying a message to an officer, jumped out of the trench and ran along the top of the parapet in full view. He was half-dressed and holding up his trousers with both hands as he ran. I refrained from shooting at him. It is true that I am a poor shot and unlikely to hit a running man at a hundred yards. Still, I did not shoot partly because of that detail about the trousers. I had come here to shoot "Fascists"; but a man who is holding up his trousers isn't a "Fascist" he is *visibly a fellow creature*, similar to yourself, and you don't feel like shooting him.[2]

Orwell was not a pacifist, but the problem he finds in this particular act of killing is akin to the problem which the pacifist finds in *all* acts of killing. That problem, the example suggests, takes the following form.

The problem with shooting the half-clothed man does not arise from the rights involved, nor is it dispensed with by showing that, yes indeed, you are justified (by your rights) in killing him. But this does not mean, as some have suggested to me, that the problem is therefore not a *moral* problem at all ("sheer sentimentality" was an objection raised by one philosopher ex-marine). Surely if Orwell had gleefully blasted away here, if he had not at least felt the tug of the other's "fellow-creaturehood," then this would have reflected badly, if not on his action, then on *him*, as a human being. The problem, in the Orwell case, is that the man's dishabille made inescapable the fact that he was a "fellow creature," and in so doing it stripped away the labels and denied the distance so necessary to murderous actions (it is not for nothing that armies give us stereotypes in thinking about the enemy). The problem, I am tempted to say, involves not so much the justification as the *possibility* of killing in such circumstances ("How could you *bring* yourself to do it?" is a natural response to one who felt no problem in such situations). And therein lies the clue to the pacifist impulse.

The pacifist's problem is that he cannot create, or does not wish to create, the necessary distance between himself and another to make the act of killing possible. Moreover, the fact that others obviously can create that distance is taken by the pacifist to reflect badly on them; they move about in the world insensitive to the half-clothed status which all humans, qua fellow creatures, share. This latter point is important to showing that the pacifist's position is indeed a moral position, and not just a personal idiosyncrasy. What should now be evident is the sense in which that moral position is motivated by a picture of the personal relationship and outlook one should maintain towards others, regardless of the actions they might take toward you. It is fitting in this regard that the debate over self-defense should come down to a personal relationship, the "negative bond" between Aggressor and Defender. For even if this negative bond renders killing in self-defense permissible, the pacifist will insist that the deeper bonds of fellow creaturehood should render it impossible. That such an outlook will be branded by others as sheer sentimentality comes to the pacifist as no surprise.

I am aware that this characterization of the pacifist's outlook may strike many as obscure, but the difficulties in characterizing that outlook themselves reflect, I think, how truly fundamental the disagreement between the pacifist and the nonpacifist really is. That disagreement far transcends the familiar problems of justice and equity; it is no surprise that the familiar terms should fail us. As to the accuracy of this characterization, I would offer as indirect support the following example of the aesthetic of fascism, which I take to be at polar ends from that of pacifism, and so illustrative in contrast of the pacifist outlook: "War is beautiful because it establishes man's dominion over the subjugated machinery by means of gas masks, terrifying megaphones, flame throwers, and small tanks. War is beautiful because it initiates the dreamt-of metalization of the human body. War is beautiful because it enriches the flowering meadow with the fiery orchids of machine guns." What the fascist rejoices in the pacifist rejects, in toto—the "metalization of the human body," the insensitivity to fellow creaturehood which the pacifist sees as the presupposition of killing.

This account of the pacifist's position suggests some obvious avenues of criticism of the more traditional sort. One could naturally ask whether killing necessarily presupposes objectification and distance, as the pacifist feels it does. It seems to me though that the differences between the pacifist and the nonpacifist are substantial enough that neither side is likely to produce a simple "refutation" along such lines which the other conceivably could, or logically need, accept. If any criticism of pacifism is to be forthcoming which can make any real claim to the pacifist's attention, it will be one which questions the consistency of his conclusions with what I have described as his motivating impulse. Let me suggest how such a criticism might go.

If the pacifist's intent is to acknowledge through his attitudes and actions the other person's status as a fellow creature, the problem is that violence, and even killing, are at times a means of acknowledging this as well, a way of bridging the distance between oneself and another person, a way of acknowledging one's *own* status as a person. This is one of the underlying themes of Hegel's account of conflict in the master-slave dialectic, and the important truth it contains should not be lost in its seeming glorification of conflict. That the refusal to allow others to treat one as an object is an important step to defining one's own integrity is a point well understood by revolutionary theorists such as Fannon. It is a point apparently lost to pacifists like Gandhi, who suggested that the Jews in the Warsaw Ghetto would have made the superior moral statement by committing collective suicide, since their resistance proved futile anyway. What strikes us as positively bizarre in the pacifist's suggestion, for example, that we *not* defend our loved ones when attacked is not the fact that someone's rights might be abused by our refusal to so act. Our real concern is what the refusal to intervene would express about our relationships and ourselves, for one of the ways we acknowledge the importance of a relationship is through our willingness to take such actions, and that is why the problem in such cases is how we can bring ourselves *not* to intervene (how is passivity possible).

The willingness to commit violence is linked to our love and estimation for others, just as the capacity for jealousy is an integral part of affection. The pacifist may respond that this is just a sociological or psychological fact about how our community links violence and care, a questionable connection that expresses thousands of years of macho culture. But this connection is no *more* questionable than that which views acts of violence against an aggressor as expressing hatred, or indifference, or objectification. If the pacifist's problem is that he cannot consistently live out his initial impulse—the posture he wishes to assume toward others requires that he commit violence and that he not commit violence—does this reflect badly on his position? Well, if you find his goals attractive it may well reflect badly on the position—or *fix*—we are all in. Unraveling the pacifist's logic may lead us to see that our world of violence and killing is one in which regarding some as people requires we regard others as things and that this is not a fact that can be excused or absolved through the techniques of moral philosophy. If the pacifist's error arises from the desire to smooth this all over by hewing to one side of the dilemma, he is no worse than his opponent, whose "refutation" of pacifism serves to dismiss those very intractable problems of violence of which pacifism is the anxious expression. As long as this tragic element in violence persists, pacifism will remain with us as a response; we should not applaud its demise, for it may well mark that the dilemmas of violence have simply been forgotten.

Impatience will now ask: so do we kill or don't we? It should be clear that I do not have the sort of answer to this question that a philosopher, at least, might expect., One can attend to the problems involved in either choice, but the greatest problem is that the choice does not flow naturally from a desire to acknowledge in others and in ourselves their importance and weaknesses and worth.

Endnotes

1. Narveson claims that the right to X entitles you to whatever is necessary to protect that right. It would follow that there can be no real problem about civil disobedience, since logic alone tells us that if the state infringes on our rights we can take whatever measures are required to protect them, including defying the state. But surely the problem is more complicated than this. Hence it is reasonable to reject the claim about the "logic" of rights which leads to such a facile conclusion.
2. George Orwell, "Looking Back on the Spanish Civil War." in *A Collection of Essays by George Orwell* (New York: Doubleday & Co., 1954), p. 199.
3. The quote is from Marinetti, a founder of Futurism, cited in Walter Benjamin's essay, "The Work of Art in the Age of Mechanical Reproduction," *Illuminations* (New York: Schocken Books, 1969), p. 241.

Review Questions

1. How does Cheyney reply to Narveson's argument?
2. How does Cheyney characterize the pacifist position?

Discussion Question

1. Narveson can reply that pacifism as Cheyney characterizes it still has an inconsistency of impulse where the pacifist both does and does not wish to commit violence. Does Cheyney have an adequate response?

William V. O'Brien

The Conduct of Just and Limited War

William V. O'Brien is Professor of Government at Georgetown University, Washington, D.C. He is the author of War and/or Survival *(1969),* Nuclear War, Deterrence and Morality *(1967), and* The Conduct of Just and Limited War *(1981), from which our reading is taken.*

O'Brien divides the just war theory into two parts. The first (jus ad bello) states conditions that have to be met in order for a state to have a right to go to war. The second (jus in bello) gives prin-

ciples limiting conduct in war. There are three main conditions of jus ad bello. The war must be declared by a competent authority for a public purpose. There must be a just cause. (This condition is subdivided into the substance of the cause [e.g., self-defense], the form of pursuing it [e.g., defensive war], the requirements of proportionality, and the exhaustion of peaceful means.) Finally, there must be a right intention which aims at peace and insists on charity towards enemies.

The jus in bello gives two principles regulating conduct in war. The principle of proportion balances the total good produced from war against the total evil. The principle of discrimination prohibits intentional attacks on noncombatants and nonmilitary targets.

The original just-war doctrine of St. Augustine, St. Thomas, and other Scholastics emphasized the conditions for permissible recourse to war—the *jus ad bellum.* To this doctrine was added another branch of prescriptions regulating the conduct of war, the *jus in bello.* . . .

The *jus ad bellum* lays down conditions that must be met in order to have permissible recourse to armed coercion. They are conditions that should be viewed in the light of the fundamental tenet of just-war doctrine: the presumption is always against war. The taking of human life is not permitted to man unless there are exceptional justifications. Just-war doctrine provides those justifications, but they are in the nature of special pleadings to overcome the presumption against killing. The decision to invoke the exceptional rights of war must be based on the following criteria: there must be competent authority to order the war for a public purpose; there must be a just cause (it may be self-defense or the protection of rights by offensive war) and the means just be proportionate to the just cause and all peaceful alternatives must have been exhausted; and there must be right intention on the part of the just belligerent. Let us examine these criteria.

Insofar as large-scale, conventional war is concerned, the issue of competent authority is different in modern times than it was in the thirteenth century. The decentralized political system wherein public, private, and criminal violence overlapped, as well as the state of military art and science, permitted a variety of private wars. So it was important to insist that war—in which individuals would be called upon to take human lives—must be waged on the order of public authorities for public purposes. This is not a serious problem in most parts of the world today. Only states have the material capacity to wage large-scale, modern, conventional war. Two other problems do, however, exist in connection with the conditions of competent authority. First, there may be disputes as to the constitutional competence of a particular official or organ of state to initiate war. Second, civil war and revolutionary terrorism are frequently initiated by persons and organizations claiming revolutionary rights.

Most states today, even totalitarian states, have specific constitutional provisions for the declaration and termination of war. If an official or state organ violates these provisions, there may not be a valid exercise of the sovereign right to declare and wage war. In such a case the first condition of the just war might not be met. This was the charge, implicitly or explicitly, against President Johnson in the Vietnam War. Johnson never requested a declaration of war from Congress with which he shared war-making powers. War critics asserted that the undeclared war was illegal. A sufficient answer to this charge is to be found in congressional cooperation in the war effort and in the refusal of the courts to declare the war unconstitutional. . . . At this point it is sufficient to raise the issue of as illustrative of the problem of competent authority within a constitutional state.

In this connection a word should be said about declaring wars. Any examination of modern wars will show that the importance of a declaration of war has diminished greatly in international practice. Because of the split-second timing of modern war, it is often undesirable to warn the enemy by way of a formal declaration. Defense measures are geared to react to hostile behavior, not declarations. When war is declared it is often an announcement confirming a condition that has already been established. Nevertheless, if a particular state's constitution does require a formal declaration of war and one is not forthcoming, the issue of competence is raised. If a public official exceeds his authority in mobilizing the people and conducting war, there is a lack of competent authority.

The second problem, however, is by far the greatest. Today, rights of revolution are frequently invoked by organizations and individuals. They clearly do not have the authority and capacity to wage war in the conventional sense. However, they do wage revolutionary war, often on an international scale. Indeed, international terrorism is one of the most pervasive and difficult problems facing the international community.

All major ideologies and blocs or alignments of states in the international system recognize the right of revolution. Usually their interpretations will emphasize the rights of revolution against others, not themselves. . . . Logically, there should be an elaborate *jus ad bellum* and *jus in bello* for revolutionary war, but development of such a doctrine has never been seriously attempted. As a result, the issues of revolutionary war tend to be treated on an ad hoc basis as special cases vaguely related to the regular categories of just war. . . .

The differences between conventional war waged by states and revolutionary war waged by rebels against states are profound. Given the formidable power of most modern governments, particularly in regard to their comparative monopoly of armed force, revolutionary rights can be asserted mainly by covert organizations waging guerrilla warfare and terrorism. The option of organizing a portion of a state and fighting a conventional civil war in the manner of the American, Spanish, or Nigerian civil wars is seldom available.

The covert, secret character of modern revolutionary movements is such that it is often hard to judge their claims to qualify as the competent authority for oppressed people. There is a decided tendency to follow the Leninist model of revolutionary leadership wherein the self-selected revolutionary elite decides on the just revolutionary cause, the means, and the circumstances of taking the initiative, all done in the name of the people and revolutionary justice. As a revolution progresses, the task of certifying competent authority continues to be difficult. Support for the revolutionary leadership is often coerced or given under conditions where there is not popular acceptance of the revolutionary authority of that leadership or its ends and means. Recognition by foreign powers of belligerency—or even of putative governmental powers—is an unreliable guide given subjective, politicized recognition policies.

To complicate matters, individuals and small groups take up revolutionary war tactics, principally terrorism in the form of airplane hijacking, hostage kidnapping, assassination, and indiscriminate bombing attacks. These acts are performed in the name of greatly varying causes, some of which could not be considered revolutionary. Sometimes the alleged justifications are political or ideological, but, on investigation, the real motivation turns out to be personal and criminal. Since most revolutionary movements manifest themselves in behavior difficult to distinguish from that of cranks and criminals, the task of sorting out revolutionaries entitled to acceptance as competent authorities is excruciating.

Two issues need to be resolved concerning revolutionary activity. First, insofar as treating revolutionaries as belligerents in a war and not as common criminals is concerned, the ultimate answer lies in the character, magnitude, and degree of success of the revolutionaries. If they can organize a government that carries on their war in a controlled fashion (assuming a magnitude requiring countermeasures that more resemble war than ordinary police operations), and if the conflict continues for an appreciable time, the revolutionaries may have won their right to be considered a competent authority for purposes of just war. Beyond this enumeration of criteria it seems unprofitable to generalize.

Second, concerning the authority of rebel leaders to mobilize the people by ordering or coercing individuals to fight for the revolutionary cause, the conscience of the individual takes precedence. Lacking any color of authority to govern, the rebels cannot of right compel participation in their cause. Needless to say, they will very probably compel participation by intimidation.

Just Cause

. . . Authorities vary in their presentation of just cause, but it seems to break down into four subdivisions: the substance of the just cause, the forms of pursuing just cause, the requirement of proportionality of ends and means, and the requirement of exhaustion of peaceful remedies.

The substance of the just cause must, in Childress's formulation be sufficiently "serious and weighty" to overcome the presumption against killing in general and war in particular. In Childress's approach, with which I am in essential agreement, this means that there must be a "competing prima facie duty or obligation" to "the prima facie obligation not to injure and kill others." [1] Childress mentions as "serious and weighty" prima facie obligations the following: (1) "to protect the innocent from unjust attack," (2) to restore rights wrongfully denied," (3) "to re-establish a just order."

This is an adequate basis, reflective of the older just-war literature, for discussing the substance of just cause. Indeed, Childress is more explicit than many modern commentators who simply state that there should be a just cause. Still, it is only a beginning. It is unfortunate that modern moralists have generally been so concerned with the issue of putatively disproportionate means of modern war that they have neglected the prior question of the ends for which these means might have to be used (that is, just cause). In practical terms, this task of evaluating the substance of just cause leads inescapably to a comparative analysis of the characteristics of the polities or political-social systems posed in warlike confrontation. . . .

Even more difficult for those who would answer in the affirmative is the question whether the United States should intervene to protect a manifestly imperfect political-social order (South Korea, South Vietnam or, perhaps, that of a state such as Jordan, Saudi Arabia, or Pakistan). . . .

By comparison, the substantive just causes of the older just-war literature are almost insignificant. In the modern world the just cause often has to do with the survival of a way of life. Claims that this is so can be false or exaggerated, but they are often all too legitimate. They must be taken seriously in assessing the substance of just cause in modern just-war analyses.

However, passing the test of just cause is not solely a matter of positing an end that is convincingly just, although that is the indispensable starting point. It is also necessary to meet the tests posed by the other three subdivisions of just cause.

The forms of pursuing just cause are defensive and offensive wars. The justice of self-defense is generally considered to be axiomatic. Just-war doctrine, following Aristotle and St. Thomas as well as the later Scholastics, places great importance on the state as a natural institution essential for man's development. Defense of the state is prima facie of an essential social institution. So strong is the presumption in favor of the right of self-defense that the requirement of probable success, to be discussed under proportionality, is usually waived.

Offensive wars raise more complications. In classical just-war doctrine, offensive wars were permitted to protect vital rights unjustly threatened or injured. Moreover, in a form now archaic, offensive wars of vindictive justice against infidels and heretics were once permitted. Such wars disappeared with the decline of the religious, holy-war element as a cause of and rationale for wars. Thus, the forms of permissible wars today are twofold: wars of self-defense and offensive wars to enforce justice for oneself. As will be seen, even the second is now seemingly prohibited by positive international law. But in terms of basic just-war theory it remains an option. A war of vindictive justice wherein the belligerent fights against error and evil as a matter of principle and not of necessity is no longer condoned by just-war doctrine. . . .

Turning from the forms of just war we come to the heart of just cause—proportionality between the just ends and the means. This concerns the relationship between *raison d'état* (the high interests of state) and the use of the military instrument in war as the means to achieve these interests. This concept of proportionality at the level of *raison d'état* is multidimensional. To begin with, the ends held out as the just cause must be sufficiently good and important to warrant the extreme means of war, the arbitrament of arms. Beyond that, a projection of the outcome of the war is required in which the probable good expected to result from success is weighed against the probable evil that the war will cause.

The process of weighing probable good against probable evil is extremely complex. The balance sheet of good and evil must be estimated for each belligerent. Additionally, there should be a balancing of effects on individual third parties and on the international common good. International interdependence means that international conflicts are difficult to contain and that their shock waves affect third parties in a manner that must be accounted for in the calculus of probable good and evil. Moreover, the international community as such has its international common good, which is necessarily affected by any war. Manifestly, the task of performing this calculus effectively is an awesome one. But even its successful completion does not fully satisfy the demands of the just-war condition of just cause. Probing even further, the doctrine requires a responsible judgment that there is a probability of success for the just party. All of these calculations must be concluded convincingly to meet the multidimensional requirement of just cause.

Moreover, the calculus of proportionality between probable good and evil in a war is a continuing one. It should be made before the decision to go to war. It must then be reviewed at critical points along the process of waging the war. The best informed estimates about wars are often in error. They may need revision or replacement by completely new estimates. The *jus ad bellum* requirement of proportionality, then, includes these requirements:

There must be a just cause of sufficient importance to warrant its defense by recourse to armed coercion.

The probable good to be achieved by successful recourse to armed coercion in pursuit of the just cause must outweigh the probable evil that the war will produce.

The calculation of proportionality between probable good and evil must be made with respect to all belligerents, affected neutrals, and the international community as a whole before initiating a war and periodically throughout a war to reevaluate the balance of good and evil that is actually produced by war.

These calculations must be made in the light of realistic estimates of the probability of success. . . .

There is an important qualification to the requirement of probability of success. A war of self-defense may be engaged in irrespective of the prospects for success, particularly if there is a great threat to continued existence and to fundamental values. . . .

The last component of the condition of just cause is that war be employed only as a last resort after the exhaustion of peaceful alternatives. To have legitimate recourse to war, it must be the ultima ratio, the arbitrament of arms. This requirement has taken on added significance in the League of Nations-United Nations period. It was the intention of the nations that founded these international organizations to create the machinery for peace that would replace self-help in the form of recourse to war and limit the need for collective security enforcement action to extreme cases of defiance of international law and order. There are certainly adequate institutions of international negotiations, mediation, arbitration, and adjudication to accommodate any nation willing to submit its international disputes to peaceful settlement. Indeed, the existence of this machinery for peaceful settlement has prompted international lawyers and statesmen to adopt a rough rule of thumb: the state that fails to exhaust the peaceful remedies available before resorting to war is prima facie an aggressor. . . .

Right Intention

Among the elements of the concept of right intention, several points may be distinguished. First, right intention limits the belligerent to the pursuit of the avowed just cause. That pursuit may not be turned into an excuse to pursue other causes that might not meet the conditions of just cause. Thus, if the just cause is to defend a nation's borders and protect them from future aggressions, but the fortunes of war place the just belligerent in the position to conquer the unjust nation, such a conquest might show a lack of right intention and change the just war into an unjust war. The just cause would have been realized by a war of limited objectives rather than a war of total conquest.

Second, right intention requires that the just belligerent have always in mind as the ultimate object of the war a just and lasting peace. There is an implicit requirement to prepare for reconciliation even as one wages war. This is a hard saying. It will often go against the grain of the belligerents' disposition, but pursuit of a just and lasting peace is an essential characteristic of the difference between just and unjust war. Accordingly, any belligerent acts that unnecessarily increase the destruction and bitterness of war and thereby endanger the prospects for true peace are liable to condemnation as violations of the condition of right intention.

Third, underlying the other requirements, right intention insists that charity and love exist even among enemies. Enemies must be treated as human beings with rights. The thrust of this requirement is twofold. Externally, belligerents must act with charity toward their enemies. Internally, belligerents must suppress natural animosity and hatred, which can be sinful and injurious to the moral and psychological health of those who fail in charity. Gratuitous cruelty may be as harmful to those who indulge in it as to their victims.

Right intention raises difficult moral and psychological problems. It may well be that its tenets set standards that will often be unattainable insofar as the thoughts and feelings of belligerents are concerned. War often treats individuals and nations so cruelly and unfairly that it is unrealistic to expect them to banish all hatred of those who have afflicted them. We can, however, more reasonably insist that just belligerents may not translate their strong feelings into behavior that is prohibited by the rule of right intention. A nation may feel tempted to impose a **Carthaginian peace**, but it may not exceed just cause by giving in to that temptation. A nation must have good reason for feeling that the enemy deserves the full force of all means available, but the requirement to build for a just and lasting peace prohibits this kind of vengeance. The enemy may have behaved abominably, engendering righteous indignation amounting to hatred, but the actions of the just belligerent must be based on charity.

Lest this appear to be so utterly idealistic as to warrant dismissal as irrelevant to the real world, let it be recalled that the greatest enemies of the modern era have often been brought around in the cyclical processes of international policies to become trusted allies against former friends who are now viewed with fear and distrust. If war is to be an instrument of policy and not, in St. Augustine's words, a "vendetta," right intention is a counsel of good policy as well as of morality. . . .

The Jus in Bello

In the *jus in bello* that emerged rather late in the development of just-war doctrine, two basic limitations on the conduct of war were laid down. One was the principle of proportion requiring proportionality of military means to political and military ends. The other was the principle of discrimination prohibiting direct, intentional attacks on noncombatants and nonmilitary targets. These are the two categories of *jus in bello* limitations generally treated by modern workers on just war. . . .

The Principle of Proportion

In the preceding [discussion] the principle of proportion was discussed at the level of *raison d'état*. One of the criteria of just-war *jus in bellum* requires that the good to be achieved by the realization of the war aims be proportionate to the evil resulting from the war. When the principle of proportion is again raised in the *jus in bello*, the question immediately arises as to the referent of proportionality in judging the means of war. Are the means to be judged in relation to the end of the war, the ends being formulated in the highest *raison d'état* terms? Or are intermediate political/military goals, referred to in the law-of-war literature as *raison de guerre,* the more appropriate referents in the calculus of proportionality as regards the conduct of a war?

There is no question that the ultimate justification for all means in war lies in the just cause that is a political purpose, *raison d'état.* But there are difficulties in making the ends of *raison d'état* the sole referent in the *jus in bello* calculus of proportionality. First, relation of all means to the highest ends of the war gives little rationale for or justification of discrete military means. If all means are simply lumped together as allegedly necessary for the war effort, one has to accept or reject them wholly in terms of the just cause, leaving no morality of means. The calculus of proportionality in just cause is the total good to be expected if the war is successful balanced against the total evil the war is likely to cause.

Second, it is evident that a discrete military means could, when viewed independently on the basis of its intermediary military end (*raison de guerre*), be proportionate or disproportionate to that military end for which it was used, irrespective of the ultimate end of the war at the level of *raison d'état.* If such a discrete military means were proportionate in terms of its military end, it would be a legitimate belligerent act. If it were disproportionate to the military end, it would be immoral and legally impermissible. Thus, an act could be proportionate or disproportionate to a legitimate military end regardless of the legitimacy of the just-cause end of *raison d'état.*

Third, there is the need to be realistic and fair in evaluating individual command responsibility for belligerent acts. The need to distinguish higher political ends from intermediate military ends was acute in the war-crimes trial after World War II. It is the law of Nuremberg, generally accepted in international law, that the *raison d'état* ends of Nazi Germany were illegal aggression. But the Nuremberg and other war-crimes tribunals rejected the argument that all military actions taken by the German armed forces were war crimes per se because they were carried out in pursuance of aggressive war. The legitimacy of discrete acts of German forces was judged, inter alia, in terms of their proportionality to intermediate military goals, *raison de guerre.* This was a matter of justice to military commanders accused of war crimes. It was also a reasonable way to evaluate the substance of the allegations that war crimes had occurred.

The distinction is equally important when applied to a just belligerent. Assuming that in World War II the Allied forces were fighting a just war, it is clear that some of the means they employed may have been unjust (for example, strategic bombing of cities and the two atomic bomb attacks). It is not difficult to assimilate these controversial means into the total Allied war effort and pronounce that total effort proportionate to the just cause of the war. It is much more difficult and quite a different calculation to justify these means as proportionate to discrete military ends. Even in the absence of war-crimes proceedings, a just belligerent ought to respect the *jus in bello* standards by meeting the requirement of proportionality of means to military ends.

To be sure, it is ultimately necessary to transcend concern for the responsibility of individual military commanders and look at the objective permissibility of a military means. Thus, it may be possible and necessary to absolve a commander from responsibility for an action taken that is judged to have been disproportionate but that appeared to him to be a proportionate, reasonable military action in the light of his imperfect estimate of the situation. This subject will be pursued in later chapters.

It would appear that analyses of the proportionality of military means will have to take a twofold form. First, any military means must be proportionate to a discrete, legitimate military end. Second, military means proportionate to discrete, legitimate military ends must also be proportionate to the object of the war, the just cause. In judging the moral and legal responsibility of a military commander, emphasis should be placed on the proportionality of the means to a legitimate military end. In judging the ultimate normative permissibility, as well as the prudential advisability, of a means at the level of *raison d'état,* the calculation should emphasize proportionality to the just cause.

The focus of normative analysis with respect to a means of war will depend on the place of the means in the total pattern of belligerent interaction. Means may be divided roughly according to the traditional distinction between tactical and strategic levels of war. Tactical means will normally be judged in terms of their proportionality to tactical military ends (for example, the tactics of attacking or defending a fortified population center will normally be judged in terms of their proportionality to the military end of taking or holding the center). Strategic means will normally be judged in terms of their proportionality to the political/military goals of the war (for example, the strategy of attacking Japanese cities, first conventionally and then with atomic bombs, in order to force the surrender of Japan will be judged in terms of its proportionality to the just cause of war).

It remains clear, however, that the two levels overlap. A number of tactical decisions regarding battles for population centers may produce an overall strategic pattern that ought to enter into the highest calculation of the proportionality of a just war. The strategic decisions, on the other hand, have necessary tactical implications (for example, strategic conventional and atomic bombing of Japan was an alternative to an amphibious invasion) the conduct of which is essentially a tactical matter. The potential costs of such a tactical invasion strongly influenced the strategic choice to seek Japan's defeat by strategic bombing rather than ground conquest.

Insofar as judgment of proportionality in terms of military ends is concerned, there is a central concept appearing in all normative analyses of human behavior—the norm of reasonableness. Reasonableness must always be defined in specific context. However, sometimes patterns of behavior recur so that there are typical situations for which common models of reasonable behavior may be prescribed. In domestic law this norm is concretized through the device of the hypothetically reasonable man whose conduct sets the standard to be emulated by law-abiding persons. The reasonable commander is the counterpart of the reasonable man in the law of war. The construct of the reasonable commander is based upon the experience of military men in dealing with basic military problems.

Formulation of this experience into the kinds of working guidelines that domestic law provides, notably in the field of torts, has not advanced very far. Its advancement is one of the purposes of this book. We do, however, have some instances in which this approach was followed. For example, the U.S. military tribunal in the *Hostage* case found that certain retaliatory means used in the German military in occupied Europe in World War II were reasonable in view of the threat to the belligerent occupant posed by guerrilla operations and their support by the civilian population. On the other hand, in the *Calley* case a court comprised of experienced combat officers found that Lieutenant Calley's response to the situation in My Lai was altogether unreasonable, below the standard of reasonableness expected in combat in Vietnam.

The difficulty with establishing the standards of reasonableness lies in the absence of authoritative decisions that can be widely disseminated for mandatory emulation. In a domestic public order such as the United States, the legislature and the courts set standards for reasonable behavior. While the standards have supporting rationales, their greatest strength lies in the fact that they are laid down by authority and must be obeyed. With the very rare exception of some of the post-World War II war-crimes cases, authoritative standards for belligerent conduct are found primarily in general conventional and customary international-law prescriptions. . . .

The Principle of Discrimination

The principle of discrimination prohibits direct intentional attacks on noncombatants and nonmilitary targets. It holds out the potential for very great, specific limitations on the conduct of just war. Accordingly, debates over the meaning of the *principle of discrimination* have become increasingly complex and important as the character of war has become more total. It is in the nature of the principle of proportion to be elastic and to offer possibilities for justifications of means that are truly necessary for efficacious military action. However, it is in the nature of the principle of discrimination to remain rigidly opposed to various categories of means irrespective of their necessity to success in war. It is not surprising, then, that most debates about the morality of modern war have focused on the principle of discrimination.

Such debates are vastly complicated by the opportunities afforded in the defiance of the principle of discrimination to expand or contract it by interpretations of its component elements. There are debates over the meaning of *direct intentional attack, noncombatants,* and *military targets.*

In order to discuss the problem of interpreting the principle of discrimination, it is necessary to understand the origins of the principle. The most fundamental aspect of the principle of discrimination lies in its direct relation to the justification for killing in war. If the presumption against killing generally and war in particular is overcome (in the case of war by meeting the just-war conditions), the killing then permitted is limited to the enemy combatants, the aggressors. The exceptional right to take life in individual self-defense and in war is limited to the attacker in the individual case and the enemy's soldiers in the case of war. One may not attack innocent third parties as part of individual self-defense. In war the only permissible objects of direct attack are the enemy's soldiers. In both cases, the overriding moral prescription is that evil must not be done to obtain a good object. As will be seen, however, the literal application of the principle of discrimination tends to conflict with the characteristics of efficacious military action necessary to make the right of just war effective and meaningful.

However, it is important to recognize that the principle of discrimination did not find its historical origins solely or even primarily in the fundamental argument summarized above. As a matter of fact, the principle seems to have owed at least as much to codes of chivalry and to the subsequent development of positive customary laws of war. These chivalric codes and customary practices were grounded in the material characteristics of warfare during the medieval and Renaissance periods. During much of that time, the key to the conduct of war was combat between mounted knights and supporting infantry. Generally speaking, there was no military utility in attacking anyone other than the enemy knights and their armed retainers. Attacks on unarmed civilians, particularly women and children, would have been considered unchivalric, contrary to the customary law of war, and militarily gratuitous.

These multiple bases for noncombatant immunity were fortified by the growth of positive international law after the seventeenth century. In what came to be known as the Rousseau-Portalis Doctrine, war was conceived as being limited to what we could call today "counterforce warfare." Armies fought each other like athletic teams designated to represent national banners. The noncombatants were spectators to these struggles and, unless they had the bad fortune to find themselves directly on the battlefield, immune in principle from military attack. Attacks on noncombatants and nonmilitary targets were now prohibited by a rule of positive international law. Here again, the principle of discrimination was grounded in material facts, the state of the art and the limited nature of the conflicts, that continued to make possible its application. Moreover, the political philosophy of the time encouraged a separation of public armed forces and the populations they represented. All of these military and political supports for discrimination were to change with the advent of modern total war.

At this point it is necessary to clarify the status of the principle of discrimination in just-war doctrine as interpreted in this book. It is often contended that there is an absolute principle of discrimination prohibiting any use of means that kill noncombatants. It is further contended that this absolute principle constitutes the central limitation of just war and that it is based on an immutable moral imperative that may never be broken no matter how just the cause. This is the moral axiom mentioned above, that evil may never be done in order to produce a good result. In this formulation, killing noncombatants intentionally is always an inadmissible evil.

These contentions have produced two principal reactions. The first is pacifism. Pacifists rightly argue that war inevitably involves violation of the absolute principle of discrimination. If that principle is unconditionally binding, a just war is difficult if not impossible to envisage. The second reaction to the claims of an absolute principle of discrimination is to modify the principle by some form of the principle of double effect whereby the counterforce component of a military means is held to represent the intent of the belligerent, whereas the countervalue, indiscriminate component of that means is explained as a tolerable, concomitant, unintended effect—collateral damage in contemporary strategic terms.

Paul Ramsey is unquestionably the most authoritative proponent of an absolute principle of discrimination as the cornerstone of just-war *jus in bello*. No one has tried more courageously to reconcile this absolute principle with the exigencies of modern war and deterrence. [But] neither Ramsey nor anyone else can reconcile the principle of discrimination in an absolute sense with the strategic countervalue nuclear warfare that is threatened in contemporary deterrence. It is possible that Ramsey's version of discrimination could survive the pressures of military necessity at levels below that of strategic nuclear deterrence and war. But the fate of Ramsey's effort to reconcile an absolute moral principle of discrimination with the characteristics of modern war should indicate the grave difficulties inherent in this effort. . . .

The question then arises whether such heroic efforts to salvage an absolute principle of discrimination are necessary. As observed above, the principle of discrimination does not appear in the just-war *jus in bello* as a doctrinally established deduction from theological or philosophical first principles. Rather, it was historically the product of belligerent practice reflecting a mixture of moral and cultural values of earlier societies. Moreover, it is significant that in the considerable body of contemporary Catholic social teaching on war, embracing the pronouncements of Pope Pius XII and his successors and of Vatican II, the principle of discrimination is not prominent in any form, absolute or conditional. When weapons systems or forms of warfare are condemned, deplored, or reluctantly condoned, the rationales are so generalized that the judgments appear to be based on a mixed application of the principles of proportion and discrimination. If anything, these pronouncements seem more concerned with disproportionate rather than indiscriminate effects.

It is a curious kind of supreme, absolute principle of the just-war doctrine that slips almost imperceptibly into the evolving formulations of the authoritative texts and then is omitted as an explicit controlling rationale in contemporary judgments by the church framed in just-war terms. Moreover, the persistent reiteration by the contemporary church that legitimate self-defense is still morally permissible should imply that such defense is practically feasible; otherwise the recognition of the right is meaningless. But, as the pacifists rightly observe, self-defense or any kind of war is incompatible with an absolute principle of discrimination.

It is my contention that the moral, just-war principle of discrimination is not an absolute limitation on belligerent conduct. There is no evidence that such a principle was ever seriously advanced by the church, and it is implicitly rejected when the church acknowledges the continued right of legitimate self-defense, a right that has always been incompatible with observance of an absolute principle of discrimination. Accordingly, I do not distinguish an absolute, moral, just-war principle of discrimination from a more flexible and variable international-law principle of discrimination. To be sure, the moral, just-war understanding of discrimination must remain independent of that of international law at any given time. But discrimination is best understood and most effectively applied in light of the interpretations of the principle in the practice of belligerents. This, after all, was the principal origin of this part of the *jus in bello*, and the need to check moral just-war formulations against contemporary international-law versions is perennial.

Such a position is in no sense a retreat from a position of maximizing normative limitations on the conduct of war. In the first place, as Ramsey's brave but ultimately unsuccessful efforts have demonstrated, attachment to an absolute principle of discrimination leads either to a finding that all war is immoral and the demise of the just-war doctrine or to tortured efforts to reconcile the irreconcilable. Neither serves the purposes of the *jus in bello*. Second, the rejection of an absolute principle of discrimination does not mean an abandonment of efforts to limit war on moral grounds. The principle of discrimination remains a critical source of both moral and legal limitations of belligerent behavior. As Tucker has observed, there are significant points of limitation between the position that no injury must ever be done to noncombatants and the position that there are no restraints on countervalue warfare. The interpretations that follow here and in succeeding chapters will try to balance the need to protect noncombatants with the need to recognize the legitimate military necessities of modern forms of warfare. In this process one may err one way or the other, but at least some relevant, practical guidance may be offered belligerents. Adherence to an absolute principle of discrimination usually means irrelevance to the question of limiting the means of war or unconvincing casuistry.

In search of such practical guidance one may resume the examination of the principle of discrimination as interpreted both by moralists and international lawyers. Even before the principle of discrimination was challenged by the changing realities of total war, there were practical difficulties with the definition of *direct intentional attack, noncombatants,* and *nonmilitary targets*. It is useful, as a starting point for analysis, to recall a standard and authoritative exposition of the principle of discrimination by Fr. Richard McCormick.

> It is a fundamental moral principle [unanimously accepted by Catholic moralists] that it is immoral directly to take innocent human life except with divine authorization. "Direct" taking of human life implies that one performs a lethal action with the intention that death should result for himself or another. Death therefore is deliberately willed as the effect of one's action. "Indirect" killing refers to an action or omission that is designed and intended solely to achieve some other purpose(s) even though death is foreseen as a concomitant effect. Death therefore is not positively willed, but is reluctantly permitted as an unavoidable by-product.[3]

An example that is frequently used in connection with this question is the use of catapults in medieval sieges of castles. The intention—indeed, the purpose—of catapulting projectiles over the castle wall was to kill enemy defenders and perhaps to break down the defenses. If noncombatants—innocents as they were called then—were killed or injured, this constituted a "concomitant effect," an "undesired by-product."

The issues of intention, act, and multiple effects are often analyzed in terms of the principle of double effect, which Father McCormick's exposition employs without invoking the concept explicitly. After centuries of inconclusive efforts to apply the principle of double effect to the *jus in bello,* Michael Walzer has proposed his own version, which merits reflection and experimental application.

> The intention of the actor is good, that is, he aims narrowly at the acceptable effect; the evil effect is not one of his ends, nor is it a means to his ends, and, aware of the evil involved, he seeks to minimize it, accepting costs to himself.[4]

It is probably not possible to reconcile observance of the principle of discrimination with the exigencies of genuine military necessity without employing the principle of double effect in one form or another. However this distinction between primary, desired effect and secondary, concomitant, undesired by-product is often difficult to accept.

It is not so hard to accept the distinction in a case where the concomitant undesired effect was accidental (for example, a case where the attacker did not know that noncombatants were present in the target area). There would still remain in such a case, a question as to whether the attacker ought to have known that noncombatants might be present. Nor is it so hard to accept a double-effect justification in a situation where the attacker had reason to believe that there might be noncombatants present but that this was a remote possibility. If, however, the attacker knows that there are noncombatants intermingled with combatants to the point that any attack on the military target is highly likely to kill or injure noncombatants, then the death or injury to those noncombatants is certainly "intended" or "deliberately willed," in the common usage of those words.

Turning to the object of the protection of the principle of discrimination—the innocents or noncombatants—another critical question of interpretation arises. How does one define noncombatants? How does one define nonmilitary targets? The assumption of separability of military forces and the populations they represented, found in medieval theory and continued by the Rousseau-Portalis Doctrine, became increasingly less valid after the wars of the French Revolution.

As nations engaged in total mobilization, one society or system against another, it was no longer possible to distinguish sharply between the military forces and the home fronts that rightly held themselves out as critical to the war effort. By the American Civil War this modern phenomenon had assumed critical importance. The material means of supporting the Confederate war effort were attacked directly and intentionally by Union forces. War in the age of the Industrial Revolution was waged against the sources of war production. Moreover, the nature of the attacks on noncombatants was psychological as well as material. Military forces have always attempted to break the will of the opposing forces as well as to destroy or scatter them. It now became the avowed purpose of military forces to break the will of the home front as well as to destroy its resources for supporting the war. This, of course, was to become a major purpose of modern strategic aerial bombardment.

To be sure, attacks on the bases of military forces have historically often been an effective strategy. But in the simpler world before the Industrial Revolution, this was not such a prominent option. When the huge conscript armies began to fight for profound ideological causes with the means provided by modern industrial mobilization and technology, the home front and consequently the noncombatants became a critical target for direct intentional attack.

The question then arose whether a civilian could be a participant in the overall war effort to such a degree as to lose his previous noncombatant immunity. Likewise, it became harder to distinguish targets that were clearly military from targets, such as factories or railroad facilities, that were of sufficient military importance to justify their direct intentional attack. It is important to note that this issue arose before the great increase in the range, areas of impact, and destructive effects of modern weaponry, conventional and nuclear. What we may term *countervalue warfare* was carried out in the American Civil War not because it was dictated by the weapons systems but because the civilian population and war-related industries and activities were considered to be critical and legitimate targets to be attacked.

In World War I this kind of attack was carried out primarily by the belligerents with their maritime blockades. Above all, these blockades caused the apparent demise of the principle of noncombatant immunity in the positive international law of war. Other factors in this demise were developments that revealed potentials not fully realized until World War II (for example, aerial bombardment of population centers and unrestricted submarine warfare). In World War II aerial bombardment of population centers was preeminent as a source of attacks on traditional noncombatants and nonmilitary targets. By this time the concept of total mobilization had advanced so far that a plausible argument could be made that vast segments of belligerent populations and complexes of industry and housing had become so integral to the war effort as to lose their noncombatant immunity.

In summary, well before the advent of weapons systems that are usually employed in ways that do not discriminate between traditional combatants and noncombatants, military and nonmilitary targets, the distinction had eroded. The wall of separation between combatants and noncombatants had been broken down by the practice of total societal mobilization in modern total war and the resulting practice of attacking directly and intentionally that mobilization base. Given these developments, it was difficult to maintain that the principle of discrimination was still a meaningful limit on war. Those who clung to the principle tended to reject modern war altogether as inherently immoral because it inherently violates the principle. In the international law of war, distinguished publicists were reduced to stating that terror bombing of noncombatants with no conceivable proximate military utility was prohibited, but that the rights of noncombatants to protection otherwise were unclear. . . .

Endnotes

1. James F. Childress, "Just War Theories," *Theological Studies* vol. 39 (1978), pp. 428-435.
2. [For a description of the My Lai Massacre, see the Problem Cases.]
3. "Morality of War," *New Catholic Encyclopedia* 14 (1967), p. 805.
4. Michael Walzer, *Just and Unjust Wars* (New York: Basic Books, 1977), p. 155.

Review Questions

1. O'Brien states three conditions for permissible recourse to war. What are they?
2. What problems arise in trying to satisfy the first condition?
3. How does O'Brien explain the four subdivisions of the just cause condition?
4. What are the elements of the concept of right intention according to O'Brien?
5. Explain the principles of proportion and discrimination.

Discussion Questions

1. O'Brien says that offensive war remains an option in just war theory., When, if ever, would an offensive war be justified?
2. "Right intention insists that charity and love exist even among enemies." Is charity and love compatible with killing people? What would Ryan say? What do you think?
3. O'Brien thinks that the bombing of Hiroshima and Nagasaki was allowed by just war theory. What do you think? Didn't this violate the principle of discrimination?

Jeffrie G. Murphy

The Killing of the Innocent

Jeffrie G. Murphy is a member of the philosophy department at Arizona State University.

Murphy argues that the legal and moral concepts of guilt and innocence do not apply in the context of war. The concern in just war theory about protecting the innocent is really a concern to protect noncombatants. Murphy defines noncombatants as those who are not engaged in an attempt to destroy you, from the viewpoint of the one claiming self-defense.

Murder, some may suggest, is to be defined as the intentional and uncoerced killing of the innocent; and it is true by definition that murder is wrong. Yet wars, particularly modern wars, seem to require the killing of the innocent, e.g., through antimorale terror bombing. Therefore war (at least modern war) must be wrong.

The above line of argument has a certain plausibility and seems to lie behind much philosophical and theological discussion of such problem as the Just War and the nature of war crimes.[1] If accepted in full, it seems to entail the immorality of war (i.e., the position of pacifism) and the moral blameworthiness of those who participate in war (i.e., warmakers and uncoerced soldiers are all murderers). To avoid these consequences, some writers will challenge some part of the argument by maintaining (a) that there are no innocents in war or (b) that modern war does not in fact require the killing of the innocent or (c) that war involves the suspension of moral considerations and thus stands outside the domain of moral criticism entirely or (d) that contributing to the death of innocents is morally blameless so long as it is only foreseen but not intended by those involved in bringing it about (the Catholic principle of the Double Effect) or (e) that the prohibition against killing the innocent is only prima facie[2] and can be overridden by even more important moral requirements, e.g., the defense of freedom.

In this paper I want to come to terms with at least some of the important issues raised by the killing of innocents in time of war. . . .

THE CONCEPT OF INNOCENCE

The notions of innocence and guilt seem most at home in a legal context and, somewhat less comfortably, in a moral context. Legally, a man is innocent if he is not guilty, i.e. if he has not engaged in conduct explicitly prohibited by rules of the criminal law. A man may be regarded as morally innocent if his actions do not result from a mental state (e.g., malice) or a character defect (e.g., negligence) which we regard as morally blameworthy. In any civilized system of criminal law, of course, there will be a close connection between legal guilt and innocence and moral guilt and innocence, e.g., murder in the criminal law has as one of its material or defining elements the blameworthy mental state *(mens rea)* of "malice aforethought." But this close connection does not show that the legal and moral concepts are not different. The existence of strict liability criminal statutes is sufficient to show that they are different. Under a strict liability statute, a man can be guilty of a criminal offense without having, at the time of his action, any blameworthy mental state or character defect, not even negligence.[3] However, the notion of strict *moral* responsibility makes little sense; for an inquiry into moral responsibility for the most part just is an inquiry into such matters as the agent's motives, intentions, beliefs, etc.[4] Also, the issue of legal responsibility is much more easily determinable than that of moral responsibility. For example: It is noncontroversial that negligence can make one legally responsible. Anyone who doubts this may simply be given a reading assignment in any number of penal codes.[5] But whether or not negligence is a mental state or a character defect for which one is *morally* responsible is a matter about which reasonable men can disagree. No reading assignment or simple inquiry into "the facts" will lay this worry to rest.[6]

Now our reasonably comfortable ability to operate with these concepts of guilt and innocence leaves us when we attempt to apply them to the context of war. Of course, the legal notions will have application in a limited number of cases, i.e., with respect to those who are legally war criminals under international law. But this will by no means illuminate the majority of cases. For example: Those who have written on the topic of protecting innocents in war would not want to regard the killing of an enemy soldier engaged in an attack against a fortified position as a case of killing the innocent. He is surely, in the right sense (whatever that is), among the guilty (or, at least, among the non-innocent) and is thus a fitting object for violent death. But he is in no sense *legally* guilty. There are no rules of international law prohibiting what he is doing; and, even if such rules were created, they would surely not involve the setting up of a random collection of soldiers from the other side to act as judges and executioners of this law. Thus the legal notions of guilt and innocence do not serve us well here.

What, then, about moral guilt or innocence? Even to make this suggestion plausible in the context of war, we surely have to attempt to narrow it down to moral innocence or guilt *of* the war or *of* something within the war—not just immoral innocence of guilt *simpliciter*. That is, we surely do not want to say that if a bomb falls (say) on a man with a self-deceiving morally impure heart who is a civilian behind the lines that this is not, in the relevant sense, a case of killing an innocent. Similarly, I think it would be odd for us to want to say that if a soldier with a morally admirable character is killed in action that this is a case of killing an innocent and is to be condemned on those grounds. If we take this line, it would seem that national leaders should attempt to make some investigation of the motives and characters of both soldiers and civilians and kill the unjust among both classes and spare the just. (Only babes in arms would be clearly protected.) Now this sort of judgment, typically thought to be reserved for God if for anyone, is surely a very disquieting thing if advocated for generals and other war leaders. Thus the notions of moral innocence and guilt *simpliciter* must be dropped in this context.

Suppose, then, we try to make use of the notions of moral innocence *of the war* or moral guilt *of the war* (or of something within the war). Even here we find serious problems. Consider the octogenarian civilian in Dresden who is an avid supporter of Hitler's war effort (pays taxes gladly, supports warmongering political rallies, etc.) and contrast his case with that of the poor, frightened, pacifist frontline soldier who is only where he is because of duress and who intends always to fire over the heads of the enemy. It seems reasonable to say that the former is much more morally guilty of the war than the latter; and yet most writers on the topic would regard killing the former, but not the latter, as a case of killing an innocent.

What all this suggests is that the classical worry about protecting the innocent is really a worry about protecting *noncombatants*. And thus the distinction between combatants and noncombatants is what needs to be illucidated. Frontline soldiers are clearly combatants; babes in arms clearly are not. And we know this without judging their respective moral and legal guilt or innocence. And thus the worry, then, is the following: Under what circumstances is an individual truly a combatant? Wars may be viewed as games (terrible ones of course) between enemies or opponents. Who, then, is an enemy or opponent?

One suggestion for defining a combatant might be the following: Only soldiers engaged in fighting are combatants. But this does not seem adequate. For if killing an enemy soldier is right, then it would also seem to be right to kill the man who *orders* him to the frontline. If anything, the case for killing (say) a general seems better, since the soldier is presumably simply acting in some sense as his agent, i.e., the general kills *through* him. Perhaps the way to put the point, then, is as follows: The enemy is represented by those who are *engaged in an attempt* to destroy you.[7] And thus all frontline combat soldiers (though not prisoners, or soldiers on leave, or wounded soldiers, or chaplains, or medics) are enemies and all who issue orders for destruction are enemies. Thus we might try the following: Combatants are those anywhere within the *chain of command or responsibility*—from bottom to top. If this is correct, then a carefully planned attack on the seat of government, intended to destroy those civilians (and only those) directing the war effort, would not be a case of killing noncombatants or, in the relevant sense, innocents.

But what is a chain of command or responsibility? It would be wrong to regard it solely as a causal chain, though it is *at least* that. That is, the notion of responsibility has to be stronger than that expressed in the sentence "The slippery pavement was *responsible* for the accident." For to regard the chain here as solely causal in character would lead to the following consequence: If a combatant is understood solely as one who performs an action which is a causally necessary condition for the waging of war, then the following are going to be combatants: farmers, employees at a city water works, and anyone who pays taxes. Obviously a country cannot wage war if there is no food, no management of the basic affairs of its cities, and no money to pay for it. And of course the list of persons "responsible" for the war in this sense could be greatly extended. But if all these persons are in the class of combatants, then the rule "protect noncombatants" is going to amount to little more than "protect babies and the senile." But one would, I think, have more ambition for it than that, e.g., one would hope that such a rule would protect housewives even if it is true that they "help" the war effort by writing consoling letters to their soldier husbands and by feeding them and providing them with emotional and sexual relief when they are home on leave. Thus I think that it is wrong to regard the notion of chain here as merely causal in character.

What kind of chain, then, is it? Let us call it a *a chain of agency*. What I mean by this is that the links of the chain (like the links between motives and actions) are held together logically and not merely causually, i.e., all held together, in this case, under the notion of who it is that is *engaged in an attempt* to destroy you. The farmer qua farmer is, like the general, performing actions which are causally necessary conditions for your destruction; but, unlike the general, he is not necessarily engaged in an attempt to destroy you. Perhaps the point can better be put in this way: The farmer's role bears a contingent connection to the war effort whereas the general's role bears a necessary connection to the war effort, i.e., his function, unlike the farmer's, is not logically separable from the waging of war. Or, following Thomas Nagel,[8] the point can perhaps be put in yet another way: The farmer is aiding the soldier qua human being whereas the general is aiding the soldier qua soldier or fighting man. And since your enemy is the soldier qua soldier, and not qua human being, we have grounds for letting the farmer off. If we think of a justified war as one of self-defense,[9] then we must ask the question "Who can be said to be *attacking* us such that we need to defend ourselves against him?" Viewed in this way, the farmer seems an unlikely candidate for combat status.

This analysis does, of course, leave us with borderline cases. But, since there *are* borderline cases, this is a virtue of the analysis so long as it captures just the right ones. Consider workers in a munitions factory. Are they or are they not combatants? At least with certain munitions factories (making only bombs, say) it is certainly going to be odd to claim that their activities bear only a contingent connection to the war effort. What they make, unlike food, certainly supports the fighting man qua fighting man and not qua human being. Thus I should be inclined to say that they are properly to be regarded as combatants and thus properly subject to attack. But what about workers in munitions factories that only in part supply the war effort, e.g., they make rifles both for soldiers and for hunters? Or workers in nonmunitions factories that do make some war products, e.g., workers in companies, like Dow Chemical, which make both Saran Wrap and Napalm? Or workers in ball bearing factories or oil refineries, some of their product going to war machines and some not? Here, I submit, we do have genuine borderline cases. And with respect to these, what should we do? I should hope that reasonable men would accept that the burden of proof lies on those claiming that a particular group of persons are combatants and properly vulnerable. I should hope that men would accept, along with the famous principle in the criminal law, the principle "noncombatant until proven otherwise" and would attempt to look at the particular facts of each case as carefully and disinterestedly as possible. I say that I hope this, not that I expect it.

Who, then, is a combatant? I shall answer this question from the point of view of one who believes that the only legitimate defense for war is self-defense.[10] It is, in this context, important to remember that one may legitimately plead self-defense even if one's belief that one's life is being threatened is false. The only requirement is that the belief be *reasonable* given the evidence that is available. If a man comes to my door with a toy pistol and says, pointing the pistol at me, "Prepare to meet your Maker for your time has come," I act in my self-defense if I kill him even if he was joking so long as my belief was reasonable, i.e., I had no way of knowing that the gun was a toy or that he was joking. Thus: combatants may be viewed as all those in the territory or allied territory of the enemy of whom it is reasonable to believe that they are engaged in an attempt to destroy you.

What about our Dresden octogenarian? Is he a combatant on this analysis? Since he does not act *on authority,* it is at least prima facie odd to regard him as part of a chain of command literally construed—the concept of command being most at home in a context of authority. He does not, of course, have much to do with the war effort; and so we might find his claim that he is "helping to defeat the Americans" quaint on purely factual grounds. And yet none of this prevents its being true that he can properly be said to be engaged in an *attempt* to destroy the enemy. For people can attempt even the impossible so long as they do not *know* it is impossible. Thus I am prepared to say of him that he is, in fact, engaged in an attempt to destroy the enemy. But I would still say that killing him would count as a case of killing a noncombatant for the following reason: that the concept of attempt here is to be applied, not from the agent's point of view, but from the point of view of the spectator who proposes to plead self-defense in defense of his acts of killing. Combatants are all those who may *reasonably* be regarded as engaged in an attempt to destroy you. This belief is reasonable (though false) in the case of the frontline soldier who plans always to shoot over the heads of the enemy and unreasonable (even if true) in the case of our octogenarian. It would be quite unreasonable to plan a bombing raid on a nonmilitary and nonindustrial city like Dresden and say, in defense of the raid, that you are just protecting yourself or your country from all those warmongering civilians who are attempting to destroy you. For making such a judgment imposes upon you a burden of proof which, given the circumstances of war, you could not satisfy. You probably could not get *any* evidence for your claim. You certainly could not get what the law calls a "preponderance of the evidence"—much less "proof beyond a reasonable doubt."

Combatants, then, are all those of whom it is reasonable to believe that they are engaged in an attempt at your destruction. Noncombatants are all those of whom it is not reasonable to believe this. . . .

Endnotes

1. "Murder," writes Miss Anscombe, "is the deliberate killing of the innocent, whether for its own sake or as a means to some further end" ("War and Murder," p. 45). Deliberate killing of the innocent (or noncombatants) is prohibited by the Just War Theory and is a crime in international law. A traditional account of the Catholic Just War Theory may be found in Chapter 35 of Austin Fagothey's *Right and Reason: Ethics in Theory and Practice* (St. Louis: C. V. Mosby Co., 1963). A useful sourcebook for inquiry into the nature of war crimes is the anthology *Crimes of War*, ed. by Richard A. Falk, Gabriel Kilko, and Robert Jay Lifton (New York: Random House, 1971).
2. By "prima facie wrong" I mean "can be overridden by other moral requirements"—*not*, as a literal translation might suggest, "only apparently wrong."
3. For example: In the criminal offense of statutory rape, the defendant is strictly liable with respect to his knowledge of the age of a girl with whom he has had sexual relations, i.e., no matter how carefully he inquired into her age, no matter how reasonable (i.e., nonnegligent) his belief that she was of legal age of consent, he is liable if his belief is in fact mistaken. For a general discussion of such offenses, see Richard Wassertrom's "Strict Liability in the Criminal Law," *Stanford Law Review*, 12 (July 1960).
4. In discussion, Richard Wasserstrom has expressed skepticism concerning my claim that there is something unintelligible about the concept of strict moral responsibility. One could regard the *Old testament* and *Oedipus Rex* as containing a strict liability conception of morality. Now I should be inclined to argue that the primitiveness of the *Old Testament* and of *Oedipus Rex* consists in these peoples not yet being able to draw a distinction between legality and morality. However, I am prepared to admit that it might be better to weaken my claim by maintaining simply that no *civilized* or *enlightened* morality would involve strict liability.
5. In California criminal law, for example, vehicular manslaughter is defined as vehicular homicide "in the commission of an unlawful act, not amounting to felony, with gross negligence . . ." (*California Penal Code*, 192, 3, a).
6. For an excellent discussion of moral and legal responsibility for negligence, see H. L. A. Hart's "Negligence, *Mens Rea* and Criminal Responsibility," in his *Punishment and Responsibility: Essays in the Philosophy of Law* (Oxford: Oxford University Press, 1963).
7. I say "engaged in an attempt" rather than "attempting" for the following reasons: A mortar attack on an encampment of combat soldiers who happens to be sleeping is surely not a case of killing noncombatants even though persons who are asleep cannot be attempting anything. Sleeping persons can, however, be engaged in an attempt—just as sleeping persons can be accomplices in crime and parties to a criminal conspiracy. Being engaged in an attempt, unlike attempting, is not necessarily a full time job. I am grateful to Anthony Woozley for pointing this out to me.
8. Thomas Nagel, "War and Massacre," *Philosophy and Public Affairs*, 2 (Winter 1972). In the same issue, Richard Brandt replies to Nagel in his "Utilitarianism and the Rules of War." I am grateful to Professors Nagel and Brandt for allowing me to read their articles prior to publication.
9. For reasons of simplicity in later drawing upon important and instructive principles from the criminal law, I shall use the phrase "self-defense." (I shall later want to draw on the notion of *reasonable belief* in the law of self-defense.) However, what I really want to focus on is the concept of "defense" and not the concept of "self." For it seems to me that war can be justified, not just to defend oneself or one's nation, but also to defend others from threats that transcend nationality, e.g., genocide. If one wants to speak of self-defense even here, then it must be regarded as self-defense for the *human*, not just national, community. The phrase "self-defense" as it occurs in what follows should always be understood as carrying this qualification. And, of course, even clear cases of self-defense are not always necessarily justified. Given the morally debased character of Nazi Germany, it is by no means obvious

that it acted rightly in trying to defend itself near the end of World War II (i.e., after it had ceased to be an aggressor).

10. Remember that this carries the qualification stated in note 9. For a survey of the law of self-defense, the reader may consult any reliable treatise on the criminal law, e.g., pp. 883 ff. of Rollin M. Perkins's *Criminal Law* (Brooklyn, N. Y.: Foundation Press, 1957). The criminal law is a highly moralized institution, and it is useful (though by no means always definitive) for the moral philosopher in that it provides an accumulated and systematized body of reflection on vital moral matters of our culture. For my purposes, I shall in what follows focus upon the *reasonable belief* condition in the law of self-defense. Other aspects of the law of self-defense (e.g., the so-called "retreat requirement"), have, I think, interesting implications for war that I cannot pursue here.

Review Questions

1. How does Murphy explain the concepts of innocence and guilt?
2. According to Murphy, why don't these concepts apply in the context of war?
3. How does Murphy define combatant? Who is a combatant and who isn't in his view?

Discussion Questions

1. Murphy thinks that workers in a munitions factory are combatants. What do you think?
2. By Murphy's account, the pacifist soldier who intends not to kill anyone is still a combatant. Is this right?

Anthony E. Hartle

Humanitarianism and the Laws of War

Anthony E. Hartle teaches philosophy at the United States Military Academy, West Point and is a colonel in the United States Army.

According to Hartle, there are two principles which underline the laws of war, a Kantian principle that individuals deserve respect as persons, and a utilitarian principle that human suffering ought to be minimized. He argues that in cases where the two principles conflict, the Kantian principle should have priority.

That moral principles underlie and constrain the activity of members of professions such as medicine and law is generally acknowledged. Whether the same can be said of the military profession is a question likely to generate considerable uncertainty. In this paper, I shall show that, like other professions, the military profession is informed by a **moral teleology.** The source of this teleology, for the profession of arms, is manifested in the laws of war. The laws of war, in turn, reflect two humanitarian principles:

1. Individual persons deserve respect as such (HP1).
2. Human suffering ought to be minimized (HP2).

These two principles differ in terms of schemes of justification; the first is non-consequentialist and appeals to human rights, while the second is consequentialist and is based on utilitarian considerations. My argument will conclude that HP1 has priority over HP2 in the formulation of the laws of war.

I

While there are few instances of provisions of the laws of war that are obviously attributable to one and only one of the two humanitarian principles, it also appears that HP1 and HP2 are none the less distinctly different principles that can conceivably come into conflict. A classical

From Anthony E. Hartle, "Humanitarianism and the Laws of War," *Philosophy* 61 (1986). Reprinted by permission.

combat situation presenting problems of moral choice is that in which enemy soldiers are taken prisoner by a small force carrying out a critical mission behind enemy lines. By examining this type of situation carefully with respect to the two humanitarian principles, we can clarify the moral nature of the laws of war.

Consider the often discussed prisoner case filled out as follows. The success of the small force in carrying out its mission will allow the seizure of a major transportation centre without a significant battle which would affect a sizeable civilian population. If the battle does not occur, many combatant and noncombatant casualties will be avoided as well as extensive destruction of civilian property. The force carrying out the mission, however, takes several wounded enemy soldiers prisoner. The mission is such that accomplishment is not possible if the force keeps its prisoners in custody. If the prisoners are released, it is highly likely that the force will be compromised and that the mission will fail. Under the circumstances, the commander of the force must decide whether to kill the prisoners and whether such execution can be justified.

We are particularly concerned not with his decision, but with the laws of war that apply to such a situation. In the discussion that follows, the two humanitarian principles will be applied directly to situations involving choice among specific alternative actions. With respect to the laws of war as they exist, however, these two principles are the basis for *formulating* the laws. Only in situations for which there is no applicable law or in situations in which the justifiability of a particular law is being questioned would the principles be applied directly in determining appropriate choices of action.

Before examining the existing laws of war on the subject of the treatment of prisoners, we should recognize that there can be a conflict between HP1 and HP2 if we apply these humanitarian principles directly in attempting to decide what to do in a given situation. In our hypothetical example, consideration of the question under HP2 indicates that the answer is 'kill the prisoners', for in the short term this action will cause considerably less suffering than not killing them. Unless we assume some condition such that the warring party to which the capturing force belongs would inevitably lose the war and that capturing the transportation centre would only prolong the war with the result of increased suffering, the logical action under HP2 will be to execute the prisoners and carry on with the mission.

One might object by saying that allowing the execution of prisoners will in the long run be counterproductive, that suffering will thereby be increased by heightening determination not to surrender and by encouraging battles and wars of annihilation, but if the prisoners are executed only in highly exceptional circumstances such as those presented in the hypothetical case above, the objection in terms of long-term effects is not persuasive.

Under HP1, however, the decision to execute the prisoners cannot be justified. If the leader of the capturing force is to respect his prisoners as individual persons, he cannot eliminate them solely as a means of expediting his mission, which he would be doing if he executed them. The prisoners, under HP1, have a basic right not to be treated cruelly or inhumanely. Both descriptions apply to summary execution.

The two humanitarian principles appear to call for opposite courses of action in the prisoner example, a situation which indicates that different laws would be produced if one or the other of the principles were considered in framing laws concerning the treatment of prisoners. There are similar situations that can arise if the two principles are applied directly. Some of the most obvious are those involving deliberate attacks on groups of civilians, use of weapons that are considered inhumane, and resettlement of civilians in occupied territories. We can hypothesize situations in which one course of action appears to be the logical choice if we desire to minimize suffering, while a different course of action is preferable if we are to respect individual persons as such. Our concern with the prisoner example and others like it, however, is that of first determining what the actual laws of war require and then identifying which of the two foundational moral principles underlies the existing law. The answers to two questions will thus clarify the issue. First, what do the laws of war permit or prohibit? Second, from what moral principle is the applicable law of war derived?

With respect to our prisoner example, clear evidence can be found in specific national regulations which are derived from the codified laws of war. Although the American manual, *The Law of Land Warfare,* written in 1956, does not specifically prohibit killing prisoners under any and all circumstances, the wording suggests that intention:

> A commander may not put his prisoners to death because their presence retards his movements or diminishes his power of resistance. . . . It is likewise unlawful for a commander to kill his prisoners on grounds of self-preservation, even in the case of airborne or commando operations . . . (para. 85, p. 35).

The United States Air Force pamphlet, *International Law—The Conduct of Armed Conflict and Air Operations,* reflects the same position in referring to Articles 12-16 of the 1949 Geneva Convention Relative to the Treatment of Prisoners of War, but in more unequivocal terms: "These provisions prohibit killing or mistreatment of PWs whatever the military reasons . . ." (para. 13-2, p. 13-1). The laws of war, as construed by the United States, prohibit the killing of prisoners. This interpretation of the laws of war appears warranted and is shared by Geneva signatories. Thus, the laws of war that apply in the case of the captured prisoners are derived from HP1 rather than from HP2, for by applying HP2 directly, we found that killing of prisoners of war could be justified in some circumstances. We must conclude, then, that HP1 has priority over HP2 in framing the laws of war in this instance. In fact, such appears to be the case in all situations in which specific rights recognized in the laws of war are involved. In the three additional circumstances suggested above (attacks on civilians, use of inhumane weapons, and resettlement), the applicable laws of war are based upon recognition of the rights of persons and thus derive from HP1. This suggests strongly that, with respect to formulating laws of war in general, HP1 has priority over HP2. If we turn now to the fundamental documents of the codified laws of war, we will find the same moral point of view embodied there.

II

An examination of the current laws of war reveals the humanitarian concern that pervades the requirements and limitations established in their provisions. The 'Martens Clause' [1] found in the preamble to both the 1899 and 1907 Hague Conventions indicates the spirit in which those two sets of constraints on warfare were promulgated:

> Until a more complete code of the laws of war can be issued, the High Contracting parties think it expedient to declare that in cases not included in the Regulations adopted by them, populations and belligerents remain under the protection and the rule of the principles of the laws of nations, as they result from the usages established between civilized nations, from the laws of humanity, and the requirements of the public conscience. . . . [2]

The United States Air Force manual concerning the conduct of armed conflict under the laws of war refers specifically to 'the principle of humanity, which forbids the infliction of suffering, injury or destruction not actually necessary for the accomplishment of legitimate military purposes'.[3] A subsequent passage states: 'The principle of humanity also confirms the basic immunity of civilian populations and civilians from being objects of attack during armed conflict'.[4]

Through the Martens Clause, the Hague Conventions are set upon the foundation of the 'laws of humanity and the requirements of public conscience'. As the United States Air Force manual further points out, the Geneva Conventions in turn

> safeguard such fundamental rights as freedom from torture or cruel and inhuman punishment; freedom from arbitrary exile; freedom from arbitrarily imposed punishment; and right to legal remedy for any abuse; right to minimum standards of respect for human rights at all times; and right to health, family sanctity and non-abuse.[5]

The four Geneva Conventions were produced at the Diplomatic Conference of 1949, and those at the Conference affirmed that their work was 'inspired solely by humanitarian aims'.[6] The law of Geneva is specifically concerned with four primary areas under the heading of humane treatment for 'protected persons':

1. Care of the wounded, sick and shipwrecked.
2. Treatment of prisoners of war.
3. Immunity of non-combatants.
4. Treatment of the population of occupied territory.

All of the prohibitions and requirements in the Conventions can be directly related to the protection of the rights of individual persons.

The Geneva Conventions thus specify measures required by the concept of human rights, which today is the dominant manifestation of the concept of respect for persons. Respect for persons entails the ideas of equality of consideration and human dignity. Individual persons cannot be treated with respect for what they are unless they are considered equally as persons (though that consideration obviously does not further entail equal treatment). To give preferential treatment is to deny the individual discriminated against the full status of a person—a rational being capable of independent choice and thus deserving of respect from other rational beings solely on the basis of that status. Human dignity is inherent in such a concept. In terms of modern ethical theory, the preferred means of establishing a framework for assessing the actions required in order to respect the status of individual persons is the delineation of fundamental human rights.

The principle thrust of the Geneva Conventions of 1949 is the attempt to specify the rights of non-combatants. The primary categories of non-combatants are (loosely) those disabled from fighting and those not directly participating in combat. Honoring their rights as required by the Conventions is a moral and legal obligation placed upon all signatory parties.

An examination of the Hague Conventions shows that they are logically consistent with the second humanitarian principle (HP2). They are specifically concerned with the way in which war is to be waged. Article 23e, which prohibits the employment of weapons or material calculated to cause unnecessary suffering, and the Hague Regulations concerning the protection of prisoners of war and civilians were framed with the intent of ameliorating the evils of war.[7] The articles prohibiting treacherous or perfidious actions were framed to achieve the same end by avoiding the prolongation of war, which would probably occur if such actions were taken. Unless some minimal standards of conduct are mutually recognized, there will be no basis for settlement of the conflict other than the virtual annihilation of one of the warring parties. Almost every provision of the Hague Convention can be seen as a direct means of minimizing human suffering, even though the motivation for establishing the conventions of war codified at The Hague may have been largely prudential.

Observance of the law of The Hague will in most cases cause less human suffering than would be caused by its non-observance. That the law of The Hague manifests the first humanitarian principle (HP1), however, is not as clear. Whether one shoots and kills an enemy soldier with a standard 0.45 calibre round or whether one shoots and kills an enemy with a 0.45 calibre round with a notched bullet appears to have little to do with respecting his status as a person. Such a constraint does, however, clearly have to do with minimizing human suffering.

III

The foregoing discussion shows that the laws of war govern practice under moral principles; accordingly, the legal rights established in the laws of war should reflect moral rights. It is clear that such rights derive from HP1. Since the laws of war do prohibit the killing of prisoners, which is consistent with HP1, one could again conclude that the two humanitarian principles, HP1 and HP2, have a priority relationship in which HP2 is subordinate to HP1. Further, as other examples of potential conflict between the principles indicate, it appears that HP1 will have priority in all cases in which recognized rights are involved. The laws of war specifically recognize that prisoners of war have a right to be treated humanely and with respect for their persons, which must certainly include the right not to be murdered. Accordingly, the right of the prisoners not to be killed would have to be satisfied before the criterion of minimizing suffering is applied. Once the non-consequentialist principle is satisfied, if more than one alternative law remains under consideration, one turns to HP2 for further discrimination among possible laws.

HP2, applied directly to actions, functions just as the Happiness Principle (or Pleasure Principle) functions in act-utilitarian theory. Minimizing suffering is merely the converse of maximizing happiness, so that if HP2 were the sole basis for deciding what to do in situations involving moral choice in warfare, we would be concerned with a particular application of utilitarianism. Our discussion has shown this not to be the case. Further, if HP2 were the principle from which all the laws of war were derived, we would be concerned with a form of rule utilitarianism, with the laws of war being the rules which, all things considered, best served HP2 (such a situation would be the ideal, that is, though it certainly has not been achieved in a practice). This, however, is not the case, for HP1 appears to have priority over HP2 in important instances, namely, those in which the two principles conflict. While we have not examined all such cases (nor would it be possible to do so), the representative cases make this a reasonable conclusion. The point argued here is that analysis of the current laws of war reveals that HP1 has priority over HP2 in the formulation of such laws.

In sum, the moral character of the laws of war is articulated by the two humanitarian principles that separately or jointly provide the moral basis for determining specific rules of conduct. The principle that individual persons should be respected as such can, however, come in conflict with the principle that human suffering ought to be minimized. When that occurs, it appears there is a plausible argument for holding that the first principle (HP1) has priority. If HP1 provides the basis for justified participation in war, then HP1 is more fundamental than HP2. And if that is the case, only when the first is satisfied will the second principle be applied. Because the laws of war are incomplete, and will probably remain so, it is important to establish these principles and their relationship. Lastly, though some commentators such as Richard B. Brandt consider a form of utilitarian theory to be the appropriate interpretation of the moral basis of the laws of war,[8] we have seen that HP2, which in itself can be considered a limited utilitarian principle, is more appropriately viewed as subordinate to HP1, which in turn is most plausibly seen as non-consequentialist and thus not a utilitarian principle.

Endnotes

1. So called in recognition of the Russian jurist, F. F. Martens, President of the 1899 Hague Conventions (see Sidney Bailey, *Prohibitions and Restraints in War* [Oxford, 1972]).
2. Leon Friedman (ed.), *The Law of War: A Documentary History* (New York; Random House, 1972), Vol. 1, 309.
3. Department of the Air Force, *International Law—The Conduct of Armed Conflicts and Air Operations,* AF Pamphlet 110-31 (Washington, DC, 19 November 1976), 1–6.
4. AFP 110-31, p. 1-6.
5. AFP 110-31, p. 11-4.
6. Morris Greenspan, *The Modern Law of Land Warfare* (Berkeley: University of California Press, 1959), 22.
7. This point is presented clearly in the Preamble to Hague Convention No. IV (1907).
8. Richard B. Brandt, 'Utilitarianism and the Rules of War', *Philosophy and Public Affairs* 1 (Winter 1972), 145-165.

Review Questions

1. What are the two principles underlying the laws of war according to Hartle?
2. In what case do they conflict?
3. Why does Hartle think that the first principle, the Kantian principle of respect for persons, has priority over the other principle?

Discussion Questions

1. In the case Hartle discusses, why not just kill the prisoners? What would you do?
2. Is killing the prisoners really incompatible with the Kantian principle of respect for persons? Kant thought one could kill someone respectfully (in cases of capital punishment for example). Using this same principle, could one respectfully kill the prisoners?
3. Can you think of any other principles that are important in the conduct of war? What are they?

Majid Khadduri

The Doctrine of Jihād

Majid Khadduri taught international studies at Johns Hopkins University and other schools; he is currently director of research at the Middle East Institute, Washington, D. C. He is the author of several books including War and Peace in the Law of Islam *(1955),* The Gulf War *(1988), and* The Islamic Conception of Justice *(1984), from which our reading is taken.*

Jihād, as Khadduri explains the term, has a broad sense in which it means exertion in Allah's path, and a narrower sense in which it refers to holy war against unbelievers and enemies of the Islamic faith. It does not include secular war. Jihād as holy war is justified because it enforces God's law or stops transgressions against it. All other war, that is, war fought for nonreligious reasons, is prohibited.

The instrument with which Islam sought to achieve its objectives was the jihād. Islam prohibited all kinds of warfare except in the form of jihād. But the jihād, though often described as a holy war, did not necessarily call for fighting, even though a state of war existed between the two dārs—**dār al-Islam** and **dār al-Harb**—since Islam's ultimate goals might be achieved by peaceful as well as by violent means.

Strictly speaking, the word "jihād" does not mean "war" in the material sense of the word. Literally, it means "exertion," "effort" and "attempt," denoting that the individual is urged to use his utmost endeavors to fulfill a certain function or carry out a specific task.[1] Its technical meaning is the exertion of the believer's strength to fulfill a duty prescribed by the Law in "The path of God" (Q. LXI, 10-13), the path of right and justice. Thus the jihād may be defined as a religious and legal duty which must be fulfilled by each believer either by the heart and tongue in combatting evil and spreading the word of God, or by the hand and sword in the sense of participation in fighting. Only in the latter sense did Islam consider the jihād a collective duty (fard al-kifāya) which every believer was bound to fulfill, provided he was able to take the field. Believers who could not take to the field nor had the means to do so were expected to contribute in weapons or supplies in lieu of fighting with the sword. Participation in the jihād in one form or another was a highly-prized duty and the believer's recompense, if he actually took to the field, would be the achievement of salvation and reward of Paradise (Q. LXC, 10-13) in addition to material rewards.[2] Such war, called in Western legal tradition "just war" *(bellum justium)*, is the only valid kind of war. All other wars are prohibited.

The jihād was the just war of Islam. God commanded the believers to spread His word and establish His Law and Justice over the world (Q. IX, 5). The dār al-Islam was the house of the believers where Law and Justice were given practical expression, and the dār al-Harb was the house of the unbelievers and an object of the jihād. Religion, however, was and still is to be carried out by peaceful means, as there should be no compulsion in the spread of the word of God (Q. II, 257). The expansion of the state, carried out by the jihād, was an entirely different matter. Thus the jihād, a duty prescribed by Religion and Law, was surely as pious and just as *pium* and *justum* in the way described by St. Augustine and St. Thomas and later by Hugo Grotius.

In early Islam, the scholars like Abū Hanīfa (d. 150/768) and Shaybānī (d. 189/804) made no explicit declarations that the jihād was a war to be waged against non-Muslims solely on the grounds of disbelief. On the contrary, they stressed that tolerance should be shown unbelievers, especially the **scripturaries** (though not idolators and polytheists), and advised the

From Majid Khadduri, *The Islamic Conception of Justice*. The Johns Hopkins University Press, Baltimore/London, 1984, pp. 164–170.

Imām to wage war only when the inhabitants of the dār al-Harb came into conflict with Islam. It was Shāfiī (d. 204/820), founder of the school of law bearing his name, who laid down a framework for Islam's relationship with non-Muslims and formulated the doctrine that the jihād had for its intent the waging of war on unbelievers for their disbelief and not only when they entered into conflict with the Islamic state.[3] The object of the jihād, which was not necessarily an offensive war, was thereby transformed into a collective obligation enjoined on the Muslim community to fight unbelievers "wherever you may find them" (Q. IX, 5), and the distinction between offensive and defensive war became no longer relevant.

The reformulation of the jihād as a doctrine of just war without regard to its defensive or offensive character provoked a debate among Shāfiī's contemporaries and led to a division of opinion among Hanafī jurists. Some, like Tahāwī (d. 321/933), adhered more closely to the early Hanafī doctrine that fighting was obligatory only in a war with unbelievers;[4] but Sarakhsī (d. 483/1101), the great commentator on Shaybānī, accepted Shāfiī's doctrine of the jihād that fighting the unbelievers was a "duty enjoined permanently until the end of time."[5] Scholars who came afterwards, until the fall of Baghdad at the hands of the Mongols in the thirteenth century, accepted the jihād as just war without regard to its offensive or defensive character.

Should the Caliph, head of the State, be obeyed if he invoked the jihād in a situation considered contrary to justice, it may be asked? According to the Orthodox doctrine of the Imamate, not to speak of Shī'ī doctrines, the Imām had to be obeyed even if he were in error. But on matters of foreign conduct of the state, the Caliph's powers were often questioned. In a war with the Byzantines, the Caliph Harūn al-Rashīd (d. 193/809) seems to have decided to use violence against the Banū Taghlib, a Christian community near the Byzantine borders, and to revoke their treaty with Islam on the grounds of their alleged sympathy with the Byzantines. Shaybānī, who was consulted on the matter, said in no uncertain terms that the Banū Taghlib did not violate the treaty and that an attack on them was unjustified, although he did not necessarily imply that if the Caliph issued an order, his order should not be obeyed.[6] Later when Islamic power was threatened, the scholars were dubious about the Imām's conduct if he violated his undertakings with the unbelievers, but Ibn Taymīya (d. 728/1328) spoke openly his mind in defense of Christian claims to protection when they were discriminated against even at the most critical time of danger to Islam. . . .

The Jihād as Defensive War

The classical doctrine of the jihād made no distinction between defensive and offensive war, for in the pursuance of the establishment of God's Sovereignty and Justice on Earth the difference between defensive and offensive acts was irrelevant. However, although the duty of the jihād was commanded by God (Q. LXI, 10-13), it was considered to be binding only when the strength of the believers was theirs (Q. II, 233). When Islamic power began to decline, the state obviously could no longer assume a preponderant attitude without impairing its internal unity. Commentators on the jihād as a doctrine of permanent war without constraints began to reinterpret its meaning in a manner which underwent a significant adjustment to realities when conditions in the dār al-Islam changed radically. Some scholars, though still adhering to the principle that the jihād was a permanent state of war, argued that the mere preparation for the jihād would be a fulfillment of its obligation.[7] Not only did Islam become preoccupied with problems of internal security, but also its territorial integrity was exposed to dangers when foreign forces (the Crusaders and Mongols) from the dār al-Harb challenged its power and threatened its very existence.

In those altered circumstances, scholars began to change their position on the question of whether the jihād, used against believers on the grounds of their hostility to Islam, was just. The doctrine of the jihād as a duty permanently imposed upon the community to fight the unbelievers wherever they might be found retained little of its substance. Ibn Taymīya, a jurist-theologian who was gravely concerned with internal disorder, understood the futility of the classical doctrine of jihād at a time when foreign enemies (Crusaders and Mongols) were menacing at the gates of dār al-Islam. He made concessions to reality by reinterpreting the jihād to mean waging a defensive war against unbelievers whenever they threatened him. Unbelievers who made no attempt to encroach upon the dār al-Islam, he asserted, were not the objective of Islam nor should Law and Religion be imposed upon them by force. "If the unbeliever were to be killed unless he becomes a Muslim," he went on to explain, "such an action would constitute the greatest compulsion," a notion which ran contrary to the Revelation which states that "no compulsion is prescribed by Religion" (Q. II, 257). But unbelievers who consciously took the offensive and encroached upon the dār al-Islam would be in an entirely different position.[8]

No longer construed as a war against the dār al-Harb on the grounds of disbelief, the doctrine of the jihād as a religious duty became binding on believers only in the defense of Islam. It entered into a period of tranquillity and assumed a dormant position, to be revived by the Imām whenever he believed Islam was in danger. It is true that the Ottoman sultans in their conquest of European territory often invoked the jihād, but in their actions they were neither in a position to exercise the rights of the Imām nor were their ways always religious in character.[15] Moreover, at the height of their power, the sultans came to terms with the unbelievers and were prepared to make peace on the basis of equality and mutuality with Christian princes, contrary to precedents. Elated by their victories against the unbelievers of Europe, they turned to eastern Islamic lands and brought them under their control when the **Shīà** seized power in Persia at the opening of the sixteenth century, thus threatening internal unity. The Ottoman Sultan, though unable to subjugate Persia, provided leadership to Islamic lands under his control until World War I.

Just War and Secular War

In theory only the Imām, enthroned to exercise God's Sovereignty on Earth, has the power to invoke the jihād and call believers to fulfill the duty. Unless the Imām delegates his power to a subordinate, nobody has the right to exercise it without prior authorization from him. Were the jihād to be proclaimed by the governor of a province without authorization of the Imām, it would be a "secular war" and not a valid or just war. If a dissident leader, whether belonging to an orthodox or to a heterodox group, claimed the right to declare a jihād, his action would be considered disobedience to the Imām and a rebellion against the legitimate authority (Q. XLIX, 9).[16] Neither the leader nor the persons who take part in such a jihād would be rewarded with Paradise, which is granted only to those who participate in a jihād declared by the Imām.

Endnotes

1. See Zabīdī, *Tāj al-Àrūs*, ed. Hārūn, VII, 534-39.
2. The promise of eternal life in Heaven, where believers attain Divine happiness and justice, is granted to all who fulfill the basic duties, but none would enable the believer to gain Paradise as surely as martyrdom in the jihād. See Sarakhsī, *Sharh Kitāb al-Siyar al-Kabīr li . . . al-Shaybānī*, ed. Munajjid (Cairo, 1957), I, 24-25. The material reward for the jihād is a share in the spoils.
3. Shāfi', *Kitāb al-Umm*, IV, 84-85.
4. Abū Ja'far al-Tahāwī, *Kitāb al-Mukhtasar*, ed. Abū al-Wafā al-Afghānī (Cairo, 1320/1950), p. 281.
5. Sarakshī, *Kitāb al-Mabsūt (Cairo, 1324/1906), X, 2-3.*
6. Khadduri, *Islamic Law of Nations*,, pp. 34-35.
7. See Ibn Hudhayl, *Kitāb Tuhfat al-Anfus Wa Sukkān al-Andalus*, ed. Mercais (Paris, 1936), p. 15.
8. Ibn Taymīya, "Qā'ida fī Qitāl al-Kuffār," Majmū 'at Rasā'il, ed. Hamīd al-Fiqqī (Cairo, 1368/1949), pp. 115-46; and *al-Siyāsa al-Sha'ir'ya, ed. Nashshār and Atīya (Cairo, 1951), pp. 125-53.*

Review Questions

1. According to Khadduri, what does the word jihād mean?
2. Explain the classical doctrine of jihād as permanent war against unbelievers.
3. How was this classical doctrine modified?
4. What is the role of the Imām in jihād as holy war?

Discussion Questions

1. Compare the doctrine of jihād with the just war theory. How are they similar, and how different?

2. Saddam Hussein declared the Gulf War a jihād. Was this really a jihād or merely a secular war?

3. Is the doctrine of jihād acceptable to you? If not, then state and explain your objections.

PROBLEM CASES

*1. **Gandhi.*** (Gandi's life is beautifully portrayed in the movie *Gandhi* (1982), directed by Richard Attenborough, with Ben Kingsley as Gandhi. Gandhi's views on war are collected in *Nonviolence in Peace and War,* edited by Mahadev Desai, 2 vols. (Ahmedalbad: Navajivan Press, 1945).)

Mohandas Gandhi (1869-1948) was the most famous and effective pacifist of the twentieth century. After achieving reforms in the treatment of Hindus and Muslims in South Africa, he returned to India where he campaigned against British rule—resulting in the departure of the British in 1948, the same year that Gandhi was killed by an orthodox Hindu.

Gandhi was a Hindu who practiced ahimsa (nonviolence) towards all living things. (He was considered unorthodox, however, because he rejected the caste system and did not accept everything in the Vedas.) The concept of ahimsa originated in Jainism, and was accepted by both Buddhism and Hinduism. In those religions, ahimsa is understood as not harming any living being by actions of body, mind, or speech. In Jainism, ahimsa is practiced even with respect to plants, while in Hinduism and Buddhism, plants are not included, but animals are.

The most original aspect of Gandhi's teaching and methods was what he called satyagraha (literally, truth force). Satyagraha involves ahimsa and austerities such as fasting. It is supposed to purify one's soul and transform the souls of those it is used against. In practice, the methods of satyagraha developed by Gandhi included marches, sit-ins, strikes, boycotts, fasts, and prayers. These nonviolent and passive methods worked well against the British and have been widely admired and copied. In the United States, Dr. Martin Luther King, Jr. (1929-1968) used similar tactics in the civil rights struggles of the 1950s and 1960s.

Gandhi's nonviolent tactics worked against the British, but would they have been effective against someone like Hitler who was not afraid to kill millions of innocent people? Is nonviolent resistence an acceptable alternative to war? What do you think?

*2. **The Gulf War.*** For a book-length treatment of the Gulf War, including the view of it as jihād, see Kenneth L. Vaux, *Ethics and the Gulf War* (Boulder, CO: Westview Press, 1992). In August, 1990, the Iraqi army invaded and occupied Kuwait. Although the United States had received warnings, officials did not take them seriously. Saddam Hussein believed the United States would not intervene and apparently had received assurances to that effect. Hussein claimed that the invasion was justified because Kuwait had once been part of Iraq and because the Kuwaitis were exploiting the Rumaila oil field which extended into Iraq. The immediate response of the United States and its allies was to begin a ship embargo against Iraq. President George Bush, citing atrocities against the Kuwaitis, compared Hussein to Hitler. For his part, Hussein declared the war to be jihād, and threatened the mother of all battles (as he put it) if the Americans dared to intervene. Iran's Ayatollah Khomeini, certainly no friend of the United States, seconded the claim of jihād adding that anyone killed in battle would be a martyr and immediately go to paradise, the Islamic heaven.

In the months that followed, Iraq ignored repeated ultimatums to leave Kuwait. But Iraq did try to stall for time, following the Quranic teaching of "withholding your hand a little while from war." (This passage is quoted by Vaux, p. 71.) Thousands of foreign prisoners were released, and Iraq responded positively to French and Soviet peace initiatives. At the same time, Saddam Hussein continued to call it a holy war, saying that the United States was a Satanic force attacking the religious values and practices of Islam.

On January 16, 1991, after a U. N. deadline had passed, the allied forces (United States, British, French, Saudi, and Kuwaiti) launched a massive night-and-day air attack on military targets in Iraq including the capital city of Baghdad. The forty days of air war that followed was very one-sided. The allied forces were able to bomb targets at will using advanced technical weapons such as radar-seeking missles, laser-guided bombs, stealth fighters that avoided radar detection, and smart cruise missles that could adjust their course. The Iraqi air force never got off the ground, but hid or flew to Iran. The Iraqi Scud missles killed twenty-two American soldiers sleeping in Saudi Arabia and civilians in Israel but were mostly unreliable and ineffective. Finally, the ground war (Operation Desert Storm) lasted only one hundred hours before the allied forces liberated Kuwait City. The Iraqis had over 200,000 casualties (according to American estimates) while the allied forces sustained less than 200 casualties.

Can this war be justified using the just war theory? Carefully explain your answer. Keep in mind that some religious leaders at the time said that it was not a just war.

Was this a jihād, as Saddam Hussein and the Ayatollah Khomeini said? Remember that Kuwait and Saudi Arabia were also Muslim countries.

Oil presented another consideration. Kuwait had about 20 percent of the world's known oil reserves. Some said the war was really about the control and price of oil and maintained that if Kuwait had no valuable resources, the United States would not have intervened. (For example, the United States did nothing when China invaded and occupied a defenseless Tibet in 1949.)

3. The Invasion of Grenada. On November 1, 1983, United States military forces invaded and occupied the Caribbean island of Grenada with only minimal resistance. The Marines captured the Pearls airport, the only usable airstrip on the island, while the Army took an uncompleted airstrip at Point Saline on the southern tip of the island. The troops came to free some 1,000 American citizens, mostly medical citizens, who were trapped on the island after a military coup had toppled the leftist regime of Maurice Bishop.

There were objections to the operation. The military leaders of the coup insisted the American citizens were in no danger. Some of the medical students agreed saying they did not need or want to be rescued. Furthermore, if the purpose of the invasion was to rescue people, why was it necessary to occupy the airstrips and take over control of the country? Why not just rescue the people and leave?

In his address to the nation, President Ronald Reagan claimed that Grenada was a military threat to the United States; the new airstrip was going to be used to attack the United States. To prove his point, President Reagan said that a cache of Cuban and Soviet weapons had been found, and that Cuban military personnel were there. "We got there just in time," he said.

Can this invasion be justified using the just war theory? Why or why not? Explain your answer.

History provides us with various examples of invasion: Iraq invaded Kuwait, the Soviets invaded Afghanistan, China invaded Tibet, and American-supported Cuban exiles tried and failed to invade Cuba in the Bay of Pigs Invasion. If you think the invasion of Grenada was justified, then what do you think about these other invasions?

4. The My Lai Massacre. (The best movie about Vietnam is *Platoon* (1986), directed by Oliver Stone. This movie shows an attack on a village that is similar to the My Lai Massacre. There are numerous books about Vietnam, too many to mention here. Douglas P. Lackey gives a fairly brief account of the My Lai Massacre in *The Ethics of War and Peace* (Englewood Cliffs, NJ: Prentice-Hall, 1989), pp. 82-85.)

The town of My Lai is located in the northern part of South Vietnam. On March 16, 1968, two platoons of American soldiers, under orders from Captain Ernest Medina, attacked the village—first by air, and then on the ground. The first platoon of twenty-five men was commanded by Lieutenant William Calley; the second platoon was under Lieutenant Steven K. Brooks. Both platoons advanced through the village, threw hand grenades into huts, shot anyone who emerged, and rounded up everybody else. The second platoon rounded up about twenty women, made them sit in a circle, and then blew them up with hand grenades. The first platoon gathered together a larger group of about one hundred fifty women, children, and old men. (There were no young men of fighting age; presumably they were away fighting or had already been killed.) This large group was put in a ditch on the south side of the village. Lieutenant Calley and the members of the first platoon then shot everyone in the ditch except a few small children (who survived because they were shielded by their mother's bodies). One small child tried to crawl away, but the soldier's shot him and threw him back in the ditch. After the shooting stopped, over four hundred people from the village lay dead. There was one American casualty, a private who deliberately shot himself in the foot in order to avoid further duty.

Only Lieutenant Calley was court-martialed for this incident. His defense was that he was following orders and that he could not distinguish combatants from noncombatants in Vietnam.

Under international law, it is illegal to kill noncombatants in war. Thus if Captain Medina ordered Lieutenant Calley to do this (and it was never clear just what the orders were), then the orders were illegal. Should a soldier disobey illegal orders? What if an order is legal but a soldier considers it immoral? Should a soldier disobey orders he considers to be immoral? In general, what are the limits of obedience for soldiers?

Besides the problem of determining if and when to disobey orders, there is the problem of identifying combatants. Surely babies are never combatants, but what about young children, women, and old men? Is it allowable to kill them if one believes they are combatants? What about those who are already injured? Can they be killed too?

Lieutenant Calley was convicted and sentenced to life in prison, but his sentence was reduced and he only served three years. The other soldiers and officers were not punished at all. Should they have been court martialed too?

5. *Torture.* (The best philosophical article on torture is Henry Shue's "Torture," *Philosophy and Public Affairs* 7, no. 2 (Winter 1978), pp. 124-143.) Most people consider torture to be wrong; it is prohibited in all the relevant international laws of war. Yet according to Amnesty International, torture is widespread and growing, even in civilized countries. Can torture be justified in some cases? Shue thinks so. To use his example, suppose a fanatic has set a hidden nuclear bomb to explode in the heart of Paris. Wouldn't it be allowable to torture the fanatic to find out where the bomb is hidden so that it could be defused? Surely this is a better alternative that letting the bomb explode.

Shue's example, however, is a case of terrorism, not war. Can interrogational torture, torture for the purpose of extracting information, be justified in war? Consider this hypothetical example. Suppose that towards the end of World War II, when the Allied forces are fighting near Berlin, Hitler is captured trying to escape disguised as an ordinary German soldier. (We are imaging that Hitler did not commit suicide with Eva Braun in the bunker in Berlin; that was just a story made up to deceive people.) After his capture, Hitler tries to commit suicide, but he is prevented from doing so. He has valuable information about Nazi plans that could save hundreds of lives on both sides if known before the Allies' final assault on Berlin. Hitler does not want to reveal this information; he wants the Germans to fight to the death, to kill as many of the enemy as possible before being defeated. He knows, of course, that the war is lost, but he doesn't care about loss of life; he wants the defeat to be costly for both sides. Time is short; the Allied interrogators must act quickly. They have only twenty-four hours to get the information before beginning the attack on Berlin. Why not torture Hitler to get this life-saving information? Isn't this justified by the principle of proportionality? What do you think?

Suggested Readings

1. Immanuel Kant, *Perpetual Peace* (New York: Liberal Arts Press, 1957). In this classic discussion of war and peace, Kant maintains that war must not be conducted in a way that rules out future peace. Perpetual peace results when democratic countries let the people decide about going to war; Kant believes that the people will always vote for peace.

2. Henry Sidgwick, *The Elements of Politics* (London: Macmillan, 1891). Sidgwick discusses the morality of war from a utilitarian viewpoint. He gives two utilitarian principles for the moral conduct of war: first, any harm produced by the war that does not contribute to the end of victory is wrong; and second, acts that contribute only slightly to that end and produce a great deal of harm are wrong.

3. Douglas P. Lackey, *The Ethics of War and Peace* (Englewood Cliffs, NJ: Prentice-Hall, 1989). Lackey surveys different kinds of pacifism in Chapter 1 and examines the just war theory in Chapters 3 and 4. He gives detailed examples to illustrate his points and comprehensive suggestions for further readings.

4. T. R. Miles, "On the Limits to the Use of Force," *Religious Studies* 20 (1984), pp. 113-120. Miles argues that the use of force may be necessary and even morally required in medical contexts and in the defense of property, but it is neither necessary nor morally required to resolve international disputes. Thus, Miles defends a version of pacifism that is opposed to all war but not to all use of force. This kind of pacifism would require one to refuse to serve in the military, but would not rule out serving as a police officer.

5. William Earle, "In Defense of War," *The Monist*, October 1973, pp. 561-569. Earle attacks pacifism (defined as the principled opposition to all war)

and then gives a justification for the morality and rationality of war.

6. Jan Narveson, "In Defense of Peace," in *Moral Issues,* Jan Narveson, ed. (New York: Oxford University Press, 1983), pp. 59-71. Narveson replies to Earle. He does not defend pacifism; instead, he argues that whenever there is a war, at least one party is morally unjustified.

7. Jan Narveson, "Morality and Violence: War, Revolution, Terrorism," in *Matters of Life and Death: New Introductory Essays in Moral Philosophy,* Third Edition, Tom Regan, ed. (New York: McGraw-Hill, 1993), pp. 121-159. Narveson covers many different issues in this survey article; the nature and morality of violence, the right of self-defense, pacifism, just war theory, and terrorism.

8. Richard A. Wasserstrom, ed., *War and Morality* (Belmont, CA: Wadsworth Publishing Co., 1970). This is a collection of articles on the morality of war and other issues. Elizabeth Anscombe discusses the doctrine of double effect as it applies to war. Wasserstrom's article "On the Morality of War: A Preliminary Inquiry" argues that the fact innocents are inevitably killed in modern wars makes it very difficult to justify them.

9. Marshall Cohen, Thomas Nagel, and Thomas Scanlon, eds., *War and Moral Responsibility* (Princeton, NJ: Princeton University Press, 1973). This collection of articles has two parts. The first part examines restrictions on the goals and methods of war; the second part covers issues related to World War II and the Vietnam War.

10. Robert L. Phillips, *War and Justice* (Norman, OK: University of Oklahoma Press, 1984). Phillips defends just war theory. He accepts two principles of this theory: The principle of proportionality (that there be no more force than is necessary to produce the end) and the principle of discrimination which distinguishes combatants from noncombatants. This second principle, however, depends on the controversial doctrine of double effect which tries to distinguish between intending to kill and merely foreseeing that something will die as an effect of action.

11. James Johnson, *Just War Tradition and the Restraint of War* (Princeton, NJ: Princeton University Press, 1981). Johnson explains the historical development of the just war theory from the Middle Ages to the present.

12. Michael Walzer, *Just and Unjust Wars: A Moral Argument with Historical Illustrations* (New York: Basic Books, 1977). Walzer develops and defends just war theory and applies the theory to numerous historical cases, e.g., the Six-day War, the Vietnam War, the Korean War, World War II. He argues that the Vietnam War can be justified as assistance to the legitimate government of South Vietnam and as counter-intervention in response to military moves by the North Vietnamese. Critics respond that intervention in the civil war of another country, e.g., the current war in Bosnia, is unwise and unjustified.

13. Paul Ramsey, *The Just War: Force and Political Responsibility* (New York: Charles Scribner's Sons, 1968). This book is a collection of various articles, chapters, and pamphlets on the subject of the just war theory, all written by Ramsey. Ramsey is a Christian who defends a version of the just war theory that has an absolute principle of discrimination against any killing of noncombatants. Yet he claims that the war in Vietnam was justified, even though it involved killing many noncombatants. There is the appearance, at least, of inconsistency.

14. Barrie Paskins and Michael Dockrill, *The Ethics of War* (Minneapolis: University of Minnesota Press, 1979). Michael Dockrill, an historian, and Barrie Paskins, a philosopher, successfully combine history (World Wars I and II) with philosophy. Their book contains good chapters on pacifism and just war theory.

15. David Luban, "Just War and Human Rights," *Philosophy and Public Affairs* 9, no. 2 (Winter 1980), pp. 160-181. Luban argues that the morality of war should be judged in terms of human rights. A just war defends human rights, and an unjust war subverts them. By this definition, an aggressive war can be a just war.

16. George I. Mavrodes, "Conventions and the Morality of War," *Philosophy and Public Affairs* 4, no. 2 (1975), pp. 117-131. Mavrodes discusses the moral rule of war that noncombatants should not be intentionally killed. He suggests that this rule is not an independent moral rule, but rather part of a convention setting up an alternative to war. As such, it creates a special obligation not to kill innocent people.

17. Dilip Hiro, *Holy Wars: The Rise of Islamic Fundamentalism* (New York: Routledge, 1989). This useful book explains the development of Islam

from the prophet Muhammad to the Islamic Fundamentalism found today in Iran and Afghanistan. There are long chapters on both Iran and Afghanistan where Islam has emerged as a radical ideology of armed resistance.

18., R. Peters, "Jihād," in *The Encyclopedia of Religion,* (Mircea Eliade, ed. (New York: Macmillan Press, 1989). Peters explains the Islamic concept of jihād and how it applies to war.

19. A. Maalory, *The Crusaders Through Arab Eyes* (New York: Schocken Books, 1985). Maalory covers two centuries of hostility and war between Muslin Arabs and Christian Crusaders from the West (called Franks) starting with the fall of Jerusalem in 1099. It is a sad story of invasion and counter-invasion, massacres and plunder.

20. Jean Bethke Elshtain, *Women and War* (New York: Basic Books, 1987). What is the feminist view of war? According to Elshtain, some feminists are pacifists working for world peace, while others want to reject the traditional noncombatant role of women and become warriors. As a result of the second position, the United States now has a higher percentage of women in the military than any other industrialized nation, ten percent of the overall force of 2.1 million.

21. Robert Ginsberg, ed., *The Critique of War* (Chicago: Henry Regnery Company, 1969). This is a collection of readings on war. In "The Technique of Nonviolent Resistance," R. Balasurbramanian claims that Gandhi's methods are the most effective way to combat war and violence. Another article on the Hindu view is "Peace: The Hindu View," by Swami Nikhilananda.

PHILOSOPHICAL GLOSSARY

A priori Known independent of experience, as distinguished from a posteriori, known from experience. "No statement can be both true and false" is known a priori, while the statement "Some crows are black" is known a posteriori.

Act and omissions doctrine The doctrine that there is an important moral difference between acts and omissions (or failures to act): an act can be wrong, but an omission with the same effect is not wrong. As it is applied to killing and letting die, the doctrine says that killing an innocent person is wrong, but letting him or her die may not be wrong, or perhaps less wrong. The application of the doctrine to euthanasia is attacked by Rachels in the reading in Chapter 3. Glover discusses and rejects the doctrine and its application to euthanasia in Chapter 7 of his book *Causing Death and Saving Lives*. A limited defense of the doctrine as it is applied to killing and letting die can be found in Foot's "Euthanasia" and Ladd's "Positive and Negative Euthanasia" (see the Suggested Readings for Chapter 3).

Actus reas (Latin) The alleged criminal act of which the defendant stands accused in a court of law.

Analytic proposition In logic, a proposition is analytic if it is true by virtue of the meanings of the words it contains. By contrast, a proposition is synthetic if its truth or falsehood is not based on the meaning of words, but on the way the world is. "All husbands are male" is an example of a true analytic proposition. "All husbands are over two feet tall" is an example of a synthetic proposition.

Argumentum hominem (Latin: to the man) In logic, the fallacy of personally attacking one's opponent instead of responding to the opponent's arguments or claims.

Autonomy Freedom; independence of the will from others. Moral autonomy is the freedom to make up one's mind about moral matters.

AZT Azidothymidine or Zidovudine, an antiviral drug used in the treatment of AIDS. It reduces the severity of AIDS-related conditions such as pneumocystis and infections of the brain and nervous system. It does not cure these conditions, but it may improve the symptoms by reducing lymph gland swelling. Although the drug slows the progress of AIDS, relapse usually occurs after several months of treatment.

Brain dead In medicine, a person is brain dead if the entire brain including the brain stem has ceased to function. A brain-dead person can be kept alive by using machines to keep the heart and lungs functioning. Such a person is not dead in the classical sense; death in this sense does not occur until all the vital functions cease including the function of the heart and lungs. A common indicator of brain death is an EEG (electroencephalogram) reading which shows no electrical activity in the brain; this is often called a flat EEG.

Carthaginian peace Carthage was an ancient city completely destroyed and razed by the Romans. A Carthaginian peace, therefore, is an ironic way of talking about total destruction.

Categorical imperative A categorical imperative is a command in the form "Do X" or "Do not do X" and is distinguished from a hypothetical imperative which has the form "If you want X, do Y." Kant rejected the form of hypothetical imperative for rules of morality; he believed that moral rules have the form of categorical imperatives or commands which admit no exceptions and are binding on all rational beings.

Criterion (pl. criteria) A standard that provides a conclusive way of determining whether something exists, or whether a word is used correctly. In the abortion controversy, writers have tried to establish criteria for the fetus being a person, that is, features that provide logically conclusive evidence that fetuses are persons. Sometimes criteria are formulated in terms of necessary and sufficient conditions. See necessary and sufficient conditions.

Cultural relativism A theory of moral values which holds that values are relative to society. If a society approves of a certain action, then it is right; and if it disapproves of an action, then it is wrong. (This theory should not be confused with anthropological relativism, the factual thesis that different societies have different moral codes.) If cultural relativism is true, then it follows, supposedly, that there are no universal moral values that hold in all societies at all times; and there are no objective moral values that hold independent of society. Both cultural and anthropological relativism have been popular with sociologists and anthropologists, but very few philosophers have accepted these views. Philosophers insist (with some support from anthropologists) that there are universal moral values, e.g., caring for children is morally approved in all known societies. Philosophers also want to criticize societies and reform them; this means that societies have made moral mistakes in the past and the present. If so, then acts previously approved by a society could be wrong (e.g., slavery was approved by some societies, but it is objectively wrong), and acts disapproved by a society may be right (e.g., allowing women to vote was disapproved by Western society until the 1920s, but is, nevertheless, objectively right).

Dar al-harb Literally, the territory of war. The land of the enemy or land not controlled by Muslims.

Dar al-Islam Literally, the territory of Islam. The land ruled by Muslims.

Deontological theory A theory determining the rightness or wrongness of an act by something other than its consequences, for example, by God's commands or moral intuition. This differs from teleological ethical theories, including utilitarianism and egoism, which hold that the rightness or wrongness of an act is determined by its consequences.

Deterrence In the readings, deterrence refers to the discouragement of crime. General deterrence is the discouragement of crimes that might be committed by people other than those punished, while specific deterrence is the discouragement of more crimes by the specific person punished. According to the utilitarian theory of punishment, deterrence (whether specific or general) is one of the consequences of punishment (along with reformation of the criminal and protection of innocent people) that can justify it.

Dialectics The art of asking and answering questions in order to arrive at knowledge.

Distributive justice The problem or theory of how to allocate or distribute goods and services in a society. Should there be an equal distribution, or should some people be allowed to have more goods and services than others?

Divine command theory In its standard form, the divine command theory says that an act is right if it is commanded by God, and wrong if it is forbidden by God. This theory has been defended by a few philosophers, but it faces a host of difficulties. First, it assumes that God exists and issues commands, which is very difficult to prove. The history of philosophy contains numerous attempts to prove that a personal God exists, but it is safe to say that each of these so-called proofs is controversial. Even assuming that God exists, there is the problem of finding out what God's commands are. Do we accept Jesus, Moses, or Muhammed as the prophet of God? Do we read the Old Testament, the New Testament, or the Koran? If we decide, say, that the New Testament is the word of God, we still have the problem of interpreting it. Different people interpret the Bible in different ways. For example, how are we to understand the basic commandment "Thou shalt not kill"? And why should we obey God in the first place? Surely, threats of reward or punishment are not good moral reasons for obeying. Don't we have a right and a duty to decide for ourselves what is right or wrong? Finally, there is the famous question found in Plato's dialogue the *Euthyphro,* namely: Is an act right because God commands it, or does God command it because it is right? It seems that no satisfactory answer can be given. If an act is right just because God commands it, then its being right is arbitrary. God could arbitrarily command you to murder your beloved son (as in the biblical story of Abraham and his son Issac), and that would supposedly make it right. But would it? On the other hand, if God commands an act because it is right, then a standard of rightness exists independent of God's commands. It might, perhaps, be Mill's Principle of Utility. If so, then we could discover this principle without knowing God's commands, and God's commands are unnecessary for morality.

Divine-will theory of morality See the entry on the Divine Command Theory in the Glossary for Chapter 1.

Doctrine of ensoulment The medieval doctrine that God puts an immortal soul into the body. The theory of instantaneous ensoulment that Noonan refers to holds that God puts the soul into the zygote at conception and not afterwards. This is a common Roman Catholic belief that is sometimes used to defend the conservative prohibition against abortion.

ELISA test ELISA stands for enzyme-linked immunosorbent assay. This is a laboratory test for infectious diseases. the ELISA test detects the specific antibody for the HIV virus. An antibody is a protein produced by the body's immune system to protect against invading microorganisms.

Epistemology Theory of the method or grounds of knowledge, one of the branches of traditional philosophy encompassing metaphysics, ethics, and logic.

Equivocation Using a word in two different senses. An argument commits the fallacy of equivocation by giving different meanings to one word. Jane English provides this example: A fetus is a being that is living and human, so a fetus is a human being (the word *being* is used equivocally).

Ethical egoism The standard formulation of the theory is that everyone ought to act in his or her own self-interest. My act is right if it is in my self-interest, and wrong if it is not. Your act is right if it is in your self-interest, and wrong if it is not. This version of the theory is called universal ethical egoism since it is supposed to apply to everyone equally. The standard criticism of universal ethical egoism is that it involves some sort of contradiction—but it is not so easy to find this alleged contradiction. Suppose John and Mary are in a fight. As a practicing, universal ethical egoist, I tell John to win (since that is in John's self-interest); but then I tell Mary that *she* should win (since that is in Mary's self-interest). Since they both can't win, there is something odd about this advice. Nevertheless, it is not formally self-contradictory to tell them both to try to win.

Another possible version of egoism is personal ethical egoism where I say that I ought to do those actions that most benefit me, but I have nothing to say about your actions. This is not really an ethical theory, but more like a personal philosophy of life. Still another version is individual ethical egoism where I say that you and I both ought to do what is in my self-interest. This view involves a strange asymmetry: You ought to always help me, but I should never help you, unless that benefits me.

None of these views should be confused with psychological egoism, the theory that everyone, in fact, is motivated by self-interest. Obviously, this is not an ethical theory, but a factual claim about how people act.

Ethnocentrism The belief that one's own race or ethnic group is superior to other races or ethnic groups.

Fallacy of affirming the consequent A fallacy of reasoning committed by arguments having the logical form P implies Q; Q; therefore P, where P and Q are statements that are true or false. In the conditional statement P implies Q, Q is called the consequent and P the antecedent. For example, consider this argument: If the fetus is a person, then the fetus is conscious. The fetus is conscious after the eighth week. So the fetus is a person after the eighth week. Here is an argument with the same logical form, only it is about Fido the dog: If Fido is a person, then Fido is conscious. Fido is conscious when barking; therefore Fido is a person when barking.

Free rider's principle A free rider is one who obtains or attempts to obtain a benefit without paying, for example, a worker who receives the benefits of a union contract without becoming a member of the union. Advocates of the free rider's principle maintain that one should be allowed to do this.

Free will According to the traditional theory of free will, acts that are produced by a special mental act of the will, and not by some external event, are said to be free, that is, not caused by anything else, either mental or physical. The standard example of an act of free will is the mental act of choosing between two things. The theory of free will is highly controversial; it is rejected by scientists and philosophers who believe that everything is caused, including human mental and physical acts.

Hedonism The theory saying that only pleasure is good. The theory is usually explained in terms of a distinction between intrinsic and instrumental goodness. Something is intrinsically good if it is good in itself, considered apart from anything else; while something is instrumentally good if it is a means of getting something else. Hedonism claims that only pleasure is intrinsically good, but allows that other things such as beauty and power can be instrumentally good. Hedonists typically make a further distinction between different types of pleasures. Mill, for example, held that intellectual pleasures (e.g., the pleasure one gets from reading or writing) are better than physical pleasures (e.g., the pleasure one gets from eating). As Mill puts it, "It is better to be a human being dissatisfied than a pig satisfied."

Hypothetical imperative See categorical imperative.

Ideal utilitarianism This is a nonhedonistic form of utilitarianism that accepts other things besides pleasure as being good. In the version adopted by G. E. Moore, knowledge and beauty are considered to be intrinsically good, and some pleasant states of mind can be intrinsically bad.

Imperfect duty See perfect duty.

Imām A leader of the people. The Imām is also referred to as the Caliph and is supposed to be a successor to Muhammad, e.g., Ali.

Infinite regress A series of events that continues without end—usually with the implication that this is impossible. A vicious infinite regress is one that is impossible, while a benign infinite regress is not impossible.

Instrumental value See Intrinsic value.

Intrinsic goods See Hedonism.

Intrinsic value Sometimes the term intrinsic value is used to mean intrinsic goodness, but strictly speaking, intrinsic value includes both intrinsic goodness and intrinsic badness. Something has intrinsic value if it is good or bad in itself apart from its use or consequences. By contrast, something has instrumental value (or extrinsic value) if it is good or bad depending on how it is used.

Intuitionism In general, intuitionism is the view that knowledge can be found using a special kind of apprehension called intuition that is neither sense-perception nor inferential reasoning, but a kind of mental vision whereby a truth is directly and clearly seen to be true. In ethics, intuitionism is the view that certain moral judgements are self-evident, and that any normal person will agree. For example, Ross thought it self-evident that one has a duty to keep a promise. Other than saying that this is self-evident, in a way similar to the self-evident axioms of mathematics, no further justification is needed or can be given.

Jus ad belleum Literally, right to war. In just war theory, the conditions which justify going to war.

Jus in bello Literally, right in war. In just war theory, the actions justified in war.

Law of Imperfect Selection In the writings of Charles Murray, the Law of Imperfect Selection says that any rule that defines eligibility for a social transfer program will arbitrarily exclude some persons. For example, Murray says that there are always some persons who are excluded from the Food Stamps program who are in greater need than some persons who receive Food Stamps.

Lex talionis The law of retaliation. It can be interpreted to mean exact retaliation as in the biblical saying "an eye for an eye, a tooth for a tooth, a life for a life;" or it can be interpreted to mean simply that the punishment should be appropriate for the crime, a severe punishment for a serious crime, and a lesser punishment for a less serious crime.

Maximize utility This is a technical phrase used by utilitarians as a shorthand way of talking about producing the best possible consequences for everyone affected by an act. In utilitarianism, of course, this is what one should do.

Mens rea (Latin: guilty mind) Criminal intent, or the knowledge that one's act is criminal before or while committing the act.

Metaphysical Relating to metaphysics, the branch of philosophy that answers questions about reality. In Glover's article, however, metaphysical means something transcendental or beyond the sensible world.

Meta-ethical relativism Meta-ethics is concerned with the nature and justification of moral judgements. Meta-ethical relativism is the view that there is no objective, rational way of justifying one moral judgement over another so that different and conflicting moral judgements are equally valid. One version of this view is emotivism, the theory that moral judgements are merely expressions of emotion that are neither true nor false; calling something right or good is equivalent to exclaiming "Terrific!" and saying something is wrong or bad is equivalent to "Terrible!" But these expressions of positive or negative emotion do not logically contradict each other, and one is no more justified than another. Since, in this view, moral judgements are mere expressions of emotion that have no descriptive content or true value, it is called noncognitivism.

Moral epistemology This is the theory of moral knowledge; it attempts to tell us about the nature and origin of knowledge or belief in morality. Intuitionism is an example of such a theory.

Moral teleology Teleology is the study of ends or aims; moral teleology is the study of the ends or aims in morality.

Natural law The term natural law usually refers to prescriptive moral laws that are derived from human nature (as distinguished from descriptive laws of nature such as those found in chemistry and physics).

Natural rights Rights that all human beings have because they are human, e.g., the right to life, as distinguished from rights or priviledges bestowed for certain purposes such as the right to vote.

Necessary and sufficient conditions A necessary condition for something is one without which the thing would not exist or occur. The presence of oxygen is a necessary condition for human life. Being alive is a necessary condition for being a person. A sufficient condition for something is one such that its occurrence or presence makes the thing exist or occur. Prolonged absence of oxygen is a sufficient condition for human death. Being a United States senator is a sufficient condition for being a person. Something can be a necessary condition and not a sufficient condition and vice versa.

Negative duty See positive duty.

Paradigm An ideal or standard example of something. In science, the term is used to refer to a pervasive way of regarding phenomena which dictates the way phenomena are explained.

Perfect duty In Kant's ethical theory, a perfect duty is an action which we should always perform or abstain from performing without exception. For example, Kant thought that the duty not to lie is a perfect duty which admits no exceptions. Another example of Kant's perfect duty is the duty not to kill an innocent person. An imperfect duty, by contrast, asks us to promote certain goals such as the welfare of others, but we are not required always to do this. We can choose when and how to fulfill an imperfect duty. For example, one person might give money for famine relief, while another gives money to help the homeless, but both are fulfilling the imperfect duty to help others. A person who does nothing at all to help others, however, would fail to satisfy the imperfect duty to help others.

Pneumocystis pneumonia An opportunistic infection of the lungs that is dangerous only to people with impaired resistance to infection such as people suffering from AIDS or leukemia. It is a major cause of death in people who have AIDS.

Positive duty An action which one is morally required to do, as distinguished from a negative duty which is an action one is morally forbidden to do. Some moral philosophers have held that negative duties such as the duty not to kill innocent people are stronger than positive duties such as the duty to help others.

Positive and negative duties are often correlated with positive and negative rights. A positive right implies that others have a positive duty to do something. The right to life, for example, if interpreted as a positive right, requires others to give food and other necessities for life. By contrast, a negative right implies that others have a negative duty not to do something. They are sometimes called rights of noninterference. Thus the right to life, if interpreted negatively, implies that one has a negative duty not to interfere with another's life.

Preference Utilitarianism This is a nonhedonistic form of utilitarianism holding that satisfaction of one's desires is what is good, rather than just pleasure, and not having one's desires satisfied is bad. Peter Singer is the main proponent of this theory.

Prima facie duty A moral duty or obligation which one has unless it is overridden by some other duty. *Prima facie* means literally on the face of it. The basic idea is that one prima facie duty (e.g., the mother's right of self-defense) can override another prima facie duty (e.g., the fetus' right to life). By contrast, an absolute duty is one that cannot be overridden by any other duties.

Prima facie *right* A moral right that can be overridden by another right (unlike an absolute right, which is a right that cannot be overridden by any other right).

Quid pro quo (Latin: something for something) An equivalent exchange.

Retribution See Retributivism.

Retributivism A theory of punishment which holds that punishment is done to correct an inequity or moral imbalance that the offense has created, and not because it produces any good consequences as in the utilitarian theory of punishment. Retribution or "paying back" the criminal is sometimes thought of as personal revenge or getting even, but it can also be perceived as a kind of impersonal correction of a moral imbalance.

Scripturaries Literally, those who have a religious scripture or holy book. The term usually refers to Christians and Jews, as distinguished from unbelievers who are polytheists and idolators.

Semantics The study of the meaning of signs and symbols, as distinguished from syntactics, the study of the grammatical arrangement of signs and symbols in order to convey meaning.

Shi'i A branch of Islam composed of sects that are the followers of Ali and who uphold Ali's leadership after Muhammad. As distinguished from the Sunni who appeal to sunna (custom or tradition) to determine correct behavior rather than to the imams or leaders. The Sunni are usually considered to be Orthodox Muslims.

Slippery slope arguments In general, an argument that one cannot draw a line or avoid certain consequences. For instance, if one allows some sick people to be killed, then one must allow all sick people to be killed—one will slide down a slope of killing. In the abortion controversy, one finds the argument that if an infant is a person, and the development of the infant from the zygote is a slippery slope, that is, a smooth continuous curve of development without any sharp breaks or discontinuities so that no lines can be drawn, then the zygote is a person too. This argument is attacked by Thomson and defended by Finnis in the readings.

Social constructionism The view of feminists such as MacKinnon and Dworkin that masculine and feminine gender roles which assign different tasks on the basis of biological sex are the result of factors in the environment and society, i.e., they are social constructions, and not the product of biological differences. Since these roles are changeable social constructions and not something biologically determined, females could play masculine gender roles such as providing and protecting, and males could play feminine gender roles such as caring for others.

Social contract theory The basic idea of social contract theory is that morality arises from an agreement or contract made by people that enables them to live together. In his book the *Leviathan,* the British philosopher Thomas Hobbes (1588–1679) says that people living in a state of nature apart from society would find life "solitary, poor, nasty, brutish, and short." To avoid such a life, people live together in a society. But social life is possible only if people agree to follow moral rules such as "Don't murder" and "Don't steal." Another philosopher who is associated with this theory is Jean-Jacques Rousseau (1712–1778). In his work *The Social Contract,* Rousseau asserts that humans living in a state of nature are stupid animals; they become intelligent beings only when they live together in a civilized society. The British philosopher John Locke (1632–1704) made an important contribution to social contract theory in his work *Two Treatises of Government.* He argues that in the state of nature humans are free and equal, but this does not mean that they can do anything they want. There is a law of nature, established by God, that gives each person certain natural rights: a right to life, a right to liberty, and a right to property. But to enjoy these rights, humans must live together under a social contract which establishes a government to protect these rights and settle disputes. Without a government, humans in a state of nature would infringe on each other's rights.

Subjectivism A theory of moral values holding that values are relative to a person's subjective feelings or emotions. If a person approves of an action, then it is morally right; and if the person disapproves of an action, then it is morally wrong. This theory should not be confused with the factual thesis that different people have different feelings about moral values. No doubt this factual thesis is true, but it does not follow that moral values are different for different people. An act might be right even if a person disapproves of it; and an act might be wrong even though a person approves of it. This is simply to say that people might be mistaken about what is right or wrong. If such mistakes are possible, and most philosophers insist that they are, then subjectivism cannot be true. Another standard criticism of subjectivism is that it fails to recognize the fact that there are genuine moral disagreements. Pro-life and pro-choice advocates disagree about the wrongness of abortion, but this disagreement is not just a disagreement in feeling or emotion. Both sides could emotionally disapprove of abortion, and yet still disagree about its wrongness in some cases, say rape.

Sufficient condition See Necessary condition.

Supererogation Performing an act that is morally good but beyond what is morally required, such as giving all your money to the needy.

Tautology Literally, saying the same thing. Sometimes the term is used to refer to an analytic proposition, but in logic the term is used to refer to logical truths, that is, propositions that are true by virtue of their logical form, e.g., "It is raining or it is not raining."

Teleological theory A theory that determines moral rightness or wrongness by looking at consequences of actions. The standard teleological theory in ethics, as we can see in the readings, is utilitarianism. Utilitarianism takes different forms, depending on what view about the good is adopted (for example, hedonism or some nonhedonistic view), but all versions agree that the consequences for everyone should be considered. Unlike utilitarianism, ethical egoism is a teleological theory that only considers the consequences for the agent and ignores the consequences for others. A third teleological theory is altruism; it considers consequences for others but not for the agent. More teleological theories can be formulated, depending on who is given moral consideration. One might only be concerned, say, with one's family or one's religious group.

Teleological theories are usually contrasted with deontological theories which do not look at consequences in determining moral rightness or wrongness. Kant's theory and the divine command theory are examples of deontological theories. Another example is situation ethics where one is supposed to decide what is right or wrong in concrete situations without using abstract rules for guidance. Appeals to conscience or moral intuition would also be classified as deontological.

Utilitarianism A standard theory in ethics that uses the principle of utility to determine whether an act is morally right or wrong. This principle is formulated in different ways, but a standard version is this: Everyone ought to act so as to bring about the greatest good for the greatest number. Utilitarians do not agree about what is good or bad. Some of them, called hedonists, think that only pleasure is intrinsically good (good in itself), and that only pain is intrinsically bad. For example, the classical utilitarians Jeremy Bentham (1748–1832) and John Stuart Mill (see the reading in Chapter 1) were hedonistic utilitarians. Other utilitarians believe that satisfaction of one's desires is what is good and not having them satisfied is bad. They are called preference utilitarians. (See Preference Utilitarianism.) Still another version is Ideal Utilitarianism which holds that other things are good besides pleasure such as beauty. The British philosopher G. E. Moore (1873–1958) held this theory, and it is discussed by W. D. Ross in the reading in Chapter 1. (See Ideal Utilitarianism.)

Virtue theory In general, virtue theory tells us what traits of character make a person good, and what traits make a person bad. The former are called virtues, the latter vices. As MacIntyre points out in the reading, different writers have picked out different traits of character as virtues. The Greeks emphasized virtues of soldiers such as courage; the Christians talked about theological virtues such as faith, hope, and charity; and modern moral philosophers have thought that justice and benevolence are essential virtues.

Western blot test Like the ELISA test, the Western Blot test detects the presence of antibodies for the HIV virus. It is more expensive and more accurate than the ELISA test and is usually used to confirm a positive ELISA test.

INDEX